Reading Sacred Texts:
Charity, Structure, Gospel

Reading Sacred Texts:
Charity, Structure, Gospel

Evan Fales

An Imprint of the
Global Center for Religious Research
1312 17TH Street • Suite 549
Denver, Colorado 80202

INFO@GCRR.ORG • GCRR.ORG

GCRR Press
An imprint of the Global Center for Religious Research
1312 17th Street Suite 549
Denver, CO 80202
www.gcrr.org

Copyright © 2021 by Evan Fales

DOI: 10.33929/GCRRPress.EF2021.01

All rights reserved. No part of this publication may be reproduced, stored in a retrieval system, or transmitted in any form or by any means, electronic, mechanical, photocopying, recording, or otherwise, without the prior permission of GCRR Press. For permissions, contact: info@gcrr.org.

Unless otherwise noted, Scripture quotations are from Revised Standard Version of the Bible, copyright © 1946, 1952, and 1971 National Council of the Churches of Christ in the United States of America. Used by permission. All rights reserved worldwide.

Typesetting: Holly Lipovits
Copyediting: Allison Guy
Cover Design: Darren M. Slade
Cover Image: Fritz Eichenberg, *The Book of Jonah, Ch. I–IV*, 1955. © 2021 The Estate of Fritz Eichenberg / Artists Rights Society (ARS), New York

Library of Congress Cataloging-in-Publication Data

Reading sacred texts : charity, structure, gospel / Evan Fales
p. cm.
Includes bibliographical references and indexes.
ISBN (Paperback): 978-1-7362739-0-6
ISBN (eBook): 978-1-7362739-1-3
1. Bible—Hermeneutics—Criticism, interpretation, etc.   2. Hermeneutics—Religious aspects—Christianity.   I. Title.

BS 500-534.8   .F354   2021

To Daniel,

who lit the candle.

Contents

Acknowledgments   xi

Preface   xiii

1   Language and the Task of Interpretation   1

    I. Language as a Means   1
    II. What Makes Language Possible?   2
    III. Trust Me on This   5
        A. The Epistemology of Testimony: Two Options   5
    IV. Religious Thought and Reason   10
    V. The Roles of Rules in Language   12
        A. How Rules (Semantic and Syntactic) Help Us   12
        B. Performing Performatives   13
    VI. The Greatest of These is Charity   16
        A. Rationality and Truth   17
        B. The Rationality of Religious Beliefs   20
        C. Conventions and Performatives   29
    VII. The Social vs. the Natural   34

2   In the Matter of Miracles   38

    I. A Requiem for Miracles   39
    II. Fraud and Folly   44
        A. The Dialectical Landscape   44
        B. Hume vs. Earman   46
            1. What is a miracle?   47
            2. Hume's Argument: How should testimony of a miracle be weighed?   55

                3. Earman's View: How should testimony of a miracle be weighed?   62
                4. The alien abduction and spawn of Satan   73
                5. Demolition derby   78
                6. Multiple witnesses   82
                7. To summarize   85
         C. The Importance of Miracles   85
                1. Miracles and interpretation   85
    III. A Better Explanation?   87

3   Roads Not Taken   90

    I. *A Priori* Naturalism?   90
    II. The Baneful Effects of the Fundamentalism vs. Fraud and Folly Debate   92
    III. LOJR: Aims and Methods   96
         A. History vs. Metaphysics, and the Category of Myth   97
         B. Signposts of Historicity   100
    IV. LOJR: Findings   111
         A. Healings and Exorcisms   111
         B. Multiple Attestation   114
         C. The Dead Will Hear the Voice of the Son of God   118
         D. The Criterion of Coherence   121
    V. Who Has the Burden of Proof?   123
         A. The Future of Criteria of Authenticity   126
    VI. Modern Miracles?   129
    VII. A Better Path, Also Declined   132

4   The Ontology of Social Roles   134

    I. The Metaphysics of the Social   136
         A. The Dialectic of Reduction of the Social   138
         B. Embodiment   145
         C. Social Ontology   152
    II. Religion Re-Conceived   158
         A. Action Explanations Generally Considered   158
         B. Uncharitable Explanations   160

       C. Trying to Do Better   165
       D. When is Irrationality Rational?   169
       E. Social Ontology as an Extreme Sport   173

5   Genres and the Character of Myth   184

       I. Myth   186
       II. Genre   195
          A. Genre in General   195
          B. The Gospels in Particular   199

6   Anthropological Excursions   207

       I. Lévi-Strauss   208
       II. Terrence Turner   218
       III. Rites of Passage   225
       IV. The Gift That Keeps on Giving   234
          A. There's No Free Lunch   235
          B. Some Implications   236

7   Ascending Mt. Moriah   240

       I. Stocking the Larder   243
       II. Pleasing (or Appeasing?) Our Higher Selves   246
       III. Systematizing Practice   247
       IV. We Be of One Blood   253
       V. Cleansing the Temple   256
       VI. Imbibing the Blood of the Son   260
       VII. Bris   266
       VIII. Sacrificing the Beloved Son   269
       IX. To Conclude   278

8   The Genesis of Genesis   282

       I. The Creation of the Universe   283
       II. A Platonic Paradise?   288
       III. Rest   292

IV. Jacob at the Jabbok/Wrestling with God   298
V. Out of the Mouths of Asses   303
Appendix: Sex and the City   306

9 The Road to Damascus   313

10 Matthew's Mythodology   334

I. Literary Form and the Probability of Myth   334
   A. Chiasm and Other Literary Structures in Matthew   334
   B. Literary Models for the Gospels   338
II. A Tale of Two Taxes   343
   A. Paying the Temple Tax (Matt. 17:24–27)   343
   B. Rendering unto Caesar (Matt. 22:15–22)   349

11 Matthew's Passion   359

I. Framing Matthew's Passion Narrative: Women and Structure   359
   A. St. Matthew's Passion as Myth   359
   B. The Greatest of These is Charity   365
   C. Substance and Structure, Theories and Tools   366
   D. Taming the Tehom: The Sign of Jonah in Matthew   369
   E. Death and Descent into the Chaos-Waters   373
   F. Piecing the Puzzle   378
   G. *Cherchez les Femmes*   379
   H. A Final Piece: The Chronology of Bethany   386
   I. "Something Greater than Jonah is Here"   387
II. Where My People are Laid to Rest   388
III. Concluding Reflections   402

12 Christ's Kingdom   407

I. Sanders and Wright on the Aims of Jesus   408
II. Powers and Principalities: What Was in the Air?   412
III. Wright on the Meaning of the Resurrection   421
IV. Focus on the Family   429

      V. The Good News   434
      VI. Roman Vacancies   436

Afterward   441

      I. A Divine City   442
      II. A Divine King   443
      III. A General Reaction to "Mythicism"   445
      IV. Conclusion   447

Bibliography   449

Index   482

Acknowledgments

No living species has a gestation period of forty-five years, but books on occasion do, and this book is one such example. My interest in the subject began quite by accident, and the initial development of my ideas similarly by accident. The pivotal moment, however, occurred in 1973 when a conversation with an old friend, Dan Larkin, made me realize that lessons I learned in the anthropology of religion might be applied to an understanding of the New Testament. A year later, chance threw us together for a year as apartment-mates, and long hours were devoted to teasing apart the structure of the Gospel of Matthew. Section I of Chapter 11, in particular, owes so much to those conversations that it would be impossible to tease apart which of the ideas in play are Daniel's and which are mine. To Daniel, then, I owe thanks beyond measure both for an enduring friendship and for the gift of a set of intellectual challenges worthy of a better scholar than I.

I also have an extended exchange with Lydia McGrew to thank for the tightening of my arguments in the first part of Chapter 11; she unerringly pointed out lacunae and challenged me to fill them in.

The third word of thanks goes to the Center for Philosophy of Religion at Notre Dame University, which granted me a year-long fellowship to pursue this project. Although in the intervening years I had written a few studies that form the basis of some chapters, it was my year at Notre Dame (2013–2014) that afforded me the opportunity finally to engage in a book-length study. It is hard to imagine a more satisfying setting than what was provided by the Center. Here, particular mention must be made of William (Billy) Abraham, whose historical knowledge and philosophical acumen allowed me to gain insight into theological ways of thinking not previously accessible to me; to Sam Lebens, whose knowledge of rabbinical thought and sense of humor were precious resources; to Carl Mosser for his extensive knowledge of Second Temple Judaism and the New Testament; and to Ryan Mullins for his knowledge of patristic literature. Billy, too, pointed me in the direction of some highly suggestive patristic material of which I was able to make good use. These are debts I cannot ever hope to repay, and they made an immense contribution to my quest for understanding the field of ancient Near Eastern studies.

My associate fellows at the Center were not the only contributors to the intellectual climate provided by the Center. A number of extremely able philosophy graduate students not only taught me much but made life at the Center a real pleasure. Particularly worth singling out are Nevin Climenhaga, whose expertise in formal epistemology helped me clarify, in major ways, my treatment of miracles in Chapter 2, as well as Amy Seymour, Dustin Crummett, and David Squire. (I could not, unfortunately, get them to agree to take responsibility for the errors in the book.) A number of Notre Dame philosophy faculty also participated helpfully in our colloquia, especially Robert Audi and Jim Sterba, not to mention the Center's administrators, Mike Rea and Sam Newlands. Further, let me thank the Center's secretary, Joyce Zurawsky, and the two graduate assistants, Katie Finley and Robin Dembroff. Last, but certainly not least, I owe a large debt of gratitude to my editor at GCRR, Darren Slade, for his wealth of suggestions for improving my efforts to communicate. I am eternally grateful to all of you for your patience and assistance with this project.

Preface

I have been thinking about the Bible for more than forty-five years. The thing happened quite accidentally; while pursuing graduate work in philosophy, I was led by quite different philosophical interests to take some graduate courses in anthropology on the side. That project soon receded from view as my attention became riveted by the literature, both ethnographic and theoretical, on tribal religions, which fed an interest I had even as a child: why do people believe as they do?—a question that becomes especially pressing in the face of religious beliefs.

My thinking about tribal religious beliefs was much influenced by Emile Durkheim's *Elementary Forms of the Religious Life* and by Claude Lévi-Strauss' work on the structural analysis of myths. At the same time, I found what I consider to be fundamental inadequacies in both their views. Yet, at least Lévi-Strauss was refreshingly free of the tendency, almost universal among early anthropologists of religion, to attribute to tribespeople deep cognitive errors of one kind or another. So matters stood until it dawned on me, thanks to a chance reunion in 1972 with Dan Larkin, who was studying the Gospel of Matthew with Norman Perrin at the University of Chicago, that anthropological methods could illuminate the New Testament. Back then, applying anthropological tools of analysis to the "home religions" was not commonly done. Things have changed somewhat for the better. Anthropological and sociological studies of Judeo-Christian traditions are now quite common.

In 1978, I published a couple of articles defending a principle of interpretive charity and outlining a social ontology that, I argued, could provide a conceptual framework for understanding both "native" and Judeo-Christian religious thought. Those articles, substantially revised and updated, form the backbone of Chapters 1 and 4 of this work. Since that time, I have remained largely silent on these matters, but here I aim to try and see whether I might be able to contribute something to our understanding of the Bible and of sacred writings more generally. This is, to say the least, an ambitious task; some would even say foolhardy. They have good reason: my project divides, roughly, into three parts: a philosophical part, a discussion of anthropological methods, and an examination and interpretation of illustrative biblical texts. My main philosophical tasks are to set forth and defend a strong principle of interpretive charity and a social ontology that can illuminate certain central theological categories.

Using the history of anthropology of religion as a foil for my philosophical arguments, I will then engage, often critically, further contributions from anthropologists that I take to be highly relevant: those of Lévi-Strauss, of course, but also Marcel Mauss, Arnold Van Gennep, Edmund Leach, Victor and Terry Turner, Mary Douglas, and others. From them, I shall draw and attempt to make as explicit as possible the conceptual tools I will apply to the illustrative texts. Those texts, treated in the third part, will be drawn from both the Hebrew Bible and the New Testament. I have selected them in the hope that my interpretations will be of sufficient interest to readers who have greater scholarly abilities than I to persuade them to pursue this approach further to see where it might lead.

Because my task spans three academic disciplines, it is, as I noted, inherently ambitious. Academicians stand eager to defend their turf. This is nowhere truer than in the field of Bible scholarship, and with good reason: there is perhaps no other discipline in which more nonsense has been written by zealous amateurs. As an interloper, I can only hope that I will not be summarily rejected. Critical Bible scholarship has been permeated with deep disagreements from the beginning. (Indeed, a number of philosophers—Michael Dummett, Alvin Plantinga, and Peter Van Inwagen come readily to mind—have justified dismissive attitudes toward the field on these grounds.) But differences of opinion, however disconcerting, are commonplace in any discipline. In Bible scholarship, they are in significant measure the result of two factors: too much data, and too little data. That may sound paradoxical, but of course it is not. There exist more data than any single scholar can hope to control; at the same time, there is often a frustrating *lack* of data that would allow us to settle crucial uncertainties in our reconstruction of the past. This fact recommends a steadfast counsel of caution respecting the conclusions that can be drawn. For such as myself who are philosophers, it demands an extra dose of humility.

At the same time, I shall be proposing and defending (at least) two controversial theses. The first, already noted, is a strong principle of charity, which I will spell out in Chapter 1. The second takes very seriously the view, commonplace among anthropologists, that tribal peoples do not characteristically draw conceptual boundaries between the categories of religion and politics. I shall argue for a stronger claim: that in most "primitive" cultural contexts, religious thought and practice *just is* political thought and practice. In this, I can be (and have been) accused of "reductionism" and various other sins. I shall defend the view against those accusations. I shall then apply this *just is* political view to the biblical texts. I do that in the spirit of proposing, and then testing, a hypothesis. To make the issue as clear as possible, I will formulate the hypothesis in the starkest of terms and then assess whether it can explain our data. If it bears sufficient fruit, then it deserves serious consideration; if not, then it must either be rejected or revised.

In all this, I intend to put my cards on the table from the outset. That is why half of this book will be devoted to questions of methodology. In testing my hypotheses, I shall, in general, proceed by way of reasoning to the best explanation. Such reasoning is highly fallible—not only because our data may be radically incomplete but because we may have failed to consider one or more hypotheses that are competitors to the ones we do consider. I shall have considered my project a success if I can put on the table a global hypothesis (and several corollaries) that have not heretofore been given adequate attention.

In keeping with my policy of putting my cards on the table, let me add here one final note. When I began thinking about these matters some forty-five years ago, I was an atheist. I remain an atheist to this day, but a defense of atheism was not then, and is not now, part of my agenda in pursuing these matters. My interest, then and now, is to understand what the biblical texts mean. In what follows, when I speak of the "meaning of a text," I speak mostly (making due allowance for hermeneutical complexities) of what the original tradents of that text meant to say to an intended audience. For me, author-meaning is conceptually primary—and, in any case, it is what primarily interests me. (If, as is common for these works, the text emerged from an extended period of shaping by several or many individuals, talk of author-meaning is obviously awkward.[1] I shall use the term as a stand-in for what is better understood as the meaning intended and understood by the community that shaped the ultimate form of a text as we have it.) As for the rest, let the chips fall where they may. Some will see the claim that the biblical messages were ultimately political (at their core) as corrosive to their faith. If so, I shall only plead that this is, in good measure, where the evidence seems to lead me.

---

[1] Werner H. Kelber, *Apostolic Tradition and the Form of the Gospel* (Atlanta, GA: Society of Biblical Literature, 2013), 11–32.

1

Language and the Task of Interpretation

I begin with language. My ultimate aim is to illuminate some biblical texts by approaching the task of reading them in a new way. It may seem strange to introduce such a project by offering quite general reflections on the nature of linguistic communication. But I believe this is necessary. Perhaps no text has ever been produced whose interpretation has been—and is—more widely contested than the Bible. Because of this, and the more so because of the particular interpretive tools I employ, it is essential that I put my methodological cards (and their defense) on the table at the outset.

What follows in this chapter are general reflections upon the nature and role of language as a medium of communication, as well as the hermeneutical constraints that follow from these reflections. The trajectory I then follow in pursuing certain puzzles in the biblical texts can be thought of as a spiral. Beginning with these very general reflections upon the nature and social role of language, this essay turns next to questions of social ontology, then to a critical discussion of the various theoretical approaches that have been proposed by anthropologists faced with the task of interpreting sacred texts, and finally to the Bible itself. Along the way, there will be an extended discussion of what to make of miracle stories, a topic that plays an unavoidable role in situating my project in the larger history of Bible interpretation and provides a key motivation for my interpretive strategy.

I. Language as a Means

If we are to start at the beginning to assess the tools required to understand difficult texts bequeathed to us from a distant past or distant culture, it behooves us to reflect with some care on the nature of human communication and language in particular. Language is a tool: we use it to communicate. Language can be used in other ways (as when we talk to ourselves and, as will emerge, for other purposes, as well), but its fundamental purpose is communication. Human beings are, by nature, highly social creatures. We are also (more or less) rational. These two major forces will, over the long haul, shape language into as efficient and effective a means of communication as possible. The very evolutionary processes that have made us social and rational will, we may assume, have encouraged linguistic invention, largely weeding out practices, conventions, and the like that are less effective.

It is important to remember that communication does not require language. It is present in non-human animals, to varying degrees, and makes use not only of vocalizations but gestures, facial expressions, and the like. Many of these—also in humans—are not conventional but genetically determined. Because such non-linguistic means of conveying intention can supply important clues for the deciphering of spoken language, we may assume that they offer a significant infrastructure upon which the invention of language, or entry into an existing language, can be erected. Together with reasonable inferences about communicative purposes from our knowledge of general biological needs, desires, and activities of fellow humans, such clues regularly serve to disambiguate the speech acts of others. The importance of these clues is sometimes overlooked or undervalued. The native speaker of Tsimshian, whose behavior shows that his principal interest in rabbits lies in hunting them down, is more likely to mean "rabbit" than "temporal part of a rabbit" when he points and says *g āq*.[1]

The grasping of referential intentions is essential to the introduction of conventional signs—e.g., words—to denote items in the world and their properties. More generally, the establishment of linguistic conventions of any kind requires that language learners be able to employ a grasp of the intentions conveyed by individual speech acts. Together with observations of the routine correlation between vocal sounds and sight of the scene, as well as by way of innate reasoning capacities, learners can then glean knowledge of a language's semantic rules.

II. What Makes Language Possible?

The acquisition of a natural, public language is universal among most human beings raised under typical social conditions. As just noted, the learning of a language involves a number of cognitive abilities. It requires, *inter alia*, the perceptual capacities of language teacher and neophyte to put both *en rapport* with a common perceived environment. How much our perceptual systems must have in common to represent a shared perceptual world is open to debate but, minimally, teacher and student should be able to establish common reference to some items and to some properties.[2] This is a

---

[1] The example is adapted from Willard Van Orman Quine, *Word and Object* (Boston, MA: MIT Press, 1960).

[2] For a discussion of how this happens, given a causal theory of reference, see Evan Fales, *Causation and Universals* (New York: Routledge, 1990).

sophisticated process, requiring that each party have a theory of mind that allows attributing semantic intentions to another on the basis of behavioral cues—a second capacity. Forming general associations between linguistic signs and their denotata further requires memory and innate reasoning capacities good enough to underwrite deductive and inductive inferences.

This has two immediate consequences relevant here. The first is that ascription of knowledge and use of a public language to others entails that people possess, in common with fellow humans, a range of communal empirical inputs and an arsenal of inferential procedures that are non-optional and universal among language users that share, or can share, such a public language. That is to say, people must be minimally rational.

So, in particular, it entails that those who employ rules of inference in acquiring knowledge about the world, about fellow human beings, and about a language—any language—must all minimally grasp the validity of the same basic rules of inference. It has sometimes been suggested that the basic logic and ontological frameworks that govern our conception of the world are themselves bequeathed by our culture and, thus, vary from one culture to another. But that view is flatly incoherent. For how is a culture to communicate its inferential norms and perceptual categories—i.e., those that reflect discrimination of properties and that underlie the individuation of physical objects—without relying upon a learner's pre-existent application of cognitive capacities to the data by means of which that information is conveyed? This does not show that we can know *a priori* that our fellow human beings engage the world with the same innate conceptual equipment that we possess. But it does show that we can know *a priori* that if they are public language users, then they do have that equipment. Let me emphasize here that the argument does not simply invoke conditions necessary for translation from one tongue to another; rather, it shows that those conditions, which inform my principle of charity, are essential to the learnability of any language whatsoever: without them, natives wouldn't *have* a language at all.

What I have suggested in skeleton form amounts to a "rationalistic" reconstruction of language-learning. One might object that this is unrealistic, that it portrays infants as carefully and systematically applying innate canons of reasoning to the welter of empirical data with which they are bombarded. Is this not a wildly idealized picture of what actually happens? Of course, no one thinks that one must be able to formulate abstractly an inferential rule—say *modus ponens*—in order to apply it correctly. But is there even an implicit following of such rules in the infant's mind? Surely there is. There are growing lines of evidence that suggest conceptual sophistication even in very young infants.[3] But that aside, I see no other way to explain how children learn.

It is true that certain preconscious biological capacities that mimic the functions of later cognitive processes may be in play—even necessary—to initiate learning a language. Consider how a child begins to learn vocabulary. Much of this proceeds haphazardly, but explicit early teaching typically involves demonstration associated with articulation of a word or phrase. Inductive methods of agreement and difference may allow a child to recognize that "ball" refers to objects of a certain shape and not to their color, position, size, or material composition. But in order for this to work, the child must presuppose, implicitly, that fluent informants are able to recognize correctly when balls are salient in the environment and mean to speak truly when they utter "ball." Perhaps this trust in others is not initially itself learned; perhaps such trust is instinctive. (We shall return to this in considering the grounds for trusting testimony.) We might allow, as well, that there are certain innate dispositions to mimic the speech sounds of others. Such features of our make-up may help explain causally how we come to be in a position to engage cognitively with language. We may be thrown into the language game before we really understand what is going on. But that understanding, when it is achieved, will at least require an implicit capacity to reason from data to semantic knowledge.

We are, then, constrained to conclude that all language users are equipped with certain basic cognitive faculties. It is straightaway to be recognized that they do not apply those faculties flawlessly. Both perceptual acuity and inferential sophistication come in degrees. Mastery of a language is by no means a trivial task, but it is compatible with a good deal of stupidity and other forms of un-reason. A sensible principle of interpretive charity will admit this. In the absence of good evidence to the contrary, we should, in attempting to decipher the communications of others, presume that they are in possession of run-of-the-mill rational faculties. The presumption may fail, in two directions: a language user may be displaying better-than-average intelligence or sub-standard abilities. Our principle should recognize those possibilities in the following way: if an interpretation of a communication attributes to its source either significantly more or less sophistication than the norm, then (in the absence of special evidence that supports this attribution) one ought to favor an interpretation that assigns run-of-the-mill intelligence and knowledge to the source.

This principle is unavoidably vague. It places a lower limit on intelligence: a speaker must be smart enough to have learned the language he or she uses. It does not tell us how much special evidence of brilliance or

---

[3] Evan Fales and Edward A. Wasserman, "Causal Knowledge: What Can Psychology Teach Philosophers," *The Journal of Mind and Behavior* 13, no. 1 (1992): 1–27.

bone-headedness may properly be demanded for out-of-the-ordinary interpretations. But it suffices to raise important questions about the interpretation of religious language, and it will provide a framework from which to assess, in particular, the language of such sacred texts as the Bible. We must therefore reflect upon how such a principle bears upon the interpretation of sacred texts; for texts, after all, are testimony.

III. Trust Me on This

A. The Epistemology of Testimony: Two Options

To an enormous extent, what we know is learned by way of receiving the testimony of others. Often, that is our sole source of information; at other times, it is an essential part of our evidential package. Moreover, and in particular, testimony plays an essential role in religious education, and sacred texts (oral or written) play an essential role in the religious curriculum. This is so even in religious traditions that place heavy emphasis on personal religious experience or participation in ritual. Thus, in spite even of the often-claimed ineffability of mystical experience, mystical traditions typically revere certain texts devoted to the description of such experiences. So, there is no escaping the evidential status of personal testimony, which is central to my project. Indeed, one debate that brings the evidential bona fides of testimony into focus is the question of whether, and when, one is justified in accepting historical claims, especially miracle reports—a matter to which I will devote extended attention in Chapter 2.

Current discussions of testimony as evidence tend to divide into two camps. The first is reductivists, who do not consider testimony a fundamental source of evidence. They hold that sense experience and introspection are the only ground-level sources of empirical knowledge; knowledge gained by way of testimony is almost always inferential knowledge since it relies upon reasoning to ground the reliability of the testimony.[4] Assessing the reliability of that testimony must rely upon inferences from evidence, in the form of sense experiences, as to the reliability of testimony in general and the reliability of the present testimonial source in particular. Anti-reductivists, on the other hand, hold that testimony can properly generate non-inferential or basic warranted belief; it therefore provides an independent source of knowledge.

The anti-reductivist position is a quite natural one if you are an externalist in epistemological matters. For in that case, a testifier can be seen as just one more link in the complex chain of causes and effects by means of

---

[4] There are unusual exceptions, as when someone says, "I'm talking now."

which information about the world is able to make its way into your cognitive arena. So long as that link (as well as others in the chain) is reliable or operating in such a way, and under such conditions, so as to provide accurate information, the resulting beliefs will suffer no principled epistemic demerit in comparison to those arrived at by way of other truth-tracking processes of information acquisition.[5]

As we will see, the debate between these two positions has direct relevance to the soundness of Hume's famous argument concerning the reliability of miracle testimony. The epistemological views I hold bear strong affinities to David Hume's; that is to say, I am a full-bore internalist and a full-bore foundationalist. I consider that the only non-inferential empirical knowledge to have epistemic meaning is knowledge of the (subjective) contents of personal sense experience and introspection.[6] This is not a common view, but more mainstream internalists will, or should, also question whether testimony can be a basic source of evidence. Surely our judgments about the truth of testimony rely upon inferences about the trustworthiness of testimony in general, as well as in particular cases.

But matters are not quite so simple; there is an *a priori* element in our evaluation of testimony. Moreover, although the anti-reductivist position may seem attractive to those who wish to credit factual assertions found in sacred texts, our assessment of those claims will in the end not depend very substantially upon whether our epistemic starting point is reductivist or not. To pursue these two points, let me consider first a significant defense of the anti-reductivist position by C. A. J. Coady, who makes his case in three main steps.[7] First, he demonstrates the pervasiveness and the depth/extent of our need to rely upon testimony to secure the knowledge we have of the world. Second, he argues that any attempt to justify our confidence in testimony runs up against the difficulties that (1) our non-testimonial evidence for the reliability of testimony is too thin to secure that conclusion; and (2) that reliance upon (other) testimonial evidence begs the question. Third, Coady provides an *a priori* argument to show that verbal communication presupposes the general truth of testimony.

In reply, I will note important ways in which Coady exaggerates his first point and show that a more accurate view of the evidential importance of testimony undermines his second point. But I will agree that something in the vicinity of Coady's third point is correct and then argue that this

---

[5] C. A. J. Coady, a defender of anti-reductionism, leans repeatedly on arguments that presuppose an externalist theory of justification. For example, see his approving discussion of Thomas Reid in C. A. J. Coady, *Testimony: A Philosophical Study* (Oxford: Clarendon Press, 1992), 120–130.

[6] See Evan Fales, *A Defense of the Given* (Lanham, MD: Rowman & Littlefield Publishers, 1996).

[7] Coady, *Testimony*.

furnishes us with the foundation on which to mount a somewhat different attack on Hume's assessment of testimony. It is the third point (or rather a reformulation of it) that underwrites a general principle of interpretive charity. Let us consider these points in order. First, there is no disputing our heavy reliance upon testimony as a source of knowledge. Take our knowledge that people do not (ordinarily, anyway) rise from the dead. What is the evidence for that belief? Not, surely, long graveyard vigils. It appears, rather, to derive from the fact that we would expect if people were to rise from the dead (even—or perhaps especially—rarely), then this fact would become common testimonial knowledge. Many people would know of those who have died and then returned to life. But this means that it is by way of testimony—or, in this case, by way of the absence of expected testimony— that we judge a bodily resurrection to be something extraordinary. Second, we now have sufficient knowledge of metabolic processes to understand why death is usually irreversible. But that biological understanding, if we have it, was acquired in large measure on the strength of learning from others (the biologists who contributed relevant biochemical knowledge).

There is nothing in this, however, that the reductivist cannot happily accept. For the reductivist will certainly agree that we somehow come to have grounds for accepting testimony, even as the only (or preponderant) direct evidence for many propositions we believe. When Coady points out how naturally, pervasively, and almost unthinkingly we resort to testimonial evidence, even in justifying quite ordinary beliefs, his examples often fail to acknowledge the tiered structure of such justification. Our primary justification for relying upon testimony begins to accrue even as we learn a language—more on this shortly—and gains nuance as we learn to use testimony to establish the bona fides of recognized experts whose testimony we can in turn rely upon. But a bottom-up approach to justification must genuinely begin at the bottom to gain any plausibility.

At issue, then, is whether those grounds must sometimes depend, circularly or question-beggingly, upon acceptance of testimony. No discovery, that most of what we believe can only be justified by some appeal to testimonial evidence, will serve by itself to unseat the reductivist's position. The critical question is whether our grounds for relying on testimony, in general and in particular cases, can be traced back to something more fundamental that is not itself also testimony. Now here is a natural picture of how a reductivist might argue for such a primitive grounding. The reductivist, so this story will go, relies upon a rather straightforward series of inductive inferences in assessing the epistemic bona fides of testimony. At a base level, she is able to compare what others testify about the world with her own experience of the world itself. Her brother tells her that there is some kielbasa in the refrigerator. She goes and looks and there it is. Her mother says that her father will return home from work at

5:30 and so he does. Her teacher explains that she can find such-and-such a book in the library and she does. Enough of this experiential confirmation and our observer has good grounds, absent voluminous countervailing evidence, for trusting personal testimony. Indeed, those grounds may well be strong enough, in particular cases, to override her own sense perception. Nothing in the reductivist position commits her to the silly view that her senses cannot err or that "testimony" cannot be overridden by testimony coming from the lips of others.

Over time, she discovers, in noting various instances of false testimony, that the class of testimonies can be divided into several relevance-classes along lines that have both to do with the content of the testimony and with the character of the testifier. She notices that sometimes testimony is false or dubious because of the difficulty of its subject matter; and she understands how this may lead to error. In a related fashion, she comes to factor in the competence of a testifier, if she can make such assessments, in judging the reliability of his testimony. She considers—again, if this is known or can be discovered—the integrity of the testifier: his honesty, judiciousness, possible motives for prevarication, and possible beliefs about the chances of escaping detection in a lie. All of these, so far as they can be known to her, cause her to update her posterior probability assignment for truth; singly or collectively, they may defeat her reliance upon the word of a particular testifier on a particular occasion without defeating her general reliance upon testimony.

Coady sometimes offers a caricature of this kind of reasoning as his target. He cites, for example, a study by Robert Buckhout demonstrating the low reliability of eyewitness testimony, only cheerily to note that Buckhout "reports to us on experiments not all of which he has done himself....All this would be laughable if it were not so common."[8] In somewhat more cautious remarks later, Coady acknowledges that many of Buckhout's conclusions about the unreliability of testimony must be taken seriously but condemns him for his "sweeping" condemnation of testimony.[9] But Coady's remarks ignore the context in which Buckhout was presenting his results: he was investigating the reliability of testimony about typical crime scenes and accidents for the purposes of establishing legal culpability. He was certainly not questioning, nor do any of his findings give us any reason to question, the processes by which scientific knowledge is established and transmitted in the scientific community. A reductivist will certainly protest that those techniques of transmission have been designed to be reliable, and if we have reason, testimonial or otherwise, to believe that this is so, then we (as well as Buckhout) have every right to such an inductively supported trust.

---

[8] Quoted in Coady, *Testimony*. 126–127.
[9] Ibid., 265–71.

The considerations just given in support of our principle of charity show, however, that this story is, at the very least, too simple. It is too simple, as earlier noted, in reconstructing language uptake as entirely dependent on conscious inductive inferences and, more crucially for the obvious reason, in suggesting that language-learning itself presupposes a context in which testimony is highly reliable. Absent that, no language-learner would discover the word-world regularities that she must depend upon to acquire semantic knowledge. Such massive truth-telling need not, nonetheless, permeate all of discourse. Achieving entry into a linguistic community requires regular truth-telling about a range of matters but leaves open the possibility of systematic error in more specialized domains, especially domains whose subject-matter lies at some distance from observational confirmation—that is, more theoretical claims.

What this means is that the very inductions that underwrite successful language acquisition also underwrite confidence in the pervasive veracity of testimony, at least about humdrum matters. Hence, Coady is right to observe that one could not both understand what one's interlocutors are saying and entertain, as a live possibility, that everything being said might be false and that, therefore, some further induction is required to establish the general trustworthiness of testimony.[10]

But Coady is surely being uncharitable when he takes Hume to be denying this in saying, "The reason why we place any credit in witnesses and historians, is not derived from any connexion, which we perceive a priori, between testimony and reality, but because we are accustomed to find conformity between them."[11] Clearly Hume was not considering in this context—as one might wish he had—the necessary conditions of language acquisition. Nonetheless, it is possible to construe him as making here a quite unexceptionable point: that there is no guarantee—no necessary connection—between a statement being made and that statement being true. Even if we must allow, as a condition for public discourse, the general reliability of testimonial content for a wide range of contexts and content, we cannot know *a priori*—and especially in more specialized contexts—how reliable testimony is. Experience would be our only guide.

Thus, no theory of testimony deserves to be taken seriously if it is not in accord with Hume's general common-sense observations about when testimony is to be trusted and when it is not. And this point, which for our purposes is the most essential one, holds whether a theory is reductivist or not. No one who ignores the character, reputation, and competence of a testifier (if known), as well as the nature of his access to the information

---

[10] C. A. J. Coady, *Testimony: A Philosophical Study* (Oxford: Clarendon Press, 1992), 177–230).

[11] David Hume, *An Inquiry Concerning Human Understanding*, ed. Charles W. Hendel (1748; repr., Indianapolis, IN: Bobbs-Merrill, 1955), 113.

purveyed, the presence or absence of motives for dissimulation, the likely chances of escaping fraud detection, and other such factors, could make a wise judge of the credibility of testimony.

It follows that as an objection to Hume's argument in "Of Miracles," anti-reductivism is nearly toothless. At most, it permits us to say only that a claim's being presented by way of testimony confers *prima facie* warrant for its truth. That leaves scope for overriders; and Hume's arsenal of overriders amply suffices to disarm this sort of defense of miracles. This point comes clearly into focus when we consider that a sensible man who witnesses the levitation of an Indian fakir judges reasonably that he is the intended victim of a clever deceit. Let him be as assured as Thomas Reid himself was that his eyes are God-given portals through which the world reliably reveals itself to him, let him understand that no cavil against their testimony can secure greater warrant than can be afforded by appeal to some other employment of his senses: yet that sensible man will rightly judge that the fakir has worked a trick upon his eyes. So much the more, upon merely hearing the testimony of others to the levitation, will he exercise suspicion. Moreover, it is precisely because his eyes and ears have taught him to be cautious that he is justified, by way of induction, in exercising it here. We shall have opportunity in Chapter 2 to examine much more extensively Hume's assessment of miracle reports. But there is nothing in the nature of testimony itself that undermines his argument in "Of Miracles."[12]

IV. Religious Thought and Reason

These quite general observations have implications for the study of religious language. The many complex and sophisticated uses of language have simple origins. They rely, in the first instance, upon the untutored observation of others and of the world, as well as the untutored employment of our ability to reason well, both inductively and deductively—well enough, at least, to discern and learn the conventional rules of a natural language, first by way of relying on non-conventional clues to discern the semantic intentions of the linguistically competent. That means that all the multi-layered levels of meaning that we encounter in theoretical and figurative uses of language must ultimately be explicable in a communicator's ability to make effective use of such simple cues to establish first-order conventions, and then to "play" upon those conventions

---

[12] Hume, *An Inquiry Concerning Human Understanding*, 117–41). For a further defense of this point that is neutral on the question of reductivism, see Jennifer Lackey "Religious Belief and the Epistemology of Testimony," in *The Oxford Handbook of the Epistemology of Theology*. William J. Abraham and Frederick D. Aquino, eds. (Oxford: Oxford University Press, (2017), 203–20.

in ways intelligible to others. It further means that authorial intent is primary to meaning, no matter the deviations in interpretation or application with the passage of time and changes in milieu.[13] And it means that language users must be able to exercise certain minimal capacities for rational thought, memory, and accurate observation of the world.

Religious language challenges these constraints in a variety of ways; indeed, so much so that the anthropology of religion is steeped in attempts to explain religious belief and practice that, at one point or another, impute to "primitive" people one or another species of systematic theoretical or practical irrationality. Especially during the latter half of the nineteenth century and the first half of the twentieth, such imputations of irrationality (even sheer imbecility) abounded. Savage peoples were, allegedly, prone to confuse dreams with reality,[14] or speech with the events described,[15] or to be simply incapable of reasoning as we moderns can.[16] In one way or another, these thinkers proposed explanations for one central aspect or another of religious belief that were predicated upon cognitive incapacities.

I will be arguing that the imputation of such deep kinds of cognitive failure is not congruent with what we have a right to expect of successful societies and cultures. I will also be arguing that it is not necessary to resort to such extreme measures to explain religious discourse and belief. Rather, I will argue that in many cases, we must on the contrary operate under the presumption that sacred texts display a very high degree of both rationality and general intelligence. Those arguments will, in turn, inform the methodology with which I will seek to understand sacred texts.

---

[13] See H. P. Grice, "Meaning," *The Philosophical Review* 66, no. 3 (1957): 377–88, http://doi.org/10.2307/2182440. Once linguistic conventions are in place, we can distinguish what a sentence uttered by a speaker means (its conventional meaning) from what the speaker meant to say by uttering it. Though these are ordinarily congruent, divorce from authorial intent is still possible and, sometimes, even intended—as when one jokingly makes use of a malapropism. But this merely serves to reinforce the observation that speaker intentions are primary: they are, after all, required to fix conventions in the first place, to say nothing of being fundamental to the whole point of language, which is to communicate thought.

[14] Edward B. Tylor, *Primitive Culture*, 6th ed. (New York: G. P. Putnam's Sons, 1922), 1:417–502; for a quick summary, see esp. pp. 499–502.

[15] James Frazer, *The Golden Bough: A Study in Magic and Religion*, Abridged ed. (New York: Macmillan & Co., 1922).

[16] Lucien Lévy-Bruhl, *How Natives Think*, trans. Lilian A. Clare (1910; repr., Princeton, NJ: Princeton University Press, 1985).

V. The Roles of Rules in Language

A. How Rules (Semantic and Syntactic) Help Us

But before turning to those matters, I must first say a bit more about language in general. Linguistic communication is, in its essence, governed by rules. Some of these rules are rigid, others are optional or flexible. But the rules (if we set aside features deriving from a universal "depth" grammar) are creatures of convention. Beyond the rule structures, we have pragmatics. The rules themselves provide a pragmatic solution to a practical need to gain substantial independence from pragmatic constraints. By this, I mean that conventional rules permit the use of language to "float free" of many of the contingent circumstances upon which one must rely if someone wishes to communicate in the absence of such mutually understood conventions. Absent the existence of linguistic signs whose conventional meanings one can rely upon to be understood, people are quite limited in conveying their thoughts to others. There exists no real help for this dilemma but to rely upon intimations in the environment and other non-verbal cues (e.g., gestures, facial expressions, miming of actions, and the like). Conventions—word meanings, grammatical rules, etc.—effect a radical gain in efficiency. They do so, in the first instance, by removing dependence upon context. One can communicate the danger from prowling tigers without having to be in close and visible proximity to one. Writing multiplies this efficiency since we no longer need to be next to the speaker.

These efficiencies do not defeat all pitfalls: occasional ambiguities, for example. But they also provide a platform on which second-order meanings can be erected, as with figurative uses of language. I say "second-order" because the communication of meaning here depends upon a shared understanding of literal meaning conventions, together with the presence of contextual cues that signal non-literal intentions. We need no longer be in the presence of the first-order (or literal) referents, but we do need to be "in the presence of" the first-order meaning conventions and other cues that point us both to the figure and to its intended meaning.[17] Figures, too, can become conventionalized; and third-order wordplay can help itself to this fact. And so on. Because rules can always be "played" with, there is no

---

[17] One could, with some charity, consider this to be the grain of truth that is reflected in the fundamentalist commitment to the literal truth of whatever is not obviously figurative in the Bible. But obviously, the fact that comprehension of literal meaning is essential to the comprehension of intended meaning goes little distance toward showing that the intended meaning is *merely* (and confined to) the literal meaning. It can be the exact contrary—as when an ironic tone tips us off that a speaker means to be denying what she is literally affirming. Of course, we will not know *what* she is denying unless we grasp what her sentence literally asserts.

reason to expect that a theory of language will ever be able to formalize either syntax or semantics fully. Nevertheless, intelligibility is preserved—so long as use and usage have lineages that can ultimately be traced back to the establishment of first-order meanings.

Word meaning and grammar are not the only convention-permeated aspects of language. Style and genre are two others. We shall have to pay some attention to genre, as the assignment of genre to texts such as the Gospel of Matthew will prove to be a contested, but exegetically important, matter. However, we may usefully observe here, first, that there is no *a priori* reason to think that genre distinctions will be sharp and definitive and, second, that genre conventions cannot fluctuate, change, or even be upended entirely if and when such revisions serve a creative author's purposes.

What the characteristics are that distinguish genres—and, for that matter, what genres there are—is up to a linguistic community to determine (though not necessarily by anything like deliberate choice). Genres are not natural kinds; as creatures of convention, they are artifacts whose utility in interpretation cannot but be a matter of what the relevant conventions are, how assiduously they are observed, and to what degree a linguistic community employs them to further certain communicative ends. Such a community may or may not impose sharp distinctions. One just has to see.

But even if custom imposes a clean taxonomy of genres in a given historical setting, there is no insurance that the mold would not be broken. Successfully breaking such molds—besides requiring perhaps considerable creativity and sometimes also courage—is dependent, as with the figurative use of words, upon prior shared understanding of the accepted genre-defining rules and upon the presence of contextual cues that tip an audience off that something new is afoot. An interpretation of a text as being of a mold-breaking kind should, ideally at least, specify what these cues are, how they would have pointed an intended audience to the interpretation being offered, and why the author might have wished to convey his or her meaning in this unorthodox way. But we can no more assume hide-bound adherence to genre (or other linguistic) conventions in an ancient text than we can assume with confidence that our own literary conventions will not be broken by creative contemporaries. That is most especially a possibility that should not be ruled out *a priori* when a text offers interpretive difficulties.

B. Performing Performatives

Finally, and somewhat in the same vein, we must bear in mind the uses of language for purposes other than fact-stating. It was J. L. Austin's theory of performatives that gave prominence to this point. I bring it up here because, in at least two ways, the complexities of performative force will require our attention. First, we may think of fictional discourse as having a different performative force than a fact-stating (or "constative") use of declarative sentences. But fiction, as is well known, can be used to convey truths. In some sense, then, these truths comprise part of the content of what fiction expresses, even though they may never be explicitly stated.

Indeed, the logic of fiction is complex and contested. Is the statement "Pegasus had wings" true or false? Both options are tempting. It is also tempting to judge the statement to lack a truth value—in which case it is arguably not a constative. Here, failure to have a truth value might be alleged on the grounds that "Pegasus" fails to refer to anything actual, but that would not reflect what is distinctive about fictional discourse. After all, reference-failure can occur also in non-fictional discourse. Consider, then, a fantasy in which "President George W. Bush grew wings" as a plot element. No reference failure here; yet we might still maintain that "true-in-the-fantasy" is not a truth value. "True-in-fiction" is, more nearly, a kind of performative operator since, as for performatives more generally, the saying (in the fiction) makes it true. More interesting for our purposes, however, is the consideration that the point of the fantasy might be to suggest that Mr. Bush is a saint. And that is a claim that (suitably disambiguated) is either true or false.

Second, there are performative uses of language that "overlap," in a sometimes logically uneasy but pragmatically important and powerful way, with the constative use of language. For instance, certain performative utterances, often taking the form of declarative sentences, provide institutionalized ways of inaugurating or effecting social facts—facts that the declaration also describes as obtaining. A standard example is promise-making. Another is "I pronounce you man and wife," when uttered on a suitable occasion by a suitable official to a suitable couple. The saying makes it so. Austin points out that performative uses of language are hedged about with conventions. These conventions invoke context, speaker, and hearer(s). Not just any utterance of "I promise" counts as a promise made. Like all conventions, these can be gamed in various ways to generate new performative uses of language; but ordinarily, the rules must be followed in order for the performative act to be accomplished.

But we must bear in mind a correlative fact about performative speech acts, which is that what they can achieve, in the relevant way, is only the creation of social facts—facts, like obligation or marriage—that are themselves dependent upon social conventions or norms. A saying cannot just make anything so. My saying that you have heart failure cannot make it the case that you die of a heart attack. Or at least, it cannot do so in the relevant way. And this brings out a point of some significance. The use of language can bring about all sorts of events—in particular, it can cause all sorts of effects upon those who receive the message (what Austin calls perlocutionary effects). But only some of these results will count as the sorts of things that are "done" in uttering a performative. Roughly, when something is performatively brought about, the utterance of the performative (under standard conditions) thereby (logically or conventionally) makes it the case that a certain conventionally defined result is achieved—e.g., a promise made, a bargain sealed—by *constituting* that achievement.

My saying that your heart is failing might, under special (but not conventionally defined) circumstances, give you such a fright as to induce a heart attack. Indeed, something like that is known to happen, in socially determined ways, in some cultures. For example, in some Australian Aborigine cultures, a suitable authority will place a curse on someone who has committed a terrible crime, a curse that declares the miscreant to be a "non-person" who should be absolutely shunned by fellow tribe members. The psychological effects of being cursed are so profound that recipients typically go into shock and die in a matter of days.[18]

But even though the shaman's *You are hereby accursed* (or whatever they say) is a performative utterance, in that the utterance (with ritual trappings) anathematizes the criminal, it is not a performance of the criminal's death, which is the result of a chain of causes set in motion by the anathematization. These causal connections are not defined by convention—even though it is conventional responses to the curse that cause fellow tribe members to behave in such a way that the criminal is unable to sustain himself in existence. In general, we may say that the utterance of a performative (e.g., "I promise") does not cause the performed act (e.g., a promise) to occur. It is (under convention-specified conditions) the doing of that act. Not every sort of thing that we do can be done—that is constituted—by the making of an utterance.

Nevertheless, attention to performative uses of language is of major importance to our study of religious communication. Religion, like language itself, is a deeply social phenomenon, and religious invocation, especially in ritual contexts, is surrounded by rules that determine when a performance is effective. But secondly, we must be alert to performative uses of religious language because the evaluation of performatives—their criteria for "rightness"—differ from those for constatives, which are either true or false. Constatives are the objects of belief, and properly believing a constative is a matter of having the right sort of evidence.

But performatives are neither true nor false.[19] Performative uses of language can be evaluated as being successful or unsuccessful, and they can be judged according to whether they satisfy the criteria that make them

---

[18] For documentation of this amazing phenomenon, see Walter Bradford Cannon, "'Voodoo' Death," *American Journal of Public Health* 92, no. 10 (2002): 1593–96, http://dx.doi.org/10.2105/ajph.92.10.1593.

[19] Except for certain cases, as briefly noted in Chapter 4, that occupy an uneasy middle-ground.

appropriate or misplaced. When I make you a promise, you may believe that I will (or will not) keep my word, and you may believe that I have made a promise to you. But, as Austin points out, believing either of these things is not a matter of believing what I said when I uttered "I promise." Therefore, if some religious utterances function as performatives, it would be misplaced to evaluate them along the dimensions of truth or falsehood and to evaluate acceptance of them as rational or irrational in terms of evidence. If we discover religious doctrines whose acceptance does not appear subject to the usual norms of evidential scrutiny, it will be amiss to ignore the possibility that language is here being used in a performative, not a constative, way. At the same time, not just anything can be done by means of performative uses of language. Standards of rationality still apply, but in a different way.

A primary concern, then, is with two different ways in which such evidence can be relevant to the assessment of truth-value. It will emerge that failure to consider this distinction may account for the extent to which anthropologists and philosophers have found themselves driven onto one horn or the other of the persistent dilemma which offers the choice that either the natives are irrational, or else the standards for rationality must be relativized.[20] I hope here to chart part of the course that will steer us between the Scylla of ethnocentrism and the Charybdis of unintelligibility.

This puts the matter quite abstractly. I will turn to specific cases in due course. I shall do so in the course of considering how our general observations concerning the prerequisites for linguistic communication constrain interpretation. Communication, we know, is effective because we can trust that others have a shared understanding of the rules and conventions governing our common language, as well as because we can, with good reason, expect that they are committed to the same use (and sometimes the intelligible bending) of those conventions in such a way as to make themselves understood and because we are prepared to give them the benefit of the doubt if difficulties arise. Hence, the gift of language requires of us faith, hope, and charity.

VI. The Greatest of These is Charity

The greatest rule to apply is charity because it reflects the expectation that other language users possess some level of rationality and, therefore, will deploy the rules that make linguistic communication both possible and efficient. Charity has at least three dimensions. First, a common language presupposes common perceptual access to a world of public objects, events,

---

[20] The term "native" sometimes has derogatory connotations. I do not intend those connotations here. By "native," I simply mean those who are at home in a given culture or members of a given society.

qualities, and states of affairs: a shared world of items that can be identified, re-identified, and become (presumably) identifiable by others. Otherwise, there will be no attaching linguistic signs to common referents. We need, then, to take our interlocutors to have epistemic access to our world. Second, mastery of at least simple forms of deductive reasoning is a necessary condition of learning a language.[21] Third, language learning requires a rather sophisticated ability to reason inductively. Everyone who speaks a language must, therefore, be capable of reasoning in these ways. Our principle of charity, therefore, will accomplish two things. First, it will serve to block any radical form of cultural relativism with respect to the norms of rationality and perception. And second, it will place a quite non-trivial constraint upon the task of judging the credentials of alternative interpretations of a text.

A. Rationality and Truth

All three of these abilities are essential to the ways in which we form true beliefs about the world. That many of a person's beliefs are true is, indeed, a significant test of his or her rationality.[22] It might be objected that this standard does not provide us with an objective criterion of rationality. After all, when I judge another person's beliefs, I do so by my lights; a madman will, presumably, judge that everyone is mad but him. Nevertheless, within our own culture at least, we do not have too much difficulty distinguishing those whose beliefs are for the most part true from those whose beliefs are largely false or outlandish. The mad are, among other handicaps, usually unable to fend for themselves.

The criterion of true belief becomes rather more acute when we are faced with the beliefs of people from another culture. Many such cultures systematically endorse beliefs that seem to us clearly false. However, making the claim that they are transparently false, and that their bearers are commensurately irrational, opens one to the charge of ethnocentrism. It has, therefore, been urged in some quarters that the standards for assessing rationality—among them, the means for judging whether beliefs are true or false—are context-relative, with no culture being privileged over others.[23]

---

[21] Deductive reasoning is essential to establish logical consistency (a minimal condition on coherence). And this consistency—in effect, the recognition of the opposition between truth and falsity—is a necessary condition for assertions to be used in such a way that their meaning can be discerned.

[22] Not that all beliefs count equally; some will be more significant than others. This fact is, in part, a function of the kind of evidence someone has, or ought to have, for a given belief.

[23] As by Peter Winch, *The Idea of a Social Science and Its Relation to Philosophy* (New York: Routledge and Keegan Paul, 1958); "Understanding a Primitive

But such relativism threatens to break down the notion of rationality altogether and with it the intelligibility of the proposition that public discourse must be grounded, however tenuously, in the possibility of objective criticism. The reason for this becomes apparent when we consider the conditions necessary for the learning of a language in the first place. As we just saw, language learning—indeed, learning any of the mores, conventions, and usages of a culture—requires reliable empirical access to a shared world, accurate memory, and mastery of various inference patterns. These could not themselves be learned, as any learning process presupposes them; *a fortiori*, they could not be culture-dependent contingencies. For if they were, only by learning could they be acquired. This places our thinking about other cultures under the following constraint: if we take them—as of course we do—to be language users (more generally, users of any mode of communication that depends on convention and not merely biologically-determined instincts), then it must be possible for us to learn their language. For, no matter what our cultural baggage may be, we share with them the general prerequisites for language; if it were otherwise, they could not teach their own children to communicate.

Now, shared access to a common world implies (at least) the acquisition of a large body of true beliefs about that world. That is a precondition of language learning for, unless you can discover that there are (say) pangolins in the vicinity when I point at one, you will not be in a position to discover what I mean (absent descriptors whose meanings you have previously mastered). Another prerequisite is, of course, that I (and others) are for the most part consistent in our use of the term "pangolin": we use that particular word, not others, when we refer to pangolins, and we do not blithely use "pangolin" to refer, capriciously, to pottos and potatoes.

It is indeed not sufficient that we should judge a person rational by the extent to which his or her beliefs accord with what we judge to be true. A further conceptual requirement, embedded in the very notion of rational procedure, is that both the person's beliefs and ours be subjected to the canons of control by empirical evidence.[24] As complex and as resistant to easy formulation as the rules for assessing evidential strength are, my concern here will not be with these rules. Rather, I want to point to another way in which evidence can be relevant to the assessment of utterances because I believe failure to consider this alternative has played a significant

---

Society," *American Philosophical Quarterly* 1 (1964): 307–24; and a host of postmodernists since.

[24] The exception is that those truths which can be known *a priori* and which must, at least, be subject to control by rational intuition. For more on these matters, see Martin Hollis, "Reason and Ritual," in *Rationality*, ed. Bryan R. Wilson (New York: Harper and Row, 1970), 214–20 and "The Limits of Irrationality," in *Rationality*, ed. Bryan R. Wilson (New York: Harper and Row, 1970), 221–39.

role in driving anthropologists and philosophers either to conclude certain alien cultures are irrational or that the standards of rationality must be relativized. This false dilemma becomes especially poignant when the alien culture is what gave us our own religious heritage. We need an alternative to ethnocentrism on the one hand and unintelligibility on the other.

Since it is possible for a false belief to be rationally held, it is logically possible for many (or perhaps even all empirical) beliefs that a rational person might hold to be false. However, it would not be possible for such a person to speak a public language. Clearly, the extent to which beliefs are true, used as a test of rationality, must be decidedly informal in character; similarly, ability to master a public language requires only a rather minimal, and not formally specifiable, level of rational competence. (But someone's ability to use a language well, and with sophistication, is a pretty good measure of intellectual competence and one we regularly rely upon.)

However, all this is a matter of degrees. Not only is truth by no means the only test of rationality, but we cannot say *a priori* how permeated a person's beliefs must be with falsehood before we are justified in judging him or her (more or less) irrational. However, it is indicative of the fact that truth is a relevant test. Where a person's belief is false and we wish, nevertheless, to claim that this in no way reflects adversely upon his or her rationality, we must assume the burden of explaining how he or she (reasonably) came to hold that belief. That requires consideration of the evidence a person has and so immediately forces us to consider the care with which he or she assesses the truth-value of other propositions.[25]

Because evidential support and belief both admit of degrees, we also expect rational persons to adjust their firmness of conviction to the strength of their evidence. So, evaluation of rationality places stronger emphasis on correctness concerning beliefs whose truth or falsity is easy to ascertain and as well expects people's reservations to track their difficulty of confirmation. It is just here that anthropologists have faced a dilemma. For

---

[25] There is a third facet of language that charitable interpretation must be sensitive to, one that is often under-recognized. We must attend to the various ways in which language will evolve so as to maximize, when possible, efficiency of communication. This can produce shortcuts that, taken naïvely, can appear to short-change truth. Color vocabularies (to take a trivial example) vary substantially from one language to another. That a Melanesian islander might describe both an apple and an orange as "red" in her language does not mean that she is incapable of detecting color differences—any more than our own lack of nuances in the English language. No sensible language would have a term for every discriminable shade of color. However, every natural language, so far as I know, has indexical terms, using context-sensitive rules to achieve efficiencies in reference-fixing that descriptions and proper names cannot match.

among the beliefs that natives[26] seem to accord the greatest conviction are those that seem to Westerners as the most bizarre and the least susceptible to positive confirmation. Finding themselves in this situation (and given the infirmities of relativized standards of rationality), are anthropologists to take their results as evidence for the irrationality of the natives, as suggesting the inadequacy of their analyses, or as reason to doubt their own rationality?

B. The Rationality of Religious Beliefs

As will become evident, I consider it salutary to consider the rationality of religious beliefs by beginning with beliefs that seem most alien to our own heritage. This encourages a kind of distancing that can sensitize us to puzzles and issues that might otherwise be much less visible. For this, there is no better source than the ethnographic literature and efforts of anthropologists to come to grips with the problems of interpreting native sacred stories and rituals. A large body of ethnographic data has also encouraged comparative studies and a search for cultural universals.

If all that seems removed from an understanding of Judeo-Christian traditions, then that is, in part, because of the failure of most scholars of Western religion—Bible scholars in particular—sufficiently to think about the insights that the anthropology of religion might have to offer.[27] At the very least, we should take note of the fact that Second Temple Judaism, both before and during the early formation of Christianity, was a tribal society with a largely tribal culture. It was, moreover, a culture whose distance from our own is to some extent masked by continuity of traditions—a continuity that foreshortens the lapse of time and awareness of the gradual processes that have altered that tradition's self-understanding. Let us, therefore, first think about the problems of interpretation in relation to cultures that are incontestably alien from our own.

People of (so-called) primitive cultures clearly display no lack of rationality when it comes to conducting the everyday business of their lives. What makes the anthropologist's puzzle so acute is the incongruity between this evident rationality and a startling lack of rationality with respect to those other beliefs that we call religious and magical (and that are commingled

---

[26] I will use the term "natives," without prejudice, to denote those who participate in a culture, especially in those tribal cultures that anthropologists have traditionally studied. More and more, anthropologists are directing their inquiries to more "modern" societies, if only because tribal cultures have become so badly destroyed, corrupted, or infiltrated by external influences.

[27] There are, increasingly, scholars who are attempting to correct this deficiency. I will be appealing to some of their work throughout this book. It must be said that anthropologists have, in the main, avoided examination of biblical texts.

and sometimes quite continuous with thought about the mundane.[28] Moreover, the internal evidence strongly suggests that these puzzling beliefs are construed by natives as propositions bearing (often empirically accessible) truth-values. The problems this generates are, indeed, the very same as those that, in various guises, have for two centuries formed a central dilemma for the hermeneutical tradition within our own culture.[29]

In the face of this dilemma, one extreme strategy has been to deny the idea that native thought is rational; a second has been to preserve the label "rational" at the price of relativizing the notion beyond the bounds of intelligibility. Steven Lukes and Martin Hollis have effectively disqualified both these strategies, arguing from the perspective of the possibility of radical translation.[30] The point applies with equal force when one considers, as I did above, the necessary conditions for the learning of a first language. A third maneuver has been to assign religious and magical beliefs a special logical status. They are not taken to be either true or false, but to be metaphorical or "expressive." But this strategy only postpones the day of reckoning, the time when the question must be faced: what is the metaphor a metaphor for? What is thereby being expressed? In the end, the strategy runs afoul of the fact that the natives give clear evidence of affirming or denying such propositions.

The difficulty of the problem is underscored by the fact that Lukes and Hollis themselves try to defend compromising positions, holding views that give religious beliefs a "free pass" while imposing rationality constraints upon the more mundane discourse that can serve as a "bridgehead" to understanding the native language and conceptual system. Thus, Lukes makes a distinction between context-free criteria for rationality and context-dependent ones:

> Then there are contextually-provided criteria of truth....Such criteria may apply to beliefs ... which do not satisfy rational (1) criteria in so far

---

[28] See Hollis, "The Limits of Irrationality," 238. For a typical example of the integration of religious belief with mundane affairs, see Godfrey Lienhardt, *Divinity and Experience: The Religion of the Dinka* (New York: Clarendon Press, 1961).

[29] A useful history of post-Reformation developments in hermeneutics can be found in Hans W. Frei, *The Eclipse of Biblical Narrative: A Study in Eighteenth and Nineteenth Century Hermeneutics* (New Haven, CT: Yale University Press, 1974).

[30] Steven Lukes, "Some Problems about Rationality," in *Rationality*, ed. Bryan R. Wilson (New York: Harper and Row, 1970), 194–213; Hollis, "Reason and Ritual," 214–20; "The Limits of Irrationality," 221–39. Hollis insists upon the *a priori* nature of these arguments. Given that the natives are language users—something that must, of course, be discovered empirically—these arguments follow inescapably from the conditions on the possibility of language learning that apply even to native speakers. Discovery that the vocalizations in alien cultures are linguistic is no different in principle than the parallel discovery made by someone learning a first language.

as they do not and could not correspond with 'reality': that is, in so far as they are in principle neither directly verifiable nor directly falsifiable by empirical means. (They may, of course, be said to relate to 'reality' in another sense; alternatively, they may be analyzed in terms of the coherence or pragmatist theories of truth.) This is to disagree with Leach and Beattie who seek to discount the fact that beliefs are accepted as true and argue that they must be interpreted metaphorically. But it is also to disagree with the Frazer-Tylor approach, which would simply count them false because they are 'non-objective.'[31]

In a similar vein, Hollis states,

Ritual beliefs, by contrast, do not have objectively specifiable truth-conditions. To be sure, a Yoruba, who believed a box covered with cowrie shells to be his head or soul, might take that belief to be true. But this is not to say that any fact referred to is objectively specifiable. Consequently the anthropologist cannot use the facts to get at the beliefs: he can, at best, use the beliefs to get at the facts. Here, then, is a first difference between ritual and everyday beliefs.[32]

It is not clear what facts Hollis intends the anthropologist to acquire. With respect to ritual beliefs, he considers the correspondence theory of truth to be "beside the point"[33] and suggests that the appropriate standards of assessment are those deriving from a coherence theory.

But, unsurprisingly, these strategies are unhelpful. Lukes does not offer any wisdom on how context-dependent criteria are to be discovered nor on how context is even to be specified in a neutral way. And to appeal, as Hollis does, to a coherence theory of truth makes unintelligible our access to the content of ritual beliefs. Coherence itself must be judged by content-independent criteria, so coherence does not tell us—or the natives themselves—what ritual beliefs are about. What is worse, ritual beliefs, so understood, are typically not consistent with ordinary, mundane beliefs. The Australian Aborigine who calls an emu his father knows, we may be sure, the ordinary facts of emu (and human) procreation.[34]

---

[31] Lukes, "Some Problems about Rationality," 211. Elsewhere, Lukes suggests that the latter criteria may be "parasitic" upon the former, but does not say how this occurs (Steven Lukes, "Relativism: Cognitive and Moral," *Aristotelian Society: Supplementary Volume* 48 [1974]: 165–89). Below, I offer a way of partly cashing this biological metaphor.

[32] Hollis, "The Limits of Irrationality," 223.

[33] Ibid., 235. See also, Kai Nielsen, "Rationality and Relativism," *Philosophy of the Social Sciences* 4 (1974): 324.

[34] Hollis provides no justification for the claim that ritual beliefs are not empirically accessible *except* for the claim that they are not otherwise intelligible. But

Coherence may be a more complex matter than mere consistency, though it requires at least this. Perhaps religious systems function as explanatory theories and, just as we are often able to explain away counterevidence to our own theories as "bad data," so too perhaps native theologians can rescue their religious commitments from counterevidence by means of parallel strategies. And this is how it sometimes seems, in fact, to go. In Zandeland, witches are identified by means of a ritual in which chickens are fed a poison, *benge*, made from the bark of a vine. The *benge* is instructed to kill the chicken if so-and-so is a witch; otherwise let the chicken live. The experiment is controlled: a second chicken is fed a similar dose of *benge*, which is instructed to let the chicken live if so-and-so is a witch. Only if the *benge* delivers a "guilty" verdict in both trials is the verdict (provisionally) secured. But the test is fallible; two poison oracles may give contradictory verdicts. What then? The Azande, a Sudanese tribe, will tell you that one oracle may have misfired because, for example, the poison had been improperly prepared or improperly invoked; thus, the oracle delivered bad data. The king's oracle, however, is deemed infallible.[35]

So, it appears that Azande oracle beliefs might offer something like a way of understanding how and why *benge* functions to expose witches—and why it might occasionally fail. On that sort of reading, a religious theory may indeed serve to explain experience, whatever else it does. Azande, presumably, theorize that *benge* is able—under the right conditions—to uncover witches. But an explanatory theory of this sort must at least have empirical content; even if it is the "theory as a whole" that stands before the court of empirical evidence, confirmation and disconfirmation must still be possible. Yet, Azande do not seem to countenance disconfirmation.[36]

Not only that, but Azande appear to be curiously uninterested in discovering, or even speculating about, how *benge* can identify witches (and all manner of other things). It might be that they think the poison is some kind of spirit or person. Edward Evans-Pritchard observes,

> Old men say that fully grown birds ought not to be used in oracle consultations because they are too susceptible to the poison and have a

---

why are we to take their apparent freedom from empirical control as an indication that different standards must be applied to them rather than as a sign that anthropological analysis has as yet been insufficiently penetrating? To refuse to concede relativization of rationality with respect to the rules of logic, and yet allow it with respect to the canons of evidence, surely requires some additional justification. Indeed, Hollis does *not* permit the latter kinds of relativization to infect the translation of "bridgehead" statements.

[35] See Edward Evan Evans-Pritchard, *Witchcraft, Oracles, and Magic Among the Azande* (Oxford: Clarendon Press, 1937), 258–351.

[36] For example, Azande believe that the children of a witch are also witches. Given that belief and the interrelatedness of Azande, it should follow that all of them are witches. But they draw no such inference.

> habit of dying straight away before the poison has had time to consider the matter placed before it or even to hear the full statement of the problem. On the other hand, a [young] chicken remains for a long time under the influence of the poison before it recovers or expires, so that the oracle has time to hear all the relevant details concerning the problem placed before it and to give a well-considered judgment.[37]

But Evans-Prichard goes on to deny that the Azande think of *benge* in personal terms, saying that they simply think of it as having what amounts to efficacy.[38] Now it would, to put it mildly, be a miracle if an inanimate substance—powdered bark from a vine—understood spoken questions, knew their answers, and could regulate its toxicity accordingly. But to Azande, these powers seem quite ordinary.

It is not easy, then, to imagine what, rationally speaking, the Azande could be thinking. All of the explanatory options considered thus far reflect a strained attempt to make the natives, in their religious (or magical) moments, out to be hardnosed empiricists or even to be guided by ordinary common sense. Among those who wish to rescue the natives from charges of irrationality and gullibility, we find those who would bend the notion of reason to suit the occasion (i.e., Peter Winch), and those who (rightfully) reject such freedom with the conditions of rationality but still argue that religious beliefs are rational in some special or partly defective way.

It seems, then, that we are driven to say that native religious beliefs are false—and more or less loony, to boot. But have we not given up too soon? Have we utilized all the conceptual resources that a rational society makes intelligible and available to us? There may be other possibilities not yet canvassed. Certainly, we shall have to allow people in other cultures as wide a scope for irrationality as we find (alas) in our own. But an inanimate substance that understands a foreign language (the vine does not grow in Zandeland) and discerns witches at a distance? Perhaps anthropologists have just misunderstood magical and religious beliefs (at least the ones that seem to float free of the criteria for rationality). Perhaps they have, if you will, been misinterpreting or mistranslating what the natives are saying when they express those beliefs.

It is, after all, commonplace, for example, that figurative uses of language, taken literally, do not yield truths or even plausibilities. The desert sun is, after all, not (literally) an unblinking eye. If an Australian Aborigine observes that the sun is a white cockatoo, perhaps he is indulging in

---

[37] Evans-Pritchard, *Witchcraft, Oracles, and Magic*, 282. It might be objected that the example appeals to magical beliefs, not religious ones. But the point is quite general (I could have picked an example involving religious beliefs), and it is in any case not so easy to distinguish magic from religion as some anthropologists have done.

[38] Evans-Pritchard, *Witchcraft, Oracles, and Magic*, 318–22.

metaphor—to which he has just as much right as we. The Azande, however, regulate their lives by the verdicts of their poison oracles. So, it is not enough to imagine that religious claims are only flights of poetic fancy. Their "cash value" —whatever it is—is a matter of great importance and real consequence to them.

It is of course not logically perverse to ascribe irrationality to particular people on particular occasions. That people make mistakes is commonplace; hence, no plausible principle of charity can forbid such ascriptions. But when our interpretation of native beliefs entails the ascription of systematic irrationality and ignoring all evidence to the contrary, then there is serious pressure to question the astuteness of the attribution itself. That pressure becomes particularly acute in light of the general admission that natives are quite capable of thoroughly rational behavior in other contexts.

Now there is admittedly nothing logically impossible about even systematic falsity of belief, within certain constraints. A brief reflection upon one's attitude toward one's favorite case of a misguided philosophical or political position should be sufficient to convince one of this fact. That the falsity of a set of beliefs is systematic may even enhance their appeal or, at any rate, help protect them against criticism. Nevertheless, when a native theory is understood in terms of an interpretation under which it has no evidence going for it or is subject to obvious disconfirmation, we will at least need to account for the irrationality we purport to have discovered. And this has, in live cases, not been at all easy to do without appealing to certain highly questionable assumptions about native mentality, whose only supporting evidence is often the very interpretations in question. We may conclude, then, that to the extent an interpretation enables us to avoid adding such *ad hoc* explanatory hypotheses, to that extent it should have, *prima facie*, an *a priori* claim upon our credulity.

Having said this much, let it at once be admitted that there are belief systems whose adherents exhibit varying degrees of intelligence and rationality or of stubbornness in the face of contrary evidence. Our own intellectual history is not particularly innocent on that score. And, as with "native" beliefs, it is appropriate to demand that an explanation for the tenure of such views be forthcoming. But even if we admit that there are severe dislocations between, for example, certain modern Christian ideologies and other beliefs that a scientific or even a common-sense approach to the empirical evidence would sustain, it must still be admitted that there is a sense in which, for a member of a practicing Christian society, the requisite ideology is in some ways rational—that is, "makes sense." For within the terms upon which social practice in such a society is founded, it is the relevant ideological tenets that provide the appropriate justification and guidance for action—and action so guided typically produces the desired social results within that context. For an individual to criticize these tenets themselves, on the other hand, may well have the rather drastic result of removing him or her from the arena of social effectiveness altogether.

Nevertheless, the skeptic will of course insist that the reasons the Christian uses to explain the success of her social system are not the reasons that in fact explain that success.[39] Let us say that belief in a social ideology that fails to accommodate the preponderant evidence concerning the nature of the world (social and/or natural), but that nevertheless "works" in the sense that belief in it mobilizes the appropriate and effective socialized behavior, is itself a weakly rational belief. Belief in such a theory satisfies certain pragmatic needs quite successfully for the believer, in the proper social context, even though the theory may not account for certain independent evidence that the believer would be hard-put to deny. Let us, on the other hand, call strongly rational a social ideology that reasonably justifies in terms of available evidence the social interactions that govern and make viable the social system in which that ideology functions.[40] Now of course, any believer in a social ideology will insist that her belief is rational in the strong sense. But she may be wrong. She may be wrong, for instance, in her assertion that all good deeds will be rewarded and all evil ones punished at some final day of reckoning—even though her doubting this may be irrational in the restricted sense that the viability of her social system depends upon general agreement that the claim is true.

The existence of weakly rational ideologies cannot be ruled out *a priori*. Nonetheless, our methodological preference must be for interpretations that present an ideology as being strongly rational; only if we have independent evidence to the contrary, or if such an interpretation fails on internal grounds, can resort plausibly be made to an interpretation that imputes only weak rationality to the natives. Functionalist interpretations of religion are typically of the latter kind. And, indeed, we may frequently be able to supply explanations—usually historical in nature—to show how a system, through entrenchment in an inflexible tradition, comes to embody an enfeebled rationality.[41] But it is especially hard to see how a new ideology

---

[39] For example, the Christian believes her society is blessed because the faithful pray to a God who answers; the functionalist sociologist suggests that prayer binds congregants into a cohesive group whose unity and commitment to common goals enhances the likelihood that those goals will be achieved.

[40] My terminology here coincides with that of I. C. Jarvie and Joseph Agassi, "The Problem of the Rationality of Magic," in *Rationality*, ed. Bryan R. Wilson (New York: Harper and Row, 1970), 173. However, my distinction is not theirs.

[41] Structure-functionalists have tended to see social arrangements as subject to something like Darwinian selection; there was debate over the existence of "survivals"—institutions that no longer served any useful purpose or were even deleterious. But there is no reason why in principle, like vestigial organs, institutions may not outlive their original rationale or purposes and survive, if only because change itself exacts costs.

can come initially to be adopted on grounds that supply only a weak rationality. Weak rationality generally requires the umbilical cord of tradition to sustain it. Yet at the same time, the logical status of tradition is just such as to make entrenchment-induced weak rationality harder to achieve (and strong rationality easier to achieve!) than might be supposed.

All social organizations require traditions of some sort (in the broadest sense of imposed uniformities of practice). And, though this might be disputed, I take it that the rationality (in the strong sense) of any particular system of traditions is underdetermined by the ecological situation in which a society finds itself. Past history supplies many additional constraints. Considering a society synchronically, however, against the background of external environmental constraints (and the basic requirements of survival), I think we discover that purely logical and empirical constraints are insufficient to determine uniquely an optimal set of social rules, especially when limitations in the ability of even very intelligent natives to ascertain optimality are taken into consideration. Since, however, it is surely more rational to have some particular set of rules, subject to constraints of internal coherence and the meeting of social necessities, than it is to have none, an element of conventionality must be introduced in the decisions that are made or are imposed by tradition. A failure to distinguish between such conventional aspects of social systems, which may vary quite remarkably from one society to the next, from the empirical and logical constraints that nevertheless confine such conventionality, has contributed heavily to the thinking that has led Winch and others into a position of extreme relativism.

A far more interesting and fruitful suggestion has been made by Robin Horton, who considers native religious and magical doctrines to constitute explanatory theories that exhibit strong structural parallels to our own scientific theories.[42] Horton details a number of these isomorphisms,

---

[42] Robin Horton, "African Traditional Thought and Western Science," in *Rationality*, ed. Bryan R. Wilson (New York: Harper and Row, 1970), 131–71. Horton seems to minimize the importance of one of the structural similarities between the two. Emile Duhem propounded the thesis, much emphasized in subsequent reflection on science, that scientific laws are interconnected in such a way that no single experimental result is sufficient to falsify a law: failures in prediction can be explained away by appeal to outside interference, non-standard conditions, errors regarding other laws, etc. Precisely this kind of defensive strategy is detailed by Evans-Pritchard's account of how the Azande explain the apparent failures of their poison oracles and other witchcraft practices (see Evans-Pritchard, *Witchcraft, Oracles, and Magic*, 466–78). Just where one crosses the line from reasonable defense of a theory against apparent counterevidence to stubbornness is not amenable to algorithmic determination. (But to admit this is not to open the door to the kind of radical epistemological relativism that tempted Thomas Kuhn and some others.) That African natives are more stubborn or irrational in this respect than the history of modern science bears Westerners out to be remains, I think, to

and while objections can be raised at numerous points regarding both his conception of science and his interpretation of native thought, I believe this type of approach suffers far less from the opposing sins of relativism or ethnocentrism.[43] Nevertheless, I do not think Horton's approach goes nearly far enough. This is partly due to the fact that Horton, while correctly distinguishing native theory from science, locates the grounds for the distinction in a misleading way, one that convicts the natives of a far more pervasive epistemological myopia than they may deserve.

Since I agree with Horton that there is an important distinction here, it will be useful to consider what he says about the distinction between native theory and science: "What I take to be the key difference is a very simple one. It is that in traditional cultures there is no developed awareness of alternatives to the established body of theoretical tenets; whereas in scientifically oriented cultures, such an awareness is highly developed."[44] Horton uses this lack of conceptual alternatives to explain the fact that

> A central characteristic of nearly all the traditional African world-views we know of is an assumption about the power of words, uttered under appropriate circumstances, to bring into being the events or states they stand for....
>
> Now if we take into account what I have called the basic predicament of the traditional thinker, we can begin to see why this assumption should be so deeply entrenched in life and thought. Briefly, no man can make contact with reality save through a screen of words. Hence no man can escape the tendency to see a unique and intimate link

---

be demonstrated. Such greater reluctance to scrap established doctrines as does exist among them can, I think, be better explained by the forthcoming considerations.

[43] See the important exchange between John Skorupski, "Science and Traditional Religious Thought," *Philosophy of the Social Sciences* 3 (1973): 209–30; "Comment on Professor Horton's Paradox and Explanation," *Philosophy of the Social Sciences* 5 (1975): 63–70; and Robin Horton, "Paradox and Explanation: A Reply to Mr. Skorupski," *Philosophy of the Social Sciences* 3 (1973): 231–56. I am in rough agreement with Skorupski's elucidation of the non-paradoxicality of the relationship between observable entities and the congeries of invisible subcomponents into which the scientist analyzes these, though I will not give a detailed reply to Horton's arguments concerning scientific explanation here. I agree, moreover, with Skorupski's conclusion, contra Horton, that *this* relationship is not the place to look in Western thought for a counterpart to puzzling native notions of unity-in-diversity. It does *not* follow that the only available analogy is to *paradoxical* elements in Western thought. There may be—indeed I think there are—detailed analogies to thoroughly *non*-paradoxical Western conceptual traditions. What those better analogies might be is a matter I defer to Chapter 4, where I will show how they shed light on Western religious "mysteries" and suggest—confirming one of Horton's suspicions—an original explanatory (and non-paradoxical) function for them, as well.

[44] Horton, "African Traditional Thought and Western Science," 153.

between words and things. For the traditional thinker this tendency has an overwhelming power. Since he can imagine no alternatives to his established system of concepts and words, the latter appear bound to reality in an absolute fashion. There is no way at all in which they can be seen as varying independently of the segments of reality they stand for. Hence they appear so integrally involved with their referents that any manipulation of the one self-evidently affects the other.[45]

This view is reminiscent of old "associationist" theories of magic, such as James Frazer's, and it convicts the natives of a blunder that is implausible to imagine them guilty of. Indeed, it violates one of the conditions necessary for learning a language at all: if "no man can make contact with reality save through a screen of words," then how would a newborn acquire a language at all; and how would empirical evidence-driven conceptual change be possible? If Africans are guilty of this confusion between words and world, why do they not press the conclusion further and, abandoning their labor in the fields, content themselves with a ritual description of the products of that activity? Why is it that—as Godfrey Lienhardt points out—the Dinka only pray for rain when the rainy season is about to commence? Nor is it clear on Horton's theory why the natives take their utterances to be efficacious only when uttered in certain ritual contexts and by certain designated officials. This suggests that we should seek an interpretation that can at least partially vindicate native practice by showing that their words, properly uttered, really do have power in at least some situations of fundamental concern to them. This, we shall see, is not as implausible as it seems. The result will be that, while we will have marked out a difference between scientific theory and native mythology, we will in no sense have denigrated the latter. Rather, it will be rescued from a kind of criticism that is inappropriate to it.

I want to examine therefore what sense can be given to the notion of a "socially defined truth" and of an efficacious utterance. For, conformably with the methodological constraints imposed upon anthropologists, we ought to hold native statements to be true and strongly rational whenever we have no good independent explanation as to why these people should be deceived.

C. Conventions and Performatives

In many human societies there are certain persons who are recognized as having a special power to perceive and speak the truth. A few examples, picked more or less at random, will serve to illustrate this phenomenon. Among the Dinka, the headmen of certain clans—masters of the fishing spear—are said, when possessed during certain rituals by a power or spirit

---

[45] Horton, "African Traditional Thought," 155–56.

known as Flesh, to speak the Truth concerning social matters.[46] Among the Azande, it is held that the verdicts of the king's oracle are above suspicion.[47] Similarly, the Roman Catholic pope is considered, by virtue of being in the line of apostolic succession, to be infallible when speaking *ex cathedra*.

Are these various examples all classifiable as instances of a single kind of phenomenon? If so, what sort of logical status may we assign to pronouncements of the sort illustrated? To see that there is an interesting problem here, and to forestall the quick response that such statements are simply either true or false (and by no means guaranteed to be true), I shall shortly consider a case that is closer to home. But first, it is worthy of notice that in almost all instances in which such special insight is attributed to a member of a society, that member occupies one of a number of antecedently specifiable official positions in the social organization of the group. Legitimate occupancy of such a position is itself determined by cultural norms. While general intelligence may help to qualify a person for such a position, and will often cause others to heed his or her words with particular care, intelligence is usually not a necessary (and is never a sufficient) condition. Moreover, the special status of such a person's words is conferred upon them after he or she acquires the role in question, not before.[48] Among the Dinka, one must be a member of a fishing-spear clan in order to be possessed by the spirit Flesh, and the dicta taken most seriously are those spoken by a fishing-spear master having been possessed during previous ritual ceremonies. Statements made by the pope have a similar status for Catholics only when issued under the proper formalities.

How can such practices be rational? Since investiture and insight may seem logically distinct matters, it will help if I advert to a more familiar example. Arguments over what is and what is not the law of the United States frequently turn upon points of interpretation of the Constitution; and in such matters, the Supreme Court is the established adjudicator of disputed claims. Members of the Court will ordinarily be selected on the basis of their intelligence, legal scholarship, and wisdom, but it is clear that these are neither necessary nor sufficient conditions. It is sufficient that a person be duly nominated and confirmed according to certain traditional ritual procedures. Moreover, even once he or she is confirmed, a justice's legal opinions carry neither more nor less legal force than any other citizen's, unless they are uttered in the properly ritualized way, in the proper place, and upon a suitable occasion. But more crucial to our present concern is the logical status of the properly executed verdicts of the Court. These display a curious ambivalence in character, which may be brought out by reference to

---

[46] Lienhardt, *Divinity and Experience*, 138–40.

[47] Evans-Pritchard, *Witchcraft, Oracles, and Magic*, 475.

[48] Except, perhaps, in some cases where a person may attempt, with some success, to usurp power or foment social change.

Austin's previously mentioned distinction between performative and constative uses of declarative sentences.[49]

Attending to Austin's point, we may notice that when the court hands down an opinion, it is not merely stating what the law of the land is, in the sense that an ordinary citizen might offer an opinion about this. For an ordinary citizen might be either mistaken or correct, whereas the pronouncements of the Court have the force of law. They dictate, in effect, what the law shall be. In this sense, a declaration of the Court is not a statement, capable of being straightforwardly assessed as true or false, but more aligned with such performances as "I christen thee…" and "I pronounce you man and wife." For there, as here, the sayings by the Court (under proper conditions) make it so. Here, we have a rather straightforward case, from our own culture, of the efficacy of certain ritually uttered words.[50]

But, curiously, this is not all there is to the matter, for Court rulings purport to state what the law of the land (as given by the Constitution) objectively is. As such, Court declarations appear to have the status of statements about facts, particularly about what other people (e.g., the "Founding Fathers") meant to say. Concomitantly, they require empirical justification and are open to relevant criticism and disagreement.[51] The facts of the case, social exigencies, and the probable intentions of the framers of the Constitution must all be considered.[52] Indeed not only the correctness of the decision but, ultimately, the viability of the Constitution itself is subject to rational criticism—though such ultimate questions, which may threaten the legitimacy of the Court itself, are likely to be mooted. Societies require a

---

[49] J. L. Austin, *How to Do Things with Words*, 2nd ed., ed. J. O. Urmson and Marina Sbisà (Cambridge, MA: Harvard University Press, 1975), 3–6. The fact that Austin came to view the utterance of statements—correctly—as also being a performance does not undermine the distinction between constatives and other types of performatives, such as "I promise."

[50] It may be objected that the analogy is a poor one, as Court opinions are intended to regulate social practice, whereas magic purports to have causal efficacy over natural phenomena and religious authorities claim to address or report on the wills of supernatural agents. I will return to the first of these in the next section, as well as to the second objection in Chapters 4 and 7). My analysis of ritual here has been in part anticipated by Gregory Bateson, "Conventions of Communications Where Validity Depends Upon Belief," in *Communication: The Social Matrix of Psychiatry*, ed. Jurgen Reusch and Gregory Bateson (Piscataway, NY: Transaction Publishers, 1951), 212–27 and S. J. Tambiah, "Form and Meaning of Magical Acts: A Point of View," in *Modes of Thought: Essays on Thinking in Western and Non-Western Societies*, ed. Robin Horton and Ruth Finnegan (London: Faber and Faber, 1973), 199–229. Neither author, however, recognizes the dual logical status of such utterances, mediating between their dependence for truth upon fiat and also upon fact (see below).

[51] The Court's rulings are authoritative because the Constitution says they are, but what makes the Constitution authoritative? On this, see Chapter 4n8 and §II, D.

[52] Which is why wisdom is a desirable character trait in judges.

(roughly) stable framework, and there are abundant reasons on the side of holding the Constitution sacred (even when reinterpreting it).

In recognition of this aspect of the status of Court decisions, the Court has available to it a mechanism for publishing dissenting opinion and, more importantly, a mechanism for overruling its own earlier decisions. Now when this occurs, the reversal has the effect of declaring the overturned decision to be false, in the sense that it never was the law of the land.[53] Thus, in one sense, decisions can be assigned a truth-value conformably with their status as statements. Hence, official opinions of the Court apparently have dual status: on the one hand, they are treated as performatives, effecting the situation they describe; on the other hand, they are taken to be statements that are capable of demanding justification and, therefore, capable of inadequate justification (and even falsity). This Janus-faced character may give the formal logician an uneasy turn, but clearly the dual treatment is eminently rational from a pragmatic point of view.[54]

Now, in the case of the Constitution and of Supreme Court opinions, we have specific acts of a performative character historically locatable in time. Much more typically, the origins of the religious myths and traditions which guide social practice cannot be traced to such specifically locatable events. They are, rather, phenomena which emerged out of a complex historical matrix of evolving customs, susceptible to faster or slower rates of change according as internal difficulties and environmental factors may demand.[55] Nevertheless, myths often perform very much the same sort of function as Supreme Court decisions (among other things). They establish and legitimize social customs within the framework of a justificatory and explanatory apparatus that serves both to

---

[53] As a result, violators of the earlier Court decision are held never to have broken the law. For a much more detailed discussion along somewhat similar lines, cf. H. L. A. Hart, *The Concept of Law* (New York: Oxford University Press, 1961), 100–23, 141–54.

[54] See also the somewhat more formal discussion of this matter in Chapter 4.

[55] Specification of necessary and sufficient conditions for a procedure P or a doctrine D to count as an accepted norm is an undertaking I think is unlikely to succeed. Must P (or D) govern the practice of most of the natives most of the time? Must there be feelings of guilt upon violation, and punishment or reprobation upon discovery of violation? Must there be explicit and sincere verbal espousal of P or D? None of these is a necessary condition for tradition-hood, though perhaps they are jointly sufficient. Mere general belief in the truth of a doctrine, and conformity to its demands, is not a sufficient condition for performative status, even when that general agreement brings about the truth of the claim. The fact that many people believe that the stock market is failing, and act accordingly, is bound to produce the expected result; yet it would not be accurate to assess this belief, no matter how often it is asserted or by whom, as having any performative force analogous to that of Supreme Court decisions. The criteria here are once again necessarily informal. Moreover, acceptance of a practice, and the performative force of the promulgation of a doctrine, must both admit of degrees.

accommodate the sense in which conventions are arbitrary and the sense in which reasons are relevant.[56] Moreover, in a culture in which traditions are changeable, the line of demarcation between what is charter and what is authoritative interpretation of charter may be far from sharp.

We are now in a position to see what the crucial difference between native myth and natural science is. Scientific theories, as we know them, deal exclusively with explanation and prediction. Whatever services myths may provide in that line of business,[57] they also serve to set forth action-guiding conventions of a normative character within a framework that permits both justification and, if necessary, criticism. The persons who, within a specific culture, are the sanctioned interpreters and elaborators of that tradition, do speak the "Truth" in so far as agreed-upon practice conforms to the principle that their dicta shall count as normatively binding.

It will be evident that adoption of the performative analysis of myth and ritual suggested here further places a non-trivial constraint upon the interpretation of the content of ritualized beliefs. It was the prior presumption of rationality that first led to this analysis; now we must be reminded that not just anything can count as a rational objective of performative action. It is reasonable to expect institutionalized authority to be efficacious only where the exercise of that authority is, in the primary instance, addressed to social issues whose outcome is controlled by the

---

[56] As W. E. H. Stanner explains in his discussion of aboriginal beliefs in Australia, "The tales are also a collation of what is validly known about such ordained permanencies. The blacks cite The Dreaming as a charter of absolute validity in answer to all questions of *why* and *how*. In this sense, the tales can be regarded as being, perhaps not a definition, but a 'key' of Truth. They also state ... the ways in which good men should, and bad men will, act now. In this sense they are a 'key' or guide to the norms of conduct..." (W. E. H. Stanner, "The Dreaming," in *Reader in Comparative Religion*, 3rd ed., ed. William A. Lessa and Evon Z. Vogt [New York: Joanna Colter Books, 1972], 272). Likewise, Roy Rappaport has put forward the interesting view that the purpose of religious belief is to sanctify—that is, certify the truth of—communications of certain information which are important to tribal survival. The information obtains certification within the ritual context through association with religious statements which are sacred: "Sanctity ... *is the quality of unquestionable truthfulness imputed by the faithful to unverifiable propositions*" (Roy A. Rappaport, "Ritual, Sanctity, and Cybernetics," *American Anthropologist* 73, no. 1 [1971]: 69; italics in original). But this is mysterious. Why should the truth of empirically significant propositions be certified by association with ones that appear to be either false or devoid of empirical content—unless, just conceivably, the religious statements are deliberately purified of empirical content by way of emphasizing their role in pointing to the norm of truthfulness itself? Yet, if *that* is their only purpose, it would be hard to explain both their complexity of structure and the non-random mappings between that structure and the social lives of the believers. Far more plausible is the conclusion that such statements are either non-literal discourse about social realities or else literal but mis-translated discourse about such matters.

[57] About which see the further discussion in Chapter 4.

acceptance of conventions. The fundamental role of ritual cannot, on this understanding, be directly to command nature. Mythology is in this respect *more like* political ideology than science, and native soothsayers are more like Supreme Court justices than modern natural scientists.[58]

VII. The Social vs. the Natural

My use of the expression "more like" in the preceding statement was deliberate since it cannot be denied that religious and magical practices do purport to exert control over natural, as well as social, phenomena. There are two reasons why this is less irrational, and should be less surprising, than it seems. In the first place, such control is often indirectly achieved. Horton, Lienhardt, and others[59] have pointed out the efficaciousness of witchcraft beliefs in dealing with physical illness, which is at least partially attributed to social maladjustments. Similarly, when it was said by ancient Egyptians and Hebrews that a just king causes the crops to flourish and the harvest to be bountiful, we may observe that social stability and security are essential prerequisites for the sustained and cooperative investment of labor required to produce that result. There is no reason to suppose that these people were ignorant of the relevant natural mechanisms.

But a second, and perhaps deeper, reason is this. As Claude Lévi-Strauss has pointed out, tribal theoreticians take those social relationships that structure their lives to be a model for understanding the relationships between phenomena in the natural world (and vice versa).[60] Both the natural world and the social world are viewed as structured by social relationships or something akin to these—as is, often enough, the relationship between the two realms. If this kind of thinking seems strange to those who possess our

---

[58] It would be, at best, misleading to assimilate simplistically the relationship between Supreme Court dicta (and their social results) to the relationship between natural causes and effects. Just as Horton's view, which states that native belief in the efficacy of words results from their commitment to a single conceptual scheme, unconvincingly convicts the natives of far too elementary a mistake, so too J. H. M. Beattie's interpretation of the native's confidence in the potency of ritual (while closer to the mark) fails to provide any intelligent rationale for the mistake the natives are (presumably) making (J. H. M. Beattie, "On Understanding Ritual," in *Rationality*, ed. Bryan R. Wilson [New York: Harper and Row, 1970], 240–69). What I am suggesting is that the native *may* parasitically assimilate natural relationships to social ones, which is the reverse mistake, but is at least a sophisticated mistake. Moreover, the assimilation, where it exists, is rarely an unintelligent one. The Dinka do their rain-dance only before the rainy season; and in certain societies, a man cursed by a powerful witchdoctor often does fall ill and die precisely because he has been cursed.

[59] Cannon, "'Voodoo' Death," 1593–96.

[60] Claude Lévi-Strauss, "The Structural Study of Myth," in *Structural Anthropology* (New York: Basic Books, 1963), 206–31.

own tradition, it is nevertheless, as I think I can show, the same type of thinking which characterizes much of modern scientific thought. Roughly, the difference is that for the native, social relationships provide the most accessible and comprehensible model of structured interconnections in terms of which he can attempt to explain the natural phenomena he encounters. For a modern scientist, the laws and causal relationships of physics provide the paradigm of intelligible access to phenomena. To the extent that this difference exists, it can be largely accounted for by differences in the empirical data to which natives and scientists have access. An important similarity, however, underlies their theoretical endeavors. For just as the native may sometimes attempt to reduce natural phenomena, as well as social ones, to a theoretical explanation modeled on social principles,[61] so too the tendency among scientists has been to attempt to explain social and psychological phenomena in terms of physical theories, or at least by the use of causal laws. In both cases, intellectual insight is presumed to be achievable through success at subsuming all phenomena within the embrace of a single theoretical framework, an endeavor suggesting a rather sophisticated level of rationality.[62]

It may be noteworthy that the failure, thus far, of physicalists to achieve their theoretical aims no more diminishes their faith in its ultimate achievability than native faith in their social models of reality is undermined by failure to explain apparently recalcitrant phenomena. For us moderns, the paradigms of successful and deep explanation are to be found in the physical sciences. What resists reductive explanation in such terms are, centrally, psychological and social phenomena. But it will hardly be surprising that,

---

[61] This, I believe, is the best way to understand the so-called anthropomorphism and animism which are said to characterize primitive thought. It remains to be shown, to be sure, that the primary source for the content of native ritual beliefs is their reflection upon the nature of their social system (see below).

[62] Stanner puts the point very well when speaking of the Australian Aborigines, though I will presently disagree with Stanner's de-emphasizing of Aborigine metaphysics: "Their creative 'drive' to make sense and order out of things has, for some reason, concentrated on the social rather than on the metaphysical or the material side. Consequently, there has been an unusually rich development of what the anthropologist calls 'social structure,' the network of enduring relations recognized between people. This very intricate system is an intellectual and social achievement of a high order ... it has to be compared ... with such a secular achievement as, say parliamentary government in a European society.... One may see within it ... the use of the power of abstract reason to rationalize the resultant relations into a system....It has become *the source of the dominant mode of aboriginal thinking.* The blacks ... have taken some of its fundamental principles and relations and have applied them to very much wider sets of phenomena. This tends to happen if any type of system of thought becomes truly dominant. It is, broadly, what Europeans did with 'religion' and 'science' as systems: extended their principles and categories beyond the contexts in which the systems grew" (Stanner, "The Dreaming," 274; italics in original).

for tribal peoples who lack a sophisticated physics and chemistry, the paradigm of explanation (the things that most naturally convey understanding) are roughly folk psychology and principles of social order. These principles might not be very successful at explaining physical and biological phenomena; but in the absence of any better wide-ranging theory, they would surely be worth a try. And should it prove to be the case that neither reduction can (even in principle) be effected, then both the native and the scientists will have been guilty of the same type of sophisticated conceptual error.[63] That either or both of them should be proven wrong here, however, would not convict them of holding their faiths irrationality.

If I am so far correct in this analysis of the status of traditional belief systems, then it becomes apparent that they are the products of complex and highly sophisticated attempts to deal intellectually with the world. Neither their complexity nor their sophistication has (perhaps forgivably) been adequately understood, but at least many of the methodological underpinnings which engender these systems are to be found in our own thought. To that extent, radical skepticism and radical relativism, with respect to the translation problem, are untenable positions.

I am of course well aware that the arguments offered here constitute support for only part of an adequate methodology. The argument I have furnished in support of the claim that native thought is more rational than previously thought is still incomplete in one major respect. To complete it, I will have to show that the content of these beliefs can (typically) be rationally understood, in the full sense which admits the appropriate sorts of empirical access. Since the presumption of native rationality in treating myths performatively requires that those myths be intended fundamentally as social charters, doing this would require showing several things. First, that, conformably with the principles announced here, there are *prima facie* grounds for according favored status to interpretations under which talk of deity, spirits, and other "ghostly" entities is just, at root, theoretical talk about social phenomena and norms of the requisite kinds. Second, that such talk is more conscious, literal, sophisticated, and I think more intelligible than was suggested by Durkheim or most of his followers. And third, that such talk is therefore empirically un-mysterious. Such an interpretation must vindicate the Lukes-Hollis insight that requires understanding the texts as literally as possible, without excluding on *a priori* grounds the existence of those poetic and metaphorical means of expressing a truth that are clearly part of any language user's repertoire. That project will be the task of several of the remaining chapters of this book, and it is entirely appropriate to withhold judgment about whether it leads to fruitful results until it has been

---

[63] Chapter 4 will examine the prospects for a reduction of the social to the psychological. My conclusion to this will be negative.

demonstrated through concrete engagement with a significant number of myth traditions.[64]

Before such concrete engagement can begin, however, there are theoretical underpinnings of various sorts that must occur. In Chapter 4, for example, I will set forth one of the major theoretical building blocks, a general framework for mapping some of the central vocabulary of myths onto social realities. In other chapters, I will develop other essential features of the theoretical framework. Once that is done, I will then use the theory to give analyses of biblical texts as a set of case studies.

---

[64] Some telling work in this direction has been done in recent years by biblical scholars, such as J. Z. Smith, Richard Horsley, and N. T. Wright, among others. For a good summary, see Richard Carrier, *On the Historicity of Jesus: Why We Might Have Reason for Doubt* (Sheffield, UK: Sheffield Phoenix Press, 2014). Of great interest is Edmund R. Leach, *Genesis as Myth and Other Essays* (London: Cape, 1969) and the structural analysis of the Oedipus cycle, which is a tour de force, in Terrence Turner, "Oedipus: Time and Structure in Narrative Form," in *Forms of Symbolic Action: Proceedings of the 1969 Annual Spring Meeting of the American Ethnological Society*, ed. Robert F. Spencer (Seattle, WA: University of Washington Press, 1969), 26–68. These works are of special interest inasmuch as they exhume parts of the rationale which explains the venerable myths of our *own* culture, and these have been notoriously neglected by social anthropologists.

In the Matter of Miracles

Miracles matter. How to approach accounts of miracles has historically been, unsurprisingly, a pivotal issue in biblical hermeneutics. Very roughly, we may say that opinion divides over whether credence should be given to miracle stories or not. Because of the theological importance of many of the miracles, the choice here has far-reaching implications for broader issues of interpretation. But in particular, as we will see, it is a matter that has profound significance for how charitable an exegete can be towards biblical texts.

At the outset I should forewarn readers that the debate—specifically, the debate over the credibility of reports of miraculous events—has made use of mathematical techniques in the theory of probabilities in order to estimate the evidential worth of such reports. The mathematical relations are often provided by Bayesian confirmation theory. So, perforce, I will be casting part of this chapter's argument in terms of applications of that theory. The mathematics itself is not difficult—it involves only the manipulation of fractions—but, for those unfamiliar with probabilities, the underlying reasoning may sometimes seem less than transparent.

To readers who may find themselves deterred by such matters, it will be reassuring to know that the mathematical details in this chapter can be safely skipped over provided that readers understand the twofold purpose of this chapter. First, I intend to develop an updated reformulation of David Hume's classical attack on the credibility of miracle stories, one that aims to be immune to the various objections that have been mounted against his reasoning. Second, the chapter will play an important role in the development of the central thesis of this book. I will take the defense of Hume's basic insights to show that literal reports of miracles should never be believed, except under very stringent conditions that have probably never been satisfied. Naturalistic explanations of why these reports exist are to be preferred over taking claims at face value. However, a skeptical reception of such reports ill comports with the principle of charity just propounded. That fact urges us to take seriously the search for a third way of reading the miracle stories—one that avoids the pitfalls of both naïve acceptance and wholesale skepticism. That third way, as it is developed in subsequent chapters, will have profound implications, not only for the interpretation of miracle stories but also of much else that appears in sacred texts.

I. A Requiem for Miracles

What, then, can be said about the matter of how to approach the miraculous? After all, miracles are the fish bones that stick most pertinaciously in the skeptic's craw—not only because the religious conjure salvation by invoking them but because they are flatly unbelievable and the skeptic has a suitcase-full of miracle stories that even the religious will agree are fraudulent. Although the issue does not lie at the heart of my project in this book, its position as a watershed problem is insured by the fact that it has both metaphysical and epistemological implications.

If miracles have occurred, then that surely implies something significant about the way the world is causally ordered and about what (or who) so orders it. Again, if there are or might be miracles, we must face questions about how they are to be identified: whether it is the proper business of science and historiography to do so, or whether other means must do it. And if the biblical miracle stories are false, then that may tell us something about the prospects, not only for Christian soteriology but also for assessment of the historical reliability of Scripture.

So, I must first, though with some reluctance, re-plow this stony ground. That will clear the path to a proper consideration of biblical texts as mythical (in a sense to be explained) in two ways.[1] First, the debate over miracles has traditionally left us with two primary options: either the stories are literally true (and God is in his heaven) or are fraudulent deceptions (what I call the *fraud and folly* view, which bears the indelible stamp of Hume's "Of Miracles"). Both views are, I shall argue, seriously in error. I believe the miracle stories are (essentially) true; and the intent of those who composed them was to edify, not to deceive. Moreover, those who accepted their truthfulness were generally neither credulous nor conniving. But by the very same token, they did not believe that people—even special people—could walk on water, change water into wine, or come back from the dead: at least not literally. Once we see this difference, the path is open to an understanding of what the authors of the story might really have been trying to say and how they were trying to say it. In fact, to my mind, the greatest tragedy of the traditional debate is that it has so effectively deflected

---

[1] In saying this, I mean to support a tradition going back to D. F. Strauss, which has now generally fallen out of favor in life-of-Jesus research. But we know a great deal more about the nature and function of myths in religious discourse than we did when Strauss wrote.

attention away from what (by my lights at least) are the actual, often profound, meanings of the texts.

The second reason some path-clearing is necessary is because of the rhetoric of the traditional debate itself. I have in mind here the rather shrill, and endlessly repeated, allegation that those interpreters who reject miracle stories do so only because they have an *a priori* (and unwarranted) commitment to a naturalistic world-view. That is nonsense: a refusal to accept miracle stories as literally true need not be based on any *a priori* commitments whatsoever, beyond those that may have to be invoked to ground reasoning about empirical matters generally. Rejection of miracles properly comes by way of *arguments*; and, as I see it, those arguments are of three sorts. First, there are arguments that make plausible the conclusion that miracles are metaphysically *impossible*. Second, there is Hume's epistemological argument, suitably reformulated below, that shows belief in miracles based on testimony alone to be *irrational*. And third, there is an argument from Scripture itself that, coupled with a principle of interpretive charity, leads to the same conclusion by providing an intrinsically more plausible reading of the texts.

Very briefly, the argument for metaphysical impossibility is that a miracle cannot be literally a violation of a law of nature. It might, to be sure, fall under the *ceteris paribus* (other things being equal) clause of a defeasible law: in that case other things are not equal because God intervenes by exerting a force upon some part of the natural world, a force that has no natural source. The problem with this conception is that such a force will violate Newton's Third Law (every force has an equal and opposite reaction) and the conservation of energy and momentum—laws that are not defeasible. Various attempts to skirt around this problem by declaring the natural world not to be a causally closed system, or by attempting to insert divine intervention by way of quantum indeterminacies, are (in my view) to no avail.[2] Of course, if miracles are metaphysically

---

[2] For more on the metaphysical issues, see Evan Fales, *Divine Intervention: Metaphysical and Epistemological Puzzles* (New York: Routledge, 2010), 1–56, "It is not Reasonable to Believe in Miracles," in *Debating Christian Theism*, ed. J. P. Moreland, Chad Meister, and Khaldoun A. Sweis, Oxford Contemporary Dialogues (New York: Oxford University Press, 2013), 298–310 and "Is a Science of the Supernatural Possible?," in *Philosophy of Pseudoscience: Reconsidering the Demarcation Problem*, Massimo Pigliucci and Maarten Boudry, eds. (Chicago University Press, 2013b), 247–62.

Robert Larmer has repeated his insistence that all laws of nature are defeasible (a defeasible law is one that holds in every case, other things being equal. Thus, the law that water freezes at 0° C always holds—unless the water is impure, not under normal atmospheric pressure, etc.) Larmer maintains that a naturalist who appeals to energy conservation is begging the question against the theist who claims that the universe as a whole is not a closed system (Robert A. Larmer, "Divine Intervention and the Conservation of Energy: A Reply to Evan Fales," *International Journal for Philosophy of*

impossible, not even God can perform them and the issue is, therefore, settled straightaway.

But even if the above abridged argument is mistaken, Hume's argument warns us away from accepting miracle stories. The central problem with that argument, in my view, is not that we should deny Hume's conclusion but that it forces us to suppose miracle stories are composed by deceivers whose audiences are incredibly credulous. Many skeptics are quite content with such a low opinion of human intellectual faculties, but I am not. In the case of the biblical stories, the literary quality of the texts alone forces the admission that the authors were extraordinarily gifted, and widespread acceptance by other intellectuals in an often-hostile environment ensures that belief did not spread simply as a matter of casual credulity or stupidity.

Religion 75, no. 1 [2013]: 27–38, http://doi.org/10.1007/s11153-013-9411-8). But in my more recent formulation of the argument ("It is not Reasonable to Believe in Miracles"), I find it clearer to appeal to Newton's Third Law, which is (*pace* Larmer) indefeasible and which (it can plausibly be maintained) characterizes an *essential* feature of the operation of forces. Larmer briefly considers this form of the objection; the most he can offer is that the force-law applies only to interactions between physical objects (Robert A. Larmer, "Against 'Against Miracles,'" in *Questions of Miracle*, ed. Robert A. Larmer [Montreal, Canada: McGill-Queen's University Press, 1996], 58). But this misses the point: the law implies that forces can be exerted only by things upon which forces can be exerted.

The above argument has, for simplicity's sake, been framed in terms of Newtonian Mechanics. Taking account of Quantum Mechanics and General Relativity requires some modifications, but the essential point seems to hold still. Conservation of energy is, to be sure, ill-defined for General Relativistic reasons; what is relevant is whether this permits the operation of forces acting locally to effect a miracle. Take any force that plays a significant role in the production of a miracle; if its source is not included in the "system," then just expand the system to include it. But Robin Collins mounts a similar argument. A bolder reply to the view that I endorse straightforwardly denies that energy is actually conserved in events in which an immaterial, a-spatial thing such as a soul, spirit, or mind causally influences the movement of matter (Robin Collins, "The Energy of the Soul," in *The Soul Hypothesis: Investigations Into the Existence of the Soul*, ed. Mark C. Baker and Stewart Goetz [New York: Continuum, 2011], 123–36). Larmer's position can be so interpreted. It has recently been carefully discussed and defended by J. Brian Pitts, "Conservation of Energy: Missing Features in Its Nature and Justification and Why They Matter," in "Special Issue on James Joule," special issue, *Foundations of Science* (2020): 1–45, http://doi.org/10.1007/s10699-020-09657-1. Pitts is discussing conservation of energy in mind-body causation within the human brains. There, it could be that very small, hard-to-detect additions of energy can cascade into muscle-motions that execute action-intentions. The same could not be said for miracles, such as Joshua's commanding the sun to stand still during the battle for Gibeon (Josh. 10:13) or Moses' parting of the Red Sea (Exod. 14). Moreover, Pitts' view raises the pressing question: why is a given mind confined to influencing just a particular brain, and not others? For a more extensive critique of this kind of view, see Robert Greg Cavin and Carlos A. Colombetti, "The Implausibility and Low Explanatory Power of the Resurrection Hypothesis—With a Rejoinder to Stephen T. Davis," *Socio-Historical Examination of Religion and Ministry* 2, no. 1 (Spring 2020): 37–94.

(Even Paleolithic peoples must have known that human beings cannot walk on water or turn water into, say, grape juice with a snap of the fingers.)

Hume's conclusion forces upon us an untowardly uncharitable hermeneutic. Is there a more charitable one? There is: the miracle stories might not have been meant literally. Of course, it is one thing to propose this alternative as a general possibility. It is another to give it substance and plausibility by developing a well-motivated methodology for discerning the figurative content of the texts, and then to show that this methodology has not only independent justification but yields interpretations that are coherent, mutually informing, and convey content that would both interest an intended audience and claim their allegiance. It is for this last set of claims that I will be mainly arguing here. My ultimate focus will therefore not be primarily upon miracles as such but, rather, upon selected biblical texts that serve more generally to illustrate the communicative strategies of their authors.

Although I am doubtful that miracles are possible, even for God, I shall proceed dialectically here by *accepting, arguendo,* that a deity is able (if s/he so chooses) to profoundly and dramatically affect the course of natural events. Let us then adopt the following characterization of miracles:

(M) An event E is a miracle if it occurs as a result of a special intervention by God in the workings of nature, done with the intention of influencing human beings or affecting their lives in such a manner as to promote his providential ends.[3]

It is a difficult question how in general one is to tell whether a given event—even when its occurrence is not in question—satisfies (M). I shall say more about this below. But for practical purposes, I shall count as miracle stories those passages in the New Testament (NT) that are generally regarded in this way. These include, perhaps most importantly, the virgin birth, the resurrection of Christ, Jesus' walking on water and calming storms, his feeding of the multitudes, the affirmation of his divine Sonship when baptized, his healings and raisings, and so on.

Christians who accept the biblical miracles divide on the question of how to appraise the stories. Some take them to be generally true because they believe, on other grounds, that there is a God with the requisite power and congruent providential concern for his creatures. They believe that the antecedent probability of miracles occurring such as those the Bible relates, relative to there being such a God, is high enough that the Bible's testimony,

---

[3] I would, for many purposes, accept a more minimalist definition of miracles (hence the conditional—*if*—rather than a biconditional—*if and only if*); however, in the present context, this more elaborated definition best captures the kinds of biblical events that are of interest to our discussion.

together with other relevant evidence, confers a high probability on the claim that the miracles indeed happened.[4]

Other Christians believe that the biblical testimony by itself, or together with other historical evidence, suffices to render the miracle stories probably true. Their truth, in turn, supplies evidence sufficient to confer probability on the existence of the God of Christian theology and upon the NT account of his plan of salvation.[5] There are also Christian scholars who try to diminish the "offense" of the miracle stories by naturalizing them. Healings, for example, are chalked up to psychophysical causes. Some nature miracles are explained as astonishing natural phenomena that were perhaps misunderstood or were remembered in elaborated ways. But this attitude salvages an historical core for these stories while abandoning their evidential value (for theism) and, often, their theological significance.[6]

Skeptics, who deny that miracles occur, can account for miracle reports in a variety of ways, but the most common strategies fall under what I shall call the "fraud and folly" approach. The *locus classicus* of that approach is, of course, Hume's pivotal "Of Miracles" (hereafter, OM).[7] My

---

[4] See for example, Richard Swinburne, *The Resurrection of God Incarnate* (New York: Oxford University Press, 2003), 9–31 and *Revelation: From Metaphor to Analogy* (New York: Oxford University Press, 2007). For a discussion on the issue, see R. Douglas Geivett, "The Evidential Value of Miracles," in *In Defense of Miracles: A Comprehensive Case for God's Action In*, ed. R. Douglas Geivett and Gary R. Habermas (Downers Grove, IL: InterVarsity Press, 1997), 178–95.

[5] For instance, Timothy and Lydia McGrew contend that, if some of the NT miracles can be established on historical grounds, this would provide significant evidence for Christian theism. In their paper, "The Argument from Miracles," they only essay to compute a value for the likelihood of the resurrection, given the NT data (and some background), but the astronomical number at which they arrive is clearly intended to provide ammunition for the claim that the resurrection occurred. To avoid this conclusion, the skeptic must assign an even more astronomically small prior probability to the resurrection. See Timothy McGrew and Lydia McGrew, "The Argument from Miracles: A Cumulative Case for the Resurrection," in *The Blackwell Companion to Natural Theology*, ed. William Lane Craig and J. P. Moreland (Malden, MA: Wiley-Blackwell, 2012), 593–662.

[6] Some scholars, for example, relocate the parting of the Red Sea at the Sea of Reeds (a marshy area in the Nile delta), and attribute the temporary retreat of the waters to a serendipitous tidal wave. But if the supposed tidal wave was a purely natural phenomenon, involving no divine intervention, then its convenient timing would have been no miracle but, instead, a pure (even if amazing) coincidence. For a recent defense of a different version of this strategy by hydraulic engineers, see Carl Drews and Weiqing Han, "Dynamics of Wind Setdown at Suez and the Eastern Nile Delta," *PLoS ONE* 5, no. 8 (2010): e12481, http://dx.doi.org/10.1371/journal.pone.0012481.

[7] David Hume, "On Miracles," in *An Inquiry Concerning Human Understanding*, ed. Charles W. Hendel (1748; repr., Indianapolis, IN: Bobbs-Merrill, 1955). Hume's skepticism was anticipated by others, perhaps most notably Baruch Spinoza, *Theological-Political Treatise*, trans. Samuel Shirley and Seymour Feldman

aim in this chapter is to defend Hume's attack on the reliability of miracle reports against certain criticisms but then to argue that Hume's view—and fraud and folly explanations generally—are less plausible than a different approach that better accords with a principle of charity in interpretation. It is not that I reject Hume's conclusions; but, in ways I shall presently explain, I think he fails to consider all the hermeneutical options.

We can accord the biblical miracle stories a fully serious, respectful hearing without actually having to suppose that there really existed talking donkeys, sticks turning into snakes, large bodies of water parting on command, or the like. Perhaps more importantly, the approach I will propose yields a bounty of new ways to harmonize biblical texts, to relate the concerns of their authors to real and pressing problems that their historical situations created and to which solutions were being offered, and to illuminate passages by reference to other passages. In short, I want to offer an alternative to the fraud and folly approach that I believe makes better sense of the texts and better accords with what we have reason to believe of the intelligence and integrity of the NT authors.

II. Fraud and Folly

A. The Dialectical Landscape

I shall not attempt a full dress rehearsal of Hume's argument and the objections of his detractors. It is useful, however, to consider some important issues raised by two of Hume's most sophisticated and notable recent critics, John Earman and C. A. J. Coady.[8] I have already addressed Coady's general views concerning testimony in Chapter 1. Earman, employing a Bayesian analysis of probabilities, attacks OM on the grounds that Hume has not supplied a workable conception of miracles and that he miscalculates the relevant probabilities. Coady, we saw, offers a non-reductive account of the evidential force of testimony, arguing that beliefs based on testimony are properly basic or non-inferential. Coady's claims about the epistemic status of testimony, if correct, might be thought to undermine Hume's analysis of the evidential force of miracle reports. But, as I have argued, they do little to diminish the bite of Hume's argument. Nevertheless, I shall reject Hume's account as an explanation of the biblical

---

(1670; repr., Indianapolis, IN: Hackett, 1998) and seconded by his contemporary, Thomas Payne, *The Age of Reason* (1795; repr., Secaucus, NJ: Citadel Press, 1974).

[8] John Earman, *Hume's Abject Failure: The Argument Against Miracles* (New York: Oxford University Press, 2000); C. A. J. Coady, *Testimony: A Philosophical Study* (Oxford: Clarendon Press, 1992). Earman is not a believer and so cannot be accused of religious bias. His title, *Hume's Abject Failure*, nevertheless overreaches.

miracle stories on the grounds that a better kind of explanation of these stories can be given—better (in part, but by no means entirely) because it provides a more plausibly charitable reading of Scripture.

The fact that this approach to the problem of miracle stories is preferable to Hume's does not mean that I reject his approach all together, however. For one thing, Hume's way of explaining these stories is far more plausible than the supposition that the stories, straightforwardly considered, are actually true—that is to say, walks on water, transmutations of water into wine, and resurrections from the dead actually happened in the past. Given a choice only between Hume and a literalist reading of these stories, I give the palm to Hume. But we can do better than Hume and better than fraud and folly approaches more generally.

At the same time, a partial concession to Hume's attitude toward miracle stories must be made. We are not justified in extending charity indiscriminately and too generously, for it is plain that unjustified or ill-justified belief in miracles (and sheer nonsense) is a dismayingly common feature of human psychology. A principle of charity so strict as to rule that out flies in the face of the evidence; nor would such a rigid criterion be imposed by the considerations that give charity a *prima facie* claim on interpretation. The question—and it is a difficult question—is where a proper balance is struck. I do not know a general answer to that question; here, historical judgment is called for, and cases will vary.

It is fair to say that intelligence and education are enemies of superstition; but they are not proof against it. Nevertheless, we should be more cautious about imputing irrationality to the thought of someone whose intelligence can independently be established and more cautious yet when a new ideology attracts numbers of people of high intelligence and apparent sobriety over time. This leaves ample room for the possibility that while sophisticated believers and creators will understand a tradition in a sophisticated way, the unsophisticated will see through a glass darkly.[9] That difference is familiar enough; philosophers who theorize about natural rights and the like will understand the language of the U.S. Declaration of Independence, as well as the Constitution, more deeply than average citizens who know that they have a right to private property (for example) but know almost nothing by way of an articulate answer to the question: what *is* a right?; or even: what is the basis of *this* right?

Thus, I want to leave open the question of how much primitive and early Christian *hoi polloi* (and their enemies) may have understood the full meaning of the Christian message. At the same time, I will be arguing that Christian *cognoscenti*—including, in the first instance, those who wrote and shaped the canonical texts—understood what they were claiming and doing

---

[9] That difference may have informed the Apostle Paul's distinction between spiritual milk and solid food (1 Cor. 3:2; 9:7; cf. Heb. 5:12–13).

in a way that is fundamentally different from what most contemporary Christians (and Hume) understand these texts to mean. I do not know any way to show this save by providing an alternative reading of the texts that achieves two desiderata: if it explains many textual passages that otherwise remain puzzling, and confers upon the primitive Christian thinkers a degree of insight, rationality, contemporary relevance, and knowledge commensurate with their obvious intellectual stature, then it will have earned its wages.[10] I propose, therefore, to engage the Gospel of Matthew and other biblical texts by doing my best to credit their authors' rationality and erudition. Perhaps, in the end, they will display some serious failings along these lines, but let us proceed, dialectically, by seeing just how far a presumption of rationality can be maintained in the case of these texts.

I will ultimately be arguing for the following claim: suppose, for the sake of argument, we allow that miracles can happen and may in fact have happened—suppose further that, for the sake of argument, we set entirely to one side Hume's arguments concerning the evidential hurdles faced by religious testimony to the miraculous—even given all this, it is still more likely that the biblical authors did not think the miracles they report literally occurred and did not retail the stories with the primary intention of convincing others that they occurred. In my view, the miracle stories play a very different role in the Bible. They are meant to convey messages of great importance from the authors to their contemporaries. Yet, we are likely not only to miss but to be blinded to their significance if we read them with literalist eyes. But first, let us return to Hume.

B. Hume vs. Earman

There has been a great deal of disagreement over just what Hume's central argument in Part I of OM was. It will not serve the purposes of our present inquiry to review that ground. The evaluation of Hume's argument is hampered by the fact that he did not have two sorts of later conceptual developments at his disposal. First, Hume did not have a sophisticated grasp of confirmation theory.[11] Second, he did not have a sufficiently developed conception of how we reason from observations to laws of nature. In view of these difficulties, what I propose to do is to present an updated version of Hume's argument—or better, an argument that I take to be in the spirit of

---

[10] As noted, that stature can be independently established on internal evidence, especially by noting the literary quality of many of the texts, and their authors' depth of knowledge of Jewish traditions and of contemporary Hellenistic culture.

[11] Unfortunately, Hume died only two years after Richard Price posthumously published Thomas Bayes' work on confirmation theory in 1776—much too late for Hume to have known of it when he penned OM.

Hume, possibly one he would have endorsed. I shall use a discussion of Earman's objections to Hume as a vehicle for doing this.

There are three questions that Earman's treatment of Hume forces us to consider. First, what is a miracle? Second, how are we to evaluate the probability that eyewitness testimony of a miracle is true? Third, what if we have multiple independent witnesses? I will discuss these in order.

1. What is a miracle?

A short while ago, I offered (M) as a criterion of the miraculous. That is not quite Hume's definition of a miracle, though it is fairly close. Hume says, "A miracle may be accurately defined, *a transgression of a law of nature by a particular volition of the Deity, or by the interposition of some invisible agent.*"[12] There are several things to remark about this definition. First, it does not exclude non-divine agency: Satan, for example, could on this definition be a performer of miracles if he can "violate" natural laws. Second, Hume's definition says nothing about the purposes or intentions of the agent. Third, it does not entail—as Hume notes—that a miracle must be such that human beings could identify it as miraculous. Fourth, and most crucially, Hume says almost nothing about what makes an event a transgression of a law of nature other than that it presents us with an exception to natural regularity.

First, then, Hume's definition leaves it an open question whether anyone other than God can perform miracles. If it cannot be shown that God is the one and only master over the laws of nature, then the existence of miracles does not, in itself, provide distinctive evidence of the hand of God. It might be thought that the nature of a miracle—in particular, its moral characteristics—could itself decide that question.[13] But that is overly optimistic. Our ability to discern God's moral intentions in events is called into severe question by certain forms of evil, as Hume realized.[14]

---

[12] Hume, *An Inquiry Concerning Human Understanding*, 123n7; italics in original.

[13] Cf. Matt. 12:22–37. Samuel Clarke, for one, argued that devils and angels might perform miracles while leaning heavily upon the moral argument on behalf of Jesus' miracles. Clarke also believed that every natural event occurs by way of personal agency (especially God's). Miracles have no special status on that score, being merely unusual events; but then their mere occurrence, even if associated with a putative revelation and not such as humans could manufacture, would offer much weaker evidence of special providence. Clarke thought, of course, that he had good independent grounds for his theistic presuppositions. See Samuel Clarke, "Evidences of Natural and Revealed Religion," in *The Works of Samuel Clarke* (1705; repr., New York: Garland Publishing, 1978), esp. 2: 695–701.

[14] David Hume, *Dialogues Concerning Natural Religion*, ed. Norman Kemp Smith (1779; repr., Indianapolis, IN: Bobbs-Merrill, 1947), Parts X and XI.

Conversely, we cannot assume that an evil being might not, by way of seducing us, perform actions that are facially good. Our main hope, then, is that only God can trespass upon natural law and that we are able to recognize such trespasses. But here I set this question aside and assume that any genuine miracle is a sign of divine intervention.

As to the second and third points, let us simplify here (by supposing that once a transgression of natural law has been identified) we can, from its nature and context, make reasonable inferences as to the purposes for which it was done; and, conversely, presume that, at least sometimes, God's purposes entail that he would perform miracles of a sufficiently dramatic and public nature that people would sit up and take note.

We come then to the fourth point. What is a law of nature, what would a violation of such a law consist of, and how would instances of the latter be identified? Hume does not offer much help on the question of violations. Beyond examples and some discussion of mere marvels, the one further hint he gives is that "nothing is ever esteemed a miracle if it ever happen in the common course of nature."[15] It is not even clear whether Hume means this to provide an *epistemic* condition or an ontological one. It provides what is at most a necessary condition on the miraculous. Nevertheless, construed ontologically, I believe it provides a better conception of what a miracle might be than the notion of law violation.

Earman immediately recognizes the difficulty with supposing that some actual event x violates a natural law. Suppose L is the natural law that spiders are carnivorous. On almost all accounts of what a natural law is, L entails the universal generalization that all spiders are carnivorous—that is, $(\forall x)(Sx \supset Cx)$. But then, it cannot (on pain of contradiction) *both* be the case that L is true while also true that some spider, miraculously or otherwise, is vegetarian. That would give Hume a swift, *a priori* argument against the possibility of miracles. Too swift.[16] It would render Hume's argument about testimony superfluous. So, Hume's conception of law violation must be otherwise explicated.

Earman's way of solving this problem is surprising. Understanding a law as a true law-like statement, and a miracle as a violation of a law, Earman's maneuver is to introduce the notion of a presumptive law:

> Let us call L a *presumptive law statement* just in case (i) L is a law statement and (ii) "uniform experience" ... speaks in favor of L in that many instances of L have been examined and found to be positive. Now

---

[15] Hume, *An Inquiry Concerning Human Understanding*, 122.

[16] Baruch Spinoza offered a refutation of miracle claims akin to this one (Spinoza, *Theological-Political Treatise*, 73–75, 82). Spinoza, moreover, rejects the distinction I am proposing between a violation miracle (what he calls an event "contrary to Nature") and supernatural intervention (p. 77).

define a *Hume miracle* to be an event that has a faithful description M such that M contradicts some presumptive law statement.[17]

Earman points out, rightly, that the paradigm cases that Hume had in mind, such as resurrections, are actual Humean miracles since they violate (what for Hume, at least) were presumptive laws of nature.

But this could not have been what Hume had in mind. For the violation of a presumptive law L just goes to show that L is not actually a law after all. And if L is no law, then why should a "violation" of it be counted as adequate evidence of a miracle? So what if some event disqualifies a putative law? Neither Hume nor his adversaries would have been wise to find such a thing religiously significant.[18] We must do better than this.

As Earman is right to point out, and as almost all philosophers agree, it cannot strictly be a law that all As are Bs and also happen that some A is not a B. But most laws are defeasible. That provides an escape. Chicken eggs hatch normal chickens—unless a mutation intervenes. Objects placed in water obey Archimedes' Principle—unless some extraneous force tugs vertically upon them. Other laws are indefeasible. Electrons unfailingly obey Fermi statistics, no object traveling slower than the speed of light can be accelerated to a speed greater than that of light in a vacuum, and so on. Perhaps it is an indefeasible law that squid never hatch from chicken eggs, or that spiders eschew zucchini.

A miracle occurs, according to the account I propose, when a certain kind of exception to a defeasible law occurs. A defeasible law takes the logical form "all As are Bs, when other things are equal." Other things need not always be equal; and there may be no algorithm or finite way of specifying potentially contravening factors—to say nothing of specifying when or how often they will intervene. Take a waterborne object governed by Archimedes' Principle. "Violations" of the principle occur when something extraneous exerts a force upon that object. A *miracle* occurs when God supplies that extra force—when God intervenes in a way that causes nature to behave in a way it would not have, in that circumstance,

---

[17] Earman, *Hume's Abject Failure*, 12; italics in original. Note the difficulty, under this definition, of reflecting Hume's distinction between the miraculous and the marvelous (e.g., the existence of water ice for the Indian prince who had never seen water freeze).

[18] If Earman is right, then John Locke did adopt a definition of miracles similar to Earman's. But consider the following: anyone who understands the logical incompatibility between a universal generalization and an exception to it could only, upon certain discovery of such an exception, reject the putative law rather than proclaim a divine miracle.

absent the divine intervention.[19] I propose, then, that our best account of miracles as "violations" of laws of nature yields the following specification:

> (MV) A miracle M is a "violation" of a law of nature L just in case L is a defeasible law of nature, M is an exception to L, and that exception occurred (at least in part) because of divine intervention and would not have occurred (barring causal over-determination, etc.), had God not intervened.[20]

Whether, and how, an immaterial God *can* supply such a force—which would, among other things, violate local conservation of momentum and energy (apparently indefeasible laws; see above)—is a problem I have set aside in order to keep the theist's project afloat. And in keeping with my policy of setting aside violations of L caused by other supernatural agents, I have confined (MV) to divine interventions.[21]

---

[19] Supposing that God exerts a force $\mathbf{F}_g$ on an object also acted upon by natural forces whose vector sum is $\mathbf{F}_n$, we can allow that the usual force law, $\mathbf{F}_t = \mathbf{ma}$ is obeyed by that object, where $\mathbf{F}_t$ is the vector sum of $\mathbf{F}_g$ and $\mathbf{F}_n$. It is the force $\mathbf{F}_g$ that makes for a miracle. What I am saying applies to classical systems. The story is more complex in the Relativistic and Quantum Mechanical domains, but without affecting the conclusion of my argument here.

[20] It might be thought preferable to define miracles without appealing to natural laws on the grounds that the ancients accepted miracles but lacked the concept of a natural law. I reject the underlying claim about conceptual sophistication: see my earlier remark about Paleolithic understanding. What it is to "have a concept" is itself contentious. If we recognize Plato's distinction between a capacity for practical application, and the ability to give a philosophically defensible "account," we must allow that primitive people were well aware of many of the basic workings of nature; otherwise, they would have been unable to deploy subjunctives such as, "If you were to jump off that cliff, you'd fall and probably die." This sort of thing requires implicit understanding of physical modality—thus, laws of nature. In any event, ancient Near Eastern culture had, by the first century, a well-developed notion of laws: witness Archimedes' Principle, Aristotelian physics, and so forth. My thanks to Nevin Climenhaga for raising this question.

[21] Considerable effort has been expended to show that divine intervention is compatible with contemporary physics and, relatedly, to show that Cartesian dualism is also compatible. For the former, see, Robert A. Larmer, *Water Into Wine? An Investigation of the Concept of Miracle* (Montreal, Quebec: McGill-Queen's University Press, 1988); Robert John Russell, Nancey Murphy, and C. J. Isham, eds., *Quantum Cosmology and the Laws of Nature: Scientific Perspectives On Divine Action* (Vatican City: Vatican Observatory Publications, 1999); Robert John Russell, Nancey Murphy, and Arthur R. Peacocke, eds., *Chaos and Complexity: Scientific Perspectives on Divine Action*, 2nd ed. (Vatican City: Vatican Observatory Publications, 2000); and Alvin Plantinga, "What is 'Intervention'?," *Theology and Science* 6, no. 4 (2008): 369–401, http://dx.doi.org/10.1080/14746700802396106. I have also entered the fray with Fales, *Divine Intervention* and "It is not Reasonable to Believe in Miracles." I believe many theists would agree that this is the best strategy for accommodating a metaphysically

With MV in mind, God can intervene by tugging on things. But how is a divine tug to be divined? In one of two ways: either the defeated law must be known to have no natural defeaters (though nevertheless defeasible), or else the potential natural defeaters must be known, as well as known to be absent.[22] In a word, what knowledge of a miracle requires is that all the natural causes of an event be known, as well as it be known that, absent some further causal influence, the event would not have occurred. That sort of knowledge typically requires considerable sophistication, which a uniform record of positive instances of the law may not be able to supply.

But perhaps a squid hatched from a chicken egg supplies an example. Perhaps no *natural* process could produce such a thing. But God arguably could, whom we presume could rearrange the internal atoms of the egg into new molecules and cells. Similarly, a reasonable person could grant that a man thoroughly deceased and sealed in a tomb who, after several days, emerged needing nothing more than a shower and a shave would have managed the miraculous. That is not merely because such an event has, with moral certainty, never (or almost never) been observed, but because we cannot see how, given everything we know about biological systems and the

---

genuine and religiously relevant conception of miracles (see e.g., Larmer, *Water Into Wine?*). As already noted, I do not believe that even this conception of intervention can be defended. While this is not the occasion to rehearse my reasons at length, the simplest way to put the difficulty is this: God influencing the material world entails his exerting a force upon material objects; a causing *just is* the exertion of a force. See Evan Fales, *Causation and Universals* (New York: Routledge, 1990). However, God exerting a force upon an object runs afoul of Newton's Third Law, for this requires that the object exert an equal and opposite force upon God. Because God is an immaterial substance, this equal and opposite force is not possible. As I take the laws of nature to be metaphysically necessary, it is therefore metaphysically impossible for God to exert a force upon material objects. And not even God can do the metaphysically impossible. The natural reply is to claim that Newton's Third Law has limited scope: it applies only when the cause is a physical object. This reply will not do, given that exertion of force is what causation *is*, together with the following consideration. When a law has limited scope (e.g., the Pauli Exclusion Principle applying to fermions but not bosons), this amounts to the law being defeasible: i.e., it applies when certain forces are in play and not others. But Newton's Third Law governs forces themselves; *a fortiori*, it cannot be defeasible, or limited in scope, in this way. As we might say, it holds in virtue of the very essence or nature or forces. This objection to the possibility of miracles is also, as I see it, the strongest objection to Cartesian dualism. The matter does, however, require a further discussion I shall not pursue here. See Collins, "The Energy of the Soul," 123–36 and Robert John Russell, "Divine Action and Quantum Mechanics: A Fresh Assessment," in *Philosophy, Science, and Divine Action*, ed. F. LeRon Shults, Nancey Murphy, and Robert John Russell (Leiden, The Netherlands: Brill, 1999), 351–403.

[22] This is not quite right. As noted in MV, a natural defeater might be present, and divine intervention may be present, as well, in which case what happens is doubly altered from the normal. I am ignoring cases of causal over-determination and causal pre-emption; it is hard to imagine that God would bother to intervene in such cases.

natural processes that they undergo, such a transformation could have been brought about, save by some agent who had the understanding and ability to rearrange billions of molecular structures in a corpse.[23]

We have, then, complex reasons, based upon a grasp of biological mechanisms that is itself the product of theoretical inferences from a multitude of data, for ruling out purely natural causes. People who lack this kind of biochemical sophistication might still recognize such a restoration to life as a miracle but on a slimmer evidential base. Paring matters down, we may wonder whether simple invariant constant conjunction is ever enough to go on; whether, in Hume's words, it can ever supply "proof" of a law. Perhaps, that is, establishing that L is a law requires situating it within a larger theoretical and explanatory arena, the elements of which empirical evidence must amply confirm.

But something like Hume's claim can be defended, even here. As is well known, Hume's official position is that laws of nature can only be known empirically, by way of inductive inference; that there is no cogent justification for inductive inferences; and that therefore, we never in fact can arrive at any "proof" of a law, or even at a judgment of probability.[24] But then, the question of identifying miracles cannot be so much as raised. In view of this difficulty, Hume's strategy depends upon the recognition that both the theist and the skeptic must, in order to pursue the issue, grant that our inductive procedures are *in fact* able to provide us with knowledge (or at least strongly justified beliefs) about laws of nature. Absent knowledge of the relevant laws, we would have no way of establishing that there had been a "violation" of them. Ergo, to "prove" a miracle, one must be able to "prove" the laws that tell us what *would* have happened, if only the natural forces at work in a target situation had been in play.[25]

---

[23] On the probability of such a reconstitution of Jesus' human body, see Cavin and Colombetti, "The Implausibility and Low Explanatory Power of the Resurrection Hypothesis," 37–94. Many Christians would insist that Jesus' resurrection involved something different than merely such a rearrangement since he was raised with a spiritual body (cf. 1 Cor. 15) rather than his former, more ordinary body. I leave it an exercise for the reader to determine just what kind of transformation, miraculous or otherwise, that would entail. In any event, this cavil does not apply to the raisings of others by Jesus or those performed by Elijah and Elisha.

[24] Earman takes Hume to task for this; but in so doing, fails to recognize the dialectical contours of the debate.

[25] Some skeptics insist that we can *never* rule out sufficient natural causes. They claim that there is *always* the possibility of unknown natural forces accounting for the target phenomenon, and that postulating that these exist, even if unknown and undetected, is always epistemically preferable to appeal to supernatural causes. I do not think any such strong claim as this can be defended. See, for example, Paul J. Dietl, "On Miracles," *American Philosophical Quarterly* 5 (1968): 130–34 and For fuller discussion, see Chapter 3, Sec. 1, and Fales (2013b).

The legitimacy of *some* inductive inferences, as conferring likelihood of truth upon their conclusions, is a presupposition, then, of the arguments on both sides of our question. We may put it this way:

(ML) The possibility of our having evidence for the occurrence of a miracle presupposes the possibility of our having evidence for laws of nature.

There is a corollary:

(ML*) The possibility of our being able to establish with moral certainty that a miracle has occurred on a given occasion presupposes our having established, with moral certainty, what the applicable laws of nature and antecedent physical circumstances are.

But secondly, why should we agree with Hume that the inductive procedures that yield this kind of knowledge of laws are captured by the straight rule? That is to say, the rule that says: project into the future the patterns experience has discovered in the past? In general, we should not do so. But we may usefully distinguish here between the defeasible and typically non-fundamental laws that are usually thought to apply to an investigation of alleged miracles, as well as the most fundamental laws of nature.[26] We regularly suppose that the obtaining of non-fundamental laws depends upon the obtaining of fundamental ones. Significantly, we regularly also presume that the *defeat* of a non-fundamental law can be explained by appeal to more fundamental laws. But what of the *most* fundamental laws? *Ex hypothesi*, they cannot be further explained by appeal to laws; but it is at least reasonable to hope—indeed, to expect—that they will be non-defeasible.[27] That is significant because one type of evidence that could establish such laws would be constant conjunctions (or, in the case of statistical laws, statistical regularities).

---

[26] This for two reasons. First, the course of events is typically a function of the ways in which multiple causal influences converge and combine. A law may be defeasible because a kind of force not usually present is activated in the defeating instance. The laws governing component causes/forces are, as I use the term, more fundamental. Second, events are typically composite in the sense that the constituent particulars on a given level of description are typically composed of physical parts whose properties and behaviors determine the properties and behaviors of the wholes they compose. The laws governing the parts are also, in my sense, more fundamental than (except when they are the same as) the laws governing the wholes they compose.

[27] The hope appears to be borne out if we inspect the laws, so far as they are known, that govern the realm of subatomic particles. My argument here is spelled out in more detail in Evan Fales, "Theoretical Simplicity and Defeasibility," *Philosophy of Science* 45, no. 2 (1978): 273–88, http://dx.doi.org/10.1086/288800.

Earman, therefore, improperly loads the dice against Hume at the outset. Having commended to us, on behalf of Hume, the notion of a "Hume miracle," he then admits that this notion has two "serious drawbacks":

> The first is that a proof of the nonexistence of a Hume miracle would seem to prove too much since it seems to make it impossible to overturn any presumptive law. That is correct; but that is exactly the position to which Hume's account of inductive reasoning leads him....The second apparent drawback of the proposed definition is that it seems to blur Hume's distinction between miracles and marvels, the latter being rare and unusual events.[28]

Indeed, these drawbacks provide excellent reason to decline Earman's gambit and to suppose Hume would have no truck with "Hume miracles." But the principal and decisive reason is that a Hume miracle provides no evidence whatever for the intervention of the divine in nature, and hence no evidence for the existence of God or for a supposed revelation being divinely inspired. Hume was, after all, interested in miracles primarily because he was interested in the epistemic credentials of revelation, and the tradition regularly appealed to miracles as supplying the necessary (and only) warrant. It is critical to a correct understanding of the dialectical situation, as Hume understood it, to remember that in his *Dialogues Concerning Natural Religion* (although then unpublished), he took himself to have disarmed the pretentions of natural theology. Thus, knowledge of God can come only by way of revelation, and revelation earns its credentials only by way of divine "signs." We must therefore understand miracles, as Hume explicitly says, as the effects of God's exercise of his power to interfere with the natural course of events.

---

[28] Earman, *Hume's Abject Failure*, 13. For a more extended defense of Hume (against Earman, among others), see Robert J. Fogelin, *A Defense of Hume on Miracles* (Princeton, NJ: Princeton University Press, 2003). Fogelin is more concerned to explicate Hume's actual argument, whereas I am more interested in reconstruction (see below). It is somewhat curious that Fogelin does not seem to notice, or to mind, Earman's odd definition of a "Hume miracle." Perhaps that is because of the sympathy Fogelin expresses for Don Garrett's interpretation of Hume's notions of "law" and "proof" in subjectivistic terms—terms that seem inconsistent with the intention of Hume's argument. Cf. Don Garrett, *Cognition and Commitment in Hume's Philosophy* (New York: Oxford University Press, 1997) and Fogelin, *A Defense of Hume on Miracles*, esp. 152–53). It may be true that Hume is to be read as treating rational inference in psychologistic terms, in which case Garrett's interpretation has some plausibility. But as my intent is not, in any case, to capture the exact terms of Hume's argument, I am not bound by such a conception of reason. If Hume hopes to show that belief in miracles, understood as *a priori* possible events that provide evidence of divine action, cannot be rationally justified (in the non-psychologistic sense) on the basis of testimonial evidence, then he should proceed as I have suggested. That is how I will read him.

2. Hume's Argument: How should testimony of a miracle be weighed?

We are now in a position to consider the cogency of Hume's central argument that testimony, as providing evidential support for the miraculous, can never positively outweigh our rational grounds for rejecting that testimony as false. My quarrels with Earman's mathematical treatment of the evidential strength of testimony are two. First, Earman's use of Bayesian conditionalization to assess the degree to which a miracle claim is supported by testimony is misdirected, especially since Hume's argument is best understood as involving a kind of reasoning to the best explanation that Earman's procedure does not capture. Second, even if we accept Earman's formal modeling of the probabilities, it turns out that his results actually *support* Hume's conclusion.

I take Hume to argue as follows: identification of an event as a miracle requires recognizing that it lies outside "the order of nature" (that is, that the antecedent natural conditions, operating according to the laws of nature) are insufficient to produce it. Thus, identification of a miracle presupposes knowing the relevant laws of nature or, at the very least, having established them with a high degree of probability. Rather too simplistically, Hume asserts (setting aside inductive skepticism) that when experience delivers an exceptionless regularity, we have as good an evidence—amounting to a "proof"—of a law as can be had.[29] We must, for starters, have this kind of strong evidence that the laws of nature forbid certain sorts of events, given just natural causes. What, then, if we are confronted with testimony to such an event?

As Hume has it, we must consult experience to judge the general reliability of human testimony, factoring in whatever we know about any special conditions that experience teaches us will affect that reliability (such as the reputation, motives, and competence) of the witness. But human nature, we know, never affords testimony a degree of reliability that is entire (for there is both fraud and folly—i.e., incompetence and credulity); hence, testimony cannot confer upon an alleged miracle a probability sufficient to outweigh the improbability it has relative to the known laws of nature. Hume says—again much too simply—that we weigh the evidence on each side and then "subtract" the weight of the lesser from that of the greater to reach an all-things-considered estimate of probability.

---

[29] Hume clearly assumes that our sample size is suitably large, and he may tacitly be presupposing that when human experience delivers a uniformity of nature, the occasions of exemplification of that uniformity will have been sufficiently diverse to avoid biasing the sample. In any event, Hume cannot mean by "proof" anything stronger than the strongest sort of inductive justification.

Thus put, the argument suffers from a number of infelicities.[30] But Hume's argument can be recast to avoid these problems. The most plausible way to construe Hume's case is to represent it as an inference to the best explanation.[31] We have a mass of data—often complex and inhomogeneous—respecting the obtaining of a law of nature. Some of these data may be firsthand experiences of instances of the law. Others may involve inferences to instances of the law from other data, such as testimony. Still other data—and this is regularly ignored in discussions of Hume— derive from independent tests of multiple predictions derived from a putative law in conjunction with other well-established laws and from systematic coherence with wider theories.[32]

---

[30] As a number of writers have pointed out, an initial difficulty is that much—usually the vast preponderance—of the evidence we have that bears on a putative regularity comes, not from personal experience, but precisely from testimony. Why, then, treat testimony to exceptions with prejudice? Why not just tally up the score, treating all data (other things being equal) in the same way, and arrive at a statistical law, should there be "exceptions"? Of course, that will not do in the present case; for then *no* event could be identified as a miracle. But Hume's way with the bearing of evidence on degrees of confirmation is too crude. According to Garrett, Hume's argument relies upon the idea that we antecedently possess "proof" that, say, the dead do not rise in the form of uniform experience under an enormous range of circumstances. A proof confers as much certainty as can be had in empirical matters. When this proof is now confronted with testimony to an exception, we must consider the mixed evidence for judging testimony to be veracious, which confers only a probability. Proof always trumps probability. But, as Garrett notes, one difficulty with this is that it makes the outcome sensitive to the order in which the evidence (concerning both post-mortem behavior and the reliability of testimony) is received. For it is only in view of an *antecedent* "proof" that the dead do not rise that we put under special scrutiny the testimony that someone did (Garrett, *Cognition and Commitment in Hume's Philosophy*, 160—161).

[31] Hume does not frame his argument in terms of an inference to the best explanation; his explicit methodological remarks formulate the reasoning by appeal to enumerative induction. But I think that abductive reasoning better captures Hume's central intuitions. Indeed, there is a minority of Hume scholars who have argued forcefully that Hume thought that observed law-like regularities reflect underlying causal *necessities*, even though we have no experience of those connections and, thus, can have only a kind of negative idea of them. See for example, John P. Wright, *The Sceptical Realism of David Hume* (Minneapolis, MN: University of Minnesota Press, 1983), 123–86 and Galen Strawson, *The Secret Connexion: Causation, Realism, and David Hume* (New York: Oxford University Press, 2014). If Hume indeed thought that such unknowable necessary connections *explain* the regularities (and presumably justify the methods of causal reasoning that Hume formulated; see also, John Foster, "Induction, Explanation and Natural Necessity," *Proceedings of the Aristotelian Society* 83, no. 1 [1982-83]: 87–102, http://dx.doi.org/10.1093/aristotelian/83.1.87), then perhaps Hume's *implicit* reasoning in OM is closer to my reformulation of the argument than it might otherwise appear.

[32] This is so in an informal way even when one has no developed and explicit theory. Implicit theorizing, and the learning of a systematic web of subjunctive

For example, my belief that a particular electron obeys the law that all electrons have charge *e* will derive from the outcome of some measurement procedure, the interpretation of which will rest on a knowledge of other laws (those governing the measurement process) grounded in other data. Some measurements of electron charge will have produced values wildly different from *e* (especially those made by novice physics students, such as I once was). We need to assess whether, in such a case, counterexamples to "all electrons have charge *e*" have been discovered or whether counterexamples to "all freshman physics students have impeccable experimental technique" have been discovered. It is not difficult to see, in this case, where the probabilities lie. That is because, on balance, we have overwhelming evidence (both from careful measurement and from the demands of wider well-confirmed theories) for the constancy of electron charge, as well as the ability to imagine any number of ways in which novice experimenters can and do botch a delicate experiment.[33] Faced with a choice between overturning the entire edifice of current physics, or attributing error to a junior experimenter, we have no hesitation doing the latter. That is the overwhelmingly reasonable choice, *even if we can no longer trace the particular error made by the student physicist.*

The kind of reasoning we employ here is reasoning to the best explanation. It is vastly more likely, given all the data we can bring to bear, that we have an incompetent experimenter than that we have a nonconformist electron. That judgment, we should note, is a result of assessing the implications for "total theory" of understanding our data in the one way or the other.[34] This way of employing inference in no way privileges the measurements made by highly trained experimental physicists over those made by novices *as such*. Each measurement is equally a datum. The question is whether, *all things considered* (including experimenter training and experience), we should accept the results of both experiments as equally good measurements of charge. The answer, clearly enough, is no.

---

conditionals and non-accidental regularities governing the world, begins in infancy. Were it not so, survival would be impossible.

[33] Just as Hume considers Cardinal de Retz to have justly judged, without any further investigation, that the man backed by "a cloud of witnesses" (a snide allusion to Heb. 12:1) was an imposter who claimed to have re-grown an amputated leg when the stub was anointed with Holy oil, so too can we justly attribute the freshman's novel value for the charge of an electron to mis-measurement without troubling to pinpoint the actual source of the error.

[34] By "total theory," I mean at least all those parts of science that depend, directly or indirectly, upon the constancy of electron charge, plus all those aspects of our understanding of human beings that are relevant to judgments of experimental competence (including our theory of the measurement process). Note: even *rare* "mutant" electrons would overthrow much of our most basic understanding of the physical world.

What, then, of the objection that in establishing "proof" of a law of nature, Hume relies improperly on the *collective* experience of humankind, which can be known to each of us only, for the most part, by way of testimony—a procedure that appears to be quite out of keeping with Hume's apparent insistence that one can ultimately rely only upon one's *own* experience in making empirical judgments? Further, if Hume is relying upon such testimony in establishing a law, how can he consistently turn a skeptical ear to testimony reporting exceptions?[35] But if we understand Hume to be reasoning to the best explanation, there is no contradiction here. In many cases, I rely initially upon personal experience to establish a presumption that a law (that, for example, water freezes at 0° C or that the dead do not revivify) obtains. I find this evidence buttressed by testimony that my experience of human trustworthiness teaches me is *of the right kind*, as well as by consilience with other laws that direct experience and reputable testimony teach me to be well supported.[36] All of these, taken together, can forge a strong presumption against a singular testimony in support of an exception, *even if* that testimony should also possess "the right kind" of credentials—and especially if it lacks them.[37]

It should be obvious how Hume's basic argument can be cast in these terms. We have overwhelming reason to believe, on the basis of everything we know, that complex organisms once dead do not revive, that water does not change to wine on command, and so on. We have, further, overwhelming reason to believe, on the basis of well-confirmed theories, that these things not only do not happen but *cannot* happen, given just the normal operations of physical causes. Even the scientifically ignorant have considerable reason to believe these things, though less reason than the literate. This much must be granted by the theist as necessary for the recognition of such events as candidate miracles.

We have, then, strong reason to believe that resurrections, vinification of water on command, and the like do not happen in the natural course of events. That leaves open the possibility that they may happen through divine intervention. But Hume is interested, not in discovering the likelihood *per se* of the supposition that there is a theistic God or that a given miracle would have happened, but in the appeal to miracles as evidence *for* a theistic God. *One* explanation for testimony that someone changed water to wine is that someone *did* change water to wine in the presence of the testifier

---

[35] Earman levels this charge at some length (Earman, *Hume's Abject Failure*, 33–37). On this matter, Garrett's interpretation of Hume is not only far more charitable, but it is also much more plausible.

[36] For example, laws concerning the similar behavior of other liquids, and the laws of thermodynamics, statistical mechanics, and chemistry.

[37] In other cases (concerning, say, the behavior of μ mesons or a giant squid), I must rely upon properly qualified testimony and consilience alone.

(that explains the testimony) and was able to do so because God intervened (that explains the change in the water). The alternatives, for Hume, are that the testifier was either an incompetent witness or a deceiver. The question then is, which proposal best explains the testimony? It is important to bear in mind that Hume does not think that natural theology can supply us with any secure independent knowledge of the existence of deity, so "total theory"—the background against which we judge probabilities—does not include good independent evidence for a God with interventionist proclivities.[38] Hume is attempting to discover what evidence miracle testimony can supply, independently considered, for the existence of such a God (and for the putative revelations associated with the alleged miracles).[39]

Because the evidence for the inviolability of the relevant law(s) is so strong, and because, on the other side, it is "no miracle" that men should lie or be deceived, Hume concludes that the correct assessment of miracle testimony is to disbelieve it—just as the correct assessment of the novice's measurement of an electron's charge is to disbelieve it, as well.[40] Perhaps an even better analogy is provided by the claim of having achieved cold fusion, a claim that, although made by professionals, could not be corroborated. And, though not strictly ruled out by fundamental theory, the claim made by Stanley Pons and Martin Fleischmann conflicted with strong theoretically based arguments respecting what could happen under the conditions they

---

[38] How the likelihoods would change if our total theory *did* postulate, on good evidence, an interventionist God is an interesting question. Some theists—as, for example, many of Hume's contemporaries—indeed approach the question of miracles in this way (for discussions, see Geivett, "The Evidential Value of Miracles," 178–95). Hume makes one passing remark concerning the question, *viz.*, that given the apparent rarity of even putative miracles, we must conclude that God is at best unlikely, on any given occasion, to intervene in this way. Our evidential situation would change, of course, if we could point to well confirmed reports of instances in which, under well controlled or understood conditions, events having apparently no sufficient natural causes did happen.

[39] That is, after all, the way the issue was framed by the tradition. See, for example, Thomas Aquinas, *Summa Contra Gentiles*, trans. Anton C. Pegis (New York: Doubleday, 1955), Chapters III—VI and John Locke, *Essay Concerning Human Understanding*, ed. Alexander Campbell (New York: Dover Publications, 1959), Vol. 2, Bk. IV, 415–41.

[40] It must, however, be pointed out that the analogy is not complete. A "mutant" electron would overthrow much of physical theory because any *physical* explanation (or even accommodation) of it would require such major revisions. It is not so clear that an intervention in the physical order by God would imply or require any revision of our physical theories, as here the explanation is precisely not a physical one. However, it does appear—see Fales, *Divine Intervention*, 1–7 and footnotes 19 and 20 above—that divine intervention would at a minimum force revision of the laws of conservation of energy and momentum (or, more precisely, of our conception of force), which is no small matter.

reported, conditions that should exclude fusion. A yet still better parallel is provided by the perennial reports of ESP phenomena, such as precognition and clairvoyance. For here there is *no* known *physical* mechanism that answers to the case (hence, no consilience with the rest of science); and in a further similarity, a tawdry history of incompetence and fraud has accompanied the efforts to investigate these alleged phenomena.

There are qualifications. First, Hume does allow that in principle, testimony to a miracle from enough independent witnesses, especially when they are of established competence and character, could provide evidence of sufficient weightiness to achieve at least a rough parity with our grounds for skepticism. But second, Hume denies that we have ever been placed in such an evidential situation with respect to testimonial grounds for any miracle. This is not only because we almost always lack the kind of evidence of integrity and competence that the case requires, and also lack independent testimony, but because miracle stories motivated by a religious agenda are invariably tainted by suspicion of fraud. Even theists admit this, for they necessarily assume such an attitude of suspicion against the miracle testimonies offered by adherents of other religions in support of their conflicting faiths. It is agreed by all sides, then, that witnesses to religious miracles have a checkered track record.[41]

---

[41] Hume's opponents made the ready reply that not all miracles are equally attested—and that the founding miracles of Christianity had, in fact, far superior evidential support than those of other religions or sects, such as those reported in defense of Jansenism and pilloried by Hume. Those who pointed to the exposure of the "miracles" connected with the Abbé de Paris seem to miss the point that of course Hume's purpose required an example so exposed; it would be quite another thing to show that the NT miracles had a *better* evidential pedigree (see also below). William Adams, one of Hume's opponents, retails a common view concerning the difficulty of fraud, "There is a wide difference betwixt establishing false miracles, by the help of a false religion, and establishing a false religion by the help of false miracles. Nothing is more easy than the former of these, or more difficult than the latter" (William Adams, "An Essay on Mr. Hume's Essay on Miracles [1752]," Lydia McGrew, accessed April 8, 2020, http://www.lydiamcgrew.com/AdamsEssayonHume.htm—thanks to Nevin Climenhaga for giving me this reference). Even for his day, Adams displays undue naïveté. Examples of the "difficult" cases abound: Spiritualism, Mormonism, Theosophy, and the classic Cargo Cults, to name just a few. Miracle stories hovered around the Baal Shem Tov, reputed founder of Hasidism, and the Buddha.

It is theoretically possible, of course, that certifiably sober, competent witnesses should provide multiple, convergent testimonies to the occurrence of something inexplicable by any known natural causes. Hume seems to entertain this question in his examples of an eight-day global darkness and a resurrected Queen Elizabeth, which he concedes, at least in the latter case, would put to the test our conviction that miracles never happen (see J. Houston, *Reported Miracles: A Critique of Hume* [New York: Cambridge University Press, 1994], 49–65, 151–68). What Hume denies—as an empirical finding—is that such a case has ever been found. Hume blocks the suggestion that we have independent grounds for thinking that some favored

Here two points need emphasis: (a) dialectically, both Hume and the theist have to accept inductive evidence sufficient to make morally certain the obtaining of the relevant laws; and (b) the *fundamental* laws of nature—which may all be indefeasible—may be knowable only by way of enumerative induction. In view of (b), Earman is wrong to charge Hume with a commitment to an inductive principle that makes impossible the confirmation of any law.[42] The falsity of that charge, of course, entirely congruent with an admission that Hume's account of induction is inadequate; e.g., to explicate how our knowledge of defeasible laws is arrived at in the first place.

---

testimony (i.e., the Bible) is more reliable on this score than the general run, with his ironically intended appeal to the Jansenist miracles associated with the Abbé de Paris, which were generally discounted as fraudulent though they satisfied, at least for a time, stricter evidential standards than could be claimed for the ancient biblical texts. Hume mentions that the miracles were prominently vouched for in Louis-Basile Carré de Montgeron's *La verité des miracles operés par l'intercession de M. de Paris, etc.*, but omits mention of the fact that Montgeron was roundly denounced in an exposé by Antoine Des Voeux in *Critique generale du livre de Mr. de Montgeron, etc.* and other works, including one by Hume's friend, the Reverend Robert Wallace. See Tom Beauchamp's annotations in David Hume, *An Enquiry Concerning Human Understanding*, ed. Tom L. Beauchamp (1748; repr., New York: Oxford University Press, 2000), 178–79. As Hume must have known of Des Voeux, it is an interesting question why he did not cite him (or Wallace). A plausible surmise is that, knowing his readers would probably have agreed with de Voeux, Hume considered the case of the Abbé a sure demonstration of how far deception could go, even in a skeptical climate. Montgeron was himself a skeptic who was, apparently, converted upon investigating the Abbé's miracles. The Abbé's miracles provided Hume with an especially convenient rhetorical weapon, as both mainstream Catholics and Protestants hated the Jansenists.

[42] Earman, *Hume's Abject Failure*, 13. Hume's rather disparate remarks on induction can be grouped under three headings: (1) his inductive skepticism; (2) his positive remarks on inductive inference in the *Treatise*, which anticipate J. S. Mill's methods; and (3) his adoption, in "On Miracles," of the "straight rule," associating probabilities with relative frequencies and calculating them by subtracting contrary "experiments" from supporting ones. These remarks do not, as we can agree with Earman, provide an adequate account of inductive reasoning. However, Hume's argument in OM cannot properly be rejected on these grounds. Earman points out that under Hume's straight rule, no universal generalization—and hence no law of nature—can acquire a probability greater than zero, no matter the number of positive instances on record. Even though correct, this point, as previously noted, ignores Hume's core dialectical strategy, which centers on the fact that both miracle mongers and their detractors must make appeal to knowledge of laws of nature, however acquired, absent which there is no distinguishing the miraculous from the mundane. I grant, nevertheless, that Hume's limited conception of inductive reasoning taints the way he formulates his case.

3. Earman's View: How should testimony of a miracle be weighed?

What, then, of my claim that Earman's analysis of the evidential force of testimony to a miracle does not properly capture the kind of reasoning I am alleging Hume employed in his rejection of miracle stories? We have seen that Earman's conception of Hume miracles is unhelpful and not in accord with what may reasonably be taken to be Hume's intentions. We have seen, further, that Earman's indictment of Hume's inductive procedure is misdirected. But there are other ways in which Earman misses what I think is a central aspect of Hume's thinking.

a) Hume's maxim

Hume summarizes his evaluation of the evidential challenge to belief in miracles (on the basis of testimony) in the following "maxim":[43]

> No testimony is sufficient to establish a miracle, unless the testimony be of such a kind, that its falsehood would be a more miraculous, than the fact, which it endeavours to establish. And even in that case there is mutual destruction of arguments, and the superior only gives us assurance suitable to that degree of force, which remains, after deducting the inferior.

Hume has often been criticized on the point that the computation of a miracle's probability in the face of such a clash of evidence is not given by a subtraction of probabilities. This is a rather minor point. What is clearly more essential is Hume's recognition that opposing evidences work to cancel one another, whatever the mathematical niceties. But how are the probabilities in Hume's first sentence to be understood? Earman, after rejecting several proposals, settles for the following: [44]

$$\Pr(M/t(M) \& E \& K) > \Pr(\sim M/t(M) \& E \& K),$$

where M is the statement that the miracle has occurred, $t(M)$ the statement that there is testimony to that effect, E is other evidence relevant to the case, and K is background knowledge. Earman goes on to point out that the rationality of belief in M on this condition simply amounts to the "tautology" that the evidence must favor the occurrence of the miracle over its nonoccurrence. Unfortunately, in his entire discussion of Hume's maxim, Earman says nothing about how E and K are to be specified (it is not clear, in this context, how they are even to be distinguished). There appear to be

---

[43] Hume, *An Inquiry Concerning Human Understanding*, 123.
[44] Earman, *Hume's Abject Failure*, 41.

two possibilities: that E & K recite the evidence relevant to the law that excludes M, or that, in addition, they recite the evidence relevant to the truth of testimony.[45] I suggest that neither possibility is correct; Hume seems rather to have meant something most closely approximated by the following:

$$\Pr(M/E_1) > \Pr(\sim M \ \& \ t(M)/E_2),$$

where E_1 is the evidence relevant to the truth of the law(s) that M "violates," and E_2 is the evidence relevant to evaluation of the reliability of the miracle report $t(M)$—and which, on Hume's view, must include E_1.[46] In any event, if Hume is saying that one should only believe the more probable of two alternatives, this is simply a corollary of his dictum that one should proportion strength of belief to the evidence. To say that the rationality of belief on this condition is a tautology is simply to agree that Hume understands a necessary condition on rational thought.[47]

---

[45] However, Earman offers one hint where he characterizes E as evidence that supports the putatively violated law and allows K to include descriptions of the witness (Earman, *Hume's Abject Failure*, 44).

[46] While I believe this most closely captures Hume's claim, one could simplify by combining E_1 and E_2—that is, by folding into a single E the evidence for the relevant laws and that relevant to assessing the reliability of $t(M)$.

[47] If we can take Hume to be conditionalizing on the same background—he is silent on this question—my suggestion is the same as Jordan Howard Sobel, "Hume's Theorem on Testimony Sufficient to Establish a Miracle," *The Philosophical Quarterly* 41, no. 163 (1991): 229–37, http://doi.org/10.2307/2219595. Earman rejects Sobel's view on the basis of two arguments: (1) Sobel's criterion provides only a necessary and not a sufficient condition for $\Pr(M/E \ \& \ K) > \frac{1}{2}$, whereas Hume says of the miracle-monger, "If the falsehood of his testimony would be more miraculous than the event which he relates, *then, and not till then* can he pretend to command my belief" (Hume, *Inquiry,* 124; emphasis added). That sounds as if Hume is invoking a necessary and sufficient condition. (2) Earman points out that $\Pr(\sim M \ \& \ t(M)/E \ \& \ K) = \Pr(\sim M/E \ \& \ K) \times \Pr(t(M)/\sim M \ \& \ E \ \& \ K)$; he then argues that the prior, $\Pr(\sim M/E \ \& \ K)$, "Seem[s] irrelevant to the probability of the falsehood of testimony" (Earman, *Hume's Abject Failure*, 41). *Pace* Earman, this strikes me as exactly right; the objection lacks force.

Argument (1) is harder to dispose of, especially as Hume does not employ the Bayesian formalism. Yet, introducing his "maxim" just a few sentences earlier, Hume says, "No testimony is sufficient to establish a miracle *unless* [it] be of such a kind that its falsity would be more miraculous than the fact which it endeavors to establish" (Hume, *Inquiry,* 123; emphasis added)—and *this* is most straightforwardly read as invoking only a *necessary* condition, and taking "falsehood of testimony" to be $t(M) \ \& \sim M$. Was Hume contradicting himself? Or, if he was careless, which reading should we adopt? There are good reasons—adumbrated below—for not reading Hume's criterion as a tautology. That reading is uncharitable, though it may be observed that timely reminders of tautologies do have their purposes. In any case, Hume's "then" may have been intended only as a rhetorical flourish to emphasize the "not till then."

Sobel himself carefully notes that his parsing of Hume's maxim provides only a necessary condition, and goes on to derive a necessary and sufficient condition. He reads

Indeed, much more must be said about the content of E_2. Taken generally, testimony is sometimes true and sometimes false. But, as Hume is at some pains to spell out, evaluation of a given piece of testimony must be sensitive to a variety of factors, some having to do with the content of the testimony (whether it attests something extraordinary or something difficult to know) and some with what we know of the character, reputation, competence, and motives of the testifier. The class of testimonies is inhomogeneous with respect to these relevant factors, and a just assessment of Pr ($\sim M$ & $t(M)/E_2$) will require narrowing the reference class to one as homogeneous as we can make it. Much of Part II of OM is, naturally enough, devoted to precisely the task of showing how, in the case of religious miracles, we are to do this.

b) Modeling the probabilities

In line with a tradition that began in Hume's own day, Earman makes use of Bayes' Theorem in evaluating Hume's claims. He distinguishes between a weak thesis that can be extracted from OM—which he dismisses as true but uninteresting—and a strong thesis, which he claims is false. The weak thesis is that extraordinary claims require correspondingly strong evidence and that, when in such a case the credentials of witnesses are doubtful, their testimony is not to be credited. The stronger thesis—which Earman considers to be absurd—is that in the very nature of the case (given human

---

Hume as I do. But he also points out that the logically possible "exceptions" to the maxim—that is, where the maxim is satisfied but in a way not sufficient to make the miracle more probable than not—are peculiar and hard to imagine. They are cases in which (using Earman's notation) Pr($\sim M$ & $t(M)/E$ & K) is really low—lower even than Pr(M/E & K)—even though Pr($\sim M$ & $t(M)/E$ & K) > or = Pr(M & $t(M)/E$ & K). Lying miracle reports would have to be more likely than ones resulting from the actual witnessing of a miracle. Sobel says this could occur "not because of the unlikelihood of the occurrence of certain testimony unless that testimony is true, but mainly and nearly entirely because ... the occurrence of that testimony (true or false), is already very improbable." Now it could be that, even though this is logically possible, Hume dismissed it even in the case of religious miracles. Had he used the mathematical tools we now deploy, he might have taken more explicit note of this. But in *any* case, the offending first '*then*' in the first quote is most naturally read concessively. It gives Hume's opponent an opening (theoretically) that Hume need not have granted.

Earman proceeds to the second part of Hume's maxim: "... even in that case there is a mutual destruction of arguments, and the superior only gives an assurance suitable to the degree of force, which remains, after deducting the inferior." With characteristic lack of charity, Earman accuses Hume here of "nonsense"—of illicit double counting. But that is not at all what Hume was doing. The sensible reading is that Hume was telling us that, when the testimonial evidence in favor of a miracle outweighs the evidence against it—but not, as he thinks must be the case, by much—then we should be near-agnostics, leaning toward the occurrence of the miracle but not with great confidence. And that is surely correct.

nature, that is), testimony for a religious miracle cannot outweigh the evidence against it. As we shall see, this latter thesis is not absurd at all, although strictly for his central purpose of discrediting the biblical miracles, Hume needs no more than the "uninteresting" weak thesis. But, properly considered, the two theses are not so distinct as Earman supposes.

Bayes' Theorem (BT) gives us the probability that a hypothesis H is true, in the light of some new piece of evidence E, given an antecedent probability that H is true (relative to some relevant background evidence K):

$$\text{(BT)} \quad \Pr(H/E \& K) = \frac{\Pr(H/K) \times \Pr(E/H \& K)}{\Pr(E/K)}$$

There are three difficulties with the application of Bayes' Theorem. First, we are ordinarily unable to assign numerical values (with any precision) to the likelihood of one state of affairs, given another. But this difficulty we will ignore.[48] A second difficulty concerns the well-known problem of the priors. (BT) specifies the rational way to update our assessment of the probability of H, in the light of some new evidence E, by conditionalizing on $E \& K$ in the way indicated. That requires knowing the antecedent probability $\Pr(H/K)$—the probability of H, given just K. It will have been calculated by sequential updating on the items of evidence that conjointly constitute K as they become known. But how do we update the probability with respect to the first piece of evidence—i.e., when K contains no information? We need, in effect, to assign an "intrinsic" probability to H, an *a priori* probability or one relative to an uninformative tautology: $\Pr(H/T)$.[49] Attempts to find a general way to assign objective values to such priors, as they are called, have not met with success; and Earman, on this score, agrees with subjective Bayesians that one is essentially free (within very broad constraints) to assign any priors one likes. But in the present context, I will argue that this is

---

[48] And often can ignore, as all we may need is to compare ratios of probabilities—e.g., the likelihood of miracle testimony (given that the miracle occurred) to the likelihood of that testimony (given that it did not). And often, such ratios are easier to estimate than the values of the numerator and denominator.

[49] Here I am adopting the standard Bayesian approach, as does Earman. Not everyone agrees. Brian Weatherson points out that difficulties arise when we allow evidence that is itself uncertain (Brian Weatherson, "Probability in Philosophy," *Rutgers and Arché* [2008], http://brian.weatherson.org/PL4.pdf). Logical probability theorists (e.g., John Maynard Keynes, E. T. Jaynes, H. Jeffreys) do not consider updating sequentially from $\Pr(H/T)$ to be necessary; they take certain conditional probabilities (relative to non-tautologous propositions) to be properly basic. It is not clear to me how this affects the present question. Practically speaking, I am taking the words of the biblical texts to be known, taking due care when, in fact, there are disagreements of consequence between different ancient copies. And if someone can plausibly defend a conditional probability not derived from a prior relative to tautology, then this, too, should not materially affect the argument I am mounting here.

unsatisfactory (even if, on some interpretations, a resurrected Hume, converted to a Bayesian view, might himself have been a subjectivist).

A third difficulty, less often noted, concerns the evaluation of the value of Pr (E/H & K), the probability of E, given that H is true. It is easy to think of H, here, as some isolated hypothesis—some putative law of nature, say. But, as Emile Duhem taught us long ago, hypotheses do not entail (or probabilify) empirical claims except in conjunction with other assumptions including, typically, other laws of nature. These can be built into K if we like, but how do we know them to be true, except by way of Bayesian conditionalization on further evidence and so forth, in what appears to be a kind of regress? What seems to be confirmable by evidence is not isolated hypotheses, but—to oversimplify a bit—entire bodies of theory.[50]

Finally, there is the question of what relation obtains between a hypothesis being more strongly confirmed by the evidence (in the Bayesian sense) than its rivals and a hypothesis being the best explanation of that evidence. Earman does not discuss the issue, though a passing remark indicates that he identifies best explanation with strongest confirmation.[51] This claim has been contested: here I mention just one difficulty that bedevils causal explanations specifically.[52] The difficulty shows that an

---

[50] Richard Boyd justifies often taking auxiliary hypotheses as known background. See Richard N. Boyd, "The Current Status of Scientific Realism," in *Scientific Realism*, ed. Jarett Leplin (Berkeley, CA: University of California Press, 1984), 41–82.

[51] Earman writes, "Pr (E/K & H) is called the *likelihood* of H; it is a measure of how well H explains E." (Earman, *Hume's Abject Failure*, 27)

[52] See Peter Lipton, *Inference to the Best Explanation*, 2nd ed. (New York: Routledge, 2004). See also, Wesley Salmon, *Four Decades of Scientific Explanation* (Minneapolis, MN: Minnesota University Press, 1989), §3.6 and Hugh Lehman, "Statistical Explanation," *Philosophy of Science* 39, no. 4 (1972): 500–6, http://dx.doi.org/10.1086/288471. The difficulty can be illustrated by an example that makes use of probabilistic causal processes. Suppose that A-type events can produce B and C-type events, with the following probabilities: when an A occurs, it produces only a B 10% of the time, and both a B and a C 50% of the time. 40% of As do not produce Bs. Diagrammatically:

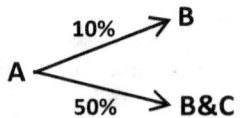

Assume that a C itself never causes a B, and that Cs and Bs are never produced, except via As. We might say that an A's producing a C is causally relevant to its production also of a B, but we cannot say that the C event itself explains any B event. Yet C events are more strongly correlated with B events than are A events. We have Pr (B/C) = Pr (B/A & C) > Pr (B/A). Nevertheless, C does not explain the occurrence of B, which it never causes.

event relative to which an event E is most likely may not be the sort of event that can cause E, and hence it cannot explain E. To be sure, Hume himself reaches his conclusions by arguing for the most likely explanation of a miracle testimony, so Earman cannot be faulted directly on that score. It remains an open question how the goodness of an explanation is related to the degree to which it is probabilified by what it explains (but that is a topic I cannot pursue further here). Let us now be more specific about the inadequacies of Earman's discussion.

The most serious mistake Earman makes in reconstructing Hume's argument is a consequence of his misunderstanding of miracles as "Hume miracles." The error is to assess the probability of a miracle, M, by assigning a (low) probability to M, relative to the evidence E that supports the law that M "violates." That, I suggest, is not the right way to think about the matter. Let L be the law(s) that M "violates," in the sense given by (MV). To keep matters simple, we assume that L is a (defeasible) deterministic law. E is all our evidence that L is a law of nature. It will in general be quite complex, as it will include facts about the consilience of L with other laws we have good evidence for, as well as the evidence for those laws and evidence for laws and other facts that underlie whatever measurement procedures are required to test L. E, therefore, provides our assurance that L really is a law and, hence, that M would not have happened under the circumstances given only natural causes. But E does not thereby provide any information on the *probability* of M's occurrence any more than it specifies probabilities for *any* of the potential defeaters of L.

We are supposing, after all, that L is not a statistical law. Defeasibility is an entirely different matter. A statistical law specifies probabilities of possible outcomes; a defeasible law does not. For there is not, in general, any *law* governing how often such a law will be defeated by a given defeater. Suppose it is a deterministic, defeasible law that spiders are carnivorous. Suppose that carnivory can be extinguished by a very unusual mutation that turns tarantulas into plant-suckers, a mutation that can be caused by cosmic rays, nuclear bomb test radiation, or some toxic wastes. There is surely no law of nature that determines with what frequency tarantulas are veganized; nor does E always tell us very much about a probability value—even if we discover a few vegetarian tarantulas. In a deterministic universe, the laws of nature, plus initial conditions, would determine the total number of tarantulas and the total number of vegetarian mutants; but not even this would make the frequency of mutants a matter of law since it would be a consequence, not only of the laws but of the initial conditions. And even allowing this much, we have no reason in general to suppose that E could provide a basis for estimating that frequency. This point is reinforced by considering the case of an indefeasible deterministic law (e.g., the law of vector addition of forces). Our body of evidence E

supplies us with a basis for judging the *epistemic* probability that L is indeed a law, which may be high but surely less than 1. But if L is indeed such a law, then the *objective* probability (i.e., chance) of a violation of L is *zero*.

We first reason, therefore, that L is indeed a law and then, if L is defeasible, we judge on the basis of ancillary information whether, on a given occasion, L applies but was defeated. It is a matter of further reasoning to show that, in all likelihood, that defeat was not produced by natural causes and, hence, can be supposed a miracle. But E, as Earman understands it, does not need to tell us this. Can we on some other basis assign an *a priori* probability to God's performing a miracle of a given sort under specified circumstances? That seems doubtful indeed.[53] In the present context—in which Hume's question is whether miracles provide us with an independent source of evidence concerning God—such an estimate would be given by assigning *a priori* probabilities both to God's existence and to his having certain fairly well-specified intentions.[54]

The issue before us therefore is not, as Earman would model it, how to evaluate testimony regarding the outcome of some process artificially constructed to generate outcomes with low objective probabilities, such as poker hands or colors of marbles drawn from an urn or lottery outcomes. In fact, recognizing this allows us to deflect one criticism commonly leveled against Hume. It is often pointed out that observation of an event easily trumps its antecedent improbability; we regularly accept the occurrence of an event upon perceiving it happen, even if it is highly improbable. Indeed, perhaps most events have very low (epistemic) antecedent probabilities if described in sufficient detail; convenient examples are a given poker hand or the winning number in a lottery. Apparently rejecting Hume's argument, we reasonably accept a newspaper report of the winning number in a large lottery. Let the chances of that number's winning be as low as you like; we still would consider it rational to accept testimony in this case.

But these examples are, in fact, not parallels to the kind of case that Hume is considering. For these cases are ones involving mere improbability. Every poker hand must contain *some* combination of cards, and every lottery has a winning number; thus, the reporting of any alternative hand/number would be a report of something equally improbable. But a miracle is not the

---

[53] Though Richard Swinburne argues in this fashion for the Incarnation (Richard Swinburne, *Miracles* [New York: Macmillan, 1989], 115–32).

[54] It depends, too, on the prior probability that God has the ability to carry out those intentions. For doubts on this score, see note 21 above. J. Houston accuses Hume of the error of supposing that regularities that provide evidence for a law are relevant to the conclusion that the law cannot be defeated—hence, cannot be defeated by divine action (this is one of two charges central to Houston's attack on Hume). See Houston, *Reported Miracles*, 133ff. Hume's conception of defeasibility is admittedly crude—he seems not to distinguish between statistical laws and defeasible ones—but that infirmity does not affect my re-casting of Hume's argument here.

outcome of a cosmic lottery. And a law of nature is not a tall probability wall over which a miracle must leap.[55] When we weigh the testimony of our senses or of the newspaper against the improbability of their report in the former cases, we rightly judge it more likely that the appearances match the facts than that we hallucinate or read in the paper a falsehood about some poker hand or lottery number no more intrinsically likely than the actual one. In this case, the improbable outcome, however small the odds, needs no special explanation. By contrast, the extraordinary does demand special explanation. This is not a matter of the odds—which may not be particularly low—but of the fact that we are presented with something that normal circumstances cannot account for. This is a distinction that Earman's analysis fails to reflect.[56]

Thus, when someone retails to us the story of a miracle, our considerations are more complex. There are three possibilities. On one side, we consider that we have no law where we thought we had one. Here, the improbability that is defeated by new evidence is not that of a law's being violated but of a putative law made probable by prior evidence being false. That makes allowance for the event but forfeits the miracle, for no law is violated. On another side, we hold fast to the law and allow the miracle. Here, the improbability, if it is one, is that God will have acted in this way on this occasion, for we are supposing that God *can* so act (if he exists, and so chooses) given the defeasibility of the law. A third hypothesis is that our witness speaks falsely.

Now we can set aside the first possibility since that vacates the question of a miracle. The contest, therefore, is between the other two options. How, then, do matters stand? As Hume sees matters (because he thinks natural theology provides essentially no evidential support for the existence of God), we are to consider the question apart from other evidence of God's existence; hence, the Bayesian will factor in only the prior probability that God exists. And relative to God's existence, what is the likelihood that he will, on the occasion in question, have wrought a miracle? Here is something perhaps largely inscrutable, but we can build into our conception of God all manner of characteristics that may make his

---

[55] Here, we may lay to rest the misguided notion that a miracle is *by nature* a kind of event that is somehow unique, or rare, or even merely unusual. What God can do once, he can do again, or often—even regularly. If the doctrine of the Real Presence in Eucharistic theology is true, then there are two sorts of miracles, one involving wafers and the other wine, which God performs millions of times every week.

[56] Recognition of this vitiates Houston's second main criticism of Hume, *viz.*, his principle that strength of evidence must be proportioned to the intrinsic (im)probability of the event being claimed to happen is false (Houston, *Reported Miracles*, 133ff). Charitably read, that is not Hume's meaning.

performance of the miracle more likely, although at the cost of lowering the prior probability of his existence.[57]

Our only real guide, it seems, is one suggested by Hume himself: how often, relative to the number of suitable occasions, have such events been known to occur? Here we must guard against begging the question, for to establish the wanted probability, we must be able to identify not only a representative class of miracle-inviting occasions but also those occasions upon which the target miracle did in fact occur. And if we rely here on testimony, we shall risk chasing in circles. However that may be, we surely must believe that the probability is very low since occasions suitable for providential miracles (so far as we can tell) are abundant indeed, relative to those we can suppose to have happened, *even if we give credence to every report of such a thing without prejudice*.[58]

This, then, we must weigh against the hypothesis that our witness speaks falsely because he is incompetent, credulous, or a cheat. Here is the state of play: we are asking miracles to provide independent evidence for the existence (and character) of God, and we want to know whether such evidential miracles have occurred. On the one side, we have all that complex evidence that makes us confident of a (defeasible) law, of how to identify its potential natural defeaters, and of the actual absence of such defeaters. On the other side, we have testimony that proposes a defeat of the law by something non-natural. But the testimony may be false (there may have been no such defeat) or the witness incompetent (the defeat may have had natural causes). In the middle, we have the (perhaps inscrutable, absent help from natural theology) *a priori* probability that God exists, and the (probably more inscrutable) probability that if he exists, he will have engineered the event in question. The latter probability is an *a priori* probability, updated by any evidence we have of the frequency with which God actually acts in the indicated way. The idea here is not that we are trying to assign some law-like probability to the laws of nature being defeated but that we are trying to use certain imputed general and stable intentions of God to judge the likelihood that he will behave in a certain way under identifiable mundane conditions, and then adjusting that probability assignment insofar as we can by observing the frequency with which God does so behave under those mundane conditions. This last item is crucial since absent hard data on such miracles, this probability is (at best!) hard to assign, especially if God's

---

[57] But see section 4 below where I generalize on Hume.

[58] Indeed, one of Craig Keener's concluding remarks in his massive tome on miracles is a lament on the paucity of providential miracles, as measured by the need for them. Keener has in mind the curing of the maimed and the sick, but of course opportunities for divine succor extend much further. See Craig S. Keener, *Miracles: The Credibility of the New Testament Accounts*, vols. 1 & 2 (Grand Rapids, MI: Baker Academic, 2011), 766–69.

designs are inscrutable. But, given an inability to provide such hard data—testimony would at this point beg the question—we can only suppose the probability to be very small indeed. The saner choice is to suppose the testimony to be mistaken.

That gives us Hume's conclusion. It is important to see that things could have been otherwise. We could, perhaps, acquire strong evidence of some other sort that God exists and that he has certain purposes. That would increase the likelihood of suitable miracles. Moreover, there is nothing in Hume's argument that rules out, in principle, the possibility of hard data, obtained through direct experience, that provides evidence for miracles of certain kinds.[59] Either of these scenarios could significantly affect the conclusion. Though he intends his conclusion to be a strong one, Hume is certainly not proposing an *a priori* proof that miracles do not happen nor that we could never, with probability, identify an event as a miracle.

c) Witness deception

Suppose, setting aside what has been said above, we perform a trial with Earman's procedure for assessing rational belief in the improbable. We begin, in this section, with a simple case; we consider the probability of a miracle M under circumstances in which a religious witness, completely honest and reliable, is certain to testify to M given the appearance of M. We are considering, then, whether or not she has been deceived, as deception provides one way her report could be false. Under these conditions, Earman gives the requisite probability as:

$$\Pr(M/t(M) \& E \& K) = \frac{1}{1 + \frac{1-\Pr(M/E \& K)}{\Pr(M/E \& K)} \times \frac{\Pr(D/{\sim}M \& E \& K)}{1-\Pr(D/M \& E \& K)}},$$

where M is the claim that the miracle occurred, E is the evidence for the governing law(s), K is background knowledge, $t(M)$ is the claim that the witness testifies that M occurred, and D says that the witness was deceived.

A rational belief in M requires that this probability be greater than 0.5. Earman assigns a very low value to $\Pr(M/E \& K)$; it follows that the first fraction in the denominator is a very large number. To arrive at $\Pr(M/t(M) \& E \& K) > .5$, the value of the second fraction in the denominator must be commensurately small—roughly the value of $\Pr(M/E \& K)$. But $\Pr(D/M \& E \& K)$, the probability that the witness thinks there is no

---

[59] Hume does not discuss the interesting question of how natural causes can be ruled out in putative cases. But, as I have mentioned, it is not too difficult to describe hypothetical scenarios in which it would be extremely hard to imagine purely natural processes being responsible for an event.

miracle, when they are in fact in the presence of one, is likely to be very small. Hence the denominator of that second fraction will be very close to 1. This means that the probability that the witness mistakenly believes a miracle to have occurred, when none did, must be extremely close to zero—near enough, it must be smaller than Pr (M/E & K).

Earman rather casually comments that, while Hume may not incline to a small value for this probability, the theist is free to deny that a witness is at all likely to imagine a miracle when none has occurred. The theist violates no stricture of subjective Bayesianism in so doing. So much the worse, then, for subjective Bayesianism. If, indeed, it is at all admissible to understand the question in terms of the probability of a miracle relative to E & K, then surely it is in general simply irrational—an irrationality that eludes our subjective Bayesian—to think that the likelihood of the miracle is larger than the likelihood that a witness has been deceived.[60]

However that may be, this result is *in agreement* with Hume's observation that it is rational to accept the testimony when its falsity would be a greater miracle than that the miraculous event should have occurred. Nevertheless, we should not lose sight of the fact that Hume *never declares himself* on the question of the likelihood that a witness should be deceived.[61] Hume's argument focuses on testimony and, hence, on the likelihood of others being deceived by alleged witnesses intent upon deceiving them.

d) Does the improbability of *M* damage the probity of *t(M)*?

Earman turns next to the claim that the improbability of the thing testified to should diminish our confidence in the testifier, given some assessment of that testifier's general reliability. Earman calls this claim the diminution principle, which is often denied by appeal to cases where we can credit testimony from a newspaper report on the winning number in a lottery. Earman considers, in turn, the possibilities that a witness to an alleged miracle is deceived, that she lies, and that she may be both deceived and deceitful. His analysis yields two kinds of cases, one in which the diminution principle operates and one in which it does not.[62] The former kind of case is analogous to testimony regarding the winning lottery number. The latter is analogous to testimony alleging a white ball was drawn from an

---

[60] Either self-deceived or deceived by others: even the ancients well understood the deceptive power of magic. Exceptions can be conceived. Given certain miraculous appearances, a naturalistic explanation may, as already noted, be implausible. See Dietl, "On Miracles," 130–34. I know of no actual event that qualifies.

[61] Though one can indeed infer something of his attitude on this from his references to Alexander of Paphlagonia.

[62] For the Bayesian details, the reader is referred to Earman, *Hume's Abject Failure*, 49–53.

urn containing a large number of black balls (and only one white). The difference hinges on the fact that, in the former case, a false testifier can provide any lottery number other than the correct one, whereas in the urn case, the only available false claim is "black" if the ball really is white.

Strangely, Earman explains this distinction for the miracles case by considering how to apply it to witness error. The analogy to the balls-in-urn case is one in which a witness hallucinates Jesus strolling across the Sea of Galilee when no one is there, and we consider ways the walker could be absent while the visual stimulus remains. The analogy to the lottery case is generated by considering how many ways a strolling Jesus could perform the feat by natural means—invisible wires or the like. The artificiality of all this only serves to reinforce the main point, which is that Hume avoids almost entirely the question of deceived witnesses.[63] Hume's interest is in fraud. But whether the case be one of folly or fraud, the reasonable way to draw the parallel is to consider all the natural events a witness might encounter as equivalent because they are like black balls drawn from an urn; the miracle is like the unlikely white ball. In that case, the proper analogy, if we accept this style of analysis, validates Hume's diminution principle.

4. The alien abduction and spawn of Satan

Following Hume's reasoning in Section 3b above, we arrived at a conclusion that is rather too narrow and not entirely fair to the theist. Hume, it will be recalled, discounts the prospect of evidential help for theism from natural theology. But what if Hume is mistaken about that? Might not a theist come, in that case, rationally to believe testimony to the miraculous? Suppose, to imagine the extreme case, that a theist thinks our natural faculties provide, independently of any miracle testimony, near (rational) certainty that God exists, can re-configure matter as he wills, and has purposes that will best be served by performing the very miracle that some witnesses attest. Given all *that*, would not it be irrational for the theist *not* to credit the testimony if the witnesses are otherwise known to be astute and sincere?

Now, given the concessions initially made, *arguendo*, on behalf of the theist—that the existence of God has a nonzero prior and that, for all we know, a being like God can directly defeat defeasible laws of nature (i.e.,

---

[63] Though he is well aware that the ancients understood the potential of magic to deceive naïve witnesses, and they often charged their opponents with such manipulations. Classic examples from Scripture include Moses' contest with the Pharaoh's magicians and Peter's conflict with Simon Magus (Acts 8:9–24). Hume himself refers to Lucien's exposure of Alexander of Paphlagonia. Here, too, there was deceit, but it was the eyes of witnesses that were taken in rather than the ears of some not present.

can push matter around)—and given that we are accepting a Bayesian view of confirmation, how should a skeptic think about the extreme case?

Perhaps the truth of the miracle testimony is the best explanation for that testimony after all, even in the absence of other testimony to similar miracles. After all, as we have observed, it is no part of a defeasible natural law that it should be defeated with a given frequency. Against this, I think the modern skeptic should respond by focusing upon the considerations that suggest a high imperviousness of miracle testimony to independent confirmation procedures. In order to explain what I have in mind, let me introduce two analogies.

The first analogy is from reports of alien abductions. Why should we not credit such (often allegedly eyewitness) testimony? The second analogy is from testimony of women who report having been either recruited or kidnapped by Satanist cults and used as breeding stock to provide babies for infant sacrifice rituals. Both sorts of reports were common in the United States a few decades ago, though they seem to have lost currency today.

Set aside the lurid, often scandalous content of the reports in question. What matters here is certain similarities in justificatory structure to miracle testimony. Why should we (as I assume we should) discredit the testimony of those who claim to have undergone alien abduction? One might assign a very low probability to the existence of alien intelligent beings. But such evidence as we have can hardly provide much assurance of that. More dispositive is the evidence that such aliens, even if far more advanced than we, could not to travel to Earth from their home planet, given the distances involved and the enormous challenge of developing propulsion systems that could enable their spacecraft to maneuver the way "flying saucers" do as commonly described. Assuming that the aliens could not achieve super-luminal velocities, it would take a very long time to travel here. More to the point, why would they bother?

Now, I do not think we are in a position to know whether it would be impossible for aliens to travel to earth, even across distances of millions of light-years. Our best physics and biology suggest that this would be remarkably difficult. But what might they know that we do not? We need, therefore, to assign a very small but still nonzero probability to such space travel. About alien purposes and motivations, we must be a good deal more uncertain. Who could fathom such a thing? But still, making allowance for very-interested-in-human-beings scenarios, it seems plausible that a strong alien desire for close acquaintance with humans is not very likely. There is a further ground for doubt. It seems not *un*likely that, over the years, physical evidence of alien presence would turn up, such as a crashed saucer, debris from artifacts, better-confirmed sightings, etc. Absence of evidence is, here, evidence of absence. And, on the other side, abductees often display psychological profiles that suggest a propensity for fabrication or confabulation. A distrust of the testimony seems in order.

The Satanic cult case is in some respects similar. It is likely that such cults exist but less likely that they have an interest in child sacrifice, whatever their rhetoric on that score might be. Yet, while the alleged victims have often been able to give very convincing testimony (convincing to some counselors and psychiatrists, at any rate), one important prediction of the kidnap hypothesis is strikingly unconfirmed. There are no records (so far as I know) of successful police investigations, arrests, or convictions on murder charges in the hundreds of alleged cases. That is decidedly unlikely, given the truth of the hypothesis. And once again, the psychological profiles of the victims raise concerns, in many cases, about competency.

In both the aliens and Satanist cases, sober reflection considers the better explanation to be deception or self-deception. Is miracle testimony in the same epistemic boat? First, it would be extremely tendentious to assume that all, or most, miracle-testifiers are not operating mentally on all four cylinders. No doubt this is not too uncommon, but we should steer shy of Hume's effort to cast belief in miracles as a kind of psychological deviance, a kind of mesmerized wonder at the absurd. We should take note, however, of a phenomenon that miracle reports often share with our analogues. They often come in "waves." Alien abduction reports (and Satanic abductions, as well) tend to arise rather suddenly, become quite "popular" for a time, and then fade away. This was not a matter of collusion. The "victims" were scattered geographically and usually not personally known to one another. However, cases were publicized, and the alleged phenomena became both widely known and sensationalized. Their stories were "in the air" and available for appropriation. As much can be said—though I shall not attempt any documentation here—for reports of (often quite stereotypical) miracles. More to our purpose, however, are the following analogies.

a) As with space alien visits, we have seen that "visits" by God can be doubted on grounds of physical impossibility. And, as with aliens, we must allow that our physics might give us imperfect knowledge of the possibilities for divine intervention. Perhaps, as Robert Russell has maintained, God can control nature without exerting forces or violating conservation laws, by somehow controlling the direction of collapse of wave-functions in causal interactions, even if we have no idea how that could be done.[64] Therefore, we must assign some nonzero, but I think still very low, probability to the proposition that God can push things around.

---

[64] Russell, "Divine Action and Quantum Mechanics," 351–403. See also, Robin Collins on the implications of General Relativity and Quantum Mechanics (Collins, "The Energy of the Soul," 123–36). For some (but inconclusive) difficulties, see Jeffrey Koperski, "Divine Action and the Quantum Amplification Problem," *Theology and Science* 13, no. 4 (2015): 379–94, http://doi.org/10.1080/14746700.2015.1082872.

b) What of divine purposes? Are they as inscrutable as those of aliens (and maybe even Satanists)? Perhaps. Christian theists take divine love and benevolence to be *general* (and necessary) features of the divine nature. But knowing what God's particular volitions are is far harder, apart from the very revelations whose provenance a miracle is supposed to certify. One can make the general argument that miracles which comport with the assumption of divine love conform to expectation. Christian apologetics sometimes go further. For example, there are arguments trying to show that God would certainly have undertaken to create the Christ event, as one uniquely suited or necessary, for human salvation.[65] These arguments are certainly met with skepticism by non-Christians. Jews, for example, regard Yom Kippur and certain other observances as the proper and sufficient means to atonement. Among other things, they do not see the Fall of Adam and Eve in the way many Christians do. There can be debate about all of this, of course. But claims to know God's particular intentions lie in tension with apophaticism and the denial that the Divine Mind is knowable by human beings. Taken all together, it appears wise to assign a rather low credence to our guesses about special divine purposes.

c) Another point of comparison concerns the availability of independent means of checking the truth of various components of an explanation. Space aliens do not seem to be generally available to us; if they were, it would be open for us to ask them about their alleged abductions. (Satanists, on the other hand, can perhaps be located and quizzed about their ritual practices or, better, can be secretly surveilled).[66] Telescopes and satellites could be deployed to look for starships. We could (actually are) listening for information-bearing interstellar radio signals. We can look to new developments in physics and astronomy for deeper wisdom into the possibility of interstellar travel. We can do psychological profiles (sometimes) of alleged abductees, and so forth. In principle, the evidence we gather could go either way, toward confirming abductee reports or (as is the case) toward infirming them.

Similar checks could, in principle, help us to assess miracle reports. However, we run into familiar barriers. We have no secure independent access to God's particular intentions, and those who have reported miracles are, for the most part, beyond the reach of independent cross-examination. Instead, we have to build into our explanatory hypothesis certain motivations imputed to God and to the alleged witnesses, thereby diminishing their priors and creating problems for theodicy. Moreover, there is not much that can be predicted about God's future behavior, in the way of publicly observable events, on the basis of the hypothesis of past self-revelation in

---

[65] Such as Swinburne, *The Resurrection of God Incarnate*, already noted.

[66] I do not mean better in the First Amendment sense but as a means for acquiring reliable evidence!

miracles. We can perhaps hope that future physics will reveal pathways by means of which an immaterial God can influence the physical world; but this remains an unfulfilled project.

Indeed, the miraculous, to the extent that it can be brought under close scrutiny, behaves disturbingly like reports of paranormal occurrences generally. In both cases, there is no good, independently verifiable theory that explains how the phenomena in question are generated. Paranormal phenomena have a disturbing tendency to vanish in the presence of trained observers, a tendency that often invites the *ad hoc* rationale that the very presence of skeptics disrupts, in unexplained ways, the operation of the paranormal forces. Miracles, similarly, tend to vanish like water mirages on a hot pavement when put to independent test. Craig Keener recounts an enormous number of contemporary miracle reports, none of which, by his own admission, meet the standards of rigorous verification.[67]

These considerations suggest that we should, indeed, assign a low prior probability to the proposition that there is a God who can intervene in physical processes, and we should be at best quite agnostic concerning the intentions of such a God with respect to the working of miracles in favor of a particular religious tradition. And, on the other hand, it is often very hard to judge the motives and sincerity of those who report the occurrence of a miracle. But on this score, there is evidence of a kind that does not bode well for belief in miracles.

d) It would surely be serendipitous, with respect to the credibility of a miracle report, if we had a string of witnesses reporting recognizably similar experiences with a high frequency of certifiably independent transmission. But this seems never to be the circumstance we face. On the contrary, as noted at the beginning of this chapter, almost everyone who accepts the miracle reports of a given religion will reject a great many reports from sources contradictory to that tradition. I shall discuss this problem in detail in the next section. What I wish to point out here is the striking frequency with which, when independent verification or falsification of a report under properly controlled conditions is actually possible and pursued, the results are negative. This evidence, too, must be brought to bear on our assessment of any given miracle report, giving due attention to relevant similarities to, and differences from, reports that have been falsified. We are not here directly comparing the frequency of deception or incompetence in human miracle-reporting with the frequency with which a natural law is defeated by some cause not physically identifiable, which is the way Hume might seem often to frame the question of whether miracle testimony should be believed. However, we must accept Hume's point that such testimony has with some regularity been shown to be unreliable.

---

[67] Cf. Darren M. Slade, "Properly Investigating Miracle Claims," in *The Case Against Miracles*, ed. John W. Loftus (United Kingdom: Hypatia Press, 2019), 114–47.

5. Demolition derby

In Part II of OM, Hume notes a further reason to withhold credence from miracle reports. It is an argument from the opposition between religions. Every religion, Hume says, cites miracles to demonstrate the truth of its own doctrines. But religious differences include doctrinal disagreements; hence, any claim that provides evidence for one religion provides evidence against some of its rivals. Because of this contest of each against all, the miraculous tales of each religion, even if their evidence were not otherwise infirmed by the arguments in Part I of OM, would be destroyed by this clamor of opposing witnesses.

Hume's argument is highly compressed. A crude statement of its central idea is this. Suppose just two religious belief systems, R_1 and R_2, are in opposition to each other. They cannot both be true. Suppose, further, that E_1 is evidence that supports R_1 and E_2 is evidence that supports R_2. Then E_1 will *dis*confirm R_2, and E_2 will disconfirm R_1. In effect, each will serve to cancel (all or some of) the evidential value of the other.

Once again, Earman is not impressed by Hume's argument. And, if it is stated as crudely as I have just put it, he has good reason. As Earman sees it, the argument needs an application of the following principle:

> (P) Let $H_1, H_2, ..., H_n$ be pairwise incompatible hypotheses, and suppose that E_i, $i = 1, 2, ..., n$, are such that (a) each E_i gives positive support to H_i and negative support to H_j for $j \neq i$, and (perhaps also) (b) the E_i are pairwise incompatible or at least probabilistically negatively relevant to one another, then it cannot be rational to assign probabilities such that Pr ($H_k/t_1(E_1)$ & $t_2(E_2)$ & ... & $t_n(E_n)$ & K) is much greater for some H_k than any competing H_j, $j \neq k$.[68]

But (P) is, Earman says, "clearly false in general." And so it is. It does not consider that the H_i need not have closely matching priors. Even worse, it ignores the fact that the evidential support for some H_i may be far stronger than that for others. But surely some E_i, or the testimony of some witnesses to them, may provide sufficient support for an H_i to knock its competitors out of the running. Moreover, Earman declares, Hume has given no reason to think that the application of (P) to the case of miracles is appropriate.

This is not a sympathetic reading of Hume. How is it a fair procedure to saddle Hume with a corrupt principle—one he nowhere articulates—and then to saddle him with the task of defending its applicability to the case of miracles? Let us see whether we can do better. We may begin by noting that Hume's strategy is to offer an *ad hominem*

---

[68] Earman, *Hume's Abject Failure*, 70.

argument here. Consider the religions of the world. Some subset of them (Hume says all, but that is over-reaching and not necessary to his purpose) offer miracle claims to show that their system is true and that competing religions are false. How is such an argument supposed to go?

In imputing arguments of this kind to religious apologists, Hume is taking it that they (and he) agree that each religious tradition is committed to some core set of doctrines (call these *kerygma*) that distinguish it from other religions. *Kerygmata* are, however, more than distinctive; they put religions at odds with one another. Let $\{R_1, ..., R_n\}$ be the set of miracle-mongering religions. We know that n > 2. Associated with each religion (R_i) is a *kerygma* (K_i) that is some conjunction of doctrines (D_{i1} & D_{i2} & ... & D_{im}). Of course, R_i may share many of its doctrines with one or another competing religion. But (we are plausibly to assume) the *kerygma* of each religion entails the negation of the *kerygmata* of the others. Taking *kerygmata* pairwise, we will find some contradiction between their constituent doctrines. For example, if R_i involves worship of a god (g_i), K_i may include the claim that g_i is the only god, or the one true god, or the one god who ought to be worshipped by everyone. That puts it into doctrinal conflict with any religion, R_j, that says the same thing about a different god, g_j.

This particular example illustrates some complications. Might g_i and g_j be the same god, even though K_i and K_j deny this? Might Allah and Yahweh be the same deity?[69] Perhaps, to take an extreme possibility, all religions worship the same divine reality, even though some postulate one god, some no personal deity at all, some many, and they disagree in manifold ways about the nature of the divine reality.

This last observation, however, makes Hume's case for him. For many worshippers *think* their god to be distinct from the gods of others; and they think this, presumably, because they think something importantly true of their god that is not true of the other gods (e.g., that the Israelites are the deity's chosen people, or that the followers of Mohammed are, or the disciples of Jesus). So, even if two religions worship what they consider to be the same god, they still are in competition over doctrinal differences.[70] However, since two religions may also *agree* with respect to certain doctrines, we must allow that a miracle that supports specifically such a

---

[69] This sort of suggestion is perennially attractive to theists who have syncretistic leanings, often motivated, in part, by precisely the concerns that Hume's argument raises.

[70] There is often another dimension of competition, though Hume does not explicitly mention it, such as competition over resources like membership. We might call this *practical* competition. It is relevant for this reason. Suppose a god sees fit to provide supportive miracles to each of two such religions. Why, knowing that these religions will come into conflict, would a god do that? *Prima facie*, such a god is either cruel or capricious and, thus, unworthy of worship. To preserve such a god's good character, one must judge that one set of miracles is non-genuine or the work of another, "false" god.

doctrine can work to support both of those religions. Hume's analysis is too crude, in part, because he seems to have taken *kerygmata* holistically rather than considering them doctrine by doctrine. Nevertheless, even this imprecision does not miss the mark by much, as I shall now directly note.

Evidential miracles would be miracles recognizable as the handiwork of a given god. How is this evidential connection to be understood? We have already discussed at length how an event might be recognized to be miraculous, but how is the author of a miracle to be identified? There are several ways this might go. Perhaps the Author of the miracle identifies him or herself to witnesses in an accompanying revelation, as with Moses and the burning bush. Or perhaps, witnesses to a miracle fix reference on its Author as "the cause of that miracle." In the latter case, if the miracle satisfies criteria that make a divinity its only possible cause, then the existence of that miracle entails the existence of that god. Of course, it remains an open whether other miracles are to be attributed to the same god.

Miracles might teach us more than the existence of (at least one) god. A miracle may display the character of its Author, such as his or her providential care or preference for a particular people. More generally—and this function is salient in the mind of Hume—such a sign can serve to seal a revelation. It does so, typically, by way of association with the shaman or prophet to whom the revelation has been given. Either the god confers upon that individual the power to work miracles or does miracles at the request of the prophet or visibly on his or her behalf. In particular, a god may do this in a contest between religions. One easily imagines that as he made his argument, Hume had in his mind such familiar examples as Elijah's contention against the priests of Baal on Mt. Carmel and Moses' competition with Pharaoh's magicians. The implications of the outcome of each of these contests were not lost on either party. Baal was impotent.[71] Ahab was abominable. Pharaoh's magicians were phony. The *reasoning* here is the very reasoning Hume purposes to turn against apologists, though it does not require the kind of open contest in which Moses or Elijah engaged. It applies generally to any miracle M_{ij} that can be used to support some distinctive dogma D_{ik}, if that dogma entails the falsity of (or more generally, is negatively relevant to) the *kerygma* of some other religion.

To be sure, one can conceive of a god who makes known distinctive *kerygmata* to different peoples and at different times and places, sealing each with suitable miracles. But worshippers almost never believe this[72]—

---

[71] Not all evidential miracles serve this kind of public apologetic function. Gideon's request for signs to confirm the divine source of his commission to lead the Israelites into battle against a superior enemy (Judges 6:36–40) does not do so, though the retelling of the tale would surely have done so.

[72] Something like this line of reasoning occurs in some apologist's efforts to make more palatable the sting of the morally rebarbative passages of the Bible. It is

why would their god sow confusion among his/her worshippers?—and, in keeping with his *ad hominem* strategy, Hume implicitly leaves out of consideration the possibility of divine deception. With this background in place, we can reparse Hume's argument as follows. Take any doctrine D_{ij} contained in the *kerygma* of R_i, and that is vouched for by testimony to various miracles, collectively denoted $t(M_{ij})$. Now, there will be a number of religions, $R_m, ..., R_n$, each of whose *kerygmata* contains doctrines negatively relevant to D_{ij} and that themselves are defended by appeal to miracles. Hume appears to be suggesting that the testimonial evidence for these opponent doctrines will, as a matter of contingent fact, almost always outweigh the testimony in favor of D_{ij}. The latter will be trumped, not only by the generally comparable quality and content of the competing testimony, but by its sheer volume.

Let us take each of these two claims in turn. First quality: Part II of OM can be read as largely devoted to an argument for the rough parity in the evidential quality—in fact the poor quality—of the testimonies for religious miracles in all ages. Hume supports that conclusion by arguing for certain universal factors that influence the creation of religious accounts of the miraculous and (again *ad hominem*) by reminding readers of their own skepticism toward the miracle reports of alien religions. And second, volume: because every religion is opposed by a multitude of others, each with some roughly comparable number of relevant miracle claims, comparably evidenced, it is a highly likely (if contingent) fact that no religion can boast of more alleged confirmatory miracles than the sum of the disconfirming testimonies of the assembled competitors.[73]

Putting the matter in Bayesian terms, the upshot is that unless our theist assigns a much higher prior to her own *kerygmatic* preferences, the weight of the negative evidence coming from the miracle testimony of competing religions will drag her posterior probability below the level of rational belief. Of course, facing a determinate evidential burden, she can save the day by ratcheting up her prior sufficiently close to 1 to produce a posterior that is greater than 0.5. Let us dub this strategy *camouflaged fideism*. It is a fideism that makes a pretense at evidentialism, while reposing

---

alleged that God's moral teachings were accommodated to the cultural milieu and level of comprehension of his people, becoming more elevated as their historical development permitted. It is, however, hard in the end to see how such a divine strategy could be justified, given God's powers and the relatively stable dimensions of human nature over the course of the millennia.

[73] It bears repeating that Hume is implicitly supposing that there is no one religious tradition that strongly outdistances the rest of the field with respect to (a) the strength of the support for its miracle claims and (b) the degree to which the reported miracles, if genuine, would support its distinctive doctrines. (To be sure, the probability of being true of even a religion decidedly superior in this way might be outstripped by that of the disjunction of its competitors.)

as much confidence in a pre-selected prior probability as required to win the game. Søren Kierkegaard would have called it bad faith; I will do so as well.

The camouflaged fideist rescues her religious commitments, but at a price. The camouflaged fideist refuses, in fact, to take miracles seriously as evidence; she does not really *need* evidence and, therefore, effectively opts out of rational debate about the matter. We may conclude that Hume was essentially right in arguing that the competition between miracle-supported religions eviscerates the force of the miraculous evidence for each of them. In a demolition derby, the premise is that one car will remain operable, if wounded, and emerge the winner. In the miracles derby, it is unlikely that there will be a winner. But there remains an important issue regarding the evidential quality of testimony.

6. Multiple witnesses

Hume recognizes the fact that agreement between independent witnesses can enormously strengthen the probity of testimony. Earman rightly argues that, however low we may estimate the antecedent probability of a miracle (if nonzero), mutually corroborating testimony from a sufficient number of independent witnesses will make it rational to believe that the event occurred. This can happen even if each of the witnesses is not very reliable.[74] But so what? How often are those conditions satisfied?[75] In particular, are they ever satisfied for the examples of primary interest to Hume—*viz.*, the Bible's miracle stories?

Commentators sometimes make note of the *literary* independence of biblical authors who relate the same miracle. Most prominently with respect to the Gospels, it is pointed out that John is independent, in this sense, of the Synoptics—though it is largely agreed that the authors of Matthew and Luke had access to, and essentially copied, significant portions of Mark. But literary independence is not the issue for us. One cannot infer independence of source information from literary distinctness. It is neither more nor less likely that two authors, independently setting out to recount a tale told to both of them by a lone witness, should differ verbally while

---

[74] Earman also considers the likelihood that at least one of several miracles has occurred where we have a witness testifying to each of them. I will not comment on this case except to remark that Earman's calculation relies upon the dubious assumption that a witness' failure to proclaim a miracle is to be counted equivalently with a pronouncement that it did not occur. That does not seem right. Silences can have very different motivations. Besides, we have no way to enumerate silences, except in cases where there is independent reason to expect a miracle, and we know the witness was in the right place at the right time.

[75] Hume himself conjures up the hypothetical case of an eight-day period of worldwide darkness, but he evidently believed there were no *actual* historical examples of this kind.

retelling essentially the same story than that they should do so, having themselves been independent witnesses of the original events. That John's writing and whatever source traditions he drew on differed verbally from, while overlapping in content with, the Synoptic authors' versions tells us nearly nothing about how those traditions originated and diverged and nothing about evidential independence. The fact of the matter is that enormous scholarly effort has been devoted to the attempt to reconstruct the history of tradition formation in the earliest phases of the Christian movement, with almost no assured results decisive for our present concern.

Nevertheless, it is worth reflecting upon the ways in which tradition formation can bear upon the issue of corroboration by independent witnesses. The complexities we actually face go well beyond anything considered by Earman. First, of course, we need to be clear about what is meant by independent witnesses to a miracle. Most of the miracles we are concerned with, if they happened at all, are passing events; they take place over the course of a few minutes at most (e.g., most of the biblical healings, raisings from the dead, exorcisms, the changing of water into wine, and so forth) to a few hours or days (e.g., the star of Bethlehem). Thus, the ordinary case will be one in which two or more witnesses (say a and b), usually in close physical and temporal proximity to one another, perceive some event M and later describe it to others. The minimum requirement for independence is that a and b in no way influence each other's understanding of what happened or way of describing it to others.[76] That, of course, does not strictly preclude their communicating with one another about M prior to testifying to others. But because mutual (or one-way) influence is so likely (and often so subtle) where there is communication, it will virtually never be rational to accept independence where witnesses have previously been in contact concerning M.[77] It would, moreover, be highly unusual for a miracle not to generate considerable immediate commentary among bystanders. Thus, the circumstances under which most alleged miracles occur do little to encourage a judgment that witness accounts are independent; and this is so even where we can rule out (as we almost never can) deliberate collusion.

Now, what about testimony that has been passed along to non-witnesses; a's testimony to c, and b's testimony to d? In that case, so long as c and d have no conversations with each other or with other parties to the transmission history, they can serve as first-generation independent hearsayers. Or, a single second party, c, can pass along, as hearsay, testimonies from independent witnesses a and b, preserving independence.

---

[76] Nor can they both have been influenced by any third party, whether himself an eyewitness or not. For further details, see Slade, "Properly Investigating Miracle Claims," 114–47.

[77] This is true, incidentally, even when a and b are in dramatic *disagreement* about M (a fact which itself suggests that one or both may have axes to grind).

So long as *c* provides faithful, unvarnished reports of the testimonies of *a* and *b*, not distorting either or both reports, *c* will be transmitting, as hearsay, two independent traditions of testimonial evidence. But neither the NT itself nor other records provide good evidence that any of these conditions were satisfied by the authors of its various books.

The internal evidence we have along these lines is twofold. First, there is some evidence of literary independence. Matthew and Luke are not independent of Mark (or of Q, if Q indeed existed) because they borrowed language and narratives from Mark and, it is generally held, from the postulated Q. But, as noted, John does appear to display such literary independence.[78]

Second, the four Gospels *disagree* on multiple points of detail. These disagreements might suggest the absence of collusion, in the sense of a deliberate and effective conspiracy to come up with a single, coherent story. Indeed, given the extensive opportunities that must have existed within the earliest Christian communities for mutual corroboration, correction, or manipulation of the witness traditions, the challenge seems to be how to explain these *differences*, rather than how to explain the agreements. And indeed, one such explanation is that independent witness traditions were preserved, without substantial editing or modification aimed at bringing them into line.[79]

But here the apologist faces two difficulties and a dilemma. The dilemma is that the evidential force of independent testimony depends upon *agreement* between the independent sources. When they *disagree*, the competence or integrity of one or both witnesses are impeached, even as the likelihood of independence is somewhat enhanced. So even the points of agreement come under suspicion, especially when the opportunity for collusion has not been decisively ruled out. (However, when the witnesses *are known* to be independent, points of agreement, not otherwise explicable, do carry significant evidential force, even when their accounts elsewhere diverge.) When (as in our case), there is partial agreement and partial disagreement, everything depends upon how the points of agreement and the points of disagreement can best be understood. The dilemma, then, is that disagreements support independence only at the cost of impugning competence and veracity, and disagreements do not support independence very strongly when other explanations are available.

The two difficulties are: (1) there exist explanations for the disagreements other than independence; and (2) the dilemma can be disabled only if it can be shown that the disagreements are on matters of relatively

---

[78] Though Richard Carrier has argued that John *did* know the Synoptics. See Richard C. Carrier, *On the Historicity of Jesus: Why We Might Have Reason for Doubt* (Sheffield, UK: Sheffield Phoenix Press, 2014), 487–90.

[79] See also Chapter 3 in this book.

unimportant (or at least not salient) details that do not impeach the reliability of the Gospels on the matters on which they agree.[80]

The truth is that we know almost nothing of importance to the issue of independence about the transmission histories of the stories about Jesus that eventuated in the formation of the canonical Gospels. There has been no dearth of speculation; but nothing I know of can aspire to provide a secure foundation upon which to build claims of independent testimony to identifiable events. I conclude that Earman's discussion of independent testimony, while possessing some intrinsic interest, is useless for an evaluation of the biblical miracle stories—and, one suspects, virtually every other miracle tale ever told.

7. To summarize

Is Hume's argument, then, an abject failure? Or has Earman failed to do Hume justice? I hope to have shown that Hume's argument has significant flaws but that these flaws can be repaired in a way that enables Hume's core insight—which is, after all, a matter of common sense that we acknowledge easily in the case of heathen miracles—to emerge unscathed. Earman's criticisms, while they are in some cases technically on the mark, suffer from a failure to capture a conception of miracles on which miracles could do the evidential work that the tradition requires of them, from a mischaracterization of the probability of miracles in terms of lottery and urn examples (rather than a recognition that what is at issue is not random processes but estimates that a defeasible law has been defeated in a certain way) to an over-simplified attempt to formalize reasoning to the best explanation in Bayesian terms. In all these ways, Earman's treatment fails to give Hume the respectful and charitable reading he deserves. Even so, as we have seen, Earman's analysis actually supports Hume's conclusions in important ways. In my judgment, therefore, Earman's attack fails to vanquish Hume's famous argument. However, there remains another important criticism of Hume, and in later chapters we will turn to it.

C. The Importance of Miracles

1. Miracles and interpretation

My extended defense of Hume—or of Hume reconstructed—will, I fear, have severely imposed upon the patience of many readers. Permit me, therefore, to emphasize the importance of this lengthy journey into laws of nature, probabilities, and testimony. Everyone recognizes, intuitively, that

---

[80] I hope to show, however, that often what may strike our ears as "unimportant details" are often far more significant than modern lay readers usually take them to be.

whether or not God intervenes miraculously in human affairs, and (for Jews and Christians) whether he did so in the ways recounted in the Bible, is of momentous importance for the interpretation of Scripture (to say nothing of its importance for salvation). The options are many, on either side of the divide, but the failure of the miracle stories to be literally true would at least force us to concede that much in the Bible that takes the form of straightforward narration is not to be accepted at "face value."

There has been a rather marked tendency, in some quarters, to characterize opposing attitudes toward miracles as a matter of differing "presuppositions," with most theists on one side and, naturally, most skeptics and atheists on the other. Such presuppositions are, if only by implication, commonly seen as unargued assumptions, among which one is free to choose. It is worth citing one extended example of this view of the matter, here expressed in the measured prose of Colin Hemer:

> It is specifically the difficulty over miracle which lies at the root of much of our present impasse over Acts [*we add: Scripture generally*]. The difficulty for the modern mind of a text embodying miracle has been the first stimulus to reinterpretation, and that reinterpretation of the text has led finally into improbabilities and the rejection of awkward collateral evidence....
>
> The factor of differing world-views cannot be avoided here. It would be comfortable to suppose that we might settle the matter empirically, and indeed it is important to try so far as possible. But presuppositions are inevitably involved. Post-Enlightenment thought may take an absolute position that miracles do not happen, and that *all* alleged instances must accordingly be either rejected or re-explained. Such a position is, however, dogmatic, not empirical. To say that is not to attack it unfairly, but to insist that we recognize the status of this doctrine. It is rooted in a specific world-view. It is none the worse for that if that world-view happens to be correct, but that is a point at issue. The same argument could equally be turned on a dogmatically supernaturalist view. Even when we strive to be scrupulously fair, we are operating here in a context of irreducibly conflicting world-views, and the attempt to be scientifically empirical must at least try to wrestle with contrary options.[81]

Hemer does not come right out and say that there is no evidentially based argument that can settle disputes of this sort between "world-views." But he seems to imply as much, or at least, to imply that no such arguments *have* been given in the dispute over miracles. Instead, the differences have

---

[81] Colin J. Hemer, *The Book of Acts in the Setting of Hellenistic History*, ed. Conrad H. Gempf (Tübingen, Germany: J.C.B. Mohr, 1989), 438–39; italics in original.

allegedly been, in the main, dogmatic. But that is flatly false. It is false, as we have seen, that Hume and his spiritual heirs simply presupposed a skeptical view of miracles. It is equally false that non-skeptical theists are unified in a dogmatic acceptance of miracles. There exists an enormous apologetic literature that argues for biblical miracles on historical grounds (though nevertheless polemically attacking the miracles of other religions and often accusing the skeptics of dogmatically accepting naturalist assumptions).

III. A Better Explanation?

I have argued that Hume offers reasons, both general and special, for not accepting the occurrence of miracles on someone's say-so. My approach was to reconstruct Hume's argument to the effect that, given what we know of human testimony generally, and of the motivations that can affect the reliability of religiously inspired miracle stories, there is a contest between two explanations for such miracle reports. One explanation—we may without prejudice call it "fundamentalist"—is that the miracles happened, more or less as described, that they were witnessed, and that these honest reports were reliably handed down to us.[82] The other is that the miracles did not occur, that what did happen was misapprehended or inaccurately transmitted or, more bluntly, that the stories were manufactured from whole cloth.[83] As between these two styles of explanation, I have agreed with Hume that the latter is by far the more likely. That conclusion, then, must of course exercise a controlling constraint upon the interpretation of texts that contain such reports.

But can we do better than this? Is the choice, in fact, between (more or less) literal truth and fraud, incompetence, and/or folly? Surely the fraud and folly school does not deserve to win by default if there are other explanations of miracle reports that merit consideration.[84] And so there are:

---

[82] By fundamentalism, I mean just the position that the texts are literally true. More explicitly, fundamentalism is the view that the primary intended meaning of a text is its literal meaning (unless a passage is obviously allegorical, poetic, parabolic, or the like), and that, taken in this way, what it says is true historically and spiritually.

[83] There is a middle ground—e.g., those explanations occupied by Rationalists that consider miracle stories to have originated from unusual natural events, which were often exaggerated in the re-telling. I exclude discussion of this option because actual explanatory attempts along these lines are so regularly *ad hoc* and range from the merely clever to the absurd. The most plausible cases are healing miracles, but "nature" miracles present a hurdle that, in my opinion, Rationalists cannot clear.

[84] Benjamin Jantzen makes the obvious and correct point that application of Bayes' Theorem is sensitive to whether one has corralled all of the relevant alternative explanations—or at least those that, *a priori*, collectively occupy the major portion of the

in particular, there is one class of explanations that cannot easily be dismissed. One thing that unites the fraud and fundamentalist interpretations is the view that the truth of miracle reports is to be assessed by taking the reports literally.[85] An alternative, clearly, is to agree with Hume that, literally, the reports are almost certainly false, but to agree with fundamentalists that the miracle stories are intended to convey important truths known to those who told them. That view is possible if we reject the assumption that the stories are to be understood literally. We may, therefore, call this third option the *figurative view*. Of course, like the other two views, it is not a single interpretive option but, rather, covers a range of possibilities that depend, among other things, upon what sort of figurative language one supposes to be in play.[86]

Our three main options, then, are fundamentalism, fraud/folly, and figuration. In the chapters that follow, I shall be arguing, in progressively more detailed ways, that these are generally, and in the absence of good evidence to the contrary, to be engaged by giving first preference to the figuration hypothesis (not just for miracles stories but, as we shall see, for much else), second preference to fraud/folly, and permitting fundamentalism to bring up the rear. More precisely, I have argued thus far for the claim that fraud/folly is to be preferred to fundamentalism; it remains to be argued that figuration can offer us a more satisfying explanation than fraud/folly. I will mount that argument in several stages. Having begun with a general examination of the nature and significance of a principle of charity in interpretation, I will presently turn to some important resources from the field of anthropology that we can exploit to strengthen that case and make it much more precise. The aim is to make it precise enough to provide specific tools for reading sacred texts figuratively, for it is one thing to announce

---

probability space. See Benjamin C. Jantzen, "Peirce on Miracles: The Failure of Bayesian Analysis," in *Probability in the Philosophy of Religion*, ed. Jake Chandler and Victoria S. Harrison (New York: Oxford University Press, 2012), 27–45.

[85] There being a range of hermeneutical methods and principles, with terminology to match, I should explain how I am using the term 'literal' in the context of Bible interpretation. I consider someone to adhere to a literal interpretation if, while heeding common sense to recognize parable, poetry, irony, satire, figures of speech and the like, they otherwise adhere to a literal understanding of Biblical texts. (Thanks to Darren Slade for alerting me to this issue.)

[86] McGrew and McGrew note the relevance of motives for veracity that may lead a witness to claim a miracle when none occurred and, conversely, to deny it when one did, emphasizing that Jesus' followers witnessed his miracles in spite of (supposed) severe threats of persecution. They suggest that, in this sort of case, a sharp distinction should be made between individuals who are willing to suffer for a false religious or political ideology (common enough) and those who risk persecution for false testimony to a specific, concrete event (McGrew and McGrew, "The Argument from Miracles," 661). But this contrast becomes specious when the story reporting the alleged event is, in fact, meant to articulate a religious or political ideology.

programmatically that a text has a figurative meaning and quite another to provide the means for discovering what those figures are and what they are figures for. Finally, to test the promise of the enterprise, I will undertake to interpret a series of pivotal passages in the Hebrew Bible and the Gospel of Matthew, attempting to assess its potential to provide a comprehensive interpretation of these texts.

Having just insisted upon the dialectical significance of the miraculous in the understanding of religious texts, let me add, at the risk of seeming to indulge in paradox, this concluding observation: *once one adopts the figurative perspective and applies the tools of structural anthropology, the miracle stories will no longer seem that "special." For much sacred narrative that seems to recount "ordinary" events can be seen to be similarly figurative and to carry just as much symbolic freight.* It becomes, therefore, a question of renewed urgency which texts (and elements of texts) can be understood as "historical" in the modern sense. To engage that question, a good deal will have to be said about the nature and function of the category of myth.

Roads Not Taken

I. *A Priori* Naturalism?

Bible critics are sometimes accused of unfair play because they allegedly approach the texts with a prior commitment to naturalism as an un-argued-for *assumption* or *presupposition* or *methodological stance* that excludes any supernatural explanations of the content of biblical texts.[1] Indeed, apologists often go on to suggest that naturalism amounts to an article of *faith*, quite on a par with the religious faith that informed traditional exegesis.

Naturalism itself, in this context, can be a metaphysical thesis or an epistemological (i.e., methodological) one. Metaphysical naturalism is here relevantly construed as a denial that there are gods, demons, angels, and other disembodied spirits, or in any case denial that these play a causal role in human and natural affairs. Methodological naturalism amounts to a refusal, as a matter of general policy, to allow explanations that appeal to the supernatural to enter on equal terms into our understanding of religious phenomena and texts.

---

[1] A recent and paradigmatic example of this apologetic strategy is Paul Rhodes Eddy and Gregory A. Boyd, *The Jesus Legend: A Case for the Historical Reliability of the Synoptic Jesus Tradition* (Grand Rapids, MI: Baker Academic, 2007); see especially their Introduction and Chapter 1: "Miracles and Method." Typical is the pronouncement (p. 80) that "we find that [the critical movement] is not quite as scientific, objective, and critical as it claims to be. To the contrary, it is largely driven by a metaphysical assumption buttressed by a form of cultural and intellectual elitism." In an effort to gain a dialectical advantage over skeptical Bible scholars, they strike a pose of open-mindedness, insisting that such scholars display a lack of objectivity in refusing to entertain seriously the possibility of the historicity of biblical miracle stories. But this plea for open-mindedness is clearly a ploy: whatever the force of some of their arguments about textual details, their work is itself a sustained exercise in apologetics. They never so much as entertain the thought that perhaps there are no miracles *even if God exists*: that miracles may be impossible even for *God* to perform. They simply *assume* that God can perform miracles and, by implication, demand that the Bible skeptic assume this, as well. But that is something that needs to be argued, not assumed (see Chapter 2 of this book and Evan Fales, *Divine Intervention: Metaphysical and Epistemological Puzzles* [New York: Routledge, 2010]). Unsurprisingly, Eddy and Boyd's discussion of Hume on miracles is familiar boilerplate and perfunctory.

The metaphysical naturalist is hardly without a rational defense of her position: she may appeal to all the various arguments that have been offered for the conclusion that there is no God and no supernatural world.[2] Nor is the methodological naturalist unable to provide a rational defense for her stance. To be sure, many of the defenses that have been mounted are *bad* arguments, but not all. Hume's "Of Miracles" is, in spite of (reparable) flaws, a *good* argument, especially when coupled with his *Natural History of Religion* and subsequent work in that area.

But more generally, methodological naturalism need not (and should not) be anything more than a provisional and pragmatic directive to look for (and to give preference to looking for) naturalistic explanations for phenomena. It should *not* be some sort of blanket proscription on supernaturalistic explanations. There is a variety of arguments to the effect that empirical science *cannot* admit of supernatural causes. But (as I said) those are mostly bad arguments.[3] There are two *good* reasons for (pragmatic) methodological naturalism: first, a track record argument; and second, a poverty-of-explanations argument.

The track record argument is simply that explanatory gaps (often with theological explanations proposed to plug the gaps) have regularly proved, on further investigation, to be eliminated with the discovery of natural explanations. The second reason is that theological explanations are regularly nothing more than explanation skeletons—that is, they amount to saying that "God did it," with so little in the way of detail as to give no

---

[2] Robert Larmer notes the influence of metaphysical naturalism on nineteenth century Bible criticism, by way of German idealism, from figures like Spinoza and Hobbes. (Robert A. Larmer, "Against 'Against Miracles,'" in *Questions of Miracle*, ed. Robert A. Larmer [Montreal, Canada: McGill-Queen's University Press, 1996], 16–23).

[3] With the exception (in my view) of the argument just rehearsed that divine intervention violates non-defeasible conservation laws. For examples of other arguments, see Stephen Jay Gould, "Non-Overlapping Magisteria," *Skeptical Inquirer* 23, no. 4 (1999): 55–61, https://skepticalinquirer.org/1999/07/non-overlapping-magisteria/; Robert T. Pennock, "Naturalism, Evidence, and Creationism: The Case of Phillip Johnson," in *Intelligent Design Creationism and Its Critics: Philosophical, Theological, and Scientific Perspectives*, ed. Robert T. Pennock (Cambridge, MA: MIT Press, 2001), 77–98; and Michael Ruse, "Methodological Naturalism Under Attack," in *Intelligent Design Creationism and Its Critics: Philosophical, Theological, and Scientific Perspectives*, ed. Robert T. Pennock (Cambridge, MA: MIT Press, 2001), 363–85. While I cannot address their arguments here, both Pennock and Ruse seem to take it, as central to their case, that scientific understanding requires explanation in terms of laws—and hence to exclude the volitions of a supernatural agent. But why, if there is a God who causes natural events? It is not as if *agency* blocks the possibility of explanation, unless one wishes to banish the human sciences as well as God. To be sure, human behavior exhibits certain regularities, but these we understand in terms of human reasons, not laws of nature. Or at the very least, the possibility of a scientific understanding of human behavior does not—*pace* some of the positivists—depend upon the invocation of laws of nature.

direction for further useful empirical investigation or testing.[4] Indeed, this whole debate should by now be something of an embarrassment—both for those who accuse skeptics of simply assuming naturalism as an article of faith and for those skeptics who aid and abet the charge by offering ill-considered defenses of naturalism that feed the fire.

The point to be insisted upon is that none of this amounts to special pleading or to an *a priori* bias or faith commitment or anything of the sort. Theists who want to refute miracle-denying Bible critics will just have to travel the hard road of offering serious arguments to counter the reasons the critics can muster to support their naturalistic perspective. There are such arguments, of course, but they are very far from decisive. In view of this, at the very least, it remains an open and important project to see what naturalistic interpretations of Scripture can yield in the way of new insights, especially when they do not confine themselves to a narrow fraud and folly reading of the texts.

II. The Baneful Effects of the Fundamentalism vs. Fraud and Folly Debate

Indeed, one of the ways in which consideration of only a limited number of hermeneutical options is harmful is the way it can skew the debate. One example is the large and contentious debate over how heavily first century Jewish culture was influenced by Hellenistic culture and religious ideas. The question has been considered momentous by some for the following reason. Put as starkly as possible, it is argued on the one hand that first century Judaism remained ideologically committed to a pure, traditional form of monotheism; and as the earliest Christian communities were Jewish, the worship of a divine-man figure could not have arisen on such soil absent a dramatic, unexpected, and shattering event such as the resurrection.[5] If, on the other hand, Jewish thought had become interpenetrated by Hellenistic thinking, in which worship of divine men (including emperors and

---

[4] This to a considerable extent explains the complaint that theistic hypotheses are in principle untestable. That is incorrect (see Evan Fales, "Is a Science of the Supernatural Possible?," in *Philosophy of Pseudoscience: Reconsidering the Demarcation Problem*, ed. Massimo Pigliucci and Maarten Boudry [Chicago, IL: Chicago University Press, 2013], 247–62 and Maarten Boudry, Stefaan Blancke, and Johan Braeckman, "How Not to Attack Intelligent Design Creationism: Philosophical Misconceptions About Methodological Naturalism," *Foundations of Science* 15, no. 3 [2010]: 227–44), but it is true enough of sufficiently hand-waving theistic explanations.

[5] This, in itself, appears already to be a mistake: see Daniel Boyarin, *The Jewish Gospels: The Story of the Jewish Christ* (New York: The New Press, 2012). Boyarin does not consider whether Hellenistic traditions may itself have informed the son of man prototype in Daniel.

sometimes heroes resurrected from the dead) and the like abounded (cf. Acts 12:22; 14:11–12; 28:6), then the notion that early Christology could have become deeply shaped by borrowings from Gentile traditions becomes plausible, and the need to posit a miraculous intrusion of divine power in the form of a resurrection becomes unnecessary to explain the sudden rise of faith in Jesus as the Christ after the disaster of the crucifixion. Unsurprisingly, some liberal Bible scholars who are doubtful about miracles have championed the latter view, while many conservatives have insisted upon the former. In the simplest terms, this is an issue that bears on the conflict between the fraud and folly camp and the literal miracles camp.[6]

The first observation I want to make is that the debate over how much first century Jews were influenced by Hellenistic ideas is, in a way, silly. That Hellenism was everywhere present in the cultural arena of first century Galilee is not in dispute; the question concerns how much it influenced Jews, especially religiously. Two things must be noted right away. The first is that, for first century Jews (and other ancient Near Eastern peoples quite generally), there was no significant conceptual distinction between religious matters and secular ones; one cannot quarantine, for these people, religious commitments into one arena of theory and practice and secular loyalties into another.[7]

---

[6] For just one example of such probable influence, see Jennifer K. Berenson Maclean, "Barabbas, the Scapegoat Ritual, and the Development of the Passion Narrative," *Harvard Theological Review* 100, no. 3 (2007): 313–21. See also, at more length, Per Beskow, *Rex Gloriae: The Kingship of Christ in the Early Church*, trans. Eric J. Sharpe (Uppsala, Sweden: Almqvist and Wiksell, 1962); Victor Paul Furnish, *Theology and Ethics in Paul* (Nashville, TN: Abingdon Press, 1968), 44–51; Wayne Meeks, *The First Urban Christians: The Social World of the Apostle Paul* (New Haven, CT: Yale University Press, 1983), 33; Daniel Boyarin, *A Radical Jew: Paul and the Politics of Identity* (Berkeley, CA: University of California Press, 1994), 6–7, 13–14, 59–69; and Richard A. Horsley, ed., *Paul and Empire: Religion and Power in Roman Imperial Society* (Harrisburg, PA: Trinity Press International, 1997). For a brief summary of the data, see Martin Goodman, "Under the Influence: Hellenism in Ancient Jewish Life," *Biblical Archaeology Review* 36, no. 1 (2010): 60–67. For a contrary view, see Louis H. Feldman, *Judaism and Hellenism Reconsidered*, Supplements to the Journal for the Study of Judaism 107 (Leiden, The Netherlands: Brill, 2006), 69–99. See also, James Barr, *The Semantics of Biblical Language* (New York: Oxford University Press, 1961) Richard C. Carrier, *On the Historicity of Jesus: Why We Might Have Reason for Doubt* (Sheffield, UK: Sheffield Phoenix Press, 2014), 96–114. For more on this question, see especially Chapter 10 of this book.

[7] This insight is of course central to the argument in Émile Durkheim, *The Rules of Sociological Method: And Selected Texts on Sociology and Its Method*, ed. Steven Lukes (1982; repr., New York: Free Press, 2013). It is an ethnographic commonplace. For its relevance to the Judeo-Christian tradition, see for example, N. T. Wright, *The New Testament and the People of God*, Christian Origins and the Question of God, vol. 1 (Minneapolis, MN: Fortress Press, 1992). For an amusing discussion of these themes, see Jonathan Z. Smith, *Drudgery Divine: On the Comparison of Early*

The second point is that, in varying degrees, it is universally the case when a traditional culture is overwhelmed by a foreign invader, there ensues a strenuous internal debate over how much to accommodate or even accept foreign ways and how much to resist or even become super-traditional in one's loyalties. This is especially the case when the subjugated are not so demoralized and dispossessed of their traditional institutions and culture to make hope of recovery impossible. First century Jews were emphatically no exception: Israel had repeatedly been invaded, was stubbornly hopeful, and repeatedly had this internal debate. During the first century, the Essenes appear to have occupied one extreme, being so alienated from Roman influence that many seemed to have left the urban centers, and took ideological refuge in a combination of extremely traditional Jewish and messianic hope for a leader who would expel the Roman armies.[8] At the other extreme—but (so I claim) with a twist!—were the post-Pauline Christians.[9]

Now the primary point is this: if the only alternatives are to suppose that the Jesus movement adopted Hellenistic ideas in constructing a Christology, or that the traditional Jewish conceptions of God and man were shattered by the appearance among them of the risen Christ, then the debate between liberal and conservative scholars is indeed one that demands to be settled in the one direction or the other—but implausibly so. Suppose, on the other hand, one were to argue—as I precisely do—that the very *point* of the Jesus movement was to construct an ideology that would show how to transform the traditional strain of tribal exclusivism and messianism of Judaism into a trans-tribal ideology. Suppose such an ideology could not only save Judaism from eclipse by a dominant culture but in the process transform the dominant culture *itself* by teaching it lessons in social order

---

Christianities and the Religions of Late Antiquity (Chicago, IL: University of Chicago Press, 1990), 85–115. I shall expand on this claim below.

[8] And yet the Qumran scrolls still reflect Hellenistic influence. Stephen Neill and Tom Wright put the matter well:
> Palestine was never in any manner an insulated country....Scholars detect in the later books of the Old Testament the influence of ideas derived from Iranian dualism. From the time of Antiochus Epiphanes the Jews had been subject to Greek influences; the elders violently repudiated them, but the efforts of the Hellenizers had not been entirely in vain. The Essenes were devoted to the study of the Old Testament; they had no unorthodox or syncretistic purposes; the whole background of their thinking is Semitic. Yet their writings are studded with phrases which, if found in any other context, would have been unhesitatingly classed as 'Hellenistic' a generation ago. It is clear that the antithesis of 'Hebrew' and 'Greek' cannot be so rigidly maintained as was at one time supposed. (Neill and Wright, *The Interpretation of The New Testament*, 329–30)

[9] It is notoriously hard to determine what the attitude of pre-Pauline Christianity toward the Romans was, but Paul's effectiveness in arguing for a mission to the Gentiles is undeniable and probably saved Christianity from early oblivion.

that it was in desperate need of. Then the problem of whether to declare early Christology a syncretistic product of domestic and foreign ideas, or a revelation breaking in upon a traditional Jewish setting, *simply vanishes*. Such an ideology must, *by virtue of its very purpose*, be deeply rooted in the tribal traditions of Israel and, at the same time, reinterpret those traditions in such a way as to make them relevant to a re-envisioning of the wider κόσμος—in this context, imperial Rome.

Other examples of the failure to consider a broad enough spectrum of hypotheses abound. Take the argument that the Easter morning story must be historical because the Gospel writers would never have recorded a fictional narrative according women pride of place as witnesses to the empty tomb (women were allegedly not considered fully competent witnesses by contemporary Jewish law).[10] This argument has been repeatedly offered.[11] Such arguments from embarrassment are weak for numerous reasons (see Richard Carrier's *Proving History* and further below), but my present point is that they take aim only at the fraud and folly hypothesis and do not touch other explanations. In particular, as I aim to show in Chapter 11, the Easter witness given by women, situated within the proper interpretive framework, is *no embarrassment at all* but a powerful symbolic marker. From the perspective of that interpretive possibility, the argument from embarrassment marches right past the boat and off the end of the pier.

In order to consider the methodological questions here systematically, it will be worth examining the critical methods of the most recent wave of life-of-Jesus research (LOJR), which rejects the older focus on the question of myth and reflects a greater optimism that an historical

---

[10] But see Richard C. Carrier, *Not the Impossible Faith: Why Christianity Didn't Need a Miracle to Succeed* (Raleigh, NC: Lulu, 2009), 297–321. And for later rabbinic opinions, see Haim Hermann Cohn, "Witness," in *Encyclopaedia Judaica*, 2nd ed., ed. Michael Berenbaum and Fred Skolnik (New York: Macmillan Reference, 2007), 21:115–16. and Sinai Yuval, "Witness," in *Encyclopaedia Judaica*, 2nd ed., ed. Michael Berenbaum and Fred Skolnik (New York: Macmillan Reference, 2007), 21:120–21.

[11] See, for example, Philipp Seidensticker, *Die Auferstehung Jesu in der Botschaft der Evangelisten: Ein Taditionsgeschichtlicher Versuch Zum Problem der Sicherung der Osterbotschaft in der Apostolischen Zeit*, Stuttgarter Bibelstudien 26 (Stuttgart, Germany: Verlag Katholisches Bibelwerk, 1967), 60; Jean Daniélou, *The Lord of History: Reflections on the Inner Meaning of History*, trans. Nigel Abercrombie (New York: The World Publishing Company, 1968b), 218, 222; Gerald O'Collins, *The Easter Jesus* (Valley Forge, PA: Judson Press, 1973), 42–43; Hermann Hendrickx, *The Resurrection Narratives of the Synoptic Gospels* (London: G. Chapman, 1984), 15; William Lane Craig, *Assessing the New Testament Evidence for the Historicity of the Resurrection of Jesus*, Studies in the Bible and Early Christianity 16 (Lewiston, NY: Edwin Mellen Press, 1989), 188–94; Stephen T. Davis, *Risen Indeed: Making Sense of the Resurrection* (Grand Rapids, MI: William B. Eerdmans Publishing Company, 1993), 73; N. T. Wright, *The Resurrection of the Son of God*, Christian Origins and the Question of God, vol. 3 (Minneapolis, MN: Fortress Press, 2003), 326.

Jesus can, after all, be recovered from the New Testament materials. A good overview of this scholarly effort is provided by Craig Evans, which (though somewhat dated) limns the main features of the approach and the way it handles miracle stories.[12] My discussion divides naturally into two parts. First, I shall consider the more theoretical claims that lie behind LOJR, as well as the criteria it employs in judging whether texts are historically reliable. Second, I shall examine specimen analyses to show how they are vulnerable to serious objections and why the alleged criteria simply cannot perform the role demanded of them.

III. LOJR: Aims and Methods

LOJR distinguishes itself as a new approach to recovering the historical figure of Jesus. It bills itself as being, unlike the First Quest, a neutral, unbiased application of objective historiographical methods that renounces theological or apologetic concerns. It also bills itself as rejecting the skepticism and naturalism originating in the Enlightenment critiques of the Bible. Consequently, it seeks to move beyond applying the category of myth to the Gospels, pioneered prominently by D. F. Strauss. In particular, then, LOJR is hospitable to the idea that historical research might uncover good evidence for the historicity of biblical miracles, especially those of Jesus. The main features of LOJR include close attention to the Jewish roots of the Jesus movement and of Jesus' own self-understanding, an emphasis on the ways in which the entire ministry of Jesus, portrayed in the Gospels (as opposed to just the resurrection event), explains the birth of the church, and a setting-aside of theological concerns.[13]

But our main focus here will be the criteria that LOJR employs to recognize historically reliable passages in the NT and, in particular, how it determines that many, or even most, of the miracle reports reflect actual events in the life of Jesus. "That miracles played a role in Jesus' ministry is," according to Evans, "no longer seriously contested."[14] How should we regard the results of this research program?

---

[12] Craig A. Evans, "Life-of-Jesus Research and the Eclipse of Mythology," *Theological Studies* 54, no. 1 (1993): 3–36.

[13] Evans asserts that *"Theology* is no longer the primary driving force behind life-of-Jesus research. Theological agenda remain operative, to be sure, but the question of 'what is relevant' tends to be deliberately bracketed off" (Evans, "Life-of-Jesus Research," 34–35; italics in original).

[14] Ibid., 34.

A. History vs. Metaphysics, and the Category of Myth

Two preliminary points must be made concerning Evans' conception of the LOJR project's aims and methods, whose importance can hardly be underestimated. The first is that, in assessing the miracle stories in the NT, Evans claims that historians need not—indeed, should not—concern themselves with philosophical debates over miracles. He writes,

> Bruce Chilton's admonition is worth quoting: "[H]istorical enquiry must ... rest content with a reasoned, exegetical account of how what is written came to be, and how that influences our appreciation of the received form of the text. *The historical question centers fundamentally on what people perceived, and how they acted on their perceptions."* The scientific or metaphysical problem of how to define a miracle is just that—a scientific and metaphysical problem. It is not an item that should bring historical inquiry to a standstill. The historian need not know just exactly how Jesus healed someone or just exactly what happened when a person was exorcized of a "demon." What the historian needs to know is whether Jesus did these sorts of things and, if he did, what they meant to his contemporaries.[15]

Evans and his colleagues clearly see this as a license to use narrowly historiographical criteria to assess the miracle reports of the Gospels. But this attempt to isolate LOJR from general metaphysical and epistemological considerations could not be more misguided. If metaphysical analysis were to show that miracles are flatly impossible—events that not even God can bring about—then obviously all bets are off, and no appeal to "criteria" of historicity will be of any interest.[16] It might remain true, of course, that Jesus did some surprising things; and it might be that these things affected how people responded to him. But here, scientific considerations are of the utmost relevance: it would be one thing for Jesus positively to influence someone suffering from mental illness or even from certain physical illnesses; it would be quite another for him to raise Lazarus from the dead, change water to wine, or perambulate across the Sea of Galilee. And besides,

---

[15] Evans, "Life-of-Jesus Research," 17; italics and ellipses in original. The quote appears in B. D. Chilton, "Exorcism and History: Mark 1:21–28," in *Gospel Perspectives*, ed. David Wenham and Craig Blomberg, vol. 6, *The Miracles of Jesus* (Sheffield, England: JSOT Press, 1986), 265.

[16] One cannot help but suspect, in fact, that behind Evans' claim that the historian "need not know just how Jesus healed someone..." is the implicit but illegitimate suggestion that if he *did* heal someone (or, perhaps more to the point, walk on water or raise the dead), then (although the historian can remain silent on the question of *how* he did these things) everyone should properly conclude that only one explanation is possible: Jesus really did perform a miracle.

no matter what wondrous deeds Jesus accomplished, and no matter what people thought about them, these events would not be miracles and, thus, not properly taken to be signs of the in-breaking of God's divine activity or of the eschaton if they were, after all, naturally explainable phenomena.[17]

Further, one cannot—much as one might like to—just ignore Hume's argument concerning the *bona fides* of testimony in this context. *For if Hume is right*—as I have argued he is—then whatever criteria LOJR scholars trot out as indicators of historicity will, in the case of miracles, have to be weighed against Hume's strictures. And that is a contest they cannot win. (I shall show shortly that they do not even come close.) However, a more general observation can be made. Texts provide us with data. When we approach them, with the aim of understanding what they are saying, the aim of understanding why and how those things came to be said, and the aim of assessing any claims to truth, we will be searching for the best available explanation of the textual deposit. Such arguments to the best explanation are invariably fraught with dangers, as we will repeatedly see, but one principle must always apply—namely, that what we are looking for is the best explanation *of all the information* relevant to the question. It will simply not do for the historian to bracket off metaphysical, scientific, or epistemological considerations on the pretext that these "lie outside the purview of the historian" when they have obvious relevance. This would be like an electrical engineer, engaged in designing computational circuitry, insisting that she need not concern herself with the physics of random-noise generation on the grounds that she is, after all, an engineer, not a physicist. It may seem an onerous demand that historians tangle with philosophical questions, but it is nowhere written that doing historical research—especially into reports of the extraordinary—would be easy.

Evans makes a second claim that is even more worrisome. He avers that, seemingly, "a realistic, relatively myth-free historical picture of Jesus can, and does, emerge from the Gospels. What makes today's scholarship so different is that it does not find it necessary to formulate a theology or hermeneutic that deals with myth."[18] But why not? Is it that the new scholarship has simply shown (many of) the Gospel miracles to have happened? Apparently, matters are not so straightforward when "a substantially altered perspective of what myth is and what relevance it has for biblical study"[19] has since developed. Unfortunately, Evans does not tell us just what this "substantially altered perspective" is or how it does not constitute a theology or hermeneutic. We are, however, offered what may be a hint, "A major problem that attends any attempt to distinguish a

---

[17] At least not in the traditional sense. One could still approach the texts with the eyes of faith in, say, Rudolf Bultmann's sense.
[18] Evans, "Life-of-Jesus Research," 36.
[19] Ibid.

mythological world view from a 'scientific' world view is that *in a certain sense all human observation and description is to some extent 'mythological.'*"[20] What could Evans mean by this extraordinary claim? In what sense and to what extent?

Evans offers some citations, but they are of little help; only one seems at all relevant. Russell Aldwinckle suggests,

> If we rigorously exclude from the scientific account of the world's origins or from the various descriptions given of the evolutionary process all those elements which contain symbolic imagery worked up into some kind of story of events, what have we left? Surely nothing that can be called a scientific *Weltanschauung*....our scientific concepts are really myths. Atomic research has only strengthened the conviction that all pictorial descriptions of natural ... happenings are inadequate....The pure symbolism of number supersedes and obliterates the symbolism of common speech....This dominance of the symbolism of number ... is certainly not myth in the sense of pictorial story-telling, but this does not support without further argument the assumption that this scientific description of the world in terms of number is more true than the "mythical" language of religion.[21]

It is not easy to know what to make of this. Is the fact that formulations of the laws of nature employ mathematical symbols supposed to be a significant indicator of some myth-like dimension? But that cannot be right: mathematical notation is symbolical only in the trivial sense that all linguistic artefacts are. Is it that we have no adequate pictorial representation of the behavior of subatomic matter? But then, we have no adequate pictorial representation of the content of most philosophical, legal, or moral discourse either. Are all these therefore somehow mythical? Perhaps Aldwinckle's view of science is a crude prefiguration of Nancy Cartwright or other contemporary anti-realist views about scientific models and laws of nature.[22] But even if Cartwright is right—and I do not think she is—the sense in which scientific representations are unrealistic (i.e., as insightful but partial or defeasible or approximate descriptions of reality) cannot be the sense of myth operative in biblical exegesis or anthropology of religion. The Exodus story, if understood and intended as a myth, is not an attempt to "approximate" something that really happened.

---

[20] Evans, "Life-of-Jesus Research," 17n53; italics added.

[21] Russell Aldwinckel, *More Than a Man: A Study in Christology* (Grand Rapids, MI: William B. Eerdmans, 1976), 269–70.

[22] See for example, Nancy Cartwright, *How the Laws of Physics Lie* (New York: Oxford University Press, 1983).

Moreover, Evans says that all human *observation* is somehow mythical or quasi-mythical, but Aldwinckle is concerned only with scientific *theories*. Perhaps Evans means to be denying the old theory/observation distinction; maybe he has in mind something like the relativisms of Thomas Kuhn and Paul Feyerabend. Would that help Evans make his case? I do not see how. On the contrary, LOJR seems to be committed to a realist conception of historical methods and, indeed, of the results thereby obtained concerning Jesus. And in any case, analytic philosophy has happily moved past this sort of relativism, though it remains a popular card to play in certain other disciplines when the chips are down. There is nothing for it, then, but for LOJR to face up to the challenges posed by philosophical and scientific criticism. Still, suppose we bracket these worries. What can be said for the historiographical criteria that LOJR invokes to sort the possibly apocryphal chaff from the historical wheat in biblical texts?

B. Signposts of Historicity

Evans provides a list of seven criteria that historians may employ to detect historical reliability (presumably for any text, not just Scripture, though the criteria were aimed at judging the history of [Jesus'] sayings). In this, he is partly following René Latourelle.[23] I shall discuss a compilation of the criteria that Evans (E) and Latourelle (L) mention:

a) *Multiple attestation* (E), (L)
b) *Dissimilarity* (E) or *Discontinuity* (L), but also
c) *Continuity* (L)
d) *Context and expectation* (E); but by contrast
e) *Embarrassment* (E)
f) *Coherence* (E) or *Internal intelligibility* (L)
g) *Principle of Embellishment* (E)
h) *Style of Jesus* (L)
i) *Divergent interpretations, substantial agreement* (L)
j) *Effect* (E)
k) *Necessary explanation* (L)

This is a substantial list. Let us consider the items in order.

a) I have already discussed this criterion in Chapter 2, §II.B6; little more needs to be said here. But Latourelle, in spite of an admission that our textual evidence stems from a common oral source, nevertheless offers five reasons to think that we find independent attestations of miracles in the NT.

---

[23] René Latourelle, *The Miracles of Jesus and the Theology of Miracles* (Mahwah, NJ: Paulist Press, 1988).

These reasons are: (1) Attestations in Acts and the Letters, as well as the Gospels; (2) the regionalism (hence relative independence) of early church communities; (3) early Christian preaching showed a "deliberate fidelity" to Jesus, evidenced by a common basic vocabulary; (4) the consistent rejection by the "first churches" of apocrypha in favor of just four Gospels; and (5) the large body of data "found not only in varied sources but also in different literary forms."[24]

These facts, individually or collectively, are supposed to confer robustness to claims of independence. Do they? That is very hard to see: they are either question-begging—(3) and (5)—why could apocryphal material not equally explain these conditions? The answer is irrelevant—(1) and (2), or demonstrably false—(4). Indeed, (2) might help account for the development of linguistic and genre differences stemming from a common source and thereby *undermine* the use of such differences as evidence of source independence.

So much for Latourelle, but what about Evans who cites Mark, Q, and John as independent sources? Here, Evans faces a dilemma, for the existence of Q can and has been disputed; so also, the independence of Luke from Matthew. And the author of John may have read one or more of the Synoptics. The principle criterion that argues for (non)independence is sameness/difference of content (e.g., we identify Q as the material common to both Matthew and Luke but absent from Mark). But then, if a miracle story is common to two such sources—e.g., the miracle reported by Matthew 8:5–13//Luke 7:1–10 on the one hand and apparently reproduced in John 4:46–54 on the other—then two alternative explanations are in the offing: actual source independence or (here) John's dependence on Matthew or Luke (or on some earlier tradition common to all three). In other words, multiple attestation provides no evidence of source independence unless we *know*, on independent grounds, that the etiologies of our texts never crossed paths after the reported event.

Both Evans and Latourelle make much of the claim that many sayings of Jesus, judged by scholars to be authentic, presuppose (i.e., make reference to) Jesus' thaumaturgic powers. But once again, we must suspect that the question is begged. On what grounds are these sayings judged to be authentic?[25]

---

[24] Latourelle, *The Miracles of Jesus and the Theology of Miracles*, 56–57.

[25] E. P. Sanders is, for example, far more circumspect about reaching conclusions regarding the authenticity of the sayings (E. P. Sanders, *Jesus and Judaism* [Philadelphia: Fortress Press, 1985], 123–41). He concludes, with respect to the central claim that Jesus understood himself to be ushering in the kingdom of God, "We never have absolute certainty of authenticity, and we probably have the original context of any given saying seldom, if ever. Facts allow us to be fairly sure that Jesus looked for a future kingdom. But to some degree conclusions about nuance and emphasis still rest on analysis of sayings, and since this analysis will always be tentative, some things about Jesus' view of the kingdom

Finally, Evans makes the popular argument that even the enemies of Christianity, while impugning Jesus' purposes, did not deny that he performed miracles (see Matt. 9:34; 12:24//Luke 11:18; Mark 3:22; also later sources such as Celsus, according to Origen, and the Talmud). But this argument presupposes that it is *true* that Jesus' opponents never denied that he was a miracle-worker; and how can we know that? What we have is Christian sources that do not mention such denials (and later sources that almost certainly relied upon Christian ones). So, the argument must be, in any case, that the Gospel stories reporting the words of Jesus' accusers are authentic and would not have been fabricated by early Christians. But why should we suppose this? Are we to assume that there would be no polemical advantage to be gained by retailing contentions between Jesus and opponents whom he defeats? But Evans also ignores an alternative explanation that neither the early Christians, nor their opponents, understood attributions of thaumaturgic power in a literal sense.

b) and c) The criterion of continuity, as Latourelle describes it, is the demand that Jesus' miracles be "continuous with" his preaching—that is, that they exemplify his message of the in-breaking of God into the world and are meaningful as harbingers of the coming of the kingdom. This criterion seems to be just a special case of criterion g), for which see below. Of course, even if Jesus did believe in, and teach about, an immanent divinely inaugurated kingdom, it does not follow that he performed miracles. The most this criterion can hope to achieve is to de-authenticate stories, if any, of miracles that appear to be at odds with the kingdom message.

To show how slippery this criterion can be in practice, it is sufficient to point out that both Evans and Sanders take precisely the opposite view—that Jesus' miracles, with rare exceptions, do not function to advance any distinctively Christian kerygma.[26] I am inclined to side with Latourelle; but here we have Evans invoking alleged dissimilarity to argue for the authenticity of the miracle stories (apparently on the grounds that they were not fabricated to support Christian teachings) and Latourelle denying dissimilarity (on which see below) to arrive at the same conclusion. So, we have a kind of inverse Catch-22: the miracles are authentic if

---

can never be known with certainty" (p. 156). In a supporting, typical analysis of one sayings tradition (I Thess. 4:15–17//Matt. 16:27–28/Matt. 24:30–34), Sanders concludes (pp. 145–46), "It seems, then, that the tradition contained in this group of passages is old, and very possibly authentic, at least in general terms. Here as elsewhere I do not feel confident of our ability to assign certain phrases to Jesus …; but it would be rash to deny to Jesus this complex of ideas (a cataclysmic end in which a heavenly figure sends angels to separate the just from the unjust)." I agree. It would be rash to deny that. But it would be rash as well to affirm it. The reasons for my thinking so will emerge in due course.

[26] Evans, "Life-of-Jesus Research," 23; Sanders, *Jesus and Judaism*, 170.

continuous and also authentic if not. This sort of result does not auger well for the epistemic credentials of these criteria.

The criterion of dissimilarity or discontinuity is a rule according to which an event can be judged historical if it is not something for which precedent can be found in earlier Jewish or Hellenistic traditions and is also independent of the "concepts" of the early church.[27] Distinctiveness, then, is a sign of authenticity. What is in play here is, apparently, an implicit argument to the best explanation: a distinctive attribution cannot easily be explained as a borrowing from earlier tradition, or as a later invention, so it must, by default, be more likely genuine. But this reasoning is puzzling, to say the least. If we took it seriously, then all those earlier traditions must themselves have (probably) originated in actual events, as the sources of the first such stories to enter the tradition. Furthermore, what explains the novel concepts that entered the later church traditions? In short, the criterion simply marginalizes the possibility of tradent-invented novelty.

What is more—and perhaps more important, this criterion is nearly useless unless we have further (justified) guidelines for judging which sorts of similarities and dissimilarities are relevant to deciding whether a Jesus miracle tradition is or is not distinctive. Absent that, a scholar is free to pick almost any feature of a miracle description as significant and dismiss others. How much does it matter, for instance, that Jewish wonder-workers like Honi and Hanina ben Dosa *pray* for miracles, whereas Jesus simply commands them? Moses, knowing that God has his back, effects multiple miracles in Egypt by stretching forth his hands, or his rod, or throwing ashes into the air. Does that provide precedent for Jesus? Elijah multiplies foodstuffs by simply announcing that it is God's will (1 Kings 17:13–14) and parts the Jordan by striking it with his mantle (2 Kings 2:8). Do these count? Elisha effects the maiming (perhaps death) of forty-two hooligans by cursing them in the name of the Lord (2 Kings 2:23–25). Again, which similarities and differences are we to count?

It must be said, however, that discernment of relevant similarities and differences is of utmost importance in understanding biblical stories—not to determine historicity but to determine meaning, which relies heavily upon the use of repeated themes and tropes. And it must be admitted that recognizing such common themes, in all their variants, is more art than science. Where possible, we should rely upon relationships made explicit in the texts themselves. When those are absent, there are often deliberate clues—e.g., identical expressions or parallel narrative structures. Sometimes, material from outside the canon, even from outside the Christian community, can provide a sense of how traditional materials could be manipulated and used—e.g., in rabbinic midrash.

---

[27] Evans, "Life-of-Jesus Research," 22; Latourelle, *The Miracles of Jesus*, 58.

d) and **e)** Like the criterion of dissimilarity, Evans employs the criterion of context and expectation to argue for authenticity. While allowing that Jesus, in some respect, follows in the footsteps of earlier Jewish miracle workers (he mentions Elijah and Elisha but ignores Moses and Joshua), Evans denies that thaumaturgy was integral to Jewish expectations for a messianic figure. Thus, the miracle stories cannot have been manufactured to satisfy such expectations in support of Jesus' claims.

Even if that were so, however, it would not follow that the miracle stories were not integral to the Christian case for other aspects of Jesus' identity. More tellingly, it would go no distance toward showing that the Gospel accounts could not have provided a narrative context in which a new messianic role for miracles would have become intelligible. On this score, as noted above, it seems to me that Latourelle is closer to the mark. For example, one characteristic of Jesus' healings and exorcisms is that they regularly bring him in contact with persons and objects that are ritually defiling or—as in a healing performed on a Sabbath—violate Jewish law. But there is no suggestion that Jesus becomes, as a result, ritually unclean. Exactly the contrary: whereas normally, pollution is a contagion that renders the pure impure on contact, the purity invested in the person of Jesus drives out impurity on contact. And that surely is meant to suggest something important about Jesus' relation to the Torah and to the forces that underlie defilement, something that can hardly be thought irrelevant to his soteriological role. Indeed, we can be more precise about what that "something important" might be. The communication of holiness from something that is pure to something that is not is seen as possible in two circumstances in the Hebrew Bible. Leviticus 6:27–29//Ezekiel 46:20 indicate that the purity of a sin-offering is communicated to anyone who touches the meat. Thus, the priests who eat of it are made holy. Jesus, then, has the same powers as a sin offering, and anyone who partakes of his flesh will be made holy. Ezekiel 44:19 tells us that the linen garments ritually worn by the priests in the inner court of the temple communicate holiness through contact—just as Jesus' robe does to the woman with the discharge.[28] It is hard, then, to see that the criterion of "dissimilarity"—if that is what we have here—has much force.

This point can be driven home by recognizing how the criterion of expectation fails, as well, in Evans' other application of it. To show that the miracle stories could not have originated in the Hellenistic churches, Evans points to Jesus' violation of the expectation that, had this been the case, Jesus would have performed dazzling miracles to prove his opposition wrong about who he was. Instead, he refuses to give a sign when challenged by them (Matt. 12:38–40//Luke 11:16, 29). But this is a wooden reading of

---

[28] Contrast Hag. 2:12–13, which rules that contact with a robe in which consecrated meat is being carried does *not* confer holiness.

the passage. Jesus has already performed many miracles—indeed, he has just performed an exorcism and been accused of having done so in the name of Beelzebub. Jesus' miracles are explicitly portrayed as proof of his credentials (e.g., John 20:30–31; Luke 7:18–23; 10:17–20, and the apocryphal Mark 16:20). Why, then, the refusal of a sign at the Pharisees' request? Jesus may have been implicitly condemning his interrogators ("You shall not test the Lord your God"; Luke 4:12); but more plausibly, he demurred because he knew that they would do their best to misinterpret whatever he did—as they just had the exorcism. There would, he nevertheless declares, be one unmistakable sign: his resurrection.

Embarrassment is a rather stronger criterion. Here, the situation is that a reported event, rather than falling outside the range of expectations, would, if it occurred, have been a positive embarrassment to Jesus' followers. We should expect, therefore, that the early church would be eager to eliminate any mention of such an occurrence, if striking it from the record were possible. Certainly, the church would never *fabricate* any such story; and the temptation to "forget" embarrassments would only be averted if there were some stronger motive for fidelity to a tradition. And what could that stronger motive be?—if not the undeniable fact that the event occurred and, perhaps, the importance of preserving authentic memories of Jesus' life.

The criterion, then, deploys two assumptions: that folk psychology can straightforwardly tell us what sorts of facts would (and would not) be embarrassing to tradents and that embarrassments will appear in the record only (or probably) because, having actually occurred, they will be difficult or impossible to erase—whereas such things would never be invented or, if invented and later found embarrassing, would have been expunged. Both assumptions are false. It is simply not true, in general, that historical accuracy is a major determinant, *tout court*, of what stories are (and are not) told and transmitted. That depends upon the purposes for which they are composed. Nor is folk psychology, by itself, a good guide, for what is or is not embarrassing is highly context-sensitive.

First, then, does historicity itself exert strong pressure on how a story is told? Certainly, there is a certain presumption in favor of truth, if a report purports to be factual (so much our principle of charity dictates). But where there is motivation to lie or omit, we know from experience how easily temptation trumps truth. In his lively autobiography, Woodie Guthrie breathes not a whisper about his first wife and family, whom he unceremoniously abandoned in Oklahoma to wander west to California (and he adds a morality tale about a boyhood "gang war" that is obviously apocryphal).[29] The efforts of the Mormon Church to obliterate parts of their history are by now well known. Saint Bonaventure, in an effort to

---

[29] Woody Guthrie, *Bound for Glory* (New York: E. P. Dutton, 1943).

"regularize" the heritage of Saint Francis a generation after his death, ordered the destruction of all biographical material written by Francis' actual companions (Brothers Elias, Leo, Rufinus, and Angelus, and Francis' first biographer, Thomas Celano).[30]

So, there can be no doubt that a movement can have little hesitancy in removing or suppressing embarrassing information from its historical record, *even if that information concerns recent events and is true*. But then, perhaps an historian ought to think twice before reasoning that an embarrassment "must" record reliable history: a likely alternative is that the "embarrassment" was not so viewed after all or even that embarrassments had their rhetorical uses. Indeed, if the latter circumstance arises—which it can if, for example, the intention is to provoke, to unsettle usual ways of thinking—there will be an incentive to make up instructive fictions.[31]

Take the story of Peter's threefold denial of his discipleship, foretold by Jesus himself (Matt. 26:69–75//Mark 14:54//Luke 22:54–62//John 18:25–27). There are striking differences between the accounts—e.g., in Luke, but not in Matthew, the denials occur in the physical presence of Jesus. In John, there are two denials, not three, while all three disagree on who questioned Peter. Perhaps most significantly, Mark makes no mention of the denials, noting only that Peter followed after the arresting party, suggesting that the other accounts are embellishments.

Embellishments or not, could the episode be *historical*? There is no question that it represents an embarrassment to Peter. Why would he have been moved to report his cowardice back to the other disciples? Out of remorse? (In which case, not only fear of being caught by the truth but other motives as well can trump embarrassment.) If he had not, how would they have known? Was some other disciple lurking in the shadows? And even if the disciples somehow knew of the episode, why would they have been moved to preserve it? Surely not because they had fear of being caught out by remaining silent. Here, then, we have the disciple upon whom Jesus had conferred the keys to the kingdom of heaven, the designated head of the

---

[30] See André Vauchez, *Francis of Assisi: The Life and Afterlife of a Medieval Saint*, trans. Michael F. Cusato (New Haven, CT: Yale University Press, 2012), 196–205. Fortunately, copies of the earlier histories of Francis were later discovered in the libraries of other religious orders.

[31] A prime example is Evans' own example of Jesus' rejection of his family (Mark 3:31–35//Matt. 12:46–50//Luke 8:19–21), for which this sort of explanation is clearly available (Evans, "Life-of-Jesus Research," 25n82); see Chapter 12 of this book. For a much more extensive (and quite incisive) argument against the effectiveness of the criterion of embarrassment, as well as over a dozen other criteria used by some bible scholars, see Richard C. Carrier, *Proving History: Bayes' Theorem and the Quest for the Historical Jesus* (Amherst, NY: Prometheus Books, 2012), 121–206. See also, Stephen Law, "Evidence, Miracles, and the Existence of Jesus," *Faith and Philosophy* 28, no. 2 (2011): 129–51.

Christian community, falling short of the standards of leadership. Yet, the story bears abundant marks of having been manufactured, *in spite of fulfilling the criterion of embarrassment.* Whatever the background that may explain inclusion of this story in three of the Gospels, we should be wary of the criterion of embarrassment.

f) I have already mentioned in passing Evans' use of the criterion of coherence in **a)** above—specifically, the appeal to "well-attested" sayings of Jesus that make reference to his miracles. Here, all the evidential weight rests on the grounds for taking the sayings to be authentic. As noted, there are grounds for considerable skepticism.[32] Indeed, this criterion is a double-edged sword. If A entails B, and B is shown to be dubious or false, then A has been shown to be dubious or false. Given Hume's strictures on miracle testimony, we should doubt that Jesus performed miracles. If sayings of Jesus entail that he performed them, we must doubt the authenticity or candor of those sayings, as well. It will not do to protest that this begs the question against supernatural causes, as Hume's argument does not beg that question.

Somewhat related is Latourelle's criterion of internal intelligibility. What Latourelle says about this criterion is puzzling:

> When a datum of the Gospel fits perfectly into its immediate or mediate context and, in addition, is completely coherent in its internal structure …, it can be assumed that the datum is authentic. The fact that a story has internal intelligibility does not, by itself, however, constitute a criterion of historical authenticity, for the fact as such is simply of the literary order.[33]

These two sentences are not consistent if by "authentic" Latourelle means "real history." Charity requires that we take Latourelle to intend what the second asserts; he goes on to say that satisfaction of the criterion must be supplemented with satisfaction of others. But then, it is hard to see what work this criterion can do, other than signal interpolations. Is it that we can weed out apocryphal stories on the supposition that they will be *incoherent*? Why should we suppose that a writer of fables will be any less interested in, or able to achieve, coherence than a conscientious historian?

g) The principle of embellishment is another popular criterion. Observing the obviously fantastical nature of miracle stories found in pagan sources and, more relevantly, in a number of apocryphal Christian gospels (most notoriously, the *Infancy Gospel of Thomas* and *Gospel of Peter*; also

---

[32] See n25 above.
[33] Latourelle, *The Miracles of Jesus*, 63–64.

differences between cognate miracle accounts in the canonical Gospels), has led Bible scholars to emphasize the (comparatively) unembellished character of what are taken to be the most primitive accounts of these miracles and the unadorned nature of the language used to describe them. But this, too, is a puzzling criterion. It acknowledges that early Christians were perfectly capable of adding fanciful elements to their miracle traditions. Why, then, should we suppose their forbearers did not fabricate the earliest accounts of those miracles? If one can invent elaborations, one can invent the root story. What licenses us to "strip away" elaborations to arrive at the simplest surviving version of a miracle story and then to summarily declare that miracle's historicity?

h) By the "style of Jesus," Latourelle means "the inimitable impress of his person on everything he says and does; it is his way of being and acting," which is marked by "simplicity, restraint, and authority."[34] If by this Latourelle means that character development in the canonical Gospels adheres to certain common and prominent traits, it can be conceded, though judgments of simplicity and restraint will surely vary (e.g., Jesus has vituperous ways of describing his opponents). If Latourelle is denying that there are significant differences of emphasis in the Gospels, then his claim can be challenged. Either way, this criterion proves nothing more than the art of the Gospel writers and the interaction of Jesus traditions that forged—in certain circles—a more or less consistent picture of Jesus' personality.

i) The idea that underlies "divergent interpretations, substantial similarity" is a variant on the criterion of agreement. It recognizes that different witnesses may substantially agree on certain matters of fact but disagree on details or on the significance ("interpretation") of commonly acknowledged events. Latourelle sees such partial disagreements as actually *enhancing* the probative force of the features of testimony that are in agreement: "Too complete agreement begets distrust, while substantial agreement despite differences inspires trust."[35] There is something to this: too precise agreement conveys an odor of collusion or copying—i.e., witnesses that are not independent. But as we have already seen, too much difference impugns the competence or integrity of one or more of the witnesses, and we are often left with little to help us sort out who, if anyone, among the witnesses is trustworthy This criterion, therefore, does not add anything to the considerations that apply to the criterion of agreement.

j) and **k)** The criteria of effect and of necessary explanation are both essentially crude versions or special cases of reasoning to the best

---

[34] Latourelle, *The Miracles of Jesus*, 61.
[35] Ibid., 66.

explanation or abduction. Evans gives only one example of the application of the criterion of effect, viz. reasoning from a known effect to its cause. Granting that Jesus would not have been crucified had he not attracted a large following, and granting that he would not have achieved this popularity without having performed miracles, we can reason backwards from the effect (the crucifixion) to the cause (miracles performed by Jesus). Now this has a certain ring of plausibility. At the same time, reasoning from effects to causes is always a risky matter; almost any event can be caused in many different ways. Here, then, the reasoning relies upon these assumptions: 1) that Jesus was crucified; 2) that the authorities would not have bothered had Jesus been unknown or uncharismatic; and 3) that a necessary component of the source of that charisma would have been miracles, rather than (say) just his teachings or personality. The last of these is the least plausible claim. There is a vastly greater number of historical figures whose charisma projected them into positions of leadership with a devoted following who did not perform miracles (Alexander the Great, Napoleon, Gandhi, William Jennings Bryan, Martin Luther, and so on). Most will not want to challenge the first assumption, but the second is surely a claim for which the most that can be said is that it has a certain plausibility.

Regarding the (oddly named) criterion of necessary explanation, Latourelle offers the following description:

> If a sizable collection of facts or data requiring a coherent and sufficient explanation are given an explanation that clarifies and harmoniously combines all the elements (which would otherwise remain puzzling), then we may conclude that we are in the presence of an authentic datum (a deed, action, attitude, or statement of Jesus). This criterion brings to bear a set of observations that derive their value from their convergence and that as a group require an intelligible explanation, a "sufficient reason": this sufficient reason is the reality of the fact or event that is the point of departure.[36]

To make sense of this, one has to see that when Latourelle refers to an "authentic datum" in the first sentence, he does not mean any member of the "collection of facts or data" referred to in that sentence. What he appears to be claiming is this: Let P be (say) a collection of biblical passages that one wants to explain. Suppose that some set of claims E (say, a reconstruction of some events in the life of Jesus) provides a "harmonious, sufficient" explanation of P. Then we may conclude that we are "in the presence of" genuine facts (in E) about (in this case) the life of Jesus.

---

[36] Latourelle, *The Miracles of Jesus*, 67.

Of course, this reasoning is straightforwardly fallacious. It is a commonplace that theory is underdetermined by the data—or, to put it more colloquially, any given state of affairs (there being texts with a certain content) can be (sufficiently) explained in more than one way. The most charitable way to understand this criterion, then, is as another awkward statement of the principle of abductive inference: given data that want explaining, look for the best explanation.

This puts all the weight on the criteria for determining what the "best" explanation is. About this, what Latourelle and Evans have to say is given, in effect, by their *other* criteria. So, we can deny that **j)** and **k)** provide additional criteria. What I should prefer to say, however, is that what is going on in every case is (attempts at) reasoning to the best explanation. This should hardly surprise us. Almost *all* historical reasoning is, by the very nature of the case, abductive reasoning. We seek to uncover the unknown past by collecting present data and asking how the world could have come to contain those data. There are several things to be said about the frailties of abductive reasoning.

First, it almost never delivers certainty. It can only do so if it can be demonstrated that some explanation E is the *only possible* explanation of some data D (and that D must have an explanation). Second, the best explanation may not even be probable. (There might be, for example, three explanations where two can each be assigned a probability of 0.3 and the third a probability of 0.4; in that case, the third is "best"—at least in the sense of being the most probable—but it still has less than a 50-50 chance of being true.) Third, what criteria shall we adopt in judging the "goodness" of an explanation? In the domain of the natural sciences, a popular, but not uncontroversial view is that we must use Bayesian, or inverse-probability, reasoning. Carrier has recently defended at length this conception of "best explanation" in historiography.[37] But at the very least, such a criterion faces the problem of assigning antecedent probabilities—even rough probabilities—to hypotheses where judgments will vary perhaps significantly. Fourth, what the failures of Evans and Latourelle's criteria should teach us is that there are no simple recipes that lead from data to a best explanation, if only because one must always take into account relevant "background" information. And there are no simple recipes for judging what ancillary information might be relevant.

Fifth—and most important of all, in my judgment—is the "missing hypotheses" problem. The Bayesian approach makes this difficulty particularly clear: to perform a Bayesian calculation properly, one must first construct the set of all *possible*, mutually exclusive explanations of some data D; to the disjunction of these hypotheses we can assign a probability of

---

[37] See Carrier, *Proving History*.

1 (i.e., their individual probabilities must always sum to 1). More informally, what this amounts to is that when we search for the best explanation for *D*, we may not ignore or fail to imagine any explanation that would account for *D*. Perhaps this will seem too stringent: surely some hypotheses will be far-fetched (i.e., intrinsically very improbable). We will not go far astray if we simply discount them (our probabilities will still sum very nearly to 1). But how can we know, if we have failed even to think of or consider a hypothesis, whether it is far-fetched or not? Indeed, it is a regular occurrence in the history of the natural sciences that a well-entrenched hypothesis is overthrown by a new one not previously considered. Nor, in the present context, is this merely a theoretical concern. I will, with some frequency, be offering new explanatory hypotheses that, so I shall argue, upset probability estimates for previous hypotheses.

It is, then, the soundness of an historian's abductive inferences that should govern our estimate of his or her work. And that depends, in significant measure, on the historian's skill and imagination in formulating a sufficiently comprehensive set of alternative explanatory hypotheses to enter into the race for the true account of the data. So much for attempts to provide formal characterizations of the criteria employed by LOJR scholars in their reconstructions of the career of Jesus. But announced methodology is one thing; actual practice is another and can display greater competence. So, it will not be amiss to examine some of the "fruits" of LOJR investigations of Gospel miracle stories. In the course of evaluating the criteria, I have already considered various illustrative examples of their deployment. The section that follows will flesh out some reasons for caution toward the results obtained by LOJR's use of these criteria.

IV. LOJR: Findings

A. Healings and Exorcisms

First, I shall consider two studies of Jesus' healing and exorcisms in relation to their cultural environment. Is LOJR able to provide good evidence of Jesus' power to heal various diseases and to exorcise demons? It is common, and perhaps useful, to distinguish between miracles of these two sorts and "nature miracles." The former have to do with human ailments; the latter have to do with manipulation, and control over, the natural world. Jesus performs both sorts of miracles, of course. However, the distinction between them is not always clear or well-motivated.

It is natural to see demonic possession as a primitive (and ancient) way of understanding various psychopathologies. On that reading, exorcisms (if successful) are really healings—healings of sick minds. Moreover, what we know about the remarkable psychosomatic interactions between mental condition and physical health encourages the view that treatments that profoundly affect a patient's state of mind may confer genuine therapeutic benefits for a wide range of physical conditions. Thus, a healer who, through cultural conditioning and ritual or personal charisma, is able to change a patient's attitudes and outlook may provide relief or achieve an actual cure without the use of interventions such as drugs or surgery. In these cases, a naturalistic explanation is in the offing. We may therefore call them "squishy miracles," by which I mean that it is unclear whether anything genuinely miraculous was involved. Thus, the healing miracles have always been popular with those exegetes who wish to maintain that Jesus worked wonders but who are discomfited by a robust sense of the miraculous.

One problem, of course, is that we do not know very much about the limits of psychosomatic medicine. However, we *do* know enough to rule out this sort of explanation for certain sorts of cures. Changes in attitude will not re-grow an amputated limb. They will almost certainly not enable a bald man to re-grow his hair or save someone with massive third-degree burns from perishing. They will not, to take a limiting case, restore a dead person to life. These sorts of restorations, then, might just as well be put in the same class as nature miracles, such as causing the waters to part, calling down fire from heaven, calming a storm with a word, or changing water into wine.

Here, I briefly consider studies of Jesus' healings and exorcisms provided by Howard Kee (1988) and Edwin Yamouchi (1986). Both these studies set, as the cultural context for understanding Jesus' healings and exorcisms, contemporary traditions in medicine, magic, and miracle-working. Both are at pains to argue that Jesus' acts fall within the category of miracles, rather than medicine or magic. And both, using the criterion of difference, wish to distinguish Jesus' acts from apparent parallels found in other contemporary cultures, especially in the Hellenistic world.

Kee differentiates between medicine, magic, and miracle in terms of the way in which their operative mechanisms were understood: the first by way of natural processes, the second by way of ritual control over evil forces, and the third by way of engaging the direct assistance of a god or gods. Kee finds Jesus' acts to conform, in the main, to the miracle paradigm, and he takes healing stories to have been part of primitive Christian belief, indeed "almost certainly a part of the historical core of that tradition."[38] Both Kee and Yamauchi are concerned to distinguish Jesus healings and exorcisms from magic. Where Morton Smith sees similarities to Hellenistic magic, Kee and Yamauchi see difference. The latter emphasize the absence of incantations in Jesus' curative acts; he cures by simple command. Smith, on the other hand, emphasizes not only the content of Jesus' miracles, but

---

[38] Howard Clark Kee, *Medicine, Miracle, and Magic in New Testament Times* (New York: Cambridge University Press, 1988), 128.

also his occasional use of gestures, or acts such as touching a patient or applying saliva to their eyes. Unfortunately, formal criteria will be little help in deciding how to settle such a difference of opinion.

Neither Kee nor Yamouchi are much help when it comes to providing reasons for thinking that the healing/exorcism stories record genuine miracles. Both are aware of the eschatological dimensions of Jesus' acts—they are seen as integral to his engagement with, and victory over, the fundamental forces of evil that plague his world (however these are to be understood)—but neither author tackles directly the question whether this opens the stories to a purely figurative interpretation.

Yamouchi, to be sure, does say a bit about this, by way of defending Jesus' claim to be engaged in a battle against demonic forces (and, *a fortiori*, defending the existence of demons). But he does this primarily by attacking scientific naturalism, and that in familiar but ill-considered terms. Thus, Yamauchi, citing Mortimer Adler, suggests that the naturalist rejection of "spiritual substances" (I take it that disembodied spiritual substances are meant) is "as much an act of faith as the religious belief in the reality of angels"—as if there were no difference between the evidence we have for naturalistic explanations (including explanations of angelic visions) and what we have for the actual existence of angels.[39] It becomes clearer where such an apologetic is headed when Yamouchi expresses his sympathy with the view that the sciences—especially the social sciences—cannot be really objective or exclude a "bias" in favor of naturalism.[40] Particularly telling is Yamouchi's use of this quote from Robert N. Bellah:

> But what came through in my lectures, I am afraid, was the assumption that social scientists understood what people are doing when they are being religious in ways deeper than they do. Those poor benighted religious people down there are sort of blindly going through their religious practices, but we social scientists with our conceptual frameworks and our functional analyses really know what is going on....What I have come to see ... is that I was not only offering an alternative religious view of my own, but a peculiarly desiccated one, because utterly conceptual, that was designed to cope with the great issues of religion mainly by screening them out in a maze of intellectualization.[41]

---

[39] Edwin Yamouchi, "Magic or Miracle? Diseases, Miracles, and Exorcisms," in *Gospel Perspectives*, ed. David Wenham and Craig Blomberg, vol. 6, *The Miracles of Jesus* (Sheffield: JSOT Press, 1986), 143.

[40] Ibid., 146–47.

[41] Robert N. Bellah, "Confessions of a Former Establishment Fundamentalist," *Theology Today* 28, no. 2 (1971): 229–30.

Now, as Chapter 1 will have made clear, I share some of Bellah's lack of sympathy for functionalist sociological analysis, with its characteristic ascription of only weak rationality (at best) to religious practitioners. But we are hardly justified in concluding, as Yamauchi wants us to, that a "deeper" understanding of the acts attributed to Jesus requires us to accept that our world is peopled by demons, as if, for starters, we—or Yamouchi—can just know without further ado what ancient people *meant* by their demon-talk.

B. Multiple Attestation

Having in hand substantially concordant testimony from two or more independent witnesses can, in principle, provide significant evidence for the historicity of an event, even a miracle. But what does it take to establish independence? In the case of Jesus' miracles, all we usually have is the Gospel parallels themselves and perhaps some ancillary texts. Parallelism is established by sameness of content; independence, for the most part, by differences in content and language. Between these, tensions might naturally arise. What balance between similarities and differences will give evidence of independent testimonies to the same event, testimonies that are in substantial enough agreement to corroborate one another without betraying dependence? Here, I consider one such case study, P. W. Barnett's attempt to establish the independence of Mark and John's accounts of the feeding of the five thousand.[42]

Respecting these parallel narratives, there are three live possibilities: 1) The author of John knew and redacted the account in Mark, 2) both John and Mark rely upon some common earlier source, or 3) John and Mark give us independent accounts of the miracle. (We are setting aside the unlikely options that Mark took his account from John, and that the accounts do not mean to report the same event.) Barnett first surveys the similarities between Mark 6 and John 6—agreement on details (crowd size, purchase price of bread, number of loaves/fishes, volume of leftovers, and grassiness of the venue), narrative events and order, and verbal similarities. Next, Barnett considers differences, both narrative and verbal.[43]

The narrative similarities and agreements of detail certainly support the conclusion that either 1) or 2) is the correct hypothesis. Verbal

---

[42] Barnett, "The Feeding of the Multitude in Mark 6/John 6," in David Wenham and Craig Blomberg, 1986: 273–93.

[43] Barnett does not discuss (and I shall set aside as irrelevant here) the logistical challenges of such a mass picnic. How would Jesus' sermon have been audible to 5,000 people? How would their number have been ascertained? How would the orderly distribution of that much food have been managed in a timely fashion (the hour was "late," Mark 6:35; at Passover, John 6:4) since it was probably close to dark)? But one assumes that if God could give Jesus the power to multiply dead fish, he could have also supplied a divine P.A. system and other props.

agreements, however, present a more complex picture: there is strong overlap in vocabulary, but similarities in phrasing are much sparser than those between Mark 6 and the cognate accounts in Matthew 14 and Luke 9. Thus, Barnett concludes that all-told, the similarities do not decisively favor 1) or 2) over 3). What about the differences, then?

Since Barnett does not place much weight on the verbal differences, I will focus on just those narrative differences that seem to him to favor independence. First, Barnett notes that John does not describe the venue as being in the wilderness, whereas Mark mentions this twice. Given John's interest in drawing parallels between Jesus and Moses, this seems surprising to Barnett on the second dependence hypotheses. But why? On hypothesis 2), Mark could have added such a detail while John missed the opportunity (yet more than making up for it in John 6:32–59).

Second, Barnett notes that Mark and John use different words to describe the fact that the multitude ate their fill. He takes this to be good evidence for independence. But why? Why could not John express this in his own words rather than following Mark as slavishly as Matthew and Luke did? There are any number of reasons why he might want to or none at all. Absent some reason to think that John would have felt some pressure to adhere closely to the language of his sources, this variance in wording shows nothing.[44] Indeed, this sort of variation in a single story can occur *even in a single book by one author, and even involve substantive difference in content*: as, for example, the differences in the description of Paul's conversion experience (a matter of considerably more importance than the verbal details of Mark 6:42//John 6:11–12) reported in Acts 9:3–30, 22:6–21, and 26:12–21. Should we conclude that these differences signal interpolations or that Luke was unaware of what he had written a few chapters before?[45] The descriptions are set in different contexts—but so are the Markan and Johannine descriptions of the feeding of the five thousand.

The importance of context is brought out by another difference between Mark and John: the latter, but not the former, recounts an attempt by the multitude, after the miracle, to coronate Jesus—an attempt Jesus rebuffs. One can hardly avoid catching the scent of a Johannine redactional interest in this insertion, but Barnett discounts that interest, seeing rather an omission from Mark "for unknown reasons":

> How do we explain its presence in John and its absence in Mark? One possibility is that John has created this detail *ex nihilo* for redactional reasons, namely to promote the view of Jesus as Prophet-King. This,

---

[44] Indeed, on hypothesis 2), the possibility exists that both Mark and John took creative liberties with a common source.

[45] Similar remarks apply to Barnett's conclusion of independence from the differences between Mark/Matt./Luke and John's descriptions of collecting the left-overs.

however, is unlikely ... since the Fourth Evangelist neither here nor elsewhere ... actively portrays Jesus as [the prophet who was to come into the world]. [46]

This reasoning is puzzling. Royal traditions of prophecy and thaumaturgy were well entrenched in both Jewish and Hellenistic lore, and John portrays Jesus as possessing the gift of prophecy and clairvoyance.[47]

Indeed, John 2:4 is directly relevant to an understanding of Jesus' refusal to be declared king by the crowd. He knows that his hour has not yet come, and they do not understand what sort of king he is to be. Even more decisively, at John 5:46, immediately preceding the miracle pericope, Jesus declares, "If you believed Moses, you would believe me, for he wrote of me"—a clear reference to Deuteronomy 18:18–20, which states,

> [18] "I will raise up for them a prophet like you from among their brothers. And I will put my words in his mouth, and he shall speak to them all that I command him.
> [19] And whoever will not listen to my words that he shall speak in my name, I myself will require it of him.
> [20] But the prophet who presumes to speak a word in my name that I have not commanded him to speak, or who speaks in the name of other gods, that same prophet shall die."

Just so, Jesus asserts in John 5:24–27,

> [24] Truly, truly, I say to you, whoever hears my word and believes him who sent me has eternal life. He does not come into judgment, but has passed from death to life.
> [25] "Truly, truly, I say to you, an hour is coming, and is now here, when the dead will hear the voice of the Son of God, and those who hear will live.
> [26] For as the Father has life in himself, so he has granted the Son also to have life in himself.
> [27] And he has given him authority to execute judgment, because he is the Son of Man.

Jesus goes on to berate certain Jews for not receiving him, who comes in the Father's name. Instead, they listen to false prophets. It is impossible not to see in this a Johannine portrayal of Jesus as a "Prophet-King." I shall, in the closing chapters of this book, have a great deal to say about what sort of a

---

[46] Barnett, "The Feeding of the Multitude in Mark 6/John 6," 280.
[47] John 1:48–51; 2:4; 4:16–26; 6:70.

king that is; although I focus on Matthew's passion, the same view is abundantly manifest in John's passion.

That Jesus' royal destiny is at the forefront of John's concern in John 6 is obvious in what follows the miracle episode; and this narrative imperative determines not only the coronation episode but the ways in which John's story diverges from Mark's in the aftermath. Barnett fails to note the controlling influence of identifying Jesus as the perfect paschal sacrifice in the Gospel of John. The impetus to carry that theme through consistently leads John, in contrast to the Synoptics, to make Good Friday the Day of Preparation, not Passover Day. Having made that alteration, he cannot set the institution of the Eucharist at the Last Supper, which is no longer a Passover Seder. Instead, he conscripts the feeding of the five thousand—which he alone describes as a Passover celebration (John 6:4)—as the occasion on which his role as the new Paschal lamb is declared to his disciples. And this entire pericope (vv. 25–65) makes explicit the connection between Jesus' role as the paschal lamb and his royal status.

As it is, Barnett concludes,

> The two accounts of the Feeding of the Multitude were, and had been throughout their pre-histories, separate, with each resting in all probability on independent eyewitness recollection....The major implication is that although the stories have been subjected to editorial redaction ... the underlying traditions are independent, thus enhancing the probable historicity of the incident.[48]

That conclusion, if sound, would rule out hypotheses 1) and 2). But the evidence Barnett offers will not support any such conclusion. 1) and 2) remain very much alive, but it is even more important to see just how weak Barnett's evidence is. Suppose we *grant* Barnett, for the sake of argument, that 1) and 2) have been called into question. It might seem, then, that 3) wins by default; but in fact, this is a complete non-sequitur. For, as the alternatives have been described, they elide the fact that 2) is ambiguous between a whole range of possible ways in which interacting and intersecting testimonial histories may lie in the background of Mark and John. Even if we were to grant that Mark and John do not both rely upon some single *proximate* source for their knowledge of the miracle, we cannot eliminate their having relied upon multiple overlapping sources, nor can we eliminate the possibility of many and complex interactions within and between the traditions that led from some single original source to the evangelists via ultimately divergent traditions. Barnett's evidence has not

---

[48] Barnett, "The Feeding of the Multitude in Mark 6/John 6," 289.

C. The Dead Will Hear the Voice of the Son of God

Murray Harris discusses the three revivification miracles recorded in the Gospels: the raising of a woman's son at Nain (Luke 7:11–16), the raising of Jairus' daughter (Matt. 9:18–26//Mark 5:21–43//Luke 8:40–56), and the raising of Lazarus (John 11:1–44). He argues for the historicity of each of these miracles.[49] I shall comment here only on the raising at Nain. In this story, Jesus and his disciples meet a funeral procession, headed out of town to bury the only son of a widow. Jesus has compassion on the mother, stops the procession by touching the bier, and commands the young man to rise—which he does. The crowd (understandably) sees Jesus to be a great prophet and a channel of divine power.

Harris notes the strong parallels between the story of the widow from Nain (N), Elijah's raising of the son of a widow of Zarapeth (Z) in 1 Kings 17:8–24, and, in passing, the cognate miracle performed by Elisha for the Shunamite woman (S) in 2 Kings 4:8–37. He notes a series of similarities, including verbal coincidences (with the Septuagint) but, characteristically, invokes a number of differences of detail to conclude that, conceding influence, it nevertheless would be "improper to claim that Luke actually created this miracle story from the OT narrative in order to portray Jesus as a new Elijah."[50]

Before commenting on this conclusion, a few words are in order concerning the relationship of the Elijah and Elisha miracle stories. Here, the parallels are too striking and numerous to deny that the Elisha miracle is modelled on that of his mentor. But there are also differences. These may reflect a desire not to slavishly copy the Elijah miracle; but they may also have a greater significance. One difference is that Z is very poor, whereas S is wealthy. Another is that Elijah meets Z's desperate need for food with a miracle of multiplying the flour and oil on hand. Such a miracle would be out of place in the story of the wealthy S; instead, Elisha cures her infertility so that she can bear a son. Yet, 2 Kings 4 repeats the miracle of multiplying oil—only this time, just before the Shunem pericope on behalf of another widow. (And Jesus effectively repeats the miracle of restoring a woman to fertility, but as an aside to the raising of Jairus' daughter; Luke 8:43–48).

---

[49] Murray J. Harris, "'The Dead are Restored to Life': Miracles of Revivification in the Gospels," in *Gospel Perspectives*, ed. David Wenham and Craig Blomberg, vol. 6, *The Miracles of Jesus* (Sheffield, England: JSOT Press, 1986), 295–326.

[50] Harris, "'The Dead are Restored to Life,'" 301. Harris goes on to consider a couple of rather far-fetched parallels in the Hellenistic literature, which I shall ignore.

It is noteworthy that Z is a foreign woman living in a foreign land (Zarapeth was located on the Mediterranean coast, about midway between Tyre and Sidon; she is thus not a citizen of Israel). Therefore, Elijah is favoring a woman who is not a subject of King Ahab's kingdom.[51] The political context of the Elisha miracle is less clear, but S tells Elisha's servant that she "dwells among [her] own people" (2 Kings 4:13), perhaps signaling that she, too, is an alien. In any event, her wealth sets up the problem of how Elisha is to repay her kindness and permits allusion to his influence in high places. N, on the other hand, appears to be an Israelite, though her nationality is given no mention. Nevertheless, the location of Nain is quite striking—a fact Harris fails to recognize, for the Shunem of the Omride dynasty in Israel is just geographically identical with first century Nain.[52] It is difficult, therefore, to avoid the conclusion that Luke means to be associating his story not only with Elijah's miracle but Elisha's, as well. What is more, the political overtones to both the Elijah and Elisha miracles should alert us to the possibility that Jesus' revivification miracles have such overtones. Such implications are not far from the surface in the story of Jairus' daughter, and they become explicit in John's story of the raising of Lazarus. Might they also be present in the story of N? It is interesting that Harris says in passing that Jesus comes to bring "emancipation from the tyranny of death" rather than that of Rome.[53] But as I eventually hope to show in Chapter 12, that supposed contrast misreads the way in which the writers of the Gospels understood the dominion of death.

Harris perceptively notes the theological significance of the raisings as indicating Jesus' messiahship, his power (especially his "conquest of death"), his compassion, and a prefiguring Jesus' own resurrection, as well as the general resurrection. But it is then surprising that he does not seriously entertain the possibility that these stories can serve just those functions without having any historical basis. Harris' analysis reflects the wooden use of *similarity* to signal influence, and of *difference* to show that a story (even if infiltrated with elements derived from other sources) must have an historical basis. This simply fails to recognize the fact that differences can (once parallelism is established) be as meaningful—and as much under the

---

[51] Luke 4:24–27 explicitly points to this precedent for Jesus' mission to the Gentiles. Conversely, Jews that refuse to respond to the gospel are to be reckoned "as Gentiles." Marcus Borg points out that Jesus' instruction to his disciples to leave any town that does not receive their teaching and "shake the dust" from their feet reflects a tradition according to which a Jew returning from a foreign land is to shake the dust from his/her feet upon re-entering Israel. See Marcus J. Borg, *Conflict, Politics, and Politics in the Teachings of Jesus*, 2nd ed. (Harrisburg, PA: Trinity Press International, 1998), 219.

[52] Biblical atlases locate them within a mile of one another. We cannot know, but it must be assumed that Nain was known to have been built on, or near, the ruins of Shunem.

[53] Harris, "'The Dead are Restored to Life,'" 295.

willing control of a creative author—as similarities. But we can say more. Often, the differences acquire their significance *precisely because of* the contrast they achieve with an earlier story to which allusion is clearly being made by way of similarities.[54]

The chief failing, then, of the procedure of enumerating differences between a text and parallels, and proceeding more or less straightaway to conclude the existence of an independent tradition or nonexistence of influence, is that often no careful attention is paid to the possible *significance* of the differences, of what distinctive meaning they might contribute in light of intended parallels. Nor are the prospects good that LOJR scholars or their heirs can develop a plausible general theory of the significance of such differences, beyond a broad hypothesis that they may sometimes betray independence.[55]

A preliminary point is this. Beyond giving free reign to a desire to express his or her creative energies—even to convey the same message as a traditional tale but in a new, perhaps more powerful way—a storyteller may quite deliberately introduce new elements into, or otherwise alter, a narrative handed down for any number of reasons: to maintain narrative flow within a larger narrative context, to combine alternative traditions, to square a narrative with things said elsewhere, to "update" language or style; or—most importantly—to pour new meaning into familiar forms (new wine into old wineskins). All of these can motivate novelty and all are consistent with not just knowledge of and being influenced by older stories but can function in the ways intended precisely because the author has—and can count on his/her audience having—those texts in mind.

Herman Melville's *Moby Dick* is a retelling of 1 Kings 16:29–22. The name of Melville's protagonist (not to mention the brief appearance of a prophetic Elijah) make that incontestable. But suppose that a critic were to protest,

> But there are far too many *differences* between 1 Kings and *Moby Dick*; not the least that Melville's Ahab is a tragic hero, whereas Ahab of old was an unalloyed villain. Melville's Elijah is a minor character, a half-cracked retailer of riddles; Elijah of old was a man of power to whom kings did obeisance. No "Ishmael" narrates the story in Kings. To be

---

[54] In Chapter 5 of this book, I shall explore the ways in which structural analysis of myth can illuminate the creative use of difference.

[55] Among the reasons for pessimism about this is the evident fact that the class of reasons that might cause a tradent to deviate from received tradition is wildly non-homogeneous. These may range from sheer carelessness or poor memory to the joy of discovering clever new ways to deploy traditional motifs, in the interest of conveying something new or conveying something old in a newly powerful or insightful way. There being no way to circumscribe such possible factors, there is little reason to hope for any uniform account of the phenomenon.

sure, there are a few suggestive similarities (besides the coinciding names)—for example, Captain Ahab's compact with a band of demons sequestered within the bowels of the *Pequod*. But these similarities can hardly be thought to illuminate the "meaning" of Melville's novel.

Should this sort of argument be persuasive? Obviously not. We can show beyond serious doubt that Melville precisely intended the Kings narrative to serve as a kind of semantic key (one of several) to the symbolic themes that permeate *Moby Dick*. It is exactly the ways that the novel is in conversation with the Hebrew Bible that reveal the novel's theology, as well as its deliberately enigmatic and deeply ironic portrayal of Yahweh as the great fish of the deep. Melville's theology is certainly not that of the author(s) of 1 Kings. But it is precisely because Melville is able to count upon his readers' recognition of the biblical references and theology that he is able to bend the emotional power of those traditions to his own purposes.

Now our critic might hasten to object that, nevertheless, my example is inapposite. It appeals to a novelist trading upon ancient *historical* records to produce *fiction*, whereas the alleged literary precursors to Gospel *history* are either *historical* narratives from the Hebrew Bible or pagan fictions. But even if that were relevant, this objection is at least premature. Indeed, it begs the question insofar as the criterion of difference is supposed to provide precisely the evidence needed for historicity.

In his concluding remarks, Harris affirms the distinction between revivification and resurrection with an immortal body: "Before Jesus' resurrection, it could be said only that the dead are restored to life....After his resurrection, it can be said that 'the dead will be raised immortal.'"[56] But the expectation of immortality certainly had precedent in Jewish eschatology (e.g., Dan. 12:1–3; 2 Macc. 7), and as for actual pre-Christian euhemerizations, we have the assumptions of Enoch and Elijah, as well as the resurrections of Caesar Augustus and Romulus. The former two did not pass through the land of the dead; the latter two did but were pagans. Should these differences matter? How should we decide? If the pagan cases are ruled out because they are "alien" to Jesus' Jewish background (which should be irrelevant to Harris' claim), then what are we to make of Moses, who died (Deut. 34:5) but then reappears (Matt. 17:1–8; Mark 9:4)?

D. The Criterion of Coherence

Craig Blomberg makes the argument that Jesus' nature miracles cohere with the teachings contained in his parables.[57] So the authenticity of the parabolic

---

[56] Harris, "'The Dead are Restored to Life,'" 321.
[57] Craig Blomberg, "The Miracles as Parables," in *Gospel Perspectives*, ed. David Wenham and Craig Blomberg, vol. 6, *The Miracles of Jesus* (Sheffield, England:

sayings confers likely historicity upon the miracle stories. Here is Blomberg's explicit line of reasoning:

> (1) A large consensus of scholars ... agrees that a basic criterion of authenticity to be applied to the Jesus-tradition is the criterion of coherence: that which is fully consistent with material authenticated by the other recognized criteria may be accepted as authentic as well. (2) Jesus' teaching about the in-breaking kingdom of God, especially in his parables, is by these criteria the most demonstrably authentic core of historical information about Jesus in the gospels. (3) The narratives of the nature miracles when examined in their earliest forms recoverable from the gospel texts depict in symbol the identical in-breaking kingdom, often with striking parallels in both imagery and significance to specific parables of Jesus....the nature miracles and the parables closely cohere with each other....it therefore follows that the earliest forms of these miracle stories should be recognized as most probably historical.[58]

Blomberg is indeed able to draw fairly persuasive parallels between particular miracles and particular parables. But then, if coherence really does transmit historical probability, the argument works both ways. If there are very strong reasons—as clearly there are—to doubt the historicity of the miracles, it follows that the parables are placed under a shadow.

On the other hand, we have seen that not much confidence can be placed on the criterion of coherence. Suppose Jesus did pronounce the parables. Suppose those parables expressed a belief in the "in-breaking of the kingdom of God" (however that might be understood). What, exactly, makes it unlikely that tradents who knew the parables would be inspired to compose miracle stories to illustrate that message and then to attribute thaumaturgic powers to Jesus?

In the concluding observations from the anthology that has provided my principle targets here, Blomberg further muddies the waters by remarking that

> Testimony can seem to cohere even when all of it is not true. But this observation cuts two ways. To the extent that a given scholar should choose to minimize the significance of arguments for historicity based on criteria of coherence, it is logically necessary that he minimize to an equal extent argument against historicity based on seemingly

---

JSOT Press, 1986), 327–59; "Concluding Reflections on Gospel Perspectives and Miracles," in *Gospel Perspectives*, ed. David Wenham and Craig Blomberg, vol. 6, *The Miracles of Jesus* (Sheffield, England: JSOT Press, 1986), 443–57.

[58] Blomberg, "The Miracles as Parables," 347.

inconsistent or incoherent testimony. Appearances may be just as deceiving in either case.[59]

Blomberg cannot seriously believe this. A witness whose testimony is incoherent betrays either confusion (hence incompetence) or a bungled attempt to deceive. Contradictions provide certainty of falsehood; lesser incoherencies reveal improbability. They both provide defeaters of the testimony. But coherence does not defeat denial of a witness's testimony: coherence is a merely necessary condition for testimony to be taken with full seriousness. Coherence and incoherence are not epistemically "on a par," as Blomberg wants to suggest. It is obvious that incoherent testimony might contain some true bits. It is equally obvious that incoherence undermines our ability to discern which bits those are. If the historical reasoning to which Blomberg subscribes can do no better than this, we had best be on our guard.

I must add however (in the light of the lessons of Chapter 1) that apparent incoherence should also put us on guard that an author's meaning may not be as straightforward as a literal reading of a text would indicate. Apparent nonsense can reveal non-literal intentions through the use of metaphor, irony, and the like. Or, sometimes, incoherence may result from a dominating effort to insert as much symbolic significance into a text as is possible (or rather not quite possible), with resulting narrative infelicities—non-sequiturs, clashing chronologies, and the like. We must, surely, be on the alert for this sort of thing. Apparent incoherence may not signal author incompetence or disingenuousness but, rather, a struggle between competing aims. In practice, unfortunately, the application of the criterion of difference leaves so many degrees of freedom in the choice of what is relevant that a scholar is free to choose almost any feature of a miracle event that may help him make his case for genuineness (or falsehood).

V. Who Has the Burden of Proof?

Perhaps something needs to be said here about burden of proof. When the historical reliability of the Bible comes under scrutiny, do the skeptics need to make their case or those who take the Bible literalistically? Or is not the sensible thing to let each side make its case and be led by the evidence?

In general, we require someone who makes a claim to have sufficient evidence for that claim. In disputed matters, we expect both sides to supply their reasons; there is no "default"—or none besides agnosticism. Matters are, however, not quite so simple. As we have seen, even a quite liberal principle of charity creates a certain presumption of truth in favor of a

---

[59] Blomberg, "Concluding Reflections," 447–48.

testifier. If there is opposite testimony, that presumption is destroyed, and we must fall back on evidence that supports one side or the other.

But there are also special cases, and history often qualifies. Modern historians as a class tend to be a skeptical lot, who regularly employ a hermeneutic of suspicion. There is reason for this; a general presumption of charity notwithstanding, the texts upon which historians must so heavily rely are often written in circumstances that provide natural opportunities and incentives for inaccuracies and fabrications. Experience teaches that the art of spin and other forms of deception are as old as the hills themselves. So—especially when we have only one source, or sources whose interests are aligned—we need to be on our guard.

In a paper titled "The Burden of Proof," Stewart Goetz and Craig Blomberg argue, to the contrary, that the burden must fall upon the skeptic. At a general level, their argument is simply the fundamental argument for charity, together with an argument that skeptics are committed to a kind of historiographical relativism that undermines their own position. The skeptic, so Goetz and Blomberg would have it, holds that the authors of our ancient texts are inexorably in the grip of culturally conditioned values, interests, and ways of perceiving and describing their world. These inevitably distort their record of the past. But if that is so, then how can we fail to apply the same skepticism to the skeptic's *own* account of the development of post-Enlightenment "objective" historiography—with corrosive results?[60]

But this argument is misdirected. It falsely assumes that the grounds for skepticism require an appeal to some sort of relativism. Skepticism has, indeed, sometimes been defended in this way. It is not, however, an appeal that Bible critics should, or generally do, make. They are guided, in a general way, precisely by the sorts of considerations enumerated by Hume for casting suspicion on testimony: evidence of incompetence, contradiction by others, motives for lying, reasons to think detection will be hard, and so on. There is no relativism here. On the contrary, the liar knows he is lying, and the incompetent are, well, just incompetent. The skeptic puts her money, *inter alia*, precisely upon certain universals of human nature. This means that where we lack independent corroboration for testimony, we must fall back upon intrinsic plausibility and whatever can be known about the character of the testifier and the circumstances in which the testimony is produced; we may not simply adopt credulity as our default.

But surely, charity should tug in the direction of a presumption of truth? We must concede this, but it leaves ample scope for there being domains of discourse in which suspicion is the watchword. It is said that there is no honor among thieves. Nor would a Montague sensibly trust a Capulet. Goetz and Blomberg's argument for the general reliability of

---

[60] Stewart C. Goetz and Craig L. Blomberg, "The Burden of Proof," *Journal for the Study of the New Testament* 4, no. 11 (1981): 54.

history falls prey to this rather simple observation, *if* there are independent reasons to suspect historians, or historians of a given age or culture, of dissembling.[61] Thus, the considerations that show general reliability to be a necessary condition of public discourse cannot yield such a simple conclusion as, "The writer of any particular piece of history *must* be assumed reliable until shown to be otherwise. The reader must make this a priori commitment if the writing of history is to be viable."[62]

The viability of historical discourse requires something rather less than Goetz and Blomberg claim: that truth-telling is a *general* feature of discourse and that we have reasons, perhaps but not always quite general, to believe that *this* discourse (or a relevant subset of it) was produced by competent, honest historians who undertook to report actual events. Most of the rest of Goetz and Blomberg's argument is devoted to arguing that the biblical authors were indeed of this sort. I will not comment on that part of their case except to observe that their making the argument, in fact, weakens the force of their claim that making such arguments is not really needed in the first place.

One final remark is in order. We need hardly remind ourselves that the skeptics have abundant *specific* grounds for suspicion. Large portions of the Hebrew Bible appear, superficially, to be relating historical events. But few Bible scholars of any persuasion now consider the "history" contained in the Torah to be reliable. Archaeology has significantly undermined the reliability of Joshua, and the narratives found in 1 and 2 Samuel (to say nothing of, for example, Esther or Daniel) remain at best seriously contested. So, we cannot escape the fact that, *insofar as the authors of the Gospels understood themselves to be interacting with Jewish traditions*, they may have inherited a similar attitude toward the writing of "history."

I have already suggested ways in which that kind of reading of the evangelists as would-be historians may be far too simple. I shall have a great deal more to say on that score presently. Here, it will be not amiss to note, first, that the authors of our canonical Gospels (and of similar Christian literature of the day) never pause to cite their sources. They never mention competing traditions that they may have heard; therefore, they never weigh evidence for and against any particular claim they make about Jesus' career—even though there must have been competing claims, as the discrepancies between the Gospels and the indications of early opposition repeatedly proclaim.[63] Nor do these writers ever express any caution or

---

[61] Where we can identify an historian's larger moral or political aims (as, for example, those of Josephus), it may well be possible to "correct" for their influence and extract much of historical value. I am not denying that this might, in principle, be possible to do with the Gospels and Acts.

[62] Goetz and Blomberg, "The Burden of Proof," 52; italics in original.

[63] These points are tellingly made in Carrier, *On the Historicity of Jesus*, 508–9.

doubt about a story they relate. In all of this, they are acting in a most peculiar way if their aim is to preserve with as much care as possible what they could know about the life of Jesus. Well before the time of Jesus, we do have historical writings (e.g., that of Thucydides that, though in some ways tendentious, do observe these basic principles of the historian's art. But we find none of this in the Gospels or in Acts (in spite of Luke's opening asseverations). How sure should we be, then, that history, as we understand it, was the evangelists' aim?

A. The Future of Criteria of Authenticity

Now mine is by no means the first voice to raise objections to the LJOR criteria, though my rejection of them is more wholesale than is usual and focuses somewhat more systematically on general theoretical considerations. It must be also noted, however, that criticism of the criteria has with some frequency been attended by the constructive suggestion that they be replaced by efforts to seek out the best explanation for all the data we have.[64] This is, of course, very much in line with the methodological orientation I am advocating. In this neighborhood are the objections of Dale Allison, who is similarly skeptical of the use of these criteria in practice and offers many examples of cases where they lead in so many conflicting directions as to ensure that they are unreliable.[65]

Allison, therefore, effectively jettisons the toolkit of criteria of authenticity. He proposes, in its place, two principles, which, taken together, constitute not so much a "method" in his view but rather an "approach" to reconstructing the life of Jesus. The first principle is just the one I have been advocating: namely, seek the best explanation for the data we have. Second, Allison recommends that, rather than seeking initially to authenticate particular sayings and deeds attributed to Jesus in the Gospels, we rely much more heavily upon general themes, leitmotifs that leave with us a vivid impression because they recur over and over again, woven into the fabric of the New Testament Jesus traditions. Allison defends this way of framing

---

[64] See, e.g., Jens Schröter, "The Historical Jesus and the Sayings Tradition: Comments on Current Research," *Neotestimentica* 30, no. 1 (1966): 151–68; Rafael Rodríguez, "Authenticating Criteria: The Use and Misuse of a Critical Method," *Journal for the Study of the Historical Jesus* 7, no. 2 (2009): 152–67; Tobias Hägerland, "The Future of Criteria in Historical Jesus Research," *Journal for the Study of the Historical Jesus* 13, no. 1 (2015): 43–65; and Jordan J. Ryan, "Jesus at the Crossroads of Inference and Imagination," *Journal for the Study of the Historical Jesus* 13, no. 1 (2015): 66–89.

[65] Dale C. Allison, "How to Marginalize the Traditional Criteria of Authenticity," in *The Handbook for the Study of the Historical Jesus*, ed. Tom Holmén and Stanley E. Porter (Boston: Brill, 2011), 1:3–30.

some general idea of who Jesus was, and what he aimed at, by pointing out that, if we are to treat the NT records as providing us any understanding of the historical Jesus, we must treat them as preserving a deposit of remembrances passed down from those who encountered him.

Reflecting, then, upon the many vagaries and mechanisms of human memory, Allison concludes that human memory, both in individuals and in communities, has evolved to economize information-storage by reconstructing a remembered past in terms of general themes of major importance, forgetting details, filling in gaps, and reimagining strands that do not well cohere. It is therefore these major motifs, that re-appear over and over, that reflect most reliably general impressions of the man Jesus, and the impression he made upon his community.

Over and over again, for example, the Jesus of the Gospels foresees and speaks of a new kingdom or age which he has been appointed to inaugurate. Surely, then, the centrality of this theme must mirror some key preoccupation that imbued Jesus with his sense of mission, whatever the details may actually have been. Against the objection that this does not take us very far by itself, Allison makes the argument that it takes us farther than might initially be imagined, and that, in the end, it, with some supplementation from other arguments, may simply be as far as historiography can bring us. He concedes, then, that many of the sayings and stories in the Gospels may be apocryphal; we have no way to make a determination, beyond judgments about what "fits" with our general reconstruction of the sort of person Jesus was.

This is not an unreasonable way to proceed; nor is the skepticism of Allison's conclusion unreasonable. However, it does not adequately address a significant difficulty, which can be captured with the question: what did Jesus actually have in mind? Suppose we grant that he almost certainly "had in mind" the advent of a new kingdom, the initiation of which he was ordained, as Son of the Father, to inaugurate and rule over. How, exactly, would he have understood such a proclamation, and how would his audience have understood it? What would he even have meant with his use of the term "kingdom" (βασιλεία), or rather its Aramaic equivalent?

We all too readily presume that a knowledge of first century koine Greek (or some guessed-at Aramaic equivalent) could settle such matters. Sometimes not: terms like "ordained," "kingdom," and "Son of God" are at least problematic in this context. Are these terms to be understood literally? Are they being used in some way that is figurative, perhaps metaphorical? And, even if they *are* meant to be taken literally, what sort of freight do they carry? After all, terms such as "inaugurate," "ordain," and "chosen" would have had more or less precise legal implications; and these vary from one society to another over space and time. So, too, would the term "kingdom;" the conception of what it was to be a legitimate king and the bounds of both power and reach over subjects have always been contested and usually carefully theorized and legally defined matters, for the simple reason that people universally care who has power over them and under what constraints. Not just any wielder of dominion would have been recognized as a king, and not just any nation would properly have been described as a kingdom.

Even if (perhaps especially if) these terms were, in context, to be understood somehow metaphorically, a grasp of their use and connotations would require a prior grasp of their literal sense, which in turn demands some understanding of the cultural and legal traditions in which they—or the original terms we translate into English as their cognates—were conceptualized in their home setting. Context regularly provides clues when there is ambiguity. But larger linguistic units that provide context are also subject to misunderstanding. Such pressures toward more holistic approaches to interpretation are well recognized and not unwelcome. Allison's practice of looking for recurrent themes is an exercise in a quite straightforward example of such a technique. I am going to argue for an even broader application of holistic considerations, one that searches for patterns in how recurrent themes interlock and interact with other recurrent themes, in ways that are essential to the production of meaning. For example, what, if anything, does the early Christian focus upon the announcement of an impending transformation of the world that will usher in an everlasting kingdom have to do with Jesus' repeated devaluation of traditional kin-relations in the Gospels? How might it be illuminated by the tenacity with which the Jesus of the Gospels emphasizes inclusion of the socially marginalized and the rejection of traditional criteria for determining who is one's "neighbor"?

Reflection upon how such different themes are woven into a patterned textile of narrative is one way to be led to a consideration of the structure of larger units of text using the tools provided by the anthropological study of religious storytelling worldwide. These techniques certainly add a layer of complexity and subtlety to the task of meaning-analysis, and they therefore are attended with uncertainties of their own. But they hold the promise of substantially sharpening our insight into what such culturally alien texts might be attempting to convey, insights that, in their turn, may provide considerable illumination of how such culture-laden terms as "king" and "kingdom" are properly to be understood—not to mention the primitive obsession with eschatology generally. Along the way, they may also give us better tools for assessing to what degree reliance upon recurrent themes may or might not provide information regarding the origins of Christianity and the Jesus of history. That is what I aim to argue in the chapters to follow. Allison envisions a rather stark choice: either the assembly of recurrent themes in the New Testament offers material from which a broad reconstruction of the historical Jesus will be possible, or nothing will. I will maintain that structural analysis offers an opportunity to see the playing-field rather differently, by shifting the focus away from life-of-Jesus reconstruction, which emerges as a highly doubtful enterprise, to a kind of understanding of the development of primitive Christianity that may, in the end, be more informative.

My position, therefore, is more radical than Allison's. I believe the whole project that drives LOJR is one that ought to be marginalized. After two centuries of effort, it is not likely to yield major new insights respecting the central figure of interest. More than that, I do not see its central aim as providing the most significant, historically illuminating new information about the early formation of the Church that we can reasonably hope to uncover, even if it achieves a consensus portrait of a historical Jesus. I propose, therefore, to make a case for a different tack, one that may yield a richer harvest, both in shedding light upon the central aims of the Christian movement as they developed by the Second Century, and in excavating new details about how primitive Christians fleshed out those aims and hoped to achieve them.

VI. Modern Miracles?

It is one thing to attempt to establish the occurrence of miracles claimed to have occurred hundreds or thousands of years ago; it should be another to establish their contemporary occurrence. And, indeed (as in Hume's day) there is no dearth of contemporary witnesses to miracles. Moreover, if we can establish on good evidential grounds that miracles occur *nowadays*, that will certainly affect the probabilities that we must assign to ancient miracles. We should, in short, be more ready, other things being equal, to accept on testimonial evidence such miracles as those attributed to Jesus. This is the argumentative strategy pursued at length by Craig Keener in his massive two-volume work of some 1200 pages.[66] Relevant here are two pieces of Keener's project: his attempt to refute Hume directly and the amassing of

---

[66] Craig S. Keener, *Miracles: The Credibility of the New Testament Accounts*, vols. 1 & 2 (Grand Rapids, MI: Baker Academic, 2011).

some hundreds of contemporary miracle reports from many quarters of the globe. A brief consideration of Keener's work is therefore in order, beginning with his engagement with Hume.

We should note that Keener is, by training, a Bible scholar, not a philosopher. Unlike many apologetically-minded Bible scholars, however, Keener gives more than perfunctory attention to Hume, whom he sees as his chief opponent. He devotes two chapters and over 100 pages to Hume and the literature on Hume.[67] It is worth, therefore, briefly summarizing and assessing what Keener has to say about the matter.

1. Keener devotes considerable attention to Hume's rejection by some contemporary scholars but says little about why. For example, he records that contemporary historians have rejected the historiography that informs Hume's *History of England*, but he says nothing about their reasons.

2. Keener ranges widely over contemporary critiques of Hume (less widely over Hume's defenders); but again, he gives only brief summaries and little engagement with Hume's actual arguments.

3. Where he does give attention to actual criticisms of Hume, Keener offers a rambling discussion of errors and fallacies of which Hume is allegedly guilty: that his argument is "a priori," defining miracles and laws of nature in such a way that it is logically impossible for miracles to occur, and that his argument is circular or question-begging. Further, he appeals on the one hand to "the uniform experience of mankind" that certain things do (or do not) happen but then simply rules out of court any testimony to the effect that they do not (or do). Moreover, Keener objects that Hume's argument is inconsistent with his official skepticism concerning inductive reasoning and that in any case, evidence that provides "proof" for a certain law of nature is largely irrelevant to the credentials for testimony for the occurrence of some extraordinary event. All this goes to show, according to Keener, that Hume's argument is possible only because he actually *presupposes* that naturalism is true; someone who believes on independent grounds that God exists, or is "open" to the occurrence of miracles, should not be moved. I hope to have shown in the previous chapter that Hume is guilty of almost none of this litany of sins and that where his argument is unclear (as with respect to his understanding of what makes an event a miracle and with respect to the allegation of question-begging), the defect can be repaired.

4. The ways in which Keener is tone-deaf to Hume's project are typical of conservative criticisms of Hume and bear reiterating. First, Hume is not presupposing that naturalism is true. Indeed, his argument is epistemological, not ontological. Second, Keener completely misses Hume's dialectical strategy. (a) Hume wants to deploy a definition of "miracle" that

---

[67] Keener, *Miracles*, 107–209.

will give the theist what she needs—namely, events that, by their nature, indicate divine action and, hence, can serve to authenticate revelation. (b) As in his *Dialogues*, Hume deliberately sidelines his skeptical worries about induction since, if those are kept in play, one can hardly focus seriously on evidence for the existence of God. Hume's question is whether, *if a rational human being can rightly help herself to all the evidential and inferential tools required to justify both common-sense realism and scientific theorizing,* she can—using those very tools (the only ones we have)—discover good grounds for thinking that God exists and has, in identifiable instances, revealed his will to us. (c) Taking himself to have shown in the *Dialogues* that there are not good grounds to think God exists independently of revelation, Hume's project in "Of Miracles" is to examine whether revelatory means of access to the divine can, as it were, stand on their own two feet. But all this is lost on Keener and, unfortunately, on many of those he cites against Hume.

5. Similarly, Keener fails to see the dialectical force of Hume's insistence upon the relevance of the evidence for natural laws. It is only by overriding a law of nature that an event gives evidence of the kind of special divine intervention that can signal an authentic revelation; it is only tenacious regularity that can inform us what laws obtain; and it is only that knowledge that will permit the identification of an event as a miracle. Thus, the theist had better agree with Hume on these matters.

6. But what should we make of the literally hundreds of contemporary miracle reports that Keener offers? Officially, Keener's primary objective is to prove that miracles continue to be reported in the present day. But that is hardly news; nor did Hume deny it. Second, Keener suggests that the sheer volume of these reports requires us to take seriously the possibility, even the likelihood, that miracles *in fact* occur. Yet only a few of these events, reported with some circumspection, are miracles that Keener claims himself to have witnessed. Others are fairly close to hand: Keener's mother-in-law is an African Christian, a healer from Braazaville-Congo, who claims to have been involved in, for example, the resurrection of a dead child. The rest come from a vast variety of sources, none of them (by Keener's own admission) properly documented or investigated.[68] Is it too much to suggest that quantity is no substitute for quality? A really large sieve holds water no better than a small sieve.

7. Finally, we may note two further unwelcome implications of Keener's investigations. Keener focuses, rather tendentiously, upon miracles that, though reported from many parts of the globe, were collected from Christian communities. Yet, Keener admits, as he must, that miracle reports

---

[68] Keener, *Miracles*, 249–54, 266–67. See most especially, Darren M. Slade, "Properly Investigating Miracle Claims," in *The Case Against Miracles*, ed. John W. Loftus (United Kingdom: Hypatia Press, 2019), 114–47.

from non-Christian cultures abound.[69] How many of these are veridical? What is more, there are competing Christian sects. Keener sidesteps the problem of determining where to draw the boundaries between Christian and non-Christian; and he entirely side-steps the question of whether any Christian sect's miracles give it an apologetic advantage.[70] What, then, of Hume's argument that one religion's miracles, apologetically deployed, provide testimony against another religion's veracity, to their mutual destruction? Here again, Keener's discussion entirely misses the thrust of Hume's argument. Hume is accused of confusing "how a phenomenon might be exploited (in this case, for apologetic purposes) with the authenticity … of its occurrence."[71] The confusion is Keener's. For good measure, Keener suggests that religions might not be all that different, that there might be multiple (demonic?) "supernatural powers" or that miracles "could be understood as [a?] supreme powers' [*sic.*?] 'goodwill' toward people of different faiths 'without necessarily endorsing' particular beliefs."[72] Granting this last point (as well as the first), Hume's conclusion—that miracles cannot provide evidence for a particular religion—equally follows. Perhaps it is the Hindu god, Brahman, who granted Jesus the power to perform miracles out of goodwill. Keener's best card is the suggestion that the miracles of one faith tradition might be better attested, though Keener himself does nothing to undertake the task of showing this to be the case. The further, and poignant, point emerges from Keener's reflection that miracles are desperately needed to alleviate suffering in this world.[73] Why, then, does God provide deserved relief in so few cases?

VII. A Better Path, Also Declined

The methodological critique that has been the focus of this chapter has been aimed primarily at the evangelical or conservative wing of efforts to reconstruct the life of Jesus. There is, however, a very substantial body of scholarship within the Third Quest that is applying socio-political methods to attempt to gain insights into the milieu of Jesus and, thereby, situate him and his ministry within an accurate historical setting.

Such an approach is much more in tune with the argument being offered in this book; and in my view, there is much to be learned from such studies, some of which I will make use of in what follows. However, I

---

[69] Keener, *Miracles*, 242–49.
[70] Ibid., 257–60.
[71] Ibid., 195.
[72] Ibid., 196, quoting from J. Houston, *Reported Miracles: A Critique of Hume* (New York: Cambridge University Press, 1994), 204.
[73] Keener, *Miracles*, 768.

diverge from many of those who pursue this line of inquiry insofar as they presume to be able to discover, in part through the application of such methods, the Jesus of history. Or, more precisely: whether or not such a Jesus can be revealed by these efforts, I do not take this to be my project and remain deeply skeptical about the prospects for success. Where I believe progress can be made is in discovering the intentions that are expressed in the NT texts themselves (and the other early Christian sources that we have).

Toward this end, an understanding of the social and cultural milieus of first century Palestine is of course essential. Indeed, since the loci of composition of the various books of the NT appear to extend well beyond the borders of Palestine, and are often contested, it is regularly a matter of concern whether and with what confidence a *Sitz im Leben* can be established for a given text. Temporal coordinates are of equal importance— the more so as the composition of the books of the NT appears to have taken place for the most part during the second half of the first century—a period that witnessed, as of first importance, the first Jewish war of revolt against the Romans and the destruction of the Second Temple. This raises the question how this development, and others that occurred subsequent to the estimated years of Jesus' life, may have informed the ways in which the authors of the NT wrote about him.

A fuller argument than the one I can flesh out in this work would have to make careful use of the various studies along these lines to investigate whether the framework within which I attempt to understand the NT—in particular certain aspects of the Gospel of Matthew—can account (in a well-integrated fashion) for the diverse ways in which the various authors of the books of the NT developed their kerygma. What is most central to my present argument is the situation of Roman subjugation under which Israel and the Jewish diaspora labored—a situation they shared with other conquered peoples of the Mediterranean basin, as well as the internal political chaos under which Rome itself labored. I shall have more to say about those matters presently.

The Ontology of Social Roles

> Surely it ought to be a principle of the science of religions that religion expresses nothing which does not exist in nature....The only question is to learn from what part of nature these realities come and what has been able to make men represent them under this singular form which is peculiar to religious thought. But if this question is to be raised, it is necessary to commence by admitting that they are real things which are thus represented.
>
> Emile Durkheim,
> *The Elementary Forms of the Religious Life*

Since Emile Durkheim expressed his views on the matter, there has emerged a considerable body of literature devoted to the question of whether the subject matter of the social sciences can be explained in terms of the actions and psychology of individual persons taken collectively, or whether these phenomena are irreducibly emergent. Some methodological individualists have held that an explanatory reduction is possible and perspicuous. I should say immediately that much of the debate, cast in terms of the prospects for reductive explanation, has been taken to be a debate over *methodology* (hence the term "methodological individualism"); but as a realist, I take explanation here to be inextricably bound to ontological commitments. Therefore, I shall proceed largely by framing the issues straightaway in ontological terms.

This chapter is divided into two parts. In Part I, the prospects for such a reduction are examined once again, and an alternative proposal for the construal of events and institutions at the social level is sketched that is ultimately naturalistic in spirit (but see below) without conceding reductionism in the intended sense. I then explore the implications such a non-reductionist stance has for the way in which we should understand the ontological status of societies, offices, and persons *qua* holders of offices.

Part II brings those results to bear upon the vexed question of what anthropologists are to make of the religious beliefs of the cultures they study. I hope there to vindicate some of Durkheim's fundamental conclusions about religious language, but I hope to show, at the same time, that we must understand the natives of those "primitive" cultures to be far less simple-minded than they have been taken to be by most social theorists (notably including Durkheim). So, I come to resurrect Durkheim, not to praise him. If I hit my mark, one consequence will be that native mythmakers must by and large be quite clever fellows indeed—as theoretically clever, perhaps, as some of us who write scholarly tomes about them.[1]

This excursion into metaphysical matters serves my larger purposes in the following way. First, I aim to show how, in a multitude of ways, an ontology that posits irreducible social entities and relations can be read into biblical texts in a way that illuminates those texts and enables us better to explain their structure and intent. In so doing, I will be arguing, *inter alia*, that the biblical authors were consciously operating with such categories. That claim, in turn, will buttress both my general analysis of the nature of myth and my more specific claim that the category of myth, so understood, is correctly and in a theoretically powerful way applicable to the biblical texts in question. Moreover, it will support my argument that biblical narratives are conducting political business: that is, they are articulating, and in theoretically informed and sophisticated ways making a case for, identifiable political solutions to identifiable social problems. If I am successful, this will allow me, finally, to make my case for the hypothesis that what the biblical texts say is, for the most part, *true*, or, if not true, then at least deeply *rational* for the authors and their intended audiences to have accepted. It will *also* explain, importantly, why ancient Jews and others would have *cared* about what these texts say—cared enough to have fought, and often died, on behalf of their ideological commitments.

Methodologically, my strategy will be to argue for the rationality hypothesis in its strongest, starkest form. That is, I want to examine what can be said in favor of the claim that the biblical authors were not only operating with a theoretically sophisticated social ontology but had good reasons for that ontology, *were fully aware of those reasons*, and also *consciously applied that ontology's categories in fashioning their texts.*[2] We will, if that is correct, be on target in attributing to them authorial intentions of this sort when we interpret what they wrote.

The strong hypothesis is provisional. If, as I think, it will falter a bit, there is ample room for weakening it in various ways. It will come under immediate suspicion, understandably, if only because the biblical narratives (and similar literature from other cultures quite generally) do not wear their philosophical underwear on their sleeves. Or at least they do not do so in ways that are familiar and easily recognized within the Western philosophical tradition. I shall have some things to say about why that might

---

[1] I shall use the term "native" simply as a convenient way to denote the members of a society or culture.

[2] It is just here that I diverge sharply from Durkheim, who supposed that primitive people somehow unconsciously "project" social realities into a supernatural realm.

be. I will also, of course, make some observations about how the strong hypothesis may have to be modified.

I. The Metaphysics of the Social

A notorious episode in U.S. history afforded a prominent example of a set of distinctions that will be profitable to examine. In defending Richard Nixon's attempt to maintain control over the White House tapes, his lawyers were careful to distinguish between Richard Nixon the private citizen and Richard Nixon the President. It was the office of the presidency which Nixon sought (ostensibly) to "protect" by keeping the tapes confidential. It was clear that, as president, Nixon had certain rights (and could perform certain duties) which, as a private citizen, he did not (and could not) perform *at the very same time* that he held the presidency. Nixon was not, during his term of office, sometimes a mere citizen and sometimes the President, Jekyll-and-Hyde fashion; rather, he was both simultaneously.

The distinction alluded to above is recognized in United States law and has been the subject of a long and complex legal tradition.[3] The questions I wish to raise here are:

(1) What is the ontological significance, if any, of this (and similar) distinctions?
(2) Are, for example, the private person and the officer that s/he "is" different substances and/or different persons?
(3) If so, in terms of what differences in properties are they to be distinguished, and how are the two related? If not, how are we to understand the composition of the person/officer?
(4) What other distinctions, if any, might belong to the same ontological family as that between a person and the officer that s/he "is"?
(5) Can there be genuine entities and ontological distinctions which are nevertheless the creatures of convention and not "natural"?

I am going to begin by offering a very general argument for the view that socially "constructed" entities of various kinds (offices and officers, their official actions, institutions, corporate entities such as tribal clans, nations, and the like—and the formally constituted relations between them that define social structure) cannot, in general, be understood as constituted by individual human beings and their non-institutional properties. I will then develop a positive ontology of such things. That

---

[3] See Ernest H. Kantorowicz, *The King's Two Bodies: A Study in Medieval Political Theology* (Princeton, NJ: Princeton University Press, 1957).

ontology will grate against the metaphysical instincts of those who love (metaphysical) desert landscapes—especially the instincts of many who are committed to certain forms of naturalism. So, I should say some things at the outset concerning my use of the contested terms "natural" and "naturalism." I will also make explicit how I understand ontological reduction.

I will use the term "natural persons" to mean (human) persons as we might identify and describe them apart from their formal roles as actors in a social environment. There are immediate complications. First, the distinction between formal roles and informal ones is ineluctably fuzzy: if you are the *de facto* leader of the pack, at what point might it become true of you (absent clear rules about the matter) that you have become *de jure* leader? I will not attempt the perhaps thankless task of precisifying the distinction. There are clear cases, and they are enough for me to make the case I want to make. Natural persons are biologically human individuals who, paradigmatically, possess the psychological attributes necessary for (moral) personhood. We are not to think of them apart from their social engagements with other persons or apart from their concepts and thoughts, including those whose content refer to social institutions. But the social engagements in question must (for the purposes of reduction) be ones that can themselves be described in a way that is free of institutional description. So, roughly, if I give you an affectionate hug, that counts as a non-institutional (hence, natural) action so long and just insofar as it can be described apart from any formal social meaning it may have (i.e., as a formal blessing of some kind). Natural properties, here, will be properties that characterize persons apart from their participation in formal social relationships, and natural facts will be facts about natural persons (and non-persons) and their natural properties.

If the notion of natural personhood is difficult to pin down, the term "naturalism" is no easier, if only because the term is used in so many ways. As *I* will use the term, however, it will mean just this: a commitment to naturalism is a commitment to the view that there are no disembodied minds. By minds, I mean things that have, or in virtue of which something that has a mind have, original intentionality.[4] That said, my caution in claiming to adhere to the "spirit" of naturalism derives from there being room, in the

---

[4] This conception is pretty closely seconded (or firsted) by Alvin Plantinga, "Introduction: The Evolutionary Argument against Naturalism," in *Naturalism Defeated? Essays On Plantinga's Evolutionary Argument Against Naturalism*, ed. James Beilby (Ithaca, NY: Cornell University Press, 2002), 1. By "original intentionality" is meant the intrinsic directedness of conscious mental acts toward some object or content—what the individual is conscious *of*. Imputed intentionality, by contrast, is the kind of directedness that non-conscious things (such as words, sentences, symbols, computer programs, and the like) can have toward objects or contents, *in virtue of the fact that conscious agents assign* these "meanings" to features of those things. Imputed intentionality, therefore, is parasitic upon the (original) intentions of conscious agents.

ontology to be developed, for entities that are (in a sense to be explained) plausibly characterized as *super*natural. These entities will typically be *persons* of a kind with *minds* (of a kind) whose intentionality is imputed, not (strictly speaking) original. Yet even that last constraint—again, in a sense to be explained—might be relaxed in the service of a kind of idealization. What is left, in the end, of naturalism (strictly speaking) is something I shall let readers decide for themselves.

A. The Dialectic of Reduction of the Social

The literature on methodological individualism was plagued, early on, by poorly formulated conditions for a successful reduction. Thus, heavy weather was made over the question whether a successful reduction could incorporate facts about the social concepts possessed by natural persons or facts about non-institutional relationships in which they stood to one another. I believe, however, that it is entirely fair for a reductionist to appeal to facts about the conceptual equipment of social actors, including their institutional concepts, so long as s/he doesn't does not appeal to descriptions of *actions*, however motivated, that presuppose institutional facts. Similarly, a reductionist may appeal to (non-institutionally described) social relations, just as a reduction in the physical sciences can appeal to relations—e.g., between atoms in atomic structures—in explaining the macroscopic properties of matter. Here, I shall follow a model of reductive explanation that has become quite standard in the philosophy of science literature.

Reductive explanations are explanations of the properties of, and changes in, a thing in terms of the properties of, and changes in, the parts of that thing. I shall call the properties of wholes *holistic properties* and the laws or principles governing changes in those properties *holistic laws or principles*. Wholes can be divided into parts in many ways, some of interest for the purposes of explanation, some not. Properties of parts, once a partition has been settled on, are *part properties*, and the laws or principles governing changes in parts are *part laws* or *part principles*. Thus, an auto mechanic understands the operation of a vehicle in terms of his knowledge of the mechanical parts of the car and how they interact to produce whole-car behavior. A *synchronic explanation* is an explanation of some property of a whole in terms of concurrent properties of its parts. A proper (synchronic) reductive explanation is effected when it can be shown that the explanandum—(the whole's having) a holistic property—can be *identified with* what I shall call (the having of) a *compositional property*, where a compositional property of a whole is a property of that whole that satisfies the schema: *being composed of such-and-such parts possessing so-and-so part properties and relations*. Thus, a car's having the holistic property of engine failure might be just the inability of its cylinders to fire because the timing belt is broken, etc. Compositional properties will often be highly determinable (as, for example, the property *being composed of molecules whose mean kinetic energy is K*, which can be satisfied in indeterminately many ways), even though the holistic property (*being at temperature T*) to which it is identical is determinate. Identity here is to be understood in the familiar Kripkean sense in which water is H_2O; the wetness of water *just is* its property of being composed of bipolar H_2O molecules weakly bound to one another. Reduction is type-type identity. We have what I shall call *weak emergence* when a given holistic property is such that some of its instances are identical to one compositional property and others of its instances to some other compositional property.[5] These, then, are cases of token-token identity or, as it is commonly in the literature, multiple realizability. We would have *strong emergence* if two doppelgangers at the compositional level had different intrinsic holistic properties. Strong emergence erases the possibility of explanation in terms of parts.

Finally, *diachronic reductions* are explanations of changes in the holistic properties of a thing in terms of changes in the properties and relations among its parts. Such an explanation will reduce holistic laws to part-laws. It proceeds by a synchronic reduction of the holistic properties of a thing X at a time t_1 to its parts and part-properties at that time (via compositional property identities), an explanation of the time-evolution of the system of parts over time to a later time t_2 by appeal to part-properties, relations, and laws, and a determination of the holistic properties of X at t_2 by way (once again but in the opposite "direction") of compositional property/holistic property identities.[6]

---

[5] Thus, auto engine failure is a weakly emergent property: a wide variety of internal conditions can constitute it.

[6] Some would reject the ordinary application of this account of reduction because they deny the existence of objects as ordinarily understood. They do so because they deny the existence of any composition-relation in virtue of which there are composite objects that have multiple parts. By their lights, the only objects there are, are simples—the elementary particles of matter. (If there are no simples, there are no objects.) Or they might, like Peter Van Inwagen, think that there are only such simples and living organisms, on the ground that the only sorts of composition-relations there are—the ones whose obtaining allows a collection of simples to constitute a complex particular—are the causal relations that make a collection of simples a living being. See Peter van Inwagen, *Material Beings* (Ithaca, NY: Cornell University Press, 1990).

To the first group of philosophers, I say: my account of reduction is committed to talk of closed systems with parts (as an abstraction), but not to an ontology of composite *objects*. Both to them and to van Inwagen, I say that, in arguing for the existence of social entities below, I am nevertheless setting aside such counter-intuitive ontologies of objects as theirs. I do so because someone who denies that there are— "really" are—photographs, black holes, lakes, and the like will surely deny also the existence of social entities, but without any special prejudices against the latter. Against the backdrop of these ontologies, the question of the existence of social entities becomes

Those reductionists who seek to construe social institutions, statuses, and roles in terms of the behaviors, beliefs, and attitudes of persons *qua* individuals—*natural persons*, as I am calling them—may have recourse to either of the two strategies that I have called synchronic and diachronic reduction.[7] An attempt to produce a synchronic reduction of statements about social phenomena occurring at a given time is an attempt to reduce such statements to statements about the behavior, beliefs, etc. of some individuals at that time. It is widely recognized that reductive programs of this simple sort cannot succeed. It is a sufficient objection to such a position to point out the conceptual possibility of a dislocation between the correct way to describe a given social state of affairs and the facts concerning the relevant beliefs and actions of the people involved. Thus, for example, a man may have broken a law even when (a) no one disapproves of his action and (b) no one knows that a law has been broken. A reductivist may retrench by saying that it is sufficient that the law is still "on the books." But that fact, as will become clear, is an institutional fact, a fact that goes beyond, for example, mere quotation of the text of the law in a forgotten newspaper archive. If so, then it could be the case that such a law is broken even when the allegedly necessary psychological conditions are absent.

A related and more general observation is that the performance of many socially significant actions requires an institutional context and the existence of constitutive rules, absent which nothing would count as an action of that kind. But the existence of those rules depends upon the *prior* rule-defined actions of other agents so that, for example, a vote by the members of Congress would not count as the passage of a new law except by virtue of the actions of those who established and legitimized the institution of Congress itself. But the actions of those founders can themselves only be understood as the actions they were by reference to an historical/legal tradition that provides their context.[8]

---

uninteresting. So, for present purposes, I am content to cast my lot with those who think, with the vulgar, that there are tables, planets, and rocks, as well as photons, trees, and natural persons. To those people, I say: you should also think that there are works of art, societies, collective institutions, and personages (see below).

[7] These strategies are considered by Maurice Mandelbaum, "Societal Facts," in *Theories of History*, ed. Patrick L. Gardiner (New York: Free Press, 1959), 476–87; Joseph Agassi, "Methodological Individualism," *The British Journal of Sociology* 11, no. 3 (1960): 255–56; Karl Popper, *The Open Society and Its Enemies*, 4th ed. (London: Routledge, 1962), 301–10; J. O. Wisdom, "Situational Individualism and the Emergent Group-Properties," in *Explanation in the Behavioral Sciences*, ed. Robert Borger and Frank Cioffi (New York: Cambridge University Press, 1970), 274–75.

[8] It is a fair question whether the founding actions that create a charter for a nation are subject to these considerations or can serve as regress-stoppers; on this, see below. The framers of the U.S. Constitution could perhaps have simply raised a militia and driven the British from their shores, but they saw themselves as needing to do something more than that. A mere mutiny against British rule, no matter how successful,

The reductionist, then, is driven to give a diachronic account of social phenomena, but once she has accepted this maneuver, it becomes apparent that she can in principle be driven as far into the historical past as we please, without finishing the required reduction.[9] At every stage, the fact that certain actions have been performed in the past is required for the very identity of subsequent social phenomena, yet at every stage, some of the very actions appealed to are constituted as the actions they are by virtue of a social milieu whose existence antedates them. We have no historical records of the beginnings of this process; thus, in a sense, the diachronic account will always be at least incomplete and not completable. This in itself will not seriously mar its attractiveness; after all, there *was* a time when there was no human culture.[10] Cultural traditions must have emerged in some evolutionary way from a pre-cultural state, and perhaps there is some way, in theory at least, to account for the creation of actions and institutional structures defined by constitutive rules from circumstances in which no such rules already exist.

Indeed, we *do* possess just such a theoretical account (indeed more than one), and in lieu of the historical details, we may heuristically permit ourselves to substitute a myth concerning the transition from a state of nature to society. Such a myth, even if historically inaccurate, can still serve the *conceptual* function of grounding the culturally transmitted chain of institutions and conventions in history by providing a way of *construing* their status relative to the possible ways in which rational agents with no cultural history might proceed to form a society.

For the sake of simplicity, it will be useful to take as a paradigm of such myths those that form the basis of the social-contract theories that were developed in the eighteenth century. Nothing I say here will depend upon which version of the myth one chooses; it is essential, however, that such myths, insofar as they can be taken seriously at all, are not to be taken as historical accounts but rather as serving to define, in a quasi-legal sense, the

---

would not have conferred upon the Revolution any legitimacy. In order to provide that,, they had to argue that the Crown had usurped its legitimate authority, and this required engagement with British legal traditions. In their Declaration of Independence, the founding fathers, for good measure, prefixed to their litany of abuses and legal violations by the British Crown a *general* defense of the right of rebellion that did *not* appeal specifically to British legal traditions.

[9] Joseph Agassi and J. O. Wisdom agree with Karl Popper that the reduction can only be carried out "piecemeal" against an unreduced cultural backdrop. But if each of the pieces can be reduced, presumably one could, by including both intended and unintended effects of human action, carry the process as far as one wished.

[10] Moreover, it will be objected that the problem I raise for the individualist is *merely epistemological*, whereas the point at issue is ontological. But if the argument is sound, it will have at least this peculiar consequence, that we cannot fully understand the very nature of our current institutional practices.

corporate status of the society in question. Hence, the rights, duties, and responsibilities in terms of which a group of persons together constitute a society are taken to derive from an act of incorporation of a certain kind.

Now, whether any such act takes place literally, or whether the nature of society is heuristically conceived for present legal purposes to be so constituted irrespective (more or less) of the historical details, the reductionist may for her purposes claim that the making of the contract consists just in the attitudes, intentions, and behaviors of a set of rational agents historically or heuristically conceived and that the consequences of this act are inherited by the sons and daughters of the founders. Then, if the individuals in a group understand themselves to be institutionally bound together as members of a society in virtue of mutual obligations conceived on the model of a social contract, an ontological reduction of social facts pertaining to that society is in the offing. The adoption of the social contract story, in effect, trumps any historical facts, whether those facts are hospitable to such a reconstruction or not. Yet, it does so in virtue of a consideration that, while facially helpful to the reductionist, can also be turned against her.

For there is a salient feature of this strategy that presents a potential obstacle to the reductionist's account. It arises in virtue of the essential fact that the formation of a social contract in the required sense presupposes the existence of rational agents capable of having, among other things, natural beliefs and intentions; moreover, the existence of the created corporate entity itself presupposes that the founding act be intentional in character and that certain "unincorporated" actors can, *in virtue of their natural intentions*, launch a corporate existence of the sort intended. Thus, the *nature* of the established entity cannot be entirely independent of the nature of the intentions conceived to have characterized the act of incorporation. Specifically, the *force* of such a contract will depend upon the contractual intentions expressed in it by its makers (as understood, if the makers are fictional, by those who create the fiction), and the nature of the social unit thus formed must, insofar as the terms and binding force of the contract determine its character, reflect the stipulations of that charter.[11]

So, in this respect, nations (and corporations of other sorts) are intentional entities. Then whether—and in what respects—their properties may be said to depend upon, or be analyzable in terms of, the properties of individual members may be determined by the way in which these entities are conceived or intended to be constituted. Here, then, a constraint upon

---

[11] Of course, the leading idea at the heart of social contract theories is that such intentions will conform to the norms of prudential rationality, so that a rationally constructed contract will be binding upon individuals, most fundamentally not because of institutional constraints but in virtue of the pre-existing constraints of rational self-interest.

admissible sociological analysis is placed upon us by the conception a people themselves have instituted of their mode of organization. The individualist can help herself to this feature of the way in which the contractarian heuristic can govern institutional ontology. But the sword is double-edged should there be societies whose founding heuristic is not contractarian; I shall argue that these are not hard to find.

Therefore, the fact that the *genesis* of a social entity may depend on certain individuals having performed certain actions with certain intentions does not entail that the social entity so created be one whose existence consists merely in what is in the hearts and minds of its members.[12] Why cannot a society institute social arrangements whose constitutive rules rule out a reductive—i.e., individualistic—analysis? That the genetic explanation and ontological status of social organizations are conceptually distinct matters is implicit in the very concession that the nature of an organization may be heuristically given by an account which, taken as literal history, bears no correspondence to the historical facts, whether or not those facts give aid and comfort to the reductionist.

However, this last consideration may seem instead to favor the reductionist, who, refusing the concession, may respond that our account of social entities is belied by the fact that (at least typically) no founding act of the sort characterized by the relevant intentions stands at their creation. But such a response must show something much stronger. It must show that no corporations *can* be created through deliberate intention or at least that such intentions could not be effective if they have as their goal the creation of something irreducible—for example, a corporation to which rights, duties, and aims may be assignable independently of individual beliefs and intentions. That the chartering myth may most conveniently be spelled out by means of a surrogate history does not mean that the corporate relationships thus placed in effect may not be synchronically conceived as acquiring the status they have in virtue of the fact that they are so defined. So, for the purpose of assigning ontological status, it is the charter that counts, and present charter may ignore present opinion. If this is right, then a diachronic account, while perhaps affording in principle a genetic explanation of the emergence of cultural entities, will not be sufficient to disallow the emergence of non-reducible social entities.[13,14]

---

[12] The nature of the "genetic fallacy," as Maurice Mandelbaum calls it, needs here to be spelled out (see below), since the nature of many social institutions *does* depend importantly upon the genetic facts. On my account, that dependence itself can depend, at least partly, upon the intentions of institution-framers to be guided by history, as they understand it.

[13] Tangential to this discussion is the general problem of the relation of actual practice to the truth of the claim that a particular convention or rule is normative for a given society. Obviously, rule-breaking practices can generate changes in the very rules themselves; but conversely, the mere fact that practice fails to live up to preachment need

As it stands, this claim is nevertheless bound to seem counterintuitive. Surely, it will be objected, a society cannot continue to exist where all its members have died. How, then, can a social system and its structural parts (e.g., institutions and offices) be anything over and above those persons, their natural properties and relations, and, perhaps, their artifacts? What is required in order to make a non-reductionist position plausible is an account of the ontological relationship between culturally emergent entities and natural persons, which can accommodate both the

---

not vitiate preachment's normative force. It is useful here to distinguish what I shall call *first-order justification* for rules from *second-order justification*. First-order justifications enable one to grade alternatively proposed rules preferentially. A second-order justification has the character of grounding an arbitrary choice among alternatives of which none can be shown to be intrinsically more preferable but, instead, where the agreement to follow some *one* rule is clearly preferable to having several or none. Thus, given a society in which automobile transportation is desirable, we find speed-limit laws to admit of first-order justifications, whereas the choice to drive on the right-hand side of the road or to use certain colors consistently for traffic lights are (so far as I am aware) decisions which require a second-order justification.

Now, both kinds of rules are normative for a society, given that they have been appropriately adopted, regardless of whether general practice conforms to them or not. However, the normative force of a rule admitting of first-order justification retains its point even when generally violated, whereas a rule justified only by second-order considerations possesses the value it has only by virtue of general conformity to it, since the achievement of some consistent practice *is* its point. Thus, especially in those cases where a social norm comes to be accepted *ad hoc* in virtue of some informal process of behavioral adjustment to a custom not admitting of first-order justification, changes in general behavior are likely to be construed as changes in what is normative.

[14] For a different but careful defense of the irreducibility of social entities and properties, see David-Hillel Ruben, *The Metaphysics of the Social World* (London: Routledge Kegan & Paul, 1985). As to the latter, Ruben offers two arguments for irreducibility. Ruben is somewhat diffident about the first, which strikes me as both the better and the more interesting argument. Its nub is that, because human institutions are creatures of convention, and there are no limits to human invention that place sufficient and principled constraints upon the institutional structures that can thereby be created, there is no good reason to expect even token-token identities between certain sorts of social properties (e.g., *being mayor*) and physical or mental facts about individuals. Ruben formulates the argument in terms of sets of nomologically sufficient conditions for possession of a social property, not in terms of property-identities (pp. 104–5). If this argument is sound, it does not deliver the conclusion that social properties are, in my terminology, *strongly emergent*, but nevertheless, shows that, no general appeal to psychological properties can explain them. Ruben's second argument appeals to the fact that such psychological explanations must often appeal to an individual's beliefs whose content itself invokes social properties; attempts to eliminate mention of those in the analysans will lead to a vicious regress. This argument suffers from two weaknesses. First, the social predicates in the analysans appear in referentially opaque contexts; thus, it is unclear whether true ascription of the beliefs requires that these predicates refer to social properties. Second, Ruben invokes what I take to be a false principle, *viz.*, that some property must correspond to every meaningful predicate expression (p. 124).

evident fact that these entities are the products of an evolutionary history beginning with the interactions of physical bodies and the fact that the existence of cultural entities at any time is dependent upon the concurrent existence of physical entities of certain sorts.[15] I wish briefly to sketch such a view—a view which is non-reductionist with respect to both ontology and explanation but is at the same time naturalist in the sense required by the pair of concessions just made.[16]

B. Embodiment

Let us take stock. So far, I have argued that institutions, whether deliberately created or the unintended result of human interaction, may be constituted for present purposes by members of a society in terms of a conceptual framework that does not admit of reduction in the individualist's intended sense. And if an institution is thus conceived, then it is not reducible. To maintain the contrary would be to suppose either that these institutions did not really exist (which seems perverse) or that "the natives" are radically mistaken about their nature (which implies that many of their legal and social sanctions are in some sense grounded in a misapprehension of the facts). Before admitting these judgments, it is incumbent upon us to see whether any coherent, more charitable alternative is available.

Societies are not merely collections of persons and artifacts; nevertheless, their existence is in some way dependent upon the existence of the latter sorts of objects. Leaving aside artifacts, territory, etc., for the sake of simplicity, let us designate as the *population* of a society that group of individuals who are, have been, or will be its members.[17] Our problem then may be viewed as one of articulating the relations between a society (and its structural components) on the one hand and its population on the other.

---

[15] Antireductionists such as Mandelbaum and Gellner both concede that the major weakness of their accounts lies in their failure to provide a positive theory of the requisite sort (see Mandelbaum, "Societal Facts," 476–87 and Ernest Gellner, "Holism versus Individualism in History and Sociology," in *Theories of History*, ed. Patrick L. Gardiner [New York: Free Press, 1959], 489–502). I will presently consider whether the "concurrent existence" condition might be relaxed. It will remain true that the existence of social entities is parasitic upon the existence, at some time, of suitable physical entities (including ordinary human beings).

[16] The view I am proposing draws heavily upon the arguments of Joseph Margolis concerning the ontological status of persons and works of art. See Joseph Margolis, "Works of Art as Physically Embodied and Culturally Emergent Entities," *The British Journal of Aesthetics* 14, no. 3 (1974): 187–96 and "The Ontological Peculiarity of Works of Art," *The Journal of Aesthetics and Art Criticism* 36, no. 1 (1977): 45–50.

[17] Problems about "partial membership" and other sorts of borderline cases are irrelevant to my purpose here.

In searching for a solution, one might be initially struck by the thought that persons are themselves emergent entities consisting of a mind and a body where the latter may be said to *embody* the former and the former to require such embodiment. I do not believe that can be the correct story—or rather, the whole of the correct story—about the relationship between human minds and bodies.[18] Yet, I take this idea to be a significant clue. Thus, although minds are not bodies and may be construed as the bearers of special non-physical properties, the criteria for the identification and individuation of (other) minds depend upon there being a publicly accessible world of material objects, including bodies of a certain complex kind that qualify as bodies of persons.[19] But to construe an entity as a person capable of having beliefs, performing actions, and so forth is to place the entity so identified under the aegis of a conceptual framework not reducible to descriptions of causally interacting physical bodies.[20] Similarly, works of art are construed as objects whose production requires the exercise of certain kinds of intentions by rational agents within a cultural milieu; as such, their existence requires that they be embodied in physical objects (blocks of marble, books, orchestra scores and performances, etc.),. But they themselves are not *identical* with their physical embodiments—if they were, then, e.g., two copies of *Moby-Dick* would be identical particulars.

I shall not fully rehearse the arguments that favor such a view, but a few remarks are in order concerning the relation of embodiment itself.[21]

---

[18] A difficulty—I take it to be the fundamental difficulty—is that the embodiment relation itself cannot explain how it is that human brains or persons can possess original intentionality. That is not to say that embodiment is not part of the story. But all the other exemplifications of embodiment relations to which I will appeal are ones in which the intentionality of the embodied entities is imputed, not original.

[19] That is at any rate the ordinary case. If a disembodied God existed, perhaps he could provide identifying information not parasitic upon our identifying a body.

[20] I do not mean to imply that placement within such a framework is an arbitrary or conventional matter; the non-reducible descriptions are, we have decisive reasons to believe, *true* of persons.

[21] See Margolis, "Works of Art," 187–96 and Andrew Harrison, "Works of Art and Other Cultural Objects," *Proceedings of the Aristotelian Society* 68, no. 1 (1968): 105–28. There is, however, a difference between Margolis' view and my own. I construe substance-hood purely formally. That is, to be a substance is to be a possible subject for individuating predications without being predicable of anything. If one grants the classical distinction between substances and "stuff," I think we may allow, formally, that minds and nations are non-material substances, although the only "stuff" is physical matter. Margolis' view, briefly, is that there is no need to posit non-material substances, but that works of art and persons are emergent particulars with both non-material properties and the material properties of the bodies in which they are embodied (Joseph Margolis, "Reductionism and Ontological Aspects of Consciousness," *Journal for the Theory of Social Behaviour* 4, no. 1 [1974]: 3–16; "The Ontological Peculiarity," 45–50). Anticipating my argument somewhat, let me observe that Margolis also holds social institutions to be fictional entities on the grounds that they are not embodied agents as

First, embodied entities are particulars, not universals (i.e., properties), and the embodiment relation is not instantiation, for embodied entities, such as works of art, can be created and destroyed but universals cannot. Moreover, not all works of art are multiply instantiable (e.g., oil paintings are not), and this is determined, in part, by certain conventions. Finally, a copy of a multiply instantiable work of art (e.g., a musical performance) can be defective without failing to be a copy; this cannot be said of instances of a universal. Joseph Margolis offers six characteristics of embodiment:

> What is meant by saying that one particular is embodied in another is: (i) that the two particulars are not identical; (ii) that the existence of the embodied particular presupposes the existence of the embodying particular; (iii) that the embodied particular possesses some of the properties of the embodying particular; (iv) that the embodied particular possesses properties that the embodying particular does not possess; (v) that the embodied particular possesses properties of a kind that the embodying particular cannot possess; (vi) that the individuation of the embodied particular presupposes the individuation of the embodying particular.[22]

To these conditions I should add two formal conditions and two essential non-formal ones. The formal conditions are: (1) anti-symmetry: if x embodies y, then, necessarily, y does not embody x; and (2) transitivity: if x embodies y and y embodies z, then x embodies z. The non-formal conditions are: (3) that embodied entities have intentional content, either original content (as in the case of natural persons or minds) or derived content as, I believe, is the case for every other sort of embodied entity; and (4) that necessarily, everything that can be embodied exists only if it is at some time embodied in one or more material bodies. The modalities here are metaphysical necessities. The second formal condition allows that an immaterial thing might be *immediately* embodied in another immaterial thing, so long as the chain of embodiments terminates in an embodier that is a material thing or things.

One further observation that will prove to be of central importance is this: many—though not all—embodied entities whose intentional content is derived (not original) gain that content by way of *performative acts*

---

persons are (Joseph Margolis, "Collective Entities and the Rules of War" [paper presented at the International Conference on War and Violence, Union, NJ, April 1974]). But if social institutions are not construed *literally* as (natural) persons (in particular, as subjects possessing original intentionality), but rather on the *model* of personhood, then the claim that they cannot be suitably embodied seems to me to require further argument—and, in fact, to be false.

[22] Margolis, "The Ontological Peculiarity of Works of Art," 48.

performed by persons, either insofar as they are natural persons or, more frequently, acting in some official capacity and against a background of socially established rules and conventions. Thus, in contemporary Western culture, at least, something does not achieve status as a work of art simply by virtue of having been fashioned by someone and declared to be a work of art, if that is done independently of the conventions and concurrence of the "art world." There might be cultures in which *there is no such thing* as a work of art because such a context is absent.[23]

I am a realist about works of art. I do not take *Crime and Punishment* or Michelangelo's *David* to be merely "cultural fictions"—whatever that might mean. If this is a plausible view concerning works of art, then it seems equally plausible to suppose—and for rather similar reasons[24]—that a society may be realistically conceived as consisting of a social structure and a population where the social structure is embodied in the population (and artifacts), just as the people (and artifacts) are themselves embodied, in turn, in physical objects of certain kinds. Ultimately, then, social institutions and roles may be taken to be embodied in physical objects of these kinds so that the existence of the former is ontologically dependent on the existence of the latter. And this embodiment relation is mediated by the existence of rational agents who, while serving as embodiers, are themselves embodied. Like works of art and artifacts generally, social roles and institutions are culturally emergent entities; indeed, they are the culturally emergent entities *par excellence*. Moreover, just as the fact that social entities are created by and embodied in individuals does not entail that the entities so created are analyzable into noninstitutional facts about individuals, so too the fact that an oil painting is made from oil

---

[23] John Searle emphasizes the centrality of such acts ("declarations," in his terminology) in the creation of social realities, as have I. See John R. Searle, *The Construction of Social Reality* (New York: Simon & Schuster, 1995); *Making the Social World: The Structure of Human Civilization* (New York: Oxford University Press, 2010); and Evan Fales, "Truth, Tradition, and Rationality," *Philosophy of the Social Sciences* 6, no. 2 (1976): 97–113.

[24] A specific parallel may help to fix ideas. To say that the novel *War and Peace*, exists is not to say that such and such particular *copies* of the novel exist, nor that the original manuscript does; similarly, many properties of this novel (its style, coherence, and display of insight) are not explainable in terms of the physical properties of those copies. But were it not for the copies (or some other form of physical embodiment), we would not have the novel; nor are its attributes determinable save by virtue of physical attributes of its copies. Rather similarly, to say that we have a Supreme Court is not to say that such and such persons (Justice Ginsberg et al.) exist, nor that a certain building does. It is more nearly to say that certain executed laws exist and that laws, like novels, are not marks on paper, though laws and courts could neither exist nor have the properties they do were it not for the existence of marks, persons, buildings, and so on.

paints and canvas does not entail that every fact about such a painting is reducible to facts about paint and canvass.[25]

The state of play, then, is this. Metaphysical individualists can, in the face of a temporal regress of institutional facts and an appeal to some permanently obscure, prehistorical, and pre-institutional human condition, defend their reductive conception of social entities and facts by appeal to a state-of-nature/social contract picture of social relationships that, though a historical fiction, can become operative as a legal reality by way of performative acts that put that picture in place as the fundamental justificatory framework in terms of which social structures are conceived and legitimated. But, *mutatis mutandis*, communitarians can invoke a holistic justificatory framework that acquires similar legal reality independently of any true or fabricated historical narrative—though such a fabrication may effectively serve heuristic ends.

Each side may, on the level of normative political theory, believe that they are in the right—that their conception of the foundations of legitimate social and political obligations is grounded in a true picture of human nature unconditioned by cultural contingencies. But, so far as human nature is relevant, it appears to me that the communitarians may have a more nearly plausible story to tell, for although the evolutionary history of the development of full human personhood on the one hand and of institutionalized social conventions and structures on the other must certainly have involved complex interrelationships, we can be sure that pre-human hominids had complex (non-institutional) societies well before either institutional structures or full-fledged human personhood appeared. Moreover, we know that it is at least a *causally* necessary condition for the development of modern human beings into normal persons that they be

---

[25] Denying that works of art—or artifacts generally—are distinct from their composing materials, Van Inwagen argues thus:
> If ... you are still inclined to believe in the statue that is distinct from the lump of clay, consider this. We have a snake, a very long, thin, tough snake....we weave it cleverly into a hammock....If we imagine our snake to be an intelligent being and imagine him to reflect on the question "Is there an object—a hammock—that is numerically distinct from me but currently spatially coincident with me?" then we do a grave disservice to the intellectual reputation of [the snake] if we make him answer this question in the affirmative. A really *intelligent* intelligent snake ... will conclude, after only a very brief moment of reflection, "No, no ... there's nothing here but me." If we, too, are intelligent, we shall agree with him. But if we do agree ... then, surely, we should also agree that the lump of clay momentarily becomes a statue. (van Inwagen, *Material Beings*, 126–27)

I do not agree with van Inwagen's hyperintelligent colubrid. If our sapient serpent refuses to unravel, even when people lounge about in its embrace (perhaps because it is not bright enough, is maladroit, or out of an excess of *noblesse oblige*), then I say (no doubt because I am not a clever serpent) that there is both one snake and one (distinct) hammock.

raised from infancy in intimate social relationships with other human beings.[26] The social-contract myth *could not have been* an historical reality, at least in its Hobbesian form.[27]

However that may be (and granting that every society must sufficiently address basic human needs), it is important to recognize that the creation of social institutions can trump whatever views we might individually have about human nature—and can do so in ways that favor communitarianism or individualism. And, of course, it matters. Individualists will have, in general, a different fundamental view of personal autonomy *vis à vis* other human beings and the state than communitarians will. As an illustrative case, compare what Hobbes, a social contractarian, has to say about correct action under the circumstance of having committed a capital offense. In Hobbes' view, such a deed destroys the contract between the criminal and his society, creating a state of war between him and the state. The binding force of that contract derives from a rational trade-off in which each citizen sacrifices certain freedoms in exchange for the advantages of cooperation and protection. When the state legitimately demands your life, that trade-off ceases to be rational. What the criminal should do, if he can, is to escape the clutches of the state, to which he is no longer bound by any obligations.

Contrast Socrates' reply to those friends who urge him to escape unjust capital punishment. As Plato represents the matter, Socrates replies to Crito's urging that he escape with these words:

> "And was that our agreement with you?" the law would say, "or were you to abide by the sentence of the State?" And if I were to express astonishment at their saying this, the law would probably add: "Answer, Socrates, …Tell us what complaint you have to make against us which justifies you in attempting to destroy us and the State? In the first place

---

[26] As shown by the infamous experiments with infant Rhesus monkeys by Harry Harlow and by the small number of documented cases of feral children, as well as the tragic results of social deprivation of babies in Rumanian orphanages. See Harry F. Harlow, "The Nature of Love," *American Psychologist* 13, no. 12 (1958): 673–85 and Charles A. Nelson, Nathan A. Fox, and Charles H. Zeanah, "Anguish of the Abandoned Child," *Scientific American* 308, no. 4 (2013): 62–67.

[27] Thomas Hobbes' starting-point is adult, rationally self-interested human beings who have been living "solitary" lives, and seem to have emerged into the world, like "swamp-men," from nowhere. (Philosophers deploy "Swamp Man" in various thought-experiments: he is imagined to be a fully formed human being who has no parents but somehow was accidentally assembled by chemical reactions in a swamp.) Locke's version of the theory is more complicated, in as much as he considers persons in the state of nature to be governed by a moral law ordained by God. The methodological individualist is, of course, free to postulate non-institutional forms of human sociality in the state of nature.

did we not bring you into existence? Your father married your mother by our aid and begat you. Say whether you have any objection to urge against those of us who regulate marriage?" None, I should reply. "Or against those of us who regulate the system of nurture and education of children in which you were trained? Were not the laws, who have the charge of this, right in commanding your father to train you in music and gymnastic?" Right, I should reply. "Well, then, since you were brought into the world and nurtured and educated by us, can you deny in the first place that you are our child and slave, as your fathers were before you? And if this is true you are not on equal terms with us; nor can you think that you have a right to do to us what we are doing to you....And because we think [it] right to destroy you, do you think that you have any right to destroy us in return, and your country as far as in you lies?....Has a philosopher like you failed to discover that our country is more to be valued and higher and holier far than mother or father or any ancestor, and more to be regarded in the eyes of the gods and of men of understanding?" (*Crito*, 50c–51b, Jowett translation)

Here, Socrates at least allows himself to imagine his country—and even its laws—to be persons that have (superior) rights and can be injured. Is this merely a figure of speech? I think not.

To be sure, a full theory of how, in principle, the performative institution of social structures could be possible *ab initio* would have to show how (at least some) performative acts—which are typically themselves governed by institutionalized constitutive rules—can arise from the soil of pre-institutional human existence. That is a task I shall not undertake here.[28]

But if, then, natural persons as agents with intentions must themselves be conceived to be emergent in a way compatible with naturalism and with their evolution from physical objects describable in terms of causal laws, we are in a position to make the same concessions with respect to societies while then understanding how it is that, given this account of natural persons, further provision for the evolutionary

---

[28] It is, however, not too difficult to imagine how certain performatives could arise in the context of natural linguistic communication. Declarations that one will in the future perform certain actions for the benefit of others would rather naturally come to engender conventions under which such declarations were commitment-creating and failure to perform was sanctionable. Moreover, promising provides the conceptual basis for contract. It is not clear that even this is required. Suppose the relevant performative acts presuppose an institutional background of conventions. It does not follow that the new institutions that *result* cannot, in effect, "trump" the history of their production (so far as understanding their *nature* goes) and serve as regress-stoppers for diachronic explanations.

development of social entities may be accommodated.[29] Moreover, we have in the process illuminated the dialectical pressures that strongly motivate political theorists to frame their views in terms of origin myths that hark back to an *Urzeit*. We can discern three reasons for this. The first is that narrativizing theoretical matters is a powerful device, both rhetorically and heuristically, for the purposes of conveying to the *hoi polloi* a working understanding of what is at issue. The second is that what is traditional has both a psychological and a pragmatic claim upon us: psychological because we are creatures of habit, pragmatic because what has withstood the test of time must have something going for it. Therefore, even political proposals that are *non*-traditional will more easily gain acceptance if they can be represented, fictionally, as rooted in past practices. And third, an originary tale, even if fictional, can serve heuristically to satisfy the need for a terminus to the legitimacy regress we have been exploring by mimicking a scene of historical origin.

C. Social Ontology

It is necessary now to examine the nature of socially emergent entities in greater detail. I shall consider the relationships between entities of the following four kinds: persons, officers, offices, and nations or societies. I have suggested that societies are structures or systems of offices embodied in persons. But strictly speaking, this seems inaccurate, for *offices* are constituted by the social functions and duties which their occupiers serve to perform, and these *functions* are not embodied in a person as such. Rather, they are embodied in his or her *actions*, insofar as those actions are of an appropriate kind. Thus, offices are more precisely construed in relation to societies on an analogy with the relation between persons and their natural functions, such as thought or nutrition. Hence, it seems necessary to construe

---

[29] My conception of natural personhood here is limited somewhat artificially to whatever conception we can form of what it is to be a human or rational agent in a "state of nature." The difficulties are that such a state is *not* natural for our species and that, as we ordinarily use the concept of personhood, it may well have inextricably built into it a social dimension. That hominids were social creatures before they were fully persons suggests that personhood, as ordinarily conceived, may itself be a culturally emergent property. But for theoretical purposes it is useful, and I think possible, to speak heuristically of a pre-social personhood in terms of at least a capacity for beliefs, intentions, certain emotions, and rational action (perhaps as they could develop under non-institutional conditions of sociability). What is relevant here is the formulability of an ontological hierarchy, not whether there existed any corresponding stages in evolutionary development. Some philosophers (e.g., Winch and perhaps Wittgenstein) have appeared to hold that all the characteristics of personhood can appear only within a social context. While I think this is a mistaken view, I am not concerned to attack it here. It does seem true that normal *human* personhood is deeply dependent upon social interaction from infancy on.

societies as consisting of offic*ers*. Officers, as performers of culturally emergent actions, are agents embodied in those persons whose performances embody the actions in question. Officerhood, then, is a culturally emergent property that an individual possesses by way of embodying a social personage.[30] And to be an officer allows one to perform actions of certain kinds, for certain reasons, and with certain intentions, which may not be available to any person *qua* private individual. Consequently, it is not implausible to take officers to be entities construed on the model of persons of a culturally emergent sort. Finally, for the same reason, societies themselves can be (and typically are, in common parlance) conceived as persons: as having wills, intentions, and the ability to perform actions embodied in the wills, intentions, and ability to act of their populations *qua* a socially organized group in the requisite ways.[31]

Thus, we may say that Nixon once was (i.e., once embodied) the President but that the President (the same personage) is presently (embodied in) Mr. Trump or Mr. Biden—that to be a President is to be accorded the rights and duties legally constituting the office of the presidency and that among the actions performed by the man or woman who is president are ones which in turn embody actions of the society as a whole, as well as those of the president.[32] For the society, though a distinct entity, may perform certain of its deeds through particular agents or representatives—if it stipulates that its actions are to be thus embodied.[33]

Yet, the implications of this conclusion will seem unacceptable: have we not handed the natives a blank check to draw on an infinite bank of ontological *possibilia*? Such potential promiscuity would seem not to dull Occam's Razor but to break it. To what extent are culturally emergent entities the creatures of convention, and to what extent is our ontology perforce expanded or contracted by the facts of social existence, independently of any intention to create entities assigned some special ontological status? It is obvious that *particular* offices, institutions, and societies can be created and destroyed indefinitely many times by intentional

---

[30] Speaking more carefully, I should saythat offices and official actions *can* be emergent as I am conceding,, *arguendo,* that they may be so constituted as to be reducible. Ruben and Searle, on the other hand, take these things *necessarily* to be emergent.

[31] For a defense of Durkheim's views on collective agency, and an examination of the anthropology of group intentions and action, see Mary Douglas, *How Institutions Think* (Syracuse, NY: Syracuse University Press, 1986).

[32] For example, concluding treaties with other nations.

[33] These ideas are of course hardly original; they were debated with skill and developed in great detail (as applied to kings) by mediaeval legal theorists. See Kantorowicz, *The King's Two Bodies.*

acts or accidentally.³⁴ The question I wish to raise concerns, rather, the extent to which the *way* in which an office or institution is conceived by a community can affect the ontological status it has. Officers and societies are, I have said, frequently assigned the status of person-like entities, and thus conceived, it seems to me that they *are* person-like.³⁵ They can gather information, form beliefs (either justified or not), and act in ways that can be explained in terms of their aims and are subject to normative evaluation as well- or ill-justified.³⁶

But the possibility that they can be created on, and treated in terms of, some other model is not a possibility that can be ignored. Why could not a group of individuals (as lately intimated) form a functioning community

---

³⁴ Such a turnover in the furniture of the world no more threatens Occam's Razor than the manufacture of new tables and chairs. It is free license to create new ontological *categories* that disturbs.

³⁵ It is commonly held in our own tradition that such "persons" are forensic "fictions"; but this seems at best misleading. They are *not* fictions, literally, in the way that Mr. Pickwick is. Nor are they in any sense treated as eliminable; they are given special legal rights, duties, and status, are said to perform identifiable actions not ascribable to individuals, and so forth. Forensic fictions need not to be ontological phantoms. Those actions by means of which new laws and institutions are declared to exist have—if enacted in the appropriate ways—performative force, as noted. In this sense, creatures of convention can be made real, regardless of whether subsequent behavior conforms or not (cf. Fales, "Truth, Tradition, and Rationality," 97–113). Agassi has argued that the central thesis of methodological individualism is that only individuals have aims. General Motors' intentions to split its stock amounts to certain individuals having that intention (Agassi, "Methodological Individualism," 244–70). But (1) these individual aims are and can be expressed only by reference to the corporate structure (as is conceded). (2) While, to be sure, GM's intention must be embodied in the intentions or actions of certain men, it is not their private identity, but their corporate identity—their position in GM's hierarchy—that is relevant. The rules governing that structure determine what officers shall be such that their intentions or actions shall *count* as GM's having some intentions. Finally, (3) the aims of an institution may be only loosely connected with the private aims of its officers. Just as a certain arm-motion at an intersection, performed by a cyclist with whatever intention, may for legal purposes count as having made a left-turn signal, so in principle a vote by the GM board to split its stock may count as effecting an intention on the part of GM, even if every member of the board privately intends, by voting *for* a split, that it shall *not* occur. (We may imagine each member privately believing and desiring that such an announcement will in fact prevent the stock split by provoking government interference—which may never materialize. The ensuing split is still an intentional act on the part of GM—*even though* the intentionality is imputed only—for which it may later be held legally responsible.)

³⁶ On group belief, see Jennifer Lackey, "What Is Justified Group Belief?," *Philosophical Review* 125, no. 3 (2016): 341–96. On Lackey's view, "Groups are epistemic agents in their own right, with justified beliefs that respond to both evidence and normative requirements that arise only at the group level, but which are nonetheless importantly constrained by the epistemic status of the beliefs of their individual members" (p. 1).

without taking themselves to have created a society with person-like attributes? In such a society, for instance, statements about the events participated in by the members of the group *could* always be described in terms of statements about the actions of individuals characterized simply as rational agents. Some sociologists, reacting against the laudable if impractical parsimony of such natives might, for the purposes of explanation, be inclined nevertheless to postulate the existence of a non-reducible social entity. But where members of a group refuse to treat their association in such terms, the postulation is either gratuitous or requires some special justification.[37] There are, nevertheless, constraints placed upon an inventive group's powers of creation; thus, for example, in spite of the looseness attached to the requirement that social phenomena be embodied,[38] one cannot create offices and institutions where the mere intention to do so is present but where all forms of embodiment are also denied.[39]

---

[37] Here, we touch on an issue to which I shall presently return: to what extent is the social scientist justified in postulating, for the purpose of explanation, structures and forces which participants in the society do not recognize or acknowledge?

[38] As is illustrated by our earlier example of an embodied law becoming (perhaps only temporarily but for all practical purposes) disembodied. Temporary disembodiment of sovereign nations offers a more interesting possibility. Consider the debate among Israelis over whether the nation is ancient Israel *redivivus*. Both left-wing secular Jews and right-wing ultra-Orthodox Jews deny this, but with differing intent. The secularists do not want a re-constituted Davidic state; the ultra-Orthodox do but envision nothing less than a full return to Torah as Israel's law. A similar but less likely case: suppose the southern U.S. states were once again to rebel; but this time, they succeed in seceding. Surely there would be a call to identify the renascent South with the Confederacy and perhaps even to declare that this nation had never truly ceased to exist, even in the absence of any formal embodiment. This last claim, on the ontology I am defending, would really be a legal fiction. No one would, surely, seriously claim the Confederacy actually existed during the last century, absent any future re-constitution. And it is implausible to say the existence of a Confederate nation during that period could somehow be brought into being simply because it is re-constituted at a future date (but see the discussion of U.S. Supreme Court decisions in Section D below).

[39] There are, no doubt, further constraints imposed by the web of conceptual connections between such notions as rational action, responsibility, rights, duties, and so on, upon the nature of entities eligible to serve as embodiers of social personhood. But through the device of legal guardianship, legal personhood can be conferred upon even non-sentient beings such as permanently comatose human beings and forests. See Christopher D. Stone, *Should Trees Have Standing? Law, Morality, and the Environment*, 3rd ed. (New York: Oxford University Press, 2010).

I am indebted to Margolis for pointing out to me a puzzle about the ontological status of social institutions. It derives from the central problem of legitimacy. For if the existence of such entities rests upon their satisfying some criteria of legitimacy, then there is room for disputes concerning existence when the criteria for legitimacy themselves are challenged or under dispute. Nor can such disputes be straightforwardly resolved in the way that disputes about the existence of physical objects can. If, for example, a secessionist movement is not recognized by the community of nations as a

What, finally, can be said in a general way about the attributes of culturally emergent entities of the sorts familiar to Westerners? I shall consider nations and institutions on the one hand and offices and officers on the other. Social institutions, as interrelated systems of officers, are, or at least can in principle be,[40] stable structures through which the members of the population "cycle" endlessly, each member being born, assuming some sequence of social positions, and finally dying, to be replaced by someone else. Such at least is the somewhat idealized static model in terms of which people for many purposes think about social structure. In this sense, persons are mortal, while societies are (potentially) immortal. Insofar as the structure does not change and the "personhood" of officers is defined in terms of a stable set of rights and duties, it is even possible, judicially, to construe officers as immortal persons each embodied in a succession of private persons.[41] Accordingly, Nixon and Trump are different persons but have been, at different times, the same personage.

Societies, with the traditions they perpetuate, are, as Durkheim observed, more powerful than individual men—and, in a sense, more powerful than their population at any time taken collectively, for that population is invariably conditioned by its history and traditions; and where those traditions have established a society as a kind of corporate person, there is conceptual room for the occurrence of dislocations between what is understood to be the corporate or general will and the individual desires of

---

new nation, but nevertheless declares itself to be such, what is its ontological status? The dispute here hinges significantly upon who gets "the say" concerning the fledgling's attempt to constitute itself; if societies are intentional entities, whether or not they exist will depend upon the intentions of the relevant people, but there may be disagreements over who is included in the relevant group. Yet, deciding *this* in turn normally depends upon authorization, which is what is at issue. The puzzle stems from the fact that the solutions offered on either side of the dispute rely upon a reflexive maneuver, which simply re-raises the question: the secessionists claim that they constitute the relevant group and that, given their decision, a new state has been born. The parent nation, in denying the authority of the secessionists, declares that no new source of authority has been created; hence, no new state exists. There appears to be, in some cases, no "objective" way to settle such disagreements on purely ideological grounds. It is at least tempting to say that in such cases, "history decides" and that, effectively, the decision rests upon the ability of either side to make good on its claims, if necessary, by coercive means. As long as the issue hangs in the balance, a neutral observer will be unable to determine whether or not a new social entity exists. But this possibility, if peculiar, is by no means unique to social institutions. Similar puzzles can be constructed for other sorts of intentional entities, such as (putative) works of art.

[40] Although they clearly do change in time, social structures are frequently or even ordinarily *conceived* in an idealized way as unchanging by those governed by them.

[41] Thus, the formula, "The King never dies"—cf. Kantorowicz, *The King's Two Bodies*, 314–450. See also, Meyer Fortes, "Ritual and Office in Tribal Society," in *Essays on the Ritual of Social Relations*, ed. Max Gluckman (New York: Manchester University Press, 1962), 53–88.

the members of the population—even where there is unanimity in those desires. A consensus among the citizens of England that the monarchy is undesirable for the promotion of their private interests would not be incompatible with the view that a rejection of the monarchy would constitute an abandonment of what is desirable and proper for England.[42]

Officers and societies are, *as* embodied entities, visible objects accessible via their embodiments to public discourse and empirical investigation. But what are embodied are, it is evident, no more visible or physical objects than minds are. The embodiment of a society is a complex matter, and some parts of its "body" may provide important foci for the manifestation of its powers; in particular, its power to act will be vested in certain persons in positions of authority, some of whose actions are taken to embody the actions of the state as a whole.

All this means that emergently constituted societies are *supernatural* entities if we understand this to mean that they are largely the children of convention and are emergent with respect to non-cultural entities. There is something more than mere metaphor in the claim that the will of such a social agent is expressed in the creation of the social order and traditions that govern social life and that it is this agent that guards the moral and legal values upon which that social organization rests. Such conclusions will seem to some to repeat Durkheim's more extravagant sins. But unlike Durkheim, I do not hold that social phenomena are *sui generis*.[43] Nor are my reasons for denying the reducibility of (some) social phenomena Durkheim's reasons.[44] I will speak more of Durkheim presently; but he was quite correct,

---

[42] Note, precisely along these lines, that Henri Rousseau, a social contractarian, nevertheless posits a "General Will" that is not reducible to the "sum" of the wills of citizens, each directed toward his or her self-interest, but is to be identified with what determines their collective good or the good of the nation.

[43] Nor, I might add, is it a consequence of this view that people are invariably the victims of impersonal social forces beyond their control; none of the liberal's moral bugbears come to roost here.

[44] Durkheim's view concerning reduction seems to me so badly confused, indeed, that some of the reasons he gives for denying this possibility would rather constitute its *point*: thus, he argues that since the properties of wholes are different from the properties of parts, social phenomena are non-reducible. But on this view, color and temperature, for instance, could not be given a microphysical explanation, which is absurd. See Durkheim, *The Rules of Sociological Method*, xlvii–lii, 102–3). The reductionist in sociology need not deny the existence of wholes any more than the physicist need deny the existence of tables; if the anti-reductionist has an interesting thesis, it is that there *are* emergent entities whose nature cannot be *explained* in terms of the properties of individual human beings. So the opponent of methodological individualism has to make some ontological commitments (cf. the debate between Leon J. Goldstein, "The Two Theses of Methodological Individualism," *The British Journal for the Philosophy of Science* 9, no. 33 (1958): 1–11; "Mr. Watkins on the Two Theses," *The British Journal for the Philosophy of Science* 10, no. 39 (1959): 240–41; J.

I believe, in seeing that such an understanding of social phenomena may have implications for the analysis of religious language and belief. That is the issue to which I now turn.

The nearly universal connection between myth structure and social structures has been too widely observed to require any comment. But I will argue for a much stronger thesis: that this connection is not only no accident but reflects the fact that people are in their myths exhibiting a theoretically explicit and far deeper awareness of the ontology of social structures than has ordinarily been held to be the case. Let us now see what might be said, in a general way, in favor of this hypothesis. (In later chapters, I will test the hypothesis against particular religious texts.)

II. Religion Re-Conceived

A. Action Explanations Generally Considered

It is useful to approach this question via a brief discussion of a much more general one: what is it to explain (or understand) human action? Whereas an adequate answer to this general question is far beyond the scope of the present essay, it is inevitable that one's views about the general theoretical framework for explanations of action and belief will provide the setting within which it is necessary to place the more specialized discussion of ritual action and religious belief. So it will be well for me to make my views explicit, even though I will not defend them here.

Fortunately, we can set aside the controversial issue of whether some reductive program for explaining human behavior can ultimately be carried through. Regardless of one's position on that, it may, I think, be conceded that we do have something like a theoretical framework for explaining such matters embedded within ordinary parlance; it is the structure of this "naïve" model ("folk psychology") that I wish partly to exhibit. I give it pride of place not only because it is not naïve but because I believe that, whatever its limitations in difficult cases, it constitutes the conceptual foundation in terms of which the very notions of action and belief are systematized and upon which any more sophisticated explanations must be built. I believe its implications have been either ignored or misunderstood by some social scientists.[45]

The model is a normative one: humans believe and do things for reasons; there are good reasons and poor ones for believing (or doing)

W. N. Watkins, "The Two Theses of Methodological Individualism," *The British Journal for the Philosophy of Science* 9, no. 36 (1959): 319–20; and "Third Reply to Mr. Goldstein," *The British Journal for the Philosophy of Science* 10, no. 39 (1959): 242–44.

[45] Notably, by Durkheim, *The Rules of Sociological Method*, 89–124.

something; and the standard of rationality in terms of which a person may be judged is a standard for evaluating reasons. For a creature to be judgeable by such a standard, it is (minimally) necessary that it be a creature to which we have grounds for ascribing beliefs, desires, needs, and an ability to think systematically and logically. Then for x to act rationally is, at first approximation, for x to have certain beliefs about the world and herself, reasonably held in the light of the available evidence, and to act in a way that can be expected, if those beliefs are true, to promote the satisfaction of her needs and wants. Normally, too, a rational agent must *know* what her reasons are and must be able to justify her belief or action by giving them, for our ability to ascribe unconscious beliefs and desires to creatures of a given kind is parasitic upon our ability correctly to ascribe to them conscious, conveyable beliefs and desires. Fully to understand a person's action is *paradigmatically* to understand how she came to hold her relevant beliefs (that is, on what evidence) and how these, together with her particular needs and desires, could constitute *reasons* for so acting.[46]

People do deviate, more or less, from the norm of rationality, but it is just to the extent that their beliefs and actions deviate that we are puzzled by them and begin resorting to various extraordinary means to bolster our explanation.[47] Indeed, it is only then that we are *justified* in doing so. Since conscious rational action constitutes the paradigm case, recognition and explanation of deviant cases as cases of action are parasitic upon this

---

[46] A bit of clarification: in one sense, we understand an action if we just know what motivation and beliefs lie behind it and see how, given those motivations, the action is sensible. But if one or more of the relevant beliefs strikes us as *crazy*, we find the action puzzling because we find the belief to be so. This puts pressure on us either to revise our estimate of what beliefs are in play or to consider whether the agent's evidence might make a "crazy" belief rational for her after all. I do not mean to suggest that a paradigmatic understanding of actions requires, in general, tracing all the evidence for all the relevant beliefs of the actor.

[47] Even here we are conceptually constrained to attempt to bring deviant behavior back within the sphere of the model of rational action. Sigmund Freud, for example, typically proceeded by ascribing to apparently irrational persons desires and beliefs which they did not themselves recognize or acknowledge but which, *if* they had them, would constitute *reasons* for their unusual behavior. The fact that these beliefs and desires are not consciously recognized is explained in turn by alluding to reasons the agent has for repressing or disguising them. But all this, whether correct or not, makes insanity intelligible exactly to the extent that it pays homage to the normative requirements of the model of rationality. To do so does not entail, of course, that the behavior of insane men *is* (as some have been tempted to claim) rational in any full-blooded sense; only that it is understood within the conceptual framework of such a model; i.e., by giving rational form to as much of the agent's motivational structure as possible. Karl Popper's notion of situational logic has affinities to the model presented here. In describing it, I. C. Jarvie makes a similar observation regarding Freud (I. C. Jarvie, *Concepts and Society* [New York: Routledge, 1972], 19–20).

framework, for it embodies the conditions of intelligibility of our conception of agents and actions.

I wish to emphasize the fact that recourse to alternative explanatory maneuvers is justified only when actions cease to conform straightforwardly to the model of rationality. Indeed, we find anthropologists resorting to various extraordinary measures at precisely that point in their discussions of other cultures where native belief and practice seem to cease being rational—most prominently, within the domain of magic and religion. But to the extent that an interpretation of such behavior does *not* require such recourse, we have reason to prefer it, other things being equal.[48]

B. Uncharitable Explanations

One prominent position concerning the way religious beliefs are to be understood has been articulated by Edmund Leach, who maintains that the meaning of religious discourse is nothing over and above what may be observed about its use in, or reference to, explicit ritual practice.[49] These rituals themselves encode various sorts of social information. Although on this view, religious statements presumably *have* a meaning, Leach hardly tells us what the meaning of specific statements is; insofar as ritual use is

---

[48] See Chapter 1 of this book and Fales, "Truth, Tradition, and Rationality," 97–113. Here, my clash with Durkheim becomes explicit, for he holds that sociological explanation, in order to be objective and intelligible, must be explanation by *causes* in a sense that excludes intentions or reasons (Durkheim, *The Rules of Sociological Method*, 78–100). Since social phenomena emerge from a matrix of human action, explanations by reasons are conceptually primary. Even when an event does not occur as the result of anyone's intention to bring *it* about (e.g., the stock market crash of 1929), it does not follow that the explanation must be causal. I am not of course denying that causal processes can affect social phenomena, but those phenomena are usually intelligible only when we grasp the intentional—even when irreducible—character of the structures involved. And I should argue that explanations in terms of reasons and intentions cannot be reduced to explanations in terms of causes (see Evan Fales, "Davidson's Compatibilism," *Philosophy and Phenomenological Research* 45, no. 2 [1984]: 227–46 and "Divine Freedom and the Choice of a World," *International Journal for Philosophy of Religion* 35, no. 2 [1994]: 65–88). To restrict the social sciences to the study of those social phenomena which are not subject to some degree of conscious control (as Durkheim and others would) is not only to impose an artificial demarcation, but is theoretically crippling. The corollary of such a view is that the model of rationality is applicable only to the domain of individual action by private persons. Thus, in contrast to J. O. Wisdom, I am convinced that the irreducibility of institutions is not simply to be attributed to the fact that they are in part the unintended and "emergent" consequences of collective human action.

[49] Edmund R. Leach, *Political Systems of Highland Burma* (London: Bloomsbury Academic, 1954), 10–16 and "Ritualization in Man in Relation to Conceptual and Social Development," in *Reader in Comparative Religion*, 3rd ed., ed. William Lessa and Evon Vogt (New York: Harper & Row, 1972), 333–37.

what is appealed to, we are not left with anything remotely like a translation into synonymous English, and such translations as are provided raise problems precisely about the cognitive content of the originals.

If religious statements are taken to be interchangeable with ritual performance as such, it is impossible to hold that they provide any *reasons* for the performance of ritual action; hence, Leach must hold that the reasons for ritual must either not be known to the natives or, if known, must be expressed in more mundane terms. It is clear that the connection between beliefs and rites is an intimate one. But, paradoxically, the natives themselves suppose that religious belief serves to *justify* ritual, and they assign to religious statements properties, such as truth-value, that cannot be plausibly assigned to ritual practice or inferred from the facts of ritual practice but, rather, suggest cognitive content in the ordinary sense.

Durkheim also held that rituals emerged earlier than (or at least should be used to explain) the beliefs that were constructed to justify them. On his view, ritual evolved, so to speak, accidentally—that is, without deliberate planning or antecedent justification. Hence, ritual is initially a case of action in the absence of reasons, which just reverses the normative order for rational action. Worse, it is hard to see how the natives' beliefs (though for Durkheim, they are at least attempts at explanation) could, in fact, constitute anything like an empirically respectable justification for the practices in question. Durkheim never considered the possibility that such beliefs express a sophisticated understanding of precisely the social facts that he claims actually cause their formation. Hence, he was forced to invent some rather remarkable intellectual gymnastics by means of which the natives, working from the experiences generated by their rituals, arrived at a badly muddled explanation of what had happened to them—an understanding focused on the character of certain subjective feelings and representing only the dimmest apprehension of the real origin of the social forces manifested in ritual activity.[50]

But even if we admit the possibility of such confused mental processes, the resultant picture deviates from the norm of rationality in the first respect mentioned. It imputes to the natives the development of elaborate rituals in the absence of any antecedent conscious justification for the trouble involved. Durkheim's admission that ritual and justification doubtless developed more or less concurrently does little to mitigate the

---

[50] Durkheim, *The Rules of Sociological Method*. It is ironic that Durkheim is forced to appeal to such processes given his opposition to Lucien Lévy-Bruhl. The Durkheimian primitive mentality is not that much less muddled than the Lévy-Bruhlian; and Durkheim's insistence that our own intellectual processes are not so very different, so far from saving his thesis, convicts him of an unpromising analysis of theoretical thinking generally.

force of this objection. The very fact that here, deliberation follows action suggests that the deliberation must be mendacious, a rationalization.

Explanatory appeals to subconscious or extraconscious processes have taken various forms. Functional explanations have frequently involved the presumption that the efficacy of social arrangements stems from causes of which the natives are unaware and that as such the robustness of these institutions is not the product of the natives' conscious intentions. Here, it is largely extra-mental facts which the natives fail to know. Claude Lévi-Strauss, on the other hand, appeals to a putative repression of contradictions and to other "deep" cognitive structures in his explanation of myths.[51] It is certain psychological facts about the native's intellect which lead to stories whose real structure and purpose those natives are unable or unwilling to articulate. Durkheim's theory is a curious blend of these two general strategies.

Such methodological gambits have the advantage that the anthropologist's analytic stance is freed from constraint by what the natives themselves can or are willing to say about their society. Such explanatory "distance" may be required at times; societies are too complex for even perceptive individuals to understand or control them fully. On the other hand, the popularity that explanations of these sorts have enjoyed stems, I think, from the fact that they are so tempting when *we* cannot make literal sense out of the natives' own explanations of what they are up to. It is not surprising, therefore, that those who are most skeptical of such sociological explanations are those (such as Peter Winch or Robin Horton) who wish to insist that the natives *do* make sense, whether it is a sense alleged to be accessible only through culture-relative criteria (Winch) or whether it is maintained that natives, using the same explanatory strategies we use, begin with different evidence (Horton). My position, like Horton's, is an intellectualist one as well, but it also concedes the obvious fact that social processes may transcend the understanding of both native and non-native scholars. Putting some distance between our own analytic tools and those used by the natives may, thus, be a salutary procedure but only, I should insist, as a court of last appeal. First, we must try to make sense out of what the natives themselves try to tell us on the presumption that this more or less fits the facts.

What then are the consequences? Despite the intimate and essentially universal connection between ritual belief and social relationships, scholars have persisted in speculating that the content of native myths constitutes almost anything but explicit, deliberate, and reasonable

---

[51] Claude Lévi-Strauss, "The Structural Study of Myth," in *Structural Anthropology* (New York: Basic Books, 1963), 19–25, 272–74. Nevertheless, Lévi-Strauss provides—see Chapter 6 of this book—a much more interesting analysis of the cognitive processes that underlie primitive mythography.

theory concerning those relationships. It is as if, while accomplishing social ends which are obviously of the utmost concern and importance to them by means of highly complex and articulated procedures that are usually well-designed to achieve those aims, the natives have nevertheless either covered over these purposes with some disguise or else supposed themselves to be aiming at something quite different and quite mysterious—that, in any case, they have failed consciously to recognize what they were really intending. Thus, the development of social organization becomes essentially a Darwinian enterprise of random variation and natural selection. Now this is, *prima facie*, just implausible. The simpler and more stable a society is, the less plausible it becomes. A regular industry of postulating more or less unusual mental processes on the part of the natives has sprung up in an attempt to account for it.[52]

I think we have simply not taken seriously enough the possibility that native myth-making is literally intelligent native thought about social existence and articulation of the legal charter for its cultural forms. We have not done so, perhaps, partly because the different nature of our own society has necessitated a political idiom importantly different in various respects and partly for another reason that I shall suggest in my concluding remarks. But why suppose that this is what myths are about? Durkheim thought it was, but he failed to see how discourse about social matters could be the literal and conscious intention of the myth-makers.[53] Martin Hollis, in a terse dismissal of the possibility, asks why, if a Zande has socio-political matters in mind when he accuses a fellow Zande of witchcraft, he does not simply *say* so.[54] But this clearly begs the question. Perhaps the Zande *is* saying so, but the idiom in which he expresses this in *his* language is one that we translate (infelicitously?) into our rather mysterious terminology of witchcraft. Certainly, insofar as witchhood may be conceived by a Zande to constitute a kind of social role or office, a statement that a *witch* has done thus and so is not simply replaceable, for explanatory purposes, by a statement that such-and-such an individual *qua* private *person* has done it.[55]

---

[52] Not just among anthropologists but, more popularly of late, among evolutionary psychologists.

[53] I suppose that the most controversial aspect of the present thesis is the reverse insistence that native thinkers must be capable of conscious analytic thought of a high degree of sophistication and intellectual penetration. Few anthropologists have gone this far; still, one cannot fail to notice the marked trend toward increasing uneasiness with, or outright rejection of, the attribution of child-like or weak mentality to natives as field techniques have improved. We will return to the question how widespread such sophistication must be in a population to account for the sorts of data we have.

[54] Martin Hollis, "The Limits of Irrationality," in *Rationality*, ed. Bryan R. Wilson (New York: Harper and Row, 1970), 226.

[55] Thus, the statement "the President signed the treaty" has explanatory force (for someone who does not know who the President is) that "Donald Trump signed the

Indeed, one might turn Hollis' question around. If "the natives" are not articulating their understanding of their social system and political beliefs by way of their "mythical beliefs," then *where are they expressing them?* Or, instead, are we to suppose that they do not reflect upon such matters?

The above remarks suffice to indicate that, whatever differences in detail there may be between native mythical representation and the analytic theory of social structure proposed in Part I, it is not unreasonable to suppose that native myth-makers are attempting to express some very similar views about their own social organization and perhaps about social organization generally. Differences here may be differences at the level of general theory or may merely reflect differences in the particular social structure being discussed. A tentative suggestion, then, is that native myths are, for the most part, *true or at least plausible* and that they express native theorizing on the nature of social reality very much in the same spirit as the speculations that I have expressed in English in Part I of this chapter. A weaker thesis, which I am prepared to defend, is that since native myths, thus interpreted, prove to express far more *rational* beliefs (true or not) than they do on alternative interpretations that have been offered, such an interpretation ought, other things being equal, to be preferred, for I hope it will at least be conceded that the *kind* of theory I have defended in Part I is, whether true or not, at least a theory that (in the realm of philosophical theorizing) a reasonable person might hold: that it is an attempt to answer problems posed by hard empirical evidence, normative concerns, and conceptual reflection on the nature of social authority and that it involves some degree of conceptual sophistication.

---

treaty" lacks. An objection similar to Hollis is made by Ernest Gellner with respect to Berber idioms surrounding the selection of a man as an *agurram,* or institutionalized "saint." See Ernest Gellner, *Saints of the Atlas* (Chicago, IL: University of Chicago Press, 1969) and "Concepts and Society," in *Rationality* (New York: Harper and Row, 1970), 18–49. Gellner can, of course, speak about the Berbers with authority and I cannot, but I do not find persuasive his argument that what we have here is a case of the social utility of absurdity. Gellner argues that although men are chosen for this office by their fellow tribesmen, and although Berbers possess and apply the idiom of election to the mode of selecting intra-clan leaders, they insist that *igurramen* are not chosen by men but by God, an absurd but useful fiction. However, there are two important differences between selection to tribal leadership as an *agurram* and election to clan chieftainhood: (1) a chief's loyalty is restricted to a specific clan or subgroup, whereas an *agurram* must mediate dispassionately between opposing subgroup interests in the interest of the society as a whole, even though he is, unavoidably, a member of one such group; and (2) an *agurram* must express not just the will of the people, synchronically conceived, but also to some extent represent that will as "speaking through" an entire history and tradition. Thus, the principles of his selection ought to, involve more than the immediate interests of his selectors, and do. As I shall show, these two differences make eminently rational a distinction between election and selection by God, if the latter idiom is suitably understood. So I cannot agree with Gellner that such talk is "absurd."

This has certain consequences. Whether or not the theory put forward in Part I is correct, it is a view that is, and could not but be, the product of conscious speculation upon the ontological problems involved. It is no more likely that one could arrive at such a theory through some mental processes other than those constituting careful intellectual deliberation than that electromagnetic theory, say, could have been concocted by James Clerk Maxwell via some process other than conscious deliberation upon the relevant questions. Secondly, if myths are the products of native speculation upon the way society is or ought to be structured, another important result follows immediately, for, in that case, mythical statements are just as open to empirical access and control as our own social ideologies are.

To the extent that myths can be interpreted as deliberate attempts to explain or justify existing social institutions and/or to provide a charter for the legitimization of such institutions, our interpretation makes native myth-making an intelligible activity because it shows it to be a rational one. So to that extent, this interpretation may be accorded a greater initial degree of plausibility than rival interpretive approaches, which imply some defectiveness in native mentality. It remains to be shown, however, that such a framework can be successfully applied to account, in some detail, for the content of mythical thought.

C. Trying to Do Better

We shall presently turn to that task, limiting our scope to certain illustrative texts from the Bible. For the present, my aim is to suggest, programmatically and in only the most general sort of way, how reading myths in terms of this sort of framework might produce an illuminating mapping from mythical discourse onto the ontology of Part I. Yet even at this general level, one cannot help but see affinities between the results of the discussion in Part I and the content of typical myths. It is my claim that detailed analysis of cases in light of what follows will repay the effort involved. Such efforts will either yield more plausible explications of a wide range of myths than are produced by rival approaches, or they will not; a method stands or falls on its results. To illustrate the initial plausibility of the view, I shall discuss two mystifying notions that are central to most such mythical traditions: the existence of what we call souls and the existence of what we call gods.

It is perilous to attempt any general account of souls and gods, if only because there is reason to think that the terms drawn from various traditions and languages translated by ethnographers into English as "soul" and "god," respectively, name many conceptually distinct sorts of entities. We cannot just assume that a single English term marks out congruent categories across cultures. Nevertheless, I think there are certain features that mark off at least a significant range of ideas as sharing central features that justify grouping them together as soul-ideas and divinity-ideas, respectively.[56] Souls (within one such grouping) characteristically are invisible, immaterial entities that can perform or direct actions, are somehow intimately connected with individual persons and their social destinies, and can be variously "inherited," reincarnated, or resurrected according to certain prescribed rules. The fact that these rules are often governed by the kinship system and by a society's mechanism for achieving a suitable division of labor and social status among its members suggests immediately that a person's soul should, in such cases, be construed, quite literally, as his or her social personage.[57] A person (normally) is, *qua* private individual, the *embodiment* of one or more social role-players or officers. This, I suggest, is the nature of the link between a person and his/her soul, and it is the link that many native theoreticians are, more or less picturesquely but deliberately, trying to elucidate in their talk about souls. Clearly, officers can perform actions *if* they are suitably embodied; and, conceived apart from their embodiment, they are neither visible nor material objects. Finally, given a system of individuation for social roles, a person may embody more than one officer at the same or different times; conversely, officerhood is something that can and *must* be transferred in some regular way through the course of time.

Persons, by their nature, are born and die. A social structure, to some approximation, remains fixed and immortal. Thus, the population of a society must be "cycled through" the structure in some regular way. This has two corollaries: a single person must, at different times in his or her life, be able to step out of one role and into another; and secondly, different persons must be able (perhaps sequentially) to hold the same office. As regards the first problem, Arnold van Gennep has pointed out the pervasive idiom of death and rebirth that accompanies the ritual transference of natural *persons* from one *role* to another: here, we may say, the same person "dies to" a particular office and is reborn into a new one as a different social personage.[58] In the interlude, he or she has, in the social sense, lost personagehood—to use an unlovely neologism—and, insofar as s/he has no

---

[56] Obviously, the existence of "souls" and "gods" that do not fit the molds developed here do not provide counter-evidence to my general thesis, unless it should prove impossible to formulate accounts for them as well, using the same theoretical apparatus. Here, I simply mean to illustrate how such analyses go.

[57] A soul so understood, it goes without saying, is not to be identified with a consciousness or mind, as has become quite commonplace within the Western tradition. Nor can it be identified with the older Platonic conception of the soul as a principle organizing the constitution of natural persons. Yet, souls are in some ways *analogous* to minds—or, more nearly, persons—insofar as certain characteristic institutionally-defined sorts of obligations, intentions, and the like are assigned to them.

[58] Arnold van Gennep, *The Rites of Passage*, trans. Monika B. Vizedon and Gabrielle L. Caffee (1909; repr., Chicago, IL: University of Chicago Press, 1960).

assigned role or power, is in a time of danger, a time commonly regarded as also fraught with danger for the society at large when the filling of a socially important role is at stake.[59]

Conversely, the same officer can cease to be embodied and can become re-embodied in a different person; during the interlude, the officer and the society that depends upon the performance of his or her office are both often conceived to be endangered, even "dead." A person who steps into another person's social shoes may be said to have become the same officer. Thus interpreted, the allied idioms of reincarnation and resurrection become intelligible as something more than just falsehoods or metaphors. A few examples may serve to illustrate what is in view here. The *Ka* of pharaohs, which is functionally conceived to transmit the royal office from father to son, thereby plays a role not structurally dissimilar to that of the Holy Spirit in Christian theology (e.g., Mark 1:10–11; Matt. 3:16–17; John 1:29–34). Another example comes from many Australian aborigine tribes, which hold that when a man dies, his soul enters the body of, for example, a small fish in some nearby body of water (or a sacred stone). When—often a generation later—a pregnant woman of the same clan approaches the pond (or stone), the soul "jumps" from the fish (stone) into the fetus she is carrying. When the child is born, it is considered to replace that man (whose identity may be chosen by elders) in the social arena; i.e., it inherits his name and office.[60]

Practitioners of Voodoo in Haiti are closely associated with *loa* spirits, who serve to protect them. Exoterically, the *loas* are identified with Catholic saints; esoterically, they are identified as West African deities. Worshippers sometimes marry their *loas*, and, in any event, are frequently possessed by them. A Haitian *voudun* has three (or sometimes two) souls,

---

[59] See Victor Turner's important discussion of such liminal states in Victor Turner, *The Ritual Process: Structure and Anti-Structure* (1969; repr., Piscataway, NJ: Aldine Transaction, 1995) and *The Forest of Symbols: Aspects of Ndembu Ritual* (Ithaca, NY: Cornell University Press, 1970). It is not hard to find this sort of language in the NT. So, for example, the parable of the Prodigal Son: the overjoyed father declares of his son, lost and now found, "My son was dead, and is alive again" (Luke 15:24). Having become a swineherd for a Gentile, the son had broken the Covenant and ceased to be a Jew; now he has returned to the fold. Similarly, baptism is a death and re-birth. Paul says that the living can even be baptized "on behalf of" the dead—thus conferring upon them, even dead, a new personage—membership in the community of Christians. I shall defer discussion of what the implications of this might be. Paul goes on to say, "Why are we putting ourselves in danger every hour? I die every day!" (1 Cor. 15:30–31). Paul clearly does not mean this literally. Nor can he mean that he is daily undergoing a change of social status. But he can mean that his social identity is constantly being threatened by trials he is undergoing, in a way that imitates the *kenosis* of his Lord.

[60] W. Baldwin Spencer and F. J. Gillen, *The Northern Tribes of Central Australia* (New York: Macmillan and Company, 1904), 145; See also the charming Aborigine film *Ten Canoes,* directed by Rolf de Heer and Peter Djigirr.

the *Petit* (or *Ti*) *Bon Ange*, *Gros Bon Ange*, and *met tet* (from *maître de tête*). But upon possession by a *loa*, one of these souls—the *Gros* (or *Gwo*) *Bon Ange*, departs from the Haitian's body to make room, as it were, for the *loa* spirit. At the same time, the personality and behavior of the worshipper, who has entered a trance state, undergoes dramatic changes—he or she becomes a "different person"—or, as I should prefer to say, a different personage.[61]

Among the Dinka, a southern Nilotic tribe, certain holy men who are members of the clan, Masters of the Fishing Spear, are sought out to adjudicate significant social disputes. They assume the role of judge by entering a trance in front of the aggrieved parties. While entranced, they are possessed by a spirit, the god Flesh, who "takes over" the officiant's body and pronounces a verdict through that body. Under these conditions, a Master of the Fishing Spear is infallible; he speaks the Truth—*ex cathedra*, as it were.[62]

Reportedly, Alawite Muslims hold that women lack souls.[63] The absence of a soul corresponds to the fact that Alawite women are excluded from knowledge of Alawite doctrines and effectively excluded from participation in public life. Arguably, the Apostle Paul held a version of this view of the status of women; he teaches in 1 Corinthians 11:7 that men are the image and reflection of God, whereas women are the "reflection" of men. Even though this is a dark saying, Paul seems to be arguing for a view that assigns women a derivative social status. I am not suggesting that Paul's conception of "the image" is identical to the Alawite conception of the soul, but a case can be made for significant affinities, tied to a strong gender-based division of social roles. Such examples can be multiplied *ad libitum*.

Not just individuals, but groups of individuals can also embody social agency and institutions. In my brief discussion of gods, I shall confine myself to nations or tribes taken as a whole and correlatively to supreme deities. The notions of society and culture are in any view complex theoretical concepts. If I am right in Part I, such entities are embodied through time in a population and its artifacts. They are not material entities *simpliciter*, and they are not "visible" in the way material entities are, though they may be observed insofar as their agency is made manifest in those officials whose actions embody collective social action by expressing the tradition-governed and tradition-creating will of the population.[64] In this

---

[61] See I. M. Lewis, *Ecstatic Religion: An Anthropological Study of Spirit Possession and Shamanism* (Baltimore, MD: Penguin Books, 1971), 47.

[62] Godfrey Lienhardt, *Divinity and Experience: The Religion of the Dinka* (New York: Clarendon Press, 1961), 139–46.

[63] Alawites are secretive about their doctrines and, in fact, these are taught only to Alawite men. I also recall hearing of a Muslim society in North Africa that held a similar view of women, but I have been unable to confirm this.

[64] In so far as that "will" is focused most prominently in the actions of a single officer—e.g., a king or president—who serves as an agent with respect to both his private

sense, a single corporate agent can be made visible in multiple manifestations or embodiments. Finally, the social will expressed through history in a culture's traditions is indeed the creator and guardian of present social order; it is this word that must be made flesh in order to act in history. But these are just the sorts of properties characteristically ascribed to supreme deities.

Why, then, refuse to suppose that this is what native theoreticians are consciously talking about and that translations which do not exhibit their religious discourse in these terms are poor translations or mistranslations? We shall, of course, have to allow for a great deal of metaphorical elaboration, symbolic usage, and so forth on any view, provided that the sense and motivation for those metaphors can be understood. We shall also have to allow for the fact that most natives probably do not understand what the formulas they utter "really" mean, in the same sense that most Americans do not "really" understand such concepts as property and inalienable rights in any detailed theoretical or legal sense. But with *this* much sense made of religious and ritual beliefs, it becomes far less problematic to see how, on a reasonably literal construal of the core of religious dogma, doctrine can be said to have cognitive content accessible to relevant empirical checks. It can, as well, be understood as rational discourse on a subject of intense concern to human beings, and finally to constitute genuine justification and explanation for ritual action directed at executing the business of the tribe/state or celebrating national unity. A further advantage of our view is that it provides a natural explanation for the narrative or pseudo-historical form that so many myths take, for we have seen how natural such a parable form is for expressing our own ideological formulations.

D. When is Irrationality Rational?

I want, finally, to return to two related questions. 1) Granting that only certain sorts of entities are eligible for creation by way of social practice, and granting similarly grounded constraints on their genidentity conditions, what sorts of metaphysical fictions might a society nevertheless be rationally committed to? When can pragmatic reasons justify official doctrine that defies empirical evidence or invokes metaphysical, even logical impossibilities? 2) When is it methodologically proper for the social scientist

---

will (as Nixon did in respect to his private capacity as mere citizen) and to the will of the society as *corporation sole,* it becomes possible to construe the king as expressing the will of three different "persons": the private man's, the king's *per se,* and that of the society at large. (This is not, however, a Trinitarian doctrine: I believe it possible that the Trinity was a tripartite division of the sovereign's personage; see more below.)

to override native say-so? When is it fair to credit sociological analysis as providing the truth of the matter in the face of native disavowal?

In considering these questions, it will be important to bear in mind two sorts of cases: in which the natives are quite unaware that their ideology violates the norms of respecting empirical evidence, metaphysical possibility, and logical possibility; cases in which they are well aware and deliberate in allowing the violation(s). A couple of examples will serve to illustrate just how knowing violations can serve practical rationality—*so long as the violations are not publicly acknowledged.*

Among the Azande (a tribal group in the northern Congo), witches are quite plentiful. Edward Evans-Pritchard reports that such men are typically unaware of their magical powers unless successfully accused.[65] Misfortune is usually ascribed to witchcraft, but identifying the witch is a matter of consulting an oracle whose procedure (randomly) kills, or does not kill, chickens fed a special poison.[66] If the oracle identifies S as the witch, S can apologize for his unwitting act and perform a ritual to "cool the magic." It appears that Azande witchcraft serves not so much to explain misfortune as to lubricate social relations by easing the social tensions that arise in Azande society. It serves this purpose even though the inconsistency of their witch-beliefs should be evident to any Zande. They believe, for example, that the children of a witch are witches. But given the facts about their marriage system, it should be immediately obvious to any Zande that this entails that all Azande are witches. Yet they deny this. Nor does other, quite decisive counterevidence dissuade them. Evans-Pritchard enumerates a number of maneuvers Azande may employ in defense of their beliefs, but he overlooks an obvious possibility: Azande men and women know they are promulgating a fiction, understand its usefulness, and understand further that it would cease to function if it were admitted to be a fiction. Of course, such a hypothesis would, in the nature of the case, be hard to confirm. But neither can it be summarily dismissed.

The *zar* (or *sar*) cults, common in the horn of Africa, provide an even clearer example. These cults center around demonic possession, generally of women, in a culture in which women are marginalized and often exploited. In a typical case, a disgruntled and badly treated housewife will become possessed and undergo striking personality changes. She—or rather

---

[65] Edward Evan Evans-Pritchard, *Witchcraft, Oracles, and Magic Among the Azande* (Oxford: Clarendon Press, 1937).

[66] Though in fact random, the procedure employs a controlled experiment. The poison (not the chicken) is asked a yes/no question: e.g., if so-and-so is responsible for my misfortune, then kill the chicken. The death of the chicken is insufficient; poison fed to another chicken must be consulted: if so-and-so bewitched me, then *let the chicken live*. The death of the first chicken and survival of the second delivers a guilty verdict. (If the trials are negative, more chickens can be put in play with the name of another suspect.) Verdicts can be appealed; the king's oracle has the final say.

her demonic familiar—will speak in a deep and peremptory voice like a man and will cause domestic chaos, smashing dishes and household furnishings. What is a poor husband to do? Naturally enough, the demon must be exorcized. The exorcism ritual takes the form of a hen party (with hubby absent but paying the tab). The exorcist, the head of the local *zar* cult, is, like all her fellow cult members, a woman who has previously been possessed and who has, with experience, learned how to deal with demons. She and her fellow *zarinistas* gather in the victim's house, have the party, and confront the demon. There is a negotiation; the exorcist asks the demon what his price is for leaving the victim in peace. The afflicted woman (or rather her familiar) responds with a list of demands: the husband must come straight home from the fields rather than going out drinking with the boys, he must buy the woman new clothes, be attentive to her, etc. It is telling that the familiars, though exoterically represented as demonic, are esoterically worshipped as saviors by members of the cult. A wise husband will usually accede to the demands of the "demon" in return for domestic peace (if he reneges, another demonic visit may be in the offing). He can do so while saving face: after all, while any proper man should be in control of his wife, he has no control over demons; moreover, the wife is not to blame for the domestic disruption and, hence, is not to be punished. I think it will be evident to everyone that this wonderful bit of social fiction does not require actual belief on the part of anyone in the culture. What it does require is that everyone *pretend* to believe the fiction.[67]

It might be tempting to suppose that *we*—citizens of industrialized societies—are too sophisticated to commit such blunders or engage in such social chicanery. The temptation should be resisted as nothing less than the legal doctrines that define the powers of the Supreme Court of the United States will illustrate. Consider these four legal principles. 1) The Constitution cannot be altered, except by amendments sanctified by procedures spelled out in the document itself. 2) When a constitutional question arises, a ruling by the Court determines what the Constitution says or implies (i.e., such rulings have performative force). Thus, if someone convicted under a law challenges its constitutionality, and the Court rules the law to be constitutional, the plaintiff is guilty. 3) The Court can overrule itself. If the Court later reverses, then the law *always was* unconstitutional,

---

[67] See Lewis, *Ecstatic Religion*, 75–82. Similar possession cults are quite common and have a world-wide distribution. I have elsewhere argued that Lewis' analysis can be applied quite effectively to the Christian Reformation mystics—e.g., Teresa of Avila—and even to St. Paul. See Evan Fales, "Scientific Explanations of Mystical Experiences, Part I: The Case of St. Teresa," *Religious Studies* 32, no. 2 (1996): 143–63; "Scientific Explanations of Mystical Experiences, Part II: The Challenge to Theism," *Religious Studies* 32, no. 3 (1996): 297–313; and "The Road to Damascus," *Faith and Philosophy* 22, no. 4 (2005): 442–59.

and the plaintiff in the previous suit *never was* guilty. But these principles are inconsistent; they require that the Constitution both does and does not change. The conundrum is further driven home (ironically) by a further legal principle that 4) the law is consistent.

Many will challenge Principle 1, but they should consider the consequences. First, they must deny that the Constitution says what its framers meant it to say. Second, they are committed to the view that contingent social and historical factors can determine, and change, the legal basis of social order in the United States. But this is to invite, in a potentially vicious way, the theoretical problem of sovereignty. Alternatively, one might deny the performative force of Court rulings. But that would cripple the authority of the Court. Under what constraints, in principle, does the Court then lie? A more effective protest would be that my depiction of this feature of the U.S. legal structure is seriously oversimplified. But my point stands: however such incongruencies may be resolved or papered over, they illustrate how a set of principles can be both inconsistent and yet founded upon deep requirements for effective governance.

These examples are intended to show how the exigencies of social existence can provide strong reasons for ideology to embrace various intellectual sins (abstractly considered). That means that we must be doubly circumspect before condemning the beliefs of other cultures as irrational. First, because under proper interpretation, they may not commit any intellectual sin; and secondly, because they may still exhibit practical rationality even if they do.

The Structure-Functionalist School in anthropology acknowledged the latter form of rationality but typically insisted that natives were not themselves in the know about the functional advantages of their practices. Ideology became, in effect, an epiphenomenon, a faux explanation whose only virtue was to provide a kind of intellectual façade covering unrecognized ignorance. But this, I claim, is too fast. Even when ideology embraces intellectual irregularities, native thinkers or even *hoi polloi* may be well aware of this and understand the functional grounds for maintaining their fictions. It is only when the natives—even those who are intellectual leaders—are ignorant of the functional merits of their ideologically underwritten practices, only when those practices do not establish ideological truth by performative fiat, and only when ideology commits sins of the kinds just enumerated can we properly judge that the natives are wrong and the anthropologist's understanding has the rights of the matter. But establishing that these conditions are satisfied is rarely a trivial matter.

E. Social Ontology as an Extreme Sport

Let us briefly return, in light of these remarks, to some of the doctrines that do appear to violate the constraints of theoretical (if perhaps not practical) rationality. I want particularly to revisit some doctrines that appear to violate the constraint on the existence of social entities that requires current embodiment. Souls, for example, are often held to survive disembodiment. I have in mind here not only a familiar Christian view of the afterlife but widespread views that represent social status—personagehood—as being temporarily disembodied during ritual transfer from one individual to another.[68] To be sure, the Jewish and early Christian conceptions of the soul that provide the conceptual background for the development of afterlife beliefs may not correspond well to the account of souls I have offered. But let us suppose, *arguendo*, that some of them do.

By my lights, talk of disembodied souls is, at best, a *façon de parler*. But it is not unmotivated. Ontologically, the choices are either to represent a personage as going out of and coming back into existence or as existing through one or more periods of disembodiment. And—at least insofar as one wishes to emphasize social continuity—survival has much to recommend itself over recreation. If continuity is a fiction, it is a sensible one. Christian eschatology presents, to be sure, a rather special case, inasmuch as the disembodiment of souls of the dead is projected into an indefinite future, and the *eschaton* itself will realize a new heaven and a new earth. I shall say something about this special case presently (see further Chapter 12).[69]

Perspicuously, perhaps, is the thought that ancient Jews found it natural to imagine the ideal forms of earthly institutions and personages as if embodied "in heaven" in an incorruptible matter. These heavenly particulars were then to provide a model for what should be (and in apocalyptic

---

[68] Turner, *The Ritual Process*; *The Forest of Symbols*.

[69] These thoughts encourage a further speculation (it is no more than that). How might we understand the spiritual body (*soma pneumatikon*) that Paul attributes to risen saints (1 Cor. 15:35–57), and that the Gospels appear to attribute to the risen Christ? The question is whether both Paul and the authors of the Gospels saw the need for some form of embodiment that, after death, cannot exist in an ordinary body. This might help explain the much later doctrine of the king's two bodies, though it is not easy to see how it would have been supposed to work in the early Christian context—e.g., Paul's eschatology seems to imply discontinued embodiment at death and re-embodiment at the general resurrection in a spiritual body (so, too, Revelations). Later Christian thinkers seem to have understood the raised body to be thoroughly material, even identical to one's mortal body, but with conferred immortality. Genidentity concerns seem to have played a role here, too. Either way, a spiritual body would have had to have been (on my view) a kind of (natural) fiction.

thinking, would someday come to be) the way things are on earth.[70] I think we can say more. During the Second Temple period, there flourished a Jewish deuterocanonical and pseudepigraphical literature in which the ontology of the supernatural blossomed to a sometimes baroque degree. Beyond the divine ideals, there could be found hosts of angels and assumed patriarchs inhabiting multiple heavens and much else—all occupying a region of the cosmos intermediate between the sphere of the sun, moon, and stars and the highest heaven, the abode of God. It seems clear that a welter of forces, including, surely, political turmoil, persistent engagement with the problem of evil, cosmological speculation, and philosophical influences, all played a role in the production of this literature. But one key issue may have been the theoretical need for embodiment where none was to be had in the mundane sphere. The contents of the heavens were ideal models for earthly realities; whereas the copies were made of terrestrial matter, the models were made of an incorruptible substance, often not visible to eyes of flesh.

The simple view, one that maps easily onto my ontology, squares with the mantra, let it be on earth as it is in heaven. Earthly structure embodies heavenly plans. But when mundane realities veer far enough away from the divine roadmap, disembodiment threatens. God creates an ideal world; human adventurousness throws a wrench into the works. God gives Moses, and later David, a description of a proper tabernacle/temple and proper temple service; some Jews came to see in the actual temple service a corrupt hijacking of the divine plan. But how can there be no paradise and no true worship of Israel's god, unless it be on earth?

However, these things can be stored away in heaven, embodied in an imperishable celestial stuff, waiting in readiness to restore God's kingdom at the end of the eon: a new, eternal Jerusalem descending from heaven to replace the destroyed City of David, a heavenly priesthood to perfectly administer it, and the saints, its citizens, clothed in immortal flesh. This idea had staying power. In later times, we find King Arthur and Barbarossa, who do not die but whose bodies, granted immunity from decay, lie in waiting, as if freeze-dried for the time when destiny calls them to revivification and restoration to the throne. Jewish legend itself contains stories that may have led to similar ideas about King David's semen.[71] Here, we have embodiments freed from the contingencies and corruptions of time

---

[70] For a useful treatment of various appearances of this theme in the Hebrew Bible, see, e.g., Heb. 8:1–10:25 and Paul B. Sumner, "The Heavenly Council in the Hebrew Bible and New Testament," *Hebrew Streams* (2012), http://www.hebrew-streams.org/works/hebrew/council.pdf.

[71] See G. W. Dennis, *Encyclopedia of Jewish Myth, Magic, and Mysticism* (Woodbury, MN: Llewellyn, 2007), 126 and Richard C. Carrier, *On the Historicity of Jesus: Why We Might Have Reason for Doubt* (Sheffield, UK: Sheffield Phoenix Press, 2014), 576–77.

and not subject to destruction. Such ideas permeate Jewish texts, including the writings of Philo, and they clearly inform such Christian redactions as the *Apocalypse of Isaiah*. Their influence upon Hebrews 4:14–5:10, as well as Hebrews 8 and 9, is clear as is their influence upon Paul.[72] Surely, these same ideas form the conceptual background of Paul's rather mysterious description of the *soma pneumatikon* and, arguably, they are in play in the story of the Transfiguration (Matt. 17; Mark 9; Luke 9).

I do not see how the metaphysics I have sketched here can provide safe haven for such invisible, incorruptible bodies without quite independent reasons for thinking there are such things. But even if not hospitable in this full-bodied way, the view can explain why it might be so natural to posit such substances, either as a deliberately fictional heuristic or as a speculation meant to have ontological legs. Determining whether interpretation along these lines will do justice to Jewish and New Testament thought will require close readings of the early texts before any firmer conclusions can be drawn.

A fundamental feature of Jewish theology, adopted into Christianity, is that God is an immaterial being and hence is disembodied—even, according to some traditional interpretations of Genesis, existed prior to the creation of any bodies whatever. What is more, this disembodied being stands over and against the created world, both as its *cause* and as its *judge*. Surely, such beliefs must, on my account, reflect a serious misunderstanding of the ontological possibilities. I think not, though creative metaphor plays a role in the many articulations of Yahweh's nature.

I begin, once again, with works of art: consider, this time, Brancusi's *Bird in Space*. In its purity and perfection of form, this sculpture captures, in as close an embodiment as any representation could, the idea that Brancusi wanted to capture. But Brancusi made numerous attempts at *Bird*, some of them rather ungainly. What if he had never succeeded in capturing the ideal that he did, I think, achieve? What if he understood himself to have failed? He might have had a precise mental image of his target form, but alternatively, his inspiration might have been more inchoate. Yet, there is sense to be given to the notion that, even if Brancusi's mental representations fell short of the ideal, there was, nevertheless, an ideal he was attempting to grasp and give form to. It is against the standard of that ideal, however dimly imagined, that Brancusi—and we—judge the greatness of his achievement. We might think of the ideal *Bird in Space* as something like a Platonic form, something that would exist even if Brancusi had failed, even in his imagination, to limn its precise shape, but with a difference. Like actual works of art, it is, even if multiply realizable, arguably a kind of particular that might never have existed had Brancusi not been inspired as he was. Though in this sense particular, it would be at best a figure of speech to

---

[72] 2 Corinthians 12 recounts Paul's assumption into the third heaven, the heaven that housed the heavenly model of Paradise in Jewish cosmology.

say that the ideal *Bird* is some sort of immaterial but actual sculpture residing in some sort of transcendent realm. Tempting to say, but (literally) a fiction.

Next, consider human persons. We each share a common humanity. That form is a universal. But we also exhibit individual differences, and some of these are more essential to our being who we are than a mere collection of accidents that may uniquely describe us. We have our own special talents and limitations; we may have a special calling, or at least projects, the pursuit of which constitutes a large measure of who we understand ourselves to be and whom we wish to become. Both as a participant in a common human nature and as a unique individual, our lives can be judged against norms defined by the *teloi* distinctive of humanity and the *teloi* defined by our personal aims and aspirations. Thus, the flesh and blood Evan Fales can be judged, by others and by himself, against a standard comprised not only of a conception of what human flourishing generally involves but also of a conception of what it would be for Evan Fales to live *his* particular life and to pursue *his* particular projects "to perfection." That conception is of my particular "form." One might have a mistaken conception of someone's form. But any global evaluation of someone or their life presupposes a conception of such a standard. That standard need not ever be embodied or, at least, it need never be fully embodied. The perfect *Bird* and the perfect Evan strike me as belonging to an ontological category that is distinct from universals, but in many ways akin to them.

Turn now to Yahweh. What sort of an item is he in the ontological catalog? He is, familiarly, an immaterial person, characterized by an abundance of perfections. By comparison, ancient Israel (certainly in the eyes of many of its prophets) fell abundantly short of perfection. Israel was an imperfect (corporate) person who measured herself against the standard of Torah. We can put the matter abstractly. Consider a nation N, understood as a corporate person. Normative evaluation of N presupposes the existence of a standard, the Particular Form of N (call it N*). Reflecting its normative status, it will be sensible to think of N* as stable or unchanging in some important respects, as morally foundational (at least for citizens of N), as in a sense omnipresent, as the source of all legitimacy and proper exercise of power, and as in a sense primordial—if not temporally prior, then nevertheless prior (given a communitarian conception of the state) in the order of explanation of the social order, and as its ground and justifier. The corporate intentions and actions of N are to be judged by how well they measure up to the will of N*.

Ancient Israel was henotheistic. There are passages—e.g., in Isaiah—that can be read as monotheistic, and it is natural to read Genesis 1–3 in this way. But that, I think, is a mistake. The Hebrew Bible does not, in general, deny the existence of other national gods. But it insists that

Israel's national identity is defined by its obligations to Yahweh. Its actions are to be measured against what Yahweh wills. Certain individuals rise to prominence because they are socially recognized (often with hindsight) to have successfully discerned that will.[73] They are the prophets. Is such a being *supernatural*? Even as a naturalist, I do not find that description of Yahweh unnatural. But—as with the ideal *Bird* and the ideal Evan—the quite natural tendency to reify this ideal and project it into a transcendent realm (most charitably understood as figurative) might not irrationally come to be more robustly understood. So by my lights, belief in Yahweh—perhaps even if literal reification were in play—would have been at least rational for ancient Israel and would have been rational *even if* it were conceded that such things as reified Particular Forms are, at best, fictions of a sort.[74]

This way of conceiving Yahweh offers a natural way of approaching three ancient puzzles within Christian theology: the doctrine of the Trinity, the doctrine of the incarnation, and the doctrine of the Real Presence (transubstantiation). These came to be seen as sufficiently mystifying that medieval theologians pronounced the Trinity a mystery in the strict sense (i.e., impossible for any human mind, even after beatification, to comprehend). Kierkegaard declared the incarnation to be the central "paradox"—i.e., logical impossibility—of Christian faith, and Locke rejected the Real Presence as in conflict with "sense and reason." Conceding that the doctrines are difficult—sufficiently difficult that their formulation provoked a spate of metaphysical labor and debate among the early church

---

[73] Two sorts of things need, in general, to be discerned. One is true charter: what are the social structures, laws, and principles that are to form the (theoretically) permanent structures upon which the social order is to be founded? The second is an answer to the "What do we do now?" questions, which arise in historically contingent circumstances but whose answers are to reflect the underlying principles of charter. In terms familiar in the Judeo-Christian tradition, the first can be identified as the Logos or, in Jewish traditions, with Wisdom, and the second with the words of the prophets, though for obvious reasons the distinction can become blurred.

[74] This rather abstract conception of Israel's relation to Yahweh could readily accommodate vivid imagery, such as the figure of Yahweh as Israel's husband in Hosea 2. Naturally, at the same time, a good many questions about divine agency come into view. Direct agency—the performing of miracles—is perhaps the most salient. How can such an abstract thing turn water into wine? Or single-handedly defeat Israel's enemies, as at the Red Sea or the siege of Jerusalem by Sennacherib? Clearly, this is a large forest to clear, and I can only nibble at the edges. I shall have something to say as I proceed about various biblical miracle stories. In spite of the rhetoric, we need not suppose that Israel literally thought that enemy armies were trounced without either human effort or natural disasters. About the complexities of Israel's portrayal of Yahweh as a warrior fighting on her behalf, see the nice summary by Albert C. Winn, *Ain't Gonna Study War No More: Biblical Ambiguity and the Abolition of War* (Louisville, KY: Westminster John Knox Press, 1993), 27–65.

fathers—we can nevertheless outline rather straightforwardly a set of suggestions about how such doctrines might be sensibly understood.[75]

Israel, on the view I have been developing, is a kind of corporate Person, institutionally embodied in the nation's populace. Yahweh is the ideal Form of that Person, a Form that Israel is to strive to embody as perfectly as possible. Such a Form can have a structure; it would be quite natural, indeed, to think of it as containing, or comprised of, those officers or personages that quintessentially represent the normative social order of the state. In a monarchy, ultimate legislative authority rests with the king, in whose official actions are embodied the actions of the state. Stable social existence requires, on one level, the orderly transferal of power from one generation to the next—ordinarily, in patrilineal societies with primogeniture, from father to firstborn son. But battles for succession are common (for example, and most notoriously for Israel, over the successor to David); and sometimes a biological firstborn is unfit. Hence, it is imperative (in an ideal world) to have the choice of a successor confirmed by the idealized will of the nation. In this way, the agent who exercises that will may be represented as the father of the king—the ultimate source of legitimacy. The *transmission* of that legitimacy, in the thinking of ancient Israel, regularly takes place through the agency of a personage whose function it is to perform that office: the Holy Spirit, sent from Father to Son. Thus, investiture by the Holy Spirit confers royal authority upon first Saul and then David—and afterward to Jesus, of the seed of David.[76]

On this understanding, then, it makes sense for the Godhead to be comprised of three personages, all ideally embodied in the ongoing life of the community. At the level of the monarchy itself, we have the mechanics of succession from father to firstborn son; in that context, the king embodies Yahweh *qua* father, and authority passes from him to his son upon his death by means of a transfer of the Spirit. At the same time, the king (and his nation) are conceived of as sons of God, in the sense that it is in virtue of conferral of authority by the Sovereign Will of the "ideal" nation that this individual legitimately rules and that his subjects are also God's chosen. The Hebrew scriptures did not, to be sure, develop such a Trinitarian doctrine as this in any explicit way, but the conceptual materials for that development were in place. The Godhead, then, is a normative ideal for Israel, and it is

---

[75] Complications arise in the theologies and Christologies of the fathers, not only because ontological precision in the formulation of the doctrines is philosophically non-trivial, but because in the background of the struggles surrounding the various formulae rest not only the demands of philosophical adequacy but faithfulness to scripture and liturgical traditions, and—most importantly in my opinion—political differences and a recognition of the political content of the competing options.

[76] Though not explicitly mentioned in connection with the election of Solomon, divine selection, presumably by way of the action of the Holy Spirit, is repeatedly implied (1 Ki. 1:22–48; 1 Chron. 17:11–14, 28).

fundamentally comprised, as Christian theology developed the idea, of three personages—Father, Son (the Christ), and Holy Ghost—that are to become properly embodied in the New Israel, the kingdom of God.[77]

It now becomes not difficult—again in principle—to understand the dual nature of the Christ. While complications abound in the historical development of the doctrine, the central idea, if I am right, is that *Christos* names a personage, the very personage to be embodied by a legitimate ruler of the kingdom of God; hence it is available for multiple (successive) embodiments. Further, it is the embodiment relation itself that unites a natural person with this personage and the actions of that natural person with the official acts of the king. If this is correct, moreover, it should be possible to explain at least some of the patristic controversies—and the heat that accompanied them—as a reflection of contested views concerning the exact source and extent of sovereign authority to be invested in an earthly monarchy that was to govern an earthly kingdom of God.

It will probably be insisted that such a conception of Yahweh suffers shipwreck in light of the Genesis account of the creation of the cosmos. There is far more to be said about the opening chapters of Genesis than I will say here. In my view, the overriding concern of Genesis (and Exodus), taken as a whole, is to theorize the nature of the social in general and the social identity of Israel in particular. Genesis 1 and 2 are integral to this project. I do maintain that Yahweh can properly be conceived as immune to the vicissitudes of the passage of time—he is, in principle at least, immortal—but that, strictly speaking, his existence is parasitic upon the historical existence of Israel, which partially embodied him in the sense in which I embody the ideal Evan Fales. There is, at the same time, a dialectical advantage to be gained by the fiction—and it is a fiction—that Yahweh created the physical cosmos. For if so, it is his real estate. If it is his property, then he is free to allocate its resources as he will. He can, in particular, legitimately promise *eretz Israel* to his chosen people. We can see in this conception of Yahweh the legal basis for Israel's claim upon the land of Canaan.[78]

---

[77] This schema had, as noted, an already ancient lineage, being visible in the Egyptian triumvirate of pharaoh (=Osiris upon death), crown prince (=Horus upon succession to the throne), and the pharaoh's Ka (=the Spirit that transfers authority from the one to the other). This reconstruction is subject to the objection that it commits the error of Sabellianism, by identifying Father and Son as the same person. But clearly, it does not. H. E. Baber provides a clear response to this objection in H. E. Baber, "Sabellianism Reconsidered," *Sophia* 41, no. 2 (2002): 1–18.

[78] As elsewhere, it turns out that I have been anticipated in this reasoning by the rabbis; so Rashi:

> It was not necessary to begin the Torah except from "This month is to you" (Ex. 12:2), which is the first commandment that the Israelites were commanded. Now for what reason did He commence with "In the beginning"? Because of [the verse] "The

Moreover, there is a strong dialectical motivation for maintaining that Yahweh's existence is prior to the existence of Israel, even prior to Israel's cultural pre-history, as it were. As is by now familiar, it is natural to transmute the abstract notion of ontological priority into a narrativizable (and narrated) temporal priority. The dialectical payoff is a response to the question of legitimacy in the form of a regress-stopper that terminates the quest for an ultimate legitimating act that does not itself demand prior legitimation. In Israel's case, the narrative is the narrative of the Torah, with its ultimate beginning in a divine kingdom whose citizens are Adam and Eve, a kingdom representing the embodied ideal, though corruptible. On this reading, the story in Genesis 1 and 2 is not an exercise in physical cosmology, or not primarily so. The ancient authors had no business speculating about such matters, and though they must have wondered about them, they must also have known them to be beyond reach. What was not beyond reach, and must certainly have been of preeminent concern, is the securing of a conceptually adequate justification of their basic social arrangements and offices.

If this is on the right track, then it must be possible to read the book of Genesis, from beginning to end, as a work whose central concern is the creation of social order, not the creation of physical order. It would have been natural to search for analogies between the two orders; it would have

---

strength of His works He related to His people, to give them the inheritance of the nations" (Ps. 111:6). For if the nations of the world should say to Israel, "You are robbers, for you conquered by force the lands of the seven nations [of Canaan]," they will reply, "The entire earth belongs to the Holy One, blessed be He; He created it and gave it to whomever He deemed proper. When He wished, He gave it to them, and when He wished, He took it away from them and gave it to us. Rashi, Parashat Bereishit Commentary on Genesis 1:1.

There are, as hinted above, other deep motivations for thinking of Yahweh as creator of the physical cosmos; see Chapter 1. And for a reading of Genesis as an exercise in social ontology, see Chapter 8. The social ontology I have sketched here makes possible the construction of models for the doctrines of the Trinity, Incarnation, and Real Presence that are not beset by many of the conceptual difficulties that have historically bedeviled these notions. How to do this is left as an exercise for the reader (see Chapter 7 for more on the Real Presence). Whether such models are congruent with the intentions of the framers of the ecumenical creeds (or of other early Christian theologians) is of great interest but beyond the scope of my present project. A hint concerning the doctrine of Christ's two natures: there is one strand in early Christian thinking—to be found in Theodore of Mopsuestia and his follower Nestorius—according to which the indwelling Logos is united to the humanity of Jesus Christ, not according to *ousia* (as two merged substances), nor according to nature (as soul and body), but according to "person" (πρόσωπον)—see Jaroslav Pelikan, *The Christian Tradition: A History of the Development of Doctrine*, vol. 1, *The Emergence of the Catholic Tradition (100–600)* (Chicago, IL: University of Chicago Press, 1971), 251–52. The root meaning of *prosopon* is "mask" or "face;" it acquired various derived meanings. Of particular interest here is its use in Matt. 22:16 where it can only mean "personage."

been natural, perhaps, to try whether explanations for the social might somehow be extended to natural phenomena; and it would have been natural, at least, to find patterns in nature that could usefully be modeled on social structures or that would guide social interaction with the physical world, as Mary Douglas has persuasively argued can be seen to underlie the abominations of Leviticus.[79] It is perhaps worth remarking, in light of the foregoing, that the various declarations in the New Testament that God laid the foundations of the "world" (= κόσμος = political or social order), and that the Son of God will usher in a new κόσμος, can be read in this way and, so read, yield a much richer and more relevant interpretation than that resulting from a "physical-world" reading. So, also, the correlative claim that the Christ—the λοΥος made flesh—pre-existed the creation, a claim modeled upon the Jewish idea that Wisdom did so (e.g., Prov. 3:19–20, 8:22–31).

At the same time, it must be recognized that such a conceptually "clean" reading of the biblical texts—and certainly of the subsequent patristic debates—is almost certain to run up against historical complexities that will muddy the waters. To take just one example: debates over the doctrine of divine creation led ultimately to the view that God is responsible for the existence even of matter, space, and time, clearly a radical doctrine of *creatio ex nihilo* of the physical universe. But in the background of that discussion seems to have been, among other things at least, a need by the second century CE to counter Gnostic ideas concerning the intrinsically fallen and corruptible nature of the material world and its origins in the working of a demiurge. And those Gnostic notions were, I suspect, themselves deeply bound up with an articulation of Gnostic conceptions of the human condition in general and of the political circumstances of the Hellenistic world. But I shall not pursue those questions here.

A word will be in order to clarify the claims I am making respecting the semantic content (on my interpretation) of religious texts. The primary claim is that a range of religious terms, ordinarily taken by "us" (Western moderns) to refer to supernatural beings as we understand them, were used by the authors of those texts to refer to—and did, in fact, refer to—social entities of various kinds. Such discourse, then, is (if we are to remain true to authorial intentions) to be taken to be literally and referentially meant. But (of course) not all religious discourse is literal. Parables are fictional, and

---

[79] Mary Douglas, *Purity and Danger: An Analysis of Concepts of Pollution and Taboo* (New York: Frederick A. Praeger, 1966). For a somewhat different approach that takes structure seriously but conceives it differently than Lévi-Strauss (and also considers natural analogies between humans and animal symbols, as well as the possibility that a myth may *mis*represent social realities as natural in essence or origin), see Terrence Turner, "Animal Symbolism, Totemism, and the Structure of Myth," in *Animal Myths and Metaphors in South America*, ed. Gary Urton (Salt Lake City, UT: University of Utah Press, 1985), 49–106.

figures of speech abound. We see this in our own political discourse: the social contract, if understood historically, is a fiction. I have suggested that certain religious conceptions—e.g., of social entities that are embodied in some immaterial substance, or (arguably) disembodied—should also be regarded as failing of (literal) reference. Here it is useful to distinguish between *communicative* fictions (as, for example, parables), whose purpose is the vivid conveyance of important ideas, and *conceptual* fictions, whose introduction is driven by theoretical or ideological considerations (such as disembodied gods and heavens populated by particulars made of immaterial stuff). Of course, a fiction might serve both purposes, but those purposes should be distinguished. And conceptual fictions may not be understood to be fictions. But if they are taken to be real, the mistake is a philosophically sophisticated one.

In my concluding remarks, I return to the methodological problem of avoiding cultural prejudice in interpretation. I have insisted (in Chapter 1) that a norm of rationality necessarily provides the conceptual foundation for our understanding of human behavior in any culture and that at the core of that norm stand certain criteria which are not subject to cultural modification. It follows from this that *prima facie* preference must be given to explanations of phenomena in our culture and others according to the extent to which they are able to construe human action as conforming to these universal conditions of intelligibility. As such, the view I have proposed seems, if it can be made to fit the ethnographic data, to fare better than many alternatives. One should be puzzled, then, at the reluctance to take seriously an interpretation which has, after all, been rather strongly suggested by the work of Durkheim and others. In part, this may reflect older cultural prejudices that weaken Durkheim's own view—specifically, a disinclination to ascribe to primitives a capacity for serious intellectual penetration—but more centrally, I think, it may betray the presence of a skeleton hidden in our own intellectual closet.

For whatever the evidence that more primitive cultures do not draw any sharp line between recognizably political discourse and recognizably religious discourse, it is clear that our own culture *does* do so—and that, to the extent that it does, the alleged epistemological and ontological problematicality of their religious beliefs certainly pervades our own. We do not wish to convict ourselves of a greater degree of irrationality than we impute to them. But it is fairly clear that this kind of conceptual distinction was not present at earlier times in our own culture's history either. It is not within my province to speculate upon what historical processes have been responsible for the rift with its attendant problems (but my Aftermath offers some suggestions). What I wish to point out is that we may have to reassess our insistence upon construing the religious idioms of other cultures in terms of the contemporary mysterious and problematic conceptions of our own.

Precisely because I am prepared to reject the kind of radical cultural relativism which has often been suggested as a solution to this problem, I am also prepared to conclude that cultural blinders of various sorts have plagued anthropologists—but ones whose removal is made in principle possible by appeal to those standards of intelligibility which are not subject to cultural variation or constraint.

A hypothesis earns its chops by providing insight and prophecy—that is, powerful explanations and good predictions. I shall put the ontological claims pressed above to the test throughout my discussion of the biblical texts. Perhaps it is not too much to suggest here, tentatively, that it is partly because we have been afraid to make sense of the origins of our own religious heritage in political terms that we have persisted in assimilating the myths of other cultures to some of our own epistemologically insecure ideas and have succeeded in thereby foisting upon them a set of beliefs whose connection to reality is as mysterious as that of Christianity, as currently construed by *its* natives.

Genres and the Character of Myth

I shall shortly be examining a number of biblical texts and arguing that their function lies in the realm of the mythical. I shall not, of course, be attempting anything so audacious as trying to show that the Bible is pervasively mythical. But I hope, by means of selected examples, to make plausible the view that myth plays a much larger role, and a much more essential role, in the way the ancient authors chose to communicate what was on their minds than more orthodox scholarship would want to allow. Thus, I shall be examining the selected texts using tools of myth analysis derived from the work of structural anthropologists. I intend to show that those texts are indeed amenable to that type of analysis. The proof, if proof is to be had, will be in the pudding—in showing that the use of these analytic tools can yield new insights and suggest new avenues of further investigation. As for prophets, so too for interpretive techniques: by their fruits shall we know them.

Even so, a fair amount of stage-setting must precede this investigation. Not only must I explain what the relevant analytic tools are, but I must also say some general things about interpretation. When a work has become as contested as the Bible, when interpretations have been offered by serious scholars that run through virtually every conceivable possibility, it becomes necessary to step back and reflect, in a general way, about the enterprise of interpretation. In particular, it becomes necessary to consider by what criteria we will judge the adequacy, and the plausibility, of competing interpretations and interpretive approaches. That, at a suitably general level, is a properly philosophical task, and with it we have commenced our investigation. My plan now is to spiral inward, as it were, from such matters of greatest generality (which are the most properly philosophical) to matters of least generality (which are the most directly concerned with scholarly issues in the interpretation of specific texts).

Because of the scale of the enterprise, parts of my argument will inevitably remain sketches or unfinished. Nevertheless, I hope to illustrate, adequately enough that readers can evaluate its promise as a theoretical approach to sacred texts, its applicability to the biblical passages.

At this stage, it is necessary to say something about genre and, indeed, something about myth. I do so partly because the proper conception of myth is highly contested and partly because there is in particular an apologetic strategy that makes use of the claim that the Gospels fit within the genre of Greco-Roman βίοι, or biographies. From this, some conclude that they cannot be fictions and, hence, that the category of myth is inapplicable to them. The argument might be roughly stated as follows:

> B1. The Gospels display numerous features that are typical of Greco-Roman βίοι.
> B2. Therefore, the genre of the Gospels is that of (Greco-Roman) biography.
> B3. Biographies are meant by their authors to be (in the main) factually correct.
> B4. Therefore, the Gospels are not intended as fiction.
> B5. Myth is a genre of fiction.
> B6. Therefore, the Gospels cannot be interpreted in terms of the categories specific to understanding myths.

In effect, this argument takes biography and myth—as they were understood in the ancient world—to be mutually exclusive literary genres, and so it takes evidence that the Gospels fall into the first genre to show that they do not fall into the second. I shall not be arguing here that the composition of the Gospels was not influenced by Hellenistic conventions in the writing of biographies. Indeed, that does seem fairly likely (see Chapter 10)—and indeed has implications that conservative apologists will not so readily want to endorse. But I shall challenge both B3 and B5—and hence, B4 and B6. For, as we shall see, ancient biographies could contain a great deal of fiction and, conversely, myths could (and I think primarily did) aim to express the truth—albeit typically in somewhat figurative language. And, most of all, there is therefore no reason whatever to think that the two styles of composition excluded each other.

Here, we must deflect a terminological objection. Suppose one conceives genre distinctions in taxonomic terms—that is, in such a way that genres cannot cut across one another. If you think of a genre classification as excluding other genres, then there is no such genre as myth. Nor will the appearance of the mythical signal a particular genre, for it can be present in works that fall into many different genres. We can identify myth, for example, in epic poetry and saga, in biography, history, comic and tragic theater, and—even—in philosophical dialogue.[1] But for my money, nothing very much hangs on this point.

---

[1] Thus, Richard Carrier says, "Myth is not really a literary 'genre' in the standard sense, since it crosses all genres of literary composition. Plutarch's biography of Romulus is entirely myth, for example, yet written in the genre of historical biography….Most attempts at identifying the genre of the Gospels consists of comparing

I. Myth

Before I turn to arguing that myth is compatible with biography, I must say something about the contested notions of genre and myth. First, myth. The term has multiple connotations—for example, those of fantasy and of falsity—that will make up no part of the meaning of the term as I shall use it. Even in the scholarly literature, "myth" is understood in importantly different ways, and it will be essential to bear in mind the sense in which I shall understand the term. For example, the *Encyclopedia of Cultural Anthropology*, acknowledging the variable use of the term, characterizes myths as stories about the sacred that "are set initially in a previous age that is qualitatively different from the present age."[2] Similarly, the *Dictionary of Jesus and the Gospels* insists that a myth is "a narrative of origins, a study of the beginning of all things, a story of primordial time."[3] But if myths can only refer to a "primordial" time, or perhaps to a "timeless" era, then of course the Gospel stories are disqualified immediately.[4]

However, though many myths do at least appear to concern a different, perhaps remote era, I do not take this feature to be essential to myth, at least as I shall understand myths. Nor must myths be stories of origin, though they often are. Nor, for that matter, must mythical stories of origin, that on their face appear to refer to an *Urzeit*, be understood as literally recalling such an era. Reference to an *Urzeit* is, I suggest, an important and powerful literary device. As I argued in Chapter 4, it is used to establish the credentials of social customs, institutions, and ideologies by (a) assigning to them the luster and time-tested effectiveness of enduring tradition and, even more fundamentally, by (b) using the metaphor of temporal priority to represent their foundational status and legitimacy with respect to a society's institutional arrangements.[5]

[them] to other literary forms, but this has only resulted in either unresolved disagreement of classifying the Gospels as a unique genre of their own, which unhelpfully eliminates the opportunity to interpret them ... by comparison with documents of similar genre" (Richard C. Carrier, *On the Historicity of Jesus: Why We Might Have Reason for Doubt* [Sheffield, UK: Sheffield Phoenix Press, 2014], 389) Radcliffe Edmonds agrees with this non-genre conception of myth (Radcliffe G. Edmonds III, *Myths of the Underworld Journey: Plato, Aristophanes, and the 'Orphic' Gold Tablets* [New York: Cambridge University Press, 2004], 7).

[2] David Levinson and Melvin Ember, eds., *Encyclopedia of Cultural Anthropology* (New York: Henry Holt and Company, 1996), s.v. "Myth."

[3] James D. G. Dunn, "Myth," in *Dictionary of Jesus and the Gospels*, ed. Joel B. Green, Scot McKnight, and I. Howard Marshall (Downers Grove, IL: InterVarsity Press, 1992), 566–69.

[4] Though, notably, John 1:1–18 does do so, albeit with great compression.

[5] On this theme, cf. Charles H. Talbert, who wrote,

First, *myth* can be shown to be a clue to the cultic *Sitz im Leben* of certain biographies. Before this is possible, however, we must break out of the box of the

So, as we have already noted, the social contract theorists of the seventeenth and eighteenth centuries (such as Thomas Hobbes, John Locke, and Emile Rousseau) regularly spoke of an originary "state of nature" as the backdrop against which to imagine the conditions for which a (rational, legitimate) social contract between individuals could have been struck. Though this story posits a kind of *Urzeit*, no serious reader of these theorists would have taken such a story literally. It was a heuristic device for thinking about the basis of legitimate governance. And by my lights, this story qualifies as a myth.

If the essential purpose of myth is to explore, in narrative terms, fundamental human and cultural concerns, then there is no reason why the form should be bound by a convention that situates the narrative in an *Urzeit*. As we have seen, there are often good reasons for doing so—but there may also be good reasons for not doing so. An example is Virgil's *Aeneid*, an epic poem that begins in the distant past but traces the history of Rome to Virgil's own time, albeit "prophetically" by way of revelations provided to Aeneas during his sojourn in Hades. Or, to take an example from a very different culture, consider the myths invented by the Melanesian millenarian cargo cults, which include events from the recent past (from the experiences of those cultures in World War II). Millenarian movements—and Christianity certainly became such a movement early on—would be especially prone to devise myths that contain reference to the recent past, for it is in the crucible of recent events that such movements emerge.

Nor need we rummage ancient civilizations to obtain examples, for myths are stories, and storytellers are quite willing to cobble together whatever serves their purposes. Take two (more or less) contemporary examples. The famed Depression-era folk-songster, Woody Guthrie, wrote an autobiography that provides two cases worth pondering. It is striking, for

---

view of myth characteristic of much modern Bible scholarship. Exegesis today often works from a conception of myth that sees it as an involuntary conceptual form typical of a stage in human intellectual history which has now been superseded....

From Bronislaw Malinowski and Mircea Eliade has come a view of myth that sees it as a narrative telling how, through the deeds of supernatural beings, a reality came into existence, be it the whole Universe or some part of it, like an institution. Myth is a statement of primeval reality by which the present life of mankind is determined. It, furthermore, reveals the exemplary models for all human activities here and now. In this view, myth functions primarily to offer legitimation rather than explanation....So [referring to the Classical world] the noun ἀρχή means not only "beginning" but also "sovereignty." (Charles H. Talbert, *What Is a Gospel? The Genre of the Canonical Gospels* [Philadelphia, PA: Fortress Press, 1977], 99–100; italics in original)

See also Jean-Louis Ska, who shows how biblical claims to antiquity is used to argue legitimacy or authority (Jean-Louis Ska, *Introduction to Reading the Pentateuch*, trans. Sr. Pascale Dominique [Winona Lake, IN: Eisenbrauns, 2006], 165–69).

starters, that Guthrie omits any mention of his first marriage. That is understandable. Guthrie abandoned his first wife and their children to set out for California and begin the journey that ultimately brought him fame. Although Guthrie's omission of his first marriage was no doubt intended to burnish his reputation, it would hardly be appropriate to speak of Guthrie here as composing a myth.[6] Not every distortion of history qualifies.

But another episode from Guthrie's work comes much closer. First, we are treated to a brawl in which the smaller, quicker youngster Woody is forced by a crowd into a fight with a larger child whom he defeats but later patches things up with. Then follows a story in which he organizes a "gang." They build a clubhouse, but when they exclude boys from new families from joining, Woody joins the newcomers and, when efforts at mediation fail, helps lead a "war" against the homeboys that results in their defeat and a new policy of inclusion.

It is probably impossible to know whether this tale is based on incidents that actually occurred in Guthrie's youth. But Guthrie's telling of it makes it impossible to escape the conclusion that he embellished the facts.[7] Those contrivances do not merely cast Guthrie as a boy-hero. They provide the material for a morality-tale, an edifying story about moral courage versus brute force, inclusiveness versus prejudice, newcomers versus the old guard. And that is the stuff of myth, even if the story is built around some actual events or if those events or that setting are recent history (as they had to be to serve Guthrie's purpose). Real history does not manage things so neatly, and Guthrie's later biographers mention only a shack that Guthrie and a few friends more or less occupied for about a year as teenagers.

A second example is the series of books by the anthropologist Carlos Castañeda, relating his alleged apprenticeship to the Yaqi sorcerer, Don Juan. The setting, again, is contemporary. The tales are fictional.[8] As a

---

[6] Hardly, but perhaps not entirely, insofar as it may have been Guthrie's larger intention to present his life as a kind of heroic embodiment of the virtues, struggles, and courage of ordinary Depression-era folks. The work is Woody Guthrie, *Bound for Glory* (New York: E. P. Dutton, 1943). For a historically more accurate account, see Ed Cray, *Ramblin' Man: The Life and Times of Woody Guthrie* (2004; repr., New York: W. W. Norton & Company, 2006).

[7] Cray barely mentions the clubhouse, which began as an "unheated packing case." He says nothing of a gang "war" and notes, "Aware of the protective fictions he had crafted and the heroic yarns he spun, Guthrie invariably called his book 'an autobiographical novel.' Others were to assume Guthrie's fantasies were true; there lay the seeds of myth" (Cray, *Ramblin' Man*, 258).

[8] See Carlos Castañeda, *The Teachings of Don Juan: A Yaqi Way of Knowledge* (New York: Washington Square Press, 1968); *A Separate Reality* (New York: Washington Square Press, 1971); *Journey to Ixtlan* (New York: Washington Square Press, 1972); and sequels. For an exposé, see Richard DeMille, *Castañeda's Journey: The Power and the Allegory* (Santa Barbara, CA: Capra Press, 1976) and *The Don Juan Papers: Further Castañeda Controversies* (Santa Barbara, CA: Ross-Erikson, 1980).

graduate student at UCLA, Castañeda set out (he tells us in his first volume) to study the use of mind-altering substances by Yaqi Indians. His chance encounter with the Yaqi *brujo*, Don Juan, leads to an apprenticeship that includes hair-raising experiences, many defying the natural order, and "trips" induced by peyote, mescaline, and *Datura*.

But as the story unfolds, the emphasis turns decidedly and explicitly away from the use of drugs to other means of exploring a vast and surprising spiritual realm. Already by the third volume, *Journey to Ixtlan*, we are presented with a powerful and poignant allegory of loss of identity (both for Yaqis and for white Americans), of the effects of social and cultural dispossession upon both conquered and conquerors, of despoilation of the natural world, and of a new kind of reality in which both humans and animals coexist in social, if not always harmonious, relationships.

My own guess is that the notoriously secretive Castañeda set out to do a doctoral thesis, not on Yaqi religious practices but on the possibility of writing a myth that would speak to Americans of a certain generation about their condition and the manifold ills of their culture (including, ironically, the use of drugs), as well as to study the ways in which such a myth is received, appropriated, and spread. Because his narrative is quite compelling, and because its message was also compelling to a certain audience, he was fairly successful.[9] Here we have, by my lights, a modern myth whose setting is a contemporary, if partially fictionalized, region in the American Southwest and Mexico.

What, then, do I mean by myth? A myth, as I shall be using the term, is a story, a narrative that conveys, in an often figurative way, thought about fundamental questions that arise in reflection on the human condition and on the problems confronted by a society or culture at a given time. Who are we? Where did we come from, and where should we be going? How are these questions connected? How can we best live? How should we think of, and treat, our natural environment and those neighboring peoples who are not-us? Some myths justify present social arrangements; some criticize these and/or propose new ones (often under the guise of being the "original" path from which we have "strayed"). Some myths are explorations or thought-experiments: what would happen to our society if…?

But a myth is more than a socially significant, figuratively expressed narrative. Myths are typically presented to an intended audience under the rubric of history, in which the order and significance of events serves to convey a message applicable to that audience's present circumstances by way of proposing that they understand their actual history and present situation through a lens that the myth offers. The events, whose

---

[9] Thus, the dissertation—expanded into a series of "memoires"—itself constituted (and was meant to constitute) an anthropological experiment carried out upon a generation of young Americans.

significance informs the meaning of the myth, acquire their import in roughly the way words in a natural language do, by use in a given context and repetition that leads to meaning conventions.

Obviously, myths employ language; so mythmaking does not face, as language itself does, the task of constructing meaning from scratch. Thus, the intrinsic signification of mythemes—as I shall call the units of meaning out of which the meaning of a myth is constructed—is a function of the meaning of the words of the narrative. But it is also—as is the communicative content of linguistic expressions generally—a function of context and pragmatic factors. Salient among them, if not distinctive or always present, are a context of concern with socio-political and moral issues.

For a crisp characterization of myth, it is hard to do better, in my view, than the following characterization, influenced by the work of Radcliffe Edmonds, that Richard Carrier has offered:

> (1) A mythic story is a seemingly straightforward account of something that happened, yet its content and structure are carefully arranged to convey a deeper meaning than the superficial narrative might suggest. (2) This is accomplished using symbols familiar to the audience (keywords, ironies, allusions, double entendres, etc.), relying on a known database of cultural, literary, religious, grammatical, and other facts. And (3) what an author of a myth changes is often the point of the myth. For example, if the story is highly allusive to another myth, yet reverses or radically alters certain elements of that myth, the allusions indicate what myth to compare the changes to, and the changes indicate how the author's message is meant to differ from the message of the earlier myth.[10]

I should relax Carrier's condition (2) since, obviously, the author of a myth may consider it to serve his or her purposes to invent some new symbol and will surely feel free to do so while providing contextual clues of one kind or another to enable his/her audience to "decode" the import of that symbol. After all, symbols must come originally from somewhere.

I would also point to one other feature of myths, noted by Edmonds, who remarks that they can "convey meaning densely through the manipulation of mythic motifs and patterns."[11] One might capture this point with the slogan that, in a myth, there are no throw-away lines. That may be a bit hyperbolic, but I consider it a fair presumption that every sentence of a myth contributes something of significance to the myth's message. In practice, what this slogan reflects is the fact that often the most superficially "innocent" phrase

---

[10] Carrier, *On the Historicity of Jesus*, 390.
[11] Edmonds, *Myths of the Underworld Journey*, 4.

or sentence proves, upon analysis, to package an astonishing amount of semantic content. Finally, we may note that some—but certainly not all—myths are religious texts that have a narrative structure, that present stories whose content involves fantastic, bizarre, or extraordinary elements, and that appear straightforwardly to assert that content without explicit cues directing the reader to understand the story in non-literal, figurative terms. I shall call the texts I consider simply "stories," leaving it initially open whether the intention (of the authors) is to retail genuine history, history intercalated with fabrication, history interlarded with figurative material intended to convey a conception of the significance of that history, myth that incorporates some historical setting or elements, or pure myth. Before turning to the question of how to interpret myths, let us observe that such texts pose basic questions concerning how the reader is to appropriate them. In answering these questions, we will, of course, need to consider a full range of possible explanations for the shape of a text. Perhaps it *is* an unvarnished, accurate account of events—perhaps those amazing things really *did* happen as described. Or perhaps the author(s) was lying (in which case the question of a motive must be raised). Or the author may have been deceived (either by others or by him or herself). Or a text—at least the more outlandish parts of it—and perhaps other parts as well may have been shaped by the intent to convey a true message but in figurative terms. Or possibly not entirely in figurative terms but in literal ones which we have misunderstood or mistranslated.

I shall presently discuss some of the methods that have been used by anthropologists to discern the meanings of myths. For the moment, I want to emphasize that I take mythmaking to be a highly intellectual exercise, one that requires considerable abstraction, systematic thought, and, of course, skill in the construction or invention of pungent narratives. Indeed, I think of myths as a way in which the intellectual elite of a society seek not only to formulate and codify their theorizing about their world (especially their social world) but to convey the results of that thinking effectively to their less educated compatriots. That is an essential function of myth because the thinking it codifies is often not merely "academic": it is, beyond this, *prescriptive*. It encapsulates, in a memorable and readily understandable way, the social and behavioral norms (and their justification) that are essential for citizenship in the community. They serve, in other words, as social charters.

In saying this about myth, I am, of course, not giving a mere definition of myth—not even a stipulated one. But this conception of myth is one that is at home in the anthropological study of myth and that suffices for my purposes. It will be noticed that in this discussion, I have said almost nothing about the connection of myth to religion. That is intentional. Although religion provides the (or a) natural context for mythmaking, the notions of religion and religious belief are themselves sufficiently contested that invoking religion to clarify the notion of myth is not particularly helpful.

Next, let me say a word about the question of truth. As I am construing them, myths will typically not be *literally* true because of the heavy use they ordinarily make of fiction and figurative language. But a myth's truth-value must be assessed, clearly, by evaluating the message it is trying to convey, not its literal sense. On that criterion, a myth may just as easily be true as false. But, as I have argued, matters are a bit more subtle than this. For since myths often have prescriptive content, and may also have a kind of performative force, they cannot always be straightforwardly assessed for truth or falsity; they may be "true" by virtue of their functional role in instituting and maintaining the very social realities they envision.

Finally, we must consider the difference between myth and legend. Once again, we face the difficulty that there is no uniform usage of either term. I shall distinguish between them, somewhat arbitrarily, as follows. "Legends" I shall understand to be embellished stories concerning historical individuals or events, whereas a myth may or may not contain significant reference to any historical person or event. But further, I shall regard a story, whether wholly a fiction or containing historical content, to be a myth, not a legend, when it has content, either fictional or figurative, that exhibits a certain kind of structure. In brief, this structure is erected out of certain thematic elements—motifs or mythemes—that constitute a kind of symbolic vocabulary in terms of which the "message" of the myth can be expressed. Mythemes, rather like words, have semantic values that derive from a tradition of use within a cultural context.[12] Legends, by way of contrast, do not exhibit this level of semantic sophistication, or perhaps exhibit it only episodically. It will be immediately clear that the distinction is porous and admits in principle (and in fact) of borderline cases.

Myths, then, are not merely sensationalized retellings of an historical past. Whether they allude to historical individuals and events or not, their fundamental purpose is not to retell a remembered past but to create a "past" that conveys a carefully wrought message—a message about the meaning of the present, or about the human condition that implies a judgment about the present: what is right about it, or what is wrong and ought to be changed.

---

[12] The term gained currency with the work of Claude Lévi-Strauss, "The Structural Study of Myth," in *Structural Anthropology* (New York: Basic Books, 1963), 206–31. Lévi-Strauss takes mythemes to be, like phonemes (and, we may add, words), arbitrarily chosen and, therefore, impossible to explain. But this, while it may often be the case, is surely not always so. There are natural phenomena like, for example floods and deserts, that naturally lend themselves to use as symbols for, say, social disruption, as both render the earth uninhabitable (Claude Lévi-Strauss, *The Jealous Potter* [Chicago, IL: University of Chicago Press, 1988], 172).

A myth is typically a highly theorized narrative, and its vocabulary is not the merely fantastic but a symbolic world of mythemes and a symbolic "grammar" that provides principles for ordering them so as to create a meaningfully structured whole. This kind of structure is the key signature of myth. It distinguishes it from both legend and history. Legend provides a good story, but is not similarly rich in structure or meaning. Its purpose is typically limited to entertain or perhaps to celebrate some heroic deed or individual. History (the actual course of events), while it may have lessons to teach and a causal structure, characteristically lacks the symbolic structures that are diagnostic of myth.

The boundaries are not sharp. Myth and legend lie on a continuum (determined by richness of symbolic content and structure); history and legend lie on another (determined by deviation from veracity). Myth, too, may incorporate historical elements, but its narrative is organized, as history itself never is, by the principles that order mythemes into meaningful messages (that is, into a story designed to convey an understanding of who we are and what we should do about it).[13] Of course, history—what we *actually were* and *actually did about it*—can contribute fundamentally to that understanding; hence, the interest that myth has in history. But, as noted, history is messy. It often obscures more than it illuminates, or it is ambiguous in the lessons it teaches. It may even, in the eyes of the mythographer, be a snare that misleads. Its true message may be hidden from us, and its apparent lessons may be the wrong ones. A myth, then, can provide a truer perspective. Still, myth always acknowledges the idea that history *in principle* establishes who we are and how we shall proceed. That is why it takes the form, often, of a narrative that discovers origins.

When history is what we care about, but myth and legend are all we have in hand, there is a natural impetus to mine those texts for historical nuggets. This is sometimes possible, but it is a perilous enterprise—especially when we are searching for a history that will confirm our *own* meanings and understandings. For myth provides, all too readily, enough degrees of interpretive freedom to make the process of winnowing historical gold from dross fraught with danger. Our best guide, I believe, is to invoke the methodological principle that history lacks symbolic structure. If the history we recover from a myth displays such structure, the chances are we have gone astray.

Here is an illustration of this point. It is not uncommon that we encounter in Scripture what looks like a straightforward historical detail, one

---

[13] To be clear: by "history" here I mean what actually happened. In *recounting* this, the historian can (and often does) selectively trace a line of connected events and then narrate them in such a way so as to teach some lesson or other. But, unless the historian chooses to veer well away from facticity, she will not do this by assembling mythemes into a narrative structure.

that might seem on the surface to be an aside that has no theological significance and that was inserted by the author simply as a report contained in the historical traditions handed down to him. The anthropologist is always on the alert for such "innocent" details. It might seem natural to suppose, for instance, that a detail inserted into a narrative without evident thematic connection to the larger story reflects an actual occurrence. Insofar as real history presents to us a sequence of events that are causally connected but have nothing like the coherent storyline of a skillful fiction, this inference to historicity will be a natural one. But it is often a sign that one has failed to "catch" something that does in fact carry symbolic significance.

Sometimes, for instance, a figure appears on the scene with no identification that connects him or her to preceding events, performs an action or undergoes some vicissitude, and then drops entirely from view. One thinks readily of the woman who anoints Jesus' head with nard at Bethany, or of Barabbas, of Simon of Cyrene, or of Joseph of Arimathea, just in the Passion narratives alone. Sometimes, an episode involving a familiar character appears on its surface to have the hallmarks of a straightforward historical account—for example, Judas' return of the silver coins to the high priest, suicide, and then the purchase of a field with the money. I will have a good deal to say about most of these cases presently; for the moment, I can illustrate the difference in the results produced by the anthropologist and by those who look to extract an historical background from the Gospel narratives by considering the mention of mentioning Simon of Cyrene.

In Stephen Neill and N. T. Wright, Neill writes:

> Dr. H. G. Wood, one of the very few New Testament scholars who is also in his own right a trained and professional historian, adds quite a number of [Gospel stories "which can be regarded as handed down from a purely historical interest"]. The most obvious is the allusion to Simon of Cyrene as father of Alexander and Rufus (Mark 15.21); unless we are going to look for obscure typological or allegorical meanings in these names, it seems sensible to suppose that the family of Simon of Cyrene was known to the readers of the Gospel, and that the writer puts in the names to remind them of this interesting connexion between people they knew and the actual events of the crucifixion.[14]

Neill goes on to note the

> interesting fact that the name Simon is Hebrew, Alexander is Greek, and Rufus is Latin; the writer of the Gospel cannot have been unaware of the

---

[14] Stephen Neill and Tom Wright, *The Interpretation of The New Testament, 1861–1986* (New York: Oxford University Press, 1988), 276–77.

Genres and the Character of Myth 195

parallel with the three languages of the superscription on the Cross; but it is hardly necessary to suppose that this was the *reason* for which he put in the names, still less that he invented them for this purpose.

This is indeed an "interesting fact"—one that would be seen as a signal-flare by our anthropologist. No doubt it is "hardly necessary to suppose"—but what are the probabilities? As it happens, Carrier has shown that these names may be highly significant. Citing Paul's claim that Christians have crucified "the flesh with the passions and lusts thereof" (Gal. 5:24), Carrier notes that Simon's carrying of Jesus' cross may symbolize that very "flesh"; first, because the Cyrenaic school taught a materialist philosophy rejected by Christians (cf. 1 Cor. 1:20; 2:5,13; though Paul does not name the Cyrenaics specifically); and second in rejection of the use of force against the Romans by Cyrenaic Jews. Carrier goes on to suggest that "Alexander" is an intended reference to Alexander the Great, and "Rufus" to Musonius Rufus, a notable pacifist and philosopher of the day.[15] Now Carrier—who is himself uncertain—may be right about this, or he may be wrong (I am inclined to think he is right), but my present point is that such details should always incite a serious search for significance.

But this is a digression. My project is not to recover history from myth or legend. That is a minefield I leave others to cross. My project is to recover the meaning of a myth, the message it was intended to covey through its structural ordering of symbols. That project will require much more to be said about the symbols employed by myth: where they might come from, how they might be understood, and, especially, what I mean by "structure"—how it is to be discerned, and how it contributes to the creation of meanings.

Obviously, since the intended contrast between legend and myth is a matter of degree (when the subject is historical), it may not always be readily decidable whether a given story should be classified as the one or the other. In any event, we shall return to the issue in Chapter 6, where the notions of mytheme and myth structure will be more fully explored.

II. Genre

A. Genre in General

Because much debate has been devoted to the question of the genre of the Gospels, and the implications of genre identification for whether these works have mythical content, we must ask: what, then, is a genre? Most

---

[15] For further details and justification, see Carrier, *On the Historicity of Jesus*, 444–51.

generically, it is simply a classification of a group of items—specifically, human artifacts and, in our case, written works—in accordance with some feature or features that they share. But to say this is to say very little, in view of the innumerable resemblances that written works can share. We need to identify features that will tell us something of interest, something that has significance for how a written work is to be interpreted or understood. But this still is unhelpful. We can classify works by author, and knowing the author can be an aid in interpretation; so can knowing the time of composition. What is wanted, rather, is some set of intrinsic features that permit written works to be assigned to a relatively manageable number of categories that are both distinctive and that provide significant interpretive guidance. More than this, a genre is typically marked by certain conventional features or forms that are transmitted over time and indicate historical lines of influence.

How are we to discover such features? One possibility is that there are sets or clusters of features that define types into which texts just naturally fall. Something like this—with quite severe difficulties—permits biological taxonomies. But texts are artifacts, not naturally occurring items. Nevertheless, clustering of a helpful sort might occur in a couple of ways. First, there are certain distinctive natural *purposes* that a written work might address: to entertain, to inform, to move emotionally, and so forth. And there are texts—edicts, personal letters, stories, and the like—that will, in view of their function, naturally take different forms. Second, because they are produced within a cultural or literary tradition, it is possible that certain types, with identifying characteristics, are prescribed. Thus, Aristotle, in his *Poetics*, sets forth in prescriptive fashion the genres of epic, tragedy, comedy, and dithyramb. Third, distinctive types of texts may evolve willy-nilly but under pressure of the need for recognizable features that will identify how the work as a whole is to be approached or understood with respect to certain interpretive options.

We may note here that such interpretive guidance is afforded us by a variety of devices at all levels of significant communication. For example, below the level of entire works, we find division into chapters, acts, scenes, stanzas, verses, paragraphs, and the like, which provide clues as to the progression of the thoughts expressed by the work. And at the verbal level, we find ambiguities eliminated by context and the impossibility of a description's being literally true (together with the presupposition that the author is mentally competent), which provides a cue that we have encountered a figurative or fictional use of language.

Genre can often tell us much about an author's intentions and, consequently, about how a text is to be read. If a text is a poem, we should probably not read it as a piece of analytic philosophy or as a straightforward specimen of historical record. We should be on the alert for metaphor, for affective dimensions, beauty of sound, rhythm, and poetic structure. Yet, poetry comes in a wide variety of styles and subgenres. Perhaps one *could* write analytic-philosophy poems (though it is hard to see why one would want to, except as a humorous exercise). And even if poetry is not well-suited to the analytic style in philosophy, it would not follow that poetry could not be used—as indeed it has been—to express significant philosophical claims. More trenchantly, the lines between poetry and history blur, or can blur, in the spinning of sagas. Perhaps, for example, the Homeric tales or *Njal's Saga* do not contain much in the way of reliable history; but perhaps they do or could have. Thus, though a taxonomy of genres deployed in a culture can tell us something about the *ways* in which authors sought to communicate, and often tell us something about the *kinds of things* they sought thereby to communicate, there is no inferential high road that runs from the one to the other.

Nothing I have said so far about genres entails that genres cannot evolve, that they have clearly demarcated boundaries, that they cannot overlap, that a given work cannot belong to two (or more) genres that are not mutually exclusive, or that an author could not put a new "twist" on a genre, writing a work that *violates* the norms for that genre but does so in a way that (a) tips the reader off as to what genre is being violated, (b) intends the violation itself to be a meaningful element in the work, and (c) perhaps intends thereby to expand the boundaries of the genre. Indeed, this last possibility affords one of the ways in which genre provides opportunity for literary creativity. Could a work indeed fall under two genres? I have suggested that nothing rules this possibility out. A fable, for instance, could be related in rhyming couplets or some more complex poetic form. One might rule it not a fable by insisting that a fable must be written in *prose*. Or, conversely, one might rule it not a poem on the grounds that it is a story of a certain kind. But it is hard to see what theoretical gain is achieved by such gerrymanders. Or, to put the point a bit differently, we can accept the gerrymanders while remaining true to the phenomenon by describing the work as a poetically expressed fable (or a poem with fabulous content). We can preserve the classification into a single genre by allowing that features of another genre have been employed outside their "home" context. Either way, the identification of a Gospel as myth does not automatically preclude assigning it to another genre, as well, or recognizing it as displaying some of the features of another genre.

Here, it is perhaps necessary to reflect upon the relation between texts that report miracles and the mythical versus the historical. Does the presence of the miraculous automatically transport us to the land of myth? Or, alternatively, can an historical work countenance miracles? I have said nothing about miracles in my characterization of the mythical. Nor have I denied that a historical work might contain miracle reports; I have only denied, on epistemological and arguably scientific grounds, that such reports are to be trusted as literal history. Where they appear in a mythological setting, miracle stories are to be scrutinized, not for historicity but for symbolic meaning, using the tools of myth analysis. But it is not the miraculous as such—or, at any rate, by itself—that signals myth. Structure does that. (On the other hand, a symbolic interpretation of a miracle story, as an element in a myth, clearly does provide scope for a more charitable reading; thus, while not criterial, it provides a significant indicator.)

One might object that there is a fundamental methodological divide between the philosophical and scientific criteria I have deployed in assessing miracle stories and the criteria proper to history. If such a line of argument can be made out, then perhaps it is within the proper purview of the historian, after all, to assess miracle reports on purely "historical" criteria and, as may be, to pronounce them true.[16] Were that the case, then the miraculous would not serve even as a kind of independent signpost indicative of myth.

Such a view of history has commonly enough been defended. For example, Neill says,

> For it is hardly possible to imagine a greater difference than that between the temper of the historian and the temper of the philosopher. The philosopher is concerned with universals; his aim is to bring as many phenomena as possible under one single law—in this he is akin to the physical scientist….The historian, if he is a true historian, knows there are no rules. What he deals in is the unique, the unrepeatable, and the unpredictable….[The historian] is bound, of course, to accept the basic axioms of thought, and that logical law of contradiction which makes it rational and correct to speak of certain things as impossible. Beyond this he has no knowledge of the meaning of the words 'possible' and 'impossible.'
>
> Ernest Renan started out to write a life of Jesus on the assumption the supernatural does not occur; thereby he confessed in a sentence that he was not writing as an historian.[17]

Now Neill has badly overstated the freedoms of the historian. If indeed the historian is bound by "the basic axioms of thought," then he is bound—if those axioms yield the scientific conclusion that the universe is governed by

---

[16] Cf. Robert L. Webb, "The Rules of the Game: History and Historical Method in the Context of Faith: The Via Media of Methodological Naturalism," *Journal for the Study of the Historical Jesus* 9, no. 1 (2011): 59–84 and Michael R. Licona, "Historians and Miracle Claims," *Journal for the Study of the Historical Jesus* 12, no. 1/2 (2014): 106–29.

[17] Neill and Wright, *The Interpretation of The New Testament*, 300–1.

certain laws of nature—to write history in such a way that it is constrained by those laws. If reason, and our total data, yield the conclusion that it is physically impossible for a man to have a head larger than the Milky Way, then the historian must rule out historical evidence to the contrary, even though such a head is logically possible. If reason judges something to be very improbable, then history must acknowledge that improbability and look for alternative ways to give account for the data. Renan was by no means forfeiting his right to the historian's task simply because he did what every historian must do: he judged certain logical possibilities to be very improbable or even impossible and, accordingly, constrained his search for a more likely story.

But we can learn something important from the first part of the Neill quote. There are indeed recognizable differences between history and the products of the systematizing scientific or philosophical mind, the mind whose aim is to reduce the chaotic welter of experience to a few simple patterns. As Claude Lévi-Strauss has shown, the mind of the mythmaker is a systematic mind, a scientific and philosophical mind. And the products of that mind reflect an effort more nearly like that of the scientist to bring order to our understanding of reality. Because they are expressed in narrative form, however, myths occupy a region somewhere between the abstract treatises of the scientist, like Newton's *Principia*, and the works of modern historians. Here in this region they have some company; the philosophical myths of Plato and his dialogues are close in spirit (at this very general level) to myths. They are both works of theoretical penetration and works of narrative art. And, I aim to show, the same must be said for the Gospels of the New Testament.

B. The Gospels in Particular

Debate about the genre of the Gospels has gone through several phases. Nineteenth century scholars pursuing the project that Albert Schweitzer called the quest of the historical Jesus (now called the "First Quest") initially took the Gospels to be biographical accounts that contained more or less factual material from which an historically reliable life of Jesus could be reconstructed. However, even as early as the middle of the century, D. F. Strauss raised the possibility that the content of the Gospels should be viewed largely as myth. Following upon the publication of Schweitzer's *Quest*,[18] this project was largely displaced by the view that the Gospels belonged to a new and unique genre, from which could be extracted the early *kerygma* of the church, but nothing much about the life of its founder.

---

[18] Albert Schweitzer, *The Quest of the Historical Jesus*, trans. W. Montgomery (1906; repr., Mineola, NY: Dover Publications, 2005).

Rudolph Bultmann stands as perhaps the most influential figure in producing this change in orientation.

But in the second half of the twentieth century, New Testament scholars—mainly from the liberal wing—renewed the attempt to reconstruct a life of Jesus using a variety of interpretive models—for example, casting him in the mold of a Jewish magician (Morton Smith), a Cynic sage (Burton Mack), or a social revolutionary (Richard Horsley). Thus emerged a "Second Quest" for the historical Jesus, one that treated the Gospels with considerable suspicion as historical accounts but saw in them and in other ANE sources an opportunity to draw some inferences about who and what Jesus was. Partly in response to the Second Quest, more conservative scholars embarked upon a "Third Quest," one that takes the Gospel accounts to reflect more straightforwardly the historical facts of Jesus' life, including his death and resurrection. Indeed, such accounts are often directed toward establishing the historicity of the central theological claim of Christianity, namely that Jesus rose from the dead. Wolfhard Pannenberg stands as one of the principal instigators of this effort. I have critically assessed some of the methodology common to Third Questers in Chapter 3.

It is not my purpose further to review this enormous literature here but, instead, to note that one of the issues the debate highlighted was the question of the genre of the Gospels.[19] The nineteenth century largely affirmed the view that the Gospels were biographies. Bultmann denied it; but more recently, there have been scholarly efforts to rehabilitate it. Of these, perhaps the most widely recognized and respected is Richard Burridge's *What are the Gospels?*,[20] and it will serve my purpose to focus upon it in discussing the two main questions before us: whether the Gospels are biographies (more specifically, whether they classify, as Burridge argues, as the Greco-Roman βίος genre); and whether, supposing that they do, this entails that their authors are engaged in presenting historical facts about an historical person to the exclusion of myth.

Burridge begins his systematic treatment with a discussion of the notion of genre itself. He accepts several of the points I made above—for example, that the notion of genre is elastic and that genre provides a key to the interpretation of a work. After discussing the prescriptive conception of genre and the idea that genres are defined by conventional rules, Burridge settles on the view that a genre is a "conventional set of expectations." He

---

[19] I shall, however, return to some of that scholarship in Chapter 12.

[20] Richard A. Burridge, *What Are the Gospels? A Comparison with Graeco-Roman Biography*, 2nd ed. (Grand Rapids, MI: William B. Eerdmans Publishing Company, 2004). See also Craig S. Keener, *Christobiography: Memory, History, and the Reliability of the Gospels* (Grand Rapids, MI: Wm. B. Eerdmans, 2019) and Richard Bauckham, *Jesus and the Eyewitnesses: The Gospels as Eyewitness Testimony* (Grand Rapids, MI: Wm. B. Eerdmans, 2006).

must mean: something—presumably about the form of an artifact—that *generates* a set of expectations.[21]

The idea here, which is reasonable enough, is that genre is to be understood as a set of cues that function, at the level of the work as a whole, to facilitate communication by providing recipients with a certain framework within which to interpret the work—in other words, to give recipients information about the purposes the author had in writing. Such cues are useful because they allow the author to use certain conventions that make it unnecessary for him or her to step aside and *tell* the audience, in so many words, about those purposes. But Burridge pushes this idea too far. He suggests that genre, based as it is upon convention-bound practices and traditions, is *essential* to a work's being able to communicate its meaning. "We can have no idea what to expect from a *sui generic* work!"[22] This overstates the case. Meaning, and the conventions which make its transmission possible, exist on a series of levels, beginning with individual words and then sentences. It is far from obvious, indeed, that it would be impossible for a longer stretch of discourse to convey meaning even if not falling within any established genre, and without being taken by recipients to do so. Indeed, as I have suggested above, purposive *violation* of genre strictures—though parasitic upon there *being* genres—can itself convey critical meaning.

In addition to this conceptual difficulty, there are three methodological infirmities that weaken Burridge's case for classifying the Gospels as βίοι. How is genre membership to be determined? Admitting that genre classifications are vague, Burridge hits upon the idea that the members of a genre are grouped together by means of family resemblance: "Wittgenstein's term 'family resemblance' identifies the resemblance which several examples have in common."[23] Later, Burridge elucidates this by saying with respect to the Gospels:

> The genre of βίος is flexible and diverse, with variation in the pattern of features from one βίος to another. The gospels also diverge from the pattern in some aspects [*sic.*], but not to any greater degree than other βίοι; in other words, they have at least as much in common with other Greco-Roman βίοι as the βίοι have with each other. Therefore, the gospels must belong to the genre of βίος.[24]

---

[21] Burridge, *What Are the Gospels?*, 33–34.
[22] Ibid., 34. "Genre is at the heart of all attempts to communicate, a crucial component of the *filter* through which a writer's idea passes between its conception and its expression as a written word. Similarly, it is part of the filter through which written words must pass to reach the reader's understanding" (p. 48).
[23] Ibid., 38.
[24] Ibid., 250.

From this passage, we can extract the following general criterion of genre membership:

(G) Work W belongs to genre G just in case W has at least as much in common with the (other) members of G as they have with each other.

It will be seen immediately that as a criterion for determining genre membership, (G) is viciously circular: it *presupposes* that we have already identified the other members of (G). We can make the difficulty here vivid with an illustration using the color spectrum. Suppose we attempt to use a criterion parallel to (G) to classify a shade of green that is fairly near the "borderline" between the greens and the blues. It is a bluish green; as such, it bears fairly close resemblance to greenish blues. Does it resemble every shade of green at least as closely as each of these resembles other shades of green? If this means, "more closely than the most bluish of greens resembles the most yellowish of greens," then the answer is 'yes.' But our target shade of green will also resemble some (though perhaps not all) shades of blue much more closely than it resembles some shades of green. Is it, then, a shade of green or a shade of blue? Clearly, the answer to that question depends upon some antecedent choice of the boundary shades that demarcate blue and green from other colors and from each other. The situation is much more complex in the case of criteria for genres for the simple reason that classification is tied to so many different parameters, not just one as with shades of color.

In fact, Burridge's criterion has nothing to do with Wittgenstein's notion of family resemblance. It lies much closer to a criterion offered on behalf of resemblance nominalist accounts of properties. H. H. Price, for example, explores the view that something counts as red just in case it resembles the members of a certain class of exemplars—say, a glowing ember, a Burgundy apple, and a London pillar box, at least as closely as each of these resembles the others.[25] In order for this to succeed at all as a criterion of redness, the members of the exemplar class must be chosen to be as diverse as possible, except with respect to the target property. Such an account is at least not circular, though it has manifold other defects.[26]

Ignoring these, Burridge *could* nevertheless proceed by taking certain ancient writings as his exemplar βίοι. Indeed, in taking ten works widely classified as βίοι as exemplars, that is the way he *does* proceed.

---

[25] H. H. Price, *Thinking and Experience*, 2nd ed. (London: Hutchinson Publishing, 1969), 7–32.
[26] See Evan Fales, *Causation and Universals* (New York: Routledge, 1990), 160–63.

But—since the issue at hand turns on where the boundaries of the genre lie, and whether the Gospels fall inside them, proceeding in this way would be (as we will see in detail) tendentious.

However, even if Burridge's praxis does not match his methodological principles, it seems reasonable to infer that the Gospels *probably* concern an historical individual and relate some historical material from this person's life from the fact that all the βίοι in Burridge's sample do so. In fact, Burridge is remarkably circumspect in drawing either of these conclusions—especially the latter.[27] His most optimistic assessment seems to be, "Simply discovering that the gospels are βίοι does not answer all our questions about their historicity or truth, but it may give an indication of the freedom each of the evangelists has in constructing a portrait of Jesus."[28]

Yet, even this may be asking too much of Burridge's method for two reasons. First, we do not really know how representative his small sample of ten βίοι is of the range of extant Greek and Roman texts in this (somehow delineated) class. Second, and more seriously, we do not know—and probably cannot ever know—how representative the existing βίοι are of the original field of candidate texts. We do not know this because we know nothing, or at most just a bit in some cases by way of secondary references, about all those pagan texts that have been lost (many, perhaps, having been destroyed by the church after it acquired power in the fourth century). We do not know how many such texts there were; nor do we know their range of style, content, and the like; nor how clearly distinguishable they were from works in neighboring genres. Burridge deliberately chose to include, in his sample, βίοι displaying a wide range of characteristics within the genre, the better to catch in his net the Gospels. The price he pays for adopting this strategy is, as he recognizes, that his conclusions about the Gospels must be weaker. And because even this range may not reflect accurately the true variability of the ancient texts, any estimate of the relevant probabilities will be unavoidably speculative.

These problems come to a head already with even the minimal claim that the Gospels must be about an historical figure. Officially for Burridge, anything counts as a βίος if it shares enough characteristics with other βίοι (i.e., those in some reference class). How then should we classify a text that bears ample resemblance to members of the reference class but differs in not being about an historical person? Apparently, Burridge thinks that failure of the subject to be an historical person is by itself sufficient to

---

[27] So circumspect, indeed, that several critics have called Burridge's conclusions trivial—see Burridge, *What Are the Gospels?*, 255–57.
[28] Ibid., 259–60.

disqualify a work as a βίος; for it is for precisely this reason that he disqualifies several ancient texts.²⁹

One can, of course, simply *stipulate* that having an historical subject is a necessary condition for the βίος genre. But in that case, showing the Gospels to be βίοι cannot be simply a matter of showing them to share many features with other βίοι. Rather, it will have to be shown on independent grounds that their subject is historical—in which case the interesting conclusion is reached on those independent grounds, and classification as βίοι does none of the heavy lifting with respect to this issue. If one does not make such a stipulation then, of course, there is no reason why Isocrates' ecomia, *Helen*, as well as *Busiris* (and the Gospels, even if Jesus is a fiction), should not count as βίοι also.

Perhaps, however, it can be argued that the genre of the Greco-Roman βίος excludes the category of myth on the grounds that the βίος, even if it could take some liberties with the facts, was not a genre of fiction. But this will hardly convince in view of the highly fluid character of the βίος form. Burridge also admits that the boundaries between the βίος and "neighboring" genres is flexible, vague, and porous.³⁰ He concedes further that to insist upon historicity as a criterion for the genre is to impose an unfortunate "limitation."³¹ Hence, there is nothing here that would prevent the Gospel writers from building a myth (or several myths) around an historical Jesus.

But—although it is no part of my concern to argue that Jesus was, or was not, an historical figure—there is not even anything here that precludes the central figure of the Gospels from having been an invention. It will be pointed out, of course, that the two Isocratic "βίοι" concerned legendary figures from the remote past, whereas the Gospels concern a recent figure whose death is situated only half a century (or less) previously.

But why think this an impediment to such an invention? Why could the Gospel writers not have invented such a recent figure as their protagonist if it suited their purposes—and have expected their readers (at least the sophisticated ones) to understand their intent? Why, in an age that Burridge describes as one of major experimentation with the βίος form in the Roman world, would such an innovation (if indeed it was an innovation) have asked of readers too great a leap in understanding?³² And why, for that matter,

---

²⁹ For example, Isocrates' *Helen* and *Busiris* and Xenophon's *Cyropaedia*. See Burridge, *What Are the Gospels?*, 69.
³⁰ Ibid., 60–63.
³¹ Ibid., 60.
³² Indeed Charles Talbert, one of the scholars whose lead Burridge followed in developing his thesis that the Gospels are βίοι, argues that the Gospels are organized around two mythical τοποι: the Synoptics around the τοπος of the divinized hero who is

must we suppose that the Evangelists would have *wanted* all the readers and hearers of their good news to have understood this? It is not impossible that they intended some (with the eyes to see and the ears to hear) to recognize the telling of a μυθος and, indeed, to understand the Gospels in this way, as well as intend for the *hoi polloi* to receive the news with another, more literal understanding. As I shall presently argue, there are in fact reasons to guess that a rhetorical strategy of this kind would have recommended itself to the Jesus movement.

Having made these observations, I want to repeat that my case will not rest in any substantial way on whether Jesus was an historical figure, whether those that wrote and propagated the Gospels wished him to be understood in this way, or whether they did or did not consciously understand themselves to be writing biographies of Jesus in the Greco-Roman mold. Still, if, as Burridge claims, the Gospel writers *did* so understand their work, then this has implications that some of those who point to Burridge's work in support of claims of historicity will be loath to accept. To put the point succinctly: if the Gospel writers borrowed the Greco-Roman βίος *form* to convey their message (in particular, perhaps better to convey it to Gentiles), then why not seriously consider the possibility that the *content* of the Gospels may also owe something to the pagan religious traditions of the Greco-Roman world since we know that βίοι need not be strictly historical, or even historical at all? Why must we stop short of admitting influence at the level of generic form?

We should, therefore, let the texts themselves speak rather than rely upon pre-understood categories. If, for example, a miracle story appears in a context that does not provide the kind of structure and context that permit assimilating it to a mythic trope and myth-structural role, then we have reason to suppose that (whether true or false) it is meant to be a piece of historical reportage. But conversely, if it *does* lend itself to a mythological reading, then there is a strong presumption in favor of such a reading.

A concessive apologetic may find it tempting to say: Why suppose a text must be read on only one level? Why could it not be *both* reliable history and have a mythological dimension? I have already explained that

---

assumed into heaven, and John around the τοπος of the heavenly being who descends to earth and then returns to heaven:
> It would seem, therefore, that the early Christians were aware of the Mediterranean myth of the immortals and utilized it in one way or another in their proclamation of Jesus. When they employed this myth in the gospels of Matthew, Mark, and Luke-Acts as a principle by which to order the Jesus materials, they were doing what pagan and Jewish writers had already done and were doing. The sweeping statement that Graeco-Roman biographies were not mythical is inaccurate. The mythology of the immortals was used by some as the frame of their story—as do the synoptic gospels. (Talbert, *What Is a Gospel?*, 42)

history—the kind of history we can unproblematically access—does not present itself to us as having the kind of patterned structures we find in the (unproblematically) mythical. But perhaps this is not decisive. A natural response will be that in special circumstances, God choreographs history in such a way as to convey to human beings his purposes and providence. That, it must be allowed, is a hypothesis that cannot summarily be dismissed. It is, however, a hypothesis that introduces superfluous complexity, unless our data cannot be sufficiently well explained without it.

Nevertheless, readers who are sympathetic to this possibility are invited, as we proceed, to work out in detail the kind of stage-setting that God would have to engineer under the terms of the hypothesis. They will find, I think, that God will have to have done a great deal of micro-managing of historical events in order to ensure that history will unfold along the lines of the myth. Moreover, the plausibility of this approach will inevitably suffer from the need to invoke special explanations for the multitude of discrepancies between biblical accounts where more than one exists— discrepancies that, as we will see, are no obstacle for (and can often be used to advantage by) a reading that approaches the texts as myths. All-told then, this apologetic strategy will incur complexities that (other things being equal) lower its probability vis à vis the purely mythological understanding.

In this chapter, I have been repeatedly alluding to the "structural" features of myths. Those allusions are empty until specificity can be given to the claim that myths exhibit such distinctive features. The recognition that myths exhibit structural features that are key ingredients in the task of grasping their meaning is fundamentally due to the work of Lévi-Strauss on the problem of understanding myths. In the next chapter, therefore, I shall turn to a critical analysis of Lévi-Strauss' seminal contribution to the study of myth. In the next chapter, I will also present, briefly, some other work by anthropologists that is, in my view, of essential importance to the understanding of our target biblical texts, even though it is not directly concerned with the analysis of myths.

6

Anthropological Excursions

The religious myths and rituals of tribal peoples produced a set of puzzles central to the emerging discipline of anthropology in the later nineteenth century and throughout the twentieth century. It might fairly be said that, in addition to the analysis of systems of kinship, the study of the nature and origin of "primitive" religious systems was nearly an obsession among anthropologists. It was, unfortunately, characteristic of much early theorizing about the springs of religious belief that explanations appealed to irrational mental processes of one postulated kind or another. Aside from those who saw religion primarily as an outlet for emotions of some sort or as a source of social solidarity, it was recognized that religious beliefs served an explanatory purpose. But tribal peoples, it seemed, were not very good explainers. James Frazer thought magic was a kind of primitive science, founded in large measure on a confusion between spoken words and the realities to which they referred (hence the power of spells and curses). Lucien Levi-Bruhl found primitives incapable of drawing proper inferences. Edward Tylor thought men by nature tended to see in natural processes the operations of minds or spirits.[1] A more sophisticated intellectualist approach, that of Robin Horton, was discussed in Chapter 1. And in Chapter 4, we saw that Durkheim appealed to "projection" to explain the transition from felt social pressures to belief in gods and to *ex post facto* rationalization of ritual practices to flesh out primitive theologies.

Here, I shall begin with a summary and critical discussion of the work of Claude Lévi-Strauss, who perhaps more than any other anthropologist put paid to the idea that the minds of primitives are primitive. While I shall be concerned mainly with Lévi-Strauss's approach to understanding myths, I should note that his understanding of the principles underlying the complex kinship systems of Australian aborigine tribes showed that even peoples with the most primitive of material cultures are

---

[1] A broadly similar view has recently been defended by Stewart Elliot Guthrie, *Faces in the Clouds: A New Theory of Religion* (New York: Oxford University Press, 1995).

capable of abstract thought of a high order.[2] That commitment informs Lévi-Strauss's approach to the often puzzling religious myths of tribal peoples.

I. Lévi-Strauss

Like many anthropologists of religion, Lévi-Strauss steered clear of applying his analytic tools to biblical materials. His official view was that these techniques were applicable to the religious productions of "cold" societies but not "hot" ones. (Cold societies are pre-literate societies in which social and religious institutions and beliefs are stable over long periods of time. Hot societies, by contrast, change much more rapidly.) One may be skeptical of this official explanation not only because Lévi-Strauss must have known that the distinction is a rather artificial one but because he was committed to the view that the underlying mental processes are universal.[3] While we shall not be applying exactly Lévi-Strauss's methodology to biblical texts, we reject in any case his hot/cold distinction and with it the implication that structural anthropological techniques cannot yield new insights into the literary productions of ancient Israel. (Indeed, Lévi-Strauss violates his own constraint by giving—see below—a structural analysis of the Oedipus myth as a showcase example of his methods.) We examine Lévi-Strauss' work here because it provided a springboard for most of the later development of structural myth analysis. We then describe the theoretical work of Terrence Turner, which accepts some of Lévi-Strauss' central ideas but introduces major—and I think illuminating—modifications in the method.

Lévi-Strauss' project is in a way similar to Kant's: he hopes to uncover structures of thought that are universal to humankind. Kant sought structures that provided the a priori, necessary underpinnings of cognition. It is less clear whether Lévi-Strauss thinks of his quarry as necessary structures or merely contingent ones—*viz.,* understanding of what the authors of the stories might really have been trying to say and how they were trying to say it. In fact, to my mind, the greatest tragedy of the traditional debate is that it has so effectively deflected attention away from what (by my lights at least) are the actual, often profound meanings of the texts.

---

[2] For example, in his landmark Claude Lévi-Strauss, *The Elementary Structures of Kinship*, ed. Rodney Needham, trans. J. H. Bell, J. R. von Sturmer, and Rodney Needham (1949; repr., Boston, MA: Beacon Press, 1969).

[3] It is at least plausible that anthropologists' shyness with respect to the "home" religions is not merely a matter of distinguishing their turf from that of the sociologists, but it also stems from the recognition of the political implications of bringing anthropological insights to bear on Jewish and Christian traditions.

A myth cannot, in general, be understood in isolation. The procedure Lévi-Strauss advocates begins by collecting as many variants as possible of a myth. Understanding what the myth is "up to" emerges from a certain technique of collating and then dissecting into thematic components its variants. A natural starting point is a comparison of the semantics of ordinary language and the way meaning is built into a myth. Mythical meaning emerges at a higher order than ordinary linguistic meaning. We can see this, according to Lévi-Strauss, by reflecting upon two contrasts between language and myth. First, and most obviously, in myth, anything can happen.[4] That is to say, myths relate events and sequences of events that often do not tally with our ordinary experience of the world. That points us to a different level of meaning. Second, Lévi-Strauss is influenced by Ferdinand de Saussure's distinction between *langue* and *parole*. Roughly, *parole* refers to speech as a concrete event—the use of language to communicate upon particular occasions. This is the aspect of language that is "visible" to us. But underlying vocal productions is a set of rules that more or less guide the production of individual speech acts, control what can be expressed by a given choice of words, and are not under the control of individual speakers. Unlike speech, which is episodic or temporal, that system—*langue*—is fixed, atemporal. Language, which consists of *langue* and *parole*, thus has two poles, a temporal and an atemporal pole. But a myth, as Lévi-Strauss sees it, must generate meaning in a "third dimension," one that mediates between the temporal and the atemporal. It has a kind of universality but of a different order than *langue*.

Now all this is more suggestive than it is a piece of rigorous reasoning, but what it suggests to Lévi-Strauss will be of some interest. The thought is that the myth, whose variant tellings can be spread out over time and space, is a unified entity and must be studied as such if we are to decipher its meaning. A next thought, which also owes a debt to de Saussure, is that elements of a myth—the *mythemes*—are in a sense arbitrary (like phonemes or words in a language) and carry the meaning they do only in relation to other elements of the myth. As Lévi-Strauss develops this idea, the procedure is to recognize, in all the known variants of a myth, parallel or cognate elements that can be grouped together in virtue of some common theme or thread (often quite abstract) that permits them collectively to define a given mytheme and whose common principle of association determines the

---

[4] "In myth, everything becomes possible" (Claude Lévi-Strauss, "The Structural Study of Myth," in *Structural Anthropology* [New York: Basic Books, 1963], 204). This is true in one way, but also the reverse of the truth in another. A myth is a story; hence it must make some sort of narrative sense even if the world of the myth is a fantastic one. History, on the other hand, does *not* make this kind of narrative sense, except insofar as the historian selectively chooses a path that threads its way precariously through the jungle of interacting causal sequences.

meaning of the mytheme. In effect, one collapses all the variants of a myth into a single mytheme sequence.

As an initial illustration, Lévi-Strauss maps the stories comprising the Oedipus cycle onto a schema of four mythemes. The first groups together Cadmos' search for his Zeus-raped sister Europa, Oedipus' marriage with his mother, and Antigone's forbidden burial of her brother Polynices. A second mytheme has these elements: the mutual destruction of the Spartoi, Oedipus' killing of his father, Laios, and Eteocles' killing of his brother, Polynices. The third is Cadmos' slaying of the dragon and Oedipus' slaying of the Sphinx. And the fourth, three abnormal figures constituting Oedipus' line: Labadacos (Laios' father) = *lame*, Laios = *left-sided*, and Oedipus himself = *swollen-foot*. It will be seen immediately that the members of each group are not exact parallels; one must discover a common theme. For the first group this is, according to Lévi-Strauss, the "overvaluing" of blood relations (Oedipus marries too close and Antigone buries her brother illegally). By contrast, the second group displays an undervaluing of kinship. Monster mortality obviously unites group three, and the names in group four all have meanings that suggest difficulty in walking or standing.[5]

But what could be the significance of all this? We have the mythemes, but how does the repetition of their variants in the Oedipus cycle provide the material for an understanding of the meaning of the Oedipus myth? The key is a recognition of the relations in which the mythemes stand to one another. It is this relational structure that enables us to grasp the meaning of the myth, which is to "resolve" or "disarm" a contradiction. Lévi-Strauss' reasoning is, at this point, characteristically obscure. The monster killings in group three are to be understood as denials of the autochthonous origin of human beings, since both dragon and Sphinx, when alive, prevent human life. Given this (!), one can see that the significance of the fourth group lies in its *affirmation* of the ongoing autochthonous origin of human beings: Lévi-Strauss notes (citing three New-World examples) that initial lameness is a "universal characteristic of men born from the Earth." So groups three and four have conflicting significances—as do groups one and two. Lévi-Strauss continues,

> The inability to connect two kinds of relationships is overcome (or rather replaced) by the assertion that contradictory relationships are identical inasmuch as they are both self-contradictory in a similar way.
>
> [W]e may now see what [the myth] means. [It] has to do with the inability, for a culture which holds the belief that mankind is

---

[5] Lévi-Strauss omits from this group an element that might bear consideration: the solution to the Sphinx's riddle plays upon the three modes of human locomotion, two of them awkward.

autochthonous ... to find a satisfactory transition between this theory and the knowledge that human beings are born of man and woman. Although the problem obviously cannot be solved, the Oedipus myth provides a kind of logical tool which relates the original problem—born of one or two?—to the derivative problem: born from different of born from same? By a correlation of this type, the overrating of blood relations is to the underrating of blood relations as the attempt to escape autochthony is to the impossibility to succeed in it. Although experience contradicts theory, social life validates cosmology by its similarity of structure. Hence, cosmology is true.[6]

There is much to say here. First, how are the meanings of mythemes arrived at? Taking a cue from de Saussure, Lévi-Strauss holds that the meaning of a mytheme is, as the Oedipus analysis suggests, derived from the relationships between the elements of a grouping. De Saussure's view is more radical: from the fact that words have arbitrary or conventional denotations, he infers that word meaning can *only* derive from relationships between word occurrences; in other words, the rules that govern their use in linguistic contexts. That, however, is incoherent: de Saussure appears to discount the possibility of the *direct* establishment of a relation being established between a word, such as "tiger," and items in the world. But without any such initial and independent word-world anchoring, meaning floats free. Mere relations cannot pin down meaning any more than mere coherence can pin down truth conditions for sets of statements.

It is not clear that Lévi-Strauss' actual practice inherits this mistake, however, for mytheme meanings are clearly derived from the *already* given verbal meanings of the units that fall within the mytheme's group.[7] There remains, however, the serious worry that it is very far from obvious how one is to derive the meaning of a mytheme from its constituent elements—or even how one is to identify an element *as* a constituent of a group (as witness the question whether the Sphinx's riddle—or rather its answer—should be grouped together with the elements in group four—which would in turn call into question the relevance of group four to autochthony). It is not possible to give a recipe for identifying occurrences of a theme that

---

[6] Lévi-Strauss, "The Structural Study of Myth," 212.

[7] It is, however, Lévi-Strauss' official position. The linguistic parallel to mythemes is, he asserts, not the word but the phoneme. Although phoneme occurrence is "bound by certain constraints," phonemes are not bearers of meaning. Thus, the content of mythemes "consists in formal relations that, by reason of their formal nature, can accept a wide variety of different contents" (Claude Lévi-Strauss, *The Jealous Potter* [Chicago, IL: University of Chicago Press, 1988], 148–49). A wide variety indeed, so wide that one will have evacuated the mytheme of all its symbolic power. Either Lévi-Strauss is using the term "formal" in a wider sense than his official methodology allows, or he will be left with logical skeletons of little interest.

should be grouped together; this is inescapably something of an art. Some groupings are more persuasive than others, and some unifying principles or characteristics are more obvious than others. Often, those proposed by Lévi-Strauss will seem highly creative or, less charitably, far-fetched.

Next, the last two sentences quoted above put us on alert that Lévi-Strauss may in some ways not be as charitable in interpreting myths as one would hope. The Greeks were clever: but even though "experience contradicts theory [i.e., their cosmological theory]," according to Lévi-Strauss, they nevertheless accept the theory, on the grounds that it is "validated" by their social existence. What can this mean, and in what sense can it be rational? Experience teaches us that human beings are not autochthenes (thus born from one) but result from sexual reproduction (born from two). That certainly contradicts a born-from-one cosmology. One might nevertheless find such a cosmology intellectually satisfying—where did the first man and woman come from?—but why autochthony rather than some other hypothesis? Apparently, the claim is that a feature of social life—the conflicting tendencies to over- and under-value blood relationships—provides a kind of model for the conflict between being one-born and being two-born that confirms the chthonic-origin hypothesis.

It is not easy to take this line of reasoning seriously. Not only is it hard to see how through the mere existence of a kind of similar logical relation between the two pairs of items, one gets confirmation of the cosmology, but it is far from obvious that if tensions associated with blood relations can validate that hypothesis, they couldn't equally validate any number of competing hypotheses. At the very least, Lévi-Strauss owes us independent evidence for thinking that the Greeks were *worried* about the question of autochthony, and for thinking that they themselves thought that facts about blood relations would be suited to confirm certain views about that. It is likely, however, that Lévi-Strauss would have demurred in the face of such a demand, since he seems prepared to allow that myths perform their contradiction-resolving functions below the level of conscious reflection. (How else could they do this? If we *know* that we are trying to de-fang a contradiction by replacing it with a structurally similar one, why would our worries be assuaged?)[8]

---

[8] "A myth appears as a system of equations in which the symbols, never clearly perceived, are approximated by means of concrete values chosen to produce the illusion that the underlying equations are solvable. Such choices are guided by an unconscious finality, but they are made among arbitrary and contingent elements, the products of history, so that the initial choice remains as impossible to explain as the choice of a set of phonemes that come to make up a particular language" (Lévi-Strauss, *The Jealous Potter*, 172).

This brings us to a central aspect of Lévi-Strauss' project, that of uncovering universal structures of human symbolic thought, for such symbols are alleged to operate primarily unconsciously:

> If, as we believe to be the case, the unconscious activity of the mind consists in imposing forms upon content, and if these forms are fundamentally the same for all minds—ancient and modern, primitive and civilized (as the study of the symbolic function, expressed in language, so strikingly indicates)—it is necessary and sufficient to grasp the unconscious structure underlying each institution and each custom, in order to obtain a principle of interpretation valid for other institutions and other customs [and, it may be added, myths], provided of course that the analysis is carried far enough.[9]

What are these "forms" that the mind imposes? At the highest level of abstraction, Lévi-Strauss sees myth structure determined by the need to solve problems generated by the opposition between binary pairs that constitute poles of human existence: male/female, raw/cooked (more generally, the wild vs. the domesticated or civilized), earth/sky, proper/improper sexual relations, and so forth. These are characterized as "contradictories," and they are threatening both to intellectual coherence and to social functioning. But because there is no easy way to resolve or mediate such contradictions, the native mind attempts to "defuse" a nettlesome contradiction through metonymy, finding and substituting for it another contradiction that is structurally similar or identical but less troubling. This process can continue until the original contradiction is "buried" under layers of substitution and thus becomes tamer, though it is never really resolved. Thus, the force that drives the creation of myths is the need to etiolate perceived contradictions.

It is not hard to discern echoes of both Hegel and Freud in this way of understanding myths: of Hegel because we have something like a drive to resolve what are described as "contradictions," and of Freud because the mechanism for taming these contradictions sounds like a kind of (often unconscious) sublimation. Unlike Freud, Lévi-Strauss understands this process as one that entrains an intellectual if not conscious process. Lévi-Strauss' relation to Hegelian ideas is more complex. He insists that, allegedly unlike Hegelians, the anthropologist relies upon empirical data and must do so because even though the formal characteristics of human thought ultimately revealed are universal, particular myth content—both as concerns what contradictions are perceived as needing resolution and as concerns the materials available for symbolic manipulation—are matters of historical and

---

[9] Claude Lévi-Strauss, *Structural Anthropology* (New York: Basic Books, 1963), 21–22.

environmental contingencies.[10] On the other hand, Lévi-Strauss appeals to neural processing to deny that reality is ever presented to us in a way that is devoid of contributions imposed by human cognitive faculties—faculties that, once again, allegedly rely, at a pre-conscious level, upon binary oppositions; and he suggests that nature itself may embody such binary structures.

These are heavy epistemological and ontological commitments. I see no good reason to be bound by them. First, like Hegel, Lévi-Strauss uses the term "contradiction" in a clearly loose way that runs very wide of the logician's precise meaning of that term. Sometimes, Lévi-Strauss speaks instead of binary oppositions. That is better terminology, but it is hard to know what should count; the field of potential binaries is infinite. Second, it is often hard to see why the binaries that Lévi-Strauss invokes are ones that should trouble the myth-maker. There is a contrast between male and female: why should that trouble us? It is fundamental to social life and central to our lives (and even, to be sure, the source of no end of human misery), but why should there be felt pressure to disguise or bury this opposition? Some opposites are even harder to understand the threatening significance of: earth/sky, edible/inedible, food/excrement, interior/exterior, and many others. These oppositions might be interesting to "play" with intellectually, but why must they be somehow subverted? Although many have some significance for human social life, Lévi-Strauss seems sometimes to have strayed quite far from Durkheim's insight that myths focus heavily upon questions of social order.

Third, the idea that the business of myths lies in the attempted resolution of binary oppositions by substituting others creates a methodological straitjacket we will do well to jettison. It is a vestige of the Hegelian thesis/antithesis/synthesis schema. Of course, human theorizing relies essentially upon considering opposing theories and objections to a given theory. But there is no a priori reason for thinking that this dialectic is usefully understood in terms of binary oppositions. Alternatives almost always number more than one, and theory choice, we now well know, is more complex than "synthesis" between two opposed poles or replacement by some allegedly similar opposition. We should assume as much when we attempt to capture the theoretical thought that underlies the making of myths.

Fourth, there are three methodological issues that are raised by the way in which Lévi-Strauss groups together myths for the purposes of comparison. The first point is that the process of superposition of variants moves us away from the *internal* narrative logic of a given variant. The

---

[10] See Claude Lévi-Strauss, "Structuralism and Ecology," *Social Science Information* 12, no. 1 (1973): 7–23.

others concern the distribution of these myths in space, and finally, their distribution in time.

The superposition technique is meant to reflect the claim that the meaning of a mytheme can only be gleaned by the comparison and discovery of relations between its variant occurrences in related myths. As we have seen, this establishment of homologies between occurrences of allegedly the "same" mytheme relies, often, upon highly abstract similarities (e.g., "over-valuation of kinship"). More specific meanings, which may make essential contributions to the narrative of a particular version of a myth, drop out of consideration. But this is a decisive loss: it is hard to imagine that the myth-makers or their audience's appreciation of the myth are not largely riveted on this content.[11] A simple thought experiment should make this clear. Surely a myth can be heard for the first time and to a significant degree be understood? Surely the process of constructing a myth must have begun with a first version, and surely individual mythemes must have come into being without precedent but carrying on their shoulders much of the meaning that later variations might enrich? Were it not so, it is hard to see how those later variants could have been recognized by *their* creators *as* variants whose meaning might partially trade on the meaning of a predecessor. We will, therefore, do well to pay serious attention to the specific content of mythemes we encounter. This is not to say that comparison with other occurrences and variants, where they can be had, may not be illuminating—even crucial, where there is a conscious tradition of reference (implicit or explicit) to known earlier narratives.

Often, Lévi-Strauss' comparison group is gleaned from a group of tribes that lives in fairly close proximity or gives evidence of some common historical ancestry. In that event, we may suppose that structurally related myths betray a history of borrowing and diffusion. But sometimes, Lévi-Strauss assembles far-flung myths from distant geographical areas, with either no evidence for diffusion or good evidence against it. Thus, much of Lévi-Strauss' *The Jealous Potter* is devoted to myths that involve tubular configurations; a blowpipe or smoking pipe is the starting point of

> a transformation in three stages: (1) the hero's body enters a tube that contains him; (2) a tube formerly contained in the hero's body emerges from it; (3) the hero's body becomes a tube—something either goes in or comes out of it. ... there is a wide range of potential combinations within the semantic field constituted by natural tubes and their openings.

---

[11] A similar point is made in Terrence Turner, "Narrative Structure and Mythopoesis: A Critique and Reformulation of the Structuralist Concepts of Myth, Narrative, and Poetics," *Arethusa* 10 (1977): 118, 139–40.

> These openings can be at the front or back, above or below: mouth, nose, ears, vagina, anus, etc.[12]

The theme is collected from Amerindian tribes ranging from the Yukon to Amazonia. In support of the association with autochthony, Lévi-Strauss ranges even farther afield, moving from Greece to the Pueblo and Kwakiutl, Amerindian traditions where there can be no question of diffusion. If this association is somehow a human universal, we are surely owed an explanation why.

The superposition of myths without regard to chronological order raises similar concerns. In drawing upon the Freudian treatment of the Oedipus myth, Lévi-Strauss comments that "a myth remains the same as long as it is felt as such."[13] That is surely a dubious criterion, especially in oral traditions where a myth may change slowly over generations, with no possibility of comparison between contemporary and early versions. It also appears to be inconsistent with Lévi-Strauss' abstention from structural analysis of biblical myths.

Finally, the level of abstraction that separates explanatory structures from the ethnographic facts raises two significant, related concerns. One is generated by possible alternative patternings that might be read out of the data. The difficulty is not dissimilar to doubts that arise about Freud's *The Interpretation of Dreams*. When one encounters Freud's highly creative interpretations, the thought inevitably occurs to one that sufficient ingenuity would be repaid by quite different ways of understanding the same dream material upon which Freud erects psychoanalytic theory. Analogously, it is hard to escape the thought that Lévi-Strauss' elaborate interpretation of myths could, with sufficient ingenuity, be shown to be but one of many possible ways of deriving structure from data. The bravura performances that yield the elaborate analyses one finds in his *Mythologiques*[14] are reminiscent of the gematria of the rabbis. An impression, created by the very complexity of analysis, that only one pattern resides in the data can be an illusion created by failure to realize the astronomical number of degrees of freedom, absent tight constraints, in choosing structural relationships.[15]

---

[12] Lévi-Strauss, *The Jealous Potter*, 162–63.

[13] Lévi-Strauss, *Structural Anthropology*, 213.

[14] A four-volume sequence: Lévi-Strauss, *From Honey to Ashes*, trans. John Weightman and Doreen Weightman (1966; repr., New York: Harper and Row, 1973); *The Origin of Table Manners*, trans. John Weightman and Doreen Weightman (1968; repr., New York: Harper and Row, 1978); and *The Naked Man*, trans. John Weightman and Doreen Weightman (1971; repr., New York: Harper and Row, 1981).

[15] Most of these difficulties, as well as others with handling the ethnographic data, are discussed in some detail by L. L. Thomas, J. Z. Kronenfeld, and D. B. Kronenfeld, "Asdiwal Crumbles: A Critique of Lévi-Straussian Myth Analysis," *American Ethnologist* 3, no. 1 (1976): 147–73. For one of Lévi-Strauss' best-

The other concern, related to this one, is that structural analysis, as Lévi-Strauss practices it, appears to ascribe too *high* a level of intellectual industry to native thinkers and tries to moderate this difficulty by attributing much of the problem-solving attributed to mythical thought to inarticulate and subconscious processes—hence as *beneath* the level of reflective thought. Sometimes, a myth is interpreted as wrestling with what are plausibly understood to be real, lived problems faced by a society (such as, ostensibly, the social tensions created by matriliny and patrilocal marriage among the Tsimshian in the Asdiwal story). But often—as in the case of Lévi-Strauss' analysis of the Oedipus cycle—it is much harder to credit the driving "conflict" (between autochthony and sexual reproduction) with existential import. The worry arises, in short, that the peculiar genius of Lévi-Strauss' own thought processes has become universalized and projected onto the screen of human myth creation generally. There is no need here to minimize either native intellectual curiosity (which can pursue arcana for their own sakes) or creativity. But when a myth acquires a central role in the public discourse of a people, there must be a strong presumption in favor of a subject matter of commensurate importance.[16] I shall, in any case, take this to be the case with the biblical texts that I will discuss.

Given such extensive doubts about the validity of structural analyses of the sort offered by Lévi-Strauss, it will perhaps seem surprising that I regard his work on myth to be seminal and of high importance. Why do I make this evaluation? What is valuable and to be retained? What will I set aside in essaying my own analyses of biblical texts?

A first observation is that, in spite of the questions just raised about the under-determination of Lévi-Straussian analyses by the data, there are analyses that I think are suggestive and perhaps correct, even if the methodology suffers from under-specification. Other analyses—including his quick way with the Oedipus story—are less convincing. Altogether, I should hesitate to issue any blanket judgment on Lévi-Strauss' actual

---

known examples, see his structural analysis of the Tsimshian myth of Asdiwal in Claude Lévi-Strauss, "The Story of Asdiwal," in *The Structural Study of Myth and Totemism*, ed. Edmund Leach, trans. Nicholas Mann (London: Tavistock Publications Limited, 1967), 1–47.

[16] Lévi-Strauss displays some awareness of this matter, in another context (that of native thought about organization of exogamous clans). Speaking of structures that have "zero value," he writes,

> These institutions have no intrinsic property other than that of establishing the necessary preconditions for the existence of the social system to which they belong; their presence—itself devoid of significance—enables the social system to exist as a whole. Anthropology here encounters an essential problem ... with which it does not seem to have come to grips....This is the problem posed by the existence of institutions having no function other than that of giving meaning to the society in which they are found. (Claude Lévi-Strauss, "Do Dual Organizations Exist?," in *Structural Anthropology* [New York: Basic Books, 1963], 159)

analyses. But more importantly, his work has illuminated the possibility, indeed likelihood, that myths are not cesspools of intellectual confusion but encode reflections of a high order. Moreover, the project has stimulated others to develop certain basic structuralist ideas in promising directions. Here, I want to single out, as an example, another structural analysis of the Oedipus cycle, one that strikes me as far more promising.

II. Terrence Turner

In a somewhat obscure publication, Turner has done an extensive reanalysis of the Oedipus myth that is based upon a significant revision of Lévi-Straussian principles.[17] The methodological differences are two. First, and centrally, Turner pays attention to the diachronic dimension of the narratives, which Lévi-Strauss ignores. Second, Turner does a much more plausible job of connecting mytheme content to plausible social concerns, allowing us to see the myth as grappling with real, indeed existential problems (actual or potential) in Greek social organization.

Turner understands Lévi-Strauss' view that myth embodies two temporal aspects, one diachronic and one synchronic, to be a fundamental insight. But he puts this claim somewhat differently and more plausibly: diachronicity is the intrinsic concomitant of narrative structure, but the myth conveys truths that are valid for all times. He rejects Lévi-Strauss' artificial bifurcation of the diachronic aspect of myth into two dimensions, one "vertical" (the chronological ordering of events) and one "horizontal" (the ordering of the mytheme groups—groups 1/2/3/4 in our example). In the effort to synthesize the latter with the synchronic aspect of myth, the narrative dimension is left behind.

Having denied this bifurcation, Turner insists upon examining the diachronic structure of the narrative. But that structure, he rightly observes, is different from the structure of historical narrative, precisely in a way that meshes with the eternal (i.e., synchronic) truths the myth is meant to convey:

> The sequential pattern of the [myth's] narrative, although it is an irreversible form of temporal organization, is not "diachronic" in the sense of historical time (i.e., a relatively disorderly or randomized process whose organization is expressed in "statistical" rather than "mechanical" terms [Lévi-Strauss' terminology]. Narrative patterns are themselves highly structured forms, analogous in many ways to the

---

[17] Terrence Turner, "Oedipus: Time and Structure in Narrative Form," in *Forms of Symbolic Action: Proceedings of the 1969 Annual Spring Meeting of the American Ethnological Society*, ed. Robert F. Spencer (Seattle, WA: University of Washington Press, 1969), 26–68.

syntactic level of language (which is "synchronic" and part of *langue* as opposed to *parole*).[18]

The way this works, according to Turner, is that a myth is ordered as a sequence of narrative phases that stand in dialectical relations to one another. The myth begins with a stated or implied ordering of the social sphere that is (in principle) stable—a synchronically given order. Some event or action puts that order out of kilter. The point of the myth is to explore how a return to original stability can be made possible through various entrained alterations among the existing social relationships set in motion by the original perturbation: how can a de-structuring event be "erased"? A helpful analogy (not Turner's) is as follows: when an automobile suffers a breakdown, it is brought to a mechanic who takes the mechanism apart, replaces broken components, and puts it back together again. In the exercise of her skills, the mechanic enjoys a great advantage over those who would essay to repair major damage to a social system. The mechanic gets to *turn the engine off* while the repair is underway. But a disordered social system can't be similarly "turned off" during internment at a repair shop. Adjustments need to be made while the social system is running.

As a result, putting one part back in balance may require or result in putting something else into a state of disequilibrium—with the consequence that this new malfunction must in turn be brought under control (again with the "engine running"). Consequently, the Oedipus myth can be seen as a kind of social thought experiment: What would happen if a fundamental violation of social norms were to occur at the very heart of the system (attempted infanticide, actual patricide, and incestuous matrimony)? Could a social system that suffers *those* kinds of body blows somehow right itself? At what price? The narrative structure, then, will be one that describes oscillations of the social order as it careens from one sort of destabilizing malady to another. Resolution—and catharsis—is achieved when the narrative traces a path back to original order and thereby demonstrates the resilience of the system and its ability to self-heal.

It would be impossible to summarize in short order the nine-phase analysis of the Oedipus story that Turner offers. Turner does retain Lévi-Strauss' dialectical understanding of the "fuel" that drives a myth forward—only now, that dialectic is seen to play out directly in the diachronic sequence of actions in the narrative. In particular, Turner sees those actions as violating basic social norms, the ones that define synchronic order for Greek society. That order, in turn, ensures that further actions that "cancel out" the resulting disorder will violate social norms in an opposing direction, with the result that the social order teeters over into some opposing disorder,

---

[18] Turner, "Oedipus," 32.

and so on, until mediating actions result in a final restoration of order. The synchronic dimension—the social norms—in effect serves both to keep the system wobbling around a normative "center" and to guide it back to homeostasis.

In the Oedipus myth, the key social norms in play are, according to Turner, patriliny, norms governing passage from dependent childhood to independent adulthood (and then to old age), proper behavior toward kin vs. non-kin, and gender distinctions. Actions that affirm these norms are "positive"; those that violate or contradict them are "negations." In keeping with this logic, a "double negation" is said to "cancel" an original negation. To give an example, take the fifth episode in Turner's analysis—the one in which Oedipus, en route to Thebes to avoid fulfilling the oracle's prophecy that he will murder his father and marry his mother, meets his father coming in the other direction, refuses to give way, and ends by killing him.[19] Laos has a positive kin-relation to Oedipus as his (unknown) father. He has a negative relation inasmuch as he appears here as a hostile stranger who, in refusing to make way for Oedipus and striking him out of his path, is "attempting to negate Oedipus' generational and patrilineal succession." Oedipus cancels this negation by committing unwitting patricide, thereby making way for his succession to the throne at Thebes.

In the course of his analysis, Turner is able to bring into focus the symbolism inherent, *inter alia,* in two anomalous beings: the Sphinx and Teiresias. The Sphinx is anomalous in being both human (female head) and animal, in being both a creature of the air (it has wings) and of the ground (a lion's body), and as perched on a pinnacle or pillar (neither airborne nor grounded). As Turner sees it, the Sphinx is homologous, as a kind of anti-type, to Jocasta: taking the vertical spatial dimension as symbolizing generational status, we have a being that cuts young men off from generational passage by asking a riddle whose answer concerns generational passage. She (the Sphinx) keeps men "in the dark" about passage from child to adult. In this way, she perverts the mother's role, just as Jocasta perverts the wife's role. (So the Sphinx, defeated, commits suicide by casting herself down from the pillar, where she is "above" Oedipus, to his level, whereas Jocasta, having the riddle of her status vis à vis Oedipus revealed, kills herself via an elevation above ground [hanging].) Having killed his father, Oedipus is in a position to assert his manhood, even as someone whose social role has become thoroughly anomalous.

Teiresias is anomalous in being—unlike almost every other persona in the story—socially marginal as a shepherd and, more tellingly, in being a sequential hermaphrodite. He is also, like Oedipus in the final stage of certain versions of the story, a blind man who sees. Moreover, Turner

---

[19] Turner, "Oedipus," 43–44.

regards Oedipus, as committer of incest, as a social equivalent of the hermaphrodite, so there is a kind of equivalence between him and Teiresias, as there is between Jocasta and the Sphinx.

There is much more to be said about Turner's analysis of the Oedipus myth. In its favor, three remarks should be made. First, it gains considerable plausibility over Lévi-Strauss' analysis by respecting the meanings that are implicit in the narrative order itself. Second, it gains plausibility by exhibiting as the driving forces of the action concerns that lie at the heart of Greek social order (and, except for the first, in *any* society) and that Turner argues were of particular significance to Greek society during the social unrest that Greece experienced in the eighth and ninth centuries BCE—the time the Oedipus myth was composed and became a central part of the Greek canon. Third, Turner argues that this narrative achieves its effect upon individuals who hear it in part by allowing them to "identify" with Oedipus, inasmuch as it depicts struggles central to their own lived experiences and their own search for social identity and self-knowledge.

All this makes sense of the power of the Oedipus myth—not just its grip upon the ancient Greek mind but upon us as well. My reservations about Turner's analysis are primarily three. First, one might doubt some of the symbolic associations that Turner offers, and at a deeper theoretical level, the contrasted "negation" relations that he posits. The only way to judge these matters, I suggest, is holistically: How much explanatory power does Turner's reading of the myth achieve? Can analogous readings be given for (at least) other Greek myths, employing the same contrastive relations? And (of course) are there alternative mappings of the episodes in the myth onto a schema of relations and structures that are competitive in explanatory power? On this score, I will venture the opinion that at least Turner's analysis seems to be significantly more constrained by the data than Lévi-Strauss' analysis.

In spite of the apparently stronger constraints on analysis in Turner's approach—and this is my second reservation—there remain enough degrees of freedom to cast doubt upon some actual analytic moves; moreover, the effort to use structural linguistics (especially Roman Jakobson's analysis of phonemic structures) as a kind of scaffolding results in strained analogies that sometimes deploy sophisticated verbiage to say very little. An example of the latter: Turner takes the smallest narrative element for analysis to be a meaningful action, which in itself is a plausible analytic move. The simplest purposive action, Turner says, involves two interdependent components:

> One of these is the kinetic modification of the relationship between the actor and the object ... of his or her action. The other is the discrimination of the object ... in question from other possible

alternatives as an appropriate focus ... of the intentions and actions of the actor. The first (kinetic) component is metonymic or combinatorial in nature in that it initiates or modifies an association between one (or more) discrete entities; the second (discriminatory) component is metaphoric or selective. In any intentional (meaningful) act, each of these components implies the other: there can be no meaningful or intentional association without discrimination, but equally no occasion for discrimination without the dynamic context created by the requirements of effective action. The complementarity of the metaphoric and metonymic aspects of symbolic structures, and the principles on which they are based, may be a fundamental property of the general structure of the mind, as the structuralists have claimed.[20]

The obviously extended meanings of "metonymic" and "metaphorical," which Turner derives from Jakobson and Morris Halle's work,[21] are rather obscurely explained thus: A metonymic "component" or "axis" is one along which can be displayed varying combinations of two or more elements (in this case, apparently, the spatial arrangements of a scene involving actor and acted-upon). A metaphorical "component" or "axis" is one along which are displayed alternative discriminable patterns that can be identified and selected (in this case, items in an agent's environment). Even if this is not strikingly helpful, what Turner appears to be saying is that an action involves an agent's recognizing features of the situation in which she finds herself, forming relevant judgments about them, and then physically moving them by moving her body. Not only is this hardly groundbreaking, it is entirely inadequate as even a ground-level explanation of action, inasmuch as it leaves entirely out of account an agent's motivations or desires (to say nothing of her character, habits, or physical abilities). But myths are hardly unconcerned with actors' motivations. We will do better, for the most part, to stick to the homely truths of folk psychology when pursuing a ground-level comprehension of action in a myth. (At the same time, we must remember that the actions of mythical figures are highly choreographed, and motivational considerations may not always be in the forefront of the myth-maker's narrative purposes.)

A second example can be given from Turner's further treatment of a brief segment of the Oedipus myth—the usurpation of Labdacus' throne upon his death by Lycos, thereby disinheriting Laius.[22] Labdacus, Laius, and Lykos are arrayed as poles along three contrastive dimensions: adult/child, kin/non-kin, and natural/social. Their initial (normative, thus "positive")

---

[20] Turner, "Narrative Structure and Mythopoesis," 127.
[21] Roman Jakobson and Morris Halle, *Fundamentals of Language* (The Hague, Netherlands: Mouton, 1956).
[22] Turner, "Narrative Structure and Mythopoesis," 133–39.

relations are negated by the death of Labdacus. As Turner sees it, the first two contrasts have, from Laius' point of view, the metaphorical character of opposing categories; that is to say, "kin" is to "non-kin" as "natural" is to "social." Laius' relations to Labdacus and Lykos, on the other hand are, with respect to these two dimensions, "undifferentiated," hence metonymic. That is, Laius, as a non-autonomous child, has no one determinate relation to both the other characters (he is kin to one, not to the other), and thus, his place in relation to them is not determinately defined as natural or social. As Turner obscurely puts it,

> There are two adults, each embodying contrastive values as kinsman *or* non-kinsman, and predominantly natural or predominantly social; there is one child, who is not in himself differentially defined on either of the two dimensions of metaphorical contrast, but rather serves as a common focus or object of differentiated relations emanating from both of the mutually contrasted adult figures.[23]

Turner claims that the contrastive values (+, -) of all three dimensions are correlated. That is, a change—such as the death of Labdacos—that changes one relation (that of parent/child vis à vis Laius) from positive to negative will also change the other two relations similarly. (Lykos' relation to Labdacus goes from a proper non-kin relation as the king's retainer to the negative relation of usurper of the throne. His proper non-kin adult relation to Laius changes to the negative relation of dis-inheritor.) Thus, Turner writes:

> A distinction is made between what I called the "dimensional" component of content (i. e., a relation's attributes as involving kin or non-kin, child or adult, or natural or social qualities) and what I have called the "sign" or "surface" component, the positive or negative character of the relation. The point of the distinction is that ... a set of relationships of opposite signs but with the same dimensional content may still exemplify the same structure; this kind of structure-preserving transformation is ... an essential device of narrative structure, and is found in some form in all narratives, even (implicitly) in those consisting of a single episode.[24]

This last claim of Turner's is either a strikingly strong one, or in a way trivial. As a substantive generalization about *all* narratives, it would certainly require an enormous amount of empirical support—more, surely,

---

[23] Turner, "Narrative Structure and Mythopoesis," 136.
[24] Ibid., 139.

than Turner can hope to provide.[25] But there is an opposite fear: that the terms of the kind of analysis Turner is proposing remain so unconstrained that they can be tailored to fit any narrative whatsoever. And, unless Turner means really to be speaking only of myth (where the claim still remains extremely unsupported), this kind of analysis will not serve to distinguish myth from any other form of narrative discourse. This concern is not merely theoretical. Even given the dimensions which Turner chooses to use in analyzing the passage in question (and could there not be others?—for example, at the time of Labdacos' death, it would have been true that he and Lykos had speech, but the one-year-old Laius would have been speech-less, and so on), it remains unclear why he chooses to understand the contrastive relations in the way he does.

So, for example, Turner sees a relation of metaphor between the kin/non-kin and natural/social dimensions of his analysis: kin : non-kin : : natural : social. But why not see the relation between natural/social relation as metaphorically related to the child/adult relation: natural : social : : child : adult? For young children are, after all, relatively "natural" and not yet well socialized. This sort of arbitrariness in the choice of dimensions and relations between them must lead us to wonder how informative and general the kind of formal analysis Turner defends can really be.

My third reservation follows from the above concern and goes deeper. It seems clear that the Oedipus tale is an exploration in the dynamics of social crisis precipitated by norm-violation. As such, it does manifest a kind of dialectical structure, and Turner's analysis in this respect echoes Lévi-Strauss' proclivity for binary dialectical oppositions. But not all oppositions are binary (there may be more than two opponents in, say, a competition between scientific, philosophical, or political theories[26]). And it would be implausible to assume, without further argument, that all myths tangle with social polarities or wrestle as thought experiments with the implications of social violations. Turner does elsewhere provide another example, from the Kayapo of Brazil.[27] But that is a far cry from adequate support for a general claim about the business of myth.

---

[25] See also, Alan Dundes, "Binary Opposition in Myth: The Propp/Levi-Strauss Debate in Retrospect," *Western Folklore* 56, no. 1 (1997): 39–50. Like Lévi-Strauss and unlike Dundes, I am not particularly concerned to distinguish folktales from myths (as Dundes defines them), but I am in agreement with much of Dundes's critique of Lévi-Strauss.

[26] Such a competition can, trivially, be reduced to a set of binary oppositions; ,but such a reduction is typically not only cumbersome but ill reflects the sorts of holistic considerations that govern theory choice.

[27] Terrence Turner, "Animal Symbolism, Totemism, and the Structure of Myth," in *Animal Myths and Metaphors in South America*, ed. Gary Urton (Salt Lake City, UT: University of Utah Press, 1985), 49–106.

The upshot is that I shall consider myself not bound by any such presupposition in my analysis of the biblical narratives. This entails that I will not be committed to finding anything quite as abstract as the structures theorized by Lévi-Strauss or Turner. We should be on the alert for them, but we should not assume they are there. Thus, our method will be free to range over a wider set of structural possibilities. That incurs the danger that analysis will also be too unconstrained by our data, a danger we must be alive to. At the heart of our method will be the search for mythemes and their identification as symbolic markers in a narrative. We take such mythemes to gain their meaning by way of natural metaphor and prior contexts of use, and to contribute, by their placement and present contextual arrangement, to the creation of determinate intelligible meanings.

Moreover, while I consider universal claims about the aims of myth folly, I should agree that a dominant theme is systematic meditation on the norms that govern social existence. But this need not mean only affirming some normative ("synchronic") order in the face of disruptive forces. Rather than seeking a path to restoration of stasis, a myth might recommend a new, even revolutionary social order in the face of forces that have disrupted an old order, or threaten to. It might aim to condemn or demonize external enemies of a group, and so represent chauvinistic propaganda, without explicitly defending the "home" social order. It might, conversely, aim to promote or justify imperialist wars of conquest. And so on. At least one of these possibilities will engage our attention presently in connection with biblical texts. We should take things as we find them. In every case, however, we find the deployment of known mythemes, or intelligible departures from them, in the construction of a structured narrative whose meaning is a function of the sequential ordering of these mythemes.

III. Rites of Passage

In the remainder of this chapter, I will briefly present two major classic contributions to the anthropological literature, Arnold van Gennep's *The Rites of Passage* and Marcel Mauss' *The Gift*. Neither concerns the interpretation of myths as such; both will contribute in important ways, nevertheless, to our understanding of biblical narratives. Both take note of, and undertake to characterize and explain, social processes that rank among the universals of human sociality. All societies engage in rites of passage that are typically quite formalized and that exhibit certain common patterns. All human beings (unless completely isolated) engage in gift-giving, more precisely, in the exchange of gifts with other human beings. While often studiedly informal, this practice, too, turns out to run along rule-governed lines.

An understanding of the structure of rites of passage, especially initiation rites, will be of central importance to our study of certain biblical texts. Van Gennep was the first to achieve an effective classification of such rites and to note their typical tri-partite structure. Rites of passage involve, of course, a movement or transition from one realm to another, a passage that is socially marked by ritual because the realms themselves, and the distinction between them, are socially important. The movement that is marked can be physical movement from one socially defined precinct to another, as from sacred space to profane, domestic quarters to the "outside," or across jurisdictional (e.g., tribal) boundaries. More important for our purposes, however, will be transitions that mark the passage of natural persons or social groups from one social status to another. Of special significance are coming-of-age rituals that celebrate the conferral of legal majority to minors, inauguration ceremonies for kings, and the imagery associated with the birth of a new nation. These, we will see, receive particular attention in the biblical texts I will discuss.

Central to van Gennep's understanding is the view, first, that rites of passage form a genuine class of rituals, and second, that they have, with variation in emphasis, an identifiable three-part structure: *preliminal rites* (rites of separation), *liminal rites* (rites of transition), and *postliminal rites* (rites of incorporation). This structure is implicit in my discussion of transitions between social roles or positions in Chapter 4. Someone's social persona—the personage they embody—can change over time. Almost universal are rites that mark initiation into adulthood. A person is first ritually/symbolically "separated" from their existing persona and (often) correlatively from confraternal relations with a peer group of others who share that social status. Next, that individual enters a betwixt-and-between state, a state of transition during which they occupy no determinate social role and hence have no determinate social identity. This state, in turn, is accompanied by various actions and ascriptions that symbolize this fact. Finally, there is a process of incorporation into a new social identity: conferral of a new social status, new responsibilities, and, often, a new peer group.

Van Gennep notes that there are special cases, cases in which one or two of the three components of a rite of passage may be de-emphasized or submerged, usually for explicable reasons. He remarks, for example, that "first times" (e.g., a first marriage, a first initiation ceremony where there are periodic renewals) are typically celebrated with more elaboration than subsequent ones. A further caution is important for us to bear in mind.

As Radcliffe Edmonds remarks, it is important to keep in mind the distinction between rituals and narratives. A narrative may provide liturgy for a ritual, but the two are not the same.[28] We cannot assume, therefore, that narration of a rite of passage will display clearly the phases through which a celebrant must pass in an actual enacted ritual. Nevertheless, we can often detect, clearly enough, the use of rite-of-passage imagery in narrative contexts. This is most clearly apparent when a narrative helps itself to a set or system of symbols known to be characteristic of rituals of a related kind.

The symbolic language to which we will most often turn is language that is characteristic of rites of initiation. Of course, symbol systems can vary widely between cultures. Yet, there are metaphors that are surprisingly widespread—not, presumably, simply because of diffusion across cultures, but, in many cases, because of the aptness of the metaphors and the universality of the analogized experiences. So it is with rites of initiation and their representation as a process that involves a symbolic death and resurrection. I shall turn now to some examples provided by van Gennep, as well as a couple described by Victor Turner.

In rituals of adoption, the change of identity is marked in some Amerindian tribes by what van Gennep describes as reincarnation and by a change of name.[29] Again, speaking of Australian Aborigine tribes, van Gennep notes that:

> In some tribes the novice is considered dead, and he remains dead for the duration of his novitiate. It lasts for a fairly long time and consists of a physical and mental weakening which is undoubtedly intended to make him lose all recollection of his childhood existence. Then follows the positive part: instruction in tribal law and a gradual education as the novice witnesses totem ceremonies, recitations of myths, etc. The final act is a religious ceremony ... and, above all, a mutilation which varies with the tribe ... and which makes the novice forever identical with the adult members....Where the novice is considered dead, he is resurrected and taught how to live, but differently than in childhood.[30]

Similarly, in the Congo, during conferral of membership in a secret society, an initiate

> is separated from his previous environment, in relation to which he is dead, in order to be incorporated into his new one. He is taken into the forest, where he is subjected to seclusion, lustration, flagellation and

---

[28] Radcliffe G. Edmonds III, *Myths of the Underworld Journey: Plato, Aristophanes, and the 'Orphic' Gold Tablets* (New York: Cambridge University Press, 2004).

[29] Arnold van Gennep, *The Rites of Passage*, trans. Monika B. Vizedon and Gabrielle L. Caffee (1909; repr., Chicago, IL: University of Chicago Press, 1960), 38–39.

[30] Ibid., 75.

intoxication with palm wine, resulting in anesthesia. Then come transition rites, including bodily mutilation ... and painting of the body (in white [often the color of death], in red); since the novices are considered dead during their trial period, they go about naked and may neither leave their retreat nor show themselves to men....The trial period is followed by rites of reintegration into the previous environment....The initiates pretend not to know how to walk and eat and, in general, act as if they were newly born (resurrected) and must relearn all the gestures of ordinary life.[31]

Parallel cases are found by van Gennep from Melanesia, the Americas, ancient Greece, and elsewhere in Africa. Victor Turner, who makes considerable use of van Gennep's classifications, cites an interesting case from his fieldwork with the Ndembu, a tribe in northwestern Zambia. The highest rank in this society is that of the Kanongesha, the senior chieftainship. The Ndembu recognize two fundamental sources of social authority, the Kanongesha and the Kafwana, a kind of ritually potent moral leader. The Ndembu understand themselves to be an amalgam of an autochthonous group, the Mbwela, and an intruding group, the Lunda, who ultimately conquered them. The Kafwana is understood to represent the Mbwela as their headman. The installation ceremonies for a Kanongesha center around a small hut constructed some distance from a village, in which the candidate must spend a sleepless night, dressed in rags, with a ritually prescribed wife. Prior to entering the hut—understood as entering the realm of death—the candidate must undergo a severe "hazing" at the hands of his future subjects. The Kafwana wounds him and then, forcing him and his wife to sit on a mat, berates him:[32]

Be silent! You are a mean and selfish fool, one who is bad-tempered! You do not love your fellows....Meanness and theft are all you have! Yet we have called you and we say that you must succeed to the chieftainship. Put away meanness, put aside anger ... give them up immediately! We have granted you chieftainship. You must eat with your fellow men, you must live well with them....Do not be selfish, do not keep the chieftainship to yourself! You must not be killing people! You must not be ungenerous to people!

[T]oday you are born as a new chief. You must know the people....You must give up your selfish ways....You must not bring partial judgments to bear on any law case involving your people.

---

[31] van Gennep, *The Rites of Passage*, 81.
[32] Victor Turner, *The Ritual Process: Structure and Anti-Structure* (1969; repr., Piscataway, NJ: Aldine Transaction, 1995), 101.

After this, the Kanongesha-to-be must endure further humiliation at the hands of his future subjects. He must silently and patiently endure insults from anyone who has a grudge against him and wants publicly to air his or her resentments. He is regarded as a slave. He and his wife can be forced to do menial tasks. After a night spent as dead ones in the hut, they emerge to be celebrated as the new royalty. Two features of this installation rite are immediately apparent. One is that the conferral of the chieftainship involves, symbolically, a ritual killing of the candidate followed by rebirth. The other is that this ritual killing involves a dramatic repudiation of the notion that the powers of the chieftainship can be exercised for self-interested reasons. The Ndembu understand very well the temptations of power and the dangers of tyranny. Thus, they impress upon their chieftain-elect the imperative of humility and of the employment of the office in the service of those who lack power.

Paul DuChaillu reports an even more extreme example of the same kind relating to the coronation of the king of Gaboon, someone who was secretly elected:[33]

> I [DuChaillu] do not think that Njogoni had the slightest suspicion of his elevation. As he was walking on the shore ... he was suddenly set upon by the entire populace, who proceeded to a ceremony which is preliminary to the crowning and must deter any but the most ambitious man from aspiring to the crown. They surrounded him in a dense crowd, and then began to heap upon him every manner of abuse that the worst of mobs could imagine. Some spat in his face; some beat him with their fists; some kicked him; others threw disgusting objects at him; while those unlucky ones who stood on the outside, and could reach the poor fellow only with their voices, assiduously cursed him, his father, his mother, his sisters and brothers, and all his ancestors to the remotest generation. A stranger would not have given a cent for the life of him who was presently to be crowned.
>
> Amid all the noise and struggle, I caught the words which explained all this to me; for every few minutes some fellow, administering a specially severe blow or kick, would shout out, "You are not our king yet; for a little while we will do what we please with you. By-and-by we shall have to do your will."
>
> Njogoni bore himself like a man and prospective King. He kept his temper, and took all the abuse with a smiling face.

---

[33] Paul B. DuChaillu, *Explorations and Adventures in Equatorial Africa: With Accounts of the Manners and Customs of the People* (1868; repr., Ann Arbor, MI: University of Michigan Library, 2009), 43–44.

Abuse such as this both inculcates humility and reflects the idea that a king must be the servant of his subjects, willing to be first in self-sacrifice in times of danger.[34]

Turner takes the condition of liminality to be one in which an individual is reduced to a kind of minimal existence—he or she must become a kind of *"tabula rasa"*—"clay or dust, mere matter" which society then shapes into a new being.[35] The teaching imparted to a neophyte during this period is "not just an aggregation of words and sentences; it has ontological value, it refashions the very being of the neophyte." Here, without using the language I introduced in Chapter 1, Turner recognizes the performative force of these teachings within the ritual context. What, however, is the ontology of personhood that seems implicit in such rites of passage?

While the ontological commitments involved must inevitably vary from culture to culture, and a careful foray into the ethnographic literature would take us far afield, a few hints of interest can be gleaned from Turner and van Gennep. The two notions that deserve particular attention are resurrection and the loss or acquisition of a soul. Among various Australian tribes—for example, the Arunta, Kaitish, and Warramunga—a child emerges from the world of the dead, the ancestors. The Tishi on the Gulf of Guinea show a newborn various objects that belonged to dead ancestors; the object chosen by the child determines his or her identity. One can think of the choice as opening a path for that ancestor's soul to enter the child. Among the Ainu of Japan, it was held that the mother gives her child its body, and the father its soul. In a patrilineal society, this makes perfect sense if soul possession is a matter of social incorporation into the patriline, hence acquisition of a certain social status.[36]

Incorporation into a Kwakiutl totem group involves exorcism of one "spirit" and replacement by another:

> Among the Kwakiutl [a northwest Native American tribe] the previous (social) world is personified by a "spirit" which must be exorcized—a point of view which is identical to that of Christians who exorcize Satan at the time of baptism. The idea of death and resurrection is also present. Finally, for the Kwakiutl, incorporation into the group consists of the

---

[34] van Gennep instances one interesting case (the Ngente of Assam) and alludes to others in which the rites that celebrate birth exactly or partly parallel those that honor the dead. See van Gennep, *The Rites of Passage*, 49, 52.

[35] Turner, *The Ritual Process*, 103.

[36] For Ainu patriliny, see Brent L. Walker, *The Conquest of Ainu Lands: Ecology and Culture in Japanese Expansion 1590–1800* (Berkeley, CA: University of California Press, 2001), 77.

acquisition of a "spirit" who is the protector of the whole clan and is the equivalent of the Australian totem.[37]

Indeed, among various peoples, the acquisition of a soul occurs at the time a person is circumcised, baptized, or by means of some other ritual inducted into the social group. In this connection, it is of interest to consider the Greek *diamones* and the similar Roman notions concerning *genii*. The personal *genius* of a man (and *juno* of a woman) behave very much like souls, understood as social roles. They are acquired at birth, lost at death, and passed on through lines of descent. Places were associated with *genii loci*; these would not have been the same as human souls but could have been analogous insofar as places could be personified or assigned loci in social space. Strikingly, the Roman emperor's genius came to be identified with the *genius loci* of the empire as a whole, an idea that runs parallel to the identification of the medieval king's immortal body with the *corporation sole*.[38]

But if we identify the soul with a social position, it will be odd to speak of *this* as being the thing that is resurrected in an initiation rite. The initiate receives and embodies (typically reincarnates) a soul that may previously have belonged to someone else. But the individual who "dies" and is reborn is recognized as being somehow not only a new personage but also as the same person he or she once was—or so it would seem, if it is said of the initiation candidate that it is *he* (or *she*) who is then reincarnated.

It is not unlikely that van Gennep, or the ethnographers upon whose source material he depended, did not exercise sufficient conceptual care in their efforts to map native ideas onto familiar categories in Western thought. What emerges as sufficiently obvious, even so, is the recognition in all of these cultures that a ritual of initiation is marked by both continuity and discontinuity. An initiate, however temporarily disoriented he or she may psychologically become as a result of stresses induced by the rigors of initiation, remains, plainly, the same identifiable natural person from beginning to end. At the same time, that individual undergoes a profound social dislocation, entering the ritual process with one social identity, being stripped of it so as to become a "nobody," and then being clothed with a new social status—a new soul, in our parlance.

To a greater or lesser degree, such rituals articulate the extent to which social identity lies at the very core of a person's being, and they express the control that the social group asserts and exercises over the terms

---

[37] van Gennep, *The Rites of Passage*, 76–77.
[38] For the former, see *Wikipedia*, s.v. "Genius Loci," accessed June 4, 2020, https://en.wikipedia.org/wiki/Genius_loci. For the latter, see Ernest H. Kantorowicz, *The King's Two Bodies: A Study in Medieval Political Theology* (Princeton, NJ: Princeton University Press, 1957), 3–6, 379.

under which that social identity is recognized, conferred, and allowed to operate. Death-and-resurrection imagery, therefore, dramatically reflects a communitarian conception of full human personhood as fundamentally a creation of the corporate group. Indeed, it is a reflection of the fact that souls—social roles—are constituted by conventional stipulation and can have a mode of being that is determined by social rules in such a way that they need not in every instance be embodied by natural persons. Thus, we find on occasion that natural objects or artifacts can be endowed with souls or can embody the soul of a person. Both van Gennep and Mauss speak in passing of such cases.[39] Indeed, physical objects, serving as insignia of office or social position, can embody a soul and serve as an emblem or means of transfer from one holder of that social position to his or her successor. Thus, Durkheim finds exactly this role for the *churingas* (inscribed flat stones or pieces of wood) of the Aborigine tribes of central Australia. They are identified with the bodies of those who receive them upon initiation and are invested with the soul of an ancestor. Initiation transfers, or invests in a descendent, the soul of this ancestor, who previously possessed that sacred ritual object.[40]

Particularly interesting—though he is not concerned with initiation rites—is Durkheim's discussion of the Aborigine beliefs concerning the origin and fate of souls. Individuals who are members of a clan—say an emu clan—see themselves as descended from a set of original ancestors who have a mixed nature, both animal and human. When an emu-ancestor dies and goes underground, it leaves an embodiment of its immortal soul in the landscape. This can be a tree, a rock, a pool of water, etc., called a *ngarra*.[41] This soul becomes invested in soul-embryos, *ratapa*, that lie in wait, as it were, for a pregnant woman of the proper station in the emu clan to pass by, at which point one of them inserts itself into the fetus. Alternatively, the subterranean ancestor may emerge and throw a small special *churinga* (a *namatuna*, apparently invisible, as are the *ratapa*) at the woman; it burrows into the woman and becomes a fetus. According to one ethnographer, Strehlow,[42] the *namatuna* is the body of the ancestor, invested with his soul, just as the *ngarra* is. Not some *part* of that body (and soul), but the whole body-and-soul thing, which is, as it were, able to replicate itself without becoming distinct things. In this way, the child comes to be identified with

---

[39] van Gennep, *The Rites of Passage*, 51; Marcel Mauss, *The Gift: The Form and Reason for Exchange in Primitive Societies*, trans. W. D. Halls (1950; repr., New York: W. W. Norton, 2000), 44.

[40] Émile Durkheim, *The Elementary Forms of the Religious Life*, trans. J. Swain (1915; repr., New York: Free Press, 1965), 279–91.

[41] As previously mentioned in Chapter 4. See Durkheim, *The Elementary Forms of the Religious Life*, 284–85.

[42] Ibid., 287.

the ancestor who contributed the *ratapa* or *namatuna*. Of course, only one living individual can be so identified with that ancestor at a time.[43]

Now Durkheim notes an apparent contradiction between what Carl Strehlow says of the fate of the Aborigine soul and the account given by the other main ethnographers, Baldwin Spencer and Francis Gillen: the former claims that after an individual dies, the soul ceases to exist after a few peregrinations. Spencer and Gillen report a belief in immortality. Durkheim resolves the difficulty by arguing that Aborigines distinguish between two souls. One, which is immortal, transmits the "person" of the original ancestor through all successive generations of his descendants. The other consists in the unique personal characteristics—the personality as opposed to the personage, if you will—of an individual. That eventually disappears.[44]

It appears, then, that the Aborigines are in possession of an astute and perceptive anthropology. Durkheim observes,

> The churinga is at once the body of the ancestor, of the individual himself, and of the totemic animal; so ... these three beings form a "solid unity." They are almost equivalent and interchangeable terms. This is as much as to say that they are thought of as different aspects of one and the same reality, which is also defined by the distinctive attributes of the totem. Their common essence is the totemic principle. The language itself expresses this identity.[45]

---

[43] Durkheim finds similar ideas among, *inter alia*, the Native American tribes of the Pacific Northwest (Durkheim, *The Elementary Forms of the Religious Life*, 285, 287, 304). One more example beautifully illustrates the point being made here:
Among the tribes on the Pennefather River it is believed that every man has two souls: the one, called *ngai*, resides in the heart; the other, called *choi*, remains in the placenta. Soon after birth the placenta is buried in a consecrated place. A particular genius, named Anje-a, who has charge of the phenomena of procreation, comes to get this *choi* and keeps it until the child, being grown up, is married. When the time comes to give him a son, Anje-a takes a bit of the *choi* of this man, places it in the embryo he is making, and inserts it into the womb of the mother. So it is out of the soul of the father that that of the child is made. It is true that the child does not receive the paternal soul integrally at first, for the *ngai* remains in the heart of the father as long as he lives. But when he dies the *ngai*, being liberated, also incarnates itself in the bodies of the children; if there are several children it is divided equally among them. Thus there is perfect spiritual continuity between the generations; it is the same soul which is transmitted from a father to his children and from these to their children, and this unique soul, always remaining itself in spite of its successive divisions and subdivisions, is the one which animated the first ancestor at the beginning of all things (Durkheim, *The Elementary Forms of the Religious Life*, 292).

[44] Ibid., 297–302.
[45] Ibid., 290.

The language of death and resurrection, then, serves as an idiom that vividly represents social continuity—specifically, the permanence of social structures—offices and the normative rules that govern relations between them.

It is not only individuals who can be conceived as thus reborn but entire groups that incorporate for the first time, or that conceive of their corporate existence as having been transformed, or as having been dissolved and reincorporated under a new social order. Van Gennep mentions only a few cases in passing: Amerindian tribes that absorbed nearby tribes by "adoption," and rituals (European, Semitic, and Australian) that separate a group of warriors and incorporate them into a distinct social unit for the purpose of engaging in a vendetta.[46] Although the data are sparse and the claim is controversial, some biblical evidence, together with ritual texts from nearby ANE cultures, has led some scholars to speculate that in First-Temple times, the kings of Israel may have periodically performed a ritual of renewal of the kingdom and the kingship. The king is supposed to have entered the holy of holies and, seated upon Yahweh's throne and impersonating him, to have ritually reenacted the seven days of creation.[47] A number of royal psalms, certainly, appear to depict a royal descent into Sheol and resurrection. I will presently argue that both the crossing of the Red Sea and the crossing of the Jordan into Canaan can be read as narrative enactments of rites of incorporation for the new nation of Israel.

IV. The Gift That Keeps on Giving

Marcel Mauss, a nephew, pupil, and close associate of Durkheim's, first published *The Gift* in 1925 (as *Le Don*); it came to have a major impact on anthropological thinking. As Mary Douglas points out in her introduction to the English edition,[48] Mauss' work was also intended as a contribution to the debate over individualist versus communitarian conceptions of social ontology. Mauss sought nothing less than to discover the fundamental social "glue" that bound human beings together into organic unities—social groups. The individualist perspective is that this glue must be understood as fundamentally contractual in nature. Focusing on economic exchange, Mauss considered the distinction between commercial transactions (which may involve either barter or monetary purchase) and gift-giving. The former is overtly contractual ("I'll give you this if you give me that."), while the latter is, formally speaking, a voluntary transfer of goods. Mauss' insight was that gift-giving is *not in fact* "voluntary," but that, unlike contractual

---

[46] van Gennep, *The Rites of Passage*, 39–40.
[47] For further discussion, see Chapter 11, §IE.
[48] Mauss, *The Gift*, x–xvi.

relationships, it supplies a much more fundamental and pervasive means by which social groups are bound together, one that both historically and causally precedes a monetary economy.

A. There's No Free Lunch

The most basic systems of human social interaction are systems of mutual exchange of gifts, according to Mauss. The giving of a gift creates a social obligation. The nature of that obligation may vary in its details, but the underlying principles are universal. The most basic of these is that, while a gift is ostensibly given freely and without strings attached, there ought to be a reciprocal gift that is given to the giver by the recipient. Reciprocation often does not occur immediately; a delay may in fact reinforce the illusion of spontaneity.[49] More importantly, it puts donor and recipient into a temporally extended social relationship. This consequence is not incidental. Indeed, so far from being incidental, reciprocation with a return gift now places the original donor in the position of "owing" one to the original recipient, and so on. Gift-giving relationships are the structural inverses of feuds.

Such a system of on-going tit-for-tat social interactions has a number of corollaries. First, gift-exchange is the fundamental way in which human beings express friendship and the desire for social alliance. There is a constraint. Friendship as peers—social equals—requires that, *over time*, the value of the gifts given by me to thee should roughly equal the value of the gifts thee gives me. If—again over time—there is substantial disparity, one of two outcomes will occur. Either the relationship will be broken off or it will evolve into a patron/client relationship, with the superior social status accruing to the more generous giver. Honor attaches to a patron, shame to a client. An overture of friendship is effected by offering someone a gift. There is, ordinarily, not only an obligation to reciprocate but an obligation to accept the gift in the first place. To refuse a gift is to decline an offer of friendship; more sharply, it is an implied insult and often an initiation of enmity.[50]

But gift-giving itself can be a means of social warfare, or at least serious competition. Mauss found this pattern in the so-called potlatch cultures of Native American tribes of the Pacific Northwest. These tribes (e.g., the Kwakiutl, Tlingit, Tsimshian, Haida, etc.) lived in an unusually

---

[49] See Mauss, *The Gift*, 35–36. He here argues that the economic notion of credit and, indeed, of outright purchase owe their origin to such temporally delayed reciprocations.

[50] I well remember the perils of visiting the home of my mother's aunt. She emigrated from Germany to Brazil and then, after many years, to the US. If one made the mistake of admiring any of her possessions, she would insist upon giving it to one.

benign environment in which both sea and land offered abundant natural resources, and the accumulation of wealth became relatively easy, even for hunter-gatherers. Tribal chieftains competed for social status. Such status could be achieved by inviting rival chiefs and their retinues to massive feasts, with the intention of displaying generosity that could not be matched by the rivals. Given the limits of consumption, there could be escalation to displays of largess that consisted of the destruction of valuable items—for example, casting them into the sea and even a resort to burning down one's own house. A chieftain who acted in this way might reduce himself to material poverty—temporarily, at least—but he will have gained immeasurable social capital. Mauss found more muted versions of this kind of social competition for "big-man" status in Melanesian and Polynesian cultures.

Important for our purposes are the brief remarks Mauss makes about the establishment of community with the gods and the natural world through a form of gift exchange. Here, the gods (and the natural world) are necessarily the more powerful and generous gift-givers—hence, they stand in a permanent patron-relationship to humans. Nevertheless, there is reciprocity, for that is what worship is. Native Americans see the natural world as giver of game and other means to survival. In return, they make offerings that return, for example, parts of the animals they kill to the natural world to ensure its continuing fertility. A similar account can naturally be given of systems of sacrifice devoted to the deities.

If, further, I am correct in suggesting (in Chapter 4) that deities were understood to be idealized forms of a society or of aspects of that society, imperfectly embodied in the group and its members, then we can understand such worship as service given to the normative structures that sustain the social order, service given to sustain and maintain that order to which individuals owe their social being. It will be fitting that such service consists both of symbolic actions that affirm and enact social norms and of material goods necessary for the functioning of governing institutions and the support of those who devote their efforts to institutional matters.

B. Some Implications

Among the significant influences of Mauss' work, we should mention the fact that it provided the conceptual framework for Lévi-Strauss' *The Elementary Structures of Kinship*, which offered a groundbreaking theoretical advance in the study of kinship systems. Such systems are, as Lévi-Strauss was able to show, created by systems of rules that regulate the giving of women (daughters, sisters) as wives to other men, and the attendant exchange of other gifts—for example, bride-price and dowry. Such rules bind groups into more or less permanent alliances, determine social status, jural obligations and responsibilities, and govern a host of other social relationships. Since, as Lévi-Strauss notes, women are the most valuable gift one man can give to another, the giving of a woman in marriage establishes a status hierarchy that ensures a higher social status for the giver vis à vis the wife-receiver unless and until the latter provides a wife for someone in the giver's family group or clan.[51] This is, then, perhaps the most fundamental sphere of operation of the principles of reciprocity and exchange that Mauss illuminated.

The principles of reciprocity and exchange that Mauss articulated have occasional exceptions that should be noted. First, and familiarly, there are the free-riders, those who cheat. They violate the moral norms. It is in everyone's interest (except theirs) that they be caught and punished. Second, there are densely populated societies in which people are brought into close quarters but have no sense of identification or solidarity with other individuals in the crowd, whom they will probably never meet again. Such circumstances encourage, for obvious reasons, a kind of self-interested competitiveness, in which each individual tends to focus upon ensuring, as best he or she can, favorable outcomes for him or herself. At the opposite end of the spectrum is charity. Mauss himself mentions the giving of alms to the poor, who cannot reciprocate. Here, as he puts it, the morality governing gift-giving has become a principle of justice. It involves a recognition that wealth is partly a matter of luck—hence itself a gift that must be repaid— and partly something owed to society at large without which, after all, the amassing of wealth would in general be impossible (a fact that the wealthy are often all too adept at rationalizing away).[52]

In some societies, there is a principle of giving that does not expect direct reciprocation. Perhaps the best examples come from what Lévi-Strauss calls "open" kinship-systems, ones that do not involve the direct exchange of wives between moieties but the trading of wives in a "circle": Clan A gives wives to Clan B, which in turn gives wives to Clan C, and Clan C supplies Clan A with wives. Of course, bride price travels in the opposite direction around the circle, partly diminishing the debt of each clan to its wife-donor clan. Nevertheless, this kind of system, called "open" because it can in principle be expanded indefinitely by adding new clans to the circle, has the peculiar result that Clan A has superior status to Clan B, and B to C,

---

[51] A telling elaboration of these principles has been mentioned to me by a Tanzanian friend. In his culture, payment of bride-price is the norm, but the full price is not initially paid; and it is understood that the remaining debt will not—and should not— ever be completely satisfied. The reader will readily discern the cultural significance of this custom.

[52] Mauss, *The Gift*, 17–18.

but also C to A. A similar highly ritualized example involving the trading of symbolic goods is the famous *kula* circle of a group of Melanesian islands.[53]

Even more interesting are customs that mandate generalized altruism. We usually (though not always) find generalized altruism in groups where there is strong group identification and the expectation of continuing interaction, and where everyone is vulnerable to significant threats to their well-being. In such circumstances, there is an evolutionary advantage accruing to a general willingness to assist those in need, without any expectation of direct reciprocity, but with the understanding that, should the vicissitudes of life strike one down, (some) others will come to one's aid. This is the "pass it forward" principle. Masai agriculturalists provide an example.[54]

There are good reasons to expect that something as universal as reciprocity has deep genetic/evolutionary roots. We have good evidence to show that these expectations are not disappointed, in the ethological studies of altruism and a sense of fairness in the social apes and, for example, capuchin monkeys and some corvids by Frans de Waal and others. I might add, finally, that personal experience confirms the notion that we are hardwired to be able to apply these principles, even in delicate situations in which one is entirely ignorant of the relevant cultural information.[55]

This essentially completes my survey of some of the tools that anthropology can provide to the study of the Bible. I shall have occasion, hither and yon, to allude to other insights from that quarter, most especially to the work of I. M. Lewis on mystical experience in my discussion of St. Paul (summarized in due course in Chapter 9) and the work of Mary Douglas and Edmund Leach. We are now ready to apply these tools to particular biblical texts. As an opening teaser, let me mention here Abraham's acquisition, in Genesis 23, of a burial-place for his family from Ephron the Hittite. The cave was located in a field, in the land of the Hittites. When Abraham, a foreigner, asks for the cave to bury his wife Sarah, Ephron essays to give it to Abraham, thus placing Abraham in a delicate situation. Abraham does not want to establish an alliance with Ephron (much

---

[53] Studied in the classic ethnography by Bronislaw Malinowski, *Argonauts of the Western Pacific: An Account of Native Enterprise and Adventure in the Archipelagoes of Melanesian New Guinea* (1922; repr., New York: E. P. Dutton & Co., 1961).

[54] See "Giving Without Expecting Something in Return Is a Key Part of Maasai Life," The Really Big Questions, February 24, 2014, http://trbq.org/giving-without-expecting-something-in-return-is-a-key-part-maasai-life/. Insurance is, after a fashion, a commercial counterpart.

[55] As, for example, I was when, at the age of seventeen, a newfound Kenyan friend of mine offered me, quite out of the blue, his sister in marriage. That we remain good friends to this day is a testament to the ability of blind instinct to navigate such treacherous shoals.

less client status), so he must decline the gift. On the other hand, as we know, such a refusal is regularly considered to be insulting; and Abraham needs to avoid enmity. So Abraham—who wants to buy the land free and clear (in "fee simple," as we say), has to do some delicate negotiating. It is quite telling, for instance, that Ephron, in agreeing to a sale, deprecates the price of the field (which is in fact quite high: four hundred silver shekels)— as if the gift would not have been a very substantial one. We can appreciate this delicacy once we have understood the principles of reciprocity and exchange.[56] We shall have ample opportunity to return to them in our analysis of Matthew's Passion Narrative.

---

[56] I am reminded of another case in which these principles led to public denial of the value of a gift. The !Kung San, are a hunter-gatherer people living in the Kalahari Desert of southern Africa. As is quite typical of hunter-gatherer cultures, their society is radically, and insistently, egalitarian. It is extremely bad form for anyone to display any sense of entitlement or superiority over others. (If, say, one is particularly expert at making arrows, one cannot claim credit for this. In fact, there is little sense of exclusive property-rights; thus, if anyone should ask the arrow-maker for a particularly lethal arrow he has made, he is obliged to give it to them.) Although, unfortunately, I have been unable to relocate my source, the story is that an anthropologist, as a farewell gift to express his gratitude to the !Kung San for their hospitality, bought a particularly fine cow from nearby herders to be slaughtered for a parting feast—only to find the !Kung San insistently deprecating the qualities of the beast!

Ascending Mt. Moriah

"Sinai—from where did it come?" Rav Yossi said: "From Moriah. As one separates challah from a dough, so was a section of Moriah torn off from the spot where Isaac our Father was bound to the altar to serve as an offering to G-d. The Holy One, Blessed Be He, said: "Since it was upon this spot that Isaac was bound as an offering, it is fitting for his descendants to receive the Torah upon it."" [And it shall return someday to Moriah in Jerusalem.]

Midrash Tehilim 68:9

Rabbi Abbahu said: "Why do we blow on a ram's horn? The Holy One, blessed be He, said: 'Sound before Me a ram's horn so that I may remember on your behalf the binding of Isaac the son of Abraham, and account it to you as if you had bound yourselves before Me.'"

Rosh Hashana 16a

In Jewish legend, the temple stood on Mount Moriah. At the focal point at the Jewish sacrificial system, the ark and altar were situated at the very center of the *axis mundi*. Above the altar, a column of smoke (which no earthly wind could deflect) ascended to the heavens, bearing an odor pleasing to the Lord. Below it, a channel descended to the *tehom*, the chaos-waters that, but for the capstone-altar, threatened to inundate Israel. And yet, the channel was the source of the life-giving river that originally watered the Garden of Eden and divided into the four great rivers that flowed from paradise. Thus, when God parted the waters below to bring forth dry land and plant the Garden, it was precisely Mount Moriah/Zion that situated this event. King David could control the level of the waters in the channel. Early Christian mythographers moved the *axis* a couple of hundred meters to Golgotha, where the cross stood as its new capstone (and by means of that channel, of course, Jesus descended into Sheol).[1]

---

[1] See Zev Vilnay, *Legends of Jerusalem* (Philadelphia, PA: Wish Publication Society of America, 1973), 5–6, 8, 64–5, 78–80, 92. Further legendary material relates that it is through the channel penetrating Mt. Moriah that the fountains of the deep sent up the chaos-waters to overwhelm the earth in the Flood, that it was from soil scraped from the rock that God formed Adam, and that Jacob dreamed of the ladder there

I aim to trace an arc at whose proximate end stands the temple and at whose distal end stands the binding of Isaac—a story in which sacrifice and terror converge with an intensity unsurpassed in Western religious imagination. How are we to understand the *akedah*? It is—literally—appalling. Johannes Silentius, in *Fear and Trembling*, is struck dumb. Elie Wiesel strives to wrestle the God of Abraham to the ground, but unlike Jacob, achieves—at best—a standoff. There is no dearth of others who have tried.[2]

I shall offer an interpretation of the *akedah* that is, sadly—even tragically, perhaps—deflationary. What, on my reading, is lost in depth and power is, I hope, partly recompensed by moral sanity. I will approach the *akedah* through the lens of the Passover story. And I shall motivate my approach to Exodus 12–13, and consequently to Genesis 22, by borrowing insights from anthropology, notably from kinship theory, from Mauss' just-discussed work on reciprocity and exchange and from Émile Durkheim's *Elementary Forms of the Religious Life*. The key idea will be the concept of substitutionary sacrifice and the hierarchy of social authority that it establishes and maintains—in this case, in a patrilineal society with primogeniture. My plan is to show how an understanding that the firstborn is owed to God, together with the practice of substituting a ram, establishes divine authority over each *paterfamilias* and, thereby, over the entire clan structure of Israel.[3]

Clearly, for much of its complex history, the Jerusalem Temple was, for most Israelites, the focus of an elaborate system of ceremonial worship of Yahweh and the subject of a rich tradition of symbolic representation of the ways in which Israel understood the various dimensions of its relationship to its Lord. One of those dimensions—arguably the central one—was a reciprocal relationship. On the one hand, Yahweh assured the flourishing of Israel, protection against enemies and, ultimately, successful fulfillment of an aspiration to world leadership among the nations. And on the other hand, Israel swore fealty, obedience to divine commands, and a steady stream of offerings provided in thanks and as repayment for divine beneficence and forgiveness of sins, as well as maintenance of temple purity.

Yet, functionally speaking, the temple's sacrificial system served a thoroughly mundane function as well. It demanded and collected, as I should

---

(Margaret Barker, *The Gate of Heaven: The History and Symbolism of the Temple in Jerusalem* [London: SPCK, 1991], 19; and see also below). For the Christian reconfiguration, see Joachim Jeremias, *Golgotha* (Leipzig, Germany: E. Pfeiffer, 1926), 34–50.

[2] Most notably in recent years, Eleonore Stump, *Wandering in Darkness: Narrative and the Problem of Suffering* (New York: Oxford University Press, 2010).

[3] I shall use the terms "Israel" and "Israelite" to refer to the twelve tribes prior to the destruction of the Northern Kingdom by Assyria and to refer to Judea thereafter. I shall also sometimes refer to Second Temple Israelites as Jews.

put it, Israel's income tax. Most of the offerings were devoted to sustaining the Levites, who were consecrated to Israel's civil service (Josh. 13:14), but the temple also provided for the poor in times of need and served other economic functions of state.

How are we to think of the relationship between these aspects of temple worship? Is there some sort of intrinsic unity between the practical, material functions of the temple institution and the symbolic/ideological superstructure that plays such a prominent role in biblical understanding of the temple? Putting the matter in terms of a familiar dialectic: do the sacrificial practices of the temple reflect the socioeconomic realities of material production and power structures in ancient Israel, which, in turn, spawned an (arguably spurious) ideological rationale to justify the existence and maintenance of the entrenched power structures? Or, was it Israel's adoring understanding of its special closeness to a divine Father that found expression in the creation and support of a theocracy dedicated to the obedient service of its God? In trying to understand the temple, shall we be good Marxists or (perhaps less good) Hegelians?

That dichotomy, I shall argue, is a false one. I will approach the question by way of an anthropological analysis of two biblical narratives that I take to be among the foundational stories in terms of which Israel forged her self-identity. Sacrifice is central to both. Moreover, I shall argue that they are closely connected—one must be read in terms of the other—and that their connection, in turn, sheds light upon the relationship between the material and the symbolic, between the material and the spiritual (if you will) in temple worship. The two narratives I will explore are, as noted, the Passover narrative in Exodus and the *akedah*, or binding of Isaac, in Genesis 22.

I must begin with two disclaimers. First, since I am neither a Bible scholar nor an anthropologist, I will be intruding upon foreign soil with the hope of not triggering deportation proceedings. Second, an ideal argument for my view would involve providing, *inter alia*, a unified structural analysis of the ritual calendar of the temple that would show it to have reflected a conceptual landscape that articulated at least some significant features of Israel's social ontology.[4] More precisely, such a landscape would have had

---

[4] By a structural analysis, I mean in this context an analysis that identifies certain units of meaning in the Temple rituals and/or in the written and other traditions concerning them and a mapping of the relations in which those units are placed (within the totality of the rituals/narratives—the structure) to articulate a "message" so as to illuminate the underlying significance and "logic" of the traditions. The *locus classicus*, as we noted, is Claude Lévi-Strauss' analysis of myths. But such an analysis can be applied to any symbol system that is used to "spell out" "cultural messages," as ritual systems characteristically do. For a nice series of examples, see Victor Turner's classic study of Ndembu rituals in Victor Turner, *The Ritual Process: Structure and Antistructure* (1969; repr., Piscataway, NJ: Aldine Transaction, 1995).

to provide a framework for the specification and justification of a set of institutions to which at least some ancient Israelites—presumably, pro-temple partisans—were committed. But that is far too large a project for this chapter to undertake. Nor do I have such a structural analysis to offer at this point. What I can and shall attempt amounts only to an initial foray by way of a structural analysis of the law that demands devotion of the firstborn to Yahweh. First, however, I must show that the temple served as the Internal Revenue Service for ancient Israel, among the other functions it served that we now would think of as secular functions of the state.

I. Stocking the Larder

The building of the First Temple by Solomon was directly associated with the centralization and regularizing of social authority in ancient Israel, a process that was contested and perhaps never as fully accomplished as some wished. On what we think of as the secular level, we have Israel accepting the transition from charismatic judges to the kingship of Saul and contests over royal succession that appear to have been perennial.[5] On what we think of as the "religious level," we have recurrent concern over Israel's "whoring after foreign gods," both in the royal house and, in rural Israel, in the form of worship at local shrines dedicated to local and/or Canaanite deities.[6] Nevertheless, the temple was at the center of the Yahweh cult and, simultaneously, probably the most important administrative and economic institution of ancient Israel.[7]

---

[5] But with abundant second thoughts attributed to Samuel and to a succession of prophetic voices.

[6] Much prophetic anger was directed, respecting the former matter, against royal marriage with foreign wives who imported their religious cults into Israel. Such intermarriage was (and remains in many societies) a primary way to forge political alliances. Here, as I believe almost always, the religious and the political are (at a minimum) deeply intertwined. For evidence that this conjunction of the religious with the political was also a central feature of the attack on indigenous pagan worship, see Israel Finkelstein and Neil Asher Silberman, "Temple and Dynasty: Hezekiah, the Remaking of Judah and the Rise of the Pan-Israelite Ideology," *Journal for the Study of the Old Testament* 30, no. 3 (2006): 259–85, which argues that, in fact, "the cult 'reform' in the days of Hezekiah ... was actually a domestic political endeavor. It was an important step in the increasing power of the Davidic king and his entourage in Jerusalem, in the remaking of Judah in time of a demographic upheaval, and in the rise of Judah to full statehood" (p. 275).

[7] This is so even making allowance for evidence that at times in its history, the Temple was not YHWH's sole or primary abode, and that at times, he may not have been the only god worshipped there.

The scale and dimensions of the temple's economic functions in Israel are usefully surveyed by Marty Stevens.[8] Some of this requires guesswork, as the record of temple economic activity is incomplete. Where information is missing, Stevens has recourse to data from analogous institutions in other ANE societies. The temple personnel included not just priests but a wide range of laborers engaged in construction, maintenance, accounting, and other functions (from skilled craftspeople to tenant farmers who cultivated its fields and tended its herds).[9] These had to be clothed and fed. Although the temple received some income from its own lands, the bulk of its income took the form of monetary taxes, gifts, and temple sacrifices, both animal and vegetable. These included, among quite a few other offerings, payment for redemption of the firstborn son and all or part of offerings to redeem sins, peace offerings, showbread offerings, heave-offerings of dough, firstlings of domestic meat animals, and various offerings of oil, flour, wine, and grain—in short, all the various foodstuffs wanted to keep together body and soul of temple staff.[10] In return, the priests officiated over the offerings to Yahweh upon the altar (before eating much of what was thus offered) to maintain Israel's bond with its God.

But temple personnel did much else: they administered temple functions, which included serving as a national bank, collecting taxes for the king, and storing non-perishable food supplies to distribute to the poor in times of famine and presumably to hedge against attack by Israel's enemies. In short, they encompassed a major portion of the institutional structures that governed and served the needs of civil society in ancient Israel. As Stevens puts it:

> Certainly, the temple was a place for sacrifice and worship, but such actions were only a small part of the functions of the ancient temple. The temple was the central socioeconomic-religious institution in ancient Israel, combining the modern-day IRS, Supreme Court, National Cathedral, Congress, and CitiBank.[11]

Stevens concludes that

---

[8] Marty E. Stevens, *Temples, Tithes, and Taxes: The Temple and the Economic Life of Ancient Israel* (Peabody, MA: Hendrickson Publishers, 2006).

[9] Levites were excluded from the assignment of territory to each of the other eleven tribes in the Promised Land, but the Temple itself owned land, albeit illegally. See Numbers 18; Marcus J. Borg, *Conflict, Politics, and Politics in the Teachings of Jesus*, 2nd ed. (Harrisburg, PA: Trinity Press International, 1998), 14; and Stevens, *Temples, Tithes, and Taxes*, 68–9.

[10] See Alfred Edersheim, *The Temple: Its Ministry and Services as They Were at the Time of Christ* (1874; repr., Peabody, MA: Hendrickson Publishing, 1994), chap. 4, http://philologos.org/__eb-ttms/temple04.htm.

[11] Stevens, *Temples, Tithes, and Taxes*, 24.

worship is not disconnected from politics, economics, or sociology [*sic:* the social world]. If one central institution served multiple functions in ancient Israelite society, then society understood those functions to be integrated in life. Western democratic separation of church and state has artificially divided life into arenas of sacred and secular, divorcing economics from religion.[12]

That no such divide between the sacred and the secular was understood in the ancient world is now accepted wisdom, but I shall be arguing, *inter alia*, that it needs to be taken more seriously than it often is.

Though our attention tends to be drawn to the ritual/ceremonial functions performed in the temple as giving us insight to Israel's understanding of its special relationship to God, these observations suggest, at least, that a much broader conception of the temple's portfolio is in order; for, to put the matter bluntly, the priesthood served as (a major component of) the civil service of the nation, and the temple sacrifices were in-kind income tax. Even guilt offerings make sense in these materialist terms. A moral or legal transgression, after all, is an action whose visible, practical dimension is that it is in some way harmful to the social order. Damage done. Restitution is in order. Guilt offerings are like traffic fines.

Such a mundane understanding of temple worship will run up hard against our deeply entrenched ways of thinking about ancient Israel's Yahweh cult: its view of sacrifice as serving an essential role in mediating Israel's devotion to her god. In providing atonement, appeasement, and gratitude, it seems to ignore the force of sharp discrimination between the holy and the profane, between the pure and impure, between the royal power and the sacred priesthood (see, e.g., Ezek. 44:1–45:9). But this, I suggest, is a mistake: not that Israel did not make the distinctions just mentioned, much less that they were considered unimportant.

What I claim is that we tend to impose conceptual categories from our own cultural background—and especially our distinction between sacred and secular—that do not map onto ancient ways of thought. Peering through our own lens at the ancient temple, what we see is a distortion. In saying that the temple's sacrificial system served primarily as an in-kind income tax, I do not mean to be saying anything different than (I claim) an ancient Jew would have meant in speaking of devoting some of his cattle to the Lord. Thus, I am not claiming merely that the sacrifices served *functionally* as taxes (some on income, some differently gauged) but that they were so understood by Jews.

---

[12] Stevens, *Temples, Tithes, and Taxes*, 25.

II. Pleasing (or Appeasing?) Our Higher Selves

But such a narrow interpretation of the data courts various objections. One puzzle takes the form of the smoke ascending from the altar. Some portions of certain sacrifices were incinerated. An offering that has been reduced to ashes is not much use as provender for priests. And, indeed, the official story is that its purpose is to provide God with olfactory pleasure. What is the materialist to make of such an apparently wasteful disposal of valuable protein resources? The olfactory imagery suggests, on the other hand, that such offerings operate in some symbolical dimension, at home in the arena of theology. Or did Israel believe that a supreme disembodied Spirit somehow perceived and literally took sensory pleasure in the activities of the temple's functionaries?

Whatever else may be true of Israelite theology, it is indisputable that it provided Israel with a conceptual scheme in terms of which its world and its own national identity could be understood. To that extent, it stood in service to the demands of the mind and was responsive to the intellect's demand for an ontology that makes the world intelligible, coherent, to some extent predictable, and explainable by appeal to some unifying system of causes, forces, or agents. The demands of intellectual harmony are real: as Lévi-Strauss put it, speaking of clan totems, their central importance derives, not from the fact that they are "good to eat," but from the fact that they are "good to think."[13] Often, however, good to think can also be good to eat. Perhaps we can have our Marxist cruller and eat our Hegelian torte too. But there is no guarantee, and sometimes the demands of the body and those of the soul can come apart. What assurance is there, indeed, that they will hang together?

But hang together they must, at least where it matters, and it matters where theory must serve practicality. In many spheres of social life, this can be achieved by design. To the extent that a social group has control over its own institutional and legal structures, it can fashion them and the political theory that undergirds them with an eye to practical efficacy. But not every aspect of social life is malleable and amenable to creation by convention. In one domain above all others is this true: ethics. Ethics, by its very nature, must be concerned with the practical, with the consequences of human action upon human (and often non-human) life. But ethics also places theoretical demands upon us. It requires an intelligent grasp of human nature and the human condition, and it demands the systematic development of an understanding and justification of norms and general principles. Not just *any* old system of rules of behavior will meet this standard, no matter how

---

[13] Claude Lévi-Strauss, *Totemism* (Boston, MA: Beacon Press, 1963), 89.

efficacious in answering to certain practical demands, and not just any such system will withstand critical intellectual scrutiny.

So, in the domain of ethics, were certain objective demands are placed upon us that may require a good deal of practical trouble and sacrifice, things can come apart. The demands of morality may, on occasion, have dire consequences. And, on the other side, the more general demands of the intellect—the demand for a coherent, overarching conception of ourselves and of the structure of our universe—may clash with moral norms. If that happens, we have a universe that is at war with itself, a universe where meaning attacks meaning and symbols come asunder. We hope, of course, that the world in which we live is not a world of metaphysical chaos.

But then there is Abraham, who marches up Mount Moriah with his son Isaac. What are we to say? Every fiber of our being recoils against a demand to kill our own child, a child beloved as only parents can love. And anyway, we cannot just have parents going around killing their children, even if, somehow, such a demand would serve some symbolic function or align with some cosmic theory. The consequences would be ruinous, as indeed Ezekiel 20:25–26 explicitly recognizes. Here, if anywhere, the demands of the "material" world must defeat Abraham's theology. But practical matters aside, such a demand flatly violates moral norms as fundamental—and visceral—as any we know.

Yet, Abraham marches. Genesis 22 does not tell us what he thought—only that he loved Isaac, the child of his old age, the God-promised child. What on earth are we to make of this? Surely things have come unstuck? Surely, in some incomprehensible way, the system of symbols in which ancient sacrifice was situated as a meaning-conferring practice has gone off the rails with Yahweh's demand upon Abraham? Nor is that demand a strictly local imposition or Abraham its only target. We are not allowed to seek comfort in the thought that Abraham was a "special case." And not just because it is mind-numbingly hard to see how the unique features of Abraham's situation and character could make sense of *that* sort of demand, but because the demand to sacrifice the firstborn son is in any case extended to Israel generally (see Exod. 13:1–16; 22:29–30). But as we shall see, the command to Abraham must be read through the lens of the Exodus commands.

III. Systematizing Practice

Before we turn to such a difficult case as the *akedah*, where theology, ethics, and prudence appear to be at war with one another, let us first explore the hopefully more benign territory of regular sacrificial practices at the Jerusalem Temple. As we have seen, the temple's sacrificial regime was put in the service of a multitude of practical functions of the state. But all this was conceived in terms of a justifying sacred history and theology. I want, therefore, to examine the relation between theory and practice as they emerged in the Yahweh cult at the Jerusalem Temple.

In order to situate the argument within this broader context, let me reflect briefly on the conceptual dimensions of the Jerusalem Temple's sacrificial system. We will do well in this, I think, by following the lead of Jonathan Klawans, who suggests precisely that the Israelite sacrificial system must be understood as reflecting and putting into practice a conceptual system that is central to Israel's self-identity.[14] Klawans' approach is strongly influenced by Mary Douglas and by such anthropologists as Durkheim, Mauss, Lévi-Strauss, and Edmund Leach, as well as by J. Z. Smith. Klawans offers effective criticisms of much recent work that either dismisses the temple sacrifices as vestiges of a more primitive and superstitious form of worship—and often divorces an understanding of sacrifice from matters of ritual purity (e.g., William Robertson-Smith, Joseph Milgrom and others)—or positively repudiates it as a form of savagery (René Girard).

I shall not rehearse Klawans' criticisms here. What he hopes, rather, to achieve is an understanding of the temple rites that integrates sacrifice with concerns about ritual purity into a coherent symbol system that takes Douglas' work on the abominations of Leviticus as a paradigm. But the results Klawans actually achieves, while helpful, are disappointingly thin: they are at best a start. In particular, Klawans argues for two "organizing principles" that infused the priestly traditions of the Pentateuch: concern with imitating God and concern with "attracting and maintaining the presence of God within the community."[15] Thus, Klawans seeks to demonstrate that the temple and its activities were understood to be material copies of a heavenly, normative temple and that satisfactory imitation of the heavenly temple cult was considered essential to maintaining a proper relationship with Yahweh.

These are hardly novel observations. They are surely correct, as far as they go, but a much more ambitious task awaits scholarly inquiry, for Klawans leaves almost entirely out of account precisely the sorts of *details*, especially with respect to the ritual calendar, that would be expected in their content and relationships to provide a systematic representation of Israelite theology. A proper structural analysis of the temple's institutional features would show how sacrifice and purification, as actually practiced, expressed Israel's theoretical conception of its cosmos. If such a reconstruction were

---

[14] Jonathan Klawans, *Purity, Sacrifice, and the Temple: Symbolism and Supersessionism in the Study of Ancient Judaism* (New York: Oxford University Press, 2006).

[15] Klawans, *Purity, Sacrifice, and the Temple*, 48.

possible, it would then be possible to ask the further question that is posed by opposing Hegelian and Marxist explanations of culture. That is, we could press the question: are the temple ideology and the ritual practices that subserve it determined by economic forces, or do they have an independent grip upon the life of ancient Israel because they conform to some independent intellectual or spiritual demands?

Unfortunately, this task lies beyond my present competence to pursue, both because of its magnitude and because the meanings of many of the rituals are shrouded in mystery, not only perhaps in consequence of insufficient scholarly analysis but because a correct understanding may require knowledge of cultural background for which evidence no longer exists. Indeed, I must here make explicit a methodological limitation of this study. I will, for the most part, be ignoring the differences that must have existed between the rituals of the First and Second Temples.

There are two reasons for this. First, we have very little secure information about the First Temple period. The provenance of the texts from the Pentateuch upon which I shall mainly rely has been subject to intense debate as concerns authorship, dates of composition, and redaction history. There remains little consensus, but a growing number of scholars has abandoned the view that any of the sources faithfully preserve records other than short narratives from the preexilic period.[16] Furthermore, there is debate over whether to situate the Priestly, Deuteronomist, and other presumed sources in the exilic period, the postexilic time of contention over reconstruction of the temple, or after the temple had been built.

On the other hand, it would be surprising if the sacrificial regimen of the Second Temple did not substantially reflect that of the First, and equally surprising if there were no substantial differences. On the one side, it will be obvious that the First Temple must have had an organized regimen of ritual sacrifice. Moreover, it can hardly be doubted that both Judeans who returned from exile, and those who never left the land, must have retained substantial memory of First Temple practice during the roughly seventy-year period between the destruction of the First Temple in 586 BCE and the completion of the Second Temple in 516 BCE.[17] There may be some doubt over how much in the way of written records concerning First Temple history and practice ever existed (or remained after the destruction of

---

[16] See Jean-Louis Ska, *The Exegesis of the Pentateuch: Exegetical Studies and Basic Questions* (Tübingen, Germany: Mohr Siebeck, 2009), 97–164.

[17] At the same time, we must assume that the institutional structures of Judea must already have been under severe pressures during the four decades or so prior to 586, during which the nation was under serious existential threat from Assyria and then Babylon. And obviously, Temple practices would have undergone significant development during the more than 400 years that elapsed between construction of the Second Temple and its destruction in 70 CE.

Jerusalem in 586), but oral tradition would surely have kept alive memory of the traditions during the exile.

Allowing for all this, as well as the general tendency of cultures to preserve their traditions, it would however be a mistake to ignore the near-certainty that temple practices were altered in the milieu of the Second Temple, as they will have adapted to the disruption of the exile itself and to the political contest over whether the temple should be rebuilt at all. So, what was changed and what was not? Answers to that question are bound to be speculative. I will make no attempt to engage the scholarly debate over these matters. Instead, I claim that the Pentateuch *as we have it* articulates a system of temple rules and an underlying ideology or rationale that are, on certain major points, coherent and intelligible. It is a legitimate aim of scholarship to investigate these major themes and, while taking due note of such discrepancies as the texts present, attempt to uncover the explanatory cosmos within which temple sacrificial rituals played their role as expressions of ancient Jewish theology.

As I have noted, this is a much larger project than I can attempt. Here, however, are a few programmatic suggestions. To begin, we note three dimensions of the temple cult that offer material for structural analysis. First is the symbolic geography of the temple (its dimensions, orientation, layout, architecture, and component elements). Next is the symbolic history of the temple (its claim to be rooted first in a vision of Moses giving detailed instructions for the construction of the tabernacle in the desert, then in a vision given to King David, and then encompassing the many legends concerned with the construction and subsequent history of the temple, to a few of which I alluded in my opening remarks). And finally, there is the symbolic language of actual ritual (and other) practices associated with the ongoing life of the temple in relation to Israelite society.

I am, for starters, especially intrigued and puzzled by the significance of blood in ancient Israel's moral and ritual landscape. Here are a few of the facts that need accounting for: 1) Blood is sacred—hence, in some contexts polluting but in others sanctifying.[18] Contact with polluting blood must be countered with ritual purification. Above all, blood is *tref*; it must never be eaten. 2) Innocent blood spilled on the ground pollutes it. Such ground is cursed and sterile. It will not produce crops.[19] However, the

---

[18] For this dual nature of taboo substances in many cultures, see Mary Douglas, *Purity and Danger: An Analysis of Concepts of Pollution and Taboo* (New York: Frederick A. Praeger, 1966), 8–50.

[19] Raphael Patai, *On Jewish Folklore* (Detroit, MI: Wayne State University Press, 1983), 102–9. Acts 1:15–20 tells us that after his betrayal of Jesus, Judas bought a field with the blood-money and in that field, "falling headlong he burst open in the middle and all his bowels gushed out." As a result, the field, which came to be known as the Field of Blood, "became desolate." This arguably accords with the sterility tradition. Curiously, Mt. 27:3–10 provides a quite different story, even though it, too, purports to

blood of a proper sacrifice must be spilled on the ground (Deut. 12: 16, 24). 3) There are various rituals and rules that specify precisely how the blood of sacrifices in the temple is to be handled. 4) Because blood may not be eaten, its disposal or consecration to the Lord represents a significant "waste" of protein resources. Was temple sacrifice an exercise in conspicuous consumption?

Let me comment on each of these points, beginning with the last and first. Blood is not considered comestible in some societies (including our own); but in others, it is considered a delicacy or even a major source of nutrition. Blood sausage in Great Britain is highly regarded. A more extreme example is the bleeding of cattle by Masai herders in Kenya. Consumption of blood is repeatedly proscribed by the Pentateuch, and it seems that a river of blood must have flowed down the channels cut into the rock below the temple altar.[20] Wine libations flowed through another hole cut in the rock into an underground collection chamber.[21]

Why should this be? The explanation given by the texts is that the blood is the life of the animal. But why think that? And, granting it, why think it should explain the prohibition? As to the first question: one might naturally suggest that Jews inferred the connection between blood and life from the fact that the animal dies when the blood is drained from it. But this is at least hardly conclusive: death can easily result without loss of blood—for example, by strangulation. Indeed, it is through the conferring of breath ($ruach$, $n^e shâmâh$) that God vivifies animate beings.[22] But since bleeding an

---

explain the name of the field. In Matthew, Judas returns the blood-price to the chief priests and elders and then hangs himself. The priests buy the field to provide a burial-ground for foreigners. "Therefore," says Matthew, it "has been called the Field of Blood to this day." As there is no mention of anyone's blood having been spilled on the field, it is unclear how Matthew's etiology conforms to Jewish traditions concerning blood, though the episode does play a crucial structural role in Matthew's passion narrative. Matthew, of course, probably meant to suggest not that the field got its name from blood having been spilled on it but from its having been purchased with blood-money.

[20] Already in the Noahic covenant (Gen 9:4) and again at Lev. 17:10–14; 19:26; and Deut. 12:16, 23–27.

[21] Edersheim says that the blood was flushed via the subterranean channels into the River Kidron (Edersheim, *The Temple*, 31). The blood that washed up on the banks of the river was sold to farmers as fertilizer (see Mishna, *Yoma* 5.6). There having been no Environmental Protection Agency back then, this was no doubt sound practice. The dried wine was collected every seventy years and ritually burned (Tosefta, *Sukkah* 3.15).

[22] E.g. Ps. 104: 29–30. Blood and breath are of course connected in function, as engaged in transporting oxygen to body tissues. But ancient Israel did not know that. Nevertheless, the formula "the blood ($dām$) is the life ($nephesh$)" points to an intimate connection, in the eyes of the writer, between blood and breath. For the root meaning of *nephesh* is to breathe (*nâphash*); a *nephesh* is, literally, a thing that breathes. For similar speculations about the "meaning" of the blood, see William K. Gilders, *Blood Ritual in the Hebrew Bible: Meaning and Power* (Baltimore, MD: Johns Hopkins University Press, 2004), 17–24, 70–82.

animal is the specific means of sacrifice, and since the Lord, having created each animate being, can give what he wants and keep what he wants of its substance, one may imagine it convenient to suppose that he keeps the blood while permitting—after the flood—the consumption of the meat.

But still, why would God want to keep any part of the animal's substance? As it happens, Leviticus 17 provides, in this case, an explanation that hints at a quite mundane motivation for the rule. As this text elaborates upon the matter, any animal that is slaughtered for consumption must be brought to the tent of meeting (referring to the days of the tabernacle) to be offered to the Lord. Failure to do so results in bloodguilt and excommunication; conversely, the blood of a properly offered animal "makes atonement for your souls, for it is the blood that makes atonement, by reason of the life" (Lev. 17:11). This, of course, only pushes the question back a step: Why does the blood make atonement (and atonement for what, exactly?). Or, taking the further step, why does the life (of the animal) make atonement by way of its blood? This looks like a theological question. But however it is to be answered, the upshot of the rule is to secure priestly control over the consumption of meat, as the wider text makes sufficiently clear.[23] Here, then, we have another intersection between matters directly concerning social order and power relations and the ideology of justification.

---

[23] David Biale comes to the same conclusion (David Biale, *Blood and Belief: The Circulation of a Symbol between Jews and Christians* [Berkeley, CA: University of California Press, 2007], 9–43). But Biale argues, further, that *precisely the absence of a coherent rationale* for the restrictions on sacrifice shows that the priests were essentially concerned with the exercise of power (pp. 13–14). I think this gives up too easily on the idea that underlying the taboo is a coherent ideology of sacrifice. In any event, Deut. 12:10–27 clearly represents a pragmatic modification of the requirement centralizing the locus of meat consumption that reflects the expansion of Israel's territorial control: no longer could animals be transported regularly to the Temple for slaughter from everywhere in the nation. As Darren Slade has pointed out to me, many scholars translate the verb here, לְכַפֵּר, as *to purify*, applied to ritual objects, not supplicants. It is hard to see how that makes better sense of this passage, unless it is the animal itself that is cleansed. But it raises, in either case, the same question: Why does the blood purify (make ritually clean)? – all the more so, as eating it renders one unclean? And the answer, I think, is the same, whether it is the supplicant or a ritual implement used in the ceremony that makes for unfitness for contact with God.

IV. We Be of One Blood

So Mowgli to Kaa, after his rescue by the python, Bagheera, and Baloo: "We be one blood, thou and I," Mowgli answered. "I take my life from thee tonight. My kill shall be thy kill if ever thou art hungry, O Kaa."
"All thanks, Little Brother," said Kaa, though his eyes twinkled. "And what may so bold a hunter kill? I ask that I may follow when next he goes abroad."
"I kill nothing,—I am too little,—but I drive goats toward such as can use them. When thou art empty come to me and see if I speak the truth. I have some skill in these [he held out his hands], and if ever thou art in a trap, I may pay the debt which I owe to thee, to Bagheera, and to Baloo, here."

The cry for solidarity and assistance among the Hunting People in Rudyard Kipling, *The Jungle Book*. Note that the physiological image has a legal, not a biological meaning.

It is tempting to explain the elaborate priestly prescriptions and proscriptions respecting sacrifice and purity, especially as they concern sacrificial blood, as just so much window-dressing designed to obscure, or at least put a decorous face on, the exercise of power. But before we have the right to conclude that there is nothing more than authoritarian manipulation going on here, we need to consider whether there is some deeper significance to be found in the rituals and their legendary etiologies.

Let us begin by examining a ritual event that, in the eyes of a late source in Exodus, functions as the sealing of the covenant between Yahweh and his chosen.[24] Having received the Torah from God on Sinai and having taught his people, in Exodus 24, Moses secures the agreement of the Israelites to follow the Law and seals the deal with blood:

> [Moses] rose early in the morning, and built an altar at the foot of the mountain, and set up twelve pillars, corresponding to the twelve tribes of Israel. He sent young men of the people of Israel, who offered burnt offerings and sacrificed oxen as offerings of well-being to the LORD. Moses took half of the blood and put it in basins, and half of the blood he dashed against the altar. Then he took the book of the covenant, and read it in the hearing of the people; and they said, "All the words that the LORD has spoken we will do, and we will be obedient." Moses took the blood and dashed it on the people, and said, "See the blood of the covenant that the LORD has made with you in accordance with all these words." (Ex. 24:4–8)

---

[24] Cf. Jean-Louis Ska, *Introduction to Reading the Pentateuch*, trans. Sr. Pascale Dominique (Winona Lake, IN: Eisenbrauns, 2006), 201.

Considering Exodus' implication that the Children of Israel numbered well over a million souls, one imagines that the execution of this procedure must have cost Moses severe tennis elbow (he was 120 years old!). More seriously: what is the meaning of the lustration?[25] By way of contrast, we may note that the sacrifices in the temple did not involve any such sanguinary sprinkling of people.[26] Blood was cast upon the four corners of the altar, and the rest poured into channels cut below the altar. On one notable occasion, the sprinkling of blood (not on the people but arguably on God) does occur. During the Yom Kippur ritual (Lev. 16), the high priest takes blood from the bull that he has sacrificed to atone for his own sins and those of his house into the holy of holies and sprinkles it on the mercy seat and then seven times in front of the seat. He treats blood from the goat sacrificed on behalf of the people in the same manner. Then he takes blood from bull and goat and anoints the four corners of the altar as well.

Why these differences? David Biale notes that, unlike Leviticus 16, Exodus 24 makes no mention of atonement.[27] Here, rather, the blood is understood as the "blood of the covenant." But this is too hasty. There is no suggestion in Exodus that the blood expiates sin, to be sure. But we have only to recall the precise meaning of atonement—at-one-ment—to recognize that a sin offering is only one mechanism of atonement. Sin estranges, and something must be done to rectify the wrong and repair the rift. But unification need not be reunification after estrangement. It may be an act that unifies what was not properly unified to begin with.

And indeed, Biale allows that exactly this may be implied by the blood-anointment performed by Moses. We need but be reminded of the cry of the Hunting People. Moreover, Biale finds this "novel interpretation" in Philo:

---

[25] A similar act is performed by Moses upon Aaron and his sons to consecrate them for priestly service (Lev. 8:30). Moreover, Moses takes some of the blood from the sacrificed ram of ordination and smears it on Aaron's (and his sons') right earlobes, thumbs, and feet (Exod. 29:20). The meaning of this may be to consecrate bodily organs of the priest that especially pertain to liturgical functions Thanks to Darren Slade for this suggestion. The discussion in Gilders is helpful but not adequate, in my view (Gilders, *Blood Ritual in the Hebrew Bible*, 96–104). Isaiah 52:15 may contain an allusion to Exodus 24, thereby asserting that the Suffering Servant unifies (see below) the nations just as Moses unified the people of Israel with the sprinkling of blood: "So he shall sprinkle (*Heb.* nâzâh) many nations; kings shall shut their mouths because of him" (NAS). But the Hebrew is uncertain. The NRSV translation has "startle" rather than "sprinkle."

[26] With the exception of the purification ritual for a leper (Lev. 14:7), which also reunites the leper with Israel. Interestingly, another phase of the ritual duplicates the anointing of Aaron's ear, etc. (Lev. 14:14).

[27] "The blood that Moses sprinkles is not itself atoning ... but it signifies the fact that the blood of sacrifices is intended for rituals of atonement" (Biale, *Blood and Belief*, 49). Biale does not explain how this "signification" is achieved.

Why did Moses take that blood which was in the mixing bowls and sprinkle [it] over the people? By indicating that the blood of all [was] the same and that their kinship [was] the same, he wishes to show that in a certain way they were animated by one idea and nature, for on many occasions he puts the blood in the same class as the soul. Even if they are separated from one another by their bodies, they are nevertheless united by mind and thought, and they share together the divine sacrifices and victims, being brought from estrangement to community.[28]

Biale's suggestion that this understanding of the story is late strikes me as unmotivated. To be sure, Philo "spiritualizes" the basis of the unity achieved by the ritual, but let us see whether we can make some headway by understanding the symbolism in a more nearly literal way.[29]

"One blood" is a metaphor, but it uses the facts of biology to express a legal notion of social solidarity: my kin share a part of me, and we therefore share the mutual legal and moral obligations that make us "one people." Tribal societies are—by definition—societies that use kinship as the fundamental basis upon which to draw social boundaries and determine the duties that define standing as a group member and standing within the group. Though biological in origin and in root conception, kinship becomes, as noted, legally defined.[30]

If we think of the bull sacrifice ordered by Moses as a collective sacrifice representing or standing for the nation of Israel, then perhaps we may think of the blood from this collective source as joining together as "one blood" the individuals with whom that blood makes contact—which is exactly what their collective acceptance of the covenant gives legal form to. Or, to put it a bit differently: if the blood is the life of an organism, and we become one in blood, then we become one life (i.e., one organism).[31] This interpretation of Exodus 24 will appear to be, at best, rather speculative. Let

---

[28] Philo, *Questions on Exodus*, trans. Ralph Marcus (Cambridge, MA: Loeb Classical Library, 1953), 2.35.

[29] "Why does [Moses] say further, 'Behold the blood of the covenant'? Because the blood is a symbol of family kinship. And the form of kinship is twofold: one is that among men, which has its origin in ancestors, while that among souls has its origin in wisdom. Now he did not mention the kinship of ancestors and offspring, because it is also common to irrational animals, but the other as from a root grew wisdom" (Philo, *Questions on Exodus*, 2.36, pp. 77–78). Philo had his own reasons, of course, for making this move. But in so doing, he undervalued the tribal understanding of kinship: animals do not elaborate biology into legal relations.

[30] Thus, one may have a son or daughter by adoption as well as by procreation, and marriage, of course, creates affine kin. Many societies distinguish obligations to affines from those one bears toward consanguines.

[31] Curiously (perhaps) the Canaanitic god Baal, who represents his nation, is embodied in a bull.

us see, then, whether its guiding principle—that blood contact communicates the life of the blood-giver to the blood-receiver—can provide a consistent rubric for the interpretation of other sacrificial rituals in ancient Israel.

V. Cleansing the Temple

The cleansing of the temple by Jesus is reported by all four of the evangelists (Matt. 21:12–13; Mark 11:15–17; Luke 19:45–46; John 2:13–19). The episode has occasioned a good deal of scholarly debate. Here, I follow Bruce Chilton in taking Jesus primarily to have objected (as did the Pharisees) to Caiaphas' major reform of temple sacrificial practice. Caiaphas' reform concerned—at least on its face—primarily the logistics of sacrifice, and it appears, certainly in part, to have been motivated by practical problems generated by the large number of sacrifices that had to be performed and by the inefficiencies of the traditional way in which animals were brought by their owners before the altar in the inner court, given over to the priest, and then slaughtered. Most of the details need not detain us,[32] but the crucial innovation was to reassign the location of the vendors of animals for sacrifice to the temple's outer court.[33] An animal, once purchased, was handed over by the vendor directly to a priest.

This had two effects. First, it gave the priests more control over the sacrificial process. Second, it eliminated the step in the sacrificial procedure in which an Israelite, prior to giving his animal over to the priest, formally laid his hands upon it and led it into the sanctuary, thereby signifying his ownership of it. This latter might seem to be a rather minor detail. I shall argue that it was not. Certainly, many Jews of the day did not consider it minor. Chilton notes the fracas that broke out between the traditionalist Hillel and the priestly partisan Shammai over the issue.[34] The principle at

---

[32] For them, see B. D. Chilton, "Jesus' Dispute in the Temple and the Origin of the Eucharist," in *Sources of the Jesus Tradition: Separating History from Myth*, ed. R. Joseph Hoffmann (Amherst, NY: Prometheus Books, 2010), 253–71.

[33] The sale of such animals had previously taken place outside the Temple precincts (on the Mount of Olives). Animals were then escorted into the Temple by their purchasers. It will be obvious that, by the first century CE, it would have been impossible for most Jews who came from the more distant corners of Judea, not to mention the far-flung diaspora, to have driven livestock from their homes to Jerusalem—and to have arrived with blemish-free animals fit for sacrifice. Thus, the lively trade in animals that attended Temple ritual must have supplied a great majority of the animals for sacrifice.

[34] Chilton, "Jesus' Dispute in the Temple," 122–23. Carl Mosser (in conversation) has pointed out to me that Chilton's evidence for this dispute is rather thin (it comes from late sources: Babylonian Talmud tractate *Beza* 20a, b; *Tosephta Chagigah* 2:11; Jerusalem Talmud tractate *Chagigah* 2:3; *Beza* 2:4). Mosser suggests that Jesus' actions should be interpreted as an effort to enforce a strict—and disputed—position that the new Herodian outer court should, like the more interior parts of the Temple, be

stake was that one who offered a sacrifice received some benefit from the Lord in return for the offering. But this would be proper only if the giving of the gift were in fact a sacrifice for the giver (i.e., if the giver suffered the loss of something he previously owned).[35] The laying-on of hands was a ritual expression of this: it publicly said, "This that I offer is mine."

I want to argue now that it also did something more than this. My suggestion is that, in laying his hands upon the goat or sheep, a Jew was symbolically claiming to identify his own blood—his own life—with the blood of the animal.[36] The efficacy of the sacrament lay not merely in the value of the livestock as meat for the priests but as a conduit through which his life could be reconnected to the divine presence with the sprinkling of its blood upon the altar. In the pouring out of the animal's blood upon the corners of the altar, the communicant is, in a partial and symbolic way, returning his life, which he owes to God, back to God. That is why the blood must not be eaten. And that is why an animal sacrifice makes atonement, even when it is not a sin offering, for it reunites a worshipper with his god, and his god's chosen people, to whom his life is owed.

We see some hint of this idea of transference to an animal of attributes of a person in the Yom Kippur rite of laying-on of hands, in which the high priest transfers the sins of Israel—corporately understood, I think—to the scapegoat by placing his hands upon the goat's head. We find further hints of the idea of the saving transfer of human life and blood to the deity in later portrayals of God himself taking vengeance upon Israel's enemies while clad in a cloak stained red with the blood of martyrs. Already at Isaiah 63:1–2, we find:

> Who is this that comes from Edom, in crimsoned garments from Bozrah, he that is glorious in his apparel, marching in the greatness of his

---

considered sacred space where the Shabbat prohibition against work was to be observed at all times. Hence, the carrying of animals by lay-persons was forbidden. But for further details, see also B. D. Chilton, *The Temple of Jesus: His Sacrificial Program Within a Cultural History of Sacrifice* (University Park, PA: Pennsylvania State University Press, 1992), 113–36.

[35] So Alfred Edersheim: "It was a first principle that every sacrifice must be of such things as had belonged to the offerer. None other could represent him or take his place before God. Hence the Pharisees were right when, in opposition to the Sadducees, they carried it that all public sacrifices (which were offered for the nation as a whole) should be purchased, not from voluntary contributions, but from the regular Temple revenues" (Edersheim, *The Temple*, 78). See, e.g., Lev. 3:7–8; 7:29–30, *et passim*.

[36] Symbolic identification is one way to understand the relation between the celebrant's life and the blood of the animal. But I believe the connection may have been stronger than that; see below.

strength? "It is I, announcing vindication, mighty to save." Why is thy apparel red, and thy garments like his that treads in the wine press?[37]

Thus, in attacking the temple's new ritual organization, Jesus is reaffirming the principle that ownership and blood/life identity between sacrificer and sacrificed are essential to the redemptive efficacy of gifts given to God. This principle, indeed, goes on to play a crucial role in the soteriological economy of Jesus' own death. Here I aim to focus not on the ownership question but on the identity question.[38]

Chilton goes on to argue—and I would agree—that Jesus' temple action would have been in itself a lesser provocation for the temple establishment than his institution of the Eucharist at the Last Supper, for *there*, Jesus effectively does away with the institution of temple sacrifice altogether, substituting for it a redemptive ontology centered on his own being and crucifixion.[39] One might wonder, then, why Jesus even bothered to align himself with the Hillel faction in his protest in the temple. One answer: he was on a teaching mission. A better answer, I think—because it looks forward to the meaning of his own passion—is the one given above in terms of an affirmation of the ownership/life identity principle.

One might further wonder, if one were skeptically inclined, how, as Chilton's reconstruction requires, the priests would have become aware of Jesus' heresy. For—in contrast to Paul's declaration to Agrippa (Acts 26:26)—this thing *was* done in a corner, in a smoke-filled back room as it were. Chilton's natural suggestion is that Judas ratted on Jesus. But, at least if the Gospel chronologies are to be believed, the plot on Jesus' life, and the defection of Judas, are initiated before the Last Supper. A simpler solution, in my view, is to place the focus on soteriological significance rather than narrative plausibility.

---

[37] The wine/blood metonymy is obvious. Isa. 63:3 confirms it. Cf. also, Joel 3:13 and Rev. 14:19–20. In Rev. 19:11–13, the heavenly rider of the white horse wears a robe "dipped in blood." Biale comments: "Although Revelation does not specify it in this place, its reference elsewhere to martyrdom makes it likely that the blood that soaks the divine rider's cloak is the blood of the martyrs" (Biale, *Blood and Belief*, 78; for other examples from the rabbinic and patristic literature, see pp. 74–79). So, e.g., when commenting on Ps. 116:15—"Precious in the sight of the LORD is the death of his saints"—Jerome writes, "The only fitting return we can make to Him is to give blood for blood; and, as we are redeemed by the blood of Christ, gladly to lay down our lives for our Redeemer." (Jerome, *Comm. Ps.*).

[38] For the former, see Evan Fales, "Taming the Tehom: The Sign of Jonah in Matthew," in *The Empty Tomb: Jesus Beyond the Grave*, ed. Robert M. Price and Jeffrey Jay Lowder (Amherst, NY: Prometheus Books, 2005), 307–48.

[39] In this, Chilton comes close to the view of E. P. Sanders, who takes Jesus' Temple action to symbolize the destruction of the Temple (E. P. Sanders, *Jesus and Judaism* [Philadelphia: Fortress Press, 1985], 61–76).

But to return to the identification of the sacrificer's life and the blood of the sacrifice: the appearance of this kind of imagery in Christian soteriology is not only at the center of the Eucharist but permeates the early church's way of imaging the relation of union between the Christ and his church. His body is the bread of life, and the church becomes both his body and his bride. His blood is wine. At Cana, he changes water to wine, as the vine in the vineyard changes water into the blood of the grape (and, as Jesus is the vine, the disciples are his branches [e.g., John. 15:5]). In his great final sermon in John's Gospel, when his "hour has come," (cf. John 2:3–4, and note the congruence with 19:25–30), Jesus articulates a series of (partial) identity-like relations (with the connective "is in") between himself, the Father, the disciples, and the Holy Spirit.

I said above that this can be understood as symbolic—hence not literal—identity. But I believe it may be possible to understand the relation to be metaphysically more robust than that. To confine the present discussion to sacrificial atonement for sin: can the relation between the life of the human being and the blood of the animal amount to something closer than symbolic identity? Clearly, it cannot be *real* identity. But there is a different model one might apply. In Chapter 4, we considered the relation between a work of art and its material realization. Here, plainly, the work cannot be literally identical to any of its realizations. Works of art, I suggested, are particulars that are embodied in the matter by means of which they achieve realization. Some of them can be multiply embodied, others not. It is important to observe that, here at least, embodiment is a consequence of the exercise of certain intentions, constrained by social conventions and institutions of certain kinds. In other words, it's a work of art in part because someone means for it to be and because that intention is successfully exercised within (and authorized by) the conventions, traditions, and institutions of the "art world."

I am a realist about works of art. I think they exist when people create them and (appropriately) give them that status. Along with works of art, Chapter 4 identified some of the many other entities that are not natural or physical things but are immaterial things, things that exist because, to put it crudely, people say they do. With the notion of embodiment in hand, we can consider the possibility that the social context of temple rituals allows for a supplicant to affirm (arguably even truly to affirm, if "life" is understood in a certain way) that his life is multiply embodied: in his own body, of course, but also in the blood of the sacrifice. This is not as crazy as it might seem, for we ourselves can, and sometimes do, confer a kind of legal or conventional personhood to inanimate objects (e.g., flags, icons) and to living things and social institutions (ecosystems, corporations, and early-stage fetuses).

But how, in the case at hand, is the plural embodiment of life, via blood, to be understood? That is, what understanding of "life" will allow the ritual enactment in the temple to achieve its alleged end? For if the life of the supplicant is understood in the ordinary biological sense, then of course no amount of ritual hocus-pocus can transfer *that* from worshipper to animal. *Life*, however, even in our own understanding, does not always have merely a biological reference, as some of the examples given suggest. Most saliently, (human) life is something that can be given *legal* status. Murder, obviously, is a legal notion: in a hypothetical state of nature, there can be taking of human life, but no murder. Thus life, as something protected by law, has legal status; and legal status, if not the life itself, is something that is conferred institutionally and sometimes ritually. In societies in which the killing of a foreigner is not murder, this legal protection is a corollary of citizenship.

More abstractly, we may say that a living human body embodies a kind of legal personhood whose qualifying marks and associated rights are institutionally assigned. The identification of *life* with *blood* already signals that we are in the land of metaphor—even if the metaphor here is still a biological one. In the protocol of the temple, the worshipper transfers, or rather causes to be additionally embodied, *his* social/legal status, or identity, as a Jew to/in the blood of the sacrificial goat or lamb. By extension, then, there is no reason why Jesus might not have sensibly been able to claim that his blood—in other words, life—becomes embodied in the wine of the Communion.[40] But the understanding of Jesus' passion as an atoning sacrifice faces a fundamental stone of stumbling, to wit:

VI. Imbibing the Blood of the Son

Every moving thing that lives shall be food for you; and just as I gave you the green plants, I give you everything. Only, you shall not eat the flesh with its life, that is, its blood.

Gen. 9:3–4

If anyone of the house of Israel or of the aliens who reside among them eats any blood, I will set my face against that person who eats blood, and will cut that person off from the people. For the life of the flesh is in the blood;

---

[40] Some might bridle at the suggestion that Jesus—or anyway the Gospel writers—were that metaphysically sophisticated. I disagree. The church fathers were not metaphysical naïfs. Why think their predecessors were? And anyway, metaphysically complex concepts can be competently deployed by individuals who cannot provide a philosophically satisfactory account of them. (In the previous chapter, we briefly mentioned evidence that the Egyptian political class, already more than 2,000 years earlier, had been deploying such conceptual tools with great sophistication.)

and I have given it to you for making atonement for your lives on the altar; for, as life, it is the blood that makes atonement.

Lev. 17:10–11

Then he took a cup, and after giving thanks he gave it to them, saying, "Drink from it, all of you; for this is my blood of the covenant, which is poured out for many for the forgiveness of sins."

Matt. 26:27–28

Vertigo. Jesus was a Jew; and although he may have been a revolutionary Jew, it seems impossible that his teaching should have turned upside-down a command that lay at the heart of God's covenant with Noah and with Moses.[41] Orthodox Christians accept the doctrine of Hebrews 9–10: 18 that Christ is the more perfect sacrifice, made once and for all time. How can it be, then, that we are to eat the blood of that sacrifice, and to do so repeatedly? If we are to make sense of this, it must be within the framework of the concepts that explained the blood prohibition in the first place.[42]

Of course, Jesus is not your ordinary lamb. He is a Lamb with Legs. His sacrifice, as substitutionary, is obviously more valuable in being the sacrifice, not of an animal but of a man, and so (at least) equal in value to the life of a man for whom the sacrifice is made: skin for skin. I will expand upon this theme presently. But here I set it aside so as to focus upon the equivalence of wine and blood and the rebarbative notion that the blood of the Christ is to be ingested, for even if that act is "only symbolic," it would seem directly in conflict with a Jewish understanding of the mechanism of atonement.

But perhaps not. As the perfect Lamb, whose sacrifice suffices once and for all, Jesus is understood to be the Lamb for all reasons. These are two: forgiveness of sin and the creation of a new communion with a new

---

[41] Whatever that might mean in a social context in which one can perhaps not identify anything like normative Judaism.

[42] It is plainly hard—and not for want of trying—to understand how, merely in consequence of an incantation, the *substance* of the wine can come to be identical to, or replaced by, the blood of a man, which is, after all, another physical substance and evidently long-gone to boot. But there is another possibility (among others usually thought of). Could the blood of Christ (not identical to the blood of Jesus?) be a non-physical substance capable of multiple embodiment in a physical substance such as wine? Well, why not? Here, we have one application of the embodiment relation whose ontology we articulated in Chapter 4. To make this idea work, something must be said about the metaphysical status of the Christ and his relation to Jesus (see Chapters 11 and 12 and briefly below). The notion that such an understanding might be possible is at least allusively hinted at by Biale when he writes, "While the blood of Jesus [or, rather, the Christ?] might be allegorized or spiritualized into 'rational' blood or the Logos, the same could not be done as easily with the blood of those [later] mortals dying for the faith" (Biale, *Blood and Belief*, 76). See also n54 below.

covenant. The consecration of the host at the Last Supper evokes the second of these, the death on the cross the first. Let us begin with the Eucharist. Jesus' blood is "poured out for the many" as the blood of the new covenant. This clearly evokes Exodus 24. There are differences: Exodus records a once-and-for-all event, whereas Matthew 26 (and parallels) were understood by the church as inaugurating a repeatable ritual. The Exodus rite used blood—the blood of bulls—whereas the Eucharist employs a surrogate for the blood, not of an animal but a human. The atonement-conveying substance is sprinkled in the first case, imbibed in the second. Finally, Matthew adds—as Mark and Luke do not—that the blood is poured out for forgiveness of sins.

Do these differences nevertheless bespeak a consistent use of the Jewish symbol system surrounding blood to convey a sensible salvific message under the circumstances in which first century Israel found itself? I think the case can be made. Setting aside for the moment the matter of forgiveness of sin, let us focus on the theme of union under a new covenant, the form of at-one-ment achieved by the ritual in Exodus 24.[43] When Jesus pours out his blood for many, I suggest that the quantifier should be read as referring to a collective, not a mere set of individuals. But, as previously noted, this collective includes not only (parts of) the old Israel but also the Gentile nations. All these will be forged into a new Israel.[44] Just as the blood of the bulls collectively represented the "one blood" that the Israelites share after Sinai, so the one blood of Christ represents the one blood shared by Christians (cf. 1 Cor. 10:16–22; Heb. 12:24). In both cases, moreover, the ultimate source of this blood is Yahweh himself, as Leviticus 17:11 reveals. In the NT, the vehicle for that gift is the King of the new covenant community. In Exodus, it is animals that are part of God's creation. There is no space to elaborate upon the (rather familiar) implications of this, though a major implication will prove to be a natural, and sufficiently obvious, corollary of Section VIII below.

Still, why not a sprinkling with wine rather than the drinking of it? We cannot rule out the influence of nearby pagan religious practices and symbols.[45] But it may not be necessary to go so far afield. In the temple

---

[43] The play on words here is adventitious, but illuminating. The Latin root, *adunare*, means 'to unite.' The Hebrew and Greek synonyms are not cognates.

[44] Whether or not the mission to the Gentiles originated with Paul (or someone other than Jesus), it is clearly present in the Gospels.

[45] See Morton Smith, *Jesus the Magician* (New York: Harper and Row, 1978), 25, 120 and Morton Smith, "On the Wine God in Palestine," in *Salo Wittmayer Baron, Jubilee Volume* (New York: Columbia University Press, 1974), 2:815–29. For a cautiously contrary view, see Carsten Claussen, "Turning Water into Wine: Re-reading the Miracle at the Wedding in Cana," in *Jesus Research: An International Perspective*, ed. James H. Charlesworth and Petr Pokorný (Grand Rapids, MI: William B. Eerdmans Publishing Company, 2009), 73–97.

rituals, blood is a gift exchanged between God and man: God has given men and animals their blood; and some of that blood, the blood of sacrifices, is returned to God by being poured out on the altar.[46] But for Christians, the altar is no more (literally, after 70 CE).

For Christians, the new covenant community is not tied to a particular locus of homeland or worship. The temple has become portable: as Paul says, the temple is within you (1 Cor. 3:16, 6:19; cf. John 4:20–26, 6:4–63, which celebrates the Passover seder in Galilee, not Jerusalem, and punningly Mark 14:14, where Jesus asks after the location [*kataluma*] where he is to celebrate the Last Supper. The verb form *kataluō*, which means to destroy or kill, is used in Mark 13:2, 14:48, and 15:29 to refer to the destruction of the temple, now understood as Jesus' body).[47] How, then, is the blood in this new situation to be poured on the altar, which lies within communicants? Perhaps it is not unnatural to identify the act of drinking the wine with the anointing of the altar within. Nor does this conflict with the basic ground for Yahweh's prohibition of eating blood, for that purpose is to reserve the blood as a gift to be returned to the deity. But in anointing the altar within, that is what the Christian achieves—and can only achieve—precisely *by* eating the blood.

These ideas are extended and reinforced by the identification of the bread—the "bread of life" (John 6:22–59)—with Christ's body: not, I should say, with the fleshly body of Jesus but with the legally ordained body of the king,[48] for, just as a corporate nation can be focally embodied in the natural

---

[46] One explicit function of the sanguinary anointing of the altar (and of blood-sprinkling upon the mercy seat and veil) is to make atonement for both the altar and the Holy of Holies on account of the uncleanness of the people, so it appears that this is also a purification rite and that the impurity of "the people" has somehow been communicated to the sacred precincts of the Temple. But how is the impurity transferred from transgressions occurring elsewhere communicated to altar and mercy seat, and how does blood-anointing effect purification? Within the conceptual framework I am proposing, these are not difficult to understand. The Temple is built by human hands, as the central vehicle for communion with the deity. It is provided by Israel to Yahweh so that he may live among them. But if Israel has lapsed into impurity, her communion with God has been damaged. It will be natural to represent that damage as a kind of defectiveness in the vehicle of communion. This allows us to understand, further, how the gift of blood can purify, precisely by making atonement for communion-corrupting transgressions.

[47] The Markan connections are pointed out by Richard C. Carrier, *On the Historicity of Jesus: Why We Might Have Reason for Doubt* (Sheffield, UK: Sheffield Phoenix Press, 2014), 423–24n72).

[48] The history of this doctrine is complex and sometimes confusing. The early (ante-Nicene) fathers accepted several formulations, typically without much theological elaboration or explicit philosophical analysis, that had to wait until the internecine ninth-century controversy. It did not help that in the ante-Nicene era, there were deep divisions within the church over Christology. In lieu of a full-scale discussion, I offer a few observations. First, early views of the Eucharist do give some support to the view articulated above, that the consecrated host is a re-embodiment of the Christ (not the

person of a king (so that actions of this person "count" as actions of the nation), so, conversely, the king's "immortal body"—that is, the legally defined royal personage that the king embodies—can be multiply embodied in the king's subjects.[49]

What, then, of forgiveness of sin? Although Matthew includes this as an aspect of Communion, the focus here must be, I think, the literal pouring out of Christ's blood on the cross.[50] This seems to mimic the

---

human body born of Mary)—e.g., some remarks made by Irenaeus, Tertullian, Cyprian, and Theodore of Mopsuestia, the latter two holding that the bread and wine are transformed by the descent of the Holy Spirit, which invests them with the divine. Second, it appears that there were pressures on how to formulate the doctrine from various quarters: from the dialectical demands of polemical responses to opponents, from concern to avoid a view according to which Jesus' human nature *per se* becomes an object of veneration, and from the actual worship practices of the church. These worries were interconnected, and the last, I shall argue in the final chapter, bore directly on highly political questions. A good summary can be found, with relevant citations, in Jaroslav Pelikan, *The Christian Tradition: A History of the Development of Doctrine*, vol. 1, *The Emergence of the Catholic Tradition (100–600)* (Chicago, IL: University of Chicago Press, 1971), 166–171, 236–238. At the center of the later ninth-century controversy stood Berengarius of Tours, whose understanding of the Eucharist seems not to have differed much from the one I have on offer. Berengarius was anathematized. The church held that in some way, the very wafer was transformed into the very flesh that was born of Mary. Here, Berengarius had the sensible side of the argument. Orthodoxy lapsed, for whatever reason, into incoherence.

[49] These ideas are explored in detail by Ernest Kantorowicz, who traced their line of influence upon the legal theories concerning kingship during the medieval era. See Ernest H. Kantorowicz, *The King's Two Bodies: A Study in Medieval Political Theology* (Princeton, NJ: Princeton University Press, 1957). But—as Kantorowicz notes—they predate Christianity and indeed form a central part of the theory of legitimate kingship (the mortal individual who serves as king is a subject of the immortal King whom he embodies). When rulers are perceived to have violated this constraint by claiming the right to independent authority, they are seen as tyrants and invite rebellion. Notable examples include Julius Caesar, Louis XIV of France ("L'etat, c'est moi."), and Charles I of England, who was stripped of his immortal body—it was then vested in Parliament—before he was beheaded.

[50] See Matt. 26:27–8 where Jesus declares that the wine "is my blood of the covenant, which is poured out for many *for the forgiveness of sins* (εἰς ἄφεσιν ἁμαρτιῶν)." (26:28). The first part of this accords well with Exodus 24: like the bull's blood, Jesus' blood is the blood of the (new) covenant. But Exodus 24, as previously noted, makes no mention of an expiatory function. That, however, does not vitiate the parallel so much as it simply adds a further element. And, in the NT context, that additional function of forgiveness makes sense. It does not conflict with this also being the function of the cross. The language is ambiguous, but I believe the *many* in the phrase "for many" (περὶ πολλῶν) should be understood collectively. Jesus is establishing a new communion, as did Moses, but one that radically reconfigures Israel, including some (but not all) of the old Israel, and some, at least, from the Gentile nations. All of these have been heretofore "in error," hence the need for forgiveness as well as for the effecting of a new union. Here, atonement therefore carries its double meaning.

pouring of sacrificial blood on the four corners of the temple altar, for Jesus' blood flows—literally—out upon the four corners of the cross. If we are to think of the blood on the cross as a sin offering, we will do well to bear in mind that in the Torah, sin offerings atone only for violations of the Law committed unawares or accidentally—that is, not intentionally.[51]

Christians have long understood sin primarily as an individual act of willful disobedience of God. But there was a long tradition in ancient Israel of collective responsibility for collective sin—the sins of the fathers (plural).[52] Indeed, the notion of collective sin and the need for collective atonement becomes quite explicit in the setting of the Yom Kippur ritual, where the slaughter-goat is sacrificed as a sin offering for "the people" (Lev. 16:15), and Aaron places on the head of the scapegoat "all the iniquities of the people of Israel, all their transgressions."[53] What is more, it seems clear that the Passion Narratives of the Gospels intentionally mirror the Yom Kippur ritual—at least Matthew's, where some ancient manuscripts, tellingly, give the name of Barabbas as Jesus Barabbas (that is, Jesus the Son of the Father).[54]

Nor is it clear that these sins had to be intentional disobedience by all, or even any, of the parties who are collectively to take responsibility for them. Indeed, the notion of collective, unintentionally incurred guilt becomes pervasive with the Christian conception of the fall and original sin. It is perhaps echoed in Paul's plaint, "I do not do what I want, but I do the very thing I hate."[55] I have no wish to deny that in the NT there is a significant emphasis upon personal sin and personal salvation. This soteriological concern makes eminent sense in circumstances in which old social identities are radically in question and qualifications for entry into a new social order must be established. But at the same time, especially as concerns Israel's claim upon a home in the New Kingdom, a matter that clearly obsessed Paul and, I shall presently argue, also Matthew (see Chapter

---

[51] Intentional wrongdoing could not be expiated in this way.

[52] The voice of the Hebrew Bible is not unanimous on this and displays tensions in Israelite thinking on the scope of corporate responsibility. See, e.g., Deut. 24:16; Ezek. 18:20; and, notably, Gen. 18:22–33.

[53] See also, e.g., Lev. 4:4.

[54] For this (ancient) reading of the Passion narratives, with Jesus of Nazareth as the slaughter-goat and Jesus Barabbas as the scapegoat, see Chapter 11. Something analogous to the ritual transference of sin to an animal, but in the context of individual rather than collective sacrifice, appears to be at play in certain Bengali sacrifices to the Hindu goddess Kālī by members of the Hindu Śākta Tantra cult. See Suchitra Samanta, "The 'Self-Animal' and Divine Digestion: Goat Sacrifice to the Goddess Kālī in Bengal," *The Journal of Asian Studies* 53, no. 3 (1994): esp. 793, 798–99.

[55] See Rom. 7:14–25. Paul may simply have had in mind weakness of the will. But I think his notion of slavery to the law of sin may have a deeper ontology than that.

11), it would be a mistake to underestimate the degree to which corporate salvation lay at the center of early Christian reflection upon the eschaton.

And so, if we understand the blood and body of the Christ not in its biological sense—as if the personage of the King is even capable of being so understood—but rather as a socially defined personage, then it becomes intelligible that the bodies of Christian communicants can, individually and collectively, provide a housing for that being, not merely symbolically, but in a literal sense. Although the natural man Jesus is dead, the Christ has not died—it is not the sort of thing that can be killed. Rather, it has been rehoused in the church where it can remain until the Parousia; at which point it can once again be transferred to a living natural man. It can even, at the same time, remain distributively embodied in the bodies of the faithful.[56] But let us return to the theme of blood sacrifice.

VII. Bris

In one of the strangest episodes in the Bible, God attempts to assassinate Moses. He has just twisted Moses' arm, insisting upon Moses' return to Egypt to liberate his fellow Jews. Moses is camped out along the way when God attacks. The onslaught is thwarted by Moses' Midianite wife, Zipporah, who, quick as a flash, wields her stone knife to circumcise their son (Gershom? Eliezer?).[57] Then she takes the foreskin, touches it to Moses'

---

[56] H. E. Baber, deploying John Searle's notion of *declarations* in *The Construction of Social Reality* (New York: Simon & Schuster, 1995)—i.e., performative utterances socially defined by constitutive rules—comes very close to my view in suggesting that the presence of Christ in the host is an institutional fact; H. E. Baber, "Eucharist: Metaphysical Miracle or Institutional Fact?," *International Journal for Philosophy of Religion* 74, no. 3 [2013]: 333–52). But Baber takes the host to *represent*, rather than embody, the Christ, which misses the fact that Christhood is itself an office socially defined and ignores the question what it might mean that the host is consumed by communicants. E. P. Sanders wrestles with the question how Paul understood what it is to "live in Christ":
> We seem to lack a category of 'reality'—real participation in Christ, real possession of the Spirit—which lies between naïve cosmological speculation and belief in magical transference on the one hand and a revised self-understanding [i.e., existentialist] on the other. I must confess I do not have a new category of perception to propose here. This does not mean, however, that Paul did not have one. (E. P. Sanders, *Paul and Palestinian Judaism: A Comparison of Patterns of Religion* [London: SCM, 1977], 523)

Indeed, is it too much to suggest that the category Sanders is at a loss to propose is the one I have been articulating?

[57] Eliezer is not mentioned until Exodus 18:4. His birth is not mentioned at all. Presumably, he had not yet been born at the time of the Exodus 4 episode.

"feet," and says, "Surely you are a bridegroom of blood to me!" (Ex. 4:25).[58] That does the trick.

How does Zipporah know what to do? And what was it she knew that so mystifies us? It may naturally be pointed out that Moses had failed to circumcise his son(s), thereby ignoring God's command to Abraham and all his male seed. But no further mention of circumcision is made in a tale spanning 400 years of history between the story of Dinah (Gen. 34) and Moses.[59] Nor could Zipporah be expected to know the commandment on her own. She was, after all, a Midianite. Presumably, Moses *did* know the commandment. Why, then, did he ignore it? And might not God have offered him a gentler reminder?

But perhaps these are the wrong questions to ask. They are the sensible questions, given that the Exodus 4 story is to be taken at face value. But if any story is not to be taken at face value, surely we have such a story here. So, let us back up and reconnoiter. Abraham is the first Jew, the first to receive the command to be circumcised and to circumcise all the male members of his household. And where did Abraham undergo circumcision? An old tradition tells us that it was on Mount Moriah.[60] By now, this should come as no surprise. What has been said about the shedding of blood leads us to suspect something more.

Circumcision is an initiation. It brings a person—ordinarily a child—into communion with Yahweh. He becomes a citizen of Yahweh's chosen people. Like baptism and, indeed, many rites of passage, I suggest that circumcision was conceived as a ritual involving death and resurrection. Here, indeed, an individual gives part of himself to God in a way that causes it literally to die. What we have is a "small death," a baptism in blood rather than water. One is born into the nation of Israel at the price of some of one's blood—life—that is given back to God, giver of life. As we shall see in the next section, such an act can serve as a partial ransom for a debt one owes one's God. Thus, the first sacrificial act (and, after the fall of the temple, the

---

[58] Apparently a euphemism for Moses' male member—cf. Isa. 7:20.

[59] But see Josh. 5:2–9, which indicates that all Israelite males who came out of Egypt had been circumcised. That those born in the desert had not been circumcised during the wanderings, but only after entry into Canaan, is itself curious. It signifies, perhaps, that they—and the nation they are destined to refound—remain in a limnal state until they enter the promised land. They had, however, been baptized with blood (Ex. 24:8).

[60] Indeed, on the site where the Temple's altar was later constructed. See Louis Ginzberg, *The Legends of the Jews* (Philadelphia, PA: The Jewish Publication Society of America, 1946), 1:240 and 5:233–34n126. Ginzberg adds that some early sources provide a calendar date of the thirteenth or fifteenth of Nisan—i.e., at the time of the Passover. Biale notes that the *Pirkei de-Rabbi Eliezer* gives Yom Kippur as the time of Abraham's circumcision (Biale, *Blood and Belief*, 71). The rabbis seem not ever to have allowed a symbolic opportunity to slip by them.

one blood-sacrifice for which every male Jew is held to account) involves the shedding of one's own blood.

Thinking of circumcision in this way, one is naturally led to wonder how the blood from this small part of oneself—tellingly, the part that makes possible future generations of Israel—is physically handled so as to mark a ritual offering to Yahweh. Zipporah, for her part, does something rather odd: she touches the severed foreskin to the male member of the child's father, remarking that he is now truly a husband of blood to her. What might this mean? Why, for one, does she not just offer the foreskin directly to Yahweh?

Two things should be noted straight off. The first is that Moses' sons are of mixed blood: they are children of a mixed marriage. It is true that Zipporah's father Jethro acknowledges Yahweh as the greatest of the gods, but that is only much later (Ex. 18:10–12). Thus, their standing as Children (or potential Children) of Israel might be questioned. The second is that coming into the presence of the Living God is a fearsome thing. Yahweh was not displaying his gentle mercy on this occasion. Zipporah was surely wise—or certainly reasonable—in not approaching him.

But this psychologizes the story too much. More instructive, I think, would be the answer to the question why Zipporah touches Moses' groin with the foreskin. As her remark makes clear, she intends blood contact. It is hard to be sure what the symbolic dimensions of this act are. The compression and cryptic narration of the story present obstacles. But the following at least seems a reasonable guess: it is in the person of her husband that Zipporah has the surest route of transmission of her gift to God. Like the later priesthood, Moses here mediates between the divine and the human. Moreover, the contact between the son's foreskin and Moses' groin affirms that both are of "one blood," and Yahweh's implicit acceptance of the gift—he abrogates the assault—affirms that the son is accepted into the tribe of Moses.[61]

There are further resonances with Jewish sacrificial traditions. Biale notes that in rabbinic tradition, circumcision was conflated with Exodus 24.[62] In medieval times, a cloth smeared with the blood from a circumcision was hung in the door of the synagogue, in conscious imitation of the smearing of the blood of the paschal lamb upon the lintels of the Jewish doorways.[63] The meaning of the latter association will become evident in the

---

[61] The fact that the story does not bother to specify one son or the other may signal the fact that the story is operating on the plane of symbolism. Conceivably, both sons are implicitly meant. And oddly, we never hear of Gershom and Eliezer again.

[62] Biale, *Blood and Belief*, 96–98.

[63] The Hasidic Rabbi, Menachem Mendel Schneerson, makes this explicit: the purpose of circumcision is to shed "the blood of the covenant." It is instructive to quote more fully:

This [the release of "the blood of the covenant"] is required even when a child is born as if he was circumcised. [³] For even a perfect Tzaddik must manifest Mesirus

next section. The former is a kind of inversion of Exodus 24 insofar as the blood of the sacrifice is sprinkled on Moses himself. One might speculate that it marks his induction into the project of re-founding Israel itself as a newly freed people/nation, an induction that he then passes on to Israel as a whole when they agree to the new covenant, as Moses here is conformed to the older Abrahamic covenant (albeit not as an act of choice).

The commandment to sacrifice the firstborn son and redemption of the son with a lamb both declare and bring into being, I will argue in the next section, the collective fealty of Israel—Yahweh's own firstborn son—to the Lord. This declaration of Yahweh's lordship was so central that it had to be affirmed, not only in every generation by way of the consecration of firstborns but also individually for every male, as the price of membership in Israel. This is the meaning of the circumcision commandment. Failure to obey meant excommunication.[64]

VIII. Sacrificing the Beloved Son

Jon Levenson has made a strong case for the view that an impetus to sacrifice firstborn sons to Yahweh was an enduring trait of ANE religious sensibilities, both in the pagan societies that surrounded Israel and in Israel itself. The Hebrew Bible itself contains many passages that reflect, or appear to reflect, historical memory of child sacrifice in the form of hints (given that the king is the "first-born" of the nation), of royal death/resurrection rituals (e.g. Ps. 18, 22, 30, 69, 89, 116, *et passim*), and deployment of substitutionary sacrifice (e.g., Exod. 13:11–16). They include narratives—most notably, the *akedah*, but also the Passover event in Exodus, the sacrifice of Jeptha's daughter (Judges 11), and of the Moabite King Mesha's

---

Nefesh, self-sacrifice. [For this reason,] the generation who entered Eretz Yisrael were commanded to recite the Shema, because—as explained in Tanya, ch. 25—["the observance of the Torah and its Mitzvos are dependent on the constant remembrance of Mesirus Nefesh"]. The release of "the blood of the covenant" is equivalent to Mesirus Nefesh, for as our Sages commented: [4] "Of what difference does it make if one is killed entirely, or partially." This surely confirms my suggestion that circumcision was seen as a "small death." And it suggests straightaway that Paul's opposition to circumcision as a requirement on Gentile converts is not motivated merely by a wish to provide Gentile males with an easier access to Christian salvation, or even by a rejection of the tribal-membership criterion for entry into the "chosen people." His rejection of circumcision is also co-ordinate with a commitment to the idea that Christ's death is the perfect and sufficient atoning sacrifice. (quoted in Lubavitcher Rebbi, "The First Mitzvah," *Come and Hear*, accessed June 15, 2020, come-and-hear.com/editor/br-painful/)

[64] Indeed, Jewish law came to recognize and to forbid ways in which an individual, having been circumcised, might then hide the fact—e.g., by surgical manipulation of the penile sheath to create a surrogate foreskin.

(2 Kgs. 3:27) sacrifice of his son. They appear in various symbolic elaborations upon the theme—for example, representation of Israel herself as God's firstborn son (Exod. 4:21–23, Hosea and Jeremiah), or of the Levites as standing in the stead of the firstborn sons, or of the king in this role. And, finally, they appear as direct commandments (most notably, Exod. 22:28–29; see also Lev. 27:28–29 and Josh. 6:21 but contrast, e.g., Num. 18:14–16; Deut. 18:10), to say nothing of the execrations of the prophets Ezekiel and Isaiah against the practice.[65]

The view that these textual deposits reflect historical practice receives support, moreover, from archaeological evidence, especially in the form of burial urns excavated in the valley of Tophet outside Jerusalem, that contain the charred remains of infants. The interpretation of these remains is, however, contested—in particular, whether the infants were sacrificed to the pagan god Molech, or were devoted to Yahweh.[66]

Levenson traces the history of Jewish thought about the sacrifice to God of the beloved son through its various refractions in the biblical literature and then on through later developments in the Deuterocanonical literature (e.g., 2 and 4 Maccabees) and midrash. But the focal story is the story of the *akedah*, both in its influence upon other ancient—in particular biblical—sacrificial narratives and as the subject of a long history of commentary and interpretation. In all this, one of Levenson's central aims is to reject the apologetic maneuvers that permeate much modern commentary. A standard way of softening the repugnancy of Genesis 22 is to see in it a story of *rejection* of an earlier—especially pagan—practice of child sacrifice in favor of animal sacrifice. On the contrary, Levenson sees in the *akedah* a reflection of a genuine affirmation that God has the right to demand—and does demand—the immolation of the firstborn son:

---

[65] Contrast, e.g., Deut. 18:10 "No one among you shall be found who makes a son or daughter pass through fire." It is generally assumed that the reference here is to sacrificial immolation. One wonders whether another interpretation is possible; viz., reference to a kind of ritual baptism by fire (like water, a symbol of death) that may have singed but not sacrificed. That speculation would, however, have to confront the evidence from the Tophet of burial urns containing burnt bones of babies, not to mention the Carthaginian evidence. See Lawrence E. Stager and Samuel R. Wolff, "Child Sacrifice at Carthage–Religious Rite or Population Control?," *Biblical Archaeology Review* 10, no. 1 (1984): 31–51.

[66] For the latter view, see Stager and Samuel R. Wolff, "Child Sacrifice at Carthage. Levenson tentatively accepts the former view. Bennie Reynolds provides support for latter view and a good review of the complex state of the evidence (Bennie H. Reynolds, "Molek: Dead or Alive? The Meaning and Derivation of *mlk* and מלך," in *Human Sacrifice in Jewish and Christian Tradition*, ed. Karin Finsterbusch, Armin Lange, and K. F. Diethard Römheld (Boston, MA: Brill, 2007), 133–51).

As an etiology of the redemption of the first-born son through the death of the sheep, however, the aqedah is ... most ineffective. For although Abraham does indeed spot and then sacrifice a ram just after hearing the gruesome command rescinded ..., he is never actually commanded to offer the animal, as he was commanded to sacrifice his only beloved son, Isaac. And, in fact, so far as we know, Israelite tradition never explained the substitution of the sheep for the first-born son by reference to the aqedah; it was the tenth plague upon Egypt that served that role, with the paschal lamb spelling the difference between life and death for the Israelite first-born males....The sacrifice of *that* sheep is commanded emphatically and repeatedly. But more importantly, it is passing strange to condemn child sacrifice through a narrative in which a father is richly rewarded for his willingness to carry out that very practice.[67]

One might cavil that the story at least surely *implies* that Abraham is to sacrifice the ram: clearly Abraham thinks so. Otherwise, he would not have called the spot, "The Lord will provide." However, what I want to emphasize here is that for Levenson, the exegetical crux lies in the recognition that, as the angel declares in its second speech, Abraham's merit lies precisely in his willingness to sacrifice Isaac. Not in his faith that somehow God will restore Isaac to him, and certainly not in his playing the required role in a divine plan to teach Israel the wrongness of child sacrifice. On the contrary: the angel's speech implies that it is only because Abraham was prepared to pass the ultimate test of obedience (as God presumably knew he would), that God's prior promise of descendants as numerous as the stars in the sky through his son Isaac could be fulfilled. We must note further Levenson's point that substitutionary sacrifice was understood in terms of the Passover story. To this we will shortly return.

However, the Passover story is but one of many stories in the Bible that resonate with the *akedah* and provide rich material for the interweaving and playing out of theological themes centered about sacrifice of the male heir. Indeed, it is in Egypt that Yahweh declares Israel itself—that is, the corporate chosen people—as his "firstborn son." The title came to be extended to kings (e.g., Ps. 2:7; 89:27; cf. Acts 13:33), but even more foundationally, the idea plays a role in the stories of Cain and Abel, of Jacob and Esau, and of Joseph (who is cast into the "pit" and sold to descendants of Ishmael for twenty pieces of silver). Not all the sacrificial victims are eldest sons; indeed, although Isaac is Sarah's oldest (and only) child, it is Ishmael (who himself suffers near-death and is saved by Yahweh) who is

---

[67] Jon D. Levenson, *The Death and Resurrection of the Beloved Son: The Transformation of Child Sacrifice in Judaism and Christianity* (New Haven, CT: Yale University Press, 1993), 13.

Abraham's older son. Levenson has much to say about the significance of all this, including the often-contested relationship between older and younger sons for the rights of primogeniture.

Inter alia, Levenson argues against "traditional interpreters and most modern critics ... that both the context [of Exod. 22:28] and the clause itself and the manner of presentation of child sacrifice in the Hebrew Bible [as similarly in Canaanite, Phoenecian, Greek, and Punic traditions] call for a literal interpretation: the Israelite father is to sacrifice his firstborn son to YHWH." In my view, Levenson has it half right. He is correct in rejecting the moralizing readings of apologetic interpreters that would see in the *akedah* a rejection of an earlier tradition of human sacrifice. But I believe that he also has it half wrong, as does an ancient tradition that he cites. According to that tradition, Genesis 22 provides the etiology for the Passover event. But this, I now argue, has things exactly backwards.

An early text that indirectly suggests the *akedah* as the basis for the Passover event is the mid-second century BCE Book of Jubilees. In a passage that dates Abraham and Isaac's ascent of Mount Moriah on the day later assigned to the Passover and traces a seven-day festival (= Passover) to the *akedah*, Jubilees explains God's testing of Abraham as a response to a challenge from a demonic being, Prince Mastema, who impugns Abraham's love for God as playing second fiddle to his love for Isaac.[68] The parallel to Job is patent—as, to put it mildly, is the dubiousness of this late rationale for the story. The use of Genesis 22 to provide an etiology for the Passover is made clear, however, in Jubilees 18:17–19 as well as in later texts.

This connection may, given the similarities between Genesis 22 and Exodus 12–13, be much older, in Levenson's opinion. Both traditions reflect "a cultic institution, pre-Israelite in origin and evident among the Phoenicians, which allows for the substitution of an animal for the child marked for sacred slaughter....Jubilees thus only makes explicit a relationship that had always lain in the deep structure of Israelite culture."[69]

---

[68] See *Jubilees* 17–18.

[69] Levenson, *The Death and Resurrection of the Beloved Son,* 177. As Levenson vividly put it, "Abraham becomes the originator of Passover, and Passover becomes one massive footnote to the faithful obedience of the world's first Jew" (p. 179). Nevertheless, Levenson thinks that the two stories were originally independent and came to be linked only during the period of the Second Temple. (p. 184). This seems to me improbable. Yuval goes so far as to claim that Jubilees is the first point at which the connection was made, which seems even more improbable. Yuval does, however, insightfully draw out another such connection between Exod. 12:13; Gen. 22:14; and 1 Chr. 21:15 (David's purchase of Ornan's threshing-floor as the site for the Temple), which appears in the third century CE *Mekhilta.* See Israel J. Yuval, "God Will See the Blood: Sin, Punishment, and Atonement in the Jewish-Christian Discourse," in *Jewish Blood: Reality and Metaphor in History, Religion, and Culture,* ed. Mitchell B. Hart (New York: Routledge, 2009), 84–88.

And indeed, both the *akedah* and Exodus provide foundation narratives that define Israel's national identity. But of the two, I believe that the Passover narrative is the more foundational, the one that explains the symbolism and meaning of the *akedah*.

My case for that conclusion has two parts. The first argues that the *akedah* lacks a plausible rationale if we require it to "stand on its own two feet," so to speak. The second is to show that a rationale can be offered for the Passover tradition—one that transfers to Genesis 22 and makes it intelligible, whereas the *akedah* otherwise remains baffling. Jubilee's explanation of the *akedah* as the result of a provocation by Prince Mastema shows that, early on, Jews must have been puzzled about the rationale for the testing of Abraham. Why otherwise resort to such a *daemon ex machina*?

Why did God want child sacrifice in the first place? And why bother to test Abraham if he foreknew Abraham's mettle to be up to the task of passing the test? If Levenson is right that the promise of a nation of descendants to Abraham could not have been fulfilled were Abraham not worthy of the test, but that God chose Abraham precisely because he knew that Abraham *would* be worthy, then what need was there actually to go through with the ordeal?[70] Nor will it help much to point out—so Levenson—that in the eyes of ancient Israel, God would not have been countermanding his own prohibition against killing in demanding the sacrifice of Isaac, for he certainly *would* have seemed to Abraham to have been a breaker of a solemn promise.[71] And that, surely, would have been considered a violation of a binding commitment.

---

[70] Nevertheless, Gen. 18:17–19 provides strong textual support for the view that God *does* know ahead of time that Abraham is worthy of the promise. Having just promised Sarah a son (vv. 10–12, and earlier also at 17:15–19) and further declared that through this son she will give rise to nations, God says (*sotto voce*), "Shall I hide from Abraham what I am about to do, seeing that Abraham shall become a great and mighty nation…? No, for I have chosen him, that he may charge his children and his household after him to keep the way of the LORD by doing righteousness and justice; so that the LORD may bring about for Abraham what he has promised him." Here, God tells the reader what the angel later announces to Abraham; viz., that it is because of his obedience to Torah ("the way of the LORD") and his commitment to handing down to his posterity the lesson of obedience that he has been chosen father of a chosen people. Of course, he does not tell Abraham that at the outset. However, the promise is not conditional: *If* you will obey, I will make a nation; rather, it appears that God foreknows the truth of the antecedent and, therefore, issues the consequent categorically as the promise. Why, then, the need for a test? Of course, this is just the sort of puzzle that is bound to provoke a feeding frenzy among philosophers as, indeed, the angel's second speech to Abraham did from early on (for a history of the commentary upon this passage and the solutions that have been offered, see Ska, "Gen. 22 or the Testing of Abraham: An Essay on the Levels of Reading," in *The Exegesis of the Pentateuch*, 97–110).

[71] Cf. Levenson, *The Death and Resurrection of the Beloved Son*, 130.

But the most fundamental difficulty lies in the choice of the test itself. Why should God *want* the sacrifice of a son? A stiff test, to be sure: perhaps one than which none stiffer can be conceived. But why not the sacrifice of Abraham's wife Sarah? Or better, why not demand of Abraham that he sacrifice himself upon the altar?[72] Nor is there anything in the immediate literary context in which Genesis 22 recounts the testing of Abraham that suggests some further reason for the horrific command. We are, rather, left with an episode that seems to be inexplicable—unless, perhaps, help can come from another quarter.

That other quarter, I believe, is the story of the Exodus—specifically, the story of the tenth and final plague suffered by Egypt and its aftermath, a story that plays an unquestionable role in both Israel's self-understanding of its birth as a nation and in its self-understanding of the origin of the temple. In order to understand the import of this story for the *akedah*, it is necessary to note one essential common feature of both stories: in both, firstborn sons owe their lives to a miraculous intervention on the part of God. The occurrence of a divine intervention that saves Israel collectively at the Exodus works also individually elsewhere as a mark of divine selection. As has often been remarked, it is a perennial feature of the biographies of biblical heroes that God plays a direct role in their conception or in rescue from peril. Because he is miraculously conceived, Isaac owes his very existence to divine favor. What might the implications of this be?

Here, anthropology can provide us with a fundamental insight. In *The Gift*, Marcel Mauss works out the principles that govern the culturally universal practice of gift-giving. There is, we saw, a formal difference between the social interactions of buying and selling and those that involve gift-giving. Commercial relationships are contractual—you have something that is worth more to me than it is to you (and vice versa). We agree on a price or barter, and our commitments are satisfied when the goods have been exchanged. But if you approach me with a gift, then that is to be understood, as noted in Chapter 6, as an overture to friendship. If I accept, I signal receptiveness. If I reject your gift, then I am, at the least, indicating disinterest in friendship or, more seriously, hostility or insult. But if I accept,

---

[72] In later rabbinic midrash, it is indeed Isaac who, understanding how matters stand, willingly offers himself as the sacrifice upon the altar on Moriah. This idea of self-sacrifice reaches a kind of crescendo in a midrash that has Isaac in fact (momentarily) dying as the knife meets his throat:

> Rav Yehuda said, "When the sword got to his neck, Isaac's soul departed. When he heard the sound [of God's voice] from between the cherubs [who flank the Mercy Seat over the ark in the Holy of Holies of the Temple], saying, 'Do not lift your hand ...' his soul returned. He stood on his feet and ... said, 'Blessed be thou, God, who revives the dead.' Just as the nation perished at Sinai and are brought back to life, so does Isaac die, and return to life." (Pirkei D'Rrebi Eliezer, Chaps. 30–31)

the relationship has only begun. Sooner or later, the expectation is that I will reciprocate with a gift of my own—and then you respond with a further gift, and so on. Thus are social alliances forged and maintained.

But such relationships, we saw, are more carefully calibrated than this suggests. For although there is no explicit value placed upon a gift, it is understood that the reciprocity that generates friendship between peers is achieved with a return gift of roughly equal value. Moreover, it emerges that if the gifts that move in one direction between allies are in general more valuable than those given reciprocally, then the former gift-giver achieves elevated social status and authority in relation to the latter. Over time, this can stabilize into a patron/client relationship.

As we saw, for example, in many cultures, the most valuable gift one can give to another man is a sister or daughter in marriage. Typical of such cultures is the payment of a bride price by means of which the recipient of a wife seeks to ameliorate his level of indebtedness to the family that has provided the wife. But—short of the offer of a woman in exchange—the bridegroom cannot hope to equal the value of the gift he has received. Thus, he remains in debt to his in-laws and, in consequence, owes them respect, loyalty, and honor. Now, talk of bride *price* and debt might seem to suggest that such transactions are commercial ones. But that would be mistaken: marriage in these cultures is explicitly conceptualized as institutionalized mutual gift-giving. Recalling this is relevant because something quite analogous, in even more extreme form, is going on in the Exodus event.

On the Passover night, God effects a rescue of the Children of Israel from a condition of non-existence as a corporate person, even as he rescues each firstborn Israelite male child from death at the hands of the Destroyer sent to annihilate Egypt's firstborn.[73] It is important to understand that this divine act not only cuts short the lives of Egyptian children; it also cuts off Egypt itself from legal continuity as a future nation. For both Israel and Egypt, social existence and continuity are built upon a framework of family continuity, which, given a system of patrilineal primogeniture, makes each

---

[73] In the ancient world, slavery was considered a kind of legal equivalent to death, or non-personhood. See David M. Goldberg, "What Did Ham Do to Noah?" in *The Words of a Wise Man's Mouth Are gracious. (Qoh 10, 12)*, ed. Mauro Perani (New York: Walter de Gruyter, 2005), 257–65. Goldberg quotes J. Boswell: "Slavery was not simply a fate 'worse than death'—it was death in the eyes of the law, since slaves were not legally persons" (J. Boswell, *The Kindness of Strangers: The Abandonment of Children in Western Europe from Late Antiquity to the Renaissance* [Chicago, IL: Chicago University Press, 1988], 67–68). If this is right, and if killing of the Egyptian firstborn is, like the possible castration of Noah by Ham, a kind of social death for Egypt, then symbolically this turns the tables on the Egyptians, rendering them slaves just as Israel becomes free.

firstborn son the heir of the family's identity and legal standing within the community. Thus, to destroy a firstborn son is to destroy, both symbolically and in practical terms, that continued corporate existence.

In this one act, then, Yahweh restores Israel to life even as he cuts Egypt off (later completing that job with the destruction of Pharaoh and his army). In so doing, he puts Israel—corporately, family by family, and individually in the case of the firstborn males—in his debt. That debt is ultimate and peerless. Nothing can fully repay the saving of a human life. Moreover, because the continued existence of family, clan, tribe, and nation depends upon the passing of the chain of command from father to eldest son, the saving of the eldest sons is the equivalent of the salvation of the nation.

But that debt is, as I said, one that cannot ever fully be repaid—short of destroying the very people that Yahweh meant to save. Can it be partially repaid? Indeed it can: by the substitution of something less valuable—for example, an animal (and a foreskin). This does two things: it reduces the indebtedness of the one who offers the substitute. But it also leaves the debt not fully paid with the result that the debtor must acknowledge the superior status of his creditor. Sons and daughters must obey their fathers. But to whom does a father owe obedience? In a patriarchal and patrilineal society, the answer was clear; and because authority is transmitted down a chain of command, Yahweh's authority permeated Israelite society from top to bottom.[74] Thus, the Passover story provided the conceptual edifice that upheld Israel's self-understanding as ruled by Yahweh and rooted her social order.[75] Yahweh becomes, in effect, Israel's immortal king or the father of her king and establishes his will as Torah, much as social contract theory, narrativized as a story recounting a primeval negotiation between adults in a mythical state of nature, serves the same purpose for many modern constitutional democracies.

But let us return to Mount Moriah—which was sometimes identified in rabbinic midrash with Mount Sinai (no small feat, since "by definition" Moriah/Zion is located in the Land of Promise, and Sinai is located outside it)![76] God directly intervenes to cure Sarah's barrenness and

---

[74] This idea appears to be reflected in Rabbi Menahem Schneerson: "If one carries out all of the above as required, the child—the spark of holiness—becomes a viable birth, and he proceeds to the redemption of the firstborn" (quoted in Rebbi, "The First Mitzvah").

[75] The power and universality of this way of establishing obligation is attested by Robert Adams' defense of a divine command theory of moral duty: to defend (without generating a regress) the moral principle that we ought to obey our Creator, Adams appeals to the debt of gratitude we owe God for our lives and for his providence (Robert Merrihew Adams, *Finite and Infinite Goods* [New York: Oxford University Press, 2002], 252–53).

[76] To take just one example:

destines Isaac to become the father—patriarch—of Jacob/Israel and all his descendants. It is natural, then—we might even venture to say necessary—that a story be created in which Isaac is placed in a position vis á vis Yahweh parallel to that of the firstborn children of Israel who were saved in Egypt. [77] In this way, Yahweh's authority over Isaac—and by extension over all his descendants—is established by way of an insufficiently costly ransom (indeed doubly so, as God provides the very animal whose sacrifice substitutes for Isaac's).[78]

And where did Sinai come from? Rav Yossi said, "From Mount Moriah it was separated like challah, which was separated from the dough. From the place where Isaac our Forefather was bound. God said, since Isaac their Forefather was bound there, it is an appropriate place for his children to receive the Torah." (*Midrash Tehilim* 68:9, Buber edition) [And to Moriah, the midrash continues, will Sinai return.]

[77] It is perhaps noteworthy that Abraham, the first patriarch, is not himself ransomed in the same way, nor is any account given of his birth having been miraculous. Abraham earns his laurels not by a circumstantially imposed obligation of obedience, but by the merit of willing obedience. And after all, the regress implied by the Isaac story must terminate somewhere.

[78] It will not have escaped the reader's attention that this analysis reverses the order of the *akedah* and the Passover event. In the Pentateuchal chronology, the former precedes the latter. For us, the question arises: what was the order of composition of the stories? The question of literary priority is complex and difficult, as it depends upon critical source analysis of the interwoven strands of the Pentateuch. Unfortunately, Bible scholarship has been unable to arrive at a secure consensus respecting dates of composition. Certainly, it would be more congenial to my reading were the composition of the Passover story to have preceded the composition of Genesis 22. But ultimately, what is at issue here is which story is prior, or more fundamental, in the explanatory order. It is hardly likely that the general idea that underlies both stories should not have been in the air for a long time prior to the fashioning of either story, and not impossible that the story of the *akedah* should have been told first, and that the Passover story, while more fundamental, should have been constructed later, even as an afterthought. In any event, Ska, in his excellent summary of recent source research, assigns Exodus 12 to the Priestly source and Genesis 22 to a late (Post-exilic) source (see Ska, *Introduction to Reading the Pentateuch*, 132, 153). That chronology accords well with my analysis.

The reader may also wonder why Isaac is a necessary figure in the story at all. After all, Genesis devotes very little space to this Patriarch's story. Why not just have Jacob, the father of the twelve tribes, be the son of Abraham, the son whose sacrifice God demands? But Isaac is important to the Genesis narrative for at least one quite independent reason, for Isaac's story is essential to the way in which Genesis frames the genealogy of Israel in relation to neighboring tribes. This has two aspects: Isaac's marriage and his progeny. Isaac's marriage to Rebekah reflects a remarkable degree of endogamy. Rebekah is not only Isaac's half-matrilateral cross-cousin once removed, but also his patrilateral parallel cousin once removed *and* patrilateral cross-cousin twice removed! Even so, this marriage is not flatly incestuous, as is Abraham's to his half-sister Sarah. Still, Isaac repeats Abraham's ruse of calling his wife "sister" (Gen. 26:6–11; cf. 12:11–20) with similar consequences. Jacob's marriage, in turn, to Leah and Rachel is a paradigmatic matrilateral cross-cousin marriage, with the paternal line at one generation's

We have come nearly full circle. The Temple Mount is Mount Moriah. When Abraham gives tithe to the mysterious Melchizidek, king of Salem (Jerusalem?) and priest of the Most High God, he prefigures the sacrificial regimen of the temple. It is a regimen in which an unblemished lamb takes the place of the first son, a son who continues a lifetime of offerings to God and to sustain his administrators, the king and the temple priesthood. Functionally, what this means is that king and temple are able to provide for the ongoing existence of the nation, God's chosen people. Ideologically, what it means is that Israel was provided with a coherent, integrated cornucopia of conceptual tools by the use of which she was able to construct stories that gave legitimacy to her governing institutions, enabled theorizing about the proper dimensions of legitimate governance, and made possible the flexibility required by responsiveness to the vicissitudes—often daunting in Israel's case—of history and external circumstance. Shall we say that such a system of theory and practice is driven fundamentally by the demands in play in the marketplace of material goods or by the demands imposed by the marketplace of ideas? Why must we choose? Is it not, rather, that every successful society must somehow find a way to negotiate a mutually supportive set of solutions to both sets of demands?

IX. To Conclude

Blood sacrifice will inevitably seem alien to modern sensibilities. But the results of this study suggest that there is in fact nothing intrinsically outlandish or primitive about such practices, nor do the fundamental motivations and principles that explain the ritual life of the Jerusalem

---

further remove. Some of Jacob's sons, however, engage in positively exogamous marriages (Gen. 46). There is a pattern here: from too much endogamy to perhaps barely acceptable exogamy. (Esau crosses the line: he marries a Canaanite woman, then tries to back-track by marrying a daughter of Ishmael.) There are many further—and important—details (for further discussion, see Edmund R. Leach, "The Legitimacy of Solomon," in *Genesis as Myth and Other Essays* [London: Cape, 1969], 25–84), but the short of it is that there would have been no way to collapse this genealogical "history," essential to Israel's identity, into two generations, either by eliminating Isaac from the story (and changing the *akedah* to a binding of Jacob) or by somehow skipping over Jacob. The relationship between Isaac and Ishmael on the one hand, and Jacob and Esau on the other, codifies Israel's relations with the Ishmaelites, the descendants of Ishmael, and Edom, the descendants of Esau. More can be said about the essential role of Isaac, but this consideration is alone sufficient. Indeed, it is not too much to say that the question of who can count as an Israelite (or the proper wife or husband of an Israelite) is a question that bedeviled the authors of the Bible and permeated its narratives. (Perhaps unsurprisingly, Muslims have a tradition according to which it was Ishmael whom Abraham was commanded to sacrifice on the mountain!)

Temple differ in kind from those that provide the rationale for our own governing social and legal arrangements.

Even rituals that seem to us primitive and repugnant must be approached with the presumption that their content quite precisely represents or enacts significant elements of a comprehensible system of social commitments and relations.[79] In the light of what I have said about the *akedah* and child sacrifice, let us return to circumcision and, in particular, an especially unsettling feature of traditional practice, called *metzizeh b'peh*, still engaged in today by some Hassidic communities. After the *mohel* has cut off the baby's foreskin, he takes a bit of wine into his mouth, sucks vigorously upon the baby's penis, and then spits out the blood and wine.

The practice has caused considerable controversy over the years, on the grounds that it can and sometimes has transmitted serious disease to an infant. On the other hand, the practice has typically been defended on medical grounds.[80] That something more than this may be at stake for the orthodox is at least hinted at by Rabbi Schneerson's remark that

> the circumcision is the first mitzvah which Avraham, our Patriarch, the first Jew, was commanded to perform. Similarly, the circumcision is the first mitzvah performed with every Jew from the time of his birth. Thus [it can be assumed] that the mitzvah of circumcision reflects the totality of the Torah and its mitzvos, as indicated by Nedarim 32a, which states: "Great is circumcision, for it is equivalent to all the mitzvos of the Torah."

Such an equivalence might suggest that communication of blood had—and for some Jewish communities still has—religious significance. I have not been able to ascertain what that significance might be, but a possible explanation is that, as Zipporah touches the bloody foreskin of her son to

---

[79] Methodological note: in the course of digesting the textual materials and forming some sense of the ways in which the rabbis and biblical authors use their symbolic vocabulary, it is natural to make predictions about what sorts of associations and connections should underlie the texts and, therefore, about what other sorts of stories could or should be told. When these then turn up in the writings under study, it may feel deflating to discover that the idea was already long ago anticipated by the rabbis. But more positively, it provides evidence of some facility in entering into the conceptual world of those one is attempting to understand. There are larger methodological issues that lurk in the background here—e.g., the old debate between the conception of historical explanation as "empathy" or *Verstehen* and the Hempelian D-N model of scientific explanation. But I shall not engage that discussion here. See rather, Evan Fales, "Uniqueness and Historical Laws," *Philosophy of Science* 47, no. 2 (1980): 260–76; "Must Sociology Be Qualitative?" and "Reply to Professor Brown," *Qualitative Sociology* 5, no. 2 (1982): 89–105, 145–56.

[80] See, for example, Mordechai Halperin, "Metzitzah B'peh Controversy: The View from Israel," Wayback Machine, March 6, 2012.

Moses' groin to effect a communion between baby and God via the father, so the contact of an infant's blood with the mouth of the *mohel* is meant to achieve a similar union.

Something more can be said.[81] To begin with, circumcision is supposed to be performed by the father of the infant. This duty is typically (and rather understandably) delegated to a *mohel*, who stands in as the father's legal surrogate. Second, *milah* (Hebrew for circumcision) is also the Hebrew word for "word." This directly reflects the equivalence between the rite of circumcision and the sealing of the word, or covenant. But words issue from a mouth. True to form, there is an understood equivalence between the mouth and the male (and also female) sexual organs.[82] The idea is old. Exodus relates it to Moses himself: in Exodus 6:12 and 30, Moses protests his commission to the Children of Israel and Pharaoh by appealing to his inability to speak, "I am of uncircumcised lips."

Thus, there is precisely a structural homology between the *mohel*/father bringing to his lips the blood of the infant's foreskin and contact between Moses' genitals and his son's bloody foreskin. But not only that: just as the genitals are the *sine qua non* of the continued *material* life of Israel as a people, so is the propagation of the word of the covenant the essential, enduring progenitor of the *ideological* continuation of Israel as a nation. In the equivalence of the physical organs of procreation with the mouth that can speak, and of both with the sealing of the covenant through the generations, we have opened a vista upon a whole new region of the symbolic landscape. But every excursion must come to an end, and it is time to move on to other vistas.

The debate over the practice of *metzitzah* reflects, if nothing else, the durability of religious symbolism, even in a cultural environment that no longer provides the kind of context in which the practice arose. So, we should not judge its meaning simply by reference to contemporary sensibilities and conventions. It is all too easy to be blinded by those into thinking that we find, in such practices, a mentality that is fundamentally alien to our own. But this is a mistake. Of course, the maintenance of a governing bureaucracy in a small pastoral/agrarian society will take outward

---

[81] For what follows, I am largely indebted to Samuel Lebens.

[82] See Elliot R. Wolfson, "Circumcision, Vision of God, and Textual Interpretation: From Midrashic Trope to Mystical Symbol," *History of Religions* 27, no. 2 (1987): 207–15. Wolfson quotes from the *Sefer Yeẓira*: "Ten *sefirot belimah*; ten corresponding to the number of the ten fingers, five against five, and the covenant of the oneness is constituted in the center [as expressed] in the circumcision of the tongue and the mouth and in the circumcision of the foreskin" (p. 207n57). Wolfson further quotes *Sefer Yeẓira* 6:4, "Where it is said that God made a covenant with Abraham 'between the ten toes of his feet and it is the covenant of circumcision' and a covenant 'between the ten fingers of his hands which is the tongue.'"

forms different than those required in modern industrial nations. And, to be sure, governing ideologies can vary widely in response to historical accident and circumstance. But some fundamental principles remain the same. The provision of social order is a service. That service must be paid for. Effective service requires power. Vestment of that power in some group or individual must be justified. Power is always a contested commodity; and on that score, the history of ancient Israel was no exception. But, like every society, Israel thought hard about the problem of legitimate authority, and that thought generated a systematic ideology that could provide stability, some flexibility in the face of change of circumstances, and an intellectually satisfying set of conceptual tools for the very construction and revision of that ideology.

The idea that blood embodies life (both of individuals and of their community), that blood contact between persons, both human and divine, symbolizes and affirms union through gift exchange, and that such exchanges establish not only social solidarity but also authority and submission: these ideas seem to me to provide the keys to understanding the complex ideology and praxis of the Jerusalem Temple. There is no reason, in my view, to think that, in all of this, there is some necessary antagonism between the material needs of society and the need for a coherent ideology, or that either took precedence.

To be sure, these irenic observations do nothing to ameliorate the moral outrage of blood sacrifice when the victims are human beings. We can surely judge that, where such a thing became actual practice and not merely symbolism, ideology went off the rails whether or not it served some practical aim. But, lest we forget to remove the beam in our own eye when we condemn the ancients, let us be reminded of our own sins. Infanticide was a major means of population control in Medieval and early modern Europe.[83] Social ills, from slavery to modern warfare conducted for purely material gain, remain with us with little sign of abatement. Let us not turn a blind eye.

---

[83] See Boswell, *The Kindness of Strangers*.

The Genesis of Genesis

> We should observe that this approach [structural myth analysis], if it has any value, should be meaningfully applicable to the particularly important field of religious myths which usually enjoy a privileged freedom from such rational onslaughts in their secure gardens. All the world's religions rest on sacred foundations of myth. In their richness, the Jewish, Christian, Muslim, Hindu, and Buddhist mythologies ... present a luxuriant field for the mythological anthropologist that would certainly keep him busy for a long time.[1]

The title of this chapter may easily mislead. I am not going to discuss the various source hypotheses currently under discussion, nor the competing views regarding the dates of composition and redaction of the various parts of Genesis. I shall assume that Genesis received its final form sometime, perhaps not very long, after the return from exile, that parts of it may have been composed during exile, and that those parts may well have relied upon preexilic traditions. I consider it safe to assume, as well, that Genesis is not to be read as an historical record, whatever shards and fragments of the historical past may have found their way into the text in some form, but as speaking in the language of myth. It is, in fact, that language that interests me.

My plan is to offer some reflections upon selected episodes in Genesis that are informed by the tools of anthropological analysis to see whether these might shed some new light upon the structure and meaning of of the book. My focus will, however, be quite limited. First up will be a discussion of Gen. 1–3; next, an analysis of the story of the deluge and a comparison of it with the destruction of Sodom and Gomorrah; and finally, some puzzles about Jacob's combat with the angel in Genesis 32.

My overarching hypothesis, as will by now no doubt be anticipated, is that the fundamental undertaking of Genesis is to provide a theoretical underpinning for Israel's process of forging a cultural and social identity, both at the level of very general reflections upon the human social condition and, more particularly, at the level of defining and articulating what it is to

---

[1] Nur Yalman, "'The Raw : the Cooked :: Nature : Culture'—Observations on *Le Cru et le cuit*," in *The Structural Study of Myth and Totemism*, ed. Edmund R. Leach (London: Tavistock Publications, 1967), 88.

be an Israelite within the constellation of social and geopolitical circumstances that Israel's formation (or, more likely, rebirth after exile) had to negotiate. I will not, in considering only a few episodes in Genesis, be able to go very far in establishing the credentials of this large hypothesis, but I will hope to add to the initial foray undertaken with the analysis of the *akedah* in Chapter 7. And I will be suggesting, further, a relationship between the discussion there of the Exodus 4 episode and Jacob's contest with the angel in Genesis 32.

I. The Creation of the Universe

I have already briefly noted in Chapter 4 the implausibility of supposing that the creation stories in Genesis 1–3 had, as their main concern, an attempt to explain the existence and nature of the physical universe, commonplace though that view has been. I will now expand a bit on this claim. My argument in Chapter 4 was in large measure negative: considering that ancient peoples had no empirical evidence that would have supported any robust theorizing about the origins of the physical universe (and no way of acquiring such evidence), it is less than charitable to suppose them engaged primarily in such a highly speculative enterprise at the outset of the project that became the canonical laying of the foundations of Israel's understanding of her identity and destiny.

While I do not mean to exclude an interest in that subject or even a conception of the structure of the physical world that sees it as relevant to the structure of the social order, I am proposing that this is not the focus of even the first two chapters of Genesis.[2] One thing the opening chapters of Genesis do accomplish, however, is to offer a narrative that situates the foundations of the social order in an *Urgeschichte* that grounds them in the very structure of the cosmos, and thus as authoritative. I want now to offer some positive evidence for these claims.

We might begin by observing that the familiar inconsistency between the accounts of the order of creation in Genesis 1 and Genesis 2 might be ameliorated if chronology is not here at the center of attention. Both stories place the creation of man at the heart of God's creative project. Genesis 1–2:3 portray this process as one in which God first prepares a

---

[2] As noted in Chapter 4, it is possible to agree with Robin Horton that cosmogonic myths may contain elements of an attempt to explain the structure of the physical cosmos, but not (as Horton sees it) as a primitive attempt at physics. Rather, it is possible that such early explanatory efforts essentially attempted to extend the explanatory strategies of an already well-understood folk-psychological explanatory framework to the behavior of physical matter. But I do not think one needs to invoke this way of reading to understand Genesis 1 and 2.

habitation for human beings and then creates them. Genesis 2:4–25 imagines God to create the man near the beginning of the process, and then fleshing out a suitable environment, culminating in the creation of woman as his companion.

It has been proposed that both Genesis 1–2 and 2–3 exhibit chiastic structures that bind the narrative of these chapters together.[3] Such structures, if there by design, will, in controlling the order of events in the text, help to explain why the narrative order in Genesis 2 largely reverses that of Chapter 1. But in addition to that, Genesis 1 clearly emphasizes the initial stages of creation more heavily than Chapter 2, which places its emphasis upon the creation of human beings, the geography of Eden, and the relationship of man and woman. It thus sets the stage for the drama of Genesis 3.

Few scholars will deny that the early chapters of Genesis are mythical and not historical. The presence of large-scale chiastic structures, quite by itself, argues in favor of that conclusion. The reason is straightforward. Like a poet, a writer of prose fiction can shape his narrative to conform to patterns that confer aesthetic structure and unity to a work, serving often also to mediate meaning. But because narrative order is ordinarily chronological order, a history that exhibits chiastic structures would have either to be extraordinarily selective (and lucky) in the events it narrates, creatively switch the order of those events (with luck still providing matched pairs), or insert fictions that maintain the intended structure.

The only alternatives to this are chance or an Author of history who orchestrates the unfolding of events in a way that rings true to certain human artistic conventions and sensibilities. The last is (arguably) not impossible, but that explanation takes onboard heavy ontological commitments that do not burden the simple explanation that a text was composed with artistic ends in view. As for the lucky chance that history itself presents a record that displays large-scale chiastic structures: what are the odds of that?[4]

Mary Douglas has persuasively argued that the dietary restrictions imposed upon Jews by God (the so-called abominations of Leviticus 11)

---

[3] See, for example, William Shea's chiasm linking Gen. 1 and 2 ("Literary Structural Parallels between Genesis 1 and 2," *Origins* 16, no. 2 [1989]: 49–68), Joel Rosenberg for chiastic structures linking Gen. 2 to 4 and elsewhere in Genesis ("Genesis: Introduction," in *Harper-Collins Study Bible NRSV*, ed. Wayne Meeks [New York: Harper-Collins Publishers, 1993], 4–5), Roberto Ouro for a chiasm linking Gen. 2 and 3 ("The Garden of Eden Account: The Chiastic Structure of Genesis 2–3," *Andrews University Seminary Studies* 40, no. 2 [2002]: 219–43), and David Dorsey for a general introduction to Hebrew literary forms (*The Literary Structure of the Old Testament: A Commentary On Genesis–Malachi* [Grand Rapids, MI: Baker Books, 1999]).

[4] The argument does not apply to examples of small-scale chiasm (e.g., intra-sentential chiasm). I am relying here upon chiastic structures that span an entire story or narrated episode.

mirror the order God imposes upon his creation of the animal kingdom.[5] God creates the birds of the air, the four-footed beasts of the field (that is, domesticated cattle; see Gen. 1:24–25; 2:19–20), and the fish in the sea. Animals who violate these categories in certain ways are *tref*—they may not be eaten. Douglas argues that the paradigmatic animals, which for ancient Jews served as "cattle" (sheep, goats, and bovines), all shared the characteristics of chewing the cud and having cloven hooves. They could be eaten and, by extension, so could wild mammals (e.g., antelope) who were ruminants, or thought to be ruminants, with cloven hooves. Birds that lack flight (e.g., ostriches) are not "proper" birds. Eating them is forbidden. Beasts that chew the cud but have no cloven hooves (the rock badger according to ancient Israel's mistaken natural history), or have cloven hooves but do not chew the cud (pigs), violate the order of creation and cannot be eaten. Similarly, aquatic creatures that lack fins and scales are forbidden.

It seems unlikely that Jewish conceptions of the faunal order were solely dictated by prior dietary preferences (or medical considerations), and Douglas' view is much closer to Lévi-Strauss than to Marx on this question.[6] Certain ways of classifying flora and fauna are "good to think." Violators are therefore impure, polluting, and in a way, dangerous. So, Genesis 1 and 2 do have a cosmological dimension. They reflect, at least, certain divisions in the natural order as Israel conceived it and then built that order into the creation story. Even here, that natural order is also an order that structures central aspects of social life—here, diet and sacrificial ritual. Douglas has more to say about these matters, but let me turn to the larger features of biblical cosmology, which may seem sufficiently removed from social life to stand on their own as objects of theorizing about the natural cosmos.

No sooner has the suggestion been made than it becomes apparent that these features themselves all have an essential bearing on human life: day and night, dry land and water; also the moon and stars (for telling the hour, for navigation, and for geolocation), the sun (for life-giving heat) and light, minerals, and ores (as the raw materials for the making of tools and other artifacts). But why should ancient Israel have any interest in their order or manner of creation? Here, I will focus on the way in which, at the creation, God (or *Elohim*) distributes the primal waters of the "deep" (the *tehom*) that appear as the Ur-material from which the world is fashioned.

---

[5] Mary Douglas, *Purity and Danger: An Analysis of Concepts of Pollution and Taboo* (New York: Frederick A. Praeger, 1996), 51–71.

[6] For a materialist view, see Marvin Harris, *Cows, Pigs, Wars, and Witches: The Riddles of Culture* (New York: Vintage, 1989). Harris' account can possibly explain the Jewish abstinence from pork, but, unlike Douglas, his approach has little to offer by way of explaining most of the other prohibitions. And, as Douglas pointed out, neither do traditional apologetic explanations that appeal to alleged medical considerations.

The elementary act of creation is separation. God separates the waters below from the waters above, the waters that are in the times of the first creation confined to a region beyond the dome of the sky. The second act is to divide the waters below to make room for dry land. Thus, the gathering of the primal waters, waters that originally reflected chaos, results in the world below in confinement of the chaos-waters to the seas and the emergence of a *terra firma* upon which animal and plant life—but in particular, human life—is possible. The imagery is quite graphic: human social order requires the stability of land where boundaries can be fixed and not shift around. It may well be that this imagery was engendered by the experience of the large annual flooding of the fertile valleys of the great rivers of the ANE—especially the Nile, Tigris, and Euphrates. During those annual floods, the boundaries of fields were temporarily obliterated. Annually, they had to be resurveyed. Thus, social order, dependent in significant measure in an agricultural economy upon stable property distinctions, depended quite literally upon a controlled response to aquatic chaos. Repeatedly in the Hebrew Bible, the waters of the "deep" threaten to burst their boundaries and overwhelm the land. Repeatedly, God is seen as the agent who overcomes and controls them.

Contrasting with the stormy threat of the uncontrolled waters of the deep are the benign waters that sustain the lives of plants and animals. These are the rivers (when not in flood stage) and benign rain. Before the deluge, there was in fact no rain: the earth was watered by rivers—indeed, paradise contained the headwaters of four great rivers—and by temperate dew. There is a fundamental contrast, then, between the unruly chaos-waters and the *terra firma*. I shall have occasion presently to expand upon the pervasiveness of the endlessly repeated theme of divine control over the chaos-waters that threaten the earth, used throughout the Bible as a figure for control over social chaos, a figure whose meaning is sometimes made explicit. Shortly, I will be discussing the second creation of the world, a creation that God initiates when social chaos has run too rampant, by unleashing both the chaos-waters above the firmament and those heretofore confined to the "fountains of the deep."

Thus, the fundamental architecture of the cosmos, from its very inception, reflects an awareness of the foundational status of social order and stability as a condition of human existence. It is this recognition that the Genesis creation stories can be understood to express. The divine ordering of the chaos-waters poetically expresses God's role as the founder and sustainer of social order. The heavenly bodies and the air came, later, to be associated with angels and, negatively, with demonic powers and to symbolize various political realities.[7] Their regular motion may have been

---

[7] E.g., Philo, *On the Giants*, 6–16.

seen to provide a natural representation of or analogy to social stability, at least as an ideal, in the heavenly realm. Moreover, divine sovereignty over the natural world ensures the suitability of the physical environment to human life. Beyond this, as previously noted, a claim that God has created the entire world translates easily into a claim that he has the authority to give however much of it he pleases to his chosen people.

We have examined several ways in which cosmic creation stories can reflect conceptions of social order or attempts to extend folk explanations of human behavior and social relationships to the physical world. Beyond the evidence that recognition of such motivations can illuminate the Genesis creation story, we must consider the creation of a particular abode for human beings. God gives his humans authority over all the animals and provides them with vegetable food. He sets them in a garden. There are two trees of note: the tree of life and the tree of knowledge of good and evil. Genesis 2 dwells all too briefly, one might think, upon the idyllic state of existence in which Adam and Eve find themselves before Chapter 3 addresses the serious business of sin. But I should like to dwell at a bit more length upon the significance of that idyllic state.

One thing about it, and about the primal couple who inhabit it, is that they are "good." A second notable fact is that Genesis 2 is curiously ambiguous on the question of whether in this inaugural condition, Adam and Eve were intended to have children. Certainly, Genesis 1 is clear on this point: God tells Adam and Eve to "be fruitful and multiply, and fill the earth" (Gen. 1:28). Yet in Chapter 2, God places the couple in paradise, a particular district where—so it seems—they may dwell in perpetuity so long as they behave. Since the tree of life confers immortality, reproduction (assuming that their children also have access to that tree) would soon enough entail a Malthusian population crisis. Adam and Eve's prelapsarian lack of shame over their nakedness has been taken by some to imply celibacy, yet God's curse upon Eve for disobeying seems to imply that, had she not sinned, childbirth *would* have been painless for her. The story does not settle the issue for us.

Thus, the best we may be able to do is to speculate. A somewhat attractive thought, then, is that the author of Genesis 2 thought of paradise as an originary earthly instancing of a heavenly social ideal—that is, of the core model of human society stripped of all the bells and whistles and accretions derived from history and culture. It is not a state of nature, but rather the nucleus of a family placed under the laws and authority of God and provided with a secure sustenance and an absence of external threat: thus, with everything required for a perfectly stable, enduring existence. Two things, above all, can threaten this stability: human willfulness and children. If we understand the partaking of the fruit of the tree of knowledge as an attempt to usurp God's prerogative as the author of the law, then willfulness amounts to overweening pride combined with human fallibility in constructing a just and practicable legal system.

Children create two sorts of problems. First, they are themselves rebellious—that is, they display the same flaw that gets Adam and Eve into trouble in the first place. But second, they raise the problems that attend kinship systems and the predication of social status upon kin status. The problem is simple: human reproductive biology does not in general meet the desiderata of social structure. Men and women might be infertile. Or, if an heir must be male (or female), the lineage will have to make adjustment if no child of the proper gender is engendered—or too many. Thus, the unpredictability of procreation forces social systems to be elastic and to temporize. Genesis 2 might, therefore, be an exercise in thinking about how, in theory, to understand real, messy human existence as something that emerges from, hence bears some relation to, a kind of ideal that depicts the in-principle simplest, cleanest form of human social life. If so, then we can situate the first three chapters of Genesis within the ambit of fundamental social and political theory.

II. A Platonic Paradise?

Perhaps we can, therefore, consider paradise as the locus of a "Platonic form" of society, conceived as a nuclear family, potentially immortal, and under the rulership of a personified source of commanding authority *à la* Durkheim. This view is reinforced by the observation that in ANE creation stories, the emphasis is not on the creation of matter, or even on creation of the physical constituents of the universe, but on the separation of the primeval waters into functional units that bear direct relations to the creation and maintenance of social order and human wellbeing. There is linguistic evidence that Israel shared in this understanding of creation.[8]

Even more telling is the evidence, in Genesis and in its ANE cultural background generally, that the temples of the gods, and the process of their construction, parallel the cosmogonic myths. Just as Elohim (God) takes his rest on the seventh day after having created the cosmos, so too he takes his rest in the Tabernacle, where he is enthroned upon the mercy seat with the ark as his footstool (Ex. 25:17–22), which he commands to be built once Israel has defeated her enemy, Egypt. Isaiah 66:1, in which Yahweh (God) describes heaven as his throne and the earth as his footstool, repeats this theme. As in ANE cosmogonies that depend upon the defeat and separation of divine enemies representing chaos-waters—for example,

---

[8] John H. Walton, *Ancient Near Eastern Thought and the Old Testament: Introducing the Conceptual World of the Hebrew Bible* (Grand Rapids: Baker Academic, 2006), 147–72.

Marduk's splitting of Tiamat—so, too, Elohim's (God's) creation is depicted as a dividing of the chaos-waters, setting boundaries for them, and subduing the chaos-monsters, Leviathan and Rahab (see, e.g., Pss. 74; 89; Job 38:4–18, 40:15–41:34).

Who builds the First Temple? In one sense, it is clearly built by Solomon, and just as Yahweh takes seven "days" to complete his cosmos, so Solomon's workmen take seven years to complete the temple, and its dedication ceremony takes seven days (1 Kings 6:36–37; 8).[9] But, in another sense, it is Yahweh who builds this house, as is implied by Psalm 127:1. The cosmogonic dimensions of the building of the temple are reflected in Jewish legend. For example, they form the background of this delightful tale:

> When King David began to dig the foundation of the Temple, the waters of the abyss burst forth and hastened to cover the whole world. David took a fragment of pottery and wrote on it the divine Name, then threw it into the abyss. Immediately the abyss receded sixteen thousand cubits into the depths. When David saw this he said "the closer the abyss is to the earth, the more the earth drinks of its waters and is blessed thereof." What did he do? He sang the fifteen Songs of Degrees of the Book of Psalms, and the abyss rose again fifteen thousand cubits. And it remained one thousand cubits beneath the surface of the earth.[10]

Here, I shall take this interpretation to be a working hypothesis and explore what light it would shed (if true) upon Genesis.

The story, then, is about how this original, idealized state is related to the real, flesh-and-blood existence of human society in general and Israelite society in particular. The story that is central to and initiates this transformation, in its most fundamental and originary form, is the story of the fall. It is a story in which Adam and Eve, who have not yet engaged in sexual congress (or who have at least not borne any children), and who have also not yet eaten of the fruit of either the tree of life or the tree of knowledge of good and evil, are expelled from the garden in consequence of disobedience of the prohibition to eat of the second of these trees.

On its face, this story is multiply puzzling. As God has created a world that he sees to be "good," whence the conniving serpent? And how is it that this being should be given enough free reign to find opportunity to

---

[9] Years and days are often used as correlative in temporal symbolism. Thus, just as Moses rules over Israel for its forty-year sojourn in the desert (and later, Eli, David, and Solomon similarly rule for forty years), Jesus' forty-day trial in the desert after his baptism (Mark 1:13, Matt. 4:1–11, Luke 4:1–13) explicitly recapitulates Israel's "baptism" in the Red Sea and forty years in the desert. His forty-day sojourn with his disciples following his resurrection (Acts 1:3) presumably has similar significance.

[10] Zev Vilnay, *Legends of Jerusalem* (Philadelphia, PA: Wish Publication Society of America, 1973), 78–80). See b. *Sukkah* 53b.

deceive the woman? Moreover, what is the meaning of the serpent's enticement to Eve? She is told that eating the fruit will make her and her husband "like God, knowing good and evil." But why would she want to know that—and how, lacking that knowledge during her conversation with the serpent—would she be able to understand that disobedience to God's command was a sin?

Furthermore, once the deed is done, God's reason for expelling Adam and Eve from Eden is that—having indeed become like "one of us" (the gods)—there is danger that they will eat from the tree of life and become immortal, thereby evidently completing their transformation into divine beings. But what would be so terrible about that? Why would God not *want* Adam and Eve to be as much like him as possible? And why should he worry about some enduring usurpation of power on their part? After all, it is possible to understand the plural pronoun in Genesis 1–3 to refer not to other gods on a par with the Lord but to God's heavenly council. And what could be so bad about Adam and Eve's becoming equal in stature to such beings— to the angels? After all, at least from a later Christian perspective, the saints are destined not only to achieve equality with the angels but to become their superiors (Luke 20:36; 1 Cor. 6:3).

In Babylonian, Sumerian, and Assyrian epics, an enormous tree at the center of creation that spans the gap between the underworld and the heavens (and thus appears to be functionally similar to the axis mundi) is sometimes known as a tree of life.[11] In Genesis 2:9 and 3:22, the fruit of this tree confer immortality. They thus provide humans with a divine property. The fruit of the tree of knowledge of good and evil also, according to the serpent, magically confer divine qualities. But as noted, this role of the tree raises a host of questions. A number of these questions can be answered by an interpretation that has it that, in eating of the fruit, one becomes like God, not in knowledge but in assumed authority: one presumes to have authority over the law, a position that God has reserved for himself. This interpretation makes much more sense of the text.

First, the interpretation explains the sin of Adam and Eve as the sin of pride. Adam and Eve attempt to usurp God's legitimate role as the author of the law.[12] And this has two untoward consequences. First, it introduces disorder: the properly lower and subject ones try to displace the properly

---

[11] Walton, *Ancient Near Eastern Thought*, 175–76.

[12] Other readings are certainly possible—for example that, although God made Adam and Eve with fully-formed bodies, their minds were still immature and prone to misjudgment. God intended to authorize the consumption of the fruit of the tree once Adam and Eve acquired the maturity of mind necessary to handle and understand the knowledge it conferred. On this view, the sin was relatively non-culpable: it was a matter of youthful impetuousness. It does invite the question: why did God not invent the chain-link fence? (Thanks to Carl Mosser for suggesting this interpretation to me.)

superior and sovereign. Second, human beings lack the wisdom to fashion a system of laws that will reflect the perfect goodness of original creation. With some regularity, they fall into error. Ironically, as an act of disobedience, the eating of the fruit of the tree exposes exactly the ways in which humans fall short on the dimension of "knowledge" of the law. It is clear enough that God should not want that—and that, unlike a position commensurate with that of the angels, what is being contested is a standing equal to that of God himself.

This explanation leaves unanswered, so far, questions about the existence and role of the serpent. Whence this fly in the ointment, so to speak? One might speculate that the author of Genesis 2 sought some way of representing two deep features of the human condition: first, that flesh and blood are by their very nature corruptible; and second, that an affirmation of autonomy and control are deeply intrinsic to mature human nature, an affirmation always in tension with the demands and rights of community over individuals. Moreover, absent such a device as the serpent, Genesis would lack a mechanism for achieving the narrative transition from a paradise in stasis to the realities of human history. I am claiming here nothing more than that this narrative requirement may underlie the introduction of the motif of the serpent. But this is, at best, speculation. If somewhere close to correct, it might reflect a way of expressing recognition of the distinction between social stability abstractly conceived and the complications of real existence. Karel van der Toorn claims,

> An appraisal of the Babylonian conception of the person should begin with the reminder that the notion of personhood is not a universal and innate category. The modern concept of person is in fact a long way removed from the view of the ancients ... In ancient cultures, such as Mesopotamia, the human person is understood as a character or a role, rather than as a personality; the individual is not a *personne* (person) but a *personage* (character).[13]

This can be only half-right: the notion of personhood—van der Toorn means what I have called the notion of a natural person—is most surely universal (whether or not "innate"). One simply could not arrive at the notion of social personage without first developing a conception of natural personhood from which to construct that far more sophisticated notion. But van der Toorn is both right to recognize the essential place of *personage* in thinking about social order—hence its prominent appearance in ANE

---

[13] Karel van der Toorn, *Family Religion in Babylonia, Syria, and Israel: Continuity and Change in the Forms of Religious Life* (New York: Brill, 1996), 115. See also, Daniel C. Snell, "The Invention of the Individual," in *A Companion to the Ancient Near East*, ed. Daniel C. Snell (Malden, MA: Blackwell Publishing, 2005), 357–70.

mythical and political thought—and the confusion that can result when we fail to respect the distinction when we read the ancient texts. The serpent, then, may reflect or represent the inherent and eternal tension between the demands of individualism and autonomy upon the human psyche and the demands of communal existence and the subjection of individual interest to the common good.

III. Rest

My second text, from Genesis 5:28–9:28, recounts the life of Noah. We know there was no flood such as the one these chapters describe. Some great river systems in the Near East experienced annual flooding (famously, the Nile; also the Tigris and Euphrates), but nothing of Noahic dimensions (though the annual flooding may not be entirely irrelevant to the genesis of the flood symbolism). We know, then, that the story of the deluge is not an historical memory—indeed, I shall argue that it is mythical. With this in mind, we should be alert to the possibility of other narratives that share important features with the Noah story, features that may therefore indicate a story structured by mythemes. And indeed, we shall not have far to look for such a story.

Consider the similarities between this story and the story of the destruction of Sodom and Gomorrah: (a) a sinful, violent creation is destroyed by God; (b) an upright hero and his kin are saved by God; (c) while the hero is in a drunken state after rescue, his progeny sexually defile him with the consequence that (d) the transgressing son/daughters become(s) the progenitors of apostate peoples/nations who are enemies of Israel (Ham begets Canaan, Lot's first daughter begets Moab, and the second is the mother of Ben-Ammi and, thence, the Ammonites). There is also a *contrast* that appears to be significant: the Lord's post-diluvian covenant with Noah includes the promise of no future flood, but an alternative weapon of fire, rained upon Sodom, remains in play. These coincidences, I suggest, are too extensive to be merely accidental. But what is their significance?

We may begin an answer by noting two further questions that the story prompts. "Noah" means "rest," and the first question concerns Lamech's cryptic explanation for his son's name: "Out of the ground which the Lord has cursed this one shall bring us relief from our work and from the toil of our hands." Noah is described as "the first tiller of the soil" and inventor of wine (Ex. 9:20), apparently in fulfillment of Lamech's prophecy. Clearly, Lamech's prophecy contains an echo of Genesis 3:17–19. But how can Noah undo the curse the Lord placed upon Adam and Eve because of their disobedience? Surely, although he is the obedient one among the inhabitants of the earth, Noah does not reverse the human condition described in God's declaration that "in toil you shall eat of it [the fruits of the earth] all the days of your life."[14]

Moreover, we should note that Genesis 5:28 contains what appears to be a dual reference, for it also resonates with 4:10–12, where Cain is cursed for the murder of his brother. But the parallel is inexact: here, Cain is cursed *from* the ground (by Abel's blood), rather than the ground itself being explicitly cursed by God, though the effect is an intensification of the Adamic curse. For Cain, the ground becomes barren; he is driven into urban life. In any case, what is the "rest" that Noah brings to the earth?

The second puzzle is directly related to the first: how can Noah be the first tiller of the soil? For Cain had been a farmer—the very man whose sin had caused God to curse the ground a second time (Gen: 4:11–12; cf. v. 2:15).[15] There is a way to resolve the contradiction, but only if we speak of Noah as the first person to farm a "new earth." Can we make sense of this?

---

[14] Yet there is a further suggestive parallel here. Just as the fruit of the Tree of Knowledge of Good and Evil proved to be the downfall of Adam and Eve, so the fruit of the vine proved to be Noah's downfall, in this sense: just as, expelled from the garden, Adam and Eve bear a son who commits the sin of fratricide, so Noah's son Ham defiles his father. In both cases, the misdeed results in an expulsion from the lineage of the chosen people and the creation of foreign antagonists. We are not told, however, that Noah's drinking of wine was itself a sin. See further below.

[15] Like Lévi-Strauss, I take such contradictions to be key clues to interpretation. But my use of them is often the reverse of Lévi-Strauss'. Instead of taking the contradictions to be real and deeply diagnostic of an effort to resolve lived "contradictions," I apply a principle of charity that presumes contradictions to be only apparent. The project of discovering an interpretation that makes native thought consistent regularly leads to new insight into native meaning. Thus, apparent contradictions are a catalyst for deeper understanding. Where genuine contradictions appear, they are often the consequence of a mythographer's eagerness to combine narrative topoi bequeathed by the tradition in ways that generate surface-meaning contradictions or narrative incongruities but express a consistent underlying message. To illustrate with just one example, which involves a strong tension rather than flat contradiction, consider the contrast between the honorific portrait of Mary given by both Matthew and Luke's nativity narratives and Jesus' evident snubbing of his mother and brothers at Matt. 12:47–50 and Luke 8:19–21. David Sim, pointing out how Matt. 12 softens the anti-family tone of the Markan original (Mark 3:31–35), misses the real significance of the passage by trying to read it through the lens of the laudatory birth narrative (David C. Sim, *The Gospel of Matthew and Christian Judaism: The History and Social Setting of the Matthean Community* [Edinburgh, Scotland: T&T Clark, 1998], 191). Why not read it rather through the lens of Matt. 10:34–39? Even in the Matthew and Luke versions, after all, it remains that Jesus evidently cold-shoulders his (biological) family. But the difficulty is removed once we recognize that both the nativity narratives and the repeated anti-family passages in Matthew and Luke are through and through key elements in the (symbolic) formulation of a coherent worldview, one that valorizes Jesus' tribal roots but then supersedes, indeed rejects, tribalism and Jesus' status as a merely tribal king. See further in Chapter 12.

The idea that the world undergoes destruction and new (or re-) creation in Noah's time is not novel. Edmund Leach, for example, has argued as much, and he gives as part of the motive an effort to resolve another "contradiction"—*viz.*, that the original creation story implies a violation of the divine order, built into the very logic of the expulsion from the garden, since the continued existence of humanity must depend upon transgression of the incest taboo.[16] Could it be that, by way of the flood, God had created a new heaven and a new earth, an earth from which the divine curse has been lifted?[17] What can be said in favor of such a reading? The expression "new heaven and new earth" is explicitly employed twice by Isaiah (65:17; 66:22). It is quoted in Revelation 21:1, which adds that when the new heaven and earth are created, "the sea will be no more." This last reference is surely to the primal chaos-waters, the very waters out of which God fashions the world in Genesis 1 (see further below).

Once we see this, we will notice the extensive parallels between the flood narrative and the original creation narrative. Four themes stand out:

(1) The waters that produce the deluge come both from the sky and "the fountains of the deep." In the process, they effectively close in on the earth from above and below, merging into one "sea" that obliterates the earth (Gen. 7:11). Thus, they reverse God's creative process of separating the waters (vv. 1:6–10).
(2) At the end of the flood, God "made a wind (*ruach* = spirit, as in Gen. 1:2) to blow over the earth," and the waters subsided (v. 8:1; cf. Ex. 14:21—see below).
(3) Then, God commands Noah and his family to bring forth the animals and to "be fruitful and multiply" (Gen. 8:17, 9:17).
(4) Finally, God promises "never again [to] curse the ground" and to maintain the order of nature and of the seasons.

Thus, surely, the flood narrative represents an initial reversal of the creation process followed by a recreation of the habitable earth, a "new" ground from which old, sinful social structures are expunged and upon which a new social order can be constructed, even if new disordering sins are not long in coming. But more must be said about the claim that talk of chaos-waters functions in biblical narratives as a trope for social chaos and that control of those waters serves to represent establishment and maintenance of good social order as a victory over that chaos.

---

[16] Edmund R. Leach, "The Legitimacy of Solomon," in *Genesis as Myth and Other Essays* (London: Cape, 1969), 7–24.
[17] If you think a new heaven seems uncalled for, see below.

The theme of the chaos-waters, of the perennial danger of the "dry land" being overrun by them, and of the protective role of God in battling and containing them is one that recurs so often (in dozens, perhaps hundreds of passages) in Scripture that a listing is impractical. The import of the metaphor is, however, quite consistent, and a bit of attention to a few signal instances will be well repaid. Most ready to hand is Revelation 20:13–14, which understands the "sea" to be the locus of the dead (Hades, NRSV) from which they will be resurrected. Matthew 12:39–40 uses exactly the same imagery, identifying Jesus' descent into the "heart of the earth" with Jonah's descent into "the belly of the whale."[18] Second Peter 3 repeats the theme, making explicit that in the flood, the earth, which God had formed from the primal water, perished just as the earth is now to perish again (this time by fire) and make way for a new heaven and earth.

Not only heaven and earth can be made "new," however. A man's change in social status can be signaled by recreation, as Saul's investment as king (itself a new social role in Israel) is so described (1 Sam. 10:6). Heaven and earth themselves can assume a social role as "witnesses" (Deut. 31:28; 32:1. cf. 1 Mac. 2:37). Expanding on these themes, we may note that changes in social status—effected by rites of passage—are repeatedly marked by a parting or passage through the chaos-waters of the "deep" under divine protection. Signal instances occur at Israel's crossing of the Red Sea, in which Israel is constituted as a free people and then eventually re-constituted as a nation (with a repeated water-passage at the entry into Canaan across the parted waters of the Jordan, which in turn is echoed in the parting of those waters by Elijah, and as Elijah is assumed into heaven, as well as by Elisha as he inherits Elijah's prophetic role).[19]

But why are these rites of passage associated with death, and death with the chaos-waters? We have seen that rites of passage typically mark an individual's change in social status. By extension, they can mark a change in the status of an entire group. During the transition, often ceremonially recognized, individuals cease to embody one social identity and, often after a short interval, begins to embody another. During this process, then, one social personage "dies"—departs from that individual—and another is "born." During the interval, an individual is, socially speaking, "dead"—a "nobody" as well as, at least figuratively, in a dangerous social condition, a

---

[18] The allusion appears to be to the monsters of the deep (*tanninim*), which God variously creates (Gen. 1:21), controls, or defeats. They include Leviathan and Rahab (on occasion used as a derogatory name for Egypt—see Ps. 87:4). Cf. Ps. 74:13; Is. 27:1; 51:9; Ezek. 29:3; 32:2; and Job 7:12. That Jonah's language as he prays from the depths duplicates that of the death-and-resurrection Psalms makes it clear that the whale that harbors him is one of these monsters.

[19] For the crossing of the Red Sea as a passage through the chaos-waters, see Bernard F. Batto, "Red Sea or Sea of Reeds? How the Mistake Was Made and What Yam Sup Really Means," *Biblical Archaeology Review* 10, no. 4 (1984): 57–63.

condition of non-identity.[20] Thus, biological death serves as a natural metaphor and effective symbol for the passing away of a social status. Baptism, as we know, is a ritual passage through the chaos-waters of death into re-birth as a member of the Christian community. The Essenes, it seems, practiced a similar ritual in the first century CE.[21]

The other major context in which the theme appears is one in which someone of stature—characteristically a king or prophet—is plunged into the danger-waters and prays for divine rescue. What can be the meaning of the waters in these contexts? In fact, that meaning is hardly obscure, and it is made explicit in, for example, numerous Psalms, which conflate descent into the mortal dangers of the *tehom* with a condition of being in dire danger because of threats from enemies of the nation both external and internal.[22] Correlatively, divine rescue from the chaos-waters provides an idiom for expressing victory over those enemies.

Noah is not a king. However, there can be little doubt that it is these chaos-waters, the waters of "the deep" (the *tehom*), that create the flood (together with the down-pouring of the waters residing in the firmament). The flood is a time-reversal of the original process of creation in Genesis 1. Like the royal psalmist, and like Jonah, Noah is plunged into the deadly realm of the waters but, with divine instruction and protection, is able to escape in the service of the divine plan. And like Adam and Eve, Noah and his kin establish a new people and till a new earth: though not—alas!—in such a way as to make humankind henceforth immune to temptation and error.

Indeed, the anticlimax of the flood story looks suspiciously like an inversion of the Adamic indiscretion. The Original Couple's eating of a forbidden fruit confers knowledge or assumed authority.[23] Noah's misuse of a permitted fruit robs him of knowledge and proper authority. As a result, the nakedness of Adam and Eve is covered, and Noah's nakedness is

---

[20] For discussion of such liminal states as van Gennep dubbed them and their frequent representation as involving entry into the realm of death, see Victor Turner, *The Forest of Symbols: Aspects of Ndembu Ritual* (Ithaca, NY: Cornell University Press, 1970), 93–110 and *The Ritual Process: Structure and Anti-structure* (1969; repr., Piscataway, NJ: Aldine Transaction, 1995), 94–165) and the discussion in Chapter 6.

[21] Thus, e.g., 1 Pet. 3:20–21 compares baptism to the Noahic flood.

[22] So, e.g., Pss. 18, 69, 74, and 89; 2 Sam. 22; Isa. 43:2; 45:12–23; and 51:9–11; Ezek. 32:1–12; Zech. 10:6–12 *et passim*. The word *tehom* appears to be derived from the name of the Babylonian goddess of chaos and destruction, Tiamat (see Donald E. Gowan, *Genesis 1–11: From Eden to Babel* [Grand Rapids, MI: William B. Eerdmans Publishing Company, 1988], 19).

[23] On one reading, as already mentioned, what the eating of the fruit does is not confer knowledge of good and evil but, rather, reflect Adam and Eve's improperly taking into their own hands the authority to decide what is good and what is evil. This makes more sense of the story.

uncovered. The first establishes sex as an arena of action upon which restrictions and taboos must be imposed to preserve proper familial affiliation. The second violates one of those taboos and generates disaffiliation. (I am uncertain whether these [anti]parallels are intentional, but they are surely striking.)

Lamech's prophecy seems not to have been completely fulfilled, if we take "rest" to mean *complete* rest. But not even life in paradise excluded labor: Adam and Eve are to cultivate and maintain the garden (Gen. 2:15). Moreover, the Noahic covenant echoes the very phrasing of Genesis: "Be fruitful and multiply." And so, even though this time God does not start entirely "from scratch" (he has an ark-full of animals), there is a clear suggestion that Noah disembarks upon a "new earth" under a "new, rainbow-graced firmament."[24] Still, by the time God gives his new covenant to Noah, he appears to have acquired a certain wry cynicism about human nature—a cynicism that is promptly vindicated.[25]

What are the lessons that the repetitions found in these first ten chapters of Genesis are meant to teach? Among them, I should single out two, both born of reflections upon the requisites for stable social existence. One concerns the unruliness of our sexual nature, vis á vis maintaining social order. The other concerns the difficulties of accommodating changing economic activities to that order. Cain is a builder of cities, but urban life and the technical advances it fosters (and the sedentary agriculture that makes it possible) all appear to be disfavored by the authors of Genesis, apparently because they lead to social upheaval. And every one of our stories involves some sexual irregularity or change from nature (Adam and Eve become "ashamed" of their nakedness; Cain marries a woman who can

---

[24] A possible suggestion is that Noah's name echoes the culmination of the original labor of creation as the seventh day, on which the creator "rests." As John Walton explains, "rest" for ANE gods does not equate to sleep—or even snoozing—it celebrates victory over chaos and the transition to maintenance of a stable social order (Walton, *Ancient Near Eastern Thought*, 157–58). So, we can perhaps see in the day of Noah's emergence upon the "new earth" the second inaugural day of the Lord's rest. The case is weakened by the fact that (a) it is humanity, not the creator, that rests as a result of the new creation, and (b) different terms are used: *shabat* (Gen. 2:2) vs. *noach* (Gen. 5:29). It is nevertheless at least true that Noah has a hand in this second creation, in virtue of the righteousness that merits his rescue by God and his role in saving the animals. Moreover, it is also true that humanity is to rest on every seventh day in observance of the creator's rest. Thus, Lamech may be envisioning the setting in motion of the events that lead to the institution of the Sabbath for God's people during the Exodus.

[25] Genesis 8:21. The sin of Ham against Noah, like that of Adam against God, involves a usurpation of rank. Usurpation again rears its head with the building of the tower of Babel (Gen. 11), which prompts God to fragment the human community by introducing multilingualism. The reversal of the confusion of languages by the Pentecost event in Acts therefore signals the reunification of humanity, and it is telling that the nations named in Acts 2 are those said to have descended from the sons of Noah.

only be his sister; Noah's nakedness is intruded upon, in some darkly hinted way, by his son; and Sodom is the scene of gross violation of not only gender lines but rules of hospitality).

All this spells trouble, and Genesis uses these catastrophes to come to terms with the human condition and, more particularly, the circumstances plaguing Israel. The story takes turns that explain both the continuing imperfections of our existence and the origin of Israel's precarious political circumstances as a small nation surrounded by hostile neighbors.[26]

IV. Jacob at the Jabbok/Wrestling with God

In a curious but well-known episode in Genesis 32, Jacob is twice visited by the divine. Jacob is making his surreptitious escape from his maternal uncle Laban after twenty years in Laban's service, fourteen of them bride-price for the hands of Laban's two daughters, Leah and Rachel. Jacob had, therefore, consummated two matrilateral cross-cousin marriages in obedience to Isaac's wishes. The text appears to regard this form of marriage as normative for the patriarchs.[27] Laban, once a familial ally, has become hostile to Jacob and uses their association to exploit him. With God's help, Jacob has turned the tables, using his charge over Laban's flocks to increase his own herds, at Laban's expense, by magical means. Thus, Jacob, himself a cheat who has effectively stolen the birthright of his older brother Esau, has the tables turned on him by Laban and turns those tables himself in turn. At this point, Jacob receives a command from God to return to his native country near Bethel, some 400 miles to the southeast. It is a perilous journey. With Laban on his heels in pursuit, he must first negotiate a peace with his uncle and then face his older, and now powerful, brother Esau, who has every reason to hate him.

Fortunately, with his herd, wives, and children in tow, he has placated Laban (thanks to a warning God gives Laban before they meet). Just by the River Jabbok, he makes camp when he has a vision of angels and names the place, some forty miles northeast of his ultimate destination, Mahanaim. His path will run southwest, immanently through Esau's lands, and then across the Jordan. Having first sent messengers and then three successive caravans of goods ahead to entreat Esau for peace, Jacob intends to follow, but, cannily, only after Esau has been presented with the three sizeable peace-offerings. If these attempts to placate Esau fail, Jacob's plan is to retreat with his wives and children before Esau catches him. But first,

---

[26] See further the Appendix to this chapter.
[27] See Leach, *Genesis as Myth and Other Essays*, 46–48. In matrilateral cross-cousin marriage, male ego marries mother's brother's daughter. ('Ego' refers to the individual whose kin-relations are being specified.)

he spends another night at Mahanaim; and possibly (but see below) still fearing for the safety of his family, he moves them across to the other side of the Jabbok, spending the rest of the night alone.

Not quite alone. He receives a visit from a "man" who wrestles with him without further ado (nothing is said about any exchange of words till the very end of the struggle) for the remainder of the night. The "man," of course, proves to be an angel or, more precisely, an embodiment of God. Finally, at daybreak, God, having obtained no advantage in the match, dislocates Jacob's hip—an evident euphemism for an attack on his sexual organ.[28] Indeed, Jacob thereafter "walks with a limp" and has no more children. But Jacob hangs on nevertheless and refuses God's urgent demand to be released unless God blesses him. God then renames Jacob, calling him Israel, and blesses him. But he refuses to tell Jacob his own name. Jacob thanks his lucky stars: he has seen God and lived. That the intruder is God is made clear by his interpretation of the name "Israel" as "one who strives with God." In consequence, Jacob/Israel names the place "Peniel" ("the face of God").

There is much to puzzle over in this episode. For one thing, Jacob has no trouble recognizing the angels of God that meet him at Mahanaim, which he promptly identifies as God's camp. Clearly, he understands the proximity of the divine. For another, God once again blesses Jacob not very long thereafter at Bethel, then reconfers upon him the name Israel, reconfirms the covenantal promise of land and paternity of many nations, and this time provides his name as God Almighty (i.e., *El*; see Ex. 35:9–15). Indeed, Jacob has both prayed to God and received commands from him on several occasions during the narrative without the question of divine identity arising. Why, then, Jacob's ignorance of God's identity and the divine mystification in response to Jacob's request for a name?

Immediately after the encounter with God, Esau approaches with a large force of men; and Joseph, heading up the column of his wives and children, goes to meet him. There is a palaver: Joseph attempts to give Esau the gifts he sent ahead. Esau declines, but Jacob insists. Esau's final acceptance (even though he is himself wealthy) signals the formal reunion of the brothers. Joseph remains suspicious: when Esau offers to accompany him on his journey, he diplomatically declines. Esau therefore heads back to his home in Seir/Edom. Joseph's suspicion contrasts with his declaration to

---

[28] We have already encountered the use of a similar euphemism in the story of the baptism of Moses's son. Here, a helpful discussion can be found in S. H. Smith, "'Heel' and 'Thigh': The Concept of Sexuality in the Jacob-Esau Narratives," *Vetus Testamentum* 40, no. 4 (1990): 464–73. It is however surprising that Smith characterizes the divine attack upon Jacob's genitalia as a conferral of fertility: he fails to note that the attack is mounted to gain a victory in combat, that it injures Jacob, and that Jacob, in fact, ceases to sire offspring.

Esau that to see Esau's face is "like seeing the face of God ... [who] has dealt graciously with me." Stopping next at Succoth, Jacob builds a house, then proceeds to Shechem in Canaan where he purchases some land and builds an altar to the God of Israel. Eventually, after an altercation with the Shechemites over Leah's daughter Dinah, God commands Jacob to move south to Bethel. Before setting off, all of Jacob's company give him the foreign gods (i.e., images) they had, which he buries under an oak.

Now, certainly as history, this story presents a number of problems. The narrator seems to be geographically challenged. Jacob manages, in ten days, to travel some 350 miles as the crow flies, with an entourage of men, women, children, and large herds of goats and sheep. At that point, Laban, having covered the same distance in seven days, manages to catch up with him. Joseph, it seems, was able to average well over thirty-five miles a day (considering meanders in the trail), a distance that, as any hiker knows, requires considerable athleticism. More puzzling is Jacob's sending messengers to inform his brother of his arrival at a point some eighty miles (at least) to the north of Esau's home. If he feared Esau, why should he borrow trouble by giving him his travel itinerary? Why not (at least) wait till he had arrived at Shechem or Bethel? Perhaps he thought that Esau would look askance at such a return to his patrimony. But we are not told.

There are two places at which one might have expected some explanation, but the narrative remains silent. No explanation is actually given for why Jacob relocates his family to the other side of the Jabbok, apparently during the night, and then returns to his station at Mahanaim. The suggestion that he wanted to protect his family from Esau seems implausible: did he expect Esau to arrive at night?[29] More likely, this is a narrative device for isolating Jacob for his encounter with God. Second—as noted—God's onslaught appears to be unannounced and unjustified.

It is hard not to see significant parallels between this episode and the divine attack upon Moses in Exodus 4. There are notable differences, to be sure: Moses' close call occurs in the presence of his family (and a good thing, too; one imagines that he would not have survived in the absence of Zipporah and their son). God and Jacob exchange words, but in God's

---

[29] What is worse, the locations of Mahanaim and Peniel are unknown. William Ewing argues that Mahanaim was north of the Jabbok, which would mean that Jacob, in relocating his family on the south side of the stream, would have put them directly in harm's way: closer to Esau, who was traveling from the south. See William Ewing, "Mahanaim," in *International Standard Bible Encyclopedia*, ed. James Orr (Grand Rapids, MI: William B. Eerdmans Publishing Company, 1939), internationalstandardbible.com/M/mahanaim.html. For a more recent review of similar scholarly views, see W. D. Mounce, "Mahanaim," in *International Standard Bible Encyclopedia*, rev. ed., ed. Geoffrey W. Bromiley (Grand Rapids, MI: William B. Eerdmans Publishing Company, 1986), 3:222–23. If this is correct, then it is all the more likely that this detail was inserted to give Jacob a lone encounter with God.

ambush of Moses, he remains silent. Yet the similarities are striking enough to call for some explanation: 1) Both encounters occur after a divine command to return to country of origin. 2) Both involve facing a dangerous human enemy and overcoming that danger in order to fulfill the mission to bring Israel back to the land of promise. 3) Both mention an encampment at a place named Succoth after the divinely assisted escape from pursuing human opponents.[30] 4) Both involve migrations from places originally friendly but later hostile.

Here, the parallels are more complex. Jacob's ancestral home becomes hostile when he cheats Esau out of his birthright. Laban, a kinsman, is initially friendly but comes to behave toward Jacob as Jacob had behaved toward his brother (of which more below). So, Jacob flees a hostile situation only to have to confront, and resolve, a hostile situation of his own making upon his return home.

The house of Israel—Jacob's children—flees a famine and finds refuge in a welcoming Egypt (a welcome mediated by Joseph, Jacob's son, who has already arrived in Egypt as a slave because of fraternal rivalry). But Egypt turns hostile. Moses flees to an initially welcoming Midian. He marries the daughter of Midian's priest, Jethro, and, like Jacob, serves his father-in-law as a shepherd. He does not leave Jethro because Midian turns hostile, but Midian later becomes an enemy of Israel on her march from Egypt back to Canaan—though, ironically, because Midianite maidens court Israelite men! Yet, when Moses leads Israel into the wilderness, his father-in-law Jethro seeks him out, returning wife and sons (who had apparently been sent back to Midian after Moses enters Egypt), acknowledges Yahweh as Lord, and gives Moses fatherly advice (Gen. 18). Presumably, Jethro's relation to Israel is thereby somehow regularized, though there is no mention of his being circumcised. The difference between his household and the rest of the Midianites appears to be that the latter are bent upon assimilating the Jews and converting them to a worship of Baal-Peor, whereas Jethro and Zipporah become assimilated Jews.

The moral of the Jethro/Zipporah story seems to be: gentiles who come to worship Yahweh are welcomed into the fold; those that do not are actual or potential enemies. We may note that although Laban is a kinsman to Abraham, and intermarriage is normative, Laban does not ever worship Yahweh as Lord. In this way, Moses' marriage to Zipporah and Jacob's marriage to Leah and Rachel are not paradigm for opposing reasons: one is marriage to ethnic aliens who become co-religionists. The other is marriage to relatives who are not co-religionists. In both cases, purity of lineage is under threat.

---

[30] God's assistance is less spectacular in Jacob's case. It consists of a warning to Laban and, presumably, insures the success of Jacob's stratagem for breeding a better goat herd than Laban's.

It may be that the normative status of Jacob's progeny—the father of the twelve tribes—is under threat for two other reasons, *both* as concerns kinship and as concerns proper worship. On the side of kinship, Jacob's simultaneous marriage to two sisters is forbidden by the law of Moses. Though legal in Jacob's day—and, in fact, forced by a rule of female primogeniture invoked by Laban, it ceased to be normative for Judaism.[31] This difficulty may be marked in the narrative by Rachel's difficulty in getting pregnant and giving birth. She dies in giving birth to her second son, Benjamin. Indeed, Rachel never makes it all the way to Ephrath/Bethlehem, the ultimate destination of Jacob's repatriation journey. The second irregularity also involves Rachel. When Jacob prepares to flee from Laban, his wives register no complaint, remarking that Laban has spent their bride-price so that they stand to gain no inheritance from him upon his death.

But more than this, Rachel steals Laban's family gods—wooden images that would have been passed on through the patriline, presumably to Laban's eldest son, as a birthright and marker of the transmission of Laban's authority as head of family. We must assume her intention to pass these images on to her own (eldest?) son.[32] This creates not only a religious problem but a corresponding structural problem. It would entail not only the worship of foreign gods, but it would also disenfranchise all of Joseph's brothers. And indeed, one of the most poignant narratives in the Bible recounts the jealousy that developed between Joseph and his half-brothers (Benjamin, the full brother, appears to be exempt), as well as their ultimate reconciliation when Joseph renounces any claim to priority.

The first step in this equalization occurs, however, when Jacob enters what will become the Holy Land, being commanded to depart from Shechem and to journey south to Bethel. Before they set off, Jacob instructs his household to get rid of foreign gods (Gen. 35:1–4). Specific mention is not made of the gods in Rachel's possession—it is not even clear whether Jacob has learned of their presence—but the order clearly applies to them.

---

[31] Not strictly forced: both the later norms of the Mosaic covenant and Laban's rule could have been satisfied had Jacob been satisfied by a marriage to Leah only. But for him, that would have been a deal-breaker.

[32] Rachel's successful sequestration of them from Laban's attempt to find them, in a camel saddle upon which she sits, suggests a double irony. Rachel excuses herself from rising before her "Lord" because she is menstruating. For Laban to come into contact with the saddle would have been polluting. But by the same token, the images, had she in fact been menstruating, would presumably have been polluted by proximity to menstrual blood. We have here a kind of inversion of the symbolism of the Exodus 4 episode where genital blood from a son does make contact with the father's reproductive organs, something that is sanctifying, not polluting, and establishes legitimacy of the right kind (rather than being an instrument of inheritance from a rejected line). The upshot is that Laban's line is cut off and not diverted to any of Jacob's progeny.

one theory has it that the mysterious stranger who engages him during the night is none other than Esau or Esau's daemon.[36]

But that does not seem right, given Esau's tearful greeting when they meet the next day—to say nothing of the oddity, in that case, of Esau's questions regarding the two caravans of gifts that precede Jacob (and this in spite of the curious exclamation from Jacob that seeing Esau's face is like seeing that of God). Here, we may note just two points. First, Jacob's face-to-face meeting with the mysterious "man" was not unequivocally joyous—as was his reunion with Esau. Second, Jacob comments on the point of the comparison: just as God has granted him a blessing, so too Esau. Even so, the simile is striking. If we take the "man" to be an embodiment of the divine, we can understand the encounter as one in which God does, indeed, take Esau's part, exacting retribution by sterilizing Jacob, but, for all that, doing him less harm (and thus protecting him) than Esau easily might have. Jacob is not released unpunished, but he is given a reduced sentence.

Moses' liability is his failure to have circumcised his son, which may reflect divided tribal loyalties. It is, therefore, especially appropriate that rectification is effected by Zipporah, the alien wife who thereby declares her fealty to Yahweh (as her father does later). And Balaam? His case is less clear. Even having promised to deliver to Balak only what Yahweh instructs him to say, he is someone who, as he embarks on his mission, is unable properly to discern the Lord. His status as a non-Jew qualifies him as a neutral party who can be appealed to by Barak, but his alien status also calls into question his standing as a prophet of the God of Israel.

The richness of these stories suggests that there is considerably more to be said about them, both individually and in comparison, but my aim here is a limited one. It is to illustrate the plausibility and potential fruitfulness of reading biblical narratives in juxtaposition with an eye for thematic elements (and structures built out of them) that, by their strong similarities or oppositions, bespeak a deliberate intention to weave a symbolic landscape from a vocabulary of tropes that, like skeins of colored thread, can be drawn upon like the pigments on an artist's palette. We must always be alert to the danger of detecting patterns where none were intended by the authors of our texts, but once coincidence reaches a certain level of complexity, the likelihood of mere chance dwindles. An interpreter is left with two primary options. Either a divine being set himself the task of choreographing such an intricately interlinked set of histories, or else the consummate artistry of human writers intimately familiar with their culture's literary environment and traditions served, together with some social or

---

[36] So Zöe Klein, "Wrestling with Man, Not Angel," ReformJudaism.org, December 4, 2006, reformjudaism.org/wrestling-man-not-angel and Jack Miles, "Jacob's Wrestling Match: Was It an Angel or Esau?," *Bible Review* 14, no. 5 (1998): 22–23.

political need, to provoke yet another configuration of traditional meanings into contemporary reflection and ideological innovation.

Appendix: Sex and the City

Perhaps it will be well at this juncture to remind the reader of the method I am employing, as set forth in previous chapters. The first step is to search the text(s) for stories that recognizably correspond, in the sense that they contain correlated elements: episodes or themes that show parallelism or anti-parallelism. The existence of such pairs hints at the repetitive expression of mythemes—the content in virtue of which the resemblance or opposition holds. The more numerous the parallels, and the more intricate the corresponding patterns they form, the stronger the evidence that the parallel structures are intentional and the commonalities meaningful. Having isolated such presumptive mythemes, the next task is to seek their underlying content or significance. In so doing, we reason to the best explanation; and one major criterion that constrains the evaluation of alternatives must be the interpretation respects our principle of charity; we should favor interpretations that cogently engage culturally relevant issues and problems.

What appears in the main body of this chapter bears only a somewhat distant kinship to structural analysis of myths in the Lévi-Straussian mode, properly speaking.[37] I have noted repeated themes (and their patterned inversions) but have not attempted to systematize all of this material in a way that aims to bring out an overarching pattern of structures that exemplifies Lévi-Strauss' or Turner's larger concerns with the dialectics of human thought and communication in general. I have been more directly concerned with excavating the relationship of these texts to the particular cultural and historical concerns that might have exercised their authors, for example concerns over proper and improper marriage, over how to engage neighboring societies, over the creation and exercise of authority, over the creation and maintenance of cultural identity.

One might be struck, however, by a larger architectonic that these materials bring to light, a structure of interest in its own right and also suggestive of the possibility of a large-scale structural analysis. Even though

---

[37] Others who have followed Lévi-Strauss' lead in producing structural analyses—e.g., Edmund R. Leach, ed., *The Structural Study of Myth and Totemism* (London: Tavistock Publications, 1967) and Terrence Turner, "Oedipus: Time and Structure in Narrative Form," in *Forms of Symbolic Action: Proceedings of the 1969 Annual Spring Meeting of the American Ethnological Society*, ed. Robert F. Spencer (Seattle, WA: University of Washington Press, 1969)—have certainly not been slavish followers and indeed disagree (as do I) with various aspects of Lévi-Strauss' conception of how such analyses are to be performed and of what they can tell us.

I have examined only three episodes in the canon (with side references to Gen. 3–4 and to broader issues in Christian eschatology), one theme that seems to emerge (one that, if genuine, should be discoverable in many other Bible stories) is a dual concern with sexual relations and with the tension between the natural world and social order. More specifically: a concern over proper sexual relations, and the implied control over sex on the one hand, and the tension between "wilderness" and the city (mediated by control over nature in the form of farming and animal herding) on the other.

These themes seem to appear as mirror images of one another in our material. Why should that be? And how, in particular, is the dialectic that resolves the tension in the one domain reflected in the dialectic that resolves the tension in the other? For—as I hope now to indicate—there is a symmetry between the original state of the creation and the Christian eschaton that involves both themes.

My answer to these questions hinges on the claim that concern with social order is fundamental to both themes. Sex is a *natural* phenomenon, but—most emphatically in a tribal context—it is essential to the very form of social structure since tribal structures are predicated upon kinship relations. Here, several tensions are immediately evident. Sex is, by its very nature, unruly and extraordinarily difficult to regiment. Its consequences are also by nature unruly: sexual union may or may not result in a child. If it does, the sex of that child is not something that can be controlled. And whatever a child's sex, children are by their very nature unruly: they must be civilized through a long, arduous, and chancy process.[38] So sex and its consequences must be tamed.

On the other side, we may think of the need for social order in the following way. Societies are structured by means of institutions, social roles, social practices, and the legal and customary relations that govern these. For the sake of simplicity, think of a social structure as comprised of a set of social roles and jural relations between them. For such a structure to govern a smoothly running society, it must be properly embodied by social agents: ideally, every social role is filled by a competent actor. Roles are (in principle) by their nature durable. Social agents not only vary in competence but in availability—they are born, go through various stages in life often marked by changes in social status and role, and then die.

As an ongoing concern, a social structure must have a reliable "input" of new personnel to replace those whose demise or change in social position leaves a role unfilled. But Mother Nature, in the form of procreation, does this in only rather irregular and unpredictable ways. The ideal—the situation that is the "simplest (and best) to think," in Lévi-Straussian terms—is a simple, durable social structure in which the order of

---

[38] As Socrates wryly observes in the Meno—and as Huck Finn also engagingly remarks at the close of his story.

nature is itself reflected and in which nature itself is also perfectly ordered: there is no death and no need for replacement of personnel. Hence, the initial state of the garden of Eden.

That symmetry is necessarily broken when human beings procreate and try, by their own inventiveness, to regiment the results by means of human institutions. It appears that we can trace in the Bible something like a system of oppositions, reflecting ways in which things can go awry, between "good" sex and "bad" sex, and between "good" social order and "bad" that displays a recognition of the connection between the two and an attempt to explore how the problems might be overcome or at least mitigated.[39] It is not quite correct to say that the view of Genesis 2 is that the best sex is no sex: 2:24 speaks, a bit indirectly, of man and wife becoming "one flesh." But—in contrast to v. 1:28—there is no command to "be fruitful and multiply." And no multiplication is undertaken until after the expulsion. Thus, the time that Adam and Eve spend in the garden is a time of stasis and of social structure pared down to a bare minimum: Man and Wife. Nature itself is orderly; no animal kills or dies. God saw that it was good.

With God's preference of Abel's sacrifice over Cain's, we may see the first indication of a tension between sedentary farming and pastoralism, possibly reflecting an historical memory of the pastoral ways of the early Israelite communities in the highlands, in contrast to the farmer-supported urban cultures of the Canaanite lowlands. At the least, our Tanachic texts reflect a decidedly ambivalent attitude toward urbanization.[40] This becomes

---

[39] As I noted in Chapter 6, Terrence Turner, in a tour de force, shows how the Oedipus cycle can be seen as a similar thought experiment in social disorder and the possible ways to bring a social system into proper alignment again (Turner, "Oedipus," 26–68).

[40] Cain, who committed the first murder, leaves the divine presence and builds the first city. The development of urban centers, which was associated with sedentary farming, emerged over the course of several millennia and encompassed the Bronze and Early Iron ages. It is of course unthinkable that these changes, with their consequent competition over territory, would not lead to perennial conflicts. Conflict between farmers and the Canaanite cities that they supported has been suggested to explain the initial creation of the Israelite or proto-Israelite tribes that occupied the Judean hill-country (for general early urban-rural relations see Alexander Thomas, "Urbanization before Cities: Lessons for Social Theory from the Evolution of Cities," *Journal of World-Systems Research* 18, no. 2 [2012]: 211–35). As for evidence of distinct urban and rural cultural identities, Olof Pederson et al. note in passing that "Sumerian proverbs and debate literature often made use of the distinction between city and countryside. The distinction led to humorous contrasts between city dwellers and their rural counterparts, with the latter most often emerging morally superior" (Olof Pedersén et al., "Cities and Urban Landscapes in the Ancient Near East and Egypt with Special Focus on the City of Babylon," in *The Urban Mind Cultural and Environmental Dynamics*, ed. Paul J. J. Sinclair et al. [Upsala, Sweden: Upsala University Press, 2010], 131–32). It must be said, however, that current understanding of the emergence of Israel/Judah during the primitive

immediately apparent in the Noah story and its sequel. Noah and his family are chosen by God to make a fresh start. Noah, a farmer, invents wine—as always, a mixed blessing. The text is guarded concerning the offence Ham commits against him. A homosexual act is not out of the question.[41] In any event, the act serves to anathematize Ham's descendants, which include the Canaanites, whose cities of Sodom and Gomorrah have inherited Ham's impurity and amplified it.[42]

With the story of Lot's rescue from Sodom, we come to what is arguably the nadir of the corrupt sex/urban civilization complex in the Pentateuch.[43] Lot arrives in the suburbs of Sodom as a tent-dweller but becomes urbanized. By the time the two angels visit, he lives in a house in town.[44] The sexual sin involves at least rape and presumably a universal male penchant for homosexuality.[45] The social sin of violating the norms of hospitality suggests Sodom's incapacity for suitable relations with neighboring groups, which parallels the male Sodomite incapacity for proper relations to other men/women. All of Sodom (and Gomorrah for good measure) stands under divine condemnation. The un-redeemability of Sodom's sins stands in contrast to the relative excusability of the incest committed by Lot's daughters.

Just as Sodom's corruption is sufficient for her destruction, the filial incest is a necessary condition of the continuation of Lot's line since, after

---

and First Temple periods is in sufficient disarray that attempts to ground Genesis themes in social-historical conditions is unavoidably speculative. I therefore try here to confine my proposals to ones suggested by quite general social issues. For a brief summary of research into Israel's beginnings, see, e.g., Andrew Tobolowsky, "Israelite and Judahite History in Contemporary Theoretical Approaches," *Currents in Biblical Research* 17, no. 1 (2018): 33–58.

[41] It is common to deny that there was any sexual contact and to take the text at face value: Ham's sin, then, is dishonoring his father. See, for example, John Barton and John Muddiman, eds., *The Oxford Bible Commentary* (New York: Oxford University Press, 2001), 47. But other scholars disagree, and Lev. 18:6–19 is surely suggestive.

[42] The actual location of these cities is unknown, but they appear to have been situated within Canaan; see Genesis 10:19 and Numbers 34:1–6.

[43] Cf. the ghoulish tale at Judges 19:16–30.

[44] The number appears to diminish from three (Gen. 18:2) to one (Gen. 19:21–22). The textual details are difficult.

[45] There is some discussion whether the sin is general homosexuality or involves a reference to temple prostitution. Either way, Sodom has attempted a rape of divine beings, which is not only sexually improper but reverses the proper relations of power. Lot's outrageous act of offering his daughters as substitute sexual partners to the Sodomites emphasizes their dedicated homosexuality. The response to the offer itself emphasizes Lot's alien status in Sodom. The offer of a daughter or wife as a sexual partner to strangers is not an uncommon gesture, whose purpose is to mediate friendship, a declaration of peace, or social incorporation. See Arnold van Gennep, *The Rites of Passage*, trans. Monika B. Vizedon and Gabrielle L. Caffee (1909; repr., Chicago, IL: University of Chicago Press, 1960), 33–34.

escaping Sodom and after a brief sojourn in Zoar, Lot and his daughters flee to a cave in the hills: they have moved from city to wilderness.[46] The daughters become the matriarchs of Moab and Ammon, two tribes whose kinship with Israel is later attested in a divine prohibition against conquest of their territories.[47] Moreover, the tribal purity of Lot's line is preserved, and as he is the father of Moab and Ammon, they stand as cousins (once removed) through the male line to Jacob/Israel. This incest, then, mediates between extreme sexual defilement and sexual propriety.

But if there is any lesson to be learned here, it is that sex breeds trouble—especially when it is put in the service of social order. The NT offers what appears to be an extreme way out of this dilemma, one that divorces sex—or at any rate its social concomitant, marriage—from social structure. Thus, for starters, we have Jesus' surprising comment that in the resurrection, there will be no marriage (Matt. 22:30; cf. Lk. 20:36, which adds that the saints are not only like angels but cannot die). Here, we have what looks like a prophecy of return to the aboriginal social stasis. It is also—so Paul—a state in which other social distinctions (between Jew and Gentile, slave and freeman, male and female) are erased.[48] As between this state and the original paradise, there are three notable differences. One is that rather than residing in a perfectly ordered nature, the citizens of this new kingdom are to reside in a perfectly ordered city: the New Jerusalem. Second, there are more than two of them—and the model of the nuclear family has been erased. Finally, in the kingdom, an unruly nature is defeated

---

[46] D. Alan Aycock suggests that the immobilization of Lot's wife represents a mediation between no fewer than five "contradictory" events: 1) the hospitality offered by Lot to the strangers vs. the social violations of Lot's daughters in the cave; 2) the two disguised male strangers vs. the two unrecognized female intimates; 3) the destruction of Sodom vs. the creation of Moab and Ammon; 4) the initial urban location vs. the final rural one; and 5) the homosexuality of Sodom vs. the incest of the daughters (Edmund R. Leach and D. Alan Aycock, *Structural Interpretations of Biblical Myth* [New York: Cambridge University Press, 1983], 113–19). The turning of a human being to stone is a theme found in various traditions (e.g., Asdiwal in the Tsimshian myth). I cannot begin to discuss Aycock's reasoning here, which strikes me as far-fetched. Were I in a jocular mood, I would suggest yet a further mediation: just as, for Lévi-Strauss, the raw and the cooked represent the opposition between nature and culture, so salt is a mediator between raw and cooked (it is used raw, but to improve that which is cooked), and so Lot's wife mediates the opposition between city and wilderness. Here, I find the usual explanation in terms of the Dead Sea salt formations more plausible.

[47] See Deut. 2:9–22. Note, further, that Ruth, a Moabitess, is the great-grandmother of David. Yet, as Leach's detailed discussion shows, Israel's relations with Moab and Ammon were profoundly ambivalent. For instance, Solomon is condemned for taking wives from among them (1 Kings 11:1–8). See Leach, "The Legitimacy of Solomon."

[48] For more on this, see Chapter 11, Sec. 2 and Chapter 12.

and destroyed. What remains of paradise is the tree of life (Rev. 21:1: "the sea was no more," and vv. 21:22–22:5).[49]

Jesus' own origins and life presage this condition. Although he is born of woman, he has no mortal father (biologically: but as Joseph's adopted son, he becomes by adoption heir to the Davidic line). Mary's divine insemination, as it were, cuts Jesus off from original sin. Moreover, he is celibate—of a virgin born and a virgin in death. As the second Adam, Jesus mediates the conflict between nature/sex and society/ordered stasis by serving as the sexually liberated harbinger of an eschaton in which immortality vitiates the need for procreation and in which disorder—whether human or natural—is permanently banished from the city. The new paradise is a city in which sin is no longer possible.

---

[49] Cf. Ezek. 48:30–35. Revelation dramatically enhances Ezekiel's vision not only spiritually but physically.

Protagonists	Social Structures	Implications
Adam/Eve: virgin births, but not permanently celibate: sin ⇨ children.	* Paradise/social stasis; sin ⇨ social division in the form of division of labor (the sons of Cain). * Two people become many people but with no explicit tribal divisions; kinship extends across existing humans. * Opposition between farmer-urban complex and nomadic shepherd complex.	* Perfection ⇨ corruption. * Civilized wilderness ⇨ opposition between wilderness and civilization. * Procreation initially in the second generation entails incest.
Noah and his family: not virgins but sexually proper ⇨ sexual and familial impropriety/impurity: incest, homosexuality(?), dishonoring of the father.	* One people/one language ⇨ many peoples, enmity between tribes (Babel).	New validation of farmer-urban culture (rest). But the sons of Ham become fathers of enemies of Israel.
Lot and family: not virgins, sexually proper in an urban society steeped in sexual impropriety and violation of norms of hospitality (proper relations between strangers) ⇨ escape into the countryside ⇨ sexual impropriety (incest).	* Many peoples/languages but with traceable ties of kinship that lead to ambiguities in tribal boundaries and proper alliances	* Urban life leads to social and sexual corruption, violation of proper rules of hospitality and hence of relations between cities. Thus, urban life = wilderness; but abandonment of urban setting for rural setting means loss of proper husbands for the daughters of Lot. Their sons engender enemies of Israel.
Jesus/Book of Revelations: virgin birth and celibate life ⇨ no biological offspring. But all men and women, if they become disciples, are children.	* Society has become divided and corrupt; wilderness has utterly penetrated the city * But in the eschaton, all peoples are reunified into one city * Order is everywhere—both nature and society are reordered (Jesus is master of the waves, of disease). * Opposition between city and wilderness is mediated: new heaven, new earth, new Jerusalem	* Kinship becomes reconfigured in a way that divorces it completely from biology; it is now a rubric for allegiance to the King. Social glue morphs from kinship to Kingship. * In the eschaton, not only is procreation nullified but also social structures and distinctions of all kinds: no marriage (Matt. 22:30), no slavery or male/female (Gal. 3:28).

The Road to Damascus

> There is something deeply mysterious about Paul's conversion experience, something that will never be available to scientific analysis.
> Alan F. Segal[1]

It is unclear whether Segal finds Paul's conversion mysterious because Paul's descriptions of his conversion pose problems, because the historical record is so sketchy, or because Segal thinks mystical experience itself resists scientific understanding. Here are the texts from Galatians and the book of Acts:

> For I would have you know, brethren, that the gospel which was preached by me is not man's gospel. For I did not receive it from man, nor was I taught it, but it came through a revelation of Jesus Christ. For you have heard of my former life in Judaism, how I persecuted the church of God violently and tried to destroy it; and I advanced in Judaism beyond many my own age....so extremely zealous was I for the traditions of my fathers. But when he who set me apart before I was born, and called me through his grace, was pleased to reveal his Son to [*sic*: in] me, in order that I might preach him to the Gentiles, I did not confer with flesh and blood, nor did I go up to Jerusalem to those who were apostles before me, but I went away into Arabia; and again I returned to Damascus.
>
> Then after three years I went up to Jerusalem to visit Cephas, and remained with him fifteen days. But I saw none of the other apostles except James the Lord's brother. (In what I am writing to you, before God, I do not lie!) Then I went into the regions of Syria and Cilicia....
>
> Then after fourteen years I went up again to Jerusalem....I went up by revelation; and I laid before them ... the gospel which I preach among the Gentiles, lest somehow I should be running ... in vain. And ... those who were of repute added nothing to me ... and when they perceived the grace that was given to me, James and Cephas and John, who were reputed to be pillars, gave to me ... the right hand of

---

[1] Alan F. Segal, *Paul the Convert: The Apostolate and Apostasy of Saul the Pharisee* (New Haven, CT: Yale University Press, 1990), 134.

> fellowship, that we should go to the Gentiles, and they to the circumcised. (Gal. 1:11–2:9, RSV)
>
> But Saul, still breathing threats and murder against the disciples ... went to the high priest....Now as he journeyed he approached Damascus, and suddenly a light from heaven flashed about him. And he fell to the ground and heard a voice saying to him, "Saul, Saul, why do you persecute me?" And he said, "Who are you, Lord?" And he said, "I am Jesus, whom you are persecuting; but rise and enter the city, and you will be told what to do." The men who were traveling with him stood speechless, hearing the voice but seeing no one. Saul arose from the ground; and when his eyes were opened he could see nothing....And for three days he was without sight, and neither ate nor drank....
>
> [After he was cured] For several days he was with the disciples in Damascus. And in the synagogues he immediately proclaimed Jesus, saying "He is the Son of God"....When many days had passed, the Jews plotted to kill him ... but his disciples took him by night....And when he had come to Jerusalem he attempted to join the disciples; and they were all afraid of him....But Barnabas took him and brought him to the apostles, and declared to them how on the road he had seen the Lord....So he went in and out among them at Jerusalem, preaching boldly in the name of the Lord. And he spoke and disputed against the Hellenists; but they were seeking to kill him. And when the brethren knew it, they ... sent him off to Tarsus. (Acts 9:1–30)

We shall also have occasion to refer to two other accounts of Paul's conversion in Acts (Acts 22 and 26) and to his list of post-resurrection appearances of Jesus (1 Cor. 15). Here are questions: Who was Paul? What did he in fact experience? What were the consequences, for Paul, of having had this experience? What could he learn from that experience about Jesus of Nazareth? As one of the first and perhaps the single most prominent convert to Christianity, Paul stands, for Christians, as a model both of conversion and of spiritual intimacy with the risen Lord. Paul is a paradigm. What can the modern study of mystical experiences (MEs) tell us about Paul? In this chapter, I will turn to a different line of anthropological investigation than the work heretofore invoked. I will make use primarily of comparative studies of mystical traditions in contemporary tribal cultures to glean insights that, I claim, will help us to understand Paul. And I will use that exercise as a gateway to a look at a broader question: how much, in general, can we hope to learn about the phenomenology and epistemic credentials of MEs from the reports of those that have them?

To be sure, Paul does not tell us, in any extant writings, about the content, or even the circumstances, of his encounter with Jesus. For this, we must rely upon Luke, who apparently quotes Paul. Nevertheless, what Paul does say, and the contrast with the Lukan accounts, can tell us some significant things about Paul. So I shall argue. Let me alert the reader in advance that I shall, in engaging the Pauline and Lukan texts, be employing, for cause, a hermeneutics of suspicion. The reasons for this I shall shortly reveal.

Let us begin with three puzzles that concern chronology rather than the content of Paul's conversion experience. The first two puzzles have to do with Paul's post-conversion agenda. In Galatians 1, Paul tells us that he was "called" by Jesus to preach to the Gentiles and that he did not "confer with flesh and blood" to pursue this calling—in other words, he did not consult with, or seek the imprimatur of, the Jerusalem leadership of the church—but went straightaway to Arabia. Paul does not say how long he stayed in Arabia, or what he did there, but the implication is that he was engaged in preaching to the Gentiles and that this mission lasted possibly as long as three years. Only afterwards did he consult with the Jerusalem church and then only with its two leaders, Peter and James, after which time he again went away for fourteen years, confirmed in his authority to preach, to the Gentile regions of Syria and Cilicia.

This account conflicts in two striking ways with the account we find at Acts 9, for there, we are told that, after escaping an assassination plot by the Jews in Damascus, Paul went to Jerusalem, not Arabia. In Jerusalem, he spent time conferring, not just with Peter and James, but with all the apostles, convincing them of the sincerity of his conversion by preaching "against the Hellenists." Perceiving that he was under threat from these Hellenists, Paul goes to Tarsus, then Antioch (in Cilicia). In Acts 22, Luke quotes Paul confirming essentially this account in testimony before the Roman tribune, but in his testimony to Agrippa, he adds (Acts 26:20) another detail not mentioned in Galatians, namely that he preached "throughout all the country of Judea."

Did Paul preach in Arabia for some time on the sole authority of his vision before submitting himself to scrutiny by the Jerusalem church or go directly to Jerusalem from Damascus? Did Paul submit his credentials to just Peter and James or to the whole Jerusalem congregation? And—a perhaps more minor point—did his mission include all of Judea or not?

The third main puzzle is presented by 1 Corinthians 15:6, where, on the face of it, Paul is offering evidence that Jesus is risen by giving the Corinthians a chronologically ordered list of those to whom the risen Christ has appeared, beginning with Peter and ending with his own conversion experience. A noteworthy entry in this list is an appearance "to more than five hundred brethren at one time, most of whom are still alive, though some have fallen asleep." This mention of a public appearance is puzzling for two reasons. First, remarkable though it must have been, it is to my knowledge nowhere else attested in any extant ancient source. It is especially surprising not to find mention of it in Acts.² Second, it is nearly useless as evidence: Paul does not tell the Corinthians where this appearance occurred nor does he name any of the "brethren."

Furthermore, if, as we might reasonably suppose, the event took place in Judea or Galilee, it would have been something of a fool's errand for any Corinthian to attempt to confirm it. Not only are the witnesses unnamed, but Judea is some 800 miles as the crow flies distant from Corinth (an arduous journey taking perhaps a good fortnight in those days). The bearing of this passage on my argument will emerge presently. I shall suggest that Paul has something besides evidence of the resurrection in mind.³

Elsewhere, I have defended the applicability of the work of the anthropologist I. M. Lewis on mysticism to Christian mysticism—at least where mysticism "goes public."⁴ Here, I want to consider the much more

---

² Grasping at straws, some scholars have attempted to identify this appearance with the Pentecostal visitation by the Holy Spirit (Acts 2). This seems unlikely—see N. T. Wright, *The Resurrection of the Son of God*, Christian Origins and the Question of God, vol. 3 (Minneapolis, MN: Fortress Press, 2003), 324–5. But see also, Richard C. Carrier, "The Burial of Jesus in the Light of Jewish Law," in *The Empty Tomb: Jesus Beyond the Grave*, ed. Robert M. Price and Jeffrey Jay Lowder (Amherst, NY: Prometheus Books, 2005), 369–92. If Carrier is right, "five hundred" may be a copyist's misreading of "fifty" (as in "Pentecost"), which makes identity possible. Acts 2 is evidently meant to describe Jesus' predicted baptism of the brethren with the Holy Spirit and with fire (Matt. 3:11; Luke 3:16), but Jesus himself is not said to appear. If Paul *is* referring to the Pentecost event, my argument concerning 1 Cor. 15:6 will be weakened. Even so, we note that Paul places James near the end of the list. If Paul was referring to the Pentecost event, other questions immediately arise. The number of witnesses is now unknown (arguably around 120, the number reported at Acts 1:15)—but presumably well below five hundred. More crucially, either the appearance traditions Paul received contain significant error or else the early Christian community—and Paul—could understand the Pentecost visitation, by what Luke describes as the Holy Spirit, as interchangeable with encounters with the risen Jesus. In fact, Paul came close to such an identification at 2 Cor. 3:17. Indeed, Peter suggests as much in his speech following the miracle of the tongues, apparently averring that the events just transpired constitute a witnessing of the raising of Jesus by God (Acts 2:32). It raises, too, important questions about the ontological connection between infusion by the Holy Spirit and communion with the risen Christ—a matter that would lead us too far afield (but see, briefly, Chapter 12n43). The latter would arguably call into question a significant body of scholarly opinion that takes the resurrection to imply an empty tomb.

³ *Pace* Wright, *The Resurrection of the Son of God*, 325–6 and chap. 18, esp. 710–11, as well as others who have lined up behind the view that Paul is here just giving evidence—good evidence at that—for the resurrection.

⁴ See, e.g., See Evan Fales, "Scientific Explanations of Mystical Experiences, Part I: The Case of St. Teresa," *Religious Studies* 32, no. 2 (1996): 143–63; "Scientific Explanations of Mystical Experiences, Part II: The Challenge to Theism," *Religious Studies* 32, no. 3 (1996): 297–313; and "Can Science Explain Mysticism?," *Religious Studies* 35, no. 2 (1999): 213–27.

private religious experiences of many ordinary Christians as well. It is important to bear in mind, however, that the role of mystical experience in defining the public persona of an individual can come in degrees. At one end of the spectrum, we find those whose ecstasies are not only widely broadcast but play an essential part in social recognition of the mystic as a religious leader or authority. At the other end, there are no doubt individuals who have such experiences but never intimate this to anyone else. Still, if a mystic relates his or her experiences to even just one other person, this brings them—and the mystic's station as one favored by such experiences—into the social arena, even if in only a limited way. Lewis is primarily concerned with how mystical states enter into the ways social relationships are formed or altered.[5] And Paul was a public mystic if ever there was one. Accordingly, I shall begin by asking how Paul fits the models of mystical practice discovered by Lewis.

It will be necessary first to state as briefly as possible some of the central results of Lewis' comparative studies of mysticism. Looking at a broad sweep of cultures in which mystical traditions flourish, Lewis has found that mysticism has importance in two types of social contexts; and accordingly, he draws a distinction between central mysticism and peripheral mysticism. Central mysticism occurs in societies in which positions of social or political power are filled competitively on the basis of merit rather than ascriptively (i.e., rather than, for example, on the basis of the social status or position of one's parents). Merit in these contexts is a matter of acquiring charisma—the ability of a candidate individual to impress others with his or her leadership abilities, wisdom, and the like. Often, charisma is in turn connected to the ability to make convincingly the claim that one has been chosen by the gods. And here, mystical possession by the god or gods of the central cult (the "official" cult) can serve as a sure sign of divine favor.

Naturally, someone who is vying for a sought-after social status can easily come under suspicion of having manufactured such a visitation from a central god. As such status is conferred with the understanding that the position is to be used in the service of the general welfare, not for private gain, a candidate must be able to deflect such suspicion. There are several strategies for doing this. For example, those who are subject to divine visitation often describe the experience as frightening or debilitating and themselves as unwilling "victims" of the divine call. Indeed, at the time such visitations begin, the budding mystic often appears to be or to become ill or mentally disturbed, though with time—especially if the visitations are socially recognized as genuine—this helplessness is replaced with increasing mastery of the relationship with the divine (and with peers).

---

[5] I. M. Lewis, *Ecstatic Religion: An Anthropological Study of Spirit Possession and Shamanism* (Baltimore, MD: Penguin Books, 1971).

Peripheral mysticism is found among groups that are socially marginalized or dispossessed. It typically involves possession by supernatural beings that are represented to the broader society as demonic. The possessed individual is an unwilling victim. But this time, he or she typically assumes, while possessed, the persona or demeanor of someone who has social power and displays behaviors that are either disruptive or socially inappropriate for someone of lowly station—including the making of demands on behalf of the oppressed upon those who dominate them.

The cure for this malady is typically exorcism, which must be performed by someone who has previously been possessed by the demon in question and has acquired mastery over such spirits. The demon demands a *quid pro quo* as the price of eviction, and this compensation typically takes the form of better treatment of the victim by those who oppress him or her. Exorcism is often also an induction ritual that recruits the victim to the fellowship of others who have been so possessed. Thus, the cult of the demonic spirits consists of the socially dispossessed who have been supernaturally possessed. Possession is a strategy, often successful, for putting pressure on those in power to rectify wrongs that works because (a) the afflicted cannot be blamed for his or her misbehavior, and (b) the powerful can save face in acceding to the demands made upon them for, after all, these demands come not from social inferiors but from potentially dangerous demons.

The strategy can, however, fail. If the demands are too strident or overreaching, the response from those in power may be repression, using force if necessary. Thus, peripheral possession finds its natural home in social contexts in which marginalized groups are neither utterly demoralized nor driven to contemplate outright rebellion but live in an uneasy state of tension and negotiation over social resources. For obvious reasons, peripheral mysticism is viewed with suspicion—or worse—by the powers that be. And indeed, it reflects frustrations that can easily spill over into overt rebellion.[6] Also not surprisingly, the spirits that are exoterically depicted as demonic are, often enough, valorized as benign or beneficent within the esoteric ideology of their cults.

I have painted with broad strokes the stereotypical features of central and peripheral mysticism. However, mysticism does not always conform precisely to these patterns. For example, as I have elsewhere tried

---

[6] As has often occurred, or comes close to occurring, with millenarian cults such as the Melanesian Cargo Cults and the Ghost Dance Cult of the Plains Indians in the U.S. Another example is the Münzerite Movement in Reformation Germany. See Steven E. Ozment, *Mysticism and Dissent: Religious Ideology and Social Protest in the Sixteenth Century* (New Haven, CT: Yale University Press, 1973) and Andrew Weeks, *German Mysticism from Hildegard von Bingen to Ludwig Wittgenstein: A Literary and Intellectual History* (Albany, NY: SUNY Press, 1993), 152–53.

to demonstrate for Teresa of Avila and other Reformation Christian mystics, peripherals can be possessed by central deities. This is—as Teresa was acutely aware—a dangerous business.[7] But the alternative within Teresa's social context—claiming demonic possession—would have provoked almost certain and violent persecution, given her no authority, gained her nothing, and have been only somewhat less dangerous in its possible consequences.

Even so, Reformation mystics—especially women—who were too incautious in the claims they made about supernatural gifts, or too bold in the demands they made upon their oppressors, could come under attack. When they did, one available strategy was to claim that their powers and visions had in fact been produced by the devil, who had deceived them. Proper repentance did not, in general, by any means remove such a mystic entirely from blame, but it could hold at bay the flames of an *auto de fe*. Thus, the Reformation mystics (both Catholic and Protestant) were, in fact, peripheral mystics forced to deploy an unusually risky strategy.[8]

By now, my reader may have become impatient with all this talk about mystical strategies and competition for power or pressures upon those who possess it: What about the deep religious faith of the mystics? What about the profoundly significant and powerfully transformational mystical experiences themselves? I have so far said nothing about these matters— matters which will, no doubt, seem of paramount importance. But nothing I *have* said commits us to any view about this.

Nothing I have said commits us to any view as to the veridicality or evidential standing of MEs. I have only claimed—and this is supported by a substantial body of empirical evidence—that when mysticism goes public, it does so in ways that involve negotiations concerning the power, social status, or access to resources and rights for individual mystics or for groups with whose interests they identify. Direct commerce with the gods is a source of power and authority. And those who can make a socially

---

[7] Just how dangerous is vividly illustrated in an interesting paper by Gábor Klaniczay, "The Process of Trance, Heavenly and Diabolic Apparitions in Johannes Nider's *Formicarius*," in *Procession, Performance, Liturgy and Ritual: Essays in Honor of Bryan R. Gillingham*, ed. Nancy van Deusen (The Institute of Medieval Music: Ottawa, Canada, 2007), 203–58. Teresa underwent investigation by the Spanish Inquisition; and had it not been for the friendship of powerful patrons such as King Philip of Spain, she might well have fared ill. Her unusual beauty and charm, it seems, served her in good stead—not to mention an extraordinary, and canny, understanding of human psychology. Klaniczay details a series of functional correspondences between Asian shamanism and medieval/Reformation mysticism and offered evidence for possible historical links.

[8] E.g., Magdalena de la Cruz and Benedetta Carlini. For Magdalena (of whom Teresa was aware), see Stephen Clissold, *St. Teresa of Avila* (London: Sheldon Press, 1979), 46–47. For Benedetta, see Judith C. Brown, *Immodest Acts: The Life of a Lesbian Nun in Renaissance Italy* (New York: Oxford University Press, 1986).

recognized claim to such commerce do, in fact, do so in contexts in which competing social interests are at stake.

With this background in mind, let us return to Paul. The first question that Lewis' study of ecstatic religion might prompt, naturally, is how, if at all, does Paul fit the social profiles and contexts of public mysticism indicated above? As we shall see, answering this question is not an entirely easy task because Paul appears to provide an especially complex—but consequently interesting—case. We know, unfortunately, almost nothing about Paul's background prior to his conversion. What we do know must be gleaned from what little Paul tells us in his letters and indirectly via Luke. Before he converted, Paul was known as Saul of Tarsus. That suggests that he was born and raised in Tarsus, a city populated, we may assume, mainly by Gentiles and Hellenized Jews. Yet Paul tells us that he had a strict Pharisaical attitude toward Jewish law The Pharisaic Party, the most popular of the first century Jewish sects, at least in Judea, was "zealous for the law" and hence less open to Hellenistic influences than would have been true for some other groups of Jews, including the Saducean Party and many in the Diaspora.[9] That Paul could speak of himself as being "of Tarsus" also suggests that his family ranked among the more prominent in the city.[10]

These few hints do suggest, however, that Paul may well have been a young up-and-coming figure in the party of the Pharisees in Jerusalem at the time of his conversion. Certainly, he was a master polemicist and a gifted thinker. He was also deeply motivated—one might say consumed—by religious concerns (which, at the time, could not be separated from political concerns).[11] We may surmise, then, that with respect to his Jewish identity, Paul was a potential candidate for a position of influence within the chaotic Jewish political scene.

But how much room was there "at the top"? Did charisma matter? Israel's self-understanding of its history suggests a rather complex picture.[12] In the era of the judges, Israel was, by tradition, a "big man" society in

---

[9] However, Paul tells us (Acts 22:3) that as a youth, he studied the law under Gamaliel, presumably the same Gamaliel, a prominent liberal teacher in Jerusalem, who allegedly rescued the apostles from execution by the Sanhedrin (Acts 5:27–40).

[10] See Bruce J. Malina and Jerome H. Neyrey, *Portraits of Paul: An Archaeology of an Ancient Personality* (Louisville, KY: Westminster John Knox Press, 1966), 17, 24–26.

[11] See, e.g., Richard A. Horsley, ed., *Paul and Empire: Religion and Power in Roman Imperial Society* (Harrisburg, PA: Trinity Press International, 1997) and N. T. Wright, *The New Testament and the People of God*, Christian Origins and the Question of God, vol. 1 (Minneapolis, MN: Fortress Press, 1992).

[12] How accurate the histories contained in the Hebrew Bible is, of course, a matter of controversy. But what matters here is how Israel understood its history: it is its traditions, more than the actual past, that are operative for their society.

which leadership was gained through merit and charisma. The (reluctant) transition to monarchy is also marked with this feature: both Saul and David were "chosen" by God prior to public acceptance, and ascriptive kingship lasted only for one generation before rebellion split the kingdom. The prophets, likewise, achieve authority because they are singled out by God. Sometimes, like Paul, they claim to have been destined for this "in the womb."[13]

On the other hand, the priesthood was hereditary and (in theory), only Levites were admitted. There was a political furor in Israel when John Hyrcanus, who was not a Levite, assumed the role of high priest. Indeed, the Pharisees seem to have been at the center of opposition to Jonathan.[14] Yet, given the turbulent political situation in first century Judea—for example, the recurrent appearance of messianic claimants—it can safely be said that there was plenty of opportunity for sectarian movements in which leadership and charisma were closely connected.

Although he may have been a rising star within the party of the Pharisees, Paul deserted—rather suddenly, as he tells it—to the camp of an enemy sect. Here, I want to pose a question that does not admit of an easy or quick answer. Can we, quite *apart from* the revelation in which Jesus first appeared to him, make sense of Paul's conversion to Christianity? Although doing justice to this matter would take me far beyond the scope of this chapter, I want to suggest in very brief compass why I believe the answer to that question is "yes." Paul's (extra mystical) reasons for casting his lot with the Christians can illuminate, I think, both his conversion experience and his subsequent activity within the church.

A number of writers have suggested that early Christianity, and Paul's theology in particular, is in significant measure a response to the political circumstances in which Jews found themselves and cannot be separated from matters of political ideology.[15] These writers agree—and I believe they are correct—that the Pauline Christ is presented as a challenge to Caesar and that his kingdom is offered as a replacement for the Roman Imperium. I do not believe the scholars in question go far enough in pursuing the implications of this claim; but for our present purpose, it will suffice to observe that Paul's understanding of the arrival of the Messiah

---

[13] See, e.g., Jer. 1:4–5 and Isa. 49:5.

[14] See Josephus, *Ant.* 13.10.5. Josephus, however, did not describe the opposition as owing to the Maccabean lineage not being Levite.

[15] See, e.g., Horsley, *Paul and Empire*; Segal, *Paul the Convert*; and N. T. Wright, "Paul's Gospel and Caesar's Empire," in *Paul and Politics, Ekklesia, Israel, Imperium, Interpretation*, ed. Richard A. Horsley (Philadelphia, PA: Trinity Press International, 2000), 160–85. For the political implications of Jewish (e.g., Pharisaic) belief in bodily resurrection, see Wright, *The New Testament and the People of God*, 185–202 (esp. 200), 321–34 (esp. 328). The political implications of a *savior-king's* resurrection (however novel the idea) would have been strikingly more profound.

cannot be divorced from the question that dominated the Jewish political thought of his day: What does it mean that the children of Israel, the chosen people to whom Yahweh promised earthly dominion (e.g., Isa. 66), have been crushed, dispersed, and culturally overwhelmed by the enormous, apparently invincible power of Rome? How, indeed, can Jews survive as a faithful people in the face of the Roman juggernaut?

For the Pharisees, the preservation of Jewish identity was deeply dependent upon careful observance of Torah. But Paul seems to have seen in Christianity a different possibility, one that substitutes faithfulness to Torah with faithfulness to a righteous, legitimate King whose kingdom is open not just to Jews but to Gentiles—hence, to the Romans themselves. Though it is a drastic oversimplification, one might say that Paul's response to the Roman problem was: if you cannot beat them, convince them to join you.[16] In the end, this idea was actually successful—though it took nearly three centuries longer than Paul seems to have anticipated.[17]

But in this line of thought (or at least in respect of its implications for a mission to Gentiles), Paul seems to have moved significantly beyond the Jewish Christian thinking of his day and certainly beyond the views of the church leadership in Jerusalem. A proper discussion of this way of looking at Paul would have to address Paul's complex and nuanced attitude toward the Jewish law, and it would have to say much more about the political dimensions of Paul's thought and post-Pauline Christianity. The latter topic receives some attention in the remaining chapters of this volume, but the former must be for the present set aside.

---

[16] The political contrast between Paul's Pharisaic background and his newfound Christianity is dramatic. Pharisees were not entirely uninterested in welcoming Gentile converts (Segal, *Paul the Convert*, 72–114), but they saw conversion as a binding to Torah. Paul saw in Christianity the possibility of a different, more expansive principle of union between Jew and non-Jew under the lordship of Yahweh. Fellowship with Christ meant abandoning the distinction between Jew and Gentile, slave and master, even male and female (Gal. 3:28). Israel's prophetic tradition announced a day when Israel would conquer and rule a world of vassal states for Yahweh. Paul's Jesus, as a son of David (Rom. 1:3), rules a kingdom that reconfigures the tribal boundaries of Israel and relocates the temple itself within each worshipper (1 Cor. 3:16); in this way it, reconceives the vision of the prophets. Jesus, as son of a universal God, rules a kingdom that reconceives equally the hegemony of Rome, itself a tribal imperium. I shall spell this out in chapters 11 and 12.

[17] There is considerable controversy over how Paul understood the inauguration of the kingdom of Jesus in relation to contemporary events, but there is reason to think (Rom. 13:11–14; 1 Thess. 4:13–18; 5:1–9; 1 Cor. 7:29–31) that Paul anticipated (as did Jesus: Matt. 12:40) an immanent *parousia*. If so, Paul's heavenly commerce seems not to have informed him, or informed him correctly, on this important matter. On interpreting the relevant passages, see Segal, *Paul the Convert*, 161–62 and Horsley, *Paul and Empire*, 146, 166, 181.

Nevertheless, we have grounds for two important conclusions: (1) Anyone who was heavily invested, as Paul was, in first century Pharisaism would have been deeply concerned with the problem of Jewish cultural, religious, and political survival and hence very much aware of the political dimensions of rival sect ideologies. And therefore, (2) Paul would, if he came (slowly or suddenly) to recognize in Christianity a potential for a more powerful response to Roman hegemony, have had strong reason to switch his allegiance, quite aside from the experience of a celestial call. Paul did not merely convert to Christianity. He sought prominence both as a leader of the missionary effort and as a preeminent interpreter of the gospel. He faced a daunting challenge. Not only was he an outsider, a Johnny-come-lately to the fold, but he was known and feared as a former enemy. He was, one might suppose, the last sort of person to whom Christians would look for authoritative teaching.

Casting our eyes back to the social categories that Lewis associates with public mysticism, how shall we classify Paul? Paul's social position, it appears, was unusually complex. Paul was a Roman citizen hailing from a Gentile city. He was a Diaspora Jew who returned to Jerusalem to study the law. And he was a newly minted Christian. As a Roman citizen, he had a legal identity that conferred the privileges of membership in the ruling society. Yet, as a Jew, he was, vis-á-vis Rome, a member of a sometimes-despised minority, a relative "outsider." But, also as a Jew, he seems to have enjoyed "insider" status vis-á-vis the Jewish establishment in Jerusalem.

Having converted to Christianity, he was then anathema to many of those Jews—but also an object of suspicion, at best, to fellow Christians. And that suspicion must have been dramatically heightened for the Jewish Christian leadership by Paul's views about the (non)application of Torah to Gentile converts and the soteriological role of Torah generally. He seems to have had especially difficult relations with Peter and James.

What Paul most needed, if his viewpoint was to become influential, was to move from the periphery to the center in the eyes of his fellow Christians. Whatever else they did, his experience on the road to Damascus and subsequent ecstasies (if credited) would have promoted that end. It appears, indeed, that the Christian movement was at this time undergoing a gradual transition from charismatic leadership to hierarchy. As the "last" of the apostles, Paul was, in a sense, the last of those to whom (canonical) charisma had flowed directly from heaven.

In sociological terms, then, Paul was in a complexly anomalous position. In terms of Lewis' distinction between central and peripheral mysticism, it is not a straightforward matter to say what kind of mystic Paul is. His experience of a Jewish messiah maps—though awkwardly enough to be heretical—onto the central ideology of Israel.[18] For this, he immediately earns the enmity of Jews. Almost as immediately, preaching in Jerusalem, he incited, according to Luke, the animosity of the "Hellenists," apparently Jews, who, like Paul, had rejected the necessity of close adherence to ceremonial laws and temple worship but for whom accommodation with the Roman/Hellenic world possibly meant assimilation.[19] So, within the Jewish political landscape, Paul has situated himself as neither an anti-Roman nationalist nor an accommodating compromiser.

Among Christians—a peripheral Jewish sect—Paul was a newcomer with a repugnant past who had just claimed to have the kind of experience that would establish his credentials in the central cult. Within Roman society, no doubt, none of this would initially have meant much, except to those whom Paul converted and taught. Yahweh himself—to say nothing of Jesus—would from a Roman perspective have been considered a foreign deity, peripheral if not marginal, and a deity with high ambitions.

Through the complexities, however, we can see that the central theme of Lewis' work—that public mysticism mediates the struggle for recognition and authority—shines through clearly. As he enters the fold, Paul is triply marginal: as a Jewish Roman, as a Christian Jew, and as a former enemy who inserts himself into the Christian leadership with divergent, even divisive, views. Paul's hope is that he—or his soteriology—can become triply triumphant: first, as mainstream within the Christian movement; second, as a testimony to Jews; and third, as a testimony to Gentiles and the Roman Imperium.

I want now to suggest that Lewis' approach can illuminate the Pauline and Lukan presentations of his conversion—and the differences between them. Paul's most immediate problem is to gain acceptance for his teaching by the Gentiles to whom he directed his mission and to be recognized as a peer by the church elders in Jerusalem. Perhaps the latter could have forgiven his former persecutions—indeed, he must have been a prize "catch" for the movement—but Paul had sharp disagreements, at least with Peter and James, over whether circumcision and kosher food laws are to be demanded of Gentile converts. More generally, this can be understood as a dispute over the importance of obedience to Torah—that is, "works"—to salvation. Thus, it is critical for Paul to be able to claim an authority

---

[18] In *Paul the Convert*, Segal makes a strong case for the view that Paul's descriptions of his spiritual experiences owe a large debt to Jewish traditions of *Merkabah* mysticism and that his conception of Jesus as the son of man and Son of God also has deep roots in these traditions. It would, indeed, be extraordinary if Paul's experiences (or at least his descriptions of them), no matter how "revolutionary" they seem from the perspective of later Christianity, were not powerfully influenced by the mystical traditions of the culture in which he was raised.

[19] See Segal, *Paul the Convert*, 199–200.

independent of the Jerusalem church (and of Torah) and especially Peter and James.

It is exactly this that Paul claims, on behalf of his "call" on the road to Damascus, in Galatians 1. He does not preach "man's gospel;" nor was he "taught it," but he received it by revelation. The clear implication of his going away to Arabia is, surely, that he went to preach this gospel, presumably to Gentiles, *before* receiving any official approval or commission from the apostles in Jerusalem and that he *did not need* a Jerusalem imprimatur. He has clearly been challenged about this ("before God, I do not lie!"). And indeed, Luke, even while recognizing the central importance of Paul, says nothing about Arabia but has Paul go directly to Jerusalem to submit to inspection by the whole Christian congregation there.[20] As Paul would have it, he went only after three years and then only to present his already-established credentials to Peter and, secondarily, James.[21] It is, according to Paul, another fourteen years before he again traveled to Jerusalem—went "by revelation," in other words, presumably at God's behest—to be vetted by the entire congregation.

Quite similar considerations may shed some light on 1 Corinthians 15:6, which is puzzling, in part, because this appearance of the risen Christ to "more than five hundred brethren" is not elsewhere attested. Because such appearances are clearly linked to authority in the early church, it is a reasonable speculation that not just the *fact* of having been visited by Christ but the *order* in which these appearances were granted to his followers would reflect something of their relative importance within the church. Paul, omitting any mention of the women at the empty tomb, gives pride of place to Peter, as indeed he must.

With due humility, he also presents himself as the last of those to whom the divine commission has been granted—"as to one prematurely born" [*lit.*: "as to an abortion"]. What is of interest, if we look at the passage in this way, is the location of James on the list. Although he was reckoned

---

[20] Thus, Segal: "Paul's letters are full of the conflict that separated him from Peter and James. Further, almost no Pauline letter forgets to mention Paul's status as an apostle through God, underlining his constant need to establish his credentials in the face of Jesus' personal wishes in appointing only his immediate disciples as apostles" (Segal, *Paul the Convert*, 191). Moreover, Col. 4:14 and 2 Tim. 4:11 attest a close bond between Paul and the presumed author of Acts (as does the generally sympathetic portrayal of Paul in Acts). The authorship of Timothy is disputed, but supposing it at least reflects Paul's attitude toward Luke correctly, we may infer that anti-Pauline partisanship would not account for Luke's divergence from Paul's chronology.

[21] George Nickelsburg suggested to me, in conversation, that this discrepancy between Gal. 1 and Acts 9 can be explained by supposing Paul to have forgotten his first visit to the Jerusalem church (a visit during which—so Acts 9:29—Paul was under threat of death). A less plausible explanation than this is hard to imagine. Segal recognizes the authorizing force of Paul's vision (Segal, *Paul the Convert*, 70).

with Peter to be at the head of the church, here, he appears after the five hundred on the list and just barely prior to Paul himself. It is much to be wished that we had some independent account of the post-resurrection appearances with mention of James.

Should Paul have been able to expect that an appeal to his having met the Lord would gain a sympathetic hearing from the Romans? That appears more doubtful. Yet in Luke's telling, Paul did garner at least partial support from Roman officials (Acts 22, 26), even if the role of Paul's claimed theophanies in that achievement is impossible to determine. From the point of view of a Roman administrator, Paul was not a peripheral claiming demonic possession to excuse bad behavior, nor, like Teresa, was he a peripheral aspiring to be seen as possessed by a central deity. He was a semi-peripheral possessed by a peripheral deity that aspired to centrality. Lewis did not have occasion to examine this possibility. Yet it was a *topos* familiar to Israel (e.g., the stories of Joseph, Esther, and Daniel).

I have little doubt that many Christians would find the foregoing reflections upon Paul's conversion experience to be not only ungenerous but really beside the point. That point, I presume, would be directed not only to the profound change that Paul underwent but to the question whether he did not in fact see the risen Christ. But here, agreeing perhaps with Segal, I must disappoint. There is something deeply mysterious about Paul's experience, not because of its religious character but because our evidence is simply—and no doubt irremediably—too thin.[22] That is true of the phenomenal content of Paul's experience, which is described only by Luke, and by him in inconsistent ways.

In particular, Acts 9 and 22 say that Paul is told by the divine voice to rise and go into Damascus, where he will receive further instructions (from the Damascene Christians). But Acts 26 accords much more closely with Galatians 1, for there, Luke has Paul tell Agrippa that the voice itself instructed him, giving him his commission to preach to the Gentiles. Elusive brevity equally characterizes Paul's other allusions to ecstatic experience, most prominently, the heavenly journey he reports in the third person (and with ironic humility) in 2 Corinthians 12.[23]

---

[22] See again, Darren M. Slade, "Properly Investigating Miracle Claims," in *The Case Against Miracles*, ed. John W. Loftus (United Kingdom: Hypatia Press, 2019), 114–47.

[23] Some have doubted whether Paul is referring to himself. Here, I shall assume that he is. It is distantly possible that Paul's reference to the "third heaven" is a jab at the Romans. In the theology of Virgil's *Aeneid*, the third heaven is the domain of Venus, who, as the mother of Aeneas, is the patron goddess of the Caesars (this was suggested to me by Alan Nagel). It is in any event a fair surmise that Paul is referring to the third of the seven heavens known in Jewish mysticism, the heaven associated with the heavenly Jerusalem (b Talmud *Chagigah* 12b; cf. Rev. 21) and with paradise, containing a

We cannot say either whether Paul's vision provided him with good evidence that Jesus was taken alive into heaven, for we know too little about the circumstances. Prior to his Damascene encounter, did Paul know that Jesus was supposed to have been raised from the dead? It seems likely that he did. He had—so he tells us—taken upon himself the mission of persecuting the Christians; presumably, he undertook to educate himself concerning their beliefs. At 1 Corinthians 15:3–5, he repeats what many scholars suppose is a creedal formula concerning the crucifixion and resurrection, one that is thought to have originated in the earliest stratum of the Christian church. He tells us he "received" this—including the information that Jesus appeared to Peter and the twelve. But he does not tell us how much of this he knew, or had heard, before the trip to Damascus.

However, and to my mind more importantly, we do not have to suppose even that Paul *believed* he had actually seen the risen Lord in order to account for his claims about his vision. It is a further question—and one I cannot begin to enter upon here—whether Paul's conversion and subsequent career (to say nothing of 1 Cor. 15) can be explained only by supposing that he believed, in any case and for whatever reason, that Jesus was bodily raised from the dead.[24] A proper study of this question would require a much more extensive treatment of Paul's theology and its political dimensions. For present purposes, I am relying upon the work of Horsley, Segal, Wright, and others to make the case for this political dimension. To be sure, N. T. Wright thinks that Jesus did appear to Paul, and Segal thinks Paul's theology sprang out of his conversion experience.[25] But the fact that Paul had strong political reasons for his theology makes it just as possible to suppose the reverse: that

---

heavenly tree of life (*The Revelation of Moses* 37:4–5; 40:1–2. My thanks to Richard Carrier for these references).

[24] I shall be told: men do not die for a lie. However, it is nothing new that a man may well lie on behalf of a cause in whose service he is willing to die. Is Paul such a one? Perhaps: but see below.

[25] Wright, *The Resurrection of the Son of God*, 375–98, esp. 397; Segal, *Paul the Convert*, 69, 117–49. Segal thinks that, through his dying and being reborn in Christ, Paul had the experience of being set free from the law. I am suggesting that it may more nearly have been the reverse. I agree with Segal and others that the requirements of the ceremonial law (circumcision and dietary codes) set Jews apart from Gentiles, which made a mission to the Gentiles more difficult. But Paul's rejection of "works" goes much deeper. The ceremonial laws of Torah were emblematic of the standing of Israel as God's chosen people. A rejection of Torah as necessary to salvation is therefore a rejection of this distinction. The prophets envisaged a world united under Yahweh with his lordship effected through Jewish dominion. Paul envisions something different: a union among equals, where there is no master and no slave. That is one reason why the rejection of "salvation by works" has such profound political implications and why, quite apart from his mystical experiences, Paul might have arrived at such a position in a more ordinary way.

Paul had the experiences, or at any rate described them in the way he did, because he had the political insights.

In saying this, I am not accusing Paul of dishonesty, as some of my reflections below will show. What this possibility does do is to partly disarm arguments that begin with the conversion of Paul, and move on to the "sudden transformation" of the disciples after the discovery of an empty tomb, to conclude with the suggestion that the only, or best, explanation for these "facts" is an actual resurrection.[26] Whatever may have happened on the road to Damascus, Paul in some way underwent an intellectual transformation. This did not involve merely rejecting the Pharisaic response to Roman domination in favor of a (then) current Christian view but an inspired recognition that Christianity offered, in germinal form, a response that, in Paul's new understanding, could be developed and transformed into a powerful ideology and a powerful, effective social movement.

There is no good evidence for the usual assumption that this revolution in Paul's thinking *resulted from* a meeting with a risen Jesus. A fuller investigation of this point would adduce evidence, already surveyed (see also n. 4 above) to show that the introduction of revolutionary social ideas is commonly accompanied by a divine imprimatur communicated by way of MEs and that revelatory language in ancient Near Eastern societies can consistently be understood as displaying this pattern.[27] This is a perfectly natural extension of Lewis' findings of the connection between MEs and the acquisition of social authority.[28]

---

[26] This line of argument, with various bells and whistles added, is a popular current apologetic strategy for the resurrection. Subscribers include Wright, *The Resurrection of the Son of God*, 685–718; William Lane Craig, *Assessing the New Testament Evidence for the Historicity of the Resurrection of Jesus*, Studies in the Bible and Early Christianity 16 (Lewiston, NY: Edwin Mellen Press, 1989); and Gary R. Habermas, *The Historical Jesus: Ancient Evidence for the Life of Christ* (Joplin, MO: College Press Publishing Company, 1996), 152–53. Apologists will want to insist that Paul converted, and had a profound influence upon early Christianity, *because* he was commissioned and empowered by Jesus. I have not directly shown that theory to be false. But it *is* a theory; and it is not, I am arguing, the only serious explanation of the textual evidence. To my mind, the question is not even whether Paul believed the resurrection but what he *meant* by that. In a sense, we cannot assess the value of Paul's vision as evidence for the resurrection until we determine this (concerning which, see Chapter 11).

[27] Biblical examples are everywhere to be found: Abraham founds a new culture by revelation, the Law is revealed to Moses, Saul's destiny as Israel's first king is revealed to Samuel, Elijah's campaign against royal exogamy is directed by revelation, and so forth.

[28] At the same time, there is evidence that Paul's experience (if he had one)—or description of this experience as well as the one mentioned at 2 Cor. 12—owes a good deal to the tradition of *Merkabah* visions. Of particular interest vis-à-vis the latter experience is the tradition that because Abraham was taken up into the heavens and shown paradise, those who have similar visions of the third heaven are in an intimate way direct descendants. Cf. Paul's own claim at 2 Cor. 11: 22. See J. W. Bowker, *The*

Because of the role that Paul's MEs played in his career as a Christian evangelist, it is, I have suggested, not possible to know much about these experiences themselves or even about how they affected his religious understanding. Although Paul's case is a rather special one, I want, by way of recounting a couple of other more pedestrian cases, to draw the moral that without intimate knowledge of the mystic and his context, we should be very circumspect about what conclusions can be drawn concerning the evidence these experiences provide for a supernatural source of the experience.

To see that this should be a matter of concern, let us remember that philosophers are fond of quoting a few first-person descriptions of MEs, often taken conveniently from William James' *The Varieties of Religious Experience*, and proceeding straightaway to draw inferences predicated on the assumption that the cited mystics have given accurate, sincere descriptions of the phenomenology of their experience and of its effects upon them and that they are sound of mind and spirit.[29] That—to take just one example—is the procedure of Gary Gutting, who, after presenting some quotations from James and from a recent interview study by David Hay,[30] adds, "There is every reason to believe that at least a very large number of such reports are candid, that the experiences reported did in fact take place."[31] Perhaps so, but whatever reasons Gutting has in mind, they can

---

Targums and Rabbinic Literature: An Introduction to Jewish Interpretations of Scripture (New York: Cambridge University Press, 1969), 202 and J. W. Bowker, "'Merkabah' Visions and the Visions of Paul," *Journal of Semitic Studies* 16, no. 2 (1971): 157–73.

[29] Slade, "Properly Investigating Miracle Claims," 114–47.

[30] David Hay, "Religious Experience Amongst a Group of Post-Graduate Students: A Qualitative Study," *Journal for the Scientific Study of Religion* 18, no. 2 (1979): 164–82. While there is no particular reason to doubt the sincerity of Hay's informants, his methodology is open to criticism. The central question of his survey asks subjects whether they have "ever been aware of ... a presence of power, whether you call it God or not, which is different from your everyday self?" Subjects were shown a list of sample ME reports to clarify the meaning of this oddly phrased question. There is no way of determining whether or how this sample might have colored the respondents' reports of their experiences. Another key question: "Did the power seem personal or impersonal? *Clarification: did the power seem to be communicating with you as a person or not?*" (italics Hay's). Oddly, the "clarification" is grammatically ambiguous. In any case, the sample reports published by Hay are rather striking in how few and vague their characterizations of interaction with a "person" are and how unclear they are whether the interaction involved a perceptual awareness. Moreover, as many as ten or more years had elapsed in some cases since the occurrence of the reported experience. Concerning other methodological difficulties attending studies of the kind done by Hay, see Evan Fales, "Scientific Explanations of Mystical Experiences, Part II: The Challenge to Theism," *Religious Studies* 32, no. 3 (1996): 297–31, esp. 309.

[31] Gary Gutting, *Religious Belief and Religious Skepticism* (South Bend, IN: University of Notre Dame Press, 1982), 144.

hardly derive from an intimate knowledge of the individuals upon whose testimony he relies.

James' *Varieties of Religious Experience* was a pioneering work; and in its day, it did considerable service by collecting a variety of such reports. But the details of the reporters' circumstances and histories are either lost or not known except as reported by themselves. One of James' principal sources of information was a collection of data published by E. D. Starbuck.[32] Other reports were culled mainly from religious testimonials and autobiographies. (Even so, as we have seen in the case of Paul, much of interest can sometimes be gleaned from such reports. But philosophers do not in general linger over such details.)

To illustrate the potential pitfalls of simply accepting such reports, let me draw on an example from my own experience. Many years ago, we had a neighbor who, if I may so speak, was a poor white Southerner. He had moved, with his large family, from Virginia to Pennsylvania in search of a better life. But life was hard in Pennsylvania as well. He had sometime employment in a factory, as I recall, but struggled on the side to establish himself in his chosen calling, which was preaching. He told me the Holy Spirit spoke to him. In fact, it was the Spirit that had told him to relocate to Pennsylvania.

As I was interested in the phenomenology of religious experience, I asked him what it was like to hear the Holy Spirit tell him to make such a momentous move: did he literally hear a voice coming from somewhere? No, he said; it was more like a feeling inside him. What sort of feeling? Well, it seems he had been struggling for some time with the decision whether to move or not, and suddenly, he saw clearly that he should. In short, he understood this inner conviction as the work, the voice, of the Holy Spirit.

It was only later, reflecting upon this gentleman's description, that it occurred to me that not only had *he* wrestled with this difficult decision to move, but, in all likelihood, he had faced the problem of convincing a reluctant, perhaps positively resistant, family. Under these circumstances, a word from the Holy Spirit would not only seal his own inclinations but do wonders to still the doubts of wife and children. Not that his circumstances had in fact visibly improved thus far, but at least he, and his family, could feel at peace (I presume) with the risky choice he made.

Now of course I do not *know* whether my reconstruction of my neighbor's circumstances is accurate. But the evidence (together with similar examples I shall not detail) at least suggests it. Suppose I am right. Should

---

[32] E. D. Starbuck, *The Psychology of Religion: An Empirical Study of the Growth of Religious Consciousness*, 3rd ed. (New York: C. Scribner's Sons, 1912). Because he was a psychologist, Starbuck speculates about the psychodynamics of MEs but rarely provides any information about the social background of his subjects.

we conclude that Mr. X was being *disingenuous* with his family (and with me) in claiming to have heard the Holy Spirit? I think not, for something more subtle may have easily happened. People use a variety of strategies, often unconsciously, to reduce uncertainty, cognitive dissonance, and the sense of risk associated with making choices in information-poor circumstances—just the sort of situation that Mr. X faced.

Many of these strategies—for example, augury, dream interpretation, and the like, involve implicit or explicit appeal to the supernatural. It is not too much of a stretch to suppose that, in the course of agonizing over his options, Mr. X found himself leaning toward a desire to move and finally found within himself a resolve to do so, which, as he lacked any convincing external reasons for that choice, he understood in terms of the action of the God to whom he had, no doubt, been praying. I am not sure even that, under these circumstances, we can accuse Mr. X of culpable *self*-deception.

Mr. X is only one case; Gutting draws upon many. That brings with it the difficulty of significant variety of content, which Gutting, like some others, attempts to handle by taking a restricted range of MEs as evidence for a very minimal, syncretistic claim about the existence of a supernatural person.[33] But for many Christians, religious experiences serve a much more particularistic end, the end it allegedly served for Paul: because they have come personally to know Jesus, they know that he lives—hence, Jesus was resurrected.[34] As James astutely observes:

> The conversions which Dr. Starbuck ... has in mind are of course mainly those of very commonplace persons, kept true to a pre-appointed type by instruction, appeal, and example. The particular form which they affect is the result of suggestion and initiation.[35]

---

[33] E.g., John Hick, *The Fifth Dimension: An Exploration of the Spiritual Realm* (Oxford, UK: Oneworld Publications, 1999).

[34] Although he does not focus on the evidential question (which he takes as settled), Luke Timothy Johnson well exemplifies this way of appropriating the resurrection. See Luke Timothy Johnson, *Living Jesus: Learning the Heart of the Gospel* (San Francisco, CA: HarperSanFrancisco, 1998). It has been used as an argument in formal debates concerning the resurrection. The experience of a personal "presence," which Gutting focuses upon, can be produced by stimulating the temporal lobes of the brain with magnetic fields. See Michael A. Persinger et al., "The Sensed Presence as Right Hemispheric Intrusions into the Left Hemispheric Awareness of Self: An Illustrative Case Study," *Perceptual and Motor Skills* 78, no. 3 (1994): 999–1009 and Michael Persinger and Faye Healey, "Experimental Facilitation of the Sensed Presence: Possible Intercalation between the Hemispheres Induced by Complex Magnetic Fields," *Journal of Nervous and Mental Diseases* 190, no. 8 (2002): 533–41.

[35] William James, *The Varieties of Religious Experience* (New York: Macmillan, 1961), 168.

The influence of culture can be conceived in different ways. Steven Katz argues that MEs are permeated by cultural concepts. Much like Durkheim, he thinks of culture as determining the structure of thought by imbuing it with categories that, like Kant's, provide the necessary conditions for experience itself—but that, unlike Kant's, are neither *a priori* nor universal. Katz's view contrasts with James' view.

For Katz, culture and training provide the skeletal structure of thought, determining where and how thought and experience articulate reality. That suggests a rigid framework. James has it that culture and training provide *habits* of thought. The difference between them is like the difference between the biological processes that form the skeleton of a person and the training that transforms that human body into a skilled soccer player.

My position is closer to James' stance. But I want to emphasize that, beyond the role of habits of thought, we must not underestimate the capacity of the human mind to shape thought, and perhaps experience itself, in ways that are responsive to present needs, desires, and emotions. As a defender of the given in experience, I do not, in saying this, mean to suggest that experience contains no components that are distinguishable apart from concepts, or wishes, or the like. But there is perhaps no domain of human experience that is more sensitive to these influences than religion. That, indeed, helps to explain the power these experiences have in our lives.

The conclusion I mean to draw is a rather simple one. To evaluate the strength of an ME as evidence for a religious claim, we must understand the mystic's report of that experience. To understand the report, we must understand the reporter. To understand the reporter, we must ordinarily do more than simply accept, at "face value," the report itself. No one, I take it, (except possibly the Akawaio Caribs) would accept at face value an Akawaio shaman's report that he had traveled while in trance into the sky or over the mountains to consult with the spirits. I trust that most would also be hesitant to claim that it even *seemed* to the shaman, with no hint of figuration, that he was doing this. But if so, we should treat with equal caution Paul's apparent claim to have been assumed into the third heaven.

Lest I leave the impression that I am wedded to what, at the outset, I called a hermeneutics of suspicion, I should hasten to add that I in no way mean here to suggest that every ME is situated within a personal history that gives scope to the sorts of sociological influences that are analyzed by Lewis and that I have attempted to apply to the case of Paul. Indeed, I know of cases for which I find Lewis' framework not readily applicable. But absent intimate acquaintance, we should not be too quick to think ourselves entitled to draw epistemic conclusions from the reports given by our sources.

What information over and above a mystic's report of an ME one sees as relevant will be conditioned, naturally enough, by how one thinks that ME might be explained. A theist will incline toward the view that theistic MEs, at least, are produced by God for the purpose of communicating and communing with his creatures. A theist might therefore find certain facts about the mystic pertaining to moral reformation, dedication to God, and the like especially relevant.

One who is prepared to entertain purely psychological or sociological explanations will, of course, find other information significant, as well. Under the circumstances, I suggest that, faced with what is after all an essentially empirical question (viz., What causes MEs?), the responsible thing to do is to consider the available information relevant to all the explanatory hypotheses that have been brought to the table. In the case of a figure like Paul, that evidence is both frustratingly sparse and sufficiently rich to be tantalizing. I hope to have shown that any conclusions about what happened to Paul, and why, are by no means foregone. But now, let us turn our attention to an anterior question: What happened to Jesus?

Matthew's Mythodology

I. Literary Form and the Probability of Myth

A. Chiasm and Other Literary Structures in Matthew

It is a fact worthy of note that substantial stretches of biblical text were written so as to conform to established compositional formats. This is obvious in the case of the poetry, but less so, at least to modern western readers, when ring compositions are used. Rings are narratives in which the beginning and end match up. One of the most common forms is chiasmus, in which not only do a beginning and ending feature match up, but intermediate features also match up pair-wise, moving from beginning to midpoint on the one side and moving in reverse order from ending to midpoint on the other. We have already encountered ring structures in Genesis. They are pervasive in Mark and Matthew but less clear in Luke. John, though he provides evidence of being dependent upon the Synoptics, displays much less verbal closeness and does not retain their ring structures. Nevertheless, John's Gospel contains recognizable structures of its own.[1]

Of course, other sorts of literary structures can also be found. It is not uncommon, for example, for a larger ring to contain smaller ones as sub-structures, as Mary Douglas has demonstrated for a variety of literary texts, including ancient ones.[2] Here, however, I will focus primarily upon a large ring structure that can be discerned in Matthew. Indeed, the Gospel as a whole is a ring, as can be seen below.[3]

---

[1] On Johannine dependence upon the Synoptics and on literary structures in John, see Richard C. Carrier, *On the Historicity of Jesus: Why We Might Have Reason for Doubt* (Sheffield, UK: Sheffield Phoenix Press, 2014), 487–489. For a general earlier treatment of biblical ring structures, primarily in the NT, see Nils Wilhelm Lund, *Chiasmus in the New Testament: A Study in Formsgeschichte* (Chapel Hill, NC: University of North Carolina Press, 1942).

[2] See, e.g., Mary Douglas, *Thinking in Circles: An Essay on Ring Composition* (New Haven, CT: Yale University Press, 2007), esp. 31–71 and 101–14. Douglas discussed large-scale ring structures in the Hexateuch and, at some length, large-scale rings in Numbers, the *Iliad,* and the *Aeneid.*

[3] I have adapted this ring analysis from Carrier, *On the Historicity of Jesus*, 460–461, adding in particular the pairs DD' and GG'.

A Genealogy (summary of past times: 1:1–17)
B   Mary, and angel arrives, and the birth of Jesus (1:18–25)
C   Gifts of wealth at birth (magi) (2:1–2, 10–12)
D   Herod's legitimacy denied; he seeks to kill Jesus (2:3–8, 13–18)
E   Flight to Egypt, woe to the children, Jeremiah laments destruction of the First Temple (2:14–21)
F   Judea avoided (2:22–23)
G   John the Baptist curses Pharisees/Sadducees seeking baptism (3:7–10)??
H   Baptism of Jesus (3:1–17)
I   Crossing of the sea, calming the storm (8:23–27)
J   Crossing of the sea (9:1)
K   John's ministry (11:2–19)
L   Rejection of Jesus (11:20–24)
M   Secrets revealed through Jesus (11:25–30)
N   Attack of the Pharisees (12:1–13)
O Pharisees determine to kill God's servant (12:14–21)
N'   Condemnation of Pharisees (12:22–45)
M'   Secrets revealed through Jesus (13:1–52)
L'   Rejection of Jesus (13:53–58)
K'   John's death (14:1–12)
J'   Crossing the sea (14:13–14)
I'   Crossing of the sea, Jesus walks on water (14:22–33)
H'   Transfiguration of Jesus (17:1–9)
G'   Payment of the temple tax (17:24–27) ??
F'   Judea entered (19:1–20:34)
E'   March to Jerusalem, woe to the children, Jesus predicts destruction (21:1–45; 24:3–51)
D'   Caesar's coin, denial of Caesar's legitimacy (22:15–22)
C'   Gifts of wealth: nard anointing (26:6–13), tomb burial (27:57–61); attempt to thwart resurrection (Pilate, guards) (27:62–66)
B'   Mary, an angel arrives, and the resurrection of Jesus (28:1–15)
A' Commission: summary of future times (28:16–20)

As Douglas is well aware, a claim to discover such a structure—especially when it is a large-scale structure—will be met with some skepticism. Such skepticism is quite in order. We must guard against the possibility that there are so many degrees of freedom in the parsing of a text that almost any text might be regimented into a ring structure by a sufficiently ingenious pattern-finder. We have encountered this sort of worry before in connection with Lévi-Strauss' technique of structural myth analysis. Readers will have noticed the question marks I have attached to the pair GG' in the above ring diagram. They signal my awareness that this pairing may seem something of a stretch.[4] There is, unfortunately, no recipe for identifying cognate pairs in a narrative: some similarity, we know, can be found between almost any two things.

Nevertheless, such analyses are not all guesswork and gematria. Douglas herself, well aware of this criticism (she notes that it is a standard reaction among fellow anthropologists), insists that there are criteria that serve as signposts to the presence of a ring construction, and she notes that, having found a complex ring structure in Numbers, she attempted to construct a similar analysis of Leviticus—and failed. Not just any text will succumb to such a parsing. But ring construction was a well-entrenched writing technique in antiquity. And after all, if ancient writers went to the (often considerable) trouble of ordering their narratives into rings, one would expect that they would have developed ways of cluing readers in when the technique was being employed. There is no guarantee that such clues would be blatant, of course. The sophisticated appreciate subtlety and recognize both the pleasure of discovery and the practical value, in some contexts, of a message that is layered in such a way that the *hoi polloi* can grasp some of the author's meaning but not all of it.

Douglas offers seven signposts that are characteristic of ring composition. She is careful to say that they are not individually necessary conditions but that a ring should satisfy a significant number of them. It will be useful to summarize them.[5]

> 1) *Exposition or prologue:* An initial introduction sets the scene and states the theme—typically a problem of some kind. It anticipates the midpoint of the ring and the ending.
> 2) *Split into two halves:* The circle traces an "outward journey," a turning point, and a "return journey" that links to the introduction.
> 3) *Parallel sections*: In a chiasmus, each step in the outward journey is paired with a related step in the return journey, as the chiasmus above illustrates. Pairings may not be obvious. There is opportunity here for the writer to create associations that carry meanings otherwise not evident to a reader. Sometimes, one member of a pair upends or creates a reversal of the other.
> 4) *Indicators to mark individual sections*: Clearly, the structure depends upon there being identifiable building blocks. This is particularly important when pairings are not obvious and when the writer is constructing a large-scale structure. Alternations—for example,

---

[4] It may be noted, on the other side, that Herod's attempt to assassinate the (feared) newborn Jesus (part of element D) can be paired with Pilate's attempt to suppress a (feared) staged resurrection (which is part of element C').

[5] I quote her designations and paraphrase a bit of her commentary. See Douglas, *Thinking in Circles*, 36–38.

day/night or (as in Numbers) law section/narrative—offer one sort of device. Or, repeated phrases can serve as markers, and so on.

5) *Central loading:* The turning point of a ring (line O in the above example) must be well identified and should contain some reference to both the introduction and the ending of the ring. It will often contain a key that unlocks the meaning of the whole ring.

6) *Rings within rings:* As noted above, rings can contain within them smaller rings. They may even consist entirely of a series of such smaller rings. Sub-rings provide a convenient literary device for incorporating older sources and for presenting subplots.

7) *Closure at two levels:* The ring closes with an episode or passage that arrives at resolution of the original theme or problem and additionally signals closure with linguistic techniques such as repetition of key words or phrases from the introduction.

It should be clear that satisfying a significant number of the above criteria will require significant ingenuity and literary skill on the part of an author. The demonstration of such creative skill will not only provide the reader with a densely textured narrative that can convey a complexity of interwoven meanings, but it also signals the sophistication of the author.

All this suggests that, while we may be unsure of particular doublets in a chiastic pattern, we are unlikely to be in error about the existence of the structure when a significant number of highly plausible pairings can be detected. That has several methodological implications. For one thing, this kind of structural manufacturing of a text reminds us of a lesson that structural myth analysis teaches us: that different versions of a myth can reflect both a desire to adapt the story to the conveying of a more or less new set of messages (either because the composer of the variant is addressing new realities or because he or she is in some disagreement with the teaching of the myth he/she is rewriting) or because of a (perhaps playful, perhaps serious) desire to transmit the same teaching in a creatively fresh way. Such variations, therefore, are not to be taken as indicators of historical unreliability, for historical reliability is not, after all, the aim of the writer. But large-scale ring structures also place demands upon a text that mean that if one part of a source text is altered, alterations will likely have to occur elsewhere as well.

Thus, recognizing the pervasive use of such content-structuring techniques by the evangelists makes it apparent that the construction of Gospel harmonies is a misguided attempt to force this literature onto the Procrustean bed of historical realities that lacks sensitivity to authorial intentions. In composing their narratives, the authors of the Gospels each had good reasons for exercising their storytelling art in distinctive ways, drawing on common traditions and adding to, rearranging, and modifying in various ways a set of broadly similar messages built on common themes. But the artistic arsenal of the evangelists was not limited to the use of formal composition techniques such as ring composition. It appears that the great epic poems of Homer and, arguably, Virgil, which served as literary models in the ancient world, supplied inspiration, directly or indirectly, for both compositional techniques and thematic content.

B. Literary Models for the Gospels

An important question that has received some attention is whether the writers of the canonical Gospels used literary models in constructing their narratives of the life of Jesus and (in Acts) an initial history of the church. The received view has long been that the evangelists, and Paul as well, relied primarily or entirely upon Jewish scripture—usually the Septuagint— and early Christian sources that preserved the words and deeds of Jesus and of his closest followers. On this view, it follows not only that Jesus and most of those followers were Jews but that the theology that sprang from this soil is a thoroughly Jewish phenomenon.

In Chapter 3, I raised some general suspicions about this view, not to deny the profoundly Jewish roots of the Christian movement, but to question whether this fact would be incompatible with there also being quite profound Hellenistic and even Roman influences that may have contributed both to the early Christian agenda and to its modes of expression. We have had occasion—and will continue to have occasion—to note the multitude of themes that the New Testament writers derived from Hebrew Scriptures. Here, however, I want to discuss whether pagan literary models may also have played a formative role in Christian thinking and literary productions.

The two scholars who have most prominently proposed such influences are Dennis R. MacDonald and Marianne Palmer Bonz. MacDonald has argued vigorously that both Mark and Luke used Homer as a model in two ways: by borrowing verbal expressions and phrases and by borrowing larger plot elements (micro and macro *mimesis*). Bonz argues that Luke's Acts may have, in various ways, been influenced by Virgilian or neo-Virgilian epic poetry, recasting or adapting features of that genre to a prose style. In both cases, the alleged analogies and similarities are often quite subtle, and so the case for these claims is not watertight. Nevertheless, that case cannot be ignored and its implications for the historicity of the Gospels not attended to. As Marianne Bonz, commenting on the *Aeneid,* suggests,

> Yet even though the subject was historical, Virgil's epic differed markedly from contemporary historiography, not only in its poetic form, but more importantly also in the selection and arrangement of its content, which was governed not by the historian's criteria of sources and traditions but by the artist's concern for cosmic universality as it is

revealed in human particularity. In addition to the selection and arrangement of its thematic content, it is Virgil's skillful handling of narrative structures and his adherence to artistic principles of form, balance, and unity that most clearly demonstrate the *Aeneid*'s subordination of historical concerns to literary control.[6]

Bonz also notes the fluid boundaries between the genres of fiction and history. In particular, she notes that "history-telling" was understood in the ancient world as an enterprise that could be governed by the intention of conveying universal truths or lessons, using the form of a quasi-historical narrative as the vehicle. Speaking of Luke-Acts in particular, she sees that project as one that traces Christian beginnings back beyond the Jesus traditions to the prophecies of the Jewish prophets and then forward to the historical fulfillment of those prophecies. This project involved also linking Jesus to the Davidic lineage:

> The boldness of Luke's historical vision, therefore, consists of two key elements. Not only does it contain his appropriation and redirection of Israel's salvation history ... but it also includes ... Luke's perception of the gradual unfolding of Christian proclamation as divinely initiated and directed fulfillment of a universal human destiny. Both of these key Lukan elements of appropriation and universalization find their fullest and most complete expression in the great foundational epics of Mesopotamia and, subsequently, the Greco-Roman world. Indeed, unlike the various categories of Greek novels, for example, whose most significant characteristic is their flexible adaptation to an infinite variety of parochial circumstances and occasions, the great epics of antiquity have tended to appear only at significant inaugural moments in a community's or a society's corporate life.[7]

Bonz goes on to note the widespread fame of the *Aeneid*, as a result of which it came to rival Homer, at least in the Latin west, as a model of literary form. The situation was a bit different in the eastern, Greek-speaking part of the empire. Although most educated Romans understood Greek, far fewer educated individuals in the Hellenistic east knew Latin. Nonetheless, Augustus saw to it that the fame of the *Aeneid* spread across the empire. General features of the storyline would have been known, and there was, in fact, a prose translation into Greek done by Polybius, a freedman in the service of the emperor. It is fairly likely that Luke knew of the *Aeneid* (and almost certain that he had read Homer). It is not unlikely that he would have

---

[6] Marianne Palmer Bonz, *The Past as Legacy: Luke-Acts and Ancient Epic* (Minneapolis, MN: Fortress Press, 2000), 58.
[7] Bonz, *The Past as Legacy*, 16–17.

been familiar with Polybius' translation, and it is possible that he had read the Latin original.

Dennis MacDonald, acknowledging that Luke might have known the *Aeneid* or something of the *Aeneid*, remains agnostic on this matter but not on Luke's (and Mark's) knowledge of Homer. He has argued at some length that passages in both Mark's Gospel and in Acts display all the marks of *mimesis*, borrowing from identifiable episodes in both the *Illiad* and the *Odyssey*, where the similarities extend not only to similar tropes (or "inversions" of such tropes) but to identity or near-identity in verbal expression. To conclude, he then asks, provocatively, "*How much* of the New Testament imitates Homer?"[8] Bonz focuses less than MacDonald on verbal coincidences and more heavily on subtle ways in which Virgil's literary style and larger thematic structure finds echoes in Luke's Gospel and, especially, Acts.

For my part, I find it of interest to note that there are large-scale analogies between the *Aeneid* and the Christian Gospels plus Acts. The aim of the *Aeneid* is to provide a foundational history for the Roman Empire, and in particular for the Julian Caesars, and in doing so, to supply them (especially Augustus) with much-needed credentials that legitimate their rule. The history traces a journey in which a tribal leader, rescuing himself and some companions from the flames of destruction of his people, is transformed, by the will of the gods, into the founder of an empire—a trans-tribal political entity that develops, by way of conquest, from an amalgamation of two tribal peoples: the remnants of Troy and the Latin survivors of the war between the Trojans and Latium.

A marriage seals the deal (though Aeneas's royal bride, Lavinia, is never asked for her opinion respecting whom she wishes to marry). Virgil repeatedly emphasizes Aeneas' punctilious piety. Yet Aeneas is a violent man and also a cad. For this, his very piety is largely responsible. Though he possesses certain virtues, his cruel insensitivity (especially towards Dido) comes across as something of a reflection of the fact that the gods he worships and obeys are hardly paragons of virtue. As subsequent history proved, Aeneas' "descendants," the Roman Caesars, emulated all too well his less savory flaws.

Jesus is also a leader who emerges from tribal roots—again the roots of a tribe in flames or soon to experience the searing destruction of its temple and sacred city. He becomes the leader of a small band that carries his teaching and tradition into a larger, trans-tribal arena: in fact, the Roman Empire. Eventually, the Christians, while retaining their name and a certain group identity, cease to be ethnically or religiously Jewish and assume a new

---

[8] Dennis R. Macdonald, *Does the New Testament Imitate Homer? Four Cases from the Acts of the Apostles* (New Haven, CT: Yale University Press, 2003), 151; italics in original.

identification with the (now Holy) Roman Empire. But the story of Jesus is strikingly different from that of Aeneas. Though he is beloved by a number of women, he does not marry or consort with them and then jilt them, as Aeneas does Dido. His virtues are nonviolent virtues: he seeks to conquer with love. Although, through obedience to the God he worships, he aims toward a universal kingdom, his God is the anti-type of the contumacious Greek/Roman Pantheon, and the kingdom he will found is (in theory at least) an anti-type of Aeneas' kingdom.

Jesus' piety, then, is of an entirely different order. Correlatively, since his God is a very different sort of god, the kingdom he is to found is one that promises to overthrow both the rampant injustices of Roman rule and the wild instability caused by the rapacious and repeated struggles for dominion in the Roman imperium. Those had everything to do with competition for power and wealth and little to do with legitimacy. Given these (anti)parallels, it is an interesting question whether, as Bonz argues, any of the Gospel writers had Virgil and/or his Latin emulators in mind as a foil or foils in the composition of their narratives.

As with the presence of pervasive large-scale chiastic structures and other literary devices in the Gospels, the appearance that their authors derived inspiration from such sources as Homer and Virgil does not inspire confidence in the historicity of their accounts of the life of Jesus or of his disciples. Bonz takes Luke-Acts to be a prose epic adhering to conventions similar to those governing epic poetry. If that is correct, and particularly if structures and passages can be found that emulate the form and content of identifiable episodes in the *Illiad, Odyssey,* and *Aeneid*, we should be careful in assuming that their content reflects the early church's actual history.[9]

---

[9] Karl Sandnes takes aim at Bonz and more especially MacDonald, expressing doubt about whether the canonical Gospels borrow from Homer or Virgil at the level of plot elements. His study pays considerable attention to fourth- and fifth-century Christian *centones*, compositions that, following the style and copying the actual language of Homeric and Virgilian epic poetry, used the Gospels as the basis for plot content while sometimes freely inventing biographical episodes in their portrayal of Jesus. Sandnes points to the difference between those who composed *centones*, who had the Gospels to rely upon, and the Gospel writers themselves, who, according to MacDonald, relied upon Homer not only for style and language but for plot elements. Because the mimesis, if it occurred at the macro (plot) level, is so allusive, I think we must allow that the question of the extent of gospel reliance upon the epic poets remains unsettled. Sandnes himself agrees that the matter bears serious investigation, even as he argues against the suggestion that the influences of the epic poets would have overridden the evangelists' intention to remain faithful to historical traditions that they received concerning Jesus: "Mimesis Criticism rightly argues that New Testament dependence on the pagan literature cannot be limited to the quotations identified there; there is certainly a much wider dependence. Looking at Homer and Virgil from this perspective is, therefore, a most natural thing to do" (Karl Olav Sandnes, *The Gospel 'According to Homer and Virgil': Cento and Canon* [Leiden, Netherlands: Koninklijke Brill, 2011], 238).

It is not, of course, that the Greek and Latin works contain no references to historical people, places, and events. So they do. But a dutiful adherence to documentable facts concerning the past is not their aim. Such references are brought in when they serve an author's purposes. And when the preeminent purposes are the creation of a foundation myth and lessons in legitimacy, political ideology and theory, and civic virtue, the incorporation of signal events from the past are often indeed of high importance in anchoring the story to lived realities and traditions. In contributing to our understanding of "who we were," they help us understand "who we are" and "whom we should aspire to become."[10]

At the same time, history is messy and often not a good vehicle for the teaching of lessons about what the future should be. Thus, those who think hard about such matters will, while taking due note of the relevance of history, feel free to embellish, delete, and invent as best suits their pedagogical purposes. In this way, myths can be amalgams of history and story, with varying proportions of each. Clearly, Homer and Virgil stand in a tradition that created literature in this way. From such works, some history may sometimes be gleaned—as Schliemann correctly guessed the existence of a destroyed Trojan citadel. But, to the extent that the "historical" books of the New Testament evidence signs of purposes and literary techniques similar to those of the Gentile epic poets, we should apply similar interpretive standards to them as to their pagan peers. To illustrate the way in which pedagogical purposes may be in play in Matthew, even in episodes

---

[10] It is worth reminding ourselves, in this connection, of the lengths to which Matthew went to interpret the figure of Jesus by the device of comparison with major figures in Israel's self-understanding. Some of these are quite explicit, others lie only a little below the surface, and yet others are perhaps more doubtful. Among those that are explicit or nearly so, I believe we can count David, Isaac, Moses, Joshua, Elijah, Elisha, and Jonah. The connection with David is obvious, but it is perhaps worth noting that Jesus, like David, is not only the founder of the royal line to which Jesus is said to belong, but is, like David, a figure with both priestly and prophetic standing. The story of the binding of Isaac lies, of course, in the background of the sacrificial offering of Jesus on the cross. The dimensions of comparison to Moses are multiple: Jesus will lead Israel out of bondage, is the founding leader of the (new) Israel, supersedes even Moses in his closeness to God, is giver of the new covenant, and so forth. Although this typology has been disputed, Dale Allison (1993) makes what is to my mind a convincing case as well as providing an excellent summary of criteria for discerning genuine comparisons in literary texts. Joshua (= Yeshuah = Jesus) leads Israel into the Promised Land. Jesus' miracles of feeding the 5,000/4.000 and his raising of the daughter of a synagogue official (Matt. 9:18–26) as well as the transfiguration (17:3–4) echo the miracles of Elijah and Elisha and bespeak his status as even greater than that of Elijah and Moses. With great literary skill, therefore, Matthew seizes every opportunity to portray his man as the culmination and summation of the destiny toward which God has led the prophets and kings of Israel.

that invoke nothing of the miraculous, let me turn now to two passages that concern Jesus' teaching about the politically-charged topic of taxes.

II. A Tale of Two Taxes

Twice, Jesus is asked about taxes. Twice, he punts. Each reply he gives is cleverly provocative, and each proves a point. Here, we discuss tax collectors, tax payment, the temple tax, and Caesar's coin. These matters are political to the core, and, as we will see, Jesus' actions and words provide important insights into the political program that underlies the Christian gospel.

A. Paying the Temple Tax (Matt. 17:24–27)

While Jesus is preaching in Galilee, a tax collector asks Peter whether his master pays the temple tax. Peter affirms. When he returns home, Jesus clairvoyantly asks him, "From whom do kings of the earth take toll or tribute? From their sons or from others?" Peter having acknowledged that it is from others, Jesus draws the conclusion: "Then the sons are free. However, so that we do not give offense to them, go to the sea and cast a hook; take the first fish that comes up, and when you open its mouth, you will find a coin; take that and give it to them for you and me."[11]

This brief passage raises a number of questions. The tax collector is not acting in the service of Rome but of the temple establishment. Thus, the analogy Jesus draws to kings and their sons seems at first a bit jarring. It is also unclear from the context why the tax collector asks rather than simply demanding payment of the tax. Other puzzles will emerge. But as we might expect, significant attention has been paid to the miraculous fish. Are we to credit the story of a fish who serves as a kind of early ATM machine? This, I want to suggest, is precisely the wrong way to approach this tale.

Characteristic of that kind of scholarship is Richard Bauckham's treatment of the story.[12] He goes fishing around in ancient Jewish folklore. Finding several parables in which someone finds something of great worth inside a fish, he nevertheless argues for the possible historicity of the pericope in Matthew on the grounds that it is different from all these folktales in its teaching and in other details and that it lies "just outside" the boundary of the ordinary—it is wildly unlikely but not impossible that Peter

---

[11] I have replaced the gender-neutral language of the NRSV translation: "sons" for "children." In this context, it matters.
[12] Richard Bauckham, "The Coin in the Fish's Mouth," in *Gospel Perspectives: The Miracles of Jesus*, ed. David Wenham and Craig Blomberg (Sheffield, England: JSOT Press, 1986), 6:219–52.

should find a *drachma* (= 2 *didrachmas,* one to satisfy Jesus' purported obligation and a second to satisfy Peter's) in the mouth of the fish. First, this ignores the fact that Jesus knew, before Peter told him, that he had been questioned by a tax collector and *predicted* the discovery of the coin.

What is worse, Bauckham ignores the plain sense of the story. To be sure, the story tells us, as Bauckham notes, that God provides for his children. But this only scratches the surface. First, the story clearly implies that God is providing for someone who stands in a particular relation to him: his Son. Notably, the fish's beneficence extends further: it picks up the tab for Peter as well. But more pungently, when Jesus asks Peter, "From whom do the kings ($\beta\alpha\sigma\iota\lambda\epsilon\tilde{\iota}\varsigma$) of the earth ($\gamma\eta\varsigma$) take toll or tribute? From their sons or from others?" and claims, "Then the sons are free," we are meant to infer that Jesus is obliquely *asserting* that Sonship.

But then, is Peter also a Son of God? Is his inclusion just a case of generosity, perhaps, out of a sense of fairness or *noblesse oblige*? Yet Peter is not just any fellow traveler or even a random disciple. He is Christ's chosen successor. He will be given the keys to the kingdom of heaven, and "whatever you [Peter] bind on earth will be bound in heaven, and whatever you loose on earth will be loosed in heaven." (Matt. 16:19). That declaration is shortly followed by the event of the transfiguration (17:1–9), in which Peter is chosen as one of three disciples to accompany Jesus up the mountain as witnesses. There is a quite plain suggestion here that Jesus is transferring to Peter royal authority in anticipation of his own impending, repeatedly announced martyrdom (16:21; 17:9–11, 22–23).

Peter also, then, appears to have acquired special standing as a Son of God, even if in some way of diminished stature in relation to Jesus. (Telling is the progression in Peter's stature. When he essays to come to Jesus by walking across the water to his approaching master [Matt. 14:28–33], his faith falters, and Jesus must pull him from the drink. At Matthew 16:8, Jesus chides the disciples collectively for lack of faith, but when Peter declares him to be the Messiah, Son of the living God [16:16–18], he—Peter—seems to have come of age spiritually.)

Before we proceed to unwrap further layers of the story, let us return briefly to the tax collector. As noted, the tax collector's question—because it is a question—is peculiar. Was payment of the tax optional? Presumably not. Nevertheless, Jews may have refused to pay the tax either for reasons of poverty or for principled reasons. Essenes refused to pay for reasons of the latter sort. By their lights, the existing temple establishment was illegitimate and not owed fealty. Others, for principled or political reasons of their own, may have also resisted on grounds of this kind.[13]

---

[13] Richard Horsley notes that in the first century CE, the Romans exercised considerable influence on the expenditure of temple funds. Pilate aroused vigorous protest over his use of temple funds to build an aqueduct. Agrippa II, a client ruler,

Given our discussion of Jesus' overturning of the tables of the temple moneychangers, we can find it not too difficult to imagine that he could have had such principled reasons for refusal. Possibly, we are to assume that his views on the matter were already sufficiently well-known that the tax collector had heard of them and had surmised that Jesus might be a tax resistor. One can even imagine, rather improbably, that some of Jesus' political enemies put the tax collector up to asking the question in the hope of trapping Jesus. Either way, such a reconstruction is at best awkward. If Jesus had a standing policy of not paying the tax, Peter would not have answered the tax collector as he did. If Jesus is here giving Peter his rationale for tax compliance, how is it that Peter did not already know this?

Alternatively, might Jesus have been indigent? That, too, appears to be improbable. Although they are not noted by Matthew, Luke 8:2–3 indicates that Jesus had, among others, several wealthy female patrons whom he had healed. In Matthew, we do find one such woman who evidently has access to considerable wealth. She is the unnamed woman who anoints Jesus at Matthew 26:6–12. We will have much more to do presently with her. But whatever reasons Matthew expected his readers to fill in to provide a context for the tax collector's question, it is apparent that the narrative function of the question is to set up an occasion for Jesus' declaration about the paying of the tax. Let us return to that.

If Jesus is the Son of God, then God must be the King meant by the analogy at Matthew 17:25–26. But the meaning here appears to be more complex than this, a fact that is signaled by the consideration that, in the institution of the Eucharist (already foreshadowed in the teaching of Matt. 16 concerning the feeding of the five thousand), Jesus is implicitly challenging the sacerdotal authority of the temple *cultus*. Much more than that, he is replacing it with a *royal cultus*, one that strikes roots deeply into Davidic soil, implicitly repudiating the temple's client service to Rome.

Let us accept that Jesus implies that he is the Son of God. What are the structural implications of that? God is enthroned in the holy of holies. Temple taxes are therefore tributes to him as sovereign over Israel. Yahweh is not, in any ordinary sense, a "king of the earth"—though he does rule an earthly kingdom. Israel itself—or rather Judah—had not had a proper Davidic king since the exile some six hundred years previously. So in what sense could Jesus be—or have thought of himself as being—an heir to the divine throne in the holy of holies, a throne that had not in fact existed since

---

signed off on their use for street paving. Horsley concludes: "Hence the appropriation of temple funds may have been viewed as an extension of the Roman oversight of temple affairs generally" (Richard A. Horsley, *Jesus and the Spiral of Violence: Popular Jewish Resistance in Roman Palestine* [San Francisco, CA: Harper and Row, 1987], 106–7). It will be noted that I am here proceeding, *arguendo*, as if we are to suppose the incident to have been an historical one.

the destruction of the First Temple? And what would have been the political dimensions of such a claim?

First-century Jewish ideas about the monarchy, and the possibility of its restoration, were represented in a wide spectrum of views and expectations concerning a messiah. Here, it is relevant to consider what role the Messiah was expected to play vis à vis the temple and its priesthood. However, the institution of the Eucharist makes it plain that, in spite of continued worship at the temple, early Christians did not see that institution as a permanently viable conduit to the divine.[14] Indeed, aside from the deeper reasons Christians had for rejecting the preeminence of the temple, its legitimacy had been under a cloud since the Maccabean ruler, Johnathan Apphus (son of Mattatheas, the initiator of the Maccabee revolt), although not a Zadokite, enabled himself to be declared high priest.

As the Messiah, then, Jesus must properly combine in his person the sacramental role of the temple priesthood and the effective governing role of king. This is politically contested turf, perhaps because ancient Israel was rightly wary of vesting too much power in the royal office (e.g. 1 Sam. 8, 12:19). A semi-independent temple priesthood could serve as a counterbalance. King Uzziah, achieving great royal success, oversteps his bounds by seeking to offer a sacrifice on the altar of incense, located before the holy of holies where only the priesthood was permitted (2 Chron. 26:16–21). When the priests cannot deter him, the LORD afflicts him with leprosy, effectively removing him from the seat of royal power.

Saul similarly transgresses by presuming to offer a burnt offering to the LORD under strongly extenuating circumstances rather than waiting for Samuel to arrive to perform the ritual (1 Sam. 5–14).[15] Saul's punishment is a shortened reign and the extinction of his royal house after him. Yet both David and Solomon make acceptable sacrifices to the LORD (2 Sam. 24:25; 1 Chron. 21:28; 1 King. 3:3–4, 8:62–63; 2 Chron. 7:1–9).

The author of Hebrews conceives Jesus' occupancy of the former role in terms of his being a legitimate heir to Melchizedek, as King David himself was (Ps. 110:4).[16] Matthew, writing within a decade or two of that author, likely had that psalm, and other passages from Scripture as well, in mind in assimilating priestly and royal functions. At the same time (as Chapter 11 will argue), Matthew depicts the high priest Caiaphas and his

---

[14] Writing after 70 CE, Matthew would have confronted the historical reality of the temple's second destruction; but unlike many Jews, he did not hope for or anticipate its restoration as the central institution in Jesus' new kingdom.

[15] The circumstances are war against a superior Philistine army. With his own army growing hungry and deserting, Saul awaits Samuel's promised arrival for five days before finally himself offering the sacrifice.

[16] It is possible that the claim in Ps. 110 reflects a royal maneuver to perform an end run around the authority of the Aaronite priestly authority by claiming an independent lineage.

associates as effectively abdicating their legitimate claim to the positions they occupy.

If so, then Jesus is claiming himself to be also and in fact son of a "king of the earth"—a status that, in this circumstance, could only be relevant if the king whose son he claims to be is, precisely, David, also declared by Yahweh to be his son. There are repeated allusions to this idea in the Hebrew Bible. In Psalms 2, which appears to be an enthronement hymn, the LORD declares the king—by tradition David—to be both his anointed and his "begotten." The psalm is a triumphalist one: the Davidic king will conquer the nations, and they will serve the LORD with fear. Psalms 110, mentioned above, appears to strike a similar note, although the sense of v. 3, which may poetically describe a divine begetting of the king, is obscure.[17] Psalms 45, possibly a wedding hymn, repeats the theme of divine anointing. More interestingly, v. 6 can be read as identifying the royal throne with that of God.

There has been speculation that in the First Temple period, the king or high priest celebrated an annual renewal ritual in which, mounted on the divine throne in the holy of holies and serving in the role of Yahweh, he would ritually recreate the temple/cosmos (these being images of each other).[18] Such an identification, common enough in surrounding ANE cultures (and among the Roman Caesars), will strike us as anathema to ancient Israel. But, as Chapter 4 has shown, there are distinctions to be drawn here. The king *qua natural person* could hardly be identified with Yahweh. That indeed would be a serious heresy. Moreover, one must

---

[17] John Collins notes that the LXX translation (there numbered Ps. 109) translates "forthrightly" as "I have begotten you" and notes further that Hellenistic traditions of divine kingship may have influenced acceptance of this notion. See Adela Yarbro Collins and John J. Collins, *King and Messiah as the Son of God: Divine, Human, and Angelic Messianic Figures in Biblical and Related Literature* (Grand Rapids, MI: William B. Eerdmans Publishing Company, 2008), 57.

[18] See G. Widengren, "Early Hebrew Myths and their Interpretation," in *Myth, Ritual, and Kingship: Essays on the Theory and Practice of Kingship in the Ancient Near East and in Israel*, ed. S. H. Hooke (Oxford: Clarendon Press, 1958), esp. 199; Sigmund Möwinckel, *The Psalms in Israel's Worship*, trans. D. R. Ap-Thomas (New York: Abingdon Press, 1962), 1:42–80, 106–92); S. H. Hooke, "The Myth and Ritual Pattern of the Ancient East," in *Myth and Ritual: Essays on the Myth and Ritual of the Hebrews in Relation to the Culture Pattern of the Ancient East*, ed. S. H. Hooke (London: Oxford University Press, 1933), 8–14; W. O. E. Oesterley, "Early Hebrew Festival Rituals," in *Myth and Ritual: Essays on the Myth and Ritual of the Hebrews in Relation to the Culture Pattern of the Ancient East*, ed. S. H. Hooke (London: Oxford University Press, 1933), 124–26; Ivan Engnell, *A Rigid Scrutiny: Critical Essays On the Old Testament*, trans. John T. Willis (Nashville, TN: Vanderbilt University Press, 1969), 36–43, 180–84); Margaret Barker, *The Great High Priest: The Temple Roots of Christian Liturgy* (London: T&T Clark, 2003), 80–87; and Collins and Collins, *King and Messiah as the Son of God*, 1–24. According to 1 Chron. 29:23, at Solomon's (second) coronation, he sat on the throne of the LORD.

distinguish the *personage* "the King" from Yahweh. But, if we understand Yahweh, as Chapter 4 suggests, as the ideal form of a personified Israel, it is not so unthinkable that the will of the latter could in a ritualized setting speak through, be vested in, the voice of the king. And of course that officer will be embodied in some particular man. So Jesus may well be claiming here his inheritance of the Davidic throne as well as divine Sonship.[19]

At the same time, from the point of view of a messianic hope among Jews, the Caesar is a usurper of the Davidic throne. But, as I aim to show in the next section, Caesar's illegitimacy becomes, in the hands of Matthew (also Mark and Luke), a far more fundamental illegitimacy, an illegitimacy that voids rulership even of Rome itself. Before turning to the question what should be rendered unto Caesar, brief consideration is in order of the retrieval of the *drachma* from the mouth of a fish caught, we may assume, in the Sea of Galilee. While the icon of the fish came to symbolize the Christ himself, a more direct trope in the Gospel of Matthew is fishing in the Sea of Galilee as a figure for the recruitment of followers of Jesus. Jesus' first call for disciples (Matt. 4:18–22) is to fishermen—Peter and Andrew, then James and John, sons of Zebedee, whom Jesus promises to make "fishers of men."

Similarly at Matthew 13:47–50, a fishnet serves as a simile for the kingdom of God. The good catch are sorted from the bad.[20] It is also clear that the miracle of multiplication of loaves and fish (Matt. 14 and 15) symbolizes the growth of the church. Although Matthew 16:5–12 and the Eucharist emphasize the equation of bread with the body of Christ, it is plausible to think that fish, too, represent the church, the body. Does this figure shed light on the miracle of the coin?

Presumably, the fish that coughs up the coin cannot plausibly represent Christ himself. But it might represent his church, which provides tithes to meet his needs. If so, then although Jesus elects to "pass through" the tax money to the temple, it is in fact only by his authority that it is collected from his church and by his authority that its purpose is determined. The members of his church are, in effect, his proleptic subjects and the proper citizens of the new Israel, who acknowledge Jesus as the legitimate king of the new nation.

B. Rendering unto Caesar (Matt. 22:15–22)

---

[19] 2 Sam. 7:12–14 continues this theme as the LORD promises David that his royal descendants will be adopted sons forever. Isa. 9:6, typically understood by Christians to refer to Jesus, not only reiterates the theme of sonship, but addresses the royal figure as "Mighty God."

[20] At Luke 5:5–6 and John 21:6–11, the catch of fish is an explicit metaphor for an abundant catch of converts.

This famous passage appears to be a companion to Matthew 17:24–27. The first concerns Jesus' attitude toward payment of the temple tax. Here, we have his view of Roman taxation. The format is a wisdom contest: the Pharisees are hoping to set a trap for Jesus. The context is politically charged. The story is sandwiched between a saying of Jesus on the front end and, bringing up the rear, a challenge from the Sadducees that creates a puzzle about resurrection. The saying implies that those to whom God has first issued invitations to the kingdom of heaven have seen fit to pursue other ends. They will be destroyed, and vacancies thus created will be offered to a general population from which the good will be winnowed from the bad. The Sadducee challenge concerns the custom of the levirate: when a woman has successively married seven brothers, each one dying before fathering any children, whose wife is she in the resurrection?[21]

There is a wide acceptance of the view that Jesus' response to the question about the Roman tax draws a sharp distinction between temporal matters and spiritual matters. I shall argue that this misunderstands Matthew's intention. To excavate that intention, it will be important to give an attentive reading to each element of the story. Commentators not uncommonly give only cursory attention to the opening sally of the Pharisees and accompanying Herodians. That is a mistake. In my view, these words that introduce the story hold the key to its meaning.

> [The Pharisees] sent their disciples to [Jesus] along with the Herodians, saying "Teacher, we know that you are true, and teach the way of God truthfully, and care for no man; for you do not regard the position of men. Tell us, then, what you think. Is it lawful to pay taxes to Caesar of not?" (RSV: Matt. 22:16–17)[22]

Here, Jesus is ostensibly being asked to settle a politically sensitive issue that pitted those who favored paying the tax to Rome against those who found it repugnant. The law to which reference is being made is, clearly, the Jewish law, and Pharisees had a history of resisting rule over them by Roman puppets such as the Herods. Some—including presumably present company—opposed payment of the tax, whereas Herodians apparently favored paying the tax, as being preferable to direct Roman rule.[23]

---

[21] Jesus' answer—that in the resurrection, there will be no marriage and that God is not a god of the dead but of the living—raises questions I will comment on briefly below. See also Chapter 8 and Chapter 12, section IV.

[22] Here, I favor the RSV translation over the NRSV, which uses a weaker adjective: rather than having Jesus characterized (ironically) as "true," he is told that he is "sincere," which anyone might be, no matter how befuddled.

[23] Fabian Udoh has argued that such a direct Roman tax did not exist in Jesus' day, though it did after 70 CE when Matthew's Gospel was written. Thus, the story contains an anachronism. See Fabian Udoh, *To Caesar What Is Caesar's: Tribute, Taxes,*

Especially telling is the rather elaborately flattering phrasing of the introductory remark that justifies the parties' consultation with Jesus. Though we may imagine that there is an underlying tone of irony in the description of Jesus, Matthew intends the reader to understand that the description is precisely true. Indeed, refusal to "regard the position of men" is precisely a divine attribute and a behavior those in positions of authority are commanded by God to observe.[24] It is a fundamental principle of fairness: no one is to gain preferential treatment on account of social position, wealth, or power. No one is to be disadvantaged under the law for reasons of poverty or lowly status. Matthew's readers will know that Jesus is indeed a teacher who insists upon this principle.

To the question posed to him, Jesus' famous response is, "Show me the money for the tax." Given the coin, he asks, "Whose likeness and inscription is this?" Now it is of interest exactly what coin is being described in this passage. We cannot know, given only that it bears a bust of "Caesar" and an inscription. Matthew might here have been intentionally a bit vague. But the coin is specified to be a *denarius*, and we know something about the *denarii* that were minted by the empire during the era in question. And what we know is suggestive.

A number of *denarii* minted under the Roman Republic bore, on one side, an image of the Roman patron goddess Roma. Julius Caesar issued new and interestingly different *denarii* in 44 BCE when, having returned to Rome after pursuing and killing Pompey, the Senate declared him lifetime dictator. These *denarii* replaced the portrait of Roma with a bust of Caesar himself. On the reverse side were images of Venus Genatrix, his divine ancestress. The new coins caused a political uproar. They contributed to the enmity that led to Caesar's assassination months later.[25]

---

and *Imperial Administration in Early Roman Palestine (63 B.C.E.–70 C.E.)* (Providence, RI: Brown Judaic Studies, 2005), 207–43, 279–88. This does not affect my interpretation, though it clearly disconfirms historicist interpretations of the story. Udoh oddly remarks that "whether or not the saying ... is historically reliable need not be argued here" (p. 224). Yet he has in effect done just that since his findings entail that the pericope is not "historically reliable." Udoh further notes (p. 232) the archaeological evidence that makes unlikely the ready availability of Roman coinage of any kind in Judea in this period, in conflict with the general scholarly opinion that the *denarius* given to Jesus was Tiberian coinage. Of course, this makes my speculation that the coin being alluded to was the one coined by Julius even more far-fetched, if the pericope is to be taken as historical recollection. But this is not such a high barrier if we read the passage symbolically. Udoh notes that only in Matthew does Jesus identify the *denarius* as the currency with which the tax is to be paid.

[24] Of God: 2 Sam. 14:14; Rom. 2:11. Commanded by God: Lev. 19:15; Deut. 1:17, 16:19.

[25] Seth Stevenson et al. relate the incitement provoked by the coin (Seth William Stevenson, C. Roach Smith, and Frederic W. Madden, *A Dictionary of Roman Coins* [London: B. A. Seaby, 1964], 156). C. H. V. Sutherland remarks, "The denarii [of

Yet in four years, in 40 BCE, a commemorative coin depicted Julius' bust with the inscription "DIVI IVLI" ("God Julius"), an iconography that became customary for the Julio-Claudians and the Flavian emperors who followed them in the latter part of the first century CE. Thus, Augustus had coins minted designating him a divine son, and his own son, ruling at the time of Jesus' ministry, minted a *denarius* with the inscription *"Ti[berivs] Caesar Divi Avg[vsti] F[ilivs] Avgvstvs"* ("Caeasar Augustus Tiberius, son of the Divine Augustus"). The Flavians Vespasian and Titus had similar *denarii* minted in their honor. Thus, the authors of the Synoptic Gospels could safely assume that this story would bring to their readers' minds the image of a coin bearing the bust of a Caesar, with an inscription declaring that individual's deity.

But what was so incendiary about Julius Caesar's coinage? The goddess Roma was, of course, a personification of the Roman nation itself. In replacing her image with his own, and in accepting the post of dictator for life, Julius was doing two things. First, he was *identifying* himself with the Roman state and his will with that of the Roman people. But in conflating his own will with that of the state, he was, secondly, arrogating to himself the right to rule Rome in the service of his personal interests. I suggest that he was, therefore, collapsing the fundamental distinction, already well understood at the time, between personage and person.

In implying that the will of the individual Julius can functionally replace the will of Rome itself, Caesar was setting himself up as a tyrant. And this indeed would have been a political provocation of the first order. As Kantorowicz (1957) has shown, it was precisely the insistence upon this distinction by medieval political theorists (expressed in terms of the ruler's having two bodies, one mortal and private, the other immortal and identified with the nation) that permitted them to understand how a king could, *qua* private individual, be subject to the very laws that, *qua* monarch and embodier of the will of the nation, he was charged with legislating.[26]

So it was exactly this distinction between personal will and aims and those of the sovereign nation that, albeit embodied in the king, held the line between legitimate rule and descent into despotism.[27] Julius Caesar was

---

44 BCE] all bear Caesar's portrait on the obverse, with reverses given up to various representations of Venus Genatrix, his divine ancestress: at last the representation of a living Roman had been undertaken [for the first time] on the coinage of Rome, for Caesar *was* Rome" (C. H. V. Sutherland, *Roman Coins* [New York: G. P. Putnam's Sons, 1974], 95; italics in original).

[26] See also Chapter 4 on social ontology.

[27] A more complex structure can, in fact, be argued here since the natural person who "is" the sovereign embodies at least two personages, possibly three. First, he or she is simply a citizen of the nation. That is one personage. Second, he or she is king or queen—that is another. Third, he or she may be considered, on certain occasions, to embody the "person" of the nation as a whole. That is a third. In any event, the first two

not the last individual to have threatened this distinction. Particularly famous is the statement of Louis XIV of France, "*L'etat, c'est moi*," whose import had, though not for him personally, similarly disastrous consequences.[28]

We cannot be sure that the synoptic evangelists were party to a tradition that understood the *denarius* referred to in our pericope to have been one that represented the deification of the Caesars. But it is hard to think otherwise. Yet if so, then Jesus' reply to the Pharisees and Herodians has nothing to do with separating the secular from the sacred and everything to do with the distinction between a legitimate sovereign and a despot. The cardinal sin of the despot is that he does *not* "disregard the position of men." On the contrary: instead of regarding high social position as a trust, with the responsibility of fairly representing the interests of the ruled, the tyrant sees his or her position as an opportunity for self-serving oppression and exploitation. In short, the tyrant sees his or her own position as privileging him or her rather than conferring an obligation to serve the greater good.

On this reading, then, Jesus is managing to outmaneuver his opponents in two ways. First, he is affirming the principle of justice that his enemies articulate. And in doing so, he is manifesting a recognition of the very distinction between person and position that qualifies him as a proper sovereign. He has thus turned his opponents' flattery to his own advantage. But more than this: he has cleverly taken a rhetorical dagger, inserted it between Caesar's ribs, and deftly twisted it. Hearing his answer, the Pharisees and Herodians, who we may infer understood this subtle attack

---

personages are of importance in the legal theory that holds a monarch accountable for his or her official acts. For, merely *qua* natural person, one is not subject to the laws of the land. But *qua* citizen, one is. If the monarch violates his/her oath of office, (s)he may forfeit the office but, in any case, be tried as a citizen under the law. It is an empirical question whether first-century political thinkers discerned each of these distinctions. But one bit of positive evidence comes from the first century, precisely in connection with the growing trend of self-deification (in, among other things, required forms of address) by Roman emperors. Here is Pliny's expression of relief at the succession by Trajan of Nerva: "An open tribute to our Emperor demands a new form....Times are different, and our speeches must show this....Nowhere should we flatter him [Trajan] as a god; we are talking of a fellow citizen, not a tyrant, one who is our father not our over-lord" (Pliny, *Panegyricus* 2.2–3, quoted in Jonathan Bardill, *Constantine, Divine Emperor of the Christian Golden Age* [New York: Cambridge University Press, 2012], 338).

[28] Nor, evidently, was Julius Caesar the first. Akenhaten, the tenth ruler of the nineteenth dynasty in Egypt, famous for having introduced "monotheism" into Egyptian religion, appears by that maneuver to have engineered just this kind of coup to centralize his power. In rejecting the earlier tradition, which assigned to the royal god Amun the function of ordaining a new pharaoh by transferring to him the Royal *ka*—thereby forging a kind of dual Pharaoh/god being within the king —Akenhaten appears literally to have *identified* his personal being with that of the new high god, Aten. This usurpation did not survive the reign of his son, Tutankhamun. See Lanny Bell, "The New Kingdom 'Divine' Temple: The Example of Luxor," in *Temples of Ancient Egypt*, ed. Byron E. Shafer (Ithaca, NY: Cornell University Press, 1997), 180–82.

upon Caesar and the implicit contrast between Caesar and himself, must indeed have "marveled" and left in full retreat. For Jesus' answer, though extraordinarily subversive, gave every superficial appearance of innocence. The trap had backfired.[29]

So, in the end, Jesus escapes any accusation of tax dodging. Yet at the same time, Matthew's narration of Jesus' words is designed to leave no question in the minds of his readers that Jesus' teaching is deeply subversive of both the temple and its taxing authority and of Rome and the tax it levies on Judea. In both cases, that subversion is linked to a claim that the proper governing authority is neither Rome nor Jerusalem but the itinerate Jew who comes from Galilee.

Neither Matthew 17:24–27 nor 22:15–22 narrates an event that could not have happened. Yet in both cases, our suspicions ought to be aroused by the way in which the scene is set for an incisive reply from Jesus. Above, we saw that the whole of Matthew can be analyzed as a ring composition. Within that framework, it can be argued—see the diagram in section IA above—that Matthew 22:15–22 has a parallel at Matthew 2:1–18 and that perhaps Matthew 17:24–27 has a parallel at Matthew 3:7–10. As the Matthew 17 passage concerns the paying of the temple tax and its implicit critique of the legitimacy of the temple cult, so at Matthew 3:7–10, John denounces the Pharisees and Sadducees, who aligned themselves with the existing temple and its cult.

As the Matthew 22 passage aims a barbed arrow at the ideology of the Caesars, Matthew 2:1–18 portrays Jesus as the legitimate rival to the Roman puppet Herod. These identifications (especially the first one) can be challenged—they are not self-evident—but I consider the second, at least, plausible enough to add weight to the view that the taxation passages are literary inventions designed to support Matthew's portrait of Jesus.[30] But whatever evidential strength one assigns to the suggestion that the taxation

---

[29] Adela Yarbro Collins provides strong corroboration for this reading in her discussion of the political implications of the kenotic language in Phil. 2:5–7 (Collins and Collins, *King and Messiah as the Son of God*, 114–116). Jesus does not "seize" divine honors, but empties himself—concedes his humanity—and thus merits elevation to the messianic throne, in pointed contrast to Nero's self-promotion as a divine being.

[30] The following might be said in favor of pairing Matt. 3:7–10 with 17:24–27. First, 3:7–10 looks like an insertion. The text reads smoothly with it deleted. Second, it has some verbal similarity with 17:24–27: as a hook is *cast* (βάλε) into the sea to catch the fish, so an unfruitful tree is *cast* (βάλλεται) into the fire in John's tirade against the Pharisees and Sadducees. Third, there is a kind of antiparallelism in the imagery: the fish, which is fruitful, is drawn in and bound by a hook. The tree, which is unfruitful, is cut asunder by an axe. Fourth, the fruit which the tree does not bear is the fruit of repentance—the very fruit that the temple is supposed to enable by mediating between God and men. To perform penance is to do service to the temple through sacrifice or payment. But as the Pharisees and Sadducees fail to do what they should, Jesus voluntarily does what he has no legal need or obligation to do. And see further below.

passages conform to the ring pattern, the best grounds for thinking that Matthew uses these passages in the construction of a larger myth come from the way in which they contribute to the structured message I believe can be discovered in the last few chapters of Matthew. This will be the topic of our next two chapters.

Before I turn to a structural analysis of Matthew's Passion, it will be illuminating to set the confrontation over Caesar's coin in a somewhat wider context, following an insightful essay by Nicholas Townsend.[31] Townsend arrives at much the same conclusion I have—that Jesus is not merely parrying the politically loaded question by distinguishing a mundane authority from a superior one but is contrasting the authority of the proper God and of his Son with that of the overweening Caesars. My primary difference with Townsend is that I have more to say—and will say it in the remaining two chapters—about precisely who the Son and his kingdom are, something broadly hinted at in the present passage.

Townsend discusses the *denarius* passage in its somewhat simpler Markan setting, noting that the parable of the tenants (which Matthew also gives in Matt. 21) is sandwiched there between another wisdom contest on the front end and the *denarius* episode following. In the earlier verbal exchange (Matt. 21:23–27), the chief priests and elders confront Jesus in the temple and ask him by what authority he teaches and acts. Jesus replies with a question: was John's baptism divinely sanctioned or only humanly instituted? The authorities see the trap: if they denounce John, they will antagonize the crowds. Thus, they decline, and Jesus can similarly decline to claim for himself the authority he rightly has but would incite arrest for declaring.

But Jesus' provocation does not end there. Saying "What do you think?" he tells them two parables, the vineyard parable and the parable of the tenants (Matt. 21:28–45), whose meaning is transparent: God, the owner of the vineyard (which is Israel), is ill-served by the tenant caretakers (the priests and elders), who beat and murder messengers (the prophets—e.g., John) and finally God's Son. The authorities are forced to agree that the tenants ought to be put to death. Jesus adds that the kingdom of God will be taken from them and given to a (foreign) people who will produce its fruits.

Townsend uses recognition ("seeing") as an expository theme in analyzing these passages. Jesus, upon arriving in Jerusalem, is at first hiding, and then, in a gradual and controlled way, revealing his true identity—the "messianic secret"—to the authorities who can and finally will do him harm. Lacking understanding, they fail to see what the reader knows: who Jesus is. Lacking understanding, they fail to see what is being progressively unfolded

---

[31] Nicholas Townsend, "Surveillance and Seeing: A New Way of Reading Mark 12:17, 'Give Back to Caesar…',", *Studies in Christian Ethics* 27, no. 1 (2014): 79–90.

for the reader: the true locus of the Jesus' kingdom.[32] Townsend suggests that the Pharisees and Herodians who accost Jesus in the *denarius* episode are sent by the priests and elders who have been stung by Jesus' clever coyness in the exchange over authority and the tenant parable, both of which highlight their illegitimacy and ignorance of who Jesus is.

The *denarius* exchange heightens this theme of recognition. In demanding a coin and asking his interlocutors to identify the image on it (by orthodox Jewish lights a graven image[33]), Jesus dramatizes the fact that they are able to identify the emperor but unable to recognize the true son of God.[34] But then:

> What is owed to God? To see the vineyard owner's son, the messianic son, the son of God; to recognize him and to respond to the coming of God's reign. The emphatic second half of Jesus' answer is directed back to the Sanhedrin, through their covert agents. It presses on the leaders the same challenge that the [tenants] parable has just made....This was all about the fruit the tenants owe to the vineyard owner but refuse to give him....Jesus now emphasizes, 'Give back ... to God what is God's.'[35]

This seems exactly right. Moreover, it reinforces the case for identifying Matthew 3:7–10 as the chiastic double of Matthew 17: 24–27, John's execration of the Pharisees and Sadducees: "Bear fruit worthy of repentance." In echoing Jesus' own rejection of the Sanhedrin, it condemns the temple establishment and pointedly suggests that the temple tax is indeed no longer owed by the custodians of the newly inaugurated kingdom of God.[36]

---

[32] Townsend does not emphasize this second aspect of the texts, but, in the context of Matthew, I shall.

[33] The point of the prohibition on graven images is to forbid worship of false gods. The inscription on the coin—a claim of divinity—drives home the point that the coin precisely meets the criteria that render it forbidden. The Pharisees, who were punctilious about the law, would have been particularly offended by such coins.

[34] Townsend adds the nice observation that there is a play here upon the prologue to his opponents' question (Townsend, "Surveillance and Seeing, 86). The expression usually translated, "You do not regard the position of men" [or "a person's status"], literally means "You do not look at the face of a person." This, Townsend suggests, is deliberate irony: Jesus is doing exactly what his opponents flatter him for not doing. But, as we have seen, the deeper irony is precisely that Jesus is not only refusing to pay deference to Caesar's status but, rather, attacking it.

[35] Townsend, "Surveillance and Seeing, 87–88.

[36] Commenting on the tenants parable, N. T. Wright remarks: "The parable dovetails exactly into the riddle about John [i.e., whether his authority is human or divine]. In one sense, Jesus is the last of the prophetic line, coming to Israel to ask for fruit from the vineyard. In another, John was the last in the line; after the last messenger

Townsend's conclusion is that

what Jesus seems to say is: 'Dismiss the idolatrous claim on these coins, because it is false. See them for what they are. These things are merely the currency of Caesar's role, so let him have them. What really matters is what you owe God.'[37]

But if I am right, this paraphrase, while not incorrect, is much too weak: Jesus is leveling a far more insightful and theoretically powerful charge against the Caesars, a charge of tyranny. In the light of this reflection on Townsend's insightful approach of pulling into view the context of the *denarius* passages, let us now reflect briefly upon the rather more complex way in which Matthew frames this episode. To the simpler Markan narrative, Matthew adds, between the besting of the Sanhedrin and the tenants parable, another short vineyard parable and inserts also between the latter and the coin episode another parable, already briefly mentioned, about a king who invites guests to his wedding. The former parable contrasts two sons of a vineyard owner, one who refuses to do requested work but then has a change of heart and one who agrees to work but then reneges. The analogy is to a contrast between the temple establishment and the Johnny-come-latelies to the kingdom, the tax collectors and prostitutes who have accepted Jesus.

That contrast is the point as well of the wedding parable. It will be clear, I think, that these parables further serve to give shape to Jesus' kingdom. The temple establishment is out. They have forfeited their right to Yahweh's inheritance. The socially marginalized of Israel's children are—if they accept Jesus as Lord—in. But they aren't the only ones who are in. The vineyard parable itself makes a telling claim that Townsend curiously ignores: the kingdom will be given to a foreign nation.[38] We shall have opportunity to return to this signal declaration in the next two chapters.

---

comes the son" (N. T. Wright, *Jesus and the Victory of God*, Christian Origins and the Question of God [Minneapolis, MN: Fortress Press, 1996], 2:497). This only serves to reinforce further the chiasm between Matt. 3:7–10 and 17:24–27.

[37] Townsend, "Surveillance and Seeing," 90.

[38] Ched Myers, whose interesting portrayal of Jesus as a political figure Townsend makes use of, does take up the question of the identity of the "others" to whom the kingdom will be given. But rejecting the natural reading of "others"—ἔθνει—as "Gentiles" (because the coins episode displays Jesus' antipathy to Rome), Myers instead embraces the view that Jesus' aim is to inaugurate a (this-worldly) ongoing kingdom of those who reject the corrupt systems of power and exploitation of the poor and the weak. See Ched Myers, *Binding the Strong Man* (Maryknoll, NY: Orbis Books, 1988), 309–310. Thus, he concludes, "And Jesus was 'king,' but in the tradition of popular and revolutionary Israelite kingship. He was not a royal pretender to David's throne, for he repudiated the politics of imperial domination. Rather he was a 'true

On the far side of the coin controversy, Matthew adds two more confrontations (also given in Mark 12). The first is the aforementioned question, asked Jesus by the Sadducees, about the woman who had seven husbands. Jesus' puzzling answer is that "in the resurrection they neither marry nor are given in marriage, but are like angels in heaven."

The Sadducees have failed to see this because they do not know the Scriptures or the power of God. What, exactly, can this mean? What Scriptures had the Sadducees ignored? What relevant power will God exercise in the resurrection? How are the resurrected like angels, and how— even if there are no weddings "in the resurrection"—does that answer a question concerning marriages already contracted prior to the resurrection? Moreover, to what period does the phrase "in the resurrection" refer? Does it denote a temporary process of revivification or the enduring state of things in the kingdom? If there is no marriage in the kingdom, is there also no procreation?[39]

I do not intend to try to answer these questions here, but I will return to them in the final chapter. For now, we may observe that, like the parables of the tenants, the two sons, and the royal wedding feast, what Jesus says here is meant to provide clues about the shape and nature of the kingdom. So does the final contest, which again pits Jesus against the Pharisees. They ask Jesus which are the greatest commandments. He responds: love the LORD, love your neighbor as yourself. These, then, are affirmed as the ruling principles of the kingdom.

But Jesus takes opportunity to ask the Pharisees whose son the Messiah is and then quote against them the opening lines of Psalms 110: "The Lord said to my Lord, 'Sit at my right hand, until I put your enemies

---

shepherd,' anointed to lead a new tribal confederacy into a new promised land....Thus, Jesus identified with Zechariah's vision (Zech. 9:9f.), which 'evokes an image of the leader of a tribal Israel prior to the time it even possessed the more advanced military technology of horses and war chariots'" (p. 446). This is (to me at least) a very attractive reading of who Jesus was and at what he aimed. But it points Jesus in the direction of an unrecoverable distant past, and it does not bear up under the evidence. As I hope to show, Jesus is portrayed as anything but an antique tribal leader.

[39] It is conceivable that Jesus' saying refers to a tradition alluded to in the *Gospel of Philip*, according to which there was no death (and, obviously, no birth) when Eve was still a part of Adam. If, as Revelations seems to suggest, the kingdom of heaven involved a kind of symbolic return to the primal state (see also Chapter 8), then indeed "in the resurrection" there will be no male and female, no marriage, no procreation—and no death. Since this cannot have been meant literally, I take this line of interpretation, if correct, to indicate that Jesus is articulating, in a symbolic way, the idea that the kingdom of heaven will achieve a kind of "Platonic" social ideal in which somehow the vagaries of procreation, death, and generational change will no longer put at risk a stable and permanent social order. For the *Gospel of Philip*, see Coptic Gnostic Library II.3.69–73 and Barker, *The Great High Priest*, 133. See also Chapter 8 and Chapter 12 on the significance of Jesus' apparent opposition to marriage.

under your feet.'" The implicit premise is that the referent of the first occurrence of "Lord" is God, and the second must be someone whom David acknowledges as his Lord. So if the Messiah is a son of David, how can David acknowledge him as Lord? The Pharisees, of course, do not know how to answer. Defeated again in this last contest, Jesus' enemies think better of any attempt at future debate.

More to our purpose: what is the implication of the claim that David's son is his Lord? To answer that, we must first ask in what sense Jesus is David's son. Not his biological descendant, on Matthew's account.[40] It appears, then, that Jesus is a son of David by adoption (the presumption is that Joseph, a Davidic descendant, legally adopts Jesus). Is he, then, Yahweh's biological son? If he were, that might explain how he can be both David's son (by adoption) and Lord. But that does not seem to be the correct story either. Indeed, some exegetes explain Jesus' divine sonship by pointing to Matthew 3:16–17, interpreted as an act of adoption by God.

Further complicating matters is David's own adoption (and perhaps by extension, his royal descendants') by Yahweh (Ps. 2:7; cf. Ps. 89:26–27; 2 Sam. 7:14). Matthew is therefore less explicit than we might wish, but in giving Jesus a miraculous birth, he is surely suggesting some preeminent relationship with God that David lacked. This conclusion is confirmed by Jesus himself. After he performs an exorcism, the crowds wonder, "Can this be the son of David?" (Matt. 12:23; but shortly thereafter, Jesus declares to the scribes and Pharisees seeking a sign, "The queen of the South will rise up at the judgment with this generation and condemn it, because she came from the ends of the earth to listen to the wisdom of Solomon, and see, something greater than Solomon is here!" [Matt. 12:42]). All of these are strong hints, and they rise in a crescendo that points toward the Passion Narrative. We now turn to that narrative and ask how it articulates, in quite surprising detail, the nature of Jesus' conquest over the powers of evil and the shape of his kingdom and his kingship over it.

---

[40] Some exegetes have attributed the discrepancies between the genealogies of Luke and Matthew to Luke tracing Jesus' line to David through his mother. This is theologically neat but not in my view supported by the texts.

Matthew's Passion

Thou dost rule the raging of the sea;
when its waves rise, thou stillest them.
Thou didst crush Rahab like a carcass,
Thou didst scatter thy enemies with thy
mighty arm.

Psalms 89:9–10

I. Framing Matthew's Passion Narrative: Women and Structure

A. St. Matthew's Passion as Myth

It is a familiar feature of the Gospel Passion Narratives that nearly every major element of the story, in each of its differing versions, is anticipated in the Hebrew Bible (hereafter, HB)—so much so that one can virtually piece together that narrative from passages found in the Psalms, Zechariah, Jeremiah, Isaiah, and elsewhere. This is for no Gospel truer than for Matthew's. It is not that Matthew produces a pastiche of HB narratives in composing his Passion Narrative, but it is clear that a close relationship exists between almost every theme of Matthew's passion and some HB text(s).

For orthodox Christians, the explanation of this remarkable coincidence is, in essence, rather straightforward: the HB passages, reflecting God's foreknowledge and divine plan of salvation, serve as prefigurative or prophetic "hints."[1] They foreshadow the singular salvific act in which God, through the sacrifice of his Son Jesus, enters human history in the very way required to bring into the human sphere the effective workings of divine grace. To achieve this signal result, God carefully choreographed both Israelite history and the events surrounding Jesus' life, or at least, chose an historical setting that he foreknew would serve this purpose.

---

[1] This sort of claim is virtually aboriginal. We find it already at 1 Cor. 15:3–4, one of the earliest writings in the NT. Skeptics suggest rather that the early Christians scoured the Hebrew Bible for passages that could be creatively applied *ex post facto* to events in their day. I shall be suggesting a more radical understanding.

In view of the meaningful and close correspondences between the HB and the Passion Narratives—including explicit references to the HB—Matthew's use of one feature of the story of Jonah comes as something of a surprise. At Matthew 12:39–40, Jesus anticipates his passion, offering what is the most precise prediction in the NT of the chronology of his death and resurrection. As such, this verse ranks second only to his announcement of the *parousia* (especially at Matt. 16:27) as the most significant prophecy in Christian soteriology.

The surprise I wish to remark upon is not that Jesus should be able to make such a specific prophecy but that it appears to conflict strikingly with the chronology provided by Matthew's own narrative, for Jesus says that, just as Jonah was imprisoned for three days and three nights in the belly of the whale (κήτους), so too shall he be imprisoned for that period within "the heart of the earth (ἐν τῇ καρδίᾳ τῆς γῆς)."[2] Yet, Matthew's passion chronology, the most detailed of the Gospels, is quite explicit: Jesus dies at about 3 p.m. on a Friday, is buried by 6 p.m., and has risen out of the tomb sometime near or before dawn (6 a.m.) on Sunday.[3] In what follows, I shall be developing a solution to this puzzle, the puzzle created by the apparent contradiction in Matthew, and I shall argue that this solution fits the available data substantially better than other scholarly solutions that have been offered. But my broader purpose is to use this problem as a vehicle for discussing some much larger, and therefore more contentious, issues that surround biblical hermeneutics. I shall be arguing that a signal advantage of the solution I propose in explaining Matthew 12:39–40 is that it avoids convicting Matthew of an obvious contradiction and thus better minds the virtue of charity than interpretations that ignore, gloss

---

[2] Though the apparent imperviousness of the disciples to Jesus' repeated description of his fate—an obdurate incomprehension manifested in their apparent dismay at the prophecy's fulfillment—does require explanation: see, e.g., Mark 9:32/Luke 9:45, which explains the matter by saying the disciples were afraid to ask for clarification. Luke, perhaps feeling the inadequacy of Mark's explanation, invokes divine intervention! (Cf. the less explicit Luke 11:30.) Indeed, the disciples are obtuse, not only with respect to this prophecy but—especially in John—in understanding Jesus' parables and deeds. A full discussion would take us too far afield, but the pre-resurrection ignorance of the disciples serves at least the dramatic aim of highlighting and heightening the illumination and courage the disciples receive from their witness to the risen Lord. That transformation aside, it also motivates their abandonment of Jesus upon his arrest—which echoes Isa. 53:3–12 and also Pss. 22, 31, 69, and 88.

[3] According to the traditions preserved in all the Gospels, the passion took place at the time of Passover (John disagrees with the Synoptics only to the extent of placing the crucifixion on the Day of Preparation rather than on the day of Passover itself). As this falls very near the spring equinox, we can infer that the "ninth hour"—the time of death—would have struck at 3 p.m., and that daybreak occurred at 6 a.m.

over, or attempt to explain away by appeal to arcane calendrical rules the apparent discrepancy.[4]

Secondly, my solution makes central use of the idea that the Passion Narrative is a myth and that techniques of myth analysis discussed in Chapter 6 can provide new and fundamental insights into its meaning.[5] This requires appeal to the notion of myth I have articulated in Chapter 5 and will illustrate the fruitfulness of applying that category to seemingly historical passages in the Bible. It will show once again, therefore, that the utility of such an approach is by no means confined to treatment of miracle stories but can better explain, and better illuminate, the richness of meaning of much that ordinarily passes for historical recollection.

There is ample room for misunderstanding here. First, it may be remarked that the application of the category of myth to biblical exegesis has a long (and somewhat checkered) history, dating at least to the eighteenth century.[6] In the first half of the twentieth century, the notion of myth was often employed by members of the Religionsgeschichte School, which included Bultmann and Möwinckel. Some contemporary commentators, such as William Craig, dismiss myth approaches to NT studies as an old idea that has been tried and has failed.[7] There is no space here to examine this suggestion; the following remarks will have to suffice.

First, it is perhaps overly smug to allege that the investigations of the Religionsgeschichte School led to failure. Thus, H. Boers has the following to say about the results achieved by this school: "The RGS's program of biblical interpretation never came to a conclusion; it was interrupted by the rise of dialectical theology, to which even such an eminent second-generation member as Bultmann was attracted. The misfortune of this for biblical scholarship is not

---

[4] Thus, appeal is frequently made to Hos. 6:2, but Jesus is explicit in his reference to Jonah, not Hosea. As Dale Allison rightly noted: "A type should be prominent....Obscurity does not commend itself" (Dale C. Allison, *The New Moses: A Matthean Typology* [Minneapolis, MN: Fortress Press, 1993], 22).

[5] The reader may wonder whether I apply this claim to all of the Gospel accounts. I do; but here, I am confining my attention to Matthew. This approach, parenthetically, permits one to explain the contradictory details in the Gospel narratives (and elsewhere) without supposing bungled historical traditions. Variations in the story may indicate differences in theological message or emphasis or simply different ways of assembling available mythemes—see Chapters 5 and 6—to convey the same essential message—or to register disagreement, not over the historical facts, but over message content or strategies of presentation.

[6] Among the ancients, Philo Judaeus construed parts of the Hebrew Bible as myth. We find myth also in Augustine's interpretive arsenal. See St. Augustine, *Confessions* 5.14(24), 6.5(8), and all of Book 13, as well as Philo *De Posteritate Caini* 7, *De Abrahamo* 99, *The Migration of Abraham, Questions and Answers on Genesis,* and *Questions and Answers on Exodus.*

[7] See, e.g., Richard L. Purtill et al., "Replies to Evan Fales from the Contributors to in Defense of Miracle," *Philosophia Christi* 3, no. 1 (2001): 37–87.

that the answers of the RGS have been lost—to the contrary, they have been refined by sympathizers and opponents alike. The misfortune is rather that their questions have been forgotten without having been fully addressed."[8]

Even more decisive is J. Z. Smith's pointed critique of this dismissive attitude toward comparative studies. In a monograph devoted to a careful history of the anti-comparativist enterprise and analysis of its sectarian agenda, Smith remarks,

> It is, to put matters bluntly, poor method to compare and contrast a richly nuanced and historically complex understanding of Pauline Christology with a conglomerate of 'mystery texts' treated as if they were historically and ideologically simple and interchangeable; to treat the former as developmental and the latter as frozen. As long as we identify recognizable humanity with historical consciousness and openness to change with critical thought—as we do—the usual treatment of the religions of Late Antiquity, as well as the bulk of the other mythic traditions of humankind, is inhumane. (The latter is, I fear, not an unintended consequence.) The claimed ahistorical character of myth is a product of the scholar's gaze and not of some native world-view.[9]

Second, these earlier scholars were operating with conceptions of myth that were largely, or entirely, uninformed by the work of anthropologists, and—in particular—by critical attention to the work of Durkheim and Levi-Strauss, Turner, and others, which I draw heavily upon. Thus, many of the criticisms leveled against the RGS approach simply miss the mark if brought against the use I make of the category of myth.

Third, many of those criticisms are mistaken or badly defended. Here, I mention just three: (1) It is said that the genre of the Gospels is that of biography, on the strength of arguments that Acts is "clearly" an historical work, that Luke, continuous with Acts and declared by Luke 1:1–4 to be "historical," is therefore so as well, and that the other Gospels share the same genre as Luke. (2) The alleged Hellenistic mythical "parallels" to Gospel stories are not good parallels at all. (3) The figure and ideology of Jesus is thoroughly rooted in "orthodox Judaism," which rejected Hellenistic religious

---

[8] See H. Boers, "Religionsgeschichtliche Schule," in *Dictionary of Biblical Interpretation*, ed. John H. Hayes (Nashville, TN: Abingdon Press, 1999), 2:386.

[9] Jonathan Z. Smith, *Drudgery Divine: On the Comparison of Early Christianities and the Religions of Late Antiquity* (Chicago, IL: University of Chicago Press, 1990), 108–9. Smith is concerned mainly with comparison of contemporary Hellenistic cults to Christianity, whereas I am concerned more with relationships between ancient Semitic religions and the Hebrew Bible; but the methodological issues are essentially the same.

ideas. Hence, neither Jesus nor his biographers would ever have borrowed Hellenistic themes.

As against these three claims, I have already argued that: (1) This assumes that the genres of biography/history and myth are distinct (if myth is even a genre) and can readily be distinguished. But they cannot. There are clear cases but also a continuum in between. Are, for example, the stories surrounding Robin Hood biography or myth? And—to give examples from the era in question—what of the "biographies" of Aesop, Pythagoras, and Apollonius of Tyana?[10] (2) Everything depends upon which similarities and differences are considered significant. The criteria often employed, as Chapter 3 aims to show, are typically tendentious and not well motivated, for example, by any general conception of the nature of myth. (3) As N. T. Wright (1992) and others have shown, there was no such thing in the first century as "orthodox" Judaism. There were Judaisms, with strong disagreements over their attitudes toward Hellenistic ideas. It is a complete illusion to imagine that the first century Mediterranean world consisted of nations living in cultural and intellectual isolation. Furthermore, if he is anything, the Jesus of the Gospels is no traditional Jew but an innovator and rebel against the Jewish establishment of his day.

In this connection, we have noted that the basic apologetic strategy of those who take the NT miracle accounts to reflect historical events is to use arguments to the best explanation. They compare the plausibility of the explanation that these accounts should be understood as records of eyewitness experiences of the events described, with the plausibility of more skeptical hypotheses.[11] The skeptical competitors generally invoke fraud or folly (most invoke both) and can be further divided into those that imagine the early Christians to have been engaged in conscious deception and those that would involve self-deception (hallucination, exaggerated memories, and the like). The apologetic strategy, then, is to argue that the skeptical hypotheses can all be eliminated as less likely than the historical understanding of the miracle stories.

Now, argument to the best explanation is a legitimate and powerful way to reason about the unknown; often, it is our only recourse. But as we know, it is subject to the notable weakness that the strength of the argument depends upon the presumption that all eligible explanations have been

---

[10] For arguments that the genre of the Gospels is not myth, cf. Charles H. Talbert, *What Is a Gospel? The Genre of the Canonical Gospels* (Philadelphia, PA: Fortress Press, 1977).

[11] This is the consistent strategy of such evangelical apologists as William Lane Craig, Gary Habermas, and Stephen T. Davis. It is also regularly deployed by mainstream scholars such as, e.g., E. P. Sanders, *Jesus and Judaism* (Philadelphia: Fortress Press, 1985), 166–67 and N. T. Wright, *The Resurrection of the Son of God*, Christian Origins and the Question of God, vol. 3 (Minneapolis, MN: Fortress Press, 2003), 607–8 (concerning the women at the empty tomb, of which more presently)—to give just two examples.

considered. Although I believe that fraud and folly hypotheses cannot be dismissed as less probable than the occurrence of miracles, my purpose here is not to defend such hypotheses. Rather, I am going to offer an alternative that has not received sufficiently serious consideration either by apologists or by most skeptics: namely, that the passion/resurrection narrative in Matthew (and, by extension, in the other Gospels) must be understood in terms of the categories pertaining to myth, categories against which most apologetic arguments are impotent.

I am going to argue that one such strategy can help us see what is going on in the Gospel Passion Narratives and Jesus' prophetic anticipation at Matthew 12:39–40. I will make a case for the view that Matthew's understanding of the death and resurrection of Jesus cannot be correctly understood unless we recognize that much of the language the Gospel uses is figurative and that the message conveyed by the text is true—or at the least, not self-contradictory. I shall outline an interpretation that I believe offers the best explanation of the data we have—the best, indeed, *even if* we take seriously the possibilities of miracles and of folly and fraud.[12]

---

[12] The use of the category of myth in Bible scholarship has historically focused heavily upon the problem presented by miracle stories, which, from our perspective, implies far too narrow a conception of myth (see below). A typical party to this error is Craig A. Evans, "Life-of-Jesus Research and the Eclipse of Mythology," *Theological Studies* 54, no. 1 (1993): 3–36. Evans' study is ill-served by his unexplained and untutored deployment of the notion of myth. So far as one can glean a meaning from his usage, a myth is simply a story that is (literally understood?) false. Almost no anthropologist today would accept such a conception of myth (see further Chapter 3).

In any case, the authorities cited by Evans as supposedly granting the historicity of NT miracles fall roughly into three categories. There are, first, those who take the miracle reports seriously as historical data but do not invoke any supernatural agency in explaining them. Exemplifying this position is, e.g., J. D. Crossan, who is prepared to admit some naturalistically explainable events such as faith healings and exorcism but whose attitude toward nature miracles is quite different. Crossan is rather rare among Bible scholars in exhibiting some familiarity with the anthropological literature and applying its lessons to biblical miracle stories. A second treatment, exemplified by E. P. Sanders and R. H. Fuller, admits as miraculous (and emphasizes) healings and exorcisms—well documented in contemporary contexts—and simply dodges the hard cases, such as water into wine or resurrection. Finally, there are some credulous commentators. A. E. Harvey, also leaning heavily on the naturalistically explainable healings/exorcisms, extends the strategy to other effects (e.g., to Hanina's invulnerability to a poisonous serpent) by claiming paranormal powers for holy men. (Harvey is silent on the question whether it matters to which god such a man prays.) Harvey's strategy does seem, however, to tend in the direction of equal opportunity credulity. Thus, he seems to credit Josephus' fantastic yarns about portents of the fall of the temple (*The Wars of the Jews* 6.288–309). Some of the inferential leaps made by these scholars in deciding the authenticity of some NT miracle stories are breathtaking. In any case, Evans' treatment lumps together positions such as Crossan's, which is insightful and plausible, with Harvey's, which is not.

B. The Greatest of These is Charity

One consideration that guides me is the principle of interpretive charity argued for in Chapter 1. In the case at hand, we must remember that the principle gains the more bite the greater the evidence we have that an author is deeply intelligent and has an audience which includes others of great intelligence whom he or she succeeds in convincing that he or she has a serious purpose with much at stake, is sincere, and so on. On the face of it, Matthew scores high on all these measures. In particular, we have overwhelming internal evidence of his intelligence—both in his literary skill and in the mastery he has over HB texts. And ditto, in good measure, for a significant portion of his readership over the span of the first couple of centuries of church history.

It is therefore *prima facie* unlikely that Matthew would have been guilty of so significant a blunder as to put into Jesus' mouth words seriously misapprehending the temporal duration of his engagement with the forces of evil in Sheol. Of course, maybe he (or Jesus or God) understood or intended reference to Jonah's imprisonment in the whale to be merely a trope for Jesus' journey into the realm of death and marshaled it as a rhetorical ornament in reply to the Pharisees despite the strict mismatch in chronologies.[13]

But if, at least, God had intended Jonah's adventure to prefigure Christ's, it is hard to see why, considering its soteriological significance, he could not have arranged either for Jonah's captivity to have lasted a day and a half or for Jesus' battle in Sheol to have lasted a full three. This counts against a literal reading, whatever we may think of the possibility of prophecy or of resurrection.

It is one thing to suggest a tropological reading of this passage and another to say just how the trope is intended to work. The latter, naturally, requires reading in context and requires further an understanding that Matthew is speaking the language of myth. I have explained that myth, as I use the term, is a way of conceptualizing and articulating a theoretical understanding of (some features of) human existence in a largely fictionalized narrative form.[14] It may incorporate elements of the factual history of a community but typically does so only insofar as these elements subserve theoretical or pedagogical ends.

The (often true) theory a myth conveys may concern various matters, but the central and overarching purpose of religious myths is to understand,

---

[13] As we shall presently see, the rhetorical thrust of Jesus' reply cuts considerably deeper than this. Jesus in this pericope may also be alluding to the language of Ps. 74:9–17.

[14] This is, at this level of generality, congruent with a major tradition of myth interpretation within anthropology, e.g., Robin Horton, "African Traditional Thought and Western Science," in *Rationality*, ed. Bryan R. Wilson (New York: Harper and Row, 1970). As per Chapter 8, I think Horton is wrong in placing the emphasis upon myth as explanation of natural phenomena.

establish and charter, codify, and/or justify the social and institutional structures that govern the life of the community: that is, either to legitimate existing structures or to propose or legitimate a change to new ones.

C. Substance and Structure, Theories and Tools

In principle, a myth could be about almost anything. But it is religious myths that have exercised the hermeneutical imaginations of anthropologists because they have been understood to evoke a kind of fervent belief and literal-minded devotion (in contrast to fables and morality tales, with their clearly parabolical intent) and have done so in spite of, or perhaps because of, their often fantastical content. My analysis of Matthew's Passion Narrative begins from Durkheim's view that religious myths originate in, and express, social functions and institutional structures. They purport to explain the rituals, customs, and social practices of the culture in which they are at home. They do this by unconsciously (so Durkheim) concretizing social/political realities in terms of less "abstract" mental representations, first, as totem animals, and ultimately by positing a realm of supra-natural "persons"—deities, spirits, demons, and the like, whose behavior and relationships mimic the structures of social existence and who provide a source and authoritative backing for social norms.

Durkheim's account provides a natural explanation for several of the salient features of religious belief systems. It explains at a stroke their universality (all people need to understand and legitimate their social practices) and the nearly isomorphic mappings commonly found between the personae and doings of the supernatural pantheon and the institutions and processes of the social order. Moreover, the two realms are, as we have seen, analogues with respect to their *properties* to a degree that can hardly be a matter of coincidence.

Thus far, I agree with Durkheim: religion is politics. But I diverge from him on some crucial matters. The chief among these concern conscious intent and ideological flexibility. The meaning of a text is foundationally tied to authorial intent. Did the creators of primitive religious myths understand that they were really describing social and political realities? According to Durkheim, they did not. Their mythical realms are unconscious representations of their experience of the social world, imaginary constructs whose true source and content they do not understand. I have argued (in Chapter 1) that this is entirely implausible. We now reject the *general* assumption of turn-of-the-century anthropologists, that religious thinking—at least the religious thinking of "primitives"—was entirely irrational and thus required explanation by positing some irrational thought-process(es) on the part of native mythographers.

Durkheim further assumed that the *home* religions, Judaism and Christianity, were derived from the more primitive forms and were, at root, also irrational. Durkheim knew, in any case, that at least modern Jews and Christians did not consciously identify their pantheon with social or political realities. Why should one suppose that primitive peoples do? I shall, in any case, operate with the hypothesis that the business of Matthew's Passion Narrative (and of the biblical texts generally) is primarily—and self-consciously—political (and *not* "religious" as *we* understand the term).

Whether we look at the religious thought of ancient cultures or that of contemporary tribal peoples from a Durkheimian perspective, we find the notion of supernatural beings who personify idealized conceptions of social forces and corporate groups (both good and evil ones) to be pervasive. The spiritual world they populate provides a powerful way of conceptually framing thought about the needs, the dangers and opportunities faced, the mistakes and successes, and the proper courses of action of a people or nation. We must take careful note of this dualism between mundane reality and a "spirit" world of normatively idealized "representations"—"Forms"—as it will play a key role in our solution to the riddle of the sign of Jonah. Above all, we must shake ourselves free of the assumption that, because these Forms are personified just as are the social institutions for which they serve as ideals, they had to be taken to be literally conscious specters of some sort.

Let me now briefly recapitulate some of the salient issues pertaining to the structural features of myths, the contribution those features make to meaning, and the tools needed to reveal structure and uncover its semantic contribution. My approach is somewhat eclectic but recognizes the seminal importance of the work of Claude Levi-Strauss.

Human communication, everywhere and always, has availed itself of the power of compositionality in coding messages: both at the syntactic level and the semantic one, a relatively small number of symbols and meanings are deployed, through the myriad of combinatorial possibilities they admit, to spell out the indefinitely many messages we may wish to convey. (Even at the subsyntactic/subsemantic level, most languages make use of permutational possibilities to generate words from an alphabet and a small set of phonemes.) There is a trade-off between the number of basic signs/meanings employed and compression in the formulation of a message: the more basic syntactic/semantic elements employed, the shorter the string required to encode a message.

There is an analogy from logic: the fewer and simpler the axioms and rules of inference a system employs, the longer the proofs must (on average) be, and vice versa.[15] A binary code presents a limiting case: a minimum of symbols at the expense of maximal inefficiency in spelling out messages. Where compression of message is a strong desideratum, there is no reason to stick to such minimalist symbolic resources. On the contrary. We should think of mythemes as *adding* to the stock of basic semantic units. It is because of

---

[15] On the other hand, a minimalist set of axioms/rules leads to simplification at the meta-level—e.g., makes for shorter proofs of completeness and soundness.

such addition that myths can compress so great a richness of meaning into such short compass. Meaning emerges from the structured concatenation of semantic units.

Structure can (by way of analogy to rules of syntax) provide some *constraints* and can often help disambiguate content. Moreover, it is a basic insight that the semantic content of a stretch of discourse is a function *both* of the intrinsic content of its semantic elements and of their arrangement. In myth analysis, it is emphatically true that recognizing repeated occurrences of a mytheme, and comparing contexts of occurrence, can be pivotal in uncovering its significance.

What is most valuable and worth retaining in Levi-Strauss' approach are three ideas: 1) that myths represent high-level theorizing by natives about human existence and its problems,[16] 2) that they (often) contain highly organized structures of mythemes that determine the meaning of the myth (as a function of mytheme content and the way the mythemes are placed into relationship with one another), and 3) that recognition of similar mythemes and comparison of their known contexts is vital to uncovering their meanings.[17] It is a corollary that different arrangements of a set of mythemes can convey different messages or (of course) essentially the same message in different ways. It is difficult—perhaps impossible—to give rules or a general recipe for moving from myth structures to myth meanings. However, Matthew's Passion Narrative offers, as we shall see, some sterling examples for structural analysis, so it will be possible further to illustrate how the thing works in practice.

---

[16] Furthermore, Levi-Strauss is right that myths are often generated by the practical and theoretical concerns generated by social crisis or by the intellectual tensions resulting from an ideology that is inadequate to the needs of a group. That inadequacy may be either practical or conceptual (or both). But Hegelian dialectic is far too simplistic a framework for understanding how theoretical difficulties are resolved, either in science or in practical life.

[17] The matter of cross-context comparisons is somewhat delicate. The greatest purveyor of such comparisons, perhaps, was James Frazer's (1906–1915). Frazer was roundly criticized, with some justice, for running roughshod over cultural and contextual differences in assuming that a given syntactic element (e.g., lustration with water) carries the same semantic content wherever it appears. Levi-Strauss errs in going to the other extreme and making context count for everything. The wise path is to be sensitive to context, to continuities of tradition, to cultural diffusion, to cultural borrowing, and to any other historical evidence for shared significance as well as for differentiation. We may be able to illuminate a mytheme by comparison with cognates (judged initially on the basis of surface verbal, semantic, and functional similarity and ultimately as well on interpretive fecundity and explanatory fecundity) found elsewhere within a given myth, in variants of the myth, in other myths belonging to that tradition, and in myths belonging to traditions that have some historical connection to the home tradition of the myth.

D. Taming the Tehom: The Sign of Jonah in Matthew

The prefatory excursus that I have just undertaken is meant to remind the reader of the theoretical framework within which my analysis of Matthew 12:39–40 is situated. I am presupposing, as throughout, two hypotheses that are clearly controversial: that much of the Bible (here, Matthew's passion) is myth, and that such myths are (primarily) engaged in the business of social/political theorizing (and not speculations about "spooky stuff"). But it is time to return to Matthew's text, so now to business.

First, I shall review a couple of the apologetic strategies—not many are available—which have been proposed by way of reconciling Matthew 12:39–40 with the chronology of Matthew's passion story. Then we shall examine that chronology in detail, showing that it does indeed require that Jesus was crucified and died on a Friday and had emerged from the tomb by dawn on the following Sunday. This will set the stage for an analysis in which Matthew 12:39–40 offers a pivotal clue to the structure of the Passion Narrative, to a correct understanding of its employment of the theme of death and resurrection, and—as a corollary—to a resolution of the difficulty posed by the apparent discrepancy between Matthew 12:39–40 and the passion chronology.

The reader should be forewarned, however, that pursuing this lead is like tracing a thread that leads deep into a fabric whose weave connects that thread with many others leading off in multiple directions. I cannot follow all these other leads, no matter how tantalizing they may be. I can only propose that the structure is there: coherent, intricate, cohesive, weaving together a complex tapestry of mythemes in the service of a message that can indeed be deciphered and that makes good sense of what we know of the history of the early church.

Two traditional ways of handling the disparity introduced by "three days and three nights" are worth brief mention. The first of these interprets "day" and "night" in loose or figurative terms, noting that other chronological references to Jesus' interment are less specific.[18] The strategy is to cite other

---

[18] Mark characteristically uses "after" (μετά), as does Matt. 27.63. In the pericope concerning the raising of the temple, all the Gospels that contain it (Matt., Mark, and John) use (διά, ἐν), translated "in," though the former can mean "after" or "in the course of." Matt. and Luke also use "on the third" (τῇθ τρθτ ῇ). See, e.g., Michael R. Licona, *The Resurrection of Jesus: A New Historiographical Approach* (Downers Grove, IL: IVP Academic, 2014), 324–29, who uses this variability to support an argument that deploys the "vague temporal marker" strategy. I do not think we can draw that conclusion. Other factors may explain the variability. It may reflect variations in the verbal traditions that were in use in early Christian communities. It may be that Mark and Luke had not worked out the chronological symbolism with the precision that we find in Matthew: even though Matthew's own phrasing varies, Matt. 12:39f. is explicit, precise, and the signal instance in which Jesus is offering his generation a "sign" that is

contexts in which "day" and "night" are used as temporal measures for shorter or less specific durations. Thus, Delling makes the extraordinary argument that Jesus might have meant less than a twenty-four-hour period by "day and night" because the Jerusalem Talmud contains a few passages quoting rabbinical interpretations of the law that allow some part of a day to count as a day.[19] This is grasping at straws: even though Jesus was addressing scribes and Pharisees, can one seriously suppose him to have relied on such arcane, obscure, and probably contentious halachic (legal) technicalities in this context? Nor does this gloss sensibly accommodate "three *nights*."

A second strategy, ultimately more promising as we shall presently see, rejects the traditional location of Jesus' death on Friday and argues for an earlier date.[20] Evaluation of this possibility requires a careful examination of Matthew's passion chronology. Matthew's passion begins with Chapter 26. Jesus announces to his disciples that in two days, at the Passover, he will be

---

presumably intended to be decisive and unmistakably recognizable. It is highly unlikely that the chronology given there would be vague, idiomatic, or interpretable only by reference to some arcane halachic parallel. A final point is that even Matthew has difficulty working all the symbolically important details of his narrative into a chronologically coherent story that can fit into such a short time frame. As we will see, he therefore waffles just a bit on the beginning time of the three-day period. (And, e.g., in all of the Gospels the time to death on the cross is an unusually compact six hours or so. Normally, crucified individuals suffered for one or more days, though naturally a quicker demise would sometimes have occurred.)

[19] Gerhard Delling, "ἡμέρα," in *Theological Dictionary of the New Testament*, ed. Gerhard Kittel, trans. Geoffrey W. Bromiley (Grand Rapids, MI: William B. Eerdmans Publishing Company, 1964), 2.948–50. A similar strategy is used by Gleason Archer, *Encyclopedia of Bible Difficulties* (Grand Rapids, MI: Zondervan, 1982), 328 and D. A. Carson, "Matthew," in *The Expositor's Bible Commentary*, ed. Frank E. Gæbelein, vol. 8, *Matthew, Mark, Luke* (Grand Rapids, MI: Zondervan, 1984), 296. Both cite obscure passages from the Talmud (e.g., Pesahim 4a, Yerushalmi Shabbat 9:3) and the Hebrew Bible (e.g., 1 Sam. 30:1, 12; Esth. 4:16; 5:1) against which exactly the same objections are decisive. Thus, e.g., the critical temporal marker in these passages (Hebrew שו, translated "on") can mean "after" or "beyond the time." See also footnotes 4 and 18 above.

[20] A popular exponent of this view was Herbert W. Armstrong, founder of the Worldwide Church of God. See Herbert W. Armstrong, *The Resurrection was Not on Sunday* (1952; repr., n.p.: Worldwide Church of God, 1972). On Armstrong's theory, Jesus was buried on a Wednesday, late in the afternoon, and resurrected late the following Saturday afternoon. Armstrong commits—among others—the cardinal sin of using one Gospel (John) to correct another (Matt.). Armstrong was anticipated by B. F. Westcott, a nineteenth-century scholar. A variant view—that Jesus was crucified on Tuesday—was defended by W. Graham Scroggie, *A Guide to the Gospels* (London: Pickering & Inglis, 1948), 569–77. Norman Walker has, briefly and without real defense, reconciled the passage by claiming that Jesus was arrested on Tuesday and spent three days and nights in captivity: the "heart of the earth" is to be understood as a reference to prison (Norman Walker, "The Alleged Matthaean Errata," *New Testament Studies* 9, no. 4 [1963]: 393). As we shall see, this is half-right.

delivered up to be crucified. Now his enemies on the Sanhedrin conspire to arrest him but decide to delay until after the Passover meal. Jesus eats a meal at Bethany with his disciples and Simon the leper. An unnamed woman anoints him, and directly thereafter, Judas goes to the high priests and offers to betray him. Then, on the Day of Preparation, Jesus commissions his disciples to prepare a meal for him in Jerusalem: the Last Supper, which in the Synoptic Gospels is a Passover meal.[21] Later that night, after the watch in Gesthemane, he is arrested, tried by the Sanhedrin, and convicted of blasphemy. The following morning—on Passover day—he is brought before Pilate, who, failing to convince a Jewish mob of his innocence, releases Barabbas and condemns Jesus to be crucified. Meanwhile, Judas seeks to return the blood money to the Sanhedrin, who do not return it to the treasury but use it to buy a cemetery for foreigners (ξένοις).[22] Jesus is mocked by the Roman soldiers and crucified. (Mark adds the detail that this occurred at the third hour, which would have been at 9 a.m. Matthew's narrative is consonant with that hour.)

From the sixth hour (noon) till the ninth (3 p.m.), there is darkness over the land. At 3 p.m., Jesus expires, the temple veil is rent, an earthquake occurs, and the dead saints rise from their tombs and, apparently after loitering

---

[21] John's chronology differs from that of the other evangelists in placing Jesus' crucifixion on the Day of Preparation as opposed to Passover itself. This permits him consistently to carry through the theme, prominent in John, that Jesus is the Lamb of God, a lamb that must be slaughtered on the Day of Preparation (the evening of Passover: Jewish days begin at sundown). It requires John, however, to remove the Eucharistic language from his Last Supper scene (no longer a Passover meal) and associate it with the feeding of the five thousand. Here, we see already the same message—Jesus as the Passover lamb whose body is eaten by the redeemed—being conveyed by different arrangements of story elements or mythemes. Indeed, in carrying through this theme, John 19:28–30 relates that the thirsting Jesus was offered some "vinegar" (sour wine) on the cross borne by a sponge fixed to a staff of "hyssop"—evoking the hyssop that Jews were commanded to dip in the blood of the Passover lamb and employ to anoint their doorposts and lintels to ward off the Angel of Death (Exod. 12:22).

[22] Here, we meet one of the tangential threads earlier alluded to. Matthew's account of the fate of Judas—but more especially of the thirty pieces of silver paid as *quid pro quo* by the priests—limns critical elements in the economy of salvation wrought by the sacrifice of Jesus. Tracing the structure of this episode yields rich rewards and further insight into the identity of Sheol's minions (see below). On the significance of the (illegal!) purchase of land to bury foreigners, see Edmund R. Leach, "The Legitimacy of Solomon," in *Genesis as Myth and Other Essays* (London: Cape, 1969), 56–57. (There is irony in the priests' avoiding the illegality of returning the money to the treasury by using it illegally to buy the cemetery.) Leach's point about burial grounds is connected to the vineyard parable at Matt. 21. The theoretical framework for understanding the significance of the transactions involving the money is that already discussed by Marcel Mauss, *The Gift: The Form and Reason for Exchange in Primitive Societies*, trans. W. D. Halls (1950; repr., New York: W. W. Norton, 2000). Also essential, of course, are Zech. 11:7–17 and Jer. 32, where the buying of a field legally seals Israel's inheritance in its land.

there till Sunday, enter Jerusalem. Jesus is buried by Joseph of Aramathea, presumably around dusk. The next day—that is, "after the day of Preparation," according to Matthew 27:2—the chief priests obtain permission from Pilate to post a guard at the tomb "until the third day."[23] This key passage indicates that the day following Passover was a Sabbath (a holy day: cf. Mark 15:42). As the weekly Sabbath falls on a Saturday, this entails that the Passover (also a Sabbath) fell on a Friday. Ergo, Jesus was crucified on Friday—as the tradition holds. Matthew 28:1–7. says that the two Marys visited the tomb "towards the dawn of the first day of the week"—that is, near sunrise Sunday morning—only to find the tomb empty.

To summarize then: Matthew's chronology is explicit that Jesus was crucified on a Friday and died three hours before sunset that day. By Sunday sometime before daybreak, he had risen from the tomb. By anyone's count, that comes to two nights, a full day, and a bit (three hours, if you consider Jesus to have entered into the "bowels of the earth" at the moment of death rather than at the time of his entombment) of a second day—or, very nearly, half of a period of three days and three nights. What happened to the other night and two

---

[23] This passage has peculiarities. The quoted phrase (ἕως τῆς τρίτης ἡμέρας) might be intended to measure a time of two days/nights from the time the request was made, or "until the third period of daylight" from the time of Jesus' death. Licona plays this passage as the ace in his argument that the "three days" is to be taken loosely or figuratively (Licona, *The Resurrection of Jesus*, 327–28). Licona's argument is that the priests and Pharisees must have understood Jesus' prophecy to give only a vague indication of the time between death and resurrection. Otherwise, why would they have had an interest in posting the guard prior to the expiration of the full three days? Licona calls the plea of the Jewish leaders to Pilate "an odd request taken literally. For [they] are requesting that the guard remain at the tomb only during the period prior to the time when Jesus had predicted he would rise, rendering the service of the guards of minimal value … if Jesus predicted that he would be raised to life sometime after three days had passed, as the Jewish leaders were claiming, why would they request that Jesus' tomb be guarded only 'until the third day' while leaving it unguarded at the very time they should have been most concerned about body theft?" But it is Licona's argument that is odd. Since the leaders were allegedly trying to prevent body theft, why should they be concerned to protect the integrity of the tomb *only at the supposed time of resurrection*? Was their fear rather that Jesus really *would* be resurrected and precisely at the time he predicted? If they thought *that*, how could they have thought that posting a guard would somehow save the day? And surely they were not naïve enough to think that the disciples would certainly wait until the eleventh hour to execute the theft? If theft was their intent, the disciples would obviously have looked for any opportune moment (probably at night) to steal the body away. They could then have unsealed the tomb "after three days" to expose the absence of the body. Thus, having guards present during the entire three-day period (and perhaps then some) would have been the expected strategy of the Jewish leaders. What is puzzling about the story, if anything, is the time of the request: twelve or more hours after Jesus' burial. If there was concern about body theft, would they not have been afraid that by the time they tried to shut the door, the horse had already left the barn? Had they been unaware of the hour of Jesus' death?

days? Dating the crucifixion to earlier in the week is impossible on Matthew's account, as we have just seen. How, then, can this truly be the sign of Jonah, the "one sign" given to Jesus' generation?

E. Death and Descent into the Chaos-Waters

Fundamentalists hold that the Gospel Passion Narratives retail a literal dying and bodily reconstitution of the founder of the faith and that they record this event as historical.[24] Liberal Bible scholars, by contrast, often insist that the Gospels refer to an event that occurs outside of history, in some sort of "spiritual" realm. They argue—usually citing 1 Corinthians 15—that the earliest layer of the tradition knows nothing of an empty tomb and that Paul's conception of the resurrection body is not that of a physical body. But the fundamentalists typically ignore or dismiss the enormous Ancient Near Eastern (ANE) literature regarding death and resurrection (both Jewish and pagan),[25] and the liberals are forced to view the Gospel Passion Narratives not merely as later legendary accretions but as ones that appear fundamentally to misunderstand the earlier Pauline Christology—which pales beside the difficulty of making sense of trans-historical or super-historical "events."[26] Neither approach offers much help with Paul's passing remark at 1 Corinthians 15:31 that he dies every day.[27]

It is impossible here to give even an adequate summary treatment of the ways in which the theme of death and resurrection is deployed in the Hebrew Bible (HB)—to say nothing of pagan traditions. But we may take the story of Jonah as a clue. Jonah is swallowed by a "great fish (דאג)"—which for Matthew is clearly a figure for entry into the realm of death.[28] Are Matthew and

---

[24] By "fundamentalists," I mean those who subscribe to the two doctrines of biblical inerrancy and literal truth. Obviously, there is room for maneuver with respect to these doctrines. In particular, literalists readily allow for figurative uses of language in the Bible. But what seems to them straightforward historical reportage they take to be so. Though I disagree with fundamentalists, I am not using the term pejoratively.

[25] The *locus classicus* is James Frazer, *The Golden Bough: A Study in Magic and Religion*, Abridged ed. (New York: Macmillan & Co., 1922), 308–571, 802–11). See also, George W. Nickelsburg, *Resurrection, Immortality, and Eternal Life in Intertestamental Judaism* (Cambridge, MA: Harvard University Press, 1972).

[26] Paul's view is, at best, obscure. For a different reading of the critical texts, see Richard C. Carrier, "The Spiritual Body of Christ and the Legend of the Empty Tomb," in *The Empty Tomb: Jesus Beyond the Grave*, ed. Robert M. Price and Jeffrey Jay Lowder (Amherst, NY: Prometheus Books, 2005), 105–232.

[27] N. T. Wright glosses this telling remark of Paul's in his commentary by saying merely, "What matters is … the *continuity* that Paul sees between the present life and the resurrection life" (Wright, *The Resurrection of the Son of God*, 339; italics in original).

[28] This is made quite transparent by Jon. 2:2–6, which closely echoes Ps. 16:10, quoted in turn at Acts 2:27 as a proof-text for the resurrection claim.

his fellow evangelists alone in making this association? Hardly: it is one of the most pervasive mythemes in the HB.

We may, first, observe that reference to the "great fish" represents an allusion to the mythical monster that in Hebrew mythology inhabits the "deep (מְצוּלָה, *metsolah* = תְּהוֹם, *tehom*)," that is, the subterranean repository of the chaos-waters first tamed by God on the second and third days of the creation (Gen. 1:6–10) so as to make possible the bringing forth of the dry land—and with it, a stable base for human existence.[29] The HB, deuterocanonical literature, and Pseudepigrapha contain literally hundreds of references to the chaos-waters. In ordering the world, God confines them (to the oceans, but especially to Sheol, their domain), but they continually threaten to break forth and overwhelm the dry land (as they in fact do in the flood story).

Parting these unruly waters, controlling them, or walking upon them (Job 9:8) is the prerogative of God and of men upon whose shoulders God has placed the mantle of authority and leadership.[30] This power is specifically conferred upon Yahweh's king (Ps. 89:25–27). Thus, in asserting his suzerainty, Yahweh declares that he formed the earth to be inhabited and did not create a chaos (Isa. 45:18–19). Passing through the waters is a metaphor for death and rebirth, especially associated with rites of passage in which a nation is born (or reborn—Exod. 14; Josh. 3), or an individual dies to a former social existence and is reborn with a new social status.[31] There are a number of Psalms in which the Davidic king, Israel's hero, is plunged into the realm of Sheol, and the waters threaten to drown him.[32] But he is rescued by God. Rescued from what? "Chaos-waters" is clearly a figure of speech. For what does it stand?

The chaos-waters are not empty. Their most notorious denizen is, we know, the dragon or sea monster who inhabits the deep. He is sometimes

---

[29] Some may wonder whether the "great fish" is really Leviathan or just an agent of divine wrath. But these are not incompatible given the Jewish theological view that God controls even Leviathan (Job 41; Ps. 104:24–26; Isa. 45:7). Jonah's language clearly evokes the imagery we are about to elucidate: "I called to the Lord, out of my distress ... out of the belly of Sheol I cried....For thou didst cast me into the deep, into the heart of the seas, and the flood was round about me ... yet thou didst bring up my life from the Pit, O Lord my God" (Jon. 2:2–6). Furthermore, Jer. 51:34 clearly evokes the same imagery: Jeremiah is "swallowed" by the "dragon," Nebuchadrezzar/Babylon. The Rabbis carried this logic through in delightful fashion, holding that in the resurrection, the *risen dead* would feast on the body of Job's Leviathan (b. Talmud, Baba Bathra 74a–75a)! In any case, there can be no doubt that Matt. 12 understands the belly of the whale as a figure for the realm of death.

[30] E.g., Ps. 89:25. The context makes it quite clear that what is being affirmed is the king's control over the waters, a divine power delegated to him by God, his Father.

[31] Initiation into the Qumran community was understood as a passage from the realm of death into life, i.e., as a resurrection. See Nickelsburg, *Resurrection, Immortality, and Eternal Life*, 153–156.

[32] See citations, footnote 37. See also Pss. 30, 42, 86, 88, and 116.

identified as Leviathan or Rahab, and his cousins inhabit the chaos-waters/underworld of neighboring cultures: Tiamat in Babylonian myth, Yam in the Canaanite pantheon, Apophis, crocodiles, and hippopotomi in Egyptian traditions, and the seven-headed dragon Lotan (= Leviathan) in Ugaritic legend.[33] In the HB, Rahab sometimes occurs as an oblique reference to Egypt—in contexts in which Egypt is seen as a traditional enemy of Israel, indeed, as the paradigmatic denier of Israelite national identity and aspirations in Exodus (see Ps. 84:9; Isa. 51:9–11; Ez. 29:3–12).

The association of Rahab with political/military threats to Israel's existence serves as a hint; but other passages in the HB offer a much more explicit gloss of the image of the chaos-waters—notably, in some of the Psalms.[34] In these, we repeatedly see the language of chaos-waters and sea

---

[33] Cf. Ps. 74:14; G. Widengren, "Early Hebrew Myths and their Interpretation," in *Myth, Ritual, and Kingship: Essays on the Theory and Practice of Kingship in the Ancient Near East and in Israel*, ed. S. H. Hooke (Oxford: Clarendon Press, 1958), 172; and Simo Parpola, "From Whence the Beast?," *Bible Review* 15, no. 6 (1999): 24. Especially worthy of note is Widengren's argument (idem., 169–200) that YHWH may have been said to have a consort named Anat, clearly derived from Canaanite sources. Widengren speculates that there may have been a ritual drama in which the king, playing the role of Yahweh, does battle with the forces of chaos, the dragon(s) of the underworld, is mourned by Anat, reemerges from the realm of death victorious, celebrates a sacred wedding, and is enthroned as king. Widengren further connects these motifs with the theme of birth of a royal divine child. Möwinckel, in contrast, denies that the Israelite king is ever "identified with" Yahweh. See Chapter III and Chapter V—"Psalms at the Enthronement Festival of Yaweh," in Sigmund Möwinckel, *The Psalms in Israel's Worship*, trans. D. R. Ap-Thomas (New York: Abingdon Press, 1962), 1.42–80, 106–92. I believe that the conceptual framework I am suggesting here, in which YHWH is the "Platonic Form" of Israel, and in which the king—at least *qua* ideal king—embodies the corporate entity Israel, can provide considerable illumination concerning these conceptual difficulties and concerning the ideological differences that are embodied in the differing ways in which Israelites, Mesopotamian cultures, and Egypt expressed their views concerning the relationship of the king to the gods. Thus, we can begin to understand such epithets as "divine," "Son of God," "God's anointed," "God's chosen one," etc. as ways of asserting somewhat differing conceptions of the authority of a king, in terms of his jural relationship to the corporate group and its Form. This analysis effectively undermines the strained attempts of such scholars as G. E. Wright, *The Old Testament Against Its Environment* (London: SCM Press, 1950) and Henri Frankfort, *Kingship and the Gods: A Study of Near Eastern Religion as the Integration of Society and Nature* (Chicago, IL: University of Chicago Press, 1948) to demonstrate the uniquely true spirituality of Israel in contrast to the myth-dominated religions of its neighbors.

[34] See Pss. 18, 69, 74, 89, and 104. Also, 2 Sam. 22; Isa. 27, 44:26–28, 45:12–23, 51:9–11; Ezek. 32:1–12; Zech. 10:6–12; Dan. 7; and Sirach 24:5–6 (where Wisdom, the source of social order, walks upon the waves). For further examples from the intertestamental period, see Nickelsburg, *Resurrection, Immortality, and Eternal Life*. It is extraordinary that N. T. Wright virtually omits mention of the Psalms when he canvasses the Hebrew Bible for precursors to the NT conception of resurrection (Wright, *The Resurrection of the Son of God*, 85–123). What mention there is misses the essential point made here.

monsters juxtaposed with Israel's dominating concern with political survival. The realm of death/Sheol/chaos-waters/sea dragons is identified with Israel's enemies, the enemies of her king, and the threats they pose to her continued existence and autonomy. Correspondingly, God's (and his king's) ultimate victory over the waters is a figure for defeat of these enemies.[35]

If we now take this identification of chaos-waters with social/political chaos and generalize it to the less explicit passages in which the chaos-waters (and the realm of death) are invoked, we find—this should hardly come as a surprise—that we can consistently interpret those passages in terms of this metaphor: the original creation story, the Noachic Flood, the crossing of the Red Sea, and of course much more. I have already, if briefly, indicated how such readings might go. Moreover, what has been said should suffice to establish a clear parallel between two realms: the mundane realm of social and political forces that threaten social order, and, mirroring the mundane, a transcendent realm of (demonic) spiritual forces that operate within the sphere of death.

---

[35] A proper structural study of this complex of associated mythemes—chaos-waters vs. dry land, sea monsters vs. gods and royal heroes, death vs. resurrection and life, social disruption vs. stability and political flourishing—would systematically survey their occurrences and juxtapositions not only in the Bible but in the literatures of the surrounding cultures. It would look for inter- and intracultural similarities and differences, diachronic development, and association with other mythemes. That would present a daunting task, but one that I believe would reap significant insights. In his survey of pagan ANE postmortem beliefs, N. T. Wright finds little to be learned from them about the resurrection (Wright, *The Resurrection of the Son of God*, 3–84). In contrast to his earlier work, this discussion is not informed by any articulated methodological reflection of the required sort. Nor does Wright provide any theoretical framework in terms of which to assess the significance of the similarities and differences we find in the various ANE traditions. Instead, he seems just to take most of this literature as straightforwardly implying various literal postmortem beliefs. On Wright see further Chapter 12. A comparative treatment of these texts that is methodologically explicit and anthropologically informed has yet to be written, so far as I am aware. Such a treatment would, to take just one example, treat the common meanings shared by talk of victory over chaos (and the power to resist chaos) and the pan-ANE valorization of mountaintops and high places as special places of contact with the divine. The mountains rise above the floodwaters—at Ararat, Zion/Mt. Moriah, Carmel and Ebal, and, of course, Sinai (according to tradition). The Egyptian pyramids and Babylonian ziggurats were conceived as "mountains." The architecture of early Israelite "high places" (*bamah* = mountain) was modelled upon Canaanite cultic sites. See B. S. J. Isserlin, *The Israelites* (London: Thames and Hudson, 1998), 237–38. They were the focal points around which a stable civil society was organized. In ancient Jewish tradition, conquered land is "domesticated" by erecting a "high place" or sanctuary, understood as a ritual reenactment of God's creation of the cosmos. See Rabbi Yosef Kalatsky Shlita, "Parshas Terumah" (2003). Worship in Israel and in ANE cultures generally was permeated with this imagery.

In ANE royal ideologies, it is first and foremost the king who has the responsibility for meeting and holding in check the forces of dissolution that threaten his nation. Doing this successfully is a paramount requirement of kingship. The Psalms just cited clearly reflect the repeated and mortal dangers to which Israel was subjected through most of her history and the deep longing for kings who could not merely hold foreign invaders at bay but triumph over and subjugate them. Parallel royal ideologies can be found in those very enemies that Israel faced.[36]

There has been speculation that the Psalms may have played a liturgical role in Jewish ritual dramas of royal renewal in which the Davidic kings were portrayed as descending into the realm of death and then being resurrected.[37] But whether or not that was so, there can be little doubt about the use of death/resurrection imagery to capture the understanding of the king's role as first in the line of battle—and willing to be the first to sacrifice himself—in the struggle with evil.[38] Moreover, since national misfortune was often associated (reasonably enough) with internal disruptions generated by lax observance of social norms (i.e., sin), a proper king could be said to sacrifice himself, if need be, for the sins of his people.

---

[36] For Assyrian, Babylonian, and (earlier) Sumerian conceptions of the king and his obligation to control the dark forces of death represented by the Dragon, see Parpola, "From Whence the Beast?," 24 and "Sons of God: The Ideology of Assyrian Kingship," *Archaeology Odyssey* 2, no. 5 (1999): esp. 18–27). In Egypt, the royal gods Ra and Horus do battle with the dragon Apophis and sea monsters identified as crocodiles and hippopotomi, respectively (see Yves Bonnefoy, ed., *Mythologies*, trans. Wendy Doniger [Chicago, IL: University of Chicago Press, 1991], 1:93–94, 109–110). These monsters, once again, represent the enemies and disrupters of order.

[37] See, e.g., Ivan Engnell, *Studies in Divine Kingship in the Ancient Near East*, 2nd ed. (Oxford: Basil Blackwell, 1967), 35–36 and Möwinckel, *The Psalms in Israel's Worship*, 69–72, 129–30, 143–49, 239–41. Beyond this, it is certainly possible (though the evidence is indirect and contested—see J. W. Rogerson, *Myth in Old Testament Interpretation* [New York: Walter de Gruyter, 1974], esp. 66–85 and Martin Noth, *The Laws in the Pentateuch and Other Studies*, trans. D. R. Ap-Thomas [1960; repr., Philadelphia, PA: Fortress Press, 1967], 145–78) that death/resurrection imagery was at home in coronation pageants celebrating the installation of Israelite kings, as it evidently was in the coronation rituals for, e.g., Egyptian kings. It is at least not acceptable to ignore the fact that the death/resurrection motif can be found in cultures spanning the globe in association with rites of passage.

Nor has the suggestive power of this pervasive imagery been effectively disarmed as a beacon in the effort to understand the riddle of the resurrection. For the symbolic representation of rites of passage in terms of death and resurrection, see Frazer, *The Golden Bough*, as well as Arnold van Gennep, *The Rites of Passage*, trans. Monika B. Vizedon and Gabrielle L. Caffee (1909; repr., Chicago, IL: University of Chicago Press, 1960) and Victor Turner, *The Ritual Process: Structure and Anti-structure* (1969; repr., Piscataway, NJ: Aldine Transaction, 1995).

[38] The paradigms here, in the historical consciousness of Israel, are surely Saul and especially David.

F. Piecing the Puzzle

We now have in place three of the central pieces (with a fourth to follow) of the solution to our puzzle concerning the sign of Jonah: a conception of religious myth as political thought, the conceptual division of the social world into dual mirroring realms, a "transcendent" realm of Forms, and a mundane one which embodies these Forms or copies them, and third, an understanding, in particular, of kings as having the duty to engage the forces of social evil, represented in the transcendent realm by death, dragons, and the Deep. But how can these help us? The first step—and the most crucial one—is the recognition that, if the time elapsed between Jesus' death on the cross and his resurrection occupies just *half* of the period Jonah spends within the whale, then perhaps a missing half is lurking in the vicinity. If Jewish religious thought recognizes a dualism between a ("transcendent") realm of Forms or ideals and the mundane social structures under their dominion that are their imperfect copies, then why not also a dualism between a ("transcendent") realm of death and those (mundane) spheres of human activity under the dominion of the forces of evil? That is surely suggested by the chaos-waters imagery and by the notion that Satan and his minions are fallen angels. It is reinforced, as Chapter 12 will show, by first century talk of "powers of the air."

And if this is plausible, then might it not be that the passion story divides the "time of Jonah" into two equal periods? Does Jesus' engagement with Satan's domain involve not merely his descent into Sheol for a day and a half but an equal period of time during which he submits himself to the power of, but ultimately triumphs over, those mundane forces that Matthew and his church identified as the worldly embodiments of death-dealing evil?[39] Might not his victory over death be a figure for the contest and victory of a king over both the corrupt institutions that block social order and over those individuals who function in the service of these institutions? That, at any rate, is the line of thought I shall pursue.

This suggestion is at least natural enough, given Jewish dualism, and it is surely reinforced by the obvious engagement between Jesus and the governing establishment in Jerusalem that immediately precedes, and leads to, his crucifixion.[40] But can we do anything more to confirm that Matthew is

---

[39] It is important to note that, in this context, the judgment that persons or institutions are evil does not reflect a judgment on their character, that is, on whether their intentions are evil, but is rather a judgment concerning whether the policies which they pursue are socially beneficial or dangerous. Jesus' railings against the scribes and Pharisees are best understood to have that impersonal or consequentialist sense, I suggest—as (see Chapter 12) are his strident admonitions against preserving the ties of family and kinship.

[40] See, in this connection, S. G. F. Brandon, *History, Time, and Deity: A Historical and Comparative Study of the Conception of Time in Religious Thought and*

deploying a dualistic structure of this kind in constructing his passion story? I think we can. It is time to turn to the fourth, and final, piece of the puzzle.

G. *Cherchez les Femmes*

Jesus' body lies in the tomb for a day and a half. It had been anointed (though not by Joseph) and then buried by Joseph of Aramathea.[41] Matthew places two women—Mary Magdalene and Mary the mother of James and Joseph (hence, presumably, the mother of Jesus—cf. Matt. 13:55)—at the scene of the tomb at dawn on Sunday as first witnesses of the Easter event.[42] But women belonging

---

Practice (New York: Barnes & Noble, 1965), 166–72. Brandon rightly identifies the "rulers of this age" (1 Cor. 2:6–8) with the demonic powers that inhabit the "air" (Eph. 2.2), but he fails to see that these are the heavenly templates for the mundane rulers of the present age—in Jerusalem and Rome. Traditions that identify cosmic powers of evil go back at least to the book of Daniel, with roots in Deuteronomy and Judges, and ultimately bear analogy to "the cosmic myths of ancient Canaan and Mesopotamia" (see John J. Collins, "Apocalyptic Eschatology as the Transcendence of Death," *Catholic Biblical Quarterly* 36, no. 1 [1974]: 30–37, esp. 33). For more on this background to Pauline thought, see George B. Caird, *Principalities and Powers: A Study in Pauline Theology* (Oxford: Clarendon Press, 1956) and Clinton D. Morrison, *The Powers That Be: Early Rulers and Demonic Powers in Romans 13:1–7*, Studies in Biblical Theology 29 (Naperville, IL: Alec R. Allenson, Inc., 1960). All these authors understand the connections between the earthly battles with evil and the parallel battles in heaven in quasi-political terms, but they fail to see that the references to the heavenly realm do not have to be understood as reflecting a belief in a disembodied spirit realm. I shall return to this in Chapter 12.

[41] This detail is perhaps meant to echo Isa. 53:9.

[42] As we shall see, conservative exegetes who take this to reflect the basic veracity of the Easter morning traditions, on the grounds that the Evangelists would not have made up the story about the women, are fundamentally misguided. In their view, placing women at the tomb as first witnesses of Jesus' absence would have been damaging to their later disputes with the Jews, as Jewish law did not give the testimony of women the same legal standing as that of men. As the priority of the women could not have furthered the early church's polemical aims, this tradition must have been preserved only because it was known to be true. See, e.g., William Lane Craig, *Assessing the New Testament Evidence for the Historicity of the Resurrection of Jesus*, Studies in the Bible and Early Christianity 16 (Lewiston, NY: Edwin Mellen Press, 1989), 188–94; Stephen T. Davis, *Risen Indeed: Making Sense of the Resurrection* (Grand Rapids, MI: William B. Eerdmans Publishing Company, 1993), 73; and Wright, *The Resurrection of the Son of God*, 607–8). This elides the disparities between the Gospels as to the identities of the women. But more importantly, it simply misses the point of giving the women this special role, which is symbolic. Still, Matthew's wording does raise an interesting question. Why is the Virgin not identified here in the natural way as Jesus' mother? Why is she even referred to, almost insultingly, as merely "the other Mary"? Why the apparent disparagement of her blood relationship to Jesus? This is a thread that may point in the direction of Jesus' general disvaluation of familial ties (e.g., Matt. 12: 46–50) and may also suggest comparison to his dismissive treatment of Mary at the Cana wedding feast (John 2:4). The latter passage does indeed bear upon my theme here: Jesus dismisses

to Jesus' entourage do not make their first appearance in the passion story on Easter morning. They are notably present as observers of his crucifixion and mourners of his death on Friday afternoon. The two Marys follow Joseph to the burial site. Thus, the two appearances of these women who are devoted to Jesus frame Jesus' descent into the (transcendent) underworld.

If we now consider the suggestion that Jesus' sojourn into the realm of death is structurally bifurcated into two halves, the second falling between the death on the cross and the resurrection, we might wonder whether the *first* (presumably mundane) half of the sojourn is similarly demarcated by Matthew. Is it framed by women sympathetic to Jesus and ministering to him? Of course, since the two halves adjoin, we can take it that the women present at the crucifixion serve as structural markers both for the beginning of the second half and for the end of the first. But that leaves us with finding the woman or women who signal the initiation of the first half of Jesus' passion.

Before we turn to that question, we must pause to ask whether it is at all plausible in the first place to construe the presence of the women at Matthew 27:55–61 and 28:1–10 as structural signposts in a myth. That view will be significantly buttressed if we can show that the presence of sympathetic women is a common mytheme associated in ANE religious contexts with the death and resurrection of a male hero.

As it happens, there are many examples that show that Matthew would almost surely have been familiar with this motif. Ezekiel mentions women— clearly Jewish women—weeping for the Babylonian royal fertility god Tammuz (Ez. 8:14; see also Isa. 17:10–11), who undergoes an annual journey to the underworld associated with the harvesting in the fall and sprouting in the spring of the grain. Similar ideas were associated with the gods Attis/Adonis

---

Mary because his "hour has not yet come." This implies that her presence will be required when his hour *does* come. John 13:1 and 17:1 make it clear that this hour is the time of his trial and crucifixion. The changing of water to wine at Cana itself evokes the theme of death and resurrection (compare the Eucharist and the discharge of blood and water from the crucified Jesus' breast) via its association with water-to-wine rituals in nearby Dionysian cultic centers (see Morton Smith, "On the Wine God in Palestine," in *Salo Wittmayer Baron, Jubilee Volume* [New York: Columbia University Press, 1974], 2:815–29). Smith provides evidence of an equation between water and wine within Dionysian ideology, that rituals involving the "conversion" of water to wine or "creation" of wine *ex nihilo* were celebrated at Dionysian cult centers in Greece is attested by Pausanias (*Description of Greece* 6.26, for temples at Elis and Andros) in the second century and by Pliny the Elder (*Natural History* 2.231 for Andros) in the first century. A first-century treatise on hydraulics by Hero of Alexandria actually contains designs for two temple devices for performing this feat. Early Christian awareness of this Bacchic practice is attested by Epiphanius (*Panarion* 51.30.2) for Cibyra and Gerasa and is confirmed by archeological evidence for Gerasa and Corinth (C. H. Kraeling, *Gerasa, City of the Decapolis* [New Haven, CT: American Schools of Oriental Research, 1938], 63, 212 and Campbell Bonner, "A Dionysiac Miracle at Corinth," *American Journal of Archaeology* 33, no. 3 [1929]: 368–75).

and Bacchus/Dionysus. In the story of the death and revivification of the Egyptian royal god Osiris, his wife Isis is the agent who gives him life. In his battle with death (Mot), the Canaanite Baal finds an ally in his sister, Anat.[43]

What is the meaning of this motif? The stories vary, but there is enough commonality to allow us to surmise that the women in these contexts serve as symbols of parturition. Individuals who undergo death and resurrection—descent into the underworld and then reemergence—are often, as we saw, symbolically moving from one social state or status to another, a transformation regularly associated with dying and being "reborn" or—as evangelicals like to say—"born again." What more fitting way of fleshing out the symbolic representation of this idea than to have a woman or women—givers of birth—in attendance?

We must not be deterred from drawing these analogies by the commonplace objection that the story of Jesus differs in significant ways from the stories of Osiris, Tammuz, Bacchus, and the rest. Indeed, they all differ from one another, without that destroying the common significance of the mourning women motif: we must not lose sight of the fact that mythemes are semantic elements that admit of myriad arrangements and rearrangements. That, indeed, is their function: just as words bearing intrinsic semantic content are placed in sequential relation to other words to express multiple messages, so mythemes can appear in varied contexts, retaining an intrinsic meaning but contributing in manifold ways (depending upon the semantic environment) to the construction of differing (or similar!) messages. We should also bear in mind that the gospel message was being preached, not just to Jews, but to Gentiles whose cultural backgrounds would almost always have given them familiarity with, or even allegiance to, pagan myths containing this theme of parturition.

Beyond this, it is arguable that the presence of the women in the Passion Narratives would have called to mind for first century Jews the theme

---

[43] Other ANE examples are enumerated by Adela Yarbro Collins, "The Empty Tomb and the Gospel According to Mark," in *Hermes and Athena: Biblical Exegesis and Philosophical Theology*, ed. Eleonore Stump and Thomas P. Flint (Notre Dame, IN: University of Notre Dame Press, 1993), 1–10. Collins notes the role of Thetis in ministering to her son Achilles upon his death (and presumed resurrection) in the *Aithiopis*, a continuation of the *Iliad*. Matthew would surely have been familiar with the latter, which may even have served—see Dennis R. Macdonald, *The Homeric Epics and the Gospel of Mark* (New Haven, CT: Yale University Press, 2000)—as a literary model for Mark and may have known the former work. In Virgil's *Aeneid*—possibly also known to the Evangelists as already noted—Aeneus's descent into the underworld occurs under the protection of his patron goddess, Venus (*Aeneid*, Book VI, 190–207), who guides him to the golden bough, his ticket for the ferry ride across the River Styx and a required offering to Proserpina, the queen of the underworld. Another woman has a direct role in the ushering of Aeneus into and through Hades. She is a virgin priestess of Apollo, the Sibyl of Cumae, who guides his entry into the land of the shades, serves as tour guide on his journey there, and accompanies his return to the living.

of womanly travail in childbirth that appears in some of the prophetic literature as a figure for the eschatological process in which Israel is finally saved by Yahweh and made the first among nations. Here again, a rite of passage in which a "new" nation and world are created is figured in terms of death and birth.[44]

We have, then, good reason to suspect that the women whose appearances bracket Jesus' captivity within the physical bonds of death represent for Matthew a reiteration of the theme of women who, sympathetic to a fallen hero, mourn him and usher his entry into, and also his escape from, the snares of the underworld. They evoke, therefore, a familiar mythical scenario: the descent of the hero into the underworld and his return, transformed through this rite of passage into a new kind of being, that is, thereby acquiring a new social status. But Jesus' ordeal, we are guessing, has another half, an earlier one that is mundane. Where is this missing mundane half? And—as Matthew is silent about what exactly transpires while Jesus' body lies embalmed within the tomb and he himself is somehow (presumably) harrowing hell—what might parallels in this prior period tell us about the exact shape of the salvific mission accomplished by Jesus during his encounter with "Leviathan"? Would not Matthew, if he were operating with a symbol system and a set of syntactic rules governing the ordered assembly of these symbols into readable messages, mark the initiation of the first phase of Jesus' ordeal with another sympathetic woman or two?

Once the question is posed in this way, its answer virtually leaps out at us. For there is such a woman, and her actions clearly betray her role as the one who ushers in Jesus' entry into the realm of death. This woman—she is unnamed—puts in her appearance during the dinner that Jesus celebrates with his disciples at the home of Simon the leper. It is she whose special act of caring for Jesus will be "told in memory of her" wherever the gospel is

---

[44] See Hos. 13:13 and the Qumran scroll 1QH 3.6–18; esp. lines 8–10: "For the children have come to the throes of Death, and she labors in her pains who bears a Man. For amid the throes of Death she shall bring forth a man-child, and amid the pains of Hell there shall spring from her child-bearing crucible a Marvelous Mighty Counselor; and a man shall be delivered from out of the throes." See Geza Vermes, trans., *The Dead Sea Scrolls in English*, 3rd ed. (London: Penguin Books, 1987), 173f. The same symbol is repeatedly used by Micah (4:5; 6; 5:3) in a context that Matthew clearly found important, as it forms the basis for his birth-in-Bethlehem narrative (Matt. 2:6). The woman's travail brings forth a king who will "fall" and "arise" (Micah 7:8) and who will far extend the boundaries of Israel with conquest over her traditional enemies, Assyria and Egypt (Micah 7:11f.). Micah, moreover, sees this event as one in which God will pardon Israel and "cast our [Israel's] sins into the depths of the sea" (Micah 7:19). This idea is echoed by Paul in Rom. 8:19–23. See also, Richard C. Carrier, "The Spiritual Body of Christ and the Legend of the Empty Tomb," in *The Empty Tomb: Jesus Beyond the Grave*, ed. Robert M. Price and Jeffrey Jay Lowder (Amherst, NY: Prometheus Books, 2005), 216n235, 221n287, and 223n298) for more on possible symbolic dimensions.

preached. She anoints Jesus with expensive ointment.[45] There are several features of this episode that call for special attention. The first is that the disciples object to her ministering to Jesus; he replies that he will soon depart from them. They do not seem to grasp the significance of what she has done. But modern readers generally do perceive this anointing as appropriate to a declaration of Jesus as the Messiah—God's anointed king. That is part of the story.

A second significant aspect of the story may be suggested by a curious detail omitted in Matthew 26:7 but found in its cognate passage in Mark (Mark 14:3). The precious ointment is stored in an alabaster container. Matthew simply says the woman poured the ointment on Jesus' head, but Mark notes that she "crushed" (συντρίψασα) the container. Why would she do such a thing? Why not simply open the jar? It is possible that Matthew omitted this detail because of its oddity. But that seems unlikely. The detail may prove to be far from odd. Indeed, it may dovetail closely with other themes in Matthew's Passion Narrative.

A first clue to the possible significance of Mark's description can be found in Jeremiah 18–20, where the image of a potter and a clay jar is twice used (Jer. 18:1–12; 19:10–12).[46] Jeremiah is cursing Israel for her sins. The first image is of the potter whose pot is spoiled and the clay used to fashion a different pot. In the second, Jeremiah is commanded by God publicly to smash a clay pot—a symbol of the impending destruction of Israel by Nebuchadnezzar II. Especially chilling is Jeremiah 19:9, which echoes the curses for disobedience of Yahweh that accompany the covenant (Lev. 26; Deut. 28).[47] Jeremiah 20 goes on to curse the priest in charge of temple order (and who is deputy to the high priest).

Here, then, the breaking of a jar (albeit clay rather than alabaster) may figuratively represent the destruction of a wayward Israel. By contrast, the same image is used to represent the destruction of Israel's enemies and consequent rise of Israel to world dominion at Psalms 2. Jeremiah goes on to

---

[45] It was Daniel Larkin, in conversation, who, presented with the hypothesis, immediately hit upon this woman as filling the bill. Larkin further noticed the structural role of Pilate's wife, on which see below. Matthew does not give a value for the ointment, but Mark 14:5 pegs it at over 300 denarii (in today's dollars, over $18,000—hardly chump change).

[46] The LXX uses the same Greek verb at Jer. 19:10. It is of course possible (as Carl Mosser points out to me) that Mark 14:3 is describing merely the breaking off of the neck of the jar, so as to facilitate the pouring of the ointment. This, as well as Matthew's omission of *suntripsasa* (it is absent in all the variant manuscripts of Matt.), urge caution in accepting this guess as to symbolic significance.

[47] The specific curse of paedophagia is echoed at Isa. 9:20, and Zech. 11:9, where it is directed at Israel, and Isa. 49:26, where it is conversely directed at Israel's enemies. As was shown in Chapter 10, the Zechariah passage appears in turn to have echoes in Matt. 26:15.

speak of the restoration of the Israelite exiles to their homeland, and the reestablishment of the old laws of land ownership, in Jeremiah 32, which, as I will show, has resonances in the purchase of the potter's field by the chief priests in Matthew 27:7–10, resonances that in turn take us back to the parable of the evil tenants in Matthew 21. Taken together, these associations might, even in the absence of Mark's use of the verb "to crush," portray the woman's act on behalf of Jesus as one that is, wittingly or unwittingly, prophetic. If so, it seems to foreshadow both the destruction of the old Israel and the establishment of a new Israel in its place, one with some kind of world dominion, an Israel whose king is in the same act being anointed as the Messiah.

However the final, and most significant, feature of the woman's act is revealed by Jesus' own declaration of the purpose of this anointing: " ... she has done it to prepare me for burial (πρὸς τὸ ἐνταφιάσαι με ἐποίησεν)" (Matt. 26:12). This is striking, and not only because there is no direct mention of a royal inauguration.[48] In Matthew, the funeral anointing of Jesus takes place at this meal, not at any time after he is removed from the cross. One might argue that the women who attended Jesus' removal from the cross could not have anticipated that removal and would have had no time to gather and prepare burial spices and ointments. How much more remarkable, then, that this woman was able to foresee the course of events!

But the most important observations to be made are two: First, anointing for burial was an act that in Jewish custom was performed only at or after the time of death. And second, Jesus no sooner announces this burial preparation than Judas departs to betray him to the high priests, and the events of the Passion Narrative are set in motion. It is at this very moment that Jesus thus begins directly to encounter and engage the forces of death.[49] If we wish to understand what he accomplishes through this engagement, we shall have to excavate the structure and significance of his captivity at the hands of the high priests and the Romans. Jesus' "hour" has then come, the hour when he must confront, and defeat, those who exercise their power on behalf of the realm of death. Luke 22:52–53 says as much:

> Then Jesus said to the chief priests, the officers of the temple police, and the elders who came for him, "Have you come out with swords and clubs as if I were a bandit? When I was with you day after day in the temple, you did not lay hands on me. But this is your hour, and the power of darkness!"

---

[48] Though reference is certainly being made to Ps. 23:5, an enthronement motif in one of the three Davidic psalms that "prefigure" the Passion Narratives.

[49] On the close association in African and ANE kingship rituals between anointment, symbolic death/rebirth as divine, and coronation, see Raphael Patai, *On Jewish Folklore* (Detroit, MI: Wayne State University Press, 1983). See also, e.g., Luke. 22:53.

I will turn to the interpretation of this and related passages in Chapter 12, Sec. II. But, by way of announcing that there is structure aplenty to be found, I shall take note here of one such structural feature. Jesus' subjection to the power of the authorities in Jerusalem is itself marked by a basic division. He is first tried by the Jerusalem Sanhedrin. Then he is handed over to Pilate and the Romans for execution. Improbable as such a scenario would historically have been, it gives Jesus opportunity to interact with both spheres of authority that reigned over first century Jews.[50]

How is this division marked? By a woman. She is Pilate's wife, and in a dream, she receives the message that Jesus is righteous and not to be persecuted by Pilate (Matt. 27:19). That such a remarkable, and surely apocryphal, incident should be inserted by Matthew into his story is evidence that he intends, once again, to signal an important transition in the ordeal by means of which Jesus vanquishes death through his sacrifice. And so, Jesus is led to slaughter while another Jesus—Jesus Barabbas (for so some early manuscripts of Matthew name him) is, as we have seen, permitted to escape. Then, the Roman legionnaires crown him king and place upon his shoulders the mantle of the emperor, unwittingly reenacting Psalms 22, Jeremiah 30:9, and other HB passages.[51]

There are a few loose ends to be gathered up. First, when did the meal at Bethany occur? Second, who and what was redeemed by Jesus' sacrificial act? Third, could not the structures I have claimed to discover be admitted by traditional exegesis—could it not be pointed out that this is not incompatible

---

[50] Jesus' supposed crime was blasphemy. He was tried by a Jewish court and convicted under Jewish law. The question whether the Jewish authorities had and would have used the right to execute Jews convicted of capital offenses under Jewish law at this time has been disputed. If so, Jesus would have been stoned to death by the order of the Sanhedrin rather than being hauled before Pilate on a trumped-up charge of sedition. For a defense of that view, see Paul Winter, *On the Trial of Jesus* (Berlin: Walter de Gruyter, 1961), esp. 75–90 for details of the manifold historical improbabilities contained in the Gospel accounts of the trial. For a different view, see Richard C. Carrier, "The Burial of Jesus in the Light of Jewish Law," in *The Empty Tomb: Jesus Beyond the Grave*, ed. Robert M. Price and Jeffrey Jay Lowder (Amherst, NY: Prometheus Books, 2005), 369–92 and *On the Historicity of Jesus: Why We Might Have Reason for Doubt* (Sheffield, UK: Sheffield Phoenix Press, 2014), 425.

[51] In Matthew, the robe's color is given as scarlet (κοκκινος). Mark and Luke are more brazen and specify the color as purple (πορφύραν). Both are royal colors, but during this period, wearing the latter was almost exclusively the prerogative of the emperor—so Lloyd B. Jensen, "Royal Purple of Tyre," *Journal of Near Eastern Studies* 22, no. 2 (1963): 104–18. But see Meyer Reinbold, *History of Purple as a Status Symbol in Antiquity* (Brussels: Collection Latomus, 1970), who argues that the use of purple as a royal status symbol originated in the east and that it was more widespread (with, however, restrictions introduced by Nero and Caligula) in Roman times. In any case, the allusion to rulership of the Imperium seems hard to deny. We shall have a much more careful look at the implications of this symbolism, which exegesis seems rather regularly to overlook, in Chapter 12.

with supposing that Jesus did suffer (literally) a physical death and enjoy (again literally) a physical restoration to life? And what about the Easter appearances of Jesus to his disciples?

H. A Final Piece: The Chronology of Bethany

Let us begin with a brief look at the meal at Bethany, which, I claim, marks the descent of Jesus into the realm of the *tehom* (the "deep") and direct engagement with his enemies. This is the one chronological point on which one might wish Matthew to have been more explicit. Our primary clue is Jesus' declaration (Matt. 26:2) that the Passover will come "after two days." This is followed by a mention of the plottings of the chief priests and elders, something that could have occurred on the same day. Matthew continues, "Now when Jesus was at Bethany in the house of Simon the leper, a woman came ... " (Matt. 26:6–7). The "now when" leaves it vague how long after the declaration of Matthew 26:2 the Bethany meal occurred. We know this must be within the two days prior to Thursday night—hence, conceivably after dark on Tuesday as *we* reckon days, but (given the Jewish beginning of a day at sunset) more likely on Wednesday or as late as Thursday morning.

The reference to priestly plotting which follows Jesus' declaration suggests that the meal would not have occurred before Wednesday. A meal as late as midday Thursday is conceivable but would hardly have given the disciples time to walk from Bethany to Jerusalem—about an hour's journey—and make provision for the evening meal. Thus, Matthew's chronology points to a meal occurring sometime between Wednesday evening and early Thursday morning. Matthew's use of the ambiguous "ἀνα-κειμαι" unfortunately does not indicate whether the meal in question was a supper or a breakfast. It is, however, consistent with its having been an early breakfast on Thursday morning.

Matthew 26:17 introduces the events of Thursday with the temporal indicator, "Now on the first day of Unleavened Bread ... " which might be thought to suggest that Matthew places these events on the day following the Bethany meal. The Greek text, however, reads "Now on the first of unleavened ... " Matthew 26:17 is in any case initially puzzling, as the Feast of Unleavened Bread occurs immediately *after* Pesach. By the first century, however, the two feasts had been combined, and the entire seven-day period could be referred to with either feast name. Moreover, the preparations for both Pesach and the Feast of Unleavened Bread (removing of all leaven, slaughtering and roasting the sacrificial lamb) occurred during the afternoon preceding the Pesach meal.[52] Thus, it would be natural to understand Matthew 26:17 to refer to a period

---

[52] See M. Eugene Boring on Matt. 26:17 in Leander Keck, ed., *The New Interpreter's Bible* (Nashville, TN: Abingdon Press, 1995), 8.468.

beginning around midday on Thursday, which is again consistent with taking the Bethany meal to have been a Thursday breakfast.

In order for the prophecy of the sign of Jonah to be fulfilled accurately (if we assume the resurrection to have occurred just prior to the arrival of the women at the tomb), it would be necessary for Jesus to enter the *tehom* just around dawn on Thursday.[53] That is perhaps inconvenient for Matthew: it means that Jesus' anointing must occur at an early hour, at a meal occurring perhaps before dawn on Thursday. It may be because of this awkwardness that Matthew is a bit vague at this point in his chronology. Others have noted that the chronological constraints on Matthew's narrative entail other inconveniences: a midnight trial before the Sanhedrin and a very hasty burial of Jesus' body.[54] Matthew may have preferred vagueness to adding another implausibility to his tale. However that may be, our solution accepts the fact that Jesus was crucified on a Friday. But that is not when he died.

I. "Something Greater than Jonah is Here"

During the second half of the eighth century BCE, Assyria conquered and destroyed Israel, and her king, Sennacherib, made King Hezekiah of Judah a vassal after nearly laying waste to Jerusalem. With this history as background, the apocryphal story of Jonah has the reluctant prophet converting Nineveh—the capital city of Assyria. Somehow, Jonah persuades the nation that has conquered Israel to repent and obey the god of the conquered people.

Something greater than Assyria oppressed the people of Judea in the first century CE; a city greater than Nineveh dominated the Near East. Rescuing Israel would take a prophet greater than Jonah, a prophet who could teach repentance to that greater city. But whom did Jesus save?

Modern Christians believe—naturally—that Jesus came to save "the world"—a world that includes potentially all persons (at least all who hear the good news) but, in particular, that certainly includes them. Further, they quite typically think of salvation in personal terms: it is fundamentally a matter of

---

[53] Richard Carrier has suggested to me that a dawn ascent from the grave would carry considerable symbolic significance. I shall not pursue that suggestion here, but compare the imagery of Ezek. 43:1–9 and 44:1–3. For further discussion, see Carrier, "The Burial of Jesus in the Light of Jewish Law."

[54] In contravention of the standard procedures of the Great Sanhedrin: see Winter, *On the Trial of Jesus*, esp. 20–30. The difficulties of historical reconstruction are circumvented if we drop the assumption that the Evangelists were purporting to give their readers a straightforward factual narrative. Indeed, the numerous irregularities and illegalities implied by the Gospel accounts of the actions of the Jewish authorities during the passion would have served to highlight the evangelists' portrayal of the legitimacy of the Jewish hierarchy as forfeit. So far from meriting the rulership of Israel as heirs to the Mosaic covenant, they are not even competent administrators of the law.

reestablishing a right relationship between an individual and his or her God. Was that in fact Jesus' mission, as Matthew understood it?

Before I begin to essay an answer to this question in the next chapter, it will be important to bring to light two further key aspects of the structure of the Passion Narrative that contain essential ingredients in Matthew's understanding of the kingdom of God. We can uncover these critical clues by tracing with some care the careers of two figures: Barabbas and Judas. We will find that careful attention to some details, often passed over or examined in ways that make no use of anthropological tools, will yield rich meanings that point in the direction of a carefully worked-out view of the kingdom at which the first Christians were aiming.

At this point, I shall note just that the argument will provide grounds for thinking that Matthew thought of salvation primarily in corporate terms (passages apparently to the contrary notwithstanding) and that the kingdom of God, over which a royal Jesus is to preside, will be one that includes both Jews and the Gentiles of the greater Roman world. But it will also exclude. Most pointedly, it will exclude the Jewish hierarchy in Jerusalem and certain Jewish parties that are depicted as opponents of Jesus—the Pharisees and Sadducees, as well as the temple priesthood.

II. Where My People are Laid to Rest

I turn first to a familiar, but apparently rather minor, subplot in the Gospel Passion Narratives: the fate of Judas. It is natural that reflection upon Judas in the context of the Passion Narrative has focused heavily upon his relationship to, and betrayal of, Jesus. The Gospels provide several other details, but these appear almost to be afterthoughts. As such, it might seem all the more plausible to read them as historical memories that the evangelists included simply because they had survived in the traditions about Jesus' death. Yet, some of these details can hardly be ordinary historical memories: no disciple is likely to have been privy to Judas' initial negotiations with the chief priests, let alone to the subsequent incident of his attempt to return the bribe money.[55] (But more than that, it is improbable at best that the temple priesthood would have needed to rely upon help from a traitor in Jesus' inner circle: they were intent upon arresting a very public

---

[55] If that is right, then either God gave early Christians this information, they learned it by way of gossip, or else they fabricated these narrative details. The second possibility is rather unlikely on the face of it: why would someone from the inner circle of the priesthood report to anyone outside that circle (let alone directly to Jesus' disciples) about actions that, so far from doing the high priests any credit, were actually illegal? The likelihood pales to deep improbability when we consider that the details are structured—see below—to convey a message Matthew had a clear interest in purveying.

figure whose whereabouts, with his doughty band, in the narrow environs of the town of Jerusalem could hardly have been a secret.[56])

Let us review these details as they appear in Matthew's Passion Narrative. (a) Directly after Jesus is "embalmed" by the woman who anoints his body with costly ointment at the supper at Bethany, Judas departs to seek out the temple priests and betray him.[57] (b) The chief priests pay him thirty pieces of silver from the temple treasury, a sum that recalls the rather cryptic text of Zechariah 11, where God, having promised to bring the children of Israel home from exile in Egypt and Assyria, launches into a parable in which Zechariah is commanded to shepherd the flock of Israel in the service of traffickers (apparently foreign overlords) in sheep condemned to slaughter.[58] Upset with his sheep, he annuls the divine covenant with "all the peoples" and asks for his wages. He is paid thirty silver shekels, which the LORD commands him to cast into the temple treasury.[59] Finally, he voids the alliance between Judah and Israel.

All this is rather mysterious to our ears, but it clearly resonates in the story of Judas. (c) Judas betrays Jesus in the Garden of Gethsemane. (d) After Jesus' condemnation by Pilate, Judas, having second thoughts, attempts to return the bribe to the priests. When they refuse to accept, he casts the money down, departs, and hangs himself.[60] (e) The chief priests, reflecting that the bribe is "blood money" that cannot be returned to the treasury, decide to use it to buy "the field of the potter" and dedicate it as a cemetery for "strangers" (= foreigners, *xenois*). (f) This act is said to fulfill

---

[56] Which, making allowance for outlying sites like Gesthemane, still covered less than a square mile.

[57] The Greek descriptor for the anointing act is *entaphiasia*, which, as noted, in this context can only mean to embalm. Cf. Mark 14:8, John 12:7 and 19:40. Luke omits this episode, retaining only Mark's rationale for the Easter Sunday visit of the women to the tomb, which Matt. and John omit.

[58] "They shall pass through the sea of Egypt, and the waves of the sea shall be smitten....The pride of Assyria shall be laid low, and the scepter of Egypt shall depart ... " (Zech. 10:11, RSV).

[59] The Masoretic text renders the phrase rather as "Cast it to the potter." Could Matt. have been familiar also with such a reading? A pun is not out of the question: *yâtsar* (potter) vs. *'ôwtsâr* (treasury) Heb. or *kĕraměus* (potter) vs. *kŏrbanas* (treasury) Greek. Matters become even more tangled: when Matthew (mis)quotes Jeremiah at 27:9–10, he is apparently conflating Zechariah with both Jer. 18:1–10 (which uses a potter as a metaphor for God—Cf. Rom. 9) and Jer. 32:6 (which—see also below—uses the purchase of a field to secure/symbolize Israel's territorial rights to the land of the promise after the Babylonian captivity).

[60] These and the remaining details are not mentioned in the other Gospels, but Acts has Peter giving a conflicting account of the field's purchase and Judas' death in Acts 1:18. I will not digress here on the rather tortured efforts of apologists to reconcile these accounts. For an astute commentary, see John Nolland, *The Gospel of Matthew: A Commentary on the Greek Text* (Grand Rapids, MI: William B. Eerdmans Publishing Company, 2005), 1150–58.

the prophecy of Jeremiah: "And they took the thirty pieces of silver, the price of him on whom a price had been set by some of the sons of Israel, and they gave them for a potter's field ... ."[61] Although these words appear nowhere in Jeremiah, Matthew apparently intends to bring to mind Jeremiah 18:1–11 and 32:6–15, with words meant to distort Zechariah 11:12–13 so that the "price" in question can refer to that put on Jesus' head. In this highly conflated passage, it seems that Matthew also has in mind Isaiah 52:1–5 (and perhaps, by association, Gen. 37:28 and Isa. 53).[62] How is all of this to be untangled?

By my lights, we will be well advised to take to heart two anthropological principles: First, the principle of reciprocity and exchange, and its commercial analogue—when someone pays the asking price for something, they gain a right to the benefits of ownership; second, the principle that myths typically invoke well-worn themes, often alluding to them in highly compressed ways designed to form new associations and meanings. Let us begin with the shekels (or, as Deep Throat advised reporter Bob Woodward to do, let us "follow the money").

(a) First, we may recall Matthew 26:9, which omits mention of the actual value of the costly ointment used to anoint Jesus at Bethany. This is given by Mark 14:5 as more than three hundred denarii. Matthew does indicate that what the woman has done in anointing him is not only worth the price but will memorialize her forever. Although she is to be thus memorialized, it is striking that Matthew fails to relate her name. It seems possible to understand that she stands as a representative for all those Jews who have aligned themselves with Jesus as his followers, and the benefit they will gain from the performance of this service is a place in the kingdom whose king this anointing ceremonializes. If so, this gift redounds to their credit. But further financial matters impend.

(b) The thirty pieces of silver paid by the priests for Jesus' betrayal is a rather smaller sum (equivalent to about 120 denarii),[63] but it still represents a purchase of the Lamb that is to be sacrificed. Such a purchase should, of course, benefit those who have purchased it (here, the priests, in

---

[61] Matt. 27:9.

[62] Donald Senior provides a detailed investigation of the redactional history of Matt. 27:3–10. He considers Jer. 19 to be a more plausible source than Jer. 39:6–9, while not ruling the latter out (Donald P. Senior, *The Passion Narrative According to Matthew: A Redactional Study* [Louvain, Belgium: Leuven University Press, 1975], 358–62). I shall argue below that Jer. 39 is indeed a likely source. Allusion to the ominous cadences of Jer. 19, themselves reminiscent of the grim curses of Lev. 26:14–39 and Deut. 28:15–68, is also plausible. Senior's conclusion that this pericope is essentially the result of Matthew's creative elaboration of Mark seems to me likely as well.

[63] Interestingly, redemption of a man who is consecrated to Yahweh by a special vow carries a price of fifty shekels. Redemption of a woman is thirty shekels (Lev. 27:1–4). More relevant is the fact that it is the value of a slave (Exod. 21:32).

extracting the funds from the temple treasury, appear to be acting on behalf of the nation of Israel generally as well as in their own behalf[64]). Religiously speaking, such a sacrifice must serve to atone for the sins of those who pay for the sacrifice. That the temple priests benefit certainly cannot be Matthew's intention, and, as we shall see, nothing of the sort is accomplished.[65] But Matthew 26:15 plays an essential, and double, role in Matthew's plot: it sets the stage for the complex allusions to Zechariah and Jeremiah in Matthew 27, and it is central to Matthew's explanation of exactly how entry into Jesus' kingdom comes to be forfeited by the chief priests and those whom they represent.[66]

(c) The silver coins are not destined to remain in Judas' hands: undergoing a crisis of conscience, he attempts to return them to the priests. Their acceptance of the returned ransom has, effectively, cancelled their share in the atonement conferred by the sacrificial offering. (Worse, in the process, they abdicate their fundamental duty of obtaining absolution for the sins of the people: "What is that to us?" is their reply to Judas' confession that he has betrayed innocent blood. Of course, they are not portrayed as thinking in these terms, but I hold that we, the readers, are to have ears to hear.) The priests do not exactly accept the return of the ransom to the temple treasury, however: as polluted "blood-money," the ransom must be put to some other use.

(d) Put to other use it is: the priests buy the potter's field, "to bury strangers (ξένοις; that is, foreigners) in."[67] This apparently minor detail is remarkable, for in buying such a field for foreigners, the chief priests are in violation of a law that is fundamental to Yahweh's promise and covenant with Israel: namely that no territory within the boundaries of the land of promise is alienable. But it is even more remarkable because, as we shall see, the buying of a burial ground represents such an alienation in a profound sense, a sense which redefines the very boundaries of the kingdom of God and, by inference, the class of people to whom the salvation of the Christ is offered.

Tracing in this way the "path" of the ransom paid for the Lamb, what can we learn about Christ's kingdom—specifically, what can be learned about who qualifies as a citizen (or potential citizen) of the new Jerusalem? Let us begin with Israel itself. All Jews have paid taxes to the temple treasury. Hence, all have a share in the purchase of the Lamb. But

---

[64] There may well be a connection here with Jesus' execration of the sacrificial system institutionalized by Caiaphas (Matt. 21:12–13), discussed in Chapter 7.

[65] Not the least, obviously, because the "purchase" takes the form of an illegal bribe to further what amounts to an assassination plot.

[66] And by proxy, presumably, the Jerusalem leadership—i.e., the Sanhedrin—generally.

[67] Matt. 27:3–8. Acts 1:16–20 gives a conflicting explanation of how the field acquired the name "Field of Blood," but here we have to do with Matthew's account.

clearly, the temple priests have forfeited their share, not only by accepting the returned coins and putting them to another (albeit illegal)[68] use but because they abdicate their redemptive duty to Judas in washing their hands of his crime.[69]

On the other side, we may reasonably expect that those Jews who welcomed Jesus upon his royal procession into Jerusalem, hailing him as their King, as well as Jesus' loyal disciples and followers, will have a share in his kingdom. Are there other Jews who are excluded? Presumably so. One can assume that Jesus' unrepentant political opponents among the scribes, Pharisees, and Sadducees will not merit citizenship in the kingdom. But another group should not escape our attention: the unruly mob who, assembled before Pilate, demand the release of Barabbas and the crucifixion of Jesus. It appears that the populace of Jerusalem is divided between those who hail Jesus as their messiah and those who are prepared to use the title "King of the Jews" as a term of mockery.[70]

I believe we can be more precise about the status and role of this mob if we pay attention to another detail. The "robber" Barabbas—further facts about his background are minimal (Matthew describes him only as a "notorious [or notable: see Berenson Maclean (2007): 325] prisoner"[71])—is, in some ancient manuscripts of Matthew, further identified as Jesus Barabbas. Now although "Jesus" (Yeshua) was common enough a name in first-century Palestine, "Jesus Barabbas"—"Jesus the Son of the Father"—seems too striking to be mere coincidence. What can the significance of this (fictional) episode be?[72]

---

[68] See M. Av. Zar 1:8 and Lev. 25.

[69] Matt. 26:65/Mark 14:63 attribute to Caiaphas yet another crime: the high priest's rending of his garment during Jesus' trial before the Sanhedrin violates Lev. 21:10. What these items add up to is a portrayal of the temple priesthood as unfit protectors of Torah.

[70] The irony is palpable, but most readers seem unaware of the fact that the irony is double. The Roman legionnaires are not only (unwittingly) crowning Jesus the legitimate King of Israel (in a historicized rite of passage that incorporates a familiar death-and-resurrection theme) but are also crowning him Emperor of Rome. The symbolism, once noted, is quite obvious. See above, and in more detail, below.

[71] John 18:40 describes him as a robber, but Mark 15:7, Luke 23:19 (held by some scholars to be later interpolations), and Acts 3:14 agree that he was a murderer involved in a Jewish insurrection against the Romans. If so, he represents a response to Roman occupation very different from the Christian strategy.

[72] It appears rather unlikely that the Romans ever had a custom of releasing a prisoner on demand to the Jews on the occasion of Passover. Outside of the Gospels (including the Gospel of Peter), there are no historical sources mentioning such a custom, and it seems intrinsically unlikely that the Romans, or Pilate in particular, would have made such a concession to the Jews. Charles Chavel finds some evidence for such a practice in a Mishnah at Pesahim 91a, which refers to a law governing whether a Passover sacrifice is to be made on behalf of a prisoner promised release at the time of

It is of course hard to be sure, but here is a plausible suggestion. The Day of Atonement, Yom Kippur, does not coincide with the Passover, but they are conceptually linked. The Passover story articulates a fundamental aspect of Israel's understanding of her jural relationship with Yahweh. The Exodus is initiated by a divine slaughter of the firstborn sons of Egypt and the sparing of Israel (Yahweh's "first-born son"—Exod. 4:22–23) from the Angel of Death.[73] In return for the sparing of her sons, Israel "owes" her firstborn sons to Yahweh (Exod. 13:2 & 13 and 22:28; the text is not explicit here, but we may assume that the ransom is to take the form of a blemish-free sheep or goat—cf. Gen. 22:13).[74]

Because the value of this ransom can never equal the value of a son, we remember that the bargain is one that establishes a patronage relationship between the father (and, by extension, his son) and Yahweh: something is always still "owed" to God. Thus, Israel's firstborn sons—and by extension, all of Israel—are in Yahweh's debt. Devotion to him and to his covenant and acknowledgment of his authority as ruler over Israel are the natural corollaries of an insufficient sacrificial redemption.[75]

But, granting that Jesus serves as a once-for-all collective and sufficient redeeming sacrifice, how is his crucifixion connected to Yom Kippur? On Yom Kippur, the chief priest makes collective atonement for the people of Israel by offering a lamb or goat upon the altar of the temple. But

---

the festival (Charles B. Chavel, "The Releasing of a Prisoner on the Eve of Passover in Ancient Jerusalem," *Journal of Biblical Literature* 60, no. 3 [1941]: 273–78). But there is no indication that there was a *practice* of such releases—only a rule concerning what to do should a prisoner be promised release on that day. Other arguments are also quite indecisive. See also, Raymond E. Brown, *The Death of the Messiah: From Gethsemane to the Grave* (New York: Doubleday, 1994), 818–20 and Ralph Martin Novak, *Christianity and the Roman Empire: Background Texts* (Harrisburg, PA: Trinity International Press, 2001), 305.

[73] In a tribal patrilineal society with primogeniture, the firstborn sons are, of course, the inheritors of authority over family units and thus essential in the hierarchical structure of the tribe to the continuation of the social structure. To kill all the firstborn sons of Egypt is therefore, symbolically and practically, to "cut off" Egypt, to destroy its social fabric, and thus destroy Egypt itself as a continuing nation.

[74] For an extended treatment, see Jon D. Levenson, *The Death and Resurrection of the Beloved Son: The Transformation of Child Sacrifice in Judaism and Christianity* (New Haven, CT: Yale University Press, 1993). The connections to the *akedah* are profound. As I attempted to show in Chapter 7, it is precisely because Isaac is destined to become the progenitor of Israel that *his* life, too, must be represented, and most especially so, as legitimately owed to the God who gave him life and made the promise—owed, and then saved by a substitutionary (but unequal) sacrifice.

[75] For Christians, of course, the once, and for all futures sufficient, redemption comes in the form of a Lamb whose humanity makes him at least the equal of every (even blemish-free) firstborn son. Is Israel thereby freed from its client/patron relationship with Yahweh? Hardly: after all, the sacrifice is provided *by Yahweh* (as was the goat that redeemed Isaac).

that is not the entire story. In addition to the offering of the slaughter goat, there is an additional ritual in which the priest lays his hands upon a goat that is then driven into the wilderness. (Lots are drawn to pick the role for each goat.) The laying-on of the priest's hands symbolically transfers the collective sins of the people, committed during the previous year, to the head of the goat, who then carries them away and thereby serves as a sacrifice to Azazel, an apparently demonic denizen of the wilderness.[76]

But if that is the correct structure for the making of collective atonement, and Jesus is the slaughter goat, where is the scapegoat? Enter Jesus Barabbas (or so I suggest).[77] Now, if we accept this suggestion (if only for the sake of argument), what follows? Barabbas, the (alleged) insurrectionary, in carrying upon his head the collective sins of Israel, represents a response to Rome of which the Gospel writers clearly disapprove. But more: he is released—that is, "driven out into"—the mob that demands his release. The structural symmetry here identifies the mob, then, with the desert and its demon Azazel. They, we may be sure, are destined to remain outside the New Jerusalem.[78] They are the Children who have forfeited the promise.[79]

---

[76] Lev. 16: 2–22. Hence the expression "scape-goat." The wilderness, like the chaos-waters, represents a chaos, the antithesis of civilization and social order. The contrast between the desert and the *tehom* may reflect the duality of fire and water, both instruments of destruction. Civilization requires just the right amount of water: too much or too little spells death. Margaret Barker argues that the scapegoat actually "was," or represented, the demon Azazel, to whom the sins were transferred, and who was then driven out of the city into the desert and killed (Margaret Barker, *The Great High Priest: The Temple Roots of Christian Liturgy* [London: T&T Clark, 2003], 63–64). This alternative does not change the substance of the symbolism—see below—of identifying Barabbas with the scapegoat; if anything, it strengthens it. Gary Beckman indicates that there was precedent for this ceremony in second-millennium BCE Hatti (Gary Beckman, "How Religion Was Done," in *A Companion to the Ancient Near East*, ed. Daniel D. Snell [Malden, MA: Blackwell Publishing, 2005], 352).

[77] I am a johnny-come-lately with this suggestion; it can be traced back to Origen (*Homily on Leviticus* 10:2:2). For more recent commentary, see Daniel Stökl Ben Ezra, *The Impact of Yom Kippur on Early Christianity: The Day of Atonement from Second Temple Judaism to the Fifth Century* (Tübingen, Germany: Mohr Siebeck, 2003), 145–80, esp. 165–73) and Jennifer Maclean, who mentions that the *Martyrdom of Pilate* 4 links Barabbas and Judas as brothers-in-law (Jennifer K. Berenson Maclean, "Barabbas, the Scapegoat Ritual, and the Development of the Passion Narrative," *Harvard Theological Review* 100, no. 3 [2007]: 311)! However, this text dates, at the earliest, to the fifth to sixth century—too late for my argument.

[78] Michael Licona has objected to this interpretation (verbal exchange, Summer Seminar in Philosophy of Religion, St. Thomas University, 2014). The objection is that the interpretation "can't be right" (so, I suppose—see below—not only a number of contemporary scholars, but also several of the church fathers as well have made the same mistake) because in the Yom Kippur ritual, the scapegoat was driven *out* of the city, while the slaughter goat was slain *inside* the city, at the temple altar, whereas Barabbas is

Indeed, it is a curious fact that some of the early fathers of the church, though they understood this symbolism, disagreed over whether Jesus was the scapegoat or the slaughter goat. Origen—rightly—opted for the latter, but *Barnabas* 7:6–10 appears to read Jesus as the scapegoat, an error made understandable by the fact that Jesus is in fact beaten and

---

released *into* the city and Jesus led *outside* the city walls to Golgotha. And this "destroys" the intended symbolism. First, a methodological point: to require that a symbol and its referent mirror one another in *all* their particulars is to hog-tie the art of figuration. But in fact, Licona exactly misses the point. Already in early Christian lore, the *axis mundi* of Jewish lore, which had been said to be aligned with the altar in the temple, was relocated to Golgotha (see Chapter 6). So Jesus is slaughtered on precisely the new altar. And Barabbas? He is released into the new wilderness: see below. The symbolism is, indeed, careful, precise, and powerful.

[79] Cf. Matt. 22:1–10. Stökl Ben Ezra mentions a second- to fourth-century text (with a probable second-century composition date) that associates the book of Jonah with the Yom Kippur Festival (Stökl Ben Ezra, *The Impact of Yom Kippur*, 57–58). If, as Stökl Ben Ezra seems to infer, this text provides evidence that a reading of Jonah by the high priest was part of the Second Temple Yom Kippur Ritual, then a further connection between the Barabbas story and Yom Kippur suggests itself. For if, as I have argued, Jesus' three-day "death" can be divided into two parallel day-and-a-half periods, one mundane (when he is held captive by the earthly powers of evil) and one sub-mundane, as it were, when he enters Sheol (collectively described by the Jonah metaphor in Matt. 12:40 as "the belly of the whale"), then we have, apparently, a mirroring of this duality in the duality between Jesus and Barabbas. For if the ultimate soteriological destination of Jesus is the harrowing of hell, that of Barabbas is, metaphorically, becoming lost in the above-ground abode of Azazel (see also Stökl Ben Ezra, *The Impact of Yom Kippur*, 87–90 on Azazel). Berenson Maclean argues for an interpretation of Matt. 27 on which the mob demands the release of Barabbas so that they can treat him like the scapegoat—i.e., beat and kill him. Such a reading (assuming an attempt at historical realism on Matthew's part) is, among other things, incongruent with the argument, often made, that the Sanhedrin turned Jesus over to Pilate because under Roman law, it was illegal for them to execute a death sentence on a criminal. Berenson Maclean notices, significantly, that Pilate's response to the mob at 27:24 ("see to it yourselves"—i.e., the responsibility rests on you) duplicates the response of the chief priests to Judas at 27:4. But structurally, Pilate is playing the role of the officiating high priest vis-à-vis the Yom Kippur ritual. Thus—structurally—the guilt of Judas and of the mob are equated. The text seems to me rather clearly to suggest that Pilate is washing his hands of the blood of the Christ, not the blood of Barabbas. Certainly, Berenson Maclean's interpretation makes no sense if one were to take it as a reconstruction of events that actually transpired, for that would require supposing that the mob (at least) understood what was occurring on Passover as a Yom Kippur rite. Berenson Maclean does not defend the historicity of the Barabbas narrative, but she does (p. 322n61) think it is intended to be "plausible to an ancient audience." While there is no space here properly to consider all of her arguments, it will be clear that my solution to the problems raised by the text is markedly different from hers and indeed serves to illustrate the difference in methodology between the scholar who seeks a plausible reconstruction of an historical (or at least "realistic," even if invented) sequence of events that could lie behind the text and the approach of structural anthropology.

maligned as the atonement ritual dictates for that goat.[80] But that fact itself is telling.

As Carrier (2014: 407) suggests, the Jews' treatment of Jesus in this way indicates that *they* mistakenly see in Jesus the false savior, the one who bears sin, and err even more fundamentally in making the choice themselves rather than casting lots, in other words, letting God decide.[81] So this conferral in the Gospels of scapegoat-like characteristics upon Jesus the slaughter goat would have been quite intentional. Moreover, in all this, we should not lose sight of the fact that the official who performs the sacrifices (albeit in apparent collaboration with Caiaphas) is none other than the Roman prefect.[82,83]

But let us now resume our examination of Judas' story. The price of the Lamb, we are told, has gone to purchase a potter's field. In the calculus of redemption, what can this signify? What is the meaning of this detail? It is natural enough to think that it simply reflects an historical memory that quite incidentally happened to be preserved by the tradition (though only in Matt. 27:7 and Acts 1:19). Still, if we take seriously the presumption of significance and no wasted words, we may wonder about this. A burial ground, in which one's people find repose, can hardly make a trivial claim: it claims certain ground as sacred. It is not implausible to think, moreover, that

---

[80] Origen, *Homily on Leviticus* 10.2.2.

[81] Indeed, *Barnabas* also notes that, like the scapegoat around whose neck a scarlet ribbon is fastened, Jesus is arrayed in a scarlet robe. Here, he is following Matthew, who alone describes the robe as scarlet. Mark 15:17 has purple as does John 19:2. Luke 23:11 simply describes the robe as elegant and has Herod's soldiers clothe Jesus in it. For the political significance of purple, see above, footnote 51. Mark and Luke are more brazen and specify the color as purple (πορφύραν). Matthew may have thought it too dangerous a provocation to describe the robe as purple—scarlet would have been a less provocative color—but he may also have decided to alter Mark in order to reinforce the analogy between Jesus and the scapegoat. In any case, he could not have it both ways.

[82] Those who insist upon reading the Barabbas episode as true history are faced with the following choices (even assuming that the Romans did have a prisoner-release custom): either the name "Jesus Barabbas" is a remarkable coincidence, or God micromanaged certain events in first-century Palestine (locating a Barabbas family, inducing Mr. and Mrs. Barabbas to name their son "Jesus," setting this Jesus upon an insurrectionary political career, having him captured by the Romans ...). Accepting that the story plays a symbolic role in the Passion Narrative, and was composed for that purpose, requires no such assumptions. Good sense mandates the last of these explanations.

[83] I have been at pains to trace the funds that "buy" Jesus as the slaughter goat. But who provides the scapegoat? The most obvious answer is: the Romans. One might with equal justice say, however, that Barabbas, characterized by Mark 15:7 as a murderous insurrectionist, is "supplied by" the Jews—or at least by the party favoring armed rebellion against Rome and thus bearing the sins of Israel by Christian lights. But I shall not pursue the interesting implications of these suggestions.

Matthew may have had in mind Paul's description of God as the potter who makes some vessels for beauty and others for menial use—who

> has endured with much patience the objects of wrath that are made for destruction ... in order to make known the riches of his glory for the objects of mercy, which he has prepared beforehand for glory—including us whom he has called, not from the Jews only but also from the Gentiles? As indeed he says in Hosea, "Those who were not my people I will call 'my people' ... "
>
> Romans 9:22–25, NRSV

If so, then those Gentiles who have an inheritance in the promise, *in the form of a burial ground for their fathers within the land of the promise*, are among those counted as vessels whom God makes, either for destruction or for glorification—and here, glorification seems to be implied in particular, as well as judgment and predestination. It must, of course, remain a matter for speculation whether Matthew has that Pauline passage in mind, but this text from Romans certainly fleshes out the general significance of the story of the blood money, as I read it.[84]

This reading is strikingly supported by a connection between Matthew 27:7 and the story of Abraham's purchase of the cave in the field at Machpelah (Hebron), which is to serve as the sepulcher where Sarah and he, Isaac and Rebekah, and Jacob/Israel and Leah are to be buried. As Edmund Leach (1969) has shown, this purchase effectively establishes the territory as an inheritance for Israel: here is where the fathers (and mothers) are buried.[85] It is noteworthy, then, that Abraham insists upon not accepting the field as a gift from Ephron the Hittite but insists on an outright purchase that confers title "in fee simple."[86]

---

[84] See Rev. 5:8–10: "When he had taken the scroll, the four living creatures and the twenty-four elders fell before the Lamb, each holding a harp and golden bowls full of incense, which are the prayers of the saints. They sing a new song: You are worthy to take the scroll and to open its seals, for you were slaughtered and by your blood you ransomed for God saints from every tribe and language and people and nation; you have made them to be a kingdom and priests serving our God, and they will reign on earth."

[85] Some readers will perhaps be concerned that all of this insufficiently attends to the question of individual salvation. In response, let me just repeat that I believe the soteriological concerns of the NT authors involved a greater interest in corporate groups than is often recognized.

[86] The negotiations between Abraham and Ephron are delicate, and as noted in Chapter 6, a perfect exemplar of the mechanics of the principle of reciprocity and exchange. If Abraham accepts the field as a gift, then he stands in Ephron's debt as recipient of Ephron's patronage. If, however, he refuses, he is in danger of snubbing an offer of friendship. It is easy for such refusal to insult the honor of the would-be giver and turn potential friendship into actual enmity. Hence Abraham's extraordinary exercise of careful diplomacy. But although Ephron can, by Israelite lights, thus alienate a part of his

This brings us back to the mystifying "quotation" from Jeremiah at Matthew 27:9–10. It is difficult, I think, to suppose that Matthew was unaware of the liberties he took with the prophetic literature here, that his conflation of three texts was not intentional. My suggestion is that Matthew was bent upon packing as much information—as many mythemes as possible—into the short compass of this allusive passage. We have just discussed the theme of rights to the land. It is rehearsed in some detail by Jeremiah's rather elaborate discussion of his purchase of a field at the location of his birthplace, which clearly serves to assert the rights of inheritance in the face of foreign conquest. The allusion to Jeremiah 18 is also fairly transparent: just as Yahweh asserts his formative relation to Israel as potter to clay, so the purchase of the potter's field in Matthew 27 signals a reformation of Israel that is divinely ordained.[87] But what of the reference to Zechariah 11?

It is a matter of little cheer that Zechariah 9–14 and Malachi constitute, in the words of one Bible scholar, "arguably the most difficult texts for the interpreter of the Old Testament."[88] To discern Matthew's intentions in alluding to this text, we should like to know especially: Who are the "sellers of sheep"? Who are the three "bad shepherds" of whom Zechariah himself disposes? Who are they who pay his wages? Why does Yahweh command him to cast those wages into the treasury/to the potter? What does all this have to do with the breaking of the two shepherds' staffs, symbolic of the rending asunder of covenants between Yahweh and "the people" and between Israel and Judah? In fact, our task is harder in that what we are ultimately after is not what "Zechariah" meant but what Matthew thought he meant, or, more precisely, what he intended his readers to understand "Zechariah" to have meant.[89]

---

heritage, Israel cannot, in turn, similarly alienate any part of hers. See Leach, *Genesis as Myth and Other Essays*, 56–57; Gen. 17:8; and Lev. 25:23–24. Leach (p. 116n19) points out that Gen. 33:18–20, along with Acts 7:16, imply that Abraham (or Jacob?) bought the sepulcher instead from Hamor at Shechem. Because Hebron and Shechem were associated with the competing nations of Israel and Judah (David was crowned at Hebron, Jereboam at Shechem), this simply reinforces the symbolic significance of burial sites. Compare David's purchase of a Jebusite threshing floor as the site of the altar (2 Sam. 24:18–25. Cf. 1 Chron. 21:18–22:1) with David's insistence upon paying for the sacrifice himself. Interestingly, the language of 2 Sam. 24:24 echoes that of Abraham's negotiation with Ephron: here not a burial site, but a consummation of Israel's claim to the land—see Allison, *The New Moses*, 20). See also Ruth 1:15–17 for the significance of place of burial.

[87] Cf. also Isa. 45:9–13.

[88] David L. Petersen, *Zachariah 9–14 and Malachi: A Commentary* (Louisville, KY: Westminster John Knox Press, 1995), 1.

[89] I put "Zechariah" in quotes because it is almost universally agreed that Zech. 9–14—often referred to as 2 Zech.—is the product of the hand(s) of authors and editors other than those who produced Zech. 1–8.

Unfortunately, Bible scholarship is unable to answer these questions with any certainty whatever. Judgments concerning when this section of Zechariah was composed have ranged from the seventh century BCE to the period of the Maccabees, with correspondingly wide-ranging guesses as to historical background and references in the text.[90] Given these lacunae in our knowledge, we may never be able to decipher all of Matthew's meaning. But we can make some educated guesses.

Following Paul Reddit (1995), I shall assume, for the sake of argument, that the context is the Persian Period and a looked-for restoration of the houses of Judah and Joseph/Ephriam (i.e., the dispersed tribes of the Northern Kingdom) in a unified new Israel, a prophecy announced by Chapters 9 and 10 but understood by the author(s) of Chapter 11 not to have been realized. The rationale given in Chapter 11 evidently places the blame upon the bad shepherds who are "destroyed" by the prophet at 11:8, and who we may suppose were reprobate rulers of Jerusalem. In consequence, Yahweh symbolically commissions Zechariah to play the role of a shepherd who abandons the flock and annuls the promise contained in Zechariah 9–10. Then, this symbolic shepherd is paid thirty shekels by the "merchants of sheep"—apparently foreign rulers—only to be commanded by God to cast the money in the treasury.[91]

Any attempt to map this onto Matthew's narrative must be quite speculative. For starters, any attempt at such a mapping faces a dilemma. For "Zechariah," even though he is a bad shepherd, is a divinely-commissioned prophet. Jesus, who is also divinely commissioned, is the very antithesis of a bad shepherd. Like "Zechariah," Judas receives a payment of thirty shekels, but he is not a prophet and is divinely commissioned only in the sense that it might be said that his betrayal and fate are part of the divine plan. And, on the other side, thirty shekels is not Jesus' payment, but it *is* his "price."

Given these ambiguities, one could go either way, possibly identifying "Zechariah" with Jesus or with Judas! Matthew might have intended such an ambiguity, but it is at least more likely that we are missing clues that would have been available to him and his readers. In either case, we may guess that the rulers of Jerusalem—the chief priests and the Sanhedrin—are being implicated by Matthew as the three bad shepherds destroyed by "Zechariah." But then there is an inversion here: "Zechariah" is paid by the sheep-traders (= foreign powers, according to Reddit), and the money winds up in domestic hands. Judas is paid by domestic powers, and the money winds up invested in "foreign" land.

---

[90] A judicious summary of this scholarship can be found in Paul L. Reddit, *Haggai, Zecharia, and Malachi*, New Century Bible Commentary (Grand Rapids, MI: William B. Eerdmans Publishing Company, 1995), 93–105.

[91] So Reddit, *Haggai, Zecharia, and Malachi*, 126.

Thus, we find the following contrasts: "Zechariah" is a Jewish prophet figuratively shepherding Judah/Israel in the service of foreign masters, who rightly judges her leaders to have violated God's covenant. So, he voids the covenant and the alliance between the two states. His pay is cast into the temple treasury. Jesus is a Jewish prophet figuratively shepherding Israel in the service of Israel's god and sent to save her. He rightly judges her leaders to have violated God's covenant and reshapes that covenant so that they are "sold," while the true Israel—which now includes the foreign masters—is saved. His price is kept *out* of the treasury and invested in the incorporation of the foreigners. In Zechariah, Judah/Israel (brothers) are torn asunder and enslaved by foreigners. In Matthew, properly faithful Jews and Romans (enemies) are somehow to be united in a new divine promise and freed from slavery. But how?

Now the larger context of Zechariah 11—the oracles of Zechariah 9–11 and Malachi—offers an alternating juxtaposition of optimistic prophecies of divinely promised future hegemony and divinely imposed punishments upon God's people. It appears that the early hopes (so Reddit [1995: 144–145]) for a renascent unified Israel/Judah under a Davidic king, articulated in Zechariah 9 and 10, were dashed by the continued subjugation of the promised land by Persia (and later Greeks). This is reflected in Zechariah 11, which seeks to lay the blame upon Jewish misconduct. The day of promise remains affirmed (in Zech. 12–14 and Malachi), but it is indefinitely postponed. But how can Matthew, who evidently means to be suggesting that the redemption of Israel is finally at hand, have any realistic hope for such a thing in a day when Israel lay so firmly under the thumb of Roman power?

A familiar answer is that the kingdom Matthew envisions is "not of this world": he has no illusions of a (post-70 CE) military victory over Rome but is reinterpreting the messianic tradition that runs through the post-exilic prophets, a tradition that clearly envisions a Jewish empire. This, I think, is half-right. Jesus' kingdom is not of this "world" (κόσμος, i.e., social order) but of one marking the creation of a "new earth," as did the flood. I have been suggesting that Matthew's Passion Narrative maps, rather precisely, the lineaments of that kingdom. We can now see that the way in which Matthew "inverts" Zechariah 11 mirrors the way in which the shape of Jesus' kingdom "inverts" the Jewish prophetic vision of the day of the LORD. The way to achieve that day is not by the traditional means of military conquest—now clearly hopeless—but rather by a kind of ideological conquest.[92]

---

[92] The oracles of 2 Zech. and Malachi are replete with imagery that Matt. makes use of in his depiction of Jesus' final campaign: familiarly Zech. 9:9 (arguably echoing 1 King 1:33–40)/Matt. 21:5, but also probably Zech. 12:10 and Zech. 14:4–5/Matt. 27:52–54. It seems further possible to find an echo of the language of Zech.

To make this thought plausible, we should have to show how what Matthew offers to the Roman imperium is an ideological program that it might actually be sensibly attracted to and ultimately persuaded by. We can already note that two major elements of that program are these: 1) To reject tribalism as the basis of social order. The foundation of a tribal system is a social order organized along lines determined by kinship; such an order can no longer cohesively handle the social relationships implied by empire. 2) To offer as a substitute for kinship an ideology of legitimate kingship. The Roman Caesars were notoriously (and rightly) concerned about the shakiness of their claims to legitimacy. The challenge offered by the Christ is that of a model tribal king reconfigured so that he has not only legitimacy in tribal terms but is able to transcend that sphere and offer a royal ideology that combines the theme of humble service with those of divine authority and a demand for complete loyalty as the social glue that replaces kinship.

Thus, the ransom that has purchased the perfect Redeemer has been used *on behalf of the Gentiles*, to purchase for them a home within the reach of God's promise, even as it rescues the righteous remnant of Israel, making it a light unto the nations and its king the King of kings. Ideologically, Rome becomes heir to Abraham, but the practical upshot is that the New Jerusalem is moved a thousand miles to the west. I shall pursue this suggestion further in the next chapter. But fully developing this idea moves us far beyond the scope of the present volume; it would require, *inter alia*, a careful reading of the ante-Nicene church fathers, among other things.[93]

14:6–7 in Jesus' and Paul's descriptions of the eschaton (Matt. 22:30; Gal. 3:28) and of the critique of the temple sacrificial system in Zech. 14:20–21 and Malachi in Jesus' attack on the moneychangers.

[93] Lurking in the very near background is also the question of Matthew's *Sitz im Leben*. I am not for the moment taking a position on this controversial matter, but I am aware that one would have to work out the consequences of this reading of Matthew for the debate over his attitude toward Judaism and Torah. Here I shall say only this much: Matthew's Jesus was a fully legitimate Davidic king who becomes the legitimate heir to kingship over the world—i.e., the Roman Imperium. What this means for Matthew's attitude toward Torah and toward Pauline Christianity is bound to be complex, but what seems clear to me is that he rejected Tribe and Territory as boundary markers for the kingdom and probably also Torah. Matthew must have had more sympathy for Pauline Christianity—at least, in particular, for its commitment to a mission to the Gentiles—than would be allowed by some of the parties to this debate; e.g., David C. Sim, *The Gospel of Matthew and Christian Judaism: The History and Social Setting of the Matthean Community* (Edinburgh, Scotland: T&T Clark, 1998). Sim sees in Matthew an unwavering animosity toward Pauline Christianity. But it is equally possible to interpret much of the evidence he adduces for this so as to read Matthew's Jesus as undertaking to reconcile Jewish and Pauline Christianity by officially affirming every "jot and tittle" of the Law while in fact handing down a new, quite radicalized, Torah. Thus, e.g., at Matt. 7:12 Jesus offers a summary view of the law which can easily embrace the radical teachings of Matt. 5:20–48. That hypothesis is congruent with the evidence. Properly to address this question would require, *inter alia*, an extended discussion of Matt. 5:17–19,

Yet it is at least a relevant observation that the subsequent history of early Christianity in fact conveys the impression that the Romans were alternately suspicious of Christianity as a subversive movement (which it was) and one that might have something of importance to teach.

III. Concluding Reflections

There is no logical incompatibility between accepting the above analysis of Matthew's chronology and a literalist conception of Jesus' death and resurrection. Most readers will, of course, recognize the profound distance between the interpretive methodology employed here and that favored by fundamentalists. Nevertheless, one could graft a literal death and resurrection into this account of Matthew's project. Indeed, one might offer the suggestion that God is a good structuralist, crafting the sacred history of redemption of his people in just the clever ways I have imputed to the mortal Matthew.

The implausibility of this suggestion is, however, easy to see. The appeal to a divine playwright/puppeteer is otiose; it no longer does any explanatory work and has no independent grip. Not only is there little by way of evidence not otherwise explainable that favors it, but there is much, in the way of historical implausibilities, that strongly works against it. The question of miracles aside, it is the uniform experience of human affairs that their historical unfolding does *not* exhibit the kinds of structural patterns and symmetries so characteristic of myth.

To be sure, the issue I have just engaged cannot be settled on the basis of such a partial analysis of the Gospel of Matthew. I have argued that the death/resurrection motif in Matthew's passion is of a piece with death/resurrection symbolism in Jewish traditions and those of a much broader sweep of ANE traditions. And I have argued that the significance of that motif is to be sought within the arena of ancient thought about matters of political legitimacy and stability—not in terms of speculation about matters biological or "spiritual" (whatever that might mean).

But a proper evaluation of these claims clearly requires that much more be said. I have offered only the merest hints about what Matthew's

---

10:5–23, 15:22–28, and various other passages that seem to suggest that Matthew and his community were Jewish Christians. The discussion has tended to focus on these passages on the one side, and passages such as 2:1–11, 4:15, 5:13, 9:10–17, 10:18, 12:18, 21, 13:38, 15:31, 21:43, 24:14, 27:54, and 28:16–20 on the other, passages whose relevance seems fairly transparent. But it is the less obvious material I have discussed above that is, in my view, decisive. It should be added, however, that such "universalistic" passages as 2:1–11, 12:18, 21, 10:38, and 27:54, which appear to echo the nationalistic triumphalism of the prophets (especially Isaiah), must, if they are not to mislead, be tempered by the new twist that the Gospel gives to Christian universalism, as in Matt. 8:11–12 and 21:43.

political agenda might be (with some further hints yet to come). A serious proposal would have, at least, to spell that out, to show that the agenda was a plausible one for the early Christian community to have and one that could justify, and so explain, the risks it undertook to promote this ideological program. Furthermore, it would have to show in detail not only how the rest of Matthew's Gospel articulates that agenda but how the rest of the New Testament (to say nothing of other early Christian sources) can be read as proposing more or less (with some differences of emphasis or viewpoint) the same general political program. While I shall begin that task in the next chapter, much further work will remain.[94]

The hypothesis that Matthew's project is to propose a serious political program allows the approach taken here to escape other stock objections regularly raised against "liberal" and skeptical interpretations of the Gospels. Let us begin with the question of the Easter appearances of Jesus. It is regularly averred by conservative scholars that only the Easter appearances can account for the beginnings of the early church. After the crucifixion, Jesus' disciples were scattered, afraid, and above all disheartened, for they had not expected that their savior would be captured, dishonored, and killed—to say nothing of anticipating a resurrection.[95] The resurrection appearances come as a complete surprise. They galvanize the disciples, confer upon them an understanding of Jesus' mission (finally!!), and weld them into a unified movement of preachers of the good news.

The early church would indeed have seen itself as the bearer of "Good News," and there is no denying that many early Christians were prepared to take serious risks and make significant sacrifices in the service of promoting that news. But this does not at all require us to suppose that the Easter appearances occurred, or that without them, the disciples would have been at a loss and the movement abruptly aborted. Whether or not it originally formed around a teacher who was executed, the movement did not evaporate for the simple reason that it was able to formulate a political theory, strategy, and

---

[94] Initial hints about these matters have been given in footnotes 69 and 70.

[95] This in spite of the fact that, according to Matthew and the other Evangelists, Jesus has repeatedly told them what death he was to die, why he must die, and that he would be raised. Not only that: they have witnessed the raising of Lazarus and the rich man's daughter. William Craig, Stephen Davis, and many others go further and argue not only that the Easter appearances occurred but that their occurrence can only be plausibly explained by supposing that Jesus really *was* resurrected and really *did* put in a series of physical appearances. The alternatives, they think, are fraud or self-deception (i.e., multiple hallucinations). Liberal scholars often take a different tack: there was a series of post-Easter visions or "manifestations" of Jesus which restored the faith of the disciples, but these were inner, spiritual experiences whose objective basis, if any, transcends historical or scientific investigation and is an object of "faith." That there were disciples who had subjective, transformative experiences is not impossible—but this proposal is quite unnecessary.

program that spoke powerfully to the condition of many people, rich and poor, Jewish and Gentile, in Judea and across the Roman Empire.

For Judea at the time, the dominating *practical* problem was Rome's cruel hegemony and evident invincibility. For Rome itself, the preeminent *theoretical* problems were establishing the legitimacy of the Caesars and finding political principles that could coherently organize a society that had effectively lost its tribal structure and become international. Matthew, writing in the wake of Judea's failed revolt, presents, in the royal figure of Jesus, a new way of solving these enormous challenges that preoccupied conqueror and conquered alike. It is the originality and penetrating insight of this program (and presently the literary power of the expression it found in the writings of the evangelists) that held the movement together and spread its teachings.

It is not as if we have no parallels or precedents for this sort of thing. Anthropologists have been able to study a variety of millenarian movements, the contexts in which they arise, and the phenomena associated with them. Among those phenomena, a prominent role is played by purported visions, apparitions, and the like, which put leaders or would-be leaders of a movement immediately in touch with the powers and forces of the supernatural world. Such visions—or rather, the claim to have them—will confer authority upon the aspiring leader who possesses enough charisma to have his or her claims accepted.[96] There is, therefore, no reason to assume (though also no particular reason to deny) that Peter, Paul, or any other Christian leader may have had some subjective religious experience, whether involving an apparition of Jesus or some more inwardly directed ecstatic state.

Finally, then, a few words on the question whether Matthew's Gospel has some historical "core." In particular, did the Christian movement have its origin in the influence of a Jewish teacher named Jesus who was arrested by the

---

[96] Such claims and movements characteristically crop up in the context of groups that are socially marginalized or have experienced severe collective trauma of some other kind that threatens the continued existence of the group. The phenomenon has been observed across cultures, from the cargo cults of Melanesia to the Ghost Dance movement among the Plains Indians. One should not make the mistake of assuming that "acceptance" of a vision-claim made by another must involve believing that he or she has literally been in contact with some transcendent or otherworldly reality. Such claims, and their acceptance, may mean simply and precisely the recognition of an individual as capable of leading: of possessing insight into difficulties confronting the group and promising solutions and of possessing those personal qualities that make for effective leadership. For more on this subject, see I. M. Lewis, *Ecstatic Religion: An Anthropological Study of Spirit Possession and Shamanism* (Baltimore, MD: Penguin Books, 1971); Evan Fales, "Scientific Explanations of Mystical Experiences, Part I: The Case of St. Teresa," *Religious Studies* 32, no. 2 (1996): 143–63; "Scientific Explanations of Mystical Experiences, Part II: The Challenge to Theism," *Religious Studies* 32, no. 3 (1996): 297–313; and "Can Science Explain Mysticism?," *Religious Studies* 35, no. 2 (1999): 213–27. All these works contain substantial bibliographies to the literature on the neurophysiology, psychology, and sociology of mystical and visionary experiences.

Sanhedrin, tried under Pilate, and crucified by the Romans? The first thing that I should say in response to this question is that, although the answer to it matters very much to most Christians, *it does not matter very much to the project I have undertaken here.* To be sure, the question how the Christian movement arose is one whose answer will depend upon whether there was such a teacher. But the questions *I* have been trying to answer concern the meaning of Matthew's Gospel. Once one adopts the theoretical framework proposed here, one can proceed without knowing how to answer these historical questions, interesting as they might be in their own right.

There is nothing in my reading of Matthew's Gospel that excludes the possibility of an historical founder of Christianity who taught in Galilee, went to Jerusalem, and courted execution at the hands of the authorities. On the other hand, we can see clearly from the theoretical perspective I am recommending how artificial is the project of trying to separate history from legend by "peeling away" putatively apocryphal accretions to an unvarnished historical memory so as to reveal a mundane core upon which to confer the mantle of truth. For the "realistic" elements of the plot are just as integral to the message of the narrative as are the fantastical ones. If some of them are historical, that is a lucky accident; if it had served Matthew's purpose to make up realistic episodes, he would not have hesitated to do so. It is no more germane to the goal of understanding the basic meaning of Matthew's text to discern an historical core than are debates over whether Matthew used one source or two.

Was Jesus bodily raised from the tomb after a day and two nights? Anyone who accepts the interpretation offered here will recognize this question to be profoundly misguided but not because the answer must surely be "no." It is *not* that we cannot seriously entertain that possibility (and not even because it would be logically incompatible with our interpretation: it is not) but because to entertain it is to reveal a complete incomprehension of Matthew's purpose, a misunderstanding so fundamental as virtually to preclude recognition of the truths Matthew means to convey.

Those who seek a risen Jesus reveal their own religious wrestling with the problem of death. But to impose this existential concern upon the Gospel texts is to turn them into what they were never intended by their authors to be: reflections on the personal or biological fate of individuals. Their concern was with social and cultural survival.

The ANE mythographers were of course not oblivious to the universal concern over death; nor were they unmindful of the power that personal birth and death had as metaphors for larger social realities. But they no more thought of themselves as offering an escape from individual dissolution than did Ezekiel when he conjured up a vision of bone meeting bone. What transfixed Ezekiel's religious imagination was not the medical reconstruction of deceased ancestors but the reconstitution of a defeated and dispersed nation—the very image invoked in Matthew 27:51–53 by the bodies of the saints arising from the bloodstained earth at Golgotha.[97]

After a three-day ordeal in the chaos-waters of Sheol, Jonah emerges to teach Nineveh respect for the LORD. But now, an even greater imperial city rules over little Judea. To teach Rome the Way of the LORD will require a greater figure than Jonah. How could such a mission hope to succeed?

The answer to that important question belongs to the rest of the story and requires an extended analysis of the Gospels. Beyond the few hints given here and in the next chapter, that is a project for another occasion.[98]

---

[97] N. T. Wright makes it clear that the soteriological significance of belief in resurrection in first-century Judea was understood politically and in terms of the reconstitution of an independent Israel (N. T. Wright, *The New Testament and the People of God*, Christian Origins and the Question of God, vol. 1 [Minneapolis, MN: Fortress Press, 1992], esp. 188–200 and 320–34). Later, Wright claims that this also involved a belief in literal resurrection (Wright, *The Resurrection of the Son of God*). Cf.—so Richard Carrier—b. Talmud, Sanhedrin 92b.

[98] See especially footnotes 40 and 51. I will argue that the coronation of Jesus as heir-(un)apparent to the Roman throne needs to be taken seriously. Roman political theory was in disarray. The Caesars, who craved the ancient title "Rex," could not find a legal basis for assuming that role (Carin Green, personal communication). Thus, Paul announces in his opening greeting to the Romans that he is preaching "the gospel concerning his [God's] Son, who was descended from David according to the flesh, and was declared to be Son of God with power according to the spirit of holiness by resurrection from the dead, Jesus Christ our LORD, through whom we have received grace and apostleship to bring about the obedience of faith among all the Gentiles for the sake of his name, including yourselves who are called to belong to Jesus Christ." (Rom. 1:3–6, NRSV) Jesus, then, is born a Jewish messiah, has the mantle of kingship placed upon him by divine election at his baptism, and is elevated by way of a death and resurrection to a throne that places him in rulership over not just Israel, but Rome as well. It was Daniel Larkin, in conversation, who brought this central theme to my attention. He noted how pregnant with meaning was the pronouncement of the Roman centurion present at Jesus' death that he was the Son of God, a clue that opens the window to a whole iconographic complex in the Passion Narrative—and, by extension, in the gospel as a whole.

Christ's Kingdom

Over the past four decades, the diversity of views concerning who Jesus was has hardly diminished. At one pole, many evangelical scholars and scholars associated with life of Jesus research continue confidently to proclaim that the historical Jesus performed the miracles ascribed to him by the canon, that he was resurrected from the dead, and that he gave a multiplicity of other evidences of being the unique Son of God. At the other pole, there has been an increasingly intense effort to show that the "Jesus of history" is a figment, that the Jesus first, to our knowledge, proclaimed by Paul was a mythical, supernatural figure later historicized by the composers of the Gospel traditions into a first-century Jewish prophet-king whose fictional life and death inaugurated both a new age and a church.

As I have earlier stated, I have no stake in the question whether or not Jesus was an historical figure and do not tackle the problem in this book. Rather, I have sought to understand what messages certain biblical texts, as we have them, meant to convey. What can certainly be learned from the range of disagreement over Jesus is that, questions of historicity aside, it remains true that there is no stable application of agreed-upon historiographical principles that has enabled the arrival at a broad consensus about meaning. To a considerable degree, of course, this is due not only to divergences in method and reasoning but to the under-determination of conclusions by data—data that, in fact, are all too often simply and sadly missing. All of this urges modesty and caution in arriving at conclusions.

With that understood, my aim in this final chapter is to draw together various threads from the preceding chapters and, after introducing a few additional themes, to attempt to draw a picture of how the early church understood the figure of Jesus and its own mission. On my hypothesis, the early portraits of Jesus are meant to present, and argue for, a political program. Much of the persuasive force of this presentation comes through the powerfully moving narratives that draw readers and hearers into the ambit of an extraordinary figure, a truly righteous king. But it is not on a purely emotional plane that these narratives must operate. A good king is not only a charismatic leader who can move many and create deep loyalties. He, or his ministers, must also understand, and be able to offer solutions to, the most pressing and fundamental problems his kingdom faces. Such solutions often—and certainly in the present case—would require a deep theoretical understanding of social structures and the ways in which they function to create weal or woe in particular circumstances. The more fundamental the threats to social existence, the more penetrating that theoretical understanding must be.

I will argue that the NT articulates a profound grasp of the sources of social instability, not only with Israel in mind, but—and indeed unavoidably—in the ancient Mediterranean world at large. Moreover, it offers a strikingly original package of solutions to those problems and a political program for the salvation of Israel (though a redefined Israel). That program is nevertheless not entirely novel. Parts of it had been in the air (both in Israel and elsewhere) for quite some time, but the early Christian thinkers achieved a synthesis and a power of articulation that reconceived those ideas and, passing them once more through the refining fires of a novel sort of narrative, produced a new, stronger alloy. Out of that alloy were forged the weapons of a new sort of king and a vision of a new sort of kingdom. What were those weapons, who was that king, and upon what principles was his kingdom to be founded?

I. Sanders and Wright on the Aims of Jesus

We can initiate this project by considering E. P. Sanders' (1985) attempt to understand the nature of Jesus' vision of his kingdom. Sanders confronted a puzzle (as he saw it) in our data concerning Jesus. On the one hand, we can consider secure the indications that Jesus envisioned a restoration of all Israel, along the lines of John the Baptist's general call for repentance, the symbolism of "the twelve" as representing Israel's tribes, and Jesus' expectation of the replacement of the temple. On the other hand, the sayings of Jesus contain little that suggests a mission to all Israel, favoring rather the salvation of individuals in particular groups (the poor and sinners—those whose lives broke faith with the covenant).

To reconcile this tension, Sanders sees in Jesus a figure who envisioned a fundamental reconstitution of Israel but one that would not require a mass following or ordinary means of revolution. Rather, Jesus was an apolitical charismatic prophet who saw himself as proclaimer of a new Israel, whose achievement would be accomplished with the direct aid of Israel's God—a prophet whose miracles testified to God's purpose and impending eschatological activity. Jesus, in Sanders' view, did not have a worked-out plan to achieve the new kingdom. God would see to that, as John had seen to the call to Israel. What Jesus did have was charismatic gifts and a mission to the marginalized.

But unlike some contemporary Jewish freedom fighters (e.g., Theudas and the Egyptian), Jesus did not try to foment military resistance or rebellion, and he thought of the new temple and new Israel as coming to exist "in the air," similar in some ways to earthly kingdoms, yet not "of this world." In this way, Sanders hoped to account, not only for Jesus' sayings and reluctant attitude toward enthusiastic crowds, but for the incongruity of a figure who excited enough animus from the Jewish establishment and then the Roman administration to explain his execution, even though this was not then followed by any effort to arrest and execute his close companions by the Romans, as were those of other Jewish rebel leaders. But even more seriously, Sanders faces the question why the Romans would have had any interest in executing such a figure as Jesus—however much animosity he may have stirred up against himself from the Jewish religious establishment.[1] Sanders (1985: 294) states the difficulty clearly. Given that Jesus was crucified as "King of the Jews,"

> The reason the facts seem incredible is that everything we know about Jesus indicates that he sought no secular kingship. Harvey argues that 'The royal pretender must have attracted sufficient support to be capable of offering a real threat to the Roman government;' i.e., to be executed as a would-be king he must have had an army....the disciples ... claimed Jesus as Messiah and expected his return ... which was steadfastly *apolitical. Thus not only was Jesus executed as would-be king even though he had no such secular ambitions, his disciples also combined the same two points: Jesus was Messiah, but his kingdom was 'not of this world'* [Sanders' italics].

Here, Sanders makes the common mistake of reading the phrase "not of this world (κόσμος)" apolitically. Nevertheless, Jesus had no army. So, if he was in fact executed by the Romans, the threat must not have been military, even if political. (Here, one should remember that I am not in any event interested in excavating what historically occurred and so not committed to extracting from the texts any reconstructed narrative that would pass muster as historically realistic. My aim is simply to discover what message the evangelists hoped to impart in their Gospels. Historical realism may not have been on their menu, and it is not on mine.)

In any case, has Sanders given us a plausible reconstruction of the figure of Jesus? Clearly, he is walking a fine line in imagining a Jesus who is enough of a rabble-rouser to strike fear into establishment hearts while nevertheless not being seen as a leader whose followers would also merit

---

[1] Sanders takes Jesus' most serious offense to have been his challenge to the temple. As we saw in Chapter 6, it is far from clear that whatever Jesus did or said on that score would have aroused the mortal enmity of his opponents.

arrest. Moreover, Sanders' assessment of the evidence is at several points problematic. He denies the authenticity of the passages in which Jesus calls for public repentance, with his constant harping upon the obduracy of "an evil and adulterous generation," a "generation of vipers," who—unlike Nineveh—refused the call to repentance from a prophet "greater than Jonah."[2] He may be right, but we have seen how fallible the reasoning can be that lies behind such judgments.

The theme that a prophet is not honored in his own home, while contextualized to the environs of Galilee, surely had broader implications. As the Gospels represent him anyway, Jesus was not uninterested in calling Israel to repentance or providing eschatological signs. He was frustrated by the apparent refusal of a large segment of the Jewish nation to hear his message and the apparent (and facially baffling) incomprehension of his own disciples. Surely, one cannot read Jesus' teaching at Matthew 11:20/Luke 10:1–15; John 5:19–30, 6:28–59, and many other sayings as anything but a call and a warning to all of Israel. Sanders has to jettison all of this material.

By way of comparison, let us briefly consider N. T. Wright's reconstruction of Jesus' self-understanding. Chapter 10 of Wright's *Jesus and the Victory of God* deals with Jesus' conception of his kingdom and his mission as the inaugurator of the new world order.[3] On Wright's reading, Jesus' self-understanding was that he had to do battle with demonic forces that lie at the heart of the problem with the world and that blocked the ultimate triumph of God's promise to his chosen. In this battle—in which Jesus understood that he would sacrifice his own life—he had to eradicate the notion that Israel was to throw off the Roman yoke by military means. Yet, Jesus had no idea *how*, through his mission, the kingdom would be ushered in. Nor, therefore, did the disciples, who also bet their lives on success.[4]

But even if Jesus was able to perform mighty works, this is much too thin to be a plausible reconstruction of history, the more so if we cannot assume that Jesus performed miracles. And what, if not Rome and Roman occupation, were the powers of darkness against which Jesus understood himself to be arrayed? Wright is right that the Gospels diagnose the evils Israel faces partly in terms of internal political movements, movements that sought to throw off foreign domination in ways that the Jesus movement rejected. But in Wright's view, much of the battle had to be fought by Jesus as an *interior* battle, a battle against the temptations of Satan in the desert.

---

[2] E. P. Sanders, *Jesus and Judaism* (Philadelphia: Fortress Press, 1985), 110, 114.

[3] N. T. Wright, *Jesus and the Victory of God*, Christian Origins and the Question of God (Minneapolis, MN: Fortress Press, 1996), 2:443–74.

[4] Ibid., 444–45.

Yet the story of the three temptations is, as Wright well understands, permeated by a symbolism that refers to Israel's forty-year sojourn in the desert in Exodus. Surely, we have a right to expect that Jesus would have understood there to be some connection between his desert experience and the means by which his missionary activity would inaugurate his kingdom. What, beyond the symbolic evocation of Israel's original quest for nationhood, might the parallelism between the temptations Jesus surmounts and the failings of Israel in the desert teach? Wright does not seem to see how such connections are to be made. I think we can do better.

To see this, let us return to Sanders. What of Sanders' similar claim that Jesus' understanding of his mission transcended the political, which is of interest to us? Sanders takes 1 Thessalonians 4:15–17, Romans 11:15, and 1 Corinthians 15 to show that Jesus thought that the kingdom promised to him was to be founded "in the air." If taken literally, this language is at least baffling.[5] Was Paul (or Jesus) envisioning a kind of space platform?

Another reading is possible and is suggested by a similar phrase at Ephesians 2:2. Ephesians is generally agreed to be a pseudo-Pauline letter whose author was probably a contemporary of the evangelists. Though there appear to be some differences between the spiritual geography and chronology of 1 Thessalonians and Ephesians (e.g., Eph. 2:6 says that the living, through Christ's salvation, are "raised up with [God] and seated ... with him in the heavenly places in Christ Jesus;" 1 Thess. 4 envisions a future rapture), it is possible to give a coherent interpretation of the atmospheric language that appears in both epistles.

A clue is provided by the language of Ephesians 6: 11–12:

> Put on the whole armor of God, so that you may be able to stand against the wiles of the devil. For our struggle is not against enemies of blood and flesh, but against the rulers, against authorities, against the cosmic powers of this present darkness, against the spiritual forces of evil in the heavenly places.

—that is, not against "αἷμα καὶσάρκα," but against "τὰς ἀρχάς, πρὸς τς ξουσας, τοὺς κοσμοκράτοράς τοῦ σκότυδς τοῦ αἰῶνος τούτου, πρὸς τά πνευματικά τῆς προνηρίας ἐν τοῖς ἐπουρανίοις."

Here, "αἷμα καὶσάρκα" might mean simply (cf. Matt. 16:17) "human persons," but, especially in light of the way Paul himself uses "σάρξ" and "σαρκικός" to denote the carnal, even sinful or unspiritual, aspect of human nature (Rom. 7:14, 15:27; 1 Cor. 3:13, 9:11; 2 Cor. 1:12), we may surmise that the phrase here (and in Matt. 16:17) means more specifically those aspects of human nature that characterize natural persons (in the sense of

---

[5] Sanders, *Jesus and Judaism*, 228 – 36.

Chapter 4), apart from their institutionalized status as occupiers of social roles, that is, their "pneumatic" being. Then, the implied contrast in Ephesians 6:12 is with rulers and authorities, not as natural individuals, but precisely insofar as they occupy positions of institutional power.

Thus, the claim is that the Ephesians must arm themselves for struggle, not *per se* against the particular natural persons who occupy positions of power but against the power structures themselves. The critique here sees the enemy as the social structures of the present age. These are the "cosmic powers [i.e., political powers] of this present darkness," the spiritual (πνευματικά) forces of evil that occupy the "heavenly places"—in other words, the realm of idealized social structures (cf. Eph. 3:10).[6]

II. Powers and Principalities: What Was in the Air?

All of this lines up with much older traditions both in Israel and in the Hellenistic world. Moreover, the ontology of Chapter 4 permits sense to be made of these traditions, which remain at least mysterious when interpreted in terms of a kind of dualism that essays to explain the intimate connections between political realities and a spirit world filled with deities, angels, demons, and the like who are literally "spooks" with original intentionality. Thus, in the Jewish traditions, Deuteronomy 32:8 speaks of Israel's god, the "Most High," apportioning the other nations among the other gods (traditionally, there were seventy nations), later demoted to angels. We can recognize these as the personifications of those nations in parallel with Yahweh as the personification of the (ideal) Israel. When Yahweh goes to war against those gods and defeats them (as in Deut. 32:35–43), this must necessarily betoken Israel's military defeat of the nations.[7]

It will be useful to expand this discussion of the thought world in which early Christian soteriology was situated. The close connection between references to a supernatural realm of "demons," "powers," "principalities," "dominions," "world rulers," "spiritual hosts," "thrones," "angels," "elemental spirits" on the one hand and references to mundane political realities—institutional structures, authorities, political forces, and the like has been recognized for some time.[8] The question before us is how

---

[6] And cf. Luke 22:53, where Jesus addresses the Jewish authorities who have come to arrest him as "the power of darkness."

[7] So when the Deuteronomist has Yahweh declare "there is no god besides me" (Deut. 32:39), he means to be affirming not monotheism but the supremacy of Yahweh (cf. Isa. 46:21, similarly supremacist but henotheistic).

[8] E.g., George B. Caird, *Principalities and Powers: A Study in Pauline Theology* (Oxford: Clarendon Press, 1956) and Clinton D. Morrison, *The Powers That*

we are to understand this close association. So, Morrison, speaking in particular of Paul's use of *exousiai* in Romans 13, says

> It has long been obvious that this terminology [designating the spiritual powers] is shared with the concept of earthly governmental authority, and this has been explained variously, e.g. by saying that the ancients believed the spirit world to have an internal order similar to their own, or that the heavenly rulers were thought to preside over earthly affairs much as their own earthly rulers governed.[9]

This is unsatisfactory: why, exactly, would the ancients have thought that there *was* such a supernatural world, and why, further, would they have thought that its social structures mimicked those governing in human life? Morrison himself thinks there must be something more than mere analogy in play. The connection between earthly rulers and the spiritual ones is so close that their governance is "essentially one." Suggestively, Morrison observes that "It is not by accident that the terms 'principalities' and 'authorities' are used in reference to civil government, for while its power is always exercised by individuals in authority, the power exists quite apart from the character of the person, as a form of power apparent only in public office."[10] Now, Morrison is entering into a debate between some who hold that in Romans 13, Paul is using *"exousiai"* to refer to both earthly and spiritual authorities and those who hold that in Romans 13, Paul means to be referring only to temporal rulers.

In the first camp are Barth, Cullman, Dibelius, and others, and in the second, von Campenhousen, Kittel, and Brunner, among others. On the first view, the Jewish tradition in which the seventy gods that protected and governed "the nations" (and that later were demoted to angels) came to be identified with the Hellenistic "powers" and "principalities," understood in supernatural terms. Thus, Christ's victory was, in the first instance, a victory over these powers. But then how, if that victory took place at the resurrection, could it be that Christians still were confronted with the world of Roman hegemony? Was Christ's victory not yet complete? (On the second view, Christ's victory at the resurrection did not directly signal a defeat of temporal rulers.)

The issue is taken to have relevance to contemporary questions about the proper attitude of the churches to state power. I have no present wish to enter into that debate, but want to show how the positions of both sides suffer from a failure to draw on the resources of social ontology

---

Be: Early Rulers and Demonic Powers in Romans 13:1–7, Studies in Biblical Theology 29 (Naperville, IL: Alec R. Allenson, Inc., 1960).

[9] Morrison, *The Powers That Be*, 26.
[10] Ibid., 27.

presented in Chapter 4. Morrison himself attempts to resolve the disagreement by showing that the Graeco-Roman understanding of "the State in the Cosmos" formed both Paul's cultural backdrop and that of the Christians in Rome. This consisted of a matrix of ideas that Paul could assume would be understood. Hence, he did not need, in Romans 13, to make explicit reference to the transworldly powers that would have been understood to be intimately tied to public officials. Citing Roman ideas about the *comes/daimon/genius* of the emperor, Morrison notes that this sort of spiritual entity, which was thought to shadow the emperor, could lead, especially in the popular imagination, to "what is loosely called 'deification.'"[11] Yet, Morrison is unsure how to map these ancient ideas onto our own conceptual terrain:

> ... it is the idea of the *daimon* which seems basic to the Graeco-Roman conception of the emperor in his role of world ruler. But as with other terms from this period we cannot force it upon modern categories. The word appears at one time as an expression of the self, but at other times as a spiritual power which is beside the person.[12]

Faced with this conundrum, Morrison resorts to ambiguity:

> *Various as were the meanings of* daimon, *it was a single word with a fluidity of usage and capacity of bearing at one and the same time senses which we distinguish and of passing imperceptibly from one to another.*[13]

Predictably, Morrison must conclude that the ancient world could not "make radical distinctions between myth and history, material and spiritual, as we do today," and that therefore

> ... there can be no proper understanding of what early Christians, Jews, and their pagan contemporaries understood as the State, in particular as the exousiai, *apart from that world view enveloping* aeons *and* daimones, *providence and powers, in which the ruler was both divine by appointment and human by birth, and the boundaries between the spirit world, and the world of humanity and nature were fluid and often imperceptible.*[14]

---

[11] Morrison, *The Powers That Be*, 91.
[12] Ibid., 89.
[13] Ibid.; italics original.
[14] Ibid., 98–99; italics original.

From our perspective, of course, this is just confused. It is a consequence of Morrison's failure to draw upon the correct region of the modern conceptual landscape. All becomes clear if we understand the distinction at issue not as a muddled semi-conflation of the "natural" and the "spiritual" or "mythical" but as the familiar distinction between persons and personages, states and their embodiments. Interestingly, to show that the same idea world inhabited Jewish thinking, Morrison quotes Philo:[15]

> In his material substance the king is just the same as any man, but in the authority of his rank he is like God of all. For there is nothing upon earth more exalted than he. Since he is mortal, he must not vaunt himself; since he is a god, he must not give way to anger. For if he is honoured as being an image of God, yet he is at the same time fashioned from the dust of the earth, from which he should learn simplicity to all.

One could hardly ask for a passage that better appears to articulate the view for which I have been arguing. As Philo saw it, the king is a flesh-and-blood human being who must exercise a humility reflecting his common humanity, but who is also, by virtue of his rank as sovereign, "like God," and—qua office-holder—indeed a god embodied.

But Paul, in line with a long tradition of Jewish apocalyptic, saw the nations and their institutions as having become corrupted. The powers and principalities, the rulers and *daimones*, have broken free of obedience to Yahweh and created chaos. Only a new sort of kingship and a new sort of king can repair the world and set it into proper order. Revelations sees this ultimate event of restoration in terms of the descent of a new Jerusalem from a new heaven to a new earth.

So, too, the Lord's descent from heaven, and the rapture of the living to meet him "in the air" in 1 Thessalonians will be an event in which the true ruler will displace the evil rulers who presently occupy "the air." More precisely, the divinely ordained social structures of God's kingdom will replace the old, superannuated structures of the present age. For,

> You were dead through the trespasses and sins in which you once lived, following the course of this world (του κόσμου τουτου), following the ruler of the power of the air, the spirit (πνεύματος) that is now at work among those who are disobedient [i.e., the demons]. All of us once lived among them in the passions of our flesh (σαρκός), following the desires of the flesh and senses, and we were by nature children of wrath, like everyone else. But God made us alive together with Christ—by grace

---

[15] Morrison, *The Powers That Be*, 96, quoting a fragment of Philo preserved by Antony, *Melissa,* Ser. CIV, text and transl. in Erwin R. Goodenough, *The Politics of Philo Judaeus: Practice and Theory* (London: Oxford University Press, 1938), 99.

you have been saved—and raised up with him in the heavenly places of Christ Jesus." (Eph. 2:1–6)

As a result, a new temple is built in which God will dwell, built upon a foundation of prophets and apostles, Christ the cornerstone, and the rest "built together spiritually" to complete the structure (Eph. 2:20–22).[16]

So then, the Lord who was resurrected had originally descended from a region "far above the heavens" (Eph. 4:9–10) through the "air" to the lower parts of the earth, returned thence, and will descend again, "so that he might fill all things"—that is, displace the rule of the forces of evil, occupying their current turf. We have already seen some of the profoundly political dimensions of the Gospel portrayals of Jesus' career. It is my aim in this chapter, extending the results of Chapter 11, to carry this feature of the gospel message consistently through to a conclusion that will identify quite precisely what the early Christian thinkers took these forces of evil to be and what was to be done to overcome them. Unlike Sanders, I shall argue that the Gospels (and the Pauline letters) contain a quite explicit diagnosis and clear outlines of a broad strategy for defeating the forces of oppression. (I do not claim, of course, to know whether Jesus himself had worked all this out. What we can hope to excavate is the thinking that is expressed in the texts we actually have.)

The task ahead will require bringing the language of 1 Thessalonians 4 and Ephesians into relation with that of, for example, 1 Corinthians 15 and various Gospel passages. But if we provisionally accept a political reading of 1 Thessalonians and Ephesians, it will be natural to ask what authorities and cosmic powers the author of Ephesians has in mind. We may also wonder what that author and Paul meant when they envisioned a future meeting with the Lord in the air (Paul) or a present assumption of the saved into God's heavenly presence (Ephesians).

As to the former, the plausible alternatives are (a) Rome, (b) the secular Jewish rulers, or (c) the Jewish religious establishment. This I want to suggest, is, however, a false choice. The target is all three, collaboratively intertwined and constituting the system of "this age" or "κόσμος." In this sense, the Christian attack upon the establishment, and the proposed

---

[16] See Richard A. Horsley, *Jesus and the Spiral of Violence: Popular Jewish Resistance in Roman Palestine* (San Francisco, CA: Harper and Row, 1987), 168. Horsley, who correctly understands the apocalyptic sayings of the Gospels to reflect anticipation of a transformation of mundane political structures, nevertheless allows that 1 Thess. 4 may reflect a prophecy concerning the end times, an envisioned time of universal destruction/recreation not to be confused with the immanent political transformation. Marcus Borg is more nearly right, recognizing that the "cosmic" imagery can, in fact, denote deep social change (Marcus J. Borg, *Conflict, Politics, and Politics in the Teachings of Jesus*, 2nd ed. [Harrisburg, PA: Trinity Press International, 1998], 29–30). For further references, see Chapter 11 n40.

replacement, are quite general and radical. If "the establishment" was the enemy, due for replacement by the kingdom, who could enter that kingdom? Among the children of Israel, the Jesus of the Gospels pays special—even scandalous—attention to sinners and the poor. What might the significance be of Jesus' reputation for consorting with these people? Surveying various proposals, Sanders points out that the two groups should not be conflated and would not have been conflated in first-century Judea.

Moreover, Sanders points out that being a sinner meant something more than merely being in a state of impurity. A sinner was someone who, intentionally and as a matter of a way of life, engaged in behaviors forbidden by the Torah. Such a person stood outside the law and, as such, outside the community of the covenant. Here, Sanders faces two questions. First, what is the likelihood that this feature of the Gospel accounts of Jesus' ministry are historically accurate? Second, what might be the significance of this feature, or alleged feature, of Jesus' ministry?

As to the former, Sanders calls this a textbook case of historical reliability: "This is one of the instances in which the usual criteria for authenticity really work."[17] Which criteria, exactly, does Sanders see applicable here? He does not say much about this, but he mentions prominence and multiple attestation and also distinctiveness ("A high tolerance for sinners was not characteristic of the early church ... "). And we can fairly guess they would also include context and expectation (this would not be expected behavior for a messiah), and perhaps above all, embarrassment (this was an accusation hurled against Jesus by his enemies, a reputation he had to live down). In my view, this is in fact a textbook case in which these criteria for historicity can lead one astray. But this points us straightaway to the second question: what was the significance of this portrayal of Jesus as a friend to sinners and the poor? Unless we know the answer to that question, it will be hard to judge whether the allegation would have been regarded as unsavory to Christians.

A first observation is that the poor and sinners do have one thing in common: their social locus is at the margins of the community. Even if they were not despised, the poor can hardly have been thought respectable. Both groups had little to lose and potentially much to gain from an offer of salvation. Both would have experienced some degree of alienation from mainstream Jewish society. Both would likely have felt that their interests were not high on the agenda of the powerful.

It is well known that new movements often seek recruits from the socially marginal and the socially disoriented, those whose lives have gone awry, those unable through circumstance or dissipation to navigate the usual routes to social respectability, those who have "fallen between the cracks." The new cult offers them not only a welcoming new social identity but the

---

[17] Sanders, *Jesus and Judaism*, 174.

motivation for self-discipline and clear aims and guidelines for proper behavior. All this is entirely consistent with the affinity for sinners and the poor that Jesus is portrayed as having. It is certainly consistent, therefore, with Jesus actually having ministered in this way to these groups.

But it is equally consistent with his having been so depicted by the early Christian community, whether he actually behaved in this way or not. In particular, it is consistent with that community not having "a high tolerance for sinners"—in just this sense: sinners (as judged by the Torah) would be welcomed into fellowship in the Christian community but, *once members*, would be expected to toe the line in adhering to the community's rules. Indeed, Paul said exactly that in 1 Corinthians 5:9–13, where he admonishes the Corinthians not to shun immoral non-Christians because that would mean leaving "the world," but to expel immoral *Christians*—those who had converted but were now, or still, sinning—from their community. So, Sanders' criterion of distinctiveness misses its mark here. But there is more, I want to suggest, than a pattern that fits well with the known missionary psychology of small but ambitious cults.

That something more has to do with the marginal status of the poor and of sinners—but especially the latter. For, as alienated from the covenant, they are, in effect, stateless individuals, individuals who have a kind of social identity but not one that can be congenially integrated into the time-honored categories. Such individuals are by definition potentially available to anyone who seeks to overturn those traditional categories and establish new boundaries and a new communion. They are not merely individuals who have failed the Torah but individuals whom the Torah has failed. And who, in particular, are these individuals? The answer is telling.

They are regularly characterized as tax collectors, usurers, and violators of the sexual code. At first blush, these might seem to be very disparate groups. But in the context of the Christian movement, appeal to them makes particular sense. Taxpayers and usurers are individuals caught up in the necessities of an economy undreamt of by the composers of the Torah. Times had changed. Tax collectors, in particular, occupied an interstitial position that mediated between Israel and Rome. They were, therefore, neither fish nor fowl.

What of sexual irregularity? Like tax collecting, adultery and prostitution presented challenges to the very core of Jewish social identity: the first by enabling exploitation of Israel by a foreign power, the latter two by undermining the foundation of Jewish internal cohesion, a stable, well-functioning kinship system. So the named groups of sinners—the "wicked" with whom Jesus consorts and to whom he offers table fellowship and salvation—are by their very nature occupied in activities that signal and symbolize the deterioration of the old tribal order and indicate the inadequacy of the Torah as Israel confronted new realities.

We may observe here that there has been extensive inquiry into whether, and to what extent, the economic policies of Herod the Great and his sons impoverished and marginalized the lower echelons of Israelite society, especially the peasants, by concentrating land ownership among the wealthy elite through a policy of crushing taxation, leading to indebtedness, forfeiture, and tenant farming. Those, like Borg, Horsley, and Oakman, who have understood a central theme of Jesus' ministry to be an attack upon the exploitative practices of the elite have emphasized the economic hardships experienced by farmers in first-century Palestine.

Fabian Udoh, on the other hand, is skeptical of claims that the economic policies of the Herodians and Romans were ruthlessly exploitative, citing, *inter alia*, the paucity of data we have regarding their tax policies.[18] Similar questions may be asked about the economic situation in Judea once Pilate was installed as governor. But certainly, such economic wellbeing as Israel had experienced in the first half of the first century CE would have been shattered by the warfare of the late 60s and its aftermath. And whatever the economic facts may have been, it is certain that large numbers of the Jews who lived in first century Palestine viewed Roman hegemony, and the political and economic institutions that it imposed, as a threat to the very survival of a Jewish nation.

It is this existential threat, I am arguing, that the books of the NT are aimed at defeating, and it is a threat that would have been felt most acutely by those who had been pushed by their economic and political environment to the very margins of Israelite society, and for whom, therefore, the very availability of a social and political identity was a standing question. Their situation must have served, moreover, as a standing warning to their brothers and sisters who for the moment remained, institutionally, anchored in home harbor.

Sanders' failure to see either of these dimensions of Jesus' relations to the poor and to sinners is a result of his commitment to the basic historical accuracy of the Gospels and his consequent need to account, with historical realism, for how this "fact" about Jesus' ministry would have led to mortal enmity on the part of the Jewish or Roman authorities. As Sanders would have it, therefore, Jesus' offense was not that he offered absolution and salvation to sinners even before they had repented but that he offered entry into the kingdom without any requirement that they atone for their sins in accordance with the law.[19]

In response to the obvious question—why would Jesus dispense with the requirement that sinners repent?—Sanders offers only the

---

[18] Fabian Udoh, *To Caesar What Is Caesar's: Tribute, Taxes, and Imperial Administration in Early Roman Palestine (63 B.C.E.–70 C.E.)* (Providence, RI: Brown Judaic Studies, 2005).

[19] Sanders, *Jesus and Judaism*, 206 – 209.

speculation that he may have thought the time to the judgment too short for them to "create new lives for themselves."[20] But the legal requirements for acts of atonement that Sanders had just enumerated (Lev. 6:1–5; Num. 5:5–7) say nothing about the creation of a "new life." They concern monetary restitution to wronged parties and, in some cases, sacrifice and payment to a priest. Those are things that can be done in short order (at least if you are not impoverished).

Once one is freed from the shackles of trying to extract historical realities from the Gospels, and can move to the level of structure and symbol to search for historically relevant *meaning* in these texts, the kind of significance I am arguing for emerges clearly. The portrayal of Jesus' mission to the poor and sinners serves both the practical end of recruiting new members from a population likely to be receptive to a message of radical reform and the theoretical aim of shattering existing structures whose time is past to make way for the new.

But how, then, were these marginal people, who have been invited to the eschatological banquet of their king, to conceive the event of the great *parousia*? This event has long been understood along the lines of Ezekiel 37 *taken literally*. But if I am right about the meaning of the Passion Narratives, this cannot be right. In fact, the truth must lie somewhere closer to the actual, metaphorical meaning of Ezekiel 37. Even the poor and the sinners, if they accept Jesus as savior and are baptized into the Christian community, will acquire a social role that can survive their death and become re-embodied in the new Jerusalem. Those who, by their rejection of Jesus, remain outside the community of God's new chosen people, forfeit that possibility, for the social structures and roles of the present age will disappear forever. Those at the margins will gain repute. Those at the center will be cast adrift ("the first shall be last, and the last shall be first").

This may seem like a far less hopeful and attractive conception of life after death than the now-standard view. Perhaps so. But if it be thought that it would be so humdrum as to offer no help in explaining the early cohesion of the church and its eventual ability to attract large numbers of converts, then I beg to differ. I will argue that it qualifies as a central element in a new worldview of immense power, a worldview that, in the circumstances of the Roman Empire, would be well equipped to earn the fervent devotion of significant numbers of adherents. But first, we must consider what can be said in favor of the view that Jesus really was bodily raised from the dead and that this signal historical event underwrites the hope that we, too, if we are recipients of the promise, will be raised as natural persons with bodies of a new sort in the resurrection to come. Here,

---

[20] Sanders, *Jesus and Judaism*, 207.

for this purpose I shall then engage a prominent contemporary defender of this view, N. T. Wright.

III. Wright on the Meaning of the Resurrection

N. T. Wright argues at some length for the historicity of the resurrection.[21] An important part of that argument is a claim that the unique, unprecedented character of the event, as portrayed by Paul and in the Gospels, strongly supports the conclusion of historicity. Thus, Wright is invoking the criterion of discontinuity to buttress the Gospel accounts of Jesus' emergence from the tomb. Other criteria also are brought to bear, in particular, the criterion of embarrassment. In his earlier work, Wright proceeds by arguing, as is typical and proper, by reasoning to the best explanation for the data he considers relevant. The overall project is to argue that this evidence can best be explained by the supposition that Jesus rose from the dead: specifically, that the tomb was empty on Easter morning and that the disciples and others thereafter witnessed the bodily presence of Jesus. In fact, Wright argues for something much stronger: that the empty tomb and resurrection appearances are "virtually certain" and that Jesus' bodily resurrection is the only possible explanation for these facts.[22] The argument proceeds by way of a broad survey of conceptions of the afterlife, and of resurrection in particular, that existed in the cultural environment of the New Testament—in the Hellenistic/Roman world, in Jewish beliefs, and among Christians themselves (especially Paul).

I shall have to be selective in singling out disagreements with Wright's treatment of the subject. I shall note places where he seems to ignore data that should not be ignored, but more especially, places where he clearly fails to entertain other hypotheses in the offing that can explain alternatively what he thinks can be explained only in one way. Thus, he runs afoul of the chief weakness of arguments to the best explanation. (Whether my alternative explanations are better than Wright's I shall leave for the reader to judge.)

There is one large methodological issue that illustrates this difficulty. Wright is intent upon demonstrating that there were no parallel beliefs in the Greek and Latin worlds to the Christian conception of resurrection and that the Christian conception, while rooted in Jewish

---

[21] N. T. Wright, *The Resurrection of the Son of God*, Christian Origins and the Question of God, vol. 3 (Minneapolis, MN: Fortress Press, 2003); Craig A. Evans and N. T. Wright, "The Surprise of the Resurrection," in *Jesus, The Final Days: What Really Happened*, ed. Troy A. Miller (Louisville, KY: Westminster John Knox Press, 2009), 75–108.

[22] Wright, *The Resurrection of the Son of God*, 706–10, 717.

traditions, involved a radically new understanding of the notion. Thus, according to Wright, except for "certain old tales like Livy's story of Romulus," Hellenistic beliefs, whether they involve an ordinary descent into hades, the rare translation of a mortal into the realm of the gods, or metempsychosis (as in Plato), never entertain the possibility of bodily reconstitution after a period of death of the individual into an imperishable living existence.[23] Nor is the Christian conception the same as the Jewish one that, beginning with Ezekiel, understands resurrection in terms of a collective reconstitution of the nation of Israel, a view that came, under the Seleucids, to develop into one in which certain heroic martyrs, as already noted, are said (e.g., in Maccabees) to be resurrected.

In all this, Wright is keen to demonstrate the *uniqueness* of the Christian conception (and he claims it is a uniform view among the earliest Christians) of the resurrection, a conclusion he needs in order to argue, further, that this conception could not have arisen in any other way than by way of witness to both the empty tomb *and* the postmortem appearances of the risen Jesus. The methodological problem in all this is that Wright did not anywhere in his quest to prove uniqueness stop to reflect upon what sorts of similarities and differences between afterlife traditions are to be counted as significant and *how* we are to understand their significance. Thus, to dwell upon just one sort of case, Wright acknowledges that many Roman emperors, who were contemporaries of the early Christian movement (beginning with Julius Caesar and running right through the first century CE), were canonized as gods and sons of god and were sometimes said to have been assumed (in some cases in the presence of witnesses) into heaven.

That is not quite the same story as the one we have for Jesus, who is executed as a criminal and spends some quality time with his disciples after his resurrection. Is that significant? Does it show that the imperial ideology would not have influenced early Christian discourse about the post-passion appearances of Jesus? If there might have been some influence, what might its significance have been? And another case: remarkably, although Wright appeals to both Homer and Virgil to demonstrate that the Greeks and Romans denied the possibility of *anastasis* (resurrection), Virgil's *Aeneid* affirms precisely the occurrence of resurrections from the Elysian Fields in hades (6:725–50).

Virgil's view is that these individuals "roll the wheel" in hades for one thousand years, during which they are purified of all gross matter. Then they bathe in the River Lethe and forget all of the past before being reborn. The ones that father Anchises points out to his son Aeneus are to be resurrected as the major figures among his descendants who will found

---

[23] Wright, *The Resurrection of the Son of God*, 83; cf. also p. 76.

Rome and ultimately become its Caesars. They will, of course, be resurrected as mortals. Is that significant enough to deny cross-fertilization?

Of course, as I have already noted, the Gospel writers may or may not have been familiar with (this feature of) Virgil's poem, either in Latin or in the Greek paraphrase, and either directly or by way of hearsay. We have no way of knowing. Nor is the resurrection of the future descendants of Aeneus (future to his descent into hades, but past relative to Virgil's composition of the *Aeneid*, of course) exactly like the almost immediate resurrection of the slain Jesus. But what of that? Perhaps Virgil invented this device to serve his poetic ends. Perhaps such ideas about resurrection were in the air, Wright's argument to the contrary notwithstanding. But if in the air, then all the more likely that early Christians knew of them. And if invented by Virgil for literary purposes, then surely Mark, or some Christian predecessor, would have been capable of a similar invention. Either way, we can see that Wright's argument does little to gain support for his conclusion. Once again, the criterion of distinction has not much force.[24]

Certainly there are scholars (e.g., the contributors to Richard Horsley's *Paul and Empire: Religion and Power in Roman Imperial Society*) who disagree with Wright over the relevance of Roman imperial ideology. But the fundamental point is just this: we need a basic *theory* that can provide an explanatory framework in terms of which to understand all of these afterlife traditions. It is only in terms of such an explanatory theory that we can hope to understand the significance of both the differences and the similarities between such traditions. Wright lacks such a theory (he has one to explain the resurrection of Jesus but nothing much to offer for the alternative views). I have a suggestion. It is, as will be anticipated, that the social ontology developed in Chapter 4 provides the kind of framework theory that Wright's treatment of the resurrection and its ideological background lacks.

As we have seen, the claim is that kings (and emperors) are representatives of a nation (or empire) who specifically embody that state and its will in virtue of holding office and that they may be candidates for deification if they appear to articulate and bring into existence what is understood to be an ideal state of flourishing for their nation. What can "die" and be resurrected—re-embodied—is the office itself. This broad outline (which here I have articulated specifically in reference to monarchs) will, we can expect, be worked out in multifarious ways that reflect sensitivity to particular political and historical circumstances. That theory can provide the resources to explain the details of the many ways in which ANE peoples thought about the afterlife in terms of a single overarching view of personhood and its social dimensions. In the course of this volume, I have repeatedly put the theory to the test in this way.

---

[24] See also Chapter 11 n78.

As one example of a much more specific disagreement, let me single out Wright's discussion of Paul's claim that Jesus "has been raised on the third day according to scriptures" in the famous creedal formula of 1 Corinthians 15:3–5.[25] Wright recognizes, correctly enough, that Paul's claim is made with Scripture in view: Ezekiel 37 (which, given that it clearly uses metaphor to envision a collective reconstitution of Israel, is deemphasized) and Hosea 6:2. But, *because Jesus is not resurrected until Sunday morning*, Wright argues that Paul's (and early Christians') conception of what happened cannot be that it was a mere bodiless translation into heaven or a vivid way of speaking of the fulfillment of some hope. Rather, Paul must have received a tradition according to which (although Paul himself did not say this) Jesus' resurrection was *in the body*, a dateable, historical event that explains the Christian veneration of Sunday:[26]

> The phrase 'after three days', looking back mainly to Hosea 6.2, is frequently referred to in rabbinic mentions of the resurrection. This does not mean that Paul or anyone else in early Christianity supposed that it was a purely metaphorical statement, a vivid way of saying 'the biblical hope has been fulfilled'. In fact, the mention of any time-lag at all between Jesus' death and his resurrection is a further strong indication of what is meant by the latter: not only was Jesus' resurrection in principle a dateable event for the early Christians, but it was always something that took place, not immediately upon his death, but a short interval thereafter. If by Jesus' 'resurrection' the early church had meant that they believed he had attained a new state of glory with God, a special kind of non-bodily post-mortem existence, it is difficult to see why there should have been any interval at all; why should he have had to wait? If, however, the early church knew from the first that something dramatic had happened on the third day ... then not only the appeal to Hos. 6.2 ... but also the shift represented by the Christian use of Sunday as 'the lord's day', is fully explained.[27]

Wright goes on to insist upon the importance of Paul's listing of witnesses to the risen Christ (1 Cor. 15: 5–8). He avers that "despite the anguished protests of Bultmann and his followers," Paul's appeal to these witnesses can only be accounted for by supposing that indeed there *were* appearances to these five hundred-plus individuals, some of them named.[28]

---

[25] Wright, *The Resurrection of the Son of God*, 321ff.
[26] Or, at most, implies that the risen Lord had a spiritual body—whatever precisely he meant by that.
[27] Wright, *The Resurrection of the Son of God*, 322.
[28] See Ibid., 324–29.

I shall not say much about all this here. The detail concerning the three-day interval may seem relatively minor. It clearly is not. I have said much about it already in Chapter 11. One might observe, additionally, that (astonishingly), Wright simply ignores the theological theme of the harrowing of hell.[29] Here, I want to note the weakness of Wright's argument that only if the resurrection had happened immediately can we suppose that bodiless translation to heaven or glorification, and not bodily resurrection, could have been implied by what Paul said. Whether we can draw that inference *depends entirely upon whether there might be other explanations for why Paul—or his Christian sources, if any—would have insisted upon a three-day interval.* It depends, further, on whether the significance of Sunday as the Lord's Day might be otherwise explained.

And it depends most especially upon what other traditions (besides Ezekiel and Hosea) Paul might have had in view. It is noteworthy that in discussing this, Wright omits entirely reference to the most explicit Christian statement of the meaning of the three-day interval: Matthew 12: 39–40. Wright does mention Jonah 2:1, but only by citing it among other Hebrew Bible passages, and he has nothing to say about its significance for our understanding of the Gospel Passion Narratives or for Paul's understanding of the tradition he was handed. (Perhaps, of course, Wright thought that the tradition had undergone development by the time of the writing of the Gospels, but he does not argue this.)

And as for the five hundred witnesses, again, everything depends upon whether there are other—perhaps better—explanations for Paul's list at 1 Corinthians 15: 5. I think there is at least one such alternative explanation, and I believe it is one that better accounts for the data relevant to assessing this Pauline passage. My argument for that claim was presented in Chapter 9. In "The Surprise of the Resurrection," Wright explains the classical Jewish understanding of resurrection as involving (a) national restoration (Ezek. 37)—a metaphorical usage—and (b) (literally) a new embodiment for individual Jews by God at the end of time and perhaps later than the time of national restoration (e.g., the time of return from the exile).[30]

The Christians retain the notion of an end time resurrection of individuals and of the coming of the kingdom of God (both literal) but metaphorically describe baptism/holiness as a personal death and resurrection. But it looks like we have a metaphorical use of death and resurrection language for both individuals and the nation, if we think that, for individuals, what death/resurrection mean (for both Jews and Christians)

---

[29] Or does Wright imagine that Jesus could have accomplished that in the twinkling of an eye? Coronation rituals, which are rites of passage commonly involving "death/resurrection," often transpire over several days. See Chapter 4 n, ft. 57 above on the pharaohs. And on the Ndembu data, Chapter 6 §III.

[30] Wright, "The Surprise of the Resurrection," 90–91.

is that individuals "die to" their old social selves, as having embodied personages whose social identities were defined by their positions in the old Israel, and that they are "born again" as citizens of the new Israel.

And this applies equally to the traditional Jewish "literal" meaning of individual resurrection and the Christian "metaphor" describing baptism as effecting, for the living, entry into the new kingdom of God. This also may explain Paul's reference to people being baptized "on behalf of the dead" (1 Cor. 15:29; cf. 2 Macc. 12:39–45): that is, one can undergo a baptism that retroactively transfers citizenship from the old social order to the new Christian one, for a departed relative who did not convert in this life, perhaps because they died before the gospel had been preached in Corinth. That is to say, the convert sheds his/her old social identity and "puts on" a new, immortal personage, understood as citizenship in the eternal kingdom of God. And, of course, this is anticipatory in the sense that the kingdom has not yet visibly established itself on earth as a kingdom having effective dominion over all the nations. It has such dominion only proleptically. Nevertheless, there is perfect continuity in essential meaning between the understanding of the resurrection in the Jewish background and its adoption by Christians.

Wright then cites several features of the Passion Narratives that call for explanation and that can only, or best, be explained (he thinks) by supposing that "something like" a bodily resurrection of Jesus in fact occurred.[31] These are:

1) The disciples would have either disbanded or found a new messiah had Jesus been crucified and not been *bodily* raised. A more "spiritual" event would not have cut it. Nobody, including the disciples, would have understood a leader who was killed, and then stayed physically dead, as the Messiah. Nor did any Jew imagine an individual bodily resurrection that would precede the general resurrection at the end of time. Wright notes that 2 Maccabees 7 expects the future bodily resurrections of Jewish heroes martyred by Antiochus IV.[32] There is no anticipation of a general resurrection, but at least there is no claim that the heroes had already enjoyed return to life. Thus, Jesus' resurrection was a big surprise—and the jolt that brought the disciples back together as a unified movement.

2) There are plenty of citations/allusions to scriptural texts in the events leading up to Easter Sunday but none—or almost none—in the Easter day narratives.[33] Wright concedes that the tradition understands the

---

[31] See Wright, *The Resurrection of the Son of God*, 92–97.
[32] Ibid., 150–53.
[33] Cf. Ibid., 599–602.

resurrection as a fulfillment of scripture—as "according to the scriptures."[34] John 20:9 says that Peter and the other disciple who ran to the empty tomb "did not yet understand the (unspecified) scripture that he must have risen from the dead." And again, Jesus' Scripture lesson to the two disciples on the road to Emmaus (Luke 24:25–27) is related but without mentioning for which Scriptures Jesus was providing an exegesis. (Though Luke does say that Jesus interpreted to them "all the scriptures" beginning with Moses—which suggests a Bible lesson designed to show that the entirety of the Tanach had as its ultimate purpose the task of preparing the Jews for the coming of their Lord.)

Now it is perhaps not as hard as Wright makes out to guess Scriptures that these passages are meant to point to and that Luke and John would have expected their readers particularly to have brought to mind. Foremost among these, surely, will be the story of Jonah, alluded to at Matthew 12:40/Luke 11:30–32, which implies, after all, a return from the realm of death. But, in an even more detailed way, the trilogy of Psalms 22–24 provides a summary of the entire Passion Narrative, from the apparent defeat by the powers of death to the final victory. In particular, Wright fails to note the close parallels between Psalms 24 and Matthew's resurrection narrative: the meeting upon a mountain with those who have clean hands and pure hearts (= the disciples: Ps. 24:3–5; cf. Matt. 28:16), and the parallel between Psalms 24:1–2; 7–10, which declare Yahweh's dominion over the entire earth and his triumphant advent, and Matthew 28:18–19, which celebrates Christ's victory over death and the inauguration of his conquest of "all the nations."

Nor is that all: the Passion Narratives' use of Isaiah 53 also sets the scene for the Easter appearances. 1 Corinthians 15:3 describes Christ's atoning death as "according to scriptures"—presumably a reference to Isaiah 53:10.[35] The passage continues with affirmations that the suffering servant will "see his offspring," "mak[ing] many righteous." Is this not Scripture enough? Luke's language suggests that Jesus must have gone much further in instructing the two journeying disciples, no doubt with passages from Isaiah, Hosea, and the other prophets in mind, to say nothing of the Pentateuch.

Wright's inference is that we have here an historical report, not stories constructed with Scripture in view. But this is hardly persuasive. The suggestion that the dearth of explicit scriptural allusions in the Easter day narratives implies that they were not constructed out of creatively

---

[34] Wright, *The Resurrection of the Son of God*, 600.
[35] So at Luke 22:37, Jesus declares near the time of his arrest that "this scripture must be fulfilled in me, 'And he was counted among the lawless'... " a quotation of Isa. 53:12.

marshalled themes from the Hebrew Bible falls flat and with it the inference that these narratives must hark back to historical memories of Easter. Wright's reasoning ignores the fast pace required by the narrative and that the evangelists have plenty of other business to conduct in these few verses.

Much more importantly, it imagines that somehow, those verses can be torn asunder from the Passion Narratives taken as unities, with their abundant references to Scripture. It is almost as if Wright were prepared to allow (as in fact he would not be) that the Easter events took place, even though many of the symbol-laden events leading to them perhaps did not!

3) The embarrassment of women as the first witnesses to the empty tomb—a popular argument which has been disposed of in Chapter 11.

4) Jesus' resurrection involves the transformation of his ordinary human body into a new kind of immortal body. This is alleged to be radically different from both pagan conceptions—no one comes back from the dead—and traditional Jewish conceptions of resurrection, which range from resurrection as a figure for national restoration (Ezekiel) to translation into the heavens in the form of shining stars (Daniel 7). A whole range of apocryphal texts from the intertestamental period speak of a bodily resurrection, but no Jew, Wright maintains, expected such a thing to happen before all—or all who merit it—are raised together at the end of time. Jesus, in short, breaks all the molds. Such a resurrection could not have been anticipated by his disciples (even though Jesus seems several times to have given advance notice). The rare survivors of death in Jewish tradition are not resurrected, for they are translated into the presence of God without undergoing death: Enoch, Elijah, and, in some traditions, Moses and Noah. So they, too, offer no precedents for Jesus' resurrection.

But this argument suffers from both two general problems and a specific weakness. The first general difficulty is one we have met above and in Chapter 3: what kinds of difference between cases are significant, and in what ways are they significant? What sorts of similarities are significant, and in what ways? Unless we have some way of evaluating these, appeal to similarities and differences proves very little. A more specific weakness bears treatment here.

Wright disqualifies the case of Moses (and that of Noah) as precedents because, although there are Jewish and Christian traditions in which they have been translated into a heavenly realm postmortem, there are also traditions in which they did not die but underwent assumption in the mold of Enoch and Elijah. True: but in the canon, Noah and Moses both clearly died. All that matters here is that some Jews could believe them to have been resurrected *while also believing them to have died*. Is Wright claiming to know that only Jews who denied the latter believed the former? How could he know such a thing as that? Were the legends denying death composed in that way *to* allow for Moses'/Noah's ongoing existence?

The second, more general problem with Wright's reasoning is that it presupposes that we must search for an explanation for the dearth of scriptural material in the resurrection narratives under the presuppositions that Jesus was in fact crucified and buried in a known grave and that any confabulated story of a resurrection would have to adhere to Jewish (or, at the outside, Hellenistic) understandings of what a resurrection should look like. That simply discounts the possibility that Christian tradents tailored their resurrection accounts—even if constructed out of materials handed down to them from the Hebrew Bible, intertestamental Jewish sources, or pagan myths—to the specific requirements of the situation they faced and the message they meant to convey about how that situation was to be engaged. Indeed, it discounts the possibility of creativity in introducing new mythemes, if need be, to answer to the needs of time and message.

But that sort of reasoning, pushed to its logical conclusion, is, we have noted, incoherent. It would suggest that *no one* could invent new arrangements of traditional material, nor could they introduce material that is novel. Were that the case, how would the traditions themselves ever have started? Are we to suppose that they all must have their roots in actual historical events? To see that this sort of view is implausible, it is sufficient to observe the way natural languages themselves are vehicles for the formulation and communication of new ideas.

Most of this involves simply the generation of new sentences from existing vocabulary. Similarly, mythographers can draw upon an existing vocabulary of mythemes to construct myths that articulate new politics. Or, when existing vocabulary fails, we invent new words. The mythographer, in a quite parallel way, invents new mythemes. Of course, cues of various kinds must be deployed to convey new meanings. But this is commonplace. Were it not so, neither myths nor languages themselves could ever have been created in the first place. When Wright argues that the default position is historicity if we cannot find close precedents for the Jesus resurrection story in ANE myth traditions, he sits on a stool that had no legs.

IV. Focus on the Family

There is a particularly dramatic way in which the Gospels do break prior precedent, indeed, a precedent undoubtedly older than recorded human history. One of the more disturbing themes of the Gospels is the teaching concerning family solidarity. Jesus is almost uniformly portrayed as antagonistic to domestic loyalties, sometimes stridently so. Nor is this a minor or marginal motif. On the contrary, it is a recurring refrain. There are apparent exceptions—notably Matthew 19:19 and arguably Matthew 19:8/Luke 16:18 on divorce. The "anti-family" passages include Matthew 8:21 (let the dead bury the dead); 10:34–40/Luke 12:49–53; Matthew 12:46–50/Mark 3:31–35; Matthew 18:15–18; 19:10–12 (men who make themselves eunuchs for heaven); Matthew 19:29/Mark 10:29; Matthew 21:43/Mark 12:1–12/Luke 20:9–19; Matthew 23:9 (call no man your father on earth, for you have one Father, who is in heaven); Luke 2:49; 8:19–23; 11:27–28; 12:51–53; 14:26–27; and possibly John 2:4.

Most of these texts come from Matthew and Luke, but we find a few also in Mark and John. Outside the Gospels themselves, we have a passing imperative against arguing over genealogies at Titus 3:9 that seems directed against the relevance to Christians of family background and an extended argument in Hebrews 7 that identifies Jesus as a priest after the order of Melchizedek. The entire passage is one that devalues kinship. For Melchizedek, a "king of righteousness," is "Without father, without mother, without genealogy, having neither beginning of days nor end of life, but resembling the Son of God, he remains a priest forever" (Heb. 7:2–3).

From the fact that Genesis 14:17–20 supplies no genealogy for Melchizedek, the author of Hebrews infers that he had none, that he is not a kinsman of Abraham and therefore no Israelite, and even that he is immortal. Because Abraham pays him tribute, he is greater than Abraham. Similarly, "our Lord" is not a mere Levitical priest.[36] By virtue of being of the order of Melchizedek, he is someone to whom the Levitical priests owe tribute (cf. Heb. 7:9–10), and, like Melchizedek, he has neither beginning nor end. Thus, both Melchizedek and the Christ are situated above tribal identities.[37]

Among the strident anti-family sayings in the Gospels, we may single out Matthew 10:34–40/Luke 12:49–53 and Luke 14:25–27 as being particularly explicit and pungent. So Matthew 10:34–40: "Do not think that I have come to bring peace on earth; I have not come to bring peace but the sword. For I have come to set a man against his father, and a daughter against her mother-in-law... " And Luke 14:26–27: "Whoever comes to me and does not hate father and mother, wife and children ... and even life itself, cannot be my disciple." (Though one might bridle at it, the Greek term

---

[36] It is perhaps significant that here the author of Hebrews uses "our Lord" rather than "Jesus," arguably reflecting recognition of the distinction between the man and his role.

[37] Hebrews offers a clever argument: as a descendant of Judah, our Lord cannot be a priest after the order of Aaron. Being a non-Aaronite priest, our Lord is a priest under a new law (the new covenant presented in Heb. 8). This new priest has authority "not through a legal requirement concerning physical descent, but through the power of an indestructible life" (Heb. 7:16).

μισεῖν does mean "hate." But, I shall argue shortly, it does not mean here to refer to an emotional state.) What are we to make of these—certainly bracing!—teachings?

The usual apologetic is that in Matthew 10 and Luke 14, Jesus is not categorically demanding kin-hatred. Rather than expressing antipathy toward family loyalties, his remarks reflect a regretful recognition that discipleship will put many of his followers at sharp odds with their families. He is nevertheless insisting that, when the chips are down (but only then), a true disciple puts first his or her loyalty to God. And one can cite Jesus' own alienation from his family to make the point that he speaks here from painful personal experience. A number of passages speak of this alienation: his family seems to think him mad (Mark 3:21), he is rejected by his hometown (Matt. 13:57/Mark 6:4), he is distrusted by his brothers (John 7:5), and he foresees that in any case "Brother will betray brother to death, and a father his child, and children will rise against their parents and have them put to death" (Matt. 10:21–22/Mark 13:12–13/Luke 21:16–17). So, it seems that family enmity is inevitable. Yet, only a few verses later (in Matthew), Jesus says that he himself comes in order to bring about this frightful calamity. Might this be an undesired but inescapable side effect of Jesus' greater mission in ushering in his kingdom? Yet even this would not be well reflected by the language of Matthew 10:34–40 and Luke 14:25–27.

Consider, then, another astringent saying, at Matthew 8:2, where Jesus responds to a disciple who begs a few days' leave to go bury his father before following Jesus. Disturbingly, Jesus responds, "Follow me, and let the dead bury their own dead." One is naturally struck by the apparent callousness of the reply and by the question: What can Jesus mean in suggesting that the dead are to be buried by their own? It will be natural to suppose, as to this question, that Jesus means that there are some—in general those who do not follow him—that are spiritually dead. It is these who are in a position to perform the rites of burial.

While this may be Jesus' meaning, it hardly serves to remove the sting of his reply to the disciple. Why can't also disciples bury their fathers and mothers? There is hardly any more important duty that a Jew owed to his father than to afford him a proper burial. Abandoning that duty would be a serious violation of the fifth commandment (affirmed by Jesus: Matt. 19:19), the first of the commandments that do not concern the honor owed to God. Nor could it have been anything less than a radical break with Jewish religious sensibilities to oppose honor owed to parents to honor owed to God.

We can make some progress with both the rebarbativeness of Jesus' reply and the question of who "the dead" are if we see it as the purpose of the passage to signal a dramatic break in the social order, one that threatens the social practices that preserve social order at all levels. And in a tribal context, this would apply most particularly to institutional forms of continuity of families from one generation to the next. In that case, Jesus is not really expressing disdain for whatever feelings his disciple might naturally have for his departed father but is rejecting those practices situated in a now-to-be-superannuated past. To be "spiritually dead," therefore, would be to remain committed to that past. We do better, if this is correct, *not* to envision Matthew's literary purpose here to be an evocation of a realistic conversation between a bereaved disciple and his spiritual leader but as a kind of parable meant to convey a fundamental aspect of the subversive agenda that Matthew's Jesus means to teach.

As I noted, the notion that loyalty and due respect to family can somehow be in deep conflict with the worship of God was an utterly alien notion, not indeed only in ancient Israel, but in practically every known society from that day to our own in this. If Jesus had in mind what the common apologetic claims, he could hardly have found a more unfortunate way to express his point. He should (and therefore would) have rather said, respecting so delicate a matter, exactly that he had no wish to foment family disunity but understood that, sadly, his mission required of his followers commitments that might alienate family members. "Make peace with father, mother, sisters, brothers, your children, if at all you can. But if not, then the hour is short and God calls us to his wedding; make haste."

Jesus could have said that, but he did not. Rather: "Do not think that I have come to bring peace to the earth; I have not come to bring peace but a sword. For I have come to set a man against his father ... " Indeed, the "dead bury the dead" exchange can hardly be read any other way: there is no possibility for the disciple's dead father to disapprove of his commitment to Jesus. A number of other passages reinforce the insistence upon family enmity and help to pull us away from the natural impression that what Jesus is trying to promote is some kind of personal hostility towards one's kin. Their bearing in this way is more evident if one reads all these passages as commentary on structural matters—that is, upon the system of social/legal relations upon which traditional Israelite society was built.

We may begin with the sayings in which Jesus redefines his family— or, if you prefer—substitutes a new idea for the old one of kinship. Rejecting an audience with his mother and brothers, he declares: "Who is my mother, and who are my brothers?....whoever does the will of my Father in heaven is my brother and sister and mother" (Matt. 12:46–50; cf. Mark 3:31–35/Luke 8:18–21). Here, Jesus points to his disciples—those who follow him—as the ones who are the doers of the divine will. So, the old family, based upon kinship, is to be replaced by a new "family," one based upon fealty to the Father, mediated by his son, the Christ.

It is not hard to see how this could be a dangerous doctrine, a recipe for a demagogue hell-bent upon tyranny. But something deeper is actually at issue here, and we have but to be reminded of the Gospels' consistent portrayal of the Lord, who is also a servant and who is prepared above all to sacrifice himself for the sake of his subjects, to see that the kind of rulership that the Gospels mean to portray Jesus as embodying is the antithesis of despotism. Jesus is rejecting kin relations as a basis for solidarity. In their place, he is offering a substitute: a community of friendship in, and with, the Lord who mediates between his community and the Lord of heaven.

Just as he has rejected the temple as the locus of sanctity, so here he rejects blood relationship in favor of a blood that can be consecrated anywhere. Zion has been traded for a portable internal temple that can go anywhere a Christian travels. Tribal membership confined by criteria of parentage is put aside for affiliation with a king. That makes kingdom membership a matter of choice, not birth: one is "re-born," not biologically but socially. Jesus' kingdom, therefore, is one whose boundaries are defined by neither territory nor tribe.

It can hardly be overemphasized how subversive and revolutionary this cluster of ideas is. From our perspective, such a shift in thinking about the bases of national unity may seem natural, perhaps almost trivial. But that would reflect a failure to appreciate the grip of kinship as an organizing principle and social glue. A proper recognition of this is one of the insights anthropology can provide. In taking aim at sacred land and family, the Jesus of the Gospels is attacking the two most fundamental principles of social cohesion of the ancient world. What is being proposed, therefore, is a jettisoning of the only such principles that had been generally known and relied upon by human societies in the ANE's (and perhaps the human?) past and their replacement by something fundamentally new.

If this is so, then the inventive genius of the early Christian ideologues addressed the crisis of their day with a level of theoretical penetration unmatched, perhaps, by even such thinkers as John Locke or Karl Marx. Out of a tribal way of understanding the bonds of citizenship and the legal and institutional structures of an ordered society, the Christians saw a path to a new social basis for citizenship, one that was inherently elastic. Tribal membership is limited by ties of blood and marriage. And it is, in a sense, imposed rather than voluntary. In rejecting those constraints, the early Christian thinkers faced squarely a political crisis that had troubled Near-Eastern civilization for some hundreds of years: the problem of empire. When one tribe conquers (and means to retain control over) others, the choices are stark: occupation, client nation status, or extermination. The powerful nations of the ANE had hobbled along with such expedients, costly in both life and resources, for many centuries.

Rome itself had initiated the possibility for citizenship for foreigners. But it could hardly provide any deep legal theory to underwrite the *de facto* existence of a Roman order that far outstripped the theoretical resources of the tribal society that remained at the heart of Rome's identity. Virgil's *Aeneid* made a gesture at addressing the problem of trans-tribal unity in recounting a merger of two such societies: the remnants of Troy and Latium. But we do not see in the *Aeneid* any fundamental rethinking of principles of social unity. By marrying Lavinia, Aeneus becomes the crown-prince of Latium. As ever, kinship stands as a governing principle of union.

Once we see Jesus' attack upon the family for what it is—an attack upon the very foundational principle of Jewish identity—we can at the same time reasonably infer that his target is not the *affective states* of family members, the emotional content of their relationships. Although those are not in practice easily teased apart from jural and institutional relations, they are a distinct matter. Letting go of the latter need not entail hostility or even lack of love toward one's kin. Those emotions might, indeed, strongly motivate one to persuade loved ones to join in the new social order to which one has made a commitment.

But what, exactly, was the new social order into which Jesus was intent upon drawing his followers? The Matthew 21 parable of the evil tenants certainly provides a strong hint: the "vineyard"—God's chosen people, Israel—will be given to a foreign people and its ruling class deposed. Those foreigners can only have been the Romans. But Matthew cannot possibly mean to be saying that Israel will become subject to the Roman Imperium, not only because Jesus is neither turncoat nor traitor, but because Israel was already precisely under that kind of governance. What remains is the possibility that Rome itself will be conquered, not by force of arms, but by the power of a new ideology that will permit it to make sense of its own *de facto* existence and at the same time permit institutional reform that will give *de jure* legitimacy to its (reformed) political structures.

The old Rome transformed will be the new Jerusalem, and the Jewish people, as keepers of the traditions and having bestowed upon Rome its new vision, will be seen as by divine election occupying a special place in the divine providence: but only insofar as Israel itself, like all the other nations that are to be united into the new kingdom, is able to leave behind its attachment to kinship as a determiner of social identity and citizenship in God's city. On this reading, then, the parable of the evil tenants is itself one of the anti-family teachings, one that broadly hints at the rationale for Jesus' opposition to kin ties.

V. The Good News

Our task, now, is to explain why, given the circumstances of the evangelists and the message they intended to convey, it would be natural, perhaps even inevitable, that they would tell a story of a king who begins life as a village artisan (but with a royal genealogy), is unjustly murdered by the existing powers but conquers death, and who then continues to exist for a time in the presence of God in a very special kind of body. It would explain, finally, why we (or, rather, denizens of the Roman Imperium) could expect him to return in power to govern his earthly kingdom when that time has been fulfilled. We have assembled enough pieces of the puzzle to see, schematically, how such an explanation will go. Jesus is the new savior of Israel, one who was sent by Yahweh to answer to the desperate condition in which Yahweh's people found themselves. He is, therefore, a king, a messiah who will reestablish the throne of David even while unsullied by the political baggage of the current establishment.

Like several other signal saviors sent to Israel by Yahweh, he is seen as having started the process of Israel's salvation but not to have consummated the achievement of her aspirations. He has demonstrated, through his ministry—his teachings, healings, miraculous control over the chaos-waters, and enactment of victory over the powers of darkness—what his kingdom will look like. He has already come into his kingdom (but only proleptically) by being crowned the legitimate heir to the Davidic throne, a throne now transformed into the *cathedra* of the emperor in Rome.

The reality on the ground, of course, looks otherwise. Israel remains under the cruel thumb of the Imperium. But the wheels of history have been set in motion, and, through the dedicated efforts of Jesus' communicants, those wheels will lead to the overthrow of the present order and the establishment, in fully visible form, of a new Eternal City, one that will exist not only *de jure* but fully embodied on the face of the earth. In the meantime, however, the persona of the Christ must be put in cold storage, as it were, while the outpouring of the Holy Spirit upon the new material body of Christ—the church—will carry forward the divine imprimatur and new covenant. Like Enoch and Elijah, like Moses in some Jewish traditions, Jesus—or rather, the Christ—is "salted away" in heaven until his final hour, the hour of triumphant return upon the clouds, when he becomes visible to all.[38] *That* is the story, and *that* is why Jesus must "die," must undergo the mortifying battle with the powers of darkness, achieving a victory over them

---

[38] That something like this idea was in the air in Judea during the first century is supported by the development of the Danielic "son of man" tradition in Jewish texts roughly contemporaneous with the rise of Christianity. Thus, *11QMelchizedek*, the *Similitudes of Enoch*, and *4 Ezra* variously associate the expression "son of man" with Melchizedek, Enoch, or some quasi-human/divine agent who is variously "pre-existent," may have an earthly career, or may reside in heaven and exercise rulership over the earth from there as judge and sovereign. See John Collins' discussion in Adela Yarbro Collins and John J. Collins, *King and Messiah as the Son of God: Divine, Human, and Angelic Messianic Figures in Biblical and Related Literature* (Grand Rapids, MI: William B. Eerdmans Publishing Company, 2008), 79–98. Lacking an earthly, functioning royal house not in thrall to the Romans, we may speculate, Jews found attractive the idea that their ancient traditions nevertheless were preserved in a state of suspended animation (cf. Chapter 4), awaiting the opportunity to reemerge.

that has only proleptic standing until Rome has seen the error of her ways and planted her flag in the Christian camp.[39]

And, finally, *that* is why Jesus—or rather, the immortally embodied personage of the Christ—had to rise from the dead, commission his church, and then disappear into the clouds for a time. It is hard to imagine any *other* way the evangelists could have represented what they needed to convey. And so, making allowance for the interesting and significant variations in the story's details, which explore the richness of the symbolic possibilities, all of the Gospels center upon the very same fundamental vision.

VI. Roman Vacancies

Marianne Bonz gave a good summary of the political chaos that followed the reign of Augustus.[40] It was a reign that Augustan propaganda, epitomized in Virgil's *Aeneid* and many other literary efforts (including Augustus' own *Res Gestae*) tried to establish as the inauguration of a Golden Age of Roman rule over an eternal empire. This was soon proved a pipedream with the incompetency (and worse) of three of Augustus' four Julian successors, Tiberius, Caligula, and Nero, soon followed by the demise of the Julio-Claudian dynasty and the rise of the Flavians.[41]

These developments spawned works by imitators of the *Aeneid* that, in a variety of ways, walked back the original claim that the Augustan kingdom represented the culmination and fulfillment of a Roman history, guided by a destiny ordained by the gods. That destiny, history seemed now to show, had not yet come to proper fruition with Augustus. The truth is, the destiny of Rome and the legitimacy of its rulers were both at the mercy of power politics. Nothing like a settled and stable charter for the governing structures, civic virtues, or legitimate sources of authority had managed to entrench itself in the Roman's cultural consciousness or social institutions.

In spite of periods of stability under the rule of the successor Flavian Dynasty (a period that saw the composition of the four canonical Gospels), Rome might fairly be described during the first century as having been subject to recurrent inundation by the chaos-waters. This was manifested, of course, in the failure of any one dynasty to establish a secure

---

[39] Or, perhaps more accurately, until Rome has accepted the planting of the Christian flag in *its* camp—as, allegedly, Constantine did in raising the Christian banner in his decisive victories against his rival Maxentius at the battle of Milvian Bridge and subsequent battles against the rival emperor Licinius.

[40] Marianne Palmer Bonz, *The Past as Legacy: Luke-Acts and Ancient Epic* (Minneapolis, MN: Fortress Press, 2000), 61–86.

[41] Claudius, the third successor of Augustus, was at least moderately competent.

dominance over rivals and a regularized set of rules of succession. But at a deeper level, it represented a failure of the efforts of Augustus' court poets, and of those who followed in their footsteps during the reigns of his successors, to formulate an adequate and effective political ideology, one that could both command consensus and mobilize a reorganization of Roman institutions into ones insuring effective governance. In considerable measure, this appears to have been due to a strategy of backing claims to legitimacy by promoting a cult of individual greatness and uniqueness.

It might seem, at first blush, that if ever there were a group that cultivated a cult centered on the unique greatness of a particular individual, the early Christians would qualify. But, I want to argue, this assessment would misunderstand the Christian project. What is important about Jesus Christ is that he provides a model, a paradigm of correct and ideal sovereignty to which a proper king must, given the fundamental realities of the Mediterranean world during the early centuries of this era, aspire. More than that, it is essential that the legitimacy of such a king be seen in terms of a true understanding of the nature of the society over which he rules and of the kind of society it ought to become.

The Caesars all claimed descent from the gods. Some of them came to be hailed as themselves gods. But their divine progenitors were hardly models of incorruptible virtue or justice, so claims to a legitimacy rooted in descent from such mothers and fathers could not but inherit the deeper question: why should we—why should anyone—worship these gods? Why should Rome aspire to Olympus? Mere loyalty to ancient traditions was no longer a sufficient answer to that question. Still, loyalty to ancient traditions has to be part of the answer. To map a route to one's destination, one needs a proper understanding of one's present location.

It is clear enough that for the authors of the New Testament, the starting location was understood to be deeply rooted in the heritage of Judaism. It is equally clear that these authors were grappling, in insistent ways, with the question of how to come to terms with hellenization and with the realities of Roman rule. Our question is: what, in fact, did they understand their destination to be? At what terminus was their journey aimed? To say that this terminus was taken to be the *parousia*, a general resurrection and judgment, and presently, a kingdom of heaven, is to recite familiar categories but not to elucidate what, for early Christians, they might have been conceived to involve.

A good deal of effort has been devoted to determining what Jesus understood the kingdom of God to be and what he understood the scheduling of its advent to be. I have not attempted to answer either of those questions. But I have said what I think the author of Matthew thought about these matters. For Matthew—and also, I think, for Paul and the other three evangelists—the kingdom of God was to be a kingdom, essentially coinciding at the material level with the Roman Empire, governed by the god Yahweh and his earthly vicar, the Christ, who would occupy the (suitably reformed) position held by the emperor.

While recognizably Rome, the kingdom of God would be under new management and adhere to a new set of organizing principles and laws, ones rooted neither in exclusively Roman tribal identity and history nor in that of Israel (or any other ethnic group laboring under the Roman yoke). Thus, both the empire and its rulers had to be transformed. The Roman Caesars were illegitimate—the spawn of a series of coups d'etat, of corruption and violent palace intrigue, and of competing forces within the Roman army. A Davidic king would have a claim to legitimacy—in Israel—but not as the king of a polity whose membership was to be defined neither in terms of land and temple nor in terms of blood. Thus, it was imperative that the kingship itself be redefined. The sources of its legitimacy had to be conceived in a fundamentally new way, a way that abandoned blood inheritance and foregrounded the king's role as *soter*, the servant of his people, the guarantor of both peace and justice, the first to risk his own wellbeing for the sake of the nation in the face of mortal danger.

As a Davidic king and Messiah, Jesus removes the curse of corrupt Roman rule over Israel. Just as Moses leads Israel out of Egyptian bondage, just as Yahweh "brought up out of the sea the shepherds of his flock," (Isa. 63:11), so too Jesus symbolically confronts, apparently on foreign soil, a demoniac who embodies the ultimate pollution—association with pigs and tombs, an antisocial hermit, acting madly and tearing off all the constraints of civilized behavior (cf. 65:4–5). Just as God drowns Pharaoh's pursuing forces in the sea, so Jesus expels the demons—named Legion and presumably a reference to an illegitimate Roman occupying force—and drowns them in the sea.

The new kingship will be defined by new rules. Kinship does play a role in regularizing the line of succession—but as a metaphor: legitimate inheritance of the throne is through divine election as Son. The power of the king would be absolute (or rather, constrained only by the will of God)—but his rule deeply egalitarian.[42] At the same time, it was essential to see how such a kingship could emerge out of a tribal context for, fundamentally, such a context provided the one coherent and thoroughly theorized legal basis for social organization and identity that human social evolution had until this

---

[42] This appears to be the message of 1 Cor. 15: 22–28; esp. "'For God has put all things in subjection under his feet.' But when it says, 'All things are put in subjection,' it is plain that this does not include the one who puts all things in subjection under him. When all things are subjected to him, then the Son himself will also be subjected to the one who put all things in subjection under him, so that God may be all in all" (vv. 27–28). Not only is the man who fulfills the royal office subject, *qua* citizen, to the laws that, *qua* monarch, he legislates, but the royal office itself is subject to the will of God—that is, to the General Will, as Rousseau would have put it. Thus, we have in place a double hedge against tyranny.

time developed. Jesus, therefore, begins as a figure whose royal destiny emerges out of the house of David, a tribal monarch. But he ends his career by being crowned imperator—the true heir to the throne in Rome.

When was this new kingdom inaugurated? Was it already there in Jesus' day? Was it in process of being born? Or was it something future? If we think of the kingdom as I have suggested we should, we can see that these possibilities offer a false choice. Early Christians would have understood that their goal—a stable, righteously, and legitimately governed Empire—was a dream for the future. However, it would also have been understood that any realistic hope for a *de jure* future reality could only be fulfilled if the ground had been prepared by inaugurating both *de facto* changes in social relations on a large scale and *de jure* changes within smaller communities.

It is this that would have defined the mission of the early church, not only to Israel, but to Gentile communities across the empire. Paul and the Gospels attempted to give the world in which they lived a vision of what such communities would look like and of how they were to conduct outreach both to ordinary folk and to those in positions of power. As the historical record shows, they were, in the long run—considerably longer than their early rhetoric envisioned—remarkably successful in this.[43]

Although it can easily enough be denied that in the Holy Roman Empire, justice rolled down like waters, it is a remarkable fact that Christianity conquered, from within as it were, the center of the Roman state, so that Constantine himself could be depicted as the *parousia*.[44] The

---

[43] Given the magnitude of their political agenda, it seems unlikely that the leaders of the early Christian movement could seriously have entertained the possibility of achieving the intended reformation of the empire in a single lifespan (even measured from the time of the writing of the later Gospels). Whether the rhetoric was sincere or not, the prophecy of immanent overthrow of the old order fits a pattern characteristic of millenarian movements (e.g. Melanesian cargo cults, the Ghost Dance Movement among Native American tribes, and others) the world over.

[44] By Eusebius of Caesarea, *Life of Constantine*, trans. Averil Cameron and Stuart G. Hall (Oxford: Clarendon Press, 1999), 121–27; III.1.8–3.3; 4.7–8; 10; 15. These passages, which are certainly hagiographic, are at once coy and provocatively pointed. In the first, Eusebius describes in some detail a painting Constantine commissioned of himself, with the sign of the Christ above his head, and the body of the dragon, pierced by a spear, trodden beneath his feet and the feet of his sons. And in this connection, he pronounces Constantine the fulfillment of the prophecy given by Isa. 27:1. In the second passage, Eusebius describes the assembly of the bishops at Nicaea as a replica (only even better) of the Pentecostal reception of the Holy Spirit in Acts 2. One cannot but be reminded of John 15:26–16:33, where Jesus foretells his sending the Spirit to his disciples to communicate his truths until he returns; the passage ends with the triumphant "I have conquered the world!" The third passage describes Constantine's humble entrance at the council, and the fourth an imperial banquet, with all the bishops present. Eusebius remarks, "It might have been supposed that it was an imaginary representation of the kingdom of Christ, and that what was happening was 'dream, not fact'" (apparently

Christian way to salvation, and the nature of the salvation on offer, were formulated in ways that bespoke pure genius. The stories that proclaimed the kingdom enchant the deepest longings of the human heart, but, most of all, they answered the most desperate and universal needs of their own age. Few revolutions in political understanding have equaled their standard, either in conceptual depth and originality or in pastoral efficacy.

---

quoting Homer, Odyssey, 19.547 and, more significantly, Isa. 25:6–9, 26:6; Matt. 8:11, 22:1–14, 26:29/Luke 22:15–19; and Luke 13:29, which Eusebius surely meant to evoke). For other related passages in both the Hebrew Bible and NT, see Horsley, *Jesus and the Spiral of Violence*, 173–74.

Afterward

I have given a reading of the Gospel of Saint Matthew that understands it as a radical rethinking of human political existence and as a solution to a long-range political crisis in the ANE that threatened—though not for the first time—the very existence of Israel. It was a crisis caused by the process of evolution from nations with more or less cohesive tribal identities to empire. Rather than a military expulsion of Rome or the military domination of the eastern Mediterranean dreamed of by the postexilic prophets, it proposed what amounted to political subversion of an existing empire, an empire that aspired to endure the ages.

The other Gospels, each in its somewhat distinctive voice, pursued the same general agenda by portraying Jesus as a new kind of king. Paul, whether suddenly or over a period of time, came to see in the ideas of the earliest Christians a path that could be developed into a movement and an ideology powerful enough that it might, just might, unseat the apparently invincible forces of corruption that held Rome and empire in their thrall, forces that were destroying the fabric of Jewish existence and put Rome itself in a state of perennial turmoil. For him, as a committed Pharisee, this realization of what Christian ideas might achieve must have come as a wrenching sea-change, a paradigm shift.

It is hard to know what pre-Pauline, primitive Christianity looked like and how much the mind of Paul himself contributed to the ideological direction it took as it began its mission to convert the Gentile world. I have made no attempt to peel away those layers of tradition and to expose a truly "original" Christian church or an historical portrait of a founding prophet. My aim has rather been to understand the Christianity we find in the NT texts, the Christianity that, quite explicitly though in the thinly veiled language of Revelation, contemplated the destruction of the existing Roman political order—though not the destruction of its Mediterranean real estate.

This conception of the New Testament will, for most readers, seem quite alien. To read the New Testament in this way will itself require a paradigm shift. More than that, it will provoke an obvious question or objection: Since the New Testament is *not* read this way by Christians today (or at least by most Christians)—and has not been for a long time, when—and how—did such a radical reconception of these texts, the transformation from a political understanding to a "theological" (in the modern sense) interpretation take place? When, and how, did the modern reading of the New Testament as the record of an historical moment in which some of Israel received a new illumination from God (the God of modern theism) emerge and the political intentions of the New Testament authors recede and depart?

If I knew that answer to that question and undertook to provide it, this book would be many times longer than it is, for I am convinced that the process was a slow one, occurring in stages over the course of many centuries, centuries with whose history I am not intimately familiar. At the nearer end, of course, stand the ideas of John Locke, who strove to disentangle church and state, for reasons that were themselves essentially political. Near the further end stand the inception and development of the doctrine of the two swords and St. Augustine's signal *The City of God*. Here, I shall confine myself to the briefest of comments about what I see as the likely beginnings of the divorce between the church's conception of itself and its mission and the fate of the Roman Empire.

I. A Divine City

That these had been intimately bound together can hardly be denied. By the early fifth century, when Augustine wrote *The City of God*, Rome had long styled itself the "Eternal City," and Christians, it seems, must have commonly identified this city with the New Jerusalem. For had they not, how is it that Augustine felt the necessity to defend his faith against pagan derision that Christianity, having promised to found a new city that would last forever (or for a thousand years), had inherited an empire whose capital city fell to Visigoth invaders less than a century after the conversion of Constantine?[1] Augustine's defense against this scandal was (among much else in *The City of God*) a vigorous, extended argument that God's city was not to be identified with any mundane city or state.

But of course such a defense would have made little sense if the pagans had not been able to embarrass Christendom by pointing to some substantial number of Christians who saw the Christianized Roman Empire as the vindication of their eschatological prophecies. When Alaric (himself at least a nominal Christian) was beaten into a temporary retreat from his military advance on Rome by Stilicho at the battle of Pollentia (402 CE), the Christian poet Prudentius could portray the defeat as proof of the eternal

---

[1] The intervening decades had seen the more or less steady decline of the Roman Empire, which repeatedly lost territories to invading Visigoths, Vandals, and, ultimately, the Huns.

invulnerability of Christian Rome. Prudentius could go so far as to replace Romulus with Christ as the founder of Rome![2]

II. A Divine King

We can, I think, find evidence of such thinking that goes back at least to Constantine himself and the Council of Nicaea. The Nicene fathers may have held mixed views of Constantine, though they were ready enough to embrace his offer of alliance. But how, more precisely, did they envision the relationship of the emperor to the church? Opinions surely differed, but we do have a record of one father's view, a view that was evidently endorsed by Constantine himself. In his biography of Constantine, Eusebius, the first great historian of the church and an admirer, portrays Constantine as the host of the eschatological feast inaugurating the kingdom of God.[3] Now, Eusebius speaks here in figures; he does not directly declare, though he clearly implies, that Constantine is the Christ come to claim his kingdom. Yet the imagery was, one must suspect, political dynamite. For even if it does not say in so many words that Constantine is the *parousia*, it places him in the seat of the risen Christ at the banquet.[4]

Why—given, at least, my claims about who Jesus was said to be and about what, therefore, should constitute the *parousia*—might such a declaration by Eusebius be seen as politically problematic and not embraced by all of the church's bishops? We perhaps cannot know, but a guess can be made. The Gospels and the Pauline letters make it clear that the early church preached an imminent second coming, one whose time was not to be precisely revealed but that at least some living in the second half of the first

---

[2] See Gerard O'Daly, *Augustine's City of God: A Reader's Guide* (Oxford: Clarendon Press, 1999), 19–23. O'Daly goes on to note (p. 24) that Alaric's sack of Rome in 410 seems to have precipitated a resurgent interest in pagan cults and demands to remove Theodosius' edicts suppressing pagan worship. The fall of Rome had a profound effect upon the Christian community: "Jerome [exemplifying this response] compared Rome's fall with the Babylonian destruction of Jerusalem….He and others had absorbed the ideology of *Roma aeterna* to the extent that a threat to the Roman empire appeared to undermine the political and social basis upon which the Christian Church was presumed to be founded." This is the cultural sensibility that Augustine had to attack and defeat.

[3] See Eusebius of Caesarea, *Life of Constantine*, trans. Averil Cameron and Stuart G. Hall (Oxford: Clarendon Press, 1999), book III, chapter XV, and my chapter 12n43. See also, Timothy D. Barnes, *Constantine and Eusebius* (Cambridge, MA: Harvard University Press, 1981), 248–55.

[4] See Jonathan Bardill, *Constantine, Divine Emperor of the Christian Golden Age* (New York: Cambridge University Press, 2012), esp. 337–95. For evidence that Constantine himself endorsed this view, see also Paul Stephenson, *Constantine: Roman Emperor, Christian Victor* (New York: Overlook Press, 2010), 216–17 and 287–89.

century could hope to witness.[5] As it became increasingly evident that this was an overly optimistic expectation, church leaders had to backtrack on the promise (see e.g., 2 Thess. 2; 2 Pet. 3:3–10). In my view, the New Testament envisions a victory scenario in which a wholeheartedly Christian emperor is installed, presumably a leader of the church, and the empire becomes the body of Christ.

But by the fourth century, things were not so simple. Constantine, perhaps wanting to hedge his bets, was not baptized until a few months before his death in 337. By then, the church itself had become institutionalized beyond anything envisioned by the authors of the books of the New Testament. A fairly well-defined Ecclesiastical hierarchy was in place, including a pope in Rome, and the church had considerable wealth in real estate and monetary resources. Certain practicalities would have to be faced. Would the church cede its property and institutional structure to the empire? Would its hierarchy swear fealty to the emperor? Or would something like the reverse happen—Constantine's abdication of his royal authority and its transfer to the church (presumably to Pope Sylvester)?[6] It seems obvious that neither of these would have been an acceptable arrangement to both parties. Thus, plainly, the real unity of the empire as a single institution and body of people loyal to its messiah was no longer a vision that could fully be implemented.

So Eusebius' declaration was partly a natural reflection of Christian aspirations but partly inaccurate; his allusive language suggests that he recognized the need to be circumspect (or coy) in his optimism. Indeed, the Christian bishops were split on the question of the proper relationship between the emperor and God, on the one hand, and the church on the other.[7] Not a little of the political heat generated by the conflict between the Nicene bishops and the Arians over the divinity of the Christ can, in my view, be understood as a struggle intimately connected with different

---

[5] It may seem incredible, given the ambition of empire, that the early church could advertise an expectation of so rapid a takeover. Whether calculated or genuinely believed, such promises were well aimed to gain and keep a committed membership.

[6] The institutional ramifications of such a merger become quite concrete in, for example, the practices that arose in this period around the office of bishop. As representative of Christ the King, a bishop sat on a throne whose design was based on that of the imperial throne. His regalia and the manner in which he was ceremonially honored reflected the practices of the imperial court (see Per Beskow, *Rex Gloriae: The Kingship of Christ in the Early Church*, trans. Eric J. Sharpe [Uppsala, Sweden: Almqvist and Wiksell, 1962], 15). Was the church and its hierarchical structure to be absorbed into the institutional structures of the empire or vice versa?

[7] Nevertheless, Eusebius' view seems to have had staying power. Lactantius, a contemporary of Augustine's, appears to have had an at least somewhat similar conception of the relation between empire and church (see O'Daly, *Augustine's City of God*, 51).

conceptions of the authority of the emperor vis á vis the new covenant of laws handed to the church by Jesus. That debate can be seen as an heir to, and continuous with, the debates over the divinity of the emperor so effectively skewered by Jesus in the Caesar's coin episode.[8] Yet, we might say that in Constantine's conversion and adoption of Christianity as the empire's official religion, the church came as close as it ever would to the event of the *parousia*.

The fourth and early fifth centuries CE, as I see things, represent a watershed era in the transformation of the church's understanding of its own kerygma. To trace through the Medieval Period the development of the doctrine of the two swords that emerged from this period would go far beyond the project of this book, and it would require the efforts of historians to ascertain whether those developments reflect conceptual shifts that could translate what would originally have been a political ideology into something more recognizable in our day as a theology.

III. A General Reaction to "Mythicism"

Before concluding, I want to take note of an apologetic response to my arguments here that deserves at least brief consideration. One recurrent reaction to this way of approaching the biblical texts is partly conciliatory. The general thought is this: "We can accept the insights provided by applying structural myth analysis and other tools borrowed from anthropology to biblical narratives. But in suggesting that their symbolic significance is *all* these narratives mean to convey, you are over-reaching. For the symbolic meanings are entirely compatible with the view that the narratives are also literal reports of historical events, events that do indeed convey God's word and also constitute the pouring out of his grace upon a humankind in desperate need of salvation. Thus, the Bible puts us in touch with God's providence, both in the form of saving events and in the form of teachings about those events that will enable us to understand their significance for us."

This response is meant, among other things, to defend the historicity of the biblical miracles. Granting their symbolic content, the miracles nevertheless provide signs of God's actual working in human history. Indeed, if they—and for Christians, most pointedly the resurrection—were *merely* stories, their symbolism, no matter how profound, would allegedly not come close to achieving atonement for our sins and salvation for our

---

[8] For a very brief summary of this dimension of the struggles between the Athanasian and Arian parties, see Leo Donald Davis, *The First Seven Ecumenical Councils (325–787): Their History and Theology* (Wilmington, DE: Michael Glazier, Inc., 1987), 33–80, esp. 69–77.

souls. I appreciate these soteriological concerns, characteristic of theological realism, but they are inadmissible as evidence.

I have already noted, in the concluding section of Chapter 11, that there is nothing about the proposed maneuver that rules it out on purely philosophical grounds. So long as it is allowed that God can intervene in the required ways in the course of history, the addition of the historicity hypothesis to the mythicist interpretations offered here cannot in general be ruled out on grounds of logical or metaphysical incompatibility. Nevertheless, the price of adding on the theistic hypothesis is often quite steep. This is most obvious with respect to the requirements imposed by the conditions that must be met when divine providence is invoked. We have already encountered this difficulty *en passant* in a brief consideration of the sort of divine choreography that would have to lie behind the ascription of historicity to the Barabbas episode (see Chapter 11, footnotes 79 and 82). Similar problems arise, on a much grander scale, if one is to claim historicity for the chiastic structures that organize the Gospels of Mark and Matthew.

Relative to the hypothesis that God exists, such providential stage-setting on his part has a non-zero probability, obviously, but theism itself is less than certainly true. And any hypothesis about particular divine interventions in history will perforce have a lower probability still.[9] Non-Christians can afford to be rather generous here given the further asymmetries between their theory and that of the conciliatory Christian. For, consider: what will the Christian theist say about the enormous body of religious myths to be found in other cultures and religious traditions? If she is sympathetic to the anthropologist's approach, she will no doubt concede that these stories are fictions artfully composed to convey symbolically deep truths about social existence and structures. In conceding this, she is *a fortiori* conceding that human beings can, without divine inspiration or a historical record to inform them, compose stories of this kind. And—what is worse—she will have to provide *one* kind of explanation for the existence of these myths but another, rather *different* sort of explanation for her "own" myth-like traditions. This requires a kind of special pleading that someone

---

[9] Arguments such as those made by Richard Swinburne in favor of the moderate likelihood that God would engineer something like the atoning death and resurrection of Jesus of Nazareth are, in my view, decidedly over-optimistic. See Richard Swinburne, *The Resurrection of God Incarnate* (New York: Oxford University Press, 2003). This is not a proper venue for engagement with Swinburne on that matter, but it may be observed that even if Swinburne should be *correct* on that question, he will have gone little distance toward showing that *all* the central biblical narratives can be shown to relate things that God would probably have engineered. But then, the theist will have to confront the discomfort of inhomogeneous treatment of the stories: some will be allowed historical, others fictional, without any literary indication that the authors intended such a distinction.

who does not take theism onboard as an additional explanatory hypothesis has no need of.

Beyond this, there are incongruities between the specific *content* of certain mythicist interpretations of biblical stories and the way those stories are taken by the conciliatory theist. This is not in every case a problem. The theist, for example, can allow that Jesus' walking on the waters and calming the storm symbolically register his command over the forces of social chaos, while at the same time having actually occurred. Things do not always go so smoothly, however. This is true, indeed, of the resurrection itself.

As the mythicist would have it, the crucifixion of Jesus was either not a historical event, or it resulted in the death of Jesus and no resurrection (in the now generally accepted sense). Rather, the appearances of the resurrected Jesus are intended to capture the claim that a new office has been created, and put in cold storage, as it were, a kind of royalty-in-waiting, available for flesh-and-blood embodiment when the right candidate comes along. It is hard to see how this story can be stitched together with the now-orthodox conception of the resurrection, but it might, I suppose, be interesting to see whether it can be done.

IV. Conclusion

In its structural architecture, each Gospel is like an intricately folded origami piece. Once recognized, that is not easily forgotten. But the goal is not merely to appreciate this. It is to understand how the trick is done: where the folds are made, what each fold contributes to the beauty of the whole, what precisely the author meant to convey with his invention, why he would have thought it worthy of his efforts, and why his intended audience would have responded as they did. In the last three chapters, I have made an attempt to exhibit one way in which one might go about discovering how the structure is put together.

The Gospels tell a remarkable story. Most Christians consider it to be of utmost importance to know whether "all of that stuff"—or at least some of it—actually happened. My answer is that (of course) *some* of it may have: Jesus may have walked the banks of the Jordan and preached in Galilee; perhaps he was betrayed by a follower to the Romans or to the Jewish establishment. Pilate and Caiaphas did call many of the shots in the early decades of the era in Judea. But myth does not imitate real life; nor does real life imitate myth. Real life is more pedestrian, more nearly just "one damn thing after another." It lacks the precision of structure that we find in myth.[10] I have argued, using just some selected episodes, that biblical texts (I would generalize the claim to many of them) are saturated with just such structures.

Of course, my skepticism about biblical "history" is misplaced if we suppose there to be a God who somehow orchestrates history in selected times and places the way a puppeteer controls his stage.[11] That is something one may wish to believe, and many do. However, the mechanics of the requisite control, carefully considered, are extraordinarily hard to imagine, especially if allowance is made for human freedom.

Taken as an article of faith, perhaps supported by independent reasons for belief in a God whose sovereignty includes within its purview legitimate control over the course of events, both human and natural, this is a position that cannot summarily be dismissed. Nor have I been concerned directly to disqualify that possibility. Quite aside from its attractiveness apart from the explanatory work it can do, it is certainly not to be dismissed as an explanatory hypothesis on a priori grounds. But insofar as we confine our attention to historical investigation, I hope to have made a good case for the claim that, not only is such an appeal to divine providence otiose, but it comes at a heavy price to prior probabilities.

---

[10] I do not mean to suggest here, obviously, that real life is a chaos devoid of intentional human action, of the making and carrying out of plans, and the like. I do mean that all of this, both within an individual's life, respecting experience and action, and across individuals, is not coordinated into the kind of architectonic structures characteristic of myth.

[11] If, at any rate, he is a god who loves to imitate the structures of human myths.

Bibliography

Adams, Robert Merrihew. *Finite and Infinite Goods*. New York: Oxford University Press, 2002.

Adams, William. "An Essay on Mr. Hume's Essay on Miracles (1752)." Lydia McGrew. Accessed April 8, 2020. http://www.lydiamcgrew.com/AdamsEssayonHume.htm.

Agassi, Joseph. "Methodological Individualism." *The British Journal of Sociology* 11, no. 3 (1960): 244–70. http://doi.org/10.2307/586749.

Aldwinckel, Russell. *More Than a Man: A Study in Christology*. Grand Rapids, MI: William B. Eerdmans, 1976.

Allison, Dale C. "How to Marginalize the Traditional Criteria of Authenticity." In *The Handbook for the Study of the Historical Jesus*, edited by Tom Holmén and Stanley E. Porter. Vol. 1, 3–30. Boston: Brill, 2011.

———. *The New Moses: A Matthean Typology*. Minneapolis, MN: Fortress Press, 1993.

Aquinas, Thomas. *Summa Contra Gentiles*. Translated by Anton C. Pegis. New York: Doubleday, 1955.

Archer, Gleason. *Encyclopedia of Bible Difficulties*. Grand Rapids, MI: Zondervan, 1982.

Armstrong, Herbert W. *The Resurrection was Not on Sunday*. 1952. Reprint, N.p.: Worldwide Church of God, 1972.

Austin, J. L. *How to Do Things with Words*. 2nd ed. Edited by J. O. Urmson and Marina Sbisà Cambridge, MA: Harvard University Press, 1975.

Baber, H. E. "Eucharist: Metaphysical Miracle or Institutional Fact?" *International Journal for Philosophy of Religion* 74, no. 3 (2013): 333–52. http://doi.org/10.1007/s11153-012-9383-0.

———. "Sabellianism Reconsidered." *Sophia* 41, no. 2 (2002): 1–18. http://doi.org/10.1007/bf02912232.

Bardill, Jonathan. *Constantine, Divine Emperor of the Christian Golden Age*. New York: Cambridge University Press, 2012.

Barker, Margaret. *The Gate of Heaven: The History and Symbolism of the Temple in Jerusalem*. London: SPCK, 1991.

———. *The Great High Priest: The Temple Roots of Christian Liturgy*. London: T&T Clark, 2003.

Barnes, Timothy D. *Constantine and Eusebius*. Cambridge, MA: Harvard University Press, 1981.

Barnett, P. W. "The Feeding of the Multitude in Mark 6/John 6." In *Gospel Perspectives*, edited by David Wenham and Craig Blomberg. Vol. 6, *The Miracles of Jesus*, 273–93. Sheffield, England: JSOT Press, 1986.

Barr, James. *The Semantics of Biblical Language*. New York: Oxford University Press, 1961.

Barton, John, and John Muddiman, eds. *The Oxford Bible Commentary*. New York: Oxford University Press, 2001.

Bateson, Gregory. "Conventions of Communications Where Validity Depends Upon Belief." In *Communication: The Social Matrix of Psychiatry*, edited by Jurgen Reusch and Gregory Bateson, 212–27. Piscataway, NY: Transaction Publishers, 1951.

Batto, Bernard F. "Red Sea or Sea of Reeds? How the Mistake Was Made and What Yam Sup Really Means." *Biblical Archaeology Review* 10, no. 4 (1984): 57–63.

Bauckham, Richard. "The Coin in the Fish's Mouth." In *Gospel Perspectives: The Miracles of Jesus*, edited by David Wenham and Craig Blomberg. Vol. 6, 219–52. Sheffield, England: JSOT Press, 1986.

Beattie, J. H. M. "On Understanding Ritual." In *Rationality*, edited by Bryan R. Wilson, 240–69. New York: Harper and Row, 1970.

Beckman, Gary. "How Religion Was Done." In *A Companion to the Ancient Near East*, edited by Daniel D. Snell, 343–53. Malden, MA: Blackwell Publishing, 2005.

Bell, Lanny. "The New Kingdom 'Divine' Temple: The Example of Luxor." In *Temples of Ancient Egypt*, edited by Byron E. Shafer, 127–84. Ithaca, NY: Cornell University Press, 1997.

Bellah, Robert N. "Confessions of a Former Establishment Fundamentalist." *Theology Today* 28, no. 2 (1971): 229–33. http://doi.org/10.1177/004057367102800210.

Beskow, Per. *Rex Gloriae: The Kingship of Christ in the Early Church*. Translated by Eric J. Sharpe. Uppsala, Sweden: Almqvist and Wiksell, 1962.

Biale, David. *Blood and Belief: The Circulation of a Symbol between Jews and Christians*. Berkeley, CA: University of California Press, 2007.

Blomberg, Craig. "Concluding Reflections on Gospel Perspectives and Miracles." In *Gospel Perspectives*, edited by David Wenham and Craig Blomberg. Vol. 6, *The Miracles of Jesus*, 443–57. Sheffield, England: JSOT Press, 1986.

———. "The Miracles as Parables." In *Gospel Perspectives*, edited by David Wenham and Craig Blomberg. Vol. 6, *The Miracles of Jesus*, 327–59. Sheffield, England: JSOT Press, 1986.

Boers, H. "Religionsgeschichtliche Schule." In *Dictionary of Biblical Interpretation*, edited by John H. Hayes. Vol. 2, 383–87. Nashville, TN: Abingdon Press, 1999.

Bonnefoy, Yves, ed. *Mythologies*. Translated by Wendy Doniger. Vol. 1. Chicago, IL: University of Chicago Press, 1991.

Bonner, Campbell. "A Dionysiac Miracle at Corinth." *American Journal of Archaeology* 33, no. 3 (1929): 368–75. doi.org/10.2307/498351.

Bonz, Marianne Palmer. *The Past as Legacy: Luke-Acts and Ancient Epic*. Minneapolis, MN: Fortress Press, 2000.

Borg, Marcus J. *Conflict, Politics, and Politics in the Teachings of Jesus*. 2nd ed. Harrisburg, PA: Trinity Press International, 1998.

Boswell, J. *The Kindness of Strangers: The Abandonment of Children in Western Europe from Late Antiquity to the Renaissance*. Chicago, IL: Chicago University Press, 1988.

Boudry, Maarten, Stefaan Blancke, and Johan Braeckman. "How Not to Attack Intelligent Design Creationism: Philosophical Misconceptions About Methodological Naturalism." *Foundations of Science* 15, no. 3 (2010): 227–44. http://doi.org/10.1007/s10699-010-9178-7.

Bowker, J. W. "'Merkabah' Visions and the Visions of Paul." *Journal of Semitic Studies* 16, no. 2 (1971): 57–73. http://doi.org/10.1093/jss/xvi.2.157.

———. *The Targums and Rabbinic Literature: An Introduction to Jewish Interpretations of Scripture*. New York: Cambridge University Press, 1969.

Boyarin, Daniel. *The Jewish Gospels: The Story of the Jewish Christ*. New York: The New Press, 2012.

———. *A Radical Jew: Paul and the Politics of Identity*. Berkeley, CA: University of California Press, 1994.

Boyd, Richard N. "The Current Status of Scientific Realism." In *Scientific Realism*, edited by Jarett Leplin, 41–82. Berkeley, CA: University of California Press, 1984.

Brandon, S. G. F. *History, Time, and Deity: A Historical and Comparative Study of the Conception of Time in Religious Thought and Practice*. New York: Barnes & Noble, 1965.

Brown, Judith C. *Immodest Acts: The Life of a Lesbian Nun in Renaissance Italy*. New York: Oxford University Press, 1986.

Brown, Raymond E. *The Death of the Messiah: From Gethsemane to the Grave*. New York: Doubleday, 1994.

Burridge, Richard A. *What Are the Gospels? A Comparison with Graeco-Roman Biography.* 2nd ed. Grand Rapids, MI: William B. Eerdmans Publishing Company, 2004.

Caird, George B. *Principalities and Powers: A Study in Pauline Theology.* Oxford: Clarendon Press, 1956.

Cannon, Walter Bradford. "'Voodoo' Death." *American Journal of Public Health* 92, no. 10 (2002): 1593–96. http://doi.org/10.2105/ajph.92.10.1593.

Carrier, Richard C. "The Burial of Jesus in the Light of Jewish Law." In *The Empty Tomb: Jesus Beyond the Grave*, edited by Robert M. Price and Jeffrey Jay Lowder, 369–92. Amherst, NY: Prometheus Books, 2005.

———. *Not the Impossible Faith: Why Christianity Didn't Need a Miracle to Succeed.* Raleigh, NC: Lulu, 2009.

———. *On the Historicity of Jesus: Why We Might Have Reason for Doubt.* Sheffield, UK: Sheffield Phoenix Press, 2014.

———. *Proving History: Bayes' Theorem and the Quest for the Historical Jesus.* Amherst, NY: Prometheus Books, 2012.

———. "The Spiritual Body of Christ and the Legend of the Empty Tomb." In *The Empty Tomb: Jesus Beyond the Grave*, edited by Robert M. Price and Jeffrey Jay Lowder, 105–232. Amherst, NY: Prometheus Books, 2005.

Carson, D. A. "Matthew." In *The Expositor's Bible Commentary*, edited by Frank E. Gæbelein. Vol. 8, *Matthew, Mark, Luke*, 1–599. Grand Rapids, MI: Zondervan, 1984.

Cartwright, Nancy. *How the Laws of Physics Lie.* New York: Oxford University Press, 1983.

Castañeda, Carlos. *Journey to Ixtlan.* New York: Washington Square Press, 1972.

———. *A Separate Reality.* New York: Washington Square Press, 1971.

———. *The Teachings of Don Juan: A Yaqi Way of Knowledge*. New York: Washington Square Press, 1968.

Cavin, Robert Greg, and Carlos A. Colombetti. "The Implausibility and Low Explanatory Power of the Resurrection Hypothesis—With a Rejoinder to Stephen T. Davis." *Socio-Historical Examination of Religion and Ministry* 2, no. 1 (Spring 2020): 37–94. http://doi.org/10.33929/sherm.2020.vol2.no1.04.

Chavel, Charles B. "The Releasing of a Prisoner on the Eve of Passover in Ancient Jerusalem." *Journal of Biblical Literature* 60, no. 3 (1941): 273–78. http://doi.org/10.2307/3262626.

Chilton, B. D. "Exorcism and History: Mark 1:21–28." In *Gospel Perspectives*, edited by David Wenham and Craig Blomberg. Vol. 6, *The Miracles of Jesus*, 253–71. Sheffield, England: JSOT Press, 1986.

———. "Jesus' Dispute in the Temple and the Origin of the Eucharist." In *Sources of the Jesus Tradition: Separating History from Myth*, edited by R. Joseph Hoffmann, 253–71. Amherst, NY: Prometheus Books, 2010.

———. *The Temple of Jesus: His Sacrificial Program Within a Cultural History of Sacrifice*. University Park, PA: Pennsylvania State University Press, 1992.

Clarke, Samuel. "Evidences of Natural and Revealed Religion." In *The Works of Samuel Clarke*. 1705. Vol. 2. Reprint, 580–733. New York: Garland Publishing, 1978.

Claussen, Carsten. "Turning Water into Wine: Re-reading the Miracle at the Wedding in Cana." In *Jesus Research: An International Perspective*, edited by James H. Charlesworth and Petr Pokorný, 73–97. Grand Rapids, MI: William B. Eerdmans Publishing Company, 2009.

Clissold, Stephen. *St. Teresa of Avila*. London: Sheldon Press, 1979.

Coady, C. A. J. *Testimony: A Philosophical Study*. Oxford: Clarendon Press, 1992.

Cohn, Haim Hermann. "Witness." In *Encyclopaedia Judaica*. 2nd ed, edited by Michael Berenbaum and Fred Skolnik. Vol. 21. New York: Macmillan Reference, 2007.

Collins, Adela Yarbro. "The Empty Tomb and the Gospel According to Mark." In *Hermes and Athena: Biblical Exegesis and Philosophical Theology*, edited by Eleonore Stump and Thomas P. Flint, 1–10. Notre Dame, IN: University of Notre Dame Press, 1993.

Collins, Adela Yarbro, and John J. Collins. *King and Messiah as the Son of God: Divine, Human, and Angelic Messianic Figures in Biblical and Related Literature*. Grand Rapids, MI: William B. Eerdmans Publishing Company, 2008.

Collins, John J. "Apocalyptic Eschatology as the Transcendence of Death." *Catholic Biblical Quarterly* 36, no. 1 (1974): 21–43.

Collins, Robin. "The Energy of the Soul." In *The Soul Hypothesis: Investigations Into the Existence of the Soul*, edited by Mark C. Baker and Stewart Goetz, 123–36. New York: Continuum, 2011.

Craig, William Lane. *Assessing the New Testament Evidence for the Historicity of the Resurrection of Jesus*. Studies in the Bible and Early Christianity 16. Lewiston, NY: Edwin Mellen Press, 1989.

Cray, Ed. *Ramblin' Man: The Life and Times of Woody Guthrie*. 2004. Reprint, New York: W. W. Norton & Company, 2006.

Daniélou, Jean. *The Lord of History: Reflections On the Inner Meaning of History*. Translated by Nigel Abercrombie. New York: The World Publishing Company, 1968.

Davis, Leo Donald. *The First Seven Ecumenical Councils (325–787): Their History and Theology*. Wilmington, DE: Michael Glazier, Inc., 1987.

Davis, Stephen T. *Risen Indeed: Making Sense of the Resurrection*. Grand Rapids, MI: William B. Eerdmans Publishing Company, 1993.

Delling, Gerhard. "ἡμέρα." In *Theological Dictionary of the New Testament*, edited by Gerhard Kittel. Translated by Geoffrey W. Bromiley. Vol. 2, 948–50. Grand Rapids, MI: William B. Eerdmans Publishing Company, 1964.

DeMille, Richard. *Castañeda's Journey: The Power and the Allegory.* Santa Barbara, CA: Capra Press, 1976.

———. *The Don Juan Papers: Further Castañeda Controversies.* Santa Barbara, CA: Ross-Erikson Publishers, 1980.

Dennis, G. W. *Encyclopedia of Jewish Myth, Magic, and Mysticism.* Woodbury, MN: Llewellyn, 2007.

Dietl, Paul J. "On Miracles." *American Philosophical Quarterly* 5 (1968): 130–34.

Dorsey, David A. *The Literary Structure of the Old Testament: A Commentary On Genesis–Malachi.* Grand Rapids, MI: Baker Books, 1999.

Douglas, Mary. *How Institutions Think.* Syracuse, NY: Syracuse University Press, 1986.

———. *Purity and Danger: An Analysis of Concepts of Pollution and Taboo.* New York: Frederick A. Praeger, 1996.

———. *Thinking in Circles: An Essay on Ring Composition.* New Haven, CT: Yale University Press, 2007.

Drews, Carl, and Weiqing Han. "Dynamics of Wind Setdown at Suez and the Eastern Nile Delta." *PLoS ONE* 5, no. 8 (2010): e12481. http://doi.org/10.1371/journal.pone.0012481.

DuChaillu, Paul B. *Explorations and Adventures in Equatorial Africa: With Accounts of the Manners and Customs of the People.* 1868. Reprint, Ann Arbor, MI: University of Michigan Library, 2009.

Dundes, Alan. "Binary Opposition in Myth: The Propp/Levi-Strauss Debate in Retrospect." *Western Folklore* 56, no. 1 (1997): 39–50. http://doi.org/10.2307/1500385.

Dunn, James D. G. "Myth." In *Dictionary of Jesus and the Gospels*, edited by Joel B. Green, Scot McKnight, and I. Howard Marshall, 566–69. Downers Grove, IL: InterVarsity Press, 1992.

Durkheim, Émile. *The Elementary Forms of the Religious Life.* 1915. Translated by J. Swain. Reprint, New York: Free Press, 1965.

———. *The Rules of Sociological Method: And Selected Texts on Sociology and Its Method*. 1982. Edited by Steven Lukes. Reprint, New York: Free Press, 2013.

Earman, John. *Hume's Abject Failure: The Argument Against Miracles*. New York: Oxford University Press, 2000.

Eddy, Paul Rhodes, and Gregory A. Boyd. *The Jesus Legend: A Case for the Historical Reliability of the Synoptic Jesus Tradition*. Grand Rapids, MI: Baker Academic, 2007.

Edersheim, Alfred. *The Temple: Its Ministry and Services as They Were at the Time of Christ*. 1874. Reprint, Peabody, MA: Hendrickson Publishing, 1994. http://philologos.org/__eb-ttms/temple04.htm.

Edmonds, Radcliffe G. III. *Myths of the Underworld Journey: Plato, Aristophanes, and the 'Orphic' Gold Tablets*. New York: Cambridge University Press, 2004.

Engnell, Ivan. *A Rigid Scrutiny: Critical Essays On the Old Testament*. Translated by John T. Willis. Nashville, TN: Vanderbilt University Press, 1969.

———. *Studies in Divine Kingship in the Ancient Near East*. 2nd ed. Oxford: Basil Blackwell, 1967.

Eusebius of Caesarea. *Life of Constantine*. Translated by Averil Cameron and Stuart G. Hall. Oxford: Clarendon Press, 1999.

Evans, Craig A. "Life-of-Jesus Research and the Eclipse of Mythology." *Theological Studies* 54, no. 1 (1993): 3–36. http://doi.org/10.1177/004056399305400102.

Evans, Craig A. and N. T. Wright. "The Surprise of the Resurrection." In *Jesus, The Final Days: What Really Happened*, edited by Troy A. Miller, 75–108. Louisville, KY: Westminster John Knox Press, 2009.

Evans-Pritchard, Edward Evan. *Witchcraft, Oracles, and Magic Among the Azande*. Oxford: Clarendon Press, 1937.

Fairman, H. W. "The Kingship Rituals of Egypt." In *Myth, Ritual, and Kingship*, edited by S. H. Hooke, 74–104. Oxford: Clarendon Press, 1958.

Fales, Evan. "Can Science Explain Mysticism?" *Religious Studies* 35, no. 2 (1999): 213–27. http://doi.org/10.1017/s0034412599004801.

———. *Causation and Universals*. New York: Routledge, 1990.

———. "Davidson's Compatibilism." *Philosophy and Phenomenological Research* 45, no. 2 (1984): 227–46. http://doi.org/10.2307/2107426.

———. *A Defense of the Given*. Lanham, MD: Rowman & Littlefield Publishers, 1996.

———. "Divine Freedom and the Choice of a World." *International Journal for Philosophy of Religion* 35, no. 2 (1994): 65–88. doi.org/10.1007/bf01318326.

———. *Divine Intervention: Metaphysical and Epistemological Puzzles*. New York: Routledge, 2010.

———. "Is a Science of the Supernatural Possible?" In *Philosophy of Pseudoscience: Reconsidering the Demarcation Problem*, edited by Massimo Pigliucci and Maarten Boudry, 247–62. Chicago, IL: Chicago University Press, 2013.

———. "It is not Reasonable to Believe in Miracles." In *Debating Christian Theism*, edited by J. P. Moreland, Chad Meister, and Khaldoun A. Sweis. Oxford Contemporary Dialogues, 298–310. New York: Oxford University Press, 2013.

———. "Must Sociology Be Qualitative?" and "Reply to Professor Brown." *Qualitative Sociology* 5, no. 2 (1982): 89–105, 145–56. http://doi.org/10.1007/bf00987155.

———. "The Road to Damascus." *Faith and Philosophy* 22, no. 4 (2005): 442–59. http://doi.org/10.5840/faithphil200522459.

———. "Scientific Explanations of Mystical Experiences, Part I: The Case of St. Teresa." *Religious Studies* 32, no. 2 (1996): 143–63. http://doi.org/10.1017/s0034412500024203.

———. "Scientific Explanations of Mystical Experiences, Part II: The Challenge to Theism." *Religious Studies* 32, no. 3 (1996): 297–313. http://doi.org/10.1017/s0034412500024367.

———. "Taming the Tehom: The Sign of Jonah in Matthew." In *The Empty Tomb: Jesus Beyond the Grave*, edited by Robert M. Price and Jeffrey Jay Lowder, 307–48. Amherst, NY: Prometheus Books, 2005.

———. "Theoretical Simplicity and Defeasibility." *Philosophy of Science* 45, no. 2 (1978): 273–88. http://doi.org/10.1086/288800.

———. "Truth, Tradition, and Rationality." *Philosophy of the Social Sciences* 6, no. 2 (1976): 97–113. doi.org/10.1177/004839317600600201.

———. "Uniqueness and Historical Laws." *Philosophy of Science* 47, no. 2 (1980): 260–76. http://doi.org/10.1086/288932.

Fales, Evan, and Edward A. Wasserman. "Causal Knowledge: What Can Psychology Teach Philosophers." *The Journal of Mind and Behavior* 13, no. 1 (1992): 1–27.

Feldman, Louis H. *Judaism and Hellenism Reconsidered*. Supplements to the Journal for the Study of Judaism 107. Leiden, The Netherlands: Brill, 2006.

Finkelstein, Israel, and Neil Asher Silberman. "Temple and Dynasty: Hezekiah, the Remaking of Judah and the Rise of the Pan-Israelite Ideology." *Journal for the Study of the Old Testament* 30, no. 3 (2006): 259–85. http://doi.org/10.1177/0309089206063428.

Fogelin, Robert J. *A Defense of Hume on Miracles*. Princeton, NJ: Princeton University Press, 2003.

Fortes, Meyer. "Ritual and Office in Tribal Society." In *Essays on the Ritual of Social Relations*, edited by Max Gluckman, 53–88. New York: Manchester University Press, 1962.

Foster, John. "Induction, Explanation and Natural Necessity." *Proceedings of the Aristotelian Society* 83, no. 1 (1982–83): 87–102. http://doi.org/10.1093/aristotelian/83.1.87.

Frankfort, Henri. *Kingship and the Gods: A Study of Near Eastern Religion as the Integration of Society and Nature*. Chicago, IL: University of Chicago Press, 1948.

Frazer, James. *The Golden Bough: A Study in Magic and Religion*. Abridged ed. New York: Macmillan & Co., 1922.

Frei, Hans W. *The Eclipse of Biblical Narrative: A Study in Eighteenth and Nineteenth Century Hermeneutics*. New Haven, CT: Yale University Press, 1974.

Furnish, Victor Paul. *Theology and Ethics in Paul*. Nashville, TN: Abingdon Press, 1968.

Garrett, Don. *Cognition and Commitment in Hume's Philosophy*. New York: Oxford University Press, 1997.

Geivett, R. Douglas. "The Evidential Value of Miracles." In *In Defense of Miracles: A Comprehensive Case for God's Action In*, edited by R. Douglas Geivett and Gary R. Habermas, 178–95. Downers Grove, IL: InterVarsity Press, 1997.

Gellner, Ernest. "Concepts and Society." In *Rationality*, edited by Bryan R. Wilson, 18–49. New York: Harper and Row, 1970.

———. "Holism versus Individualism in History and Sociology." In *Theories of History*, edited by Patrick L. Gardiner, 489–502. New York: Free Press, 1959.

———. *Saints of the Atlas*. Chicago, IL: University of Chicago Press, 1969.

Gilders, William K. *Blood Ritual in the Hebrew Bible: Meaning and Power*. Baltimore, MD: Johns Hopkins University Press, 2004.

Ginzberg, Louis. *The Legends of the Jews*. Vol. 1. Philadelphia, PA: The Jewish Publication Society of America, 1946.

Goetz, Stewart C., and Craig L. Blomberg. "The Burden of Proof." *Journal for the Study of the New Testament* 4, no. 11 (1981): 39–63. http://doi.org/10.1177/0142064x8100401103.

Goldberg, David M. "What Did Ham Do to Noah?" In *The Words of a Wise Man's Mouth Are gracious. (Qoh 10, 12)*, edited by Mauro Perani, 257–65. New York: Walter de Gruyter, 2005. www.sas.upenn.edu/~dmg2/what%20did%20ham%20do.pdf.

Goldstein, Leon J. "Mr. Watkins on the Two Theses." *The British Journal for the Philosophy of Science* 10, no. 39 (1959): 240–41. http://doi.org/10.1093/bjps/x.39.240.

———. "The Two Theses of Methodological Individualism." *The British Journal for the Philosophy of Science* 9, no. 33 (1958): 1–11. http://doi.org/10.1093/bjps/ix.33.1.

Goodenough, Erwin R. *The Politics of Philo Judaeus: Practice and Theory*. London: Oxford University Press, 1938.

Goodman, Martin. "Under the Influence: Hellenism in Ancient Jewish Life." *Biblical Archaeology Review* 36, no. 1 (2010): 60–67.

Gould, Stephen Jay. "Non-Overlapping Magisteria." *Skeptical Inquirer* 23, no. 4 (1999): 55–61. https://skepticalinquirer.org/1999/07/non-overlapping-magisteria/.

Gowan, Donald E. *Genesis 1–11: From Eden to Babel*. Grand Rapids, MI: William B. Eerdmans Publishing Company, 1988.

Grice, H. P. "Meaning." *The Philosophical Review* 66, no. 3 (1957): 377–88. http://doi.org/10.2307/2182440.

Guthrie, Stewart Elliot. *Faces in the Clouds: A New Theory of Religion*. New York: Oxford University Press, 1995.

Guthrie, Woody. *Bound for Glory*. New York: E. P. Dutton, 1943.

Gutting, Gary. *Religious Belief and Religious Skepticism*. South Bend, IN: University of Notre Dame Press, 1982.

Habermas, Gary R. *The Historical Jesus: Ancient Evidence for the Life of Christ*. Joplin, MO: College Press Publishing Company, 1996.

Hägerland, Tobias. "The Future of Criteria in Historical Jesus Research." *Journal for the Study of the Historical Jesus* 13, no. 1 (2015): 43–65. http://doi.org/10.1163/17455197-01301003.

Halperin, Mordechai. "Metzitzah B'peh Controversy: The View from Israel." Wayback Machine. March 6, 2012. http://web.archive.org/web/20120306221308/http:/www.ou.org/jewish_action/article/8987.

Harlow, Harry F. "The Nature of Love." *American Psychologist* 13, no. 12 (1958): 673–85. http://doi.org/10.1037/h0047884.

Harris, Marvin. *Cows, Pigs, Wars, and Witches: The Riddles of Culture.* New York: Vintage, 1989.

Harrison, Andrew. "Works of Art and Other Cultural Objects." *Proceedings of the Aristotelian Society* 68, no. 1 (1968): 105–28. http://doi.org/10.1093/aristotelian/68.1.105.

Hart, H. L. A. *The Concept of Law.* New York: Oxford University Press, 1961.

Hay, David. "Religious Experience Amongst a Group of Post-Graduate Students: A Qualitative Study." *Journal for the Scientific Study of Religion* 18, no. 2 (1979): 164–82. http://doi.org/10.2307/1385938.

Hemer, Colin J. *The Book of Acts in the Setting of Hellenistic History.* Edited by Conrad H. Gempf. Tübingen, Germany: J. C. B. Mohr, 1989.

Hendrickx, Hermann. *The Resurrection Narratives of the Synoptic Gospels.* London: G. Chapman, 1984.

Hick, John. *The Fifth Dimension: An Exploration of the Spiritual Realm.* Oxford, UK: Oneworld Publications, 1999.

Hollis, Martin. "The Limits of Irrationality." In *Rationality*, edited by Bryan R. Wilson, 221–39. New York: Harper and Row, 1970.

Hooke, S. H. "The Myth and Ritual Pattern of the Ancient East." In *Myth and Ritual: Essays on the Myth and Ritual of the Hebrews in Relation to the Culture Pattern of the Ancient East*, edited by S. H. Hooke, 1–14. London: Oxford University Press, 1933.

Horsley, Richard A. *Jesus and the Spiral of Violence: Popular Jewish Resistance in Roman Palestine.* San Francisco, CA: Harper and Row, 1987.

———., ed. *Paul and Empire: Religion and Power in Roman Imperial Society*. Harrisburg, PA: Trinity Press International, 1997.

Horton, Robin. "African Traditional Thought and Western Science." In *Rationality*, edited by Bryan R. Wilson, 131–71. New York: Harper and Row, 1970.

———. "Paradox and Explanation: A Reply to Mr. Skorupski." *Philosophy of the Social Sciences* 3 (1973): 231–56.

Houston, J. *Reported Miracles: A Critique of Hume*. New York: Cambridge University Press, 1994.

Hume, David. *Dialogues Concerning Natural Religion*. 1779. Edited by Norman Kemp Smith. Reprint, Indianapolis, IN: Bobbs-Merrill, 1947.

———. *An Enquiry Concerning Human Understanding*. 1748. Edited by Tom L. Beauchamp. Reprint, New York: Oxford University Press, 2000.

———. *An Inquiry Concerning Human Understanding*. 1748. Edited by Charles W. Hendel. Reprint, Indianapolis, IN: Bobbs-Merrill, 1955.

Isserlin, B. S. J. *The Israelites*. London: Thames and Hudson, 1998.

Jakobson, Roman, and Morris Halle. *Fundamentals of Language*. The Hague, Netherlands: Mouton, 1956.

James, William. *The Varieties of Religious Experience*. New York: Macmillan, 1961.

Jantzen, Benjamin C. "Peirce on Miracles: The Failure of Bayesian Analysis." In *Probability in the Philosophy of Religion*, edited by Jake Chandler and Victoria S. Harrison, 27–45. New York: Oxford University Press, 2012.

Jarvie, I. C. *Concepts and Society*. New York: Routledge, 1972.

Jarvie, I. C., and Joseph Agassi. "The Problem of the Rationality of Magic." In *Rationality*, edited by Bryan R. Wilson, 172–93. New York: Harper and Row, 1970.

Jensen, Lloyd B. "Royal Purple of Tyre." *Journal of Near Eastern Studies* 22, no. 2 (1963): 104–18. http://doi.org/10.1086/371717.

Jeremias, Joachim. *Golgotha*. Leipzig, Germany: E. Pfeiffer, 1926.

Johnson, David Kyle. "Identifying the Conflict between Religion and Science." *Socio-Historical Examination of Religion and Ministry* 2, no. 1 (Spring 2020): 122–48. https://doi.org/10.33929/sherm.2020.vol2.no1.06.

———. "Justified Belief in Miracles is Impossible." *Science, Religion and Culture* 2, no. 2 (2015): 61–74. doi.org/10.17582/journal.src/2015/2.2.61.74.

Johnson, Luke Timothy. *Living Jesus: Learning the Heart of the Gospel*. San Francisco, CA: HarperSanFrancisco, 1998.

Kantorowicz, Ernest H. *The King's Two Bodies: A Study in Medieval Political Theology*. Princeton, NJ: Princeton University Press, 1957.

Keck, Leander, ed. *The New Interpreter's Bible*. Vol. 8. Nashville, TN: Abingdon Press, 1995.

Kee, Howard Clark. *Medicine, Miracle, and Magic in New Testament Times*. New York: Cambridge University Press, 1988.

Keener, Craig S. *Miracles: The Credibility of the New Testament Accounts*. 2 vols. Grand Rapids, MI: Baker Academic, 2011.

Kelber, Werner H. *Apostolic Tradition and the Form of the Gospel*. Atlanta, GA: Society of Biblical Literature, 2013.

Klaniczay, Gábor. "The Process of Trance, Heavenly and Diabolic Apparitions in Johannes Nider's *Formicarius*." In *Procession, Performance, Liturgy and Ritual: Essays in Honor of Bryan R. Gillingham*, edited by Nancy van Deusen, 203–58. The Institute of Medieval Music: Ottawa, Canada, 2007.

Klawans, Jonathan. *Purity, Sacrifice, and the Temple: Symbolism and Supersessionism in the Study of Ancient Judaism*. New York: Oxford University Press, 2006.

Klein, Zöe. "Wrestling with Man, Not Angel." ReformJudaism.org. December 4, 2006. https://reformjudaism.org/wrestling-man-not-angel.

Koperski, Jeffrey. "Divine Action and the Quantum Amplification Problem." *Theology and Science* 13, no. 4 (2015): 379–94. http://doi.org/10.1080/14746700.2015.1082872.

Kraeling, C. H. *Gerasa, City of the Decapolis*. New Haven, CT: American Schools of Oriental Research, 1938.

Lackey, Jennifer. "Religious Belief and the Epistemology of Testimony." In *The Oxford Handbook of the Epistemology of Theology*, edited by William J. Abraham and Frederick D. Aquino, 203–20. New York: Oxford University Press, 2017.

———. "What Is Justified Group Belief?" *Philosophical Review* 125, no. 3 (2016): 341–96. http://doi.org/10.1215/00318108-3516946.

Larmer, Robert A. "Against 'Against Miracles'." In *Questions of Miracle*, edited by Robert A. Larmer, 54–59. Montreal, Canada: McGill-Queen's University Press, 1996.

———. "Divine Intervention and the Conservation of Energy: A Reply to Evan Fales." *International Journal for Philosophy of Religion* 75, no. 1 (2013): 27–38. http://doi.org/10.1007/s11153-013-9411-8.

———. *Water Into Wine? An Investigation of the Concept of Miracle*. Montreal, Quebec: McGill-Queen's University Press, 1988.

Latourelle, René *The Miracles of Jesus and the Theology of Miracles*. Mahwah, NJ: Paulist Press, 1988.

Law, Stephen. "Evidence, Miracles, and the Existence of Jesus." *Faith and Philosophy* 28, no. 2 (2011): 129–51. http://doi.org/10.5840/faithphil20112821.

Leach, Edmund R. *Genesis as Myth and Other Essays*. London: Cape, 1969.

———. *Political Systems of Highland Burma*. London: Bloomsbury Academic, 1954.

———. "Ritualization in Man in Relation to Conceptual and Social Development." In *Reader in Comparative Religion*. 3rd ed, edited by William Lessa and Evon Vogt, 333–37. New York: Harper & Row, 1972.

———., ed. *The Structural Study of Myth and Totemism*. London: Tavistock Publications, 1967.

Leach, Edmund R., and D. Alan Aycock. *Structural Interpretations of Biblical Myth*. New York: Cambridge University Press, 1983.

Lehman, Hugh. "Statistical Explanation." *Philosophy of Science* 39, no. 4 (1972): 500–6. http://doi.org/10.1086/288471.

Levenson, Jon D. *The Death and Resurrection of the Beloved Son: The Transformation of Child Sacrifice in Judaism and Christianity*. New Haven, CT: Yale University Press, 1993.

Lévi-Strauss, Claude. *The Elementary Structures of Kinship*. 1949. Edited by Rodney Needham. Translated by J. H. Bell, J. R. von Sturmer, and Rodney Needham. Reprint, Boston, MA: Beacon Press, 1969.

———. *From Honey to Ashes*. 1966. Translated by John Weightman and Doreen Weightman. Reprint, New York: Harper and Row, 1973.

———. *The Jealous Potter*. Chicago, IL: University of Chicago Press, 1988.

———. *The Naked Man*. 1971. Translated by John Weightman and Doreen Weightman. Reprint, New York: Harper and Row, 1981.

———. *The Origin of Table Manners*. 1968. Translated by John Weightman and Doreen Weightman. Reprint, New York: Harper and Row, 1978.

———. "The Story of Asdiwal." In *The Structural Study of Myth and Totemism*, edited by Edmund Leach. Translated by Nicholas Mann, 1–47. London: Tavistock Publications Limited, 1967.

———. *Structural Anthropology*. New York: Basic Books, 1963.

———. "Structuralism and Ecology." *Social Science Information* 12, no. 1 (1973): 7–23. http://doi.org/10.1177/053901847301200101.

———. *Totemism*. Boston, MA: Beacon Press, 1963.

Levinson, David, and Melvin Ember, eds. *Encyclopedia of Cultural Anthropology*. New York: Henry Holt and Company, 1996.

Lévy-Bruhl, Lucien. *How Natives Think*. 1910. Translated by Lilian A. Clare. Reprint, Princeton, NJ: Princeton University Press, 1985.

Lewis, I. M. *Ecstatic Religion: An Anthropological Study of Spirit Possession and Shamanism*. Baltimore, MD: Penguin Books, 1971.

Licona, Michael R. "Historians and Miracle Claims." *Journal for the Study of the Historical Jesus* 12, no. 1/2 (2014): 106–29.

———. *The Resurrection of Jesus: A New Historiographical Approach*. Downers Grove, IL: IVP Academic, 2014.

Lienhardt, Godfrey. *Divinity and Experience: The Religion of the Dinka*. New York: Clarendon Press, 1961.

Lipton, Peter. *Inference to the Best Explanation*. 2nd ed. New York: Routledge, 2004.

Locke, John. *Essay Concerning Human Understanding*. Edited by Alexander Campbell. Vol. 2, Book 4. New York: Dover Publications, 1959.

Lukes, Steven. "Relativism: Cognitive and Moral." *Aristotelian Society: Supplementary Volume* 48 (1974): 165–89.

———. "Some Problems about Rationality." In *Rationality*, edited by Bryan R. Wilson, 194–213. New York: Harper and Row, 1970.

Lund, Nils Wilhelm. *Chiasmus in the New Testament: A Study in Formsgeschichte*. Chapel Hill, NC: University of North Carolina Press, 1942.

Macdonald, Dennis R. *Does the New Testament Imitate Homer? Four Cases from the Acts of the Apostles*. New Haven, CT: Yale University Press, 2003.

———. *The Homeric Epics and the Gospel of Mark*. New Haven, CT: Yale University Press, 2000.

Maclean, Jennifer K. Berenson. "Barabbas, the Scapegoat Ritual, and the Development of the Passion Narrative." *Harvard Theological Review* 100, no. 3 (2007): 309–34. http://doi.org/10.1017/s0017816007001605.

Malina, Bruce J., and Jerome H. Neyrey. *Portraits of Paul: An Archaeology of an Ancient Personality*. Louisville, KY: Westminster John Knox Press, 1966.

Malinowski, Bronislaw. *Argonauts of the Western Pacific: An Account of Native Enterprise and Adventure in the Archipelagoes of Melanesian New Guinea*. 1922. Reprint, New York: E. P. Dutton & Co., 1961.

Mandelbaum, Maurice. "Societal Facts." In *Theories of History*, edited by Patrick L. Gardiner, 476–87. New York: Free Press, 1959.

Margolis, Joseph. "Collective Entities and the Rules of War." Paper presented at the International Conference on War and Violence, Union, NJ, April 1974.

———. "The Ontological Peculiarity of Works of Art." *The Journal of Aesthetics and Art Criticism* 36, no. 1 (1977): 45–50. http://doi.org/10.2307/430748.

———. "Reductionism and Ontological Aspects of Consciousness." *Journal for the Theory of Social Behaviour* 4, no. 1 (1974): 3–16. http://doi.org/10.1111/j.1468-5914.1974.tb00327.x.

———. "Works of Art as Physically Embodied and Culturally Emergent Entities." *The British Journal of Aesthetics* 14, no. 3 (1974): 187–96. doi.org/10.1093/bjaesthetics/14.3.187.

Mauss, Marcel. *The Gift: The Form and Reason for Exchange in Primitive Societies*. 1950. Translated by W. D. Halls. Reprint, New York: W. W. Norton, 2000.

McGrew, Timothy, and Lydia McGrew. "The Argument from Miracles: A Cumulative Case for the Resurrection." In *The Blackwell Companion to Natural Theology*, edited by William Lane Craig and J. P. Moreland, 593–662. Malden, MA: Wiley-Blackwell, 2012.

Meeks, Wayne. *The First Urban Christians: The Social World of the Apostle Paul*. New Haven, CT: Yale University Press, 1983.

Miles, Jack. "Jacob's Wrestling Match: Was It an Angel or Esau?" *Bible Review* 14, no. 5 (1998): 22–23.

Morrison, Clinton D. *The Powers That Be: Early Rulers and Demonic Powers in Romans 13: 1–7*. Studies in Biblical Theology 29. Naperville, IL: Alec R. Allenson, Inc., 1960.

Mounce, W. D. "Mahanaim." In *International Standard Bible Encyclopedia*. Rev. ed, edited by Geoffrey W. Bromiley. Vol. 3, 222–23. Grand Rapids, MI: William B. Eerdmans Publishing Company, 1986.

Möwinckel, Sigmund. *The Psalms in Israel's Worship*. Translated by D. R. Ap-Thomas. Vol. 1. New York: Abingdon Press, 1962.

Murray, Harris J. "'The Dead are Restored to Life': Miracles of Revivification in the Gospels." In *Gospel Perspectives*, edited by David Wenham and Craig Blomberg. Vol. 6, *The Miracles of Jesus*, 295–326. Sheffield, England: JSOT Press, 1986.

Myers, Ched. *Binding the Strong Man*. Maryknoll, NY: Orbis Books, 1988.

Neill, Stephen, and Tom Wright. *The Interpretation Of The New Testament, 1861–1986*. New York: Oxford University Press, 1988.

Nelson, Charles A., Nathan A. Fox, and Charles H. Zeanah. "Anguish of the Abandoned Child." *Scientific American* 308, no. 4 (2013): 62–67. doi.org/10.1038/scientificamerican0413-62.

Nickelsburg, George W. *Resurrection, Immortality, and Eternal Life in Intertestamental Judaism*. Cambridge, MA: Harvard University Press, 1972.

Nielsen, Kai. "Rationality and Relativism." *Philosophy of the Social Sciences* 4 (1974): 313–31.

Nolland, John. *The Gospel of Matthew: A Commentary On the Greek Text*. Grand Rapids, MI: William B. Eerdmans Publishing Company, 2005.

Noth, Martin. *The Laws in the Pentateuch and Other Studies*. 1960. Translated by D. R. Ap-Thomas. Reprint, Philadelphia, PA: Fortress Press, 1967.

Novak, Ralph Martin. *Christianity and the Roman Empire: Background Texts*. Harrisburg, PA: Trinity International Press, 2001.

O'Collins, Gerald. *The Easter Jesus*. Valley Forge, PA: Judson Press, 1973.

O'Daly, Gerard. *Augustine's* City of God*: A Reader's Guide*. Oxford: Clarendon Press, 1999.

Oesterley, W. O. E. "Early Hebrew Festival Rituals." In *Myth and Ritual: Essays on the Myth and Ritual of the Hebrews in Relation to the Culture Pattern of the Ancient East*, edited by S. H. Hooke, 111–46. London: Oxford University Press, 1933.

Ouro, Roberto. "The Garden of Eden Account: The Chiastic Structure of Genesis 2–3." *Andrews University Seminary Studies* 40, no. 2 (2002): 219–43.

Ozment, Steven E. *Mysticism and Dissent: Religious Ideology and Social Protest in the Sixteenth Century*. New Haven, CT: Yale University Press, 1973.

Parpola, Simo. "From Whence the Beast?" *Bible Review* 15, no. 6 (1999): 24.

———. "Sons of God: The Ideology of Assyrian Kingship." *Archaeology Odyssey* 2, no. 5 (1999): 16–27.

Patai, Raphael. *On Jewish Folklore*. Detroit, MI: Wayne State University Press, 1983.

Payne, Thomas. *The Age of Reason*. 1795. Reprint, Secaucus, NJ: Citadel Press, 1974.

Pedersén, Olof, Paul J. J. Sinclair, Irmgard Hein, and Jakob Andersson. "Cities and Urban Landscapes in the Ancient Near East and Egypt with Special Focus on the City of Babylon." In *The Urban Mind Cultural and Environmental Dynamics*, edited by Paul J. J. Sinclair et al. Upsala, Sweden: Upsala University Press, 2010.

Pelikan, Jaroslav. *The Christian Tradition: A History of the Development of Doctrine*. Vol. 1, *The Emergence of the Catholic Tradition (100–600)*. Chicago, IL: University of Chicago Press, 1971.

Pennock, Robert T. "Naturalism, Evidence, and Creationism: The Case of Phillip Johnson." In *Intelligent Design Creationism and Its Critics: Philosophical, Theological, and Scientific Perspectives*, edited by Robert T. Pennock, 77–98. Cambridge, MA: MIT Press, 2001.

Persinger, Michael, and Faye Healey. "Experimental Facilitation of the Sensed Presence: Possible Intercalation between the Hemispheres Induced by Complex Magnetic Fields." *Journal of Nervous and Mental Diseases* 190, no. 8 (2002): 533–41.

Persinger, Michael A., Yves R. J. Bureau, Oksana P. Peredery, and Pauline M. Richards. "The Sensed Presence as Right Hemispheric Intrusions into the Left Hemispheric Awareness of Self: An Illustrative Case Study." *Perceptual and Motor Skills* 78, no. 3 (1994): 999–1009. doi.org/10.1177/003151259407800358.

Petersen, David L. *Zachariah 9–14 and Malachi: A Commentary*. Louisville, KY: Westminster John Knox Press, 1995.

Philo. *Questions On Exodus*. Translated by Ralph Marcus. Cambridge, MA: Loeb Classical Library, 1953.

Pitts, J. Brian. "Conservation of Energy: Missing Features in Its Nature and Justification and Why They Matter," in "Special Issue on James Joule." Special issue, *Foundations of Science* (2020): 1–45. http://doi.org/10.1007/s10699-020-09657-1.

Plantinga, Alvin. "Introduction: The Evolutionary Argument against Naturalism." In *Naturalism Defeated? Essays On Plantinga's Evolutionary Argument Against Naturalism*, edited by James Beilby, 1–12. Ithaca, NY: Cornell University Press, 2002.

———. "What is 'Intervention'?" *Theology and Science* 6, no. 4 (2008): 369–401. http://doi.org/10.1080/14746700802396106.

Popper, Karl. *The Open Society and Its Enemies*. 4th ed. London: Routledge, 1962.

Price, H. H. *Thinking and Experience*. 2nd ed. London: Hutchinson Publishing, 1969.

Purtill, Richard L., Norman L. Geisler, Francis J. Beckwith, Winfried Corduan, Ronald H. Nash, and J. P. Moreland. "Replies to Evan Fales from the Contributors to in Defense of Miracle." *Philosophia Christi* 3, no. 1 (2001): 37–87. http://doi.org/10.5840/pc2001313.

Quine, Willard Van Orman. *Word and Object*. Boston, MA: MIT Press, 1960.

Rappaport, Roy A. "Ritual, Sanctity, and Cybernetics." *American Anthropologist* 73, no. 1 (1971): 59–76.

The Really Big Questions. "Giving Without Expecting Something in Return Is a Key Part of Maasai Life." February 24, 2014. http://trbq.org/giving-without-expecting-something-in-return-is-a-key-part-maasai-life/.

Rebbi, Lubavitcher. "The First Mitzvah." *Come and Hear*. Accessed June 15, 2020. http://www.come-and-hear.com/editor/br-painful/.

Reddit, Paul L. *Haggai, Zecharia, and Malachi*. New Century Bible Commentary. Grand Rapids, MI: William B. Eerdmans Publishing Company, 1995.

Reinbold, Meyer. *History of Purple as a Status Symbol in Antiquity*. Vol. 116. Brussels: Collection Latomus, 1970.

Reynolds, Bennie H. "Molek: Dead or Alive? The Meaning and Derivation of *mlk* and מלך." In *Human Sacrifice in Jewish and Christian Tradition*, edited by Karin Finsterbusch, Armin Lange, and K. F. Diethard Römheld, 133–51. Boston, MA: Brill, 2007.

Rodríguez, Rafael. "Authenticating Criteria: The Use and Misuse of a Critical Method." *Journal for the Study of the Historical Jesus* 7, no. 2 (2009): 152–67. http://doi.org/10.1163/174551909x447374.

Rogerson, J. W. *Myth in Old Testament Interpretation*. New York: Walter de Gruyter, 1974.

Rosenberg, Joel W. "Genesis: Introduction." In *Harper-Collins Study Bible NRSV*, edited by Wayne Meeks. New York: Harper-Collins Publishers, 1993.

Ruben, David-Hillel. *The Metaphysics of the Social World*. London: Routledge Kegan & Paul, 1985.

Ruse, Michael. "Methodological Naturalism Under Attack." In *Intelligent Design Creationism and Its Critics: Philosophical, Theological, and Scientific Perspectives*, edited by Robert T. Pennock, 363–85. Cambridge, MA: MIT Press, 2001.

Russell, Robert John. "Divine Action and Quantum Mechanics: A Fresh Assessment." In *Philosophy, Science, and Divine Action*, edited by F. LeRon Shults, Nancey Murphy, and Robert John Russell, 351–403. Leiden, The Netherlands: Brill, 1999.

Russell, Robert John, Nancey Murphy, and Arthur R. Peacocke, eds. *Chaos and Complexity: Scientific Perspectives on Divine Action*. 2nd ed. Vatican City: Vatican Observatory Publications, 2000.

Russell, Robert John, Nancey Murphy, and C. J. Isham, eds. *Quantum Cosmology and the Laws of Nature: Scientific Perspectives On Divine Action*. Vatican City: Vatican Observatory Publications, 1999.

Ryan, Jordan J. "Jesus at the Crossroads of Inference and Imagination." *Journal for the Study of the Historical Jesus* 13, no. 1 (2015): 66–89. http://doi.org/10.1163/17455197-01301004.

Salmon, Wesley. *Four Decades of Scientific Explanation*. Minneapolis, MN: Minnesota University Press, 1989.

Samanta, Suchitra. "The 'Self-Animal' and Divine Digestion: Goat Sacrifice to the Goddess Kālī in Bengal." *The Journal of Asian Studies* 53, no. 3 (1994): 779–803. http://doi.org/10.2307/2059730.

Sanders, E. P. *Jesus and Judaism*. Philadelphia: Fortress Press, 1985.

———. *Paul and Palestinian Judaism: A Comparison of Patterns of Religion*. London: SCM, 1977.

Sandnes, Karl Olav. *The Gospel 'According to Homer and Virgil': Cento and Canon*. Leiden, Netherlands: Koninklijke Brill, 2011.

Schröter, Jens. "The Historical Jesus and the Sayings Tradition: Comments On Current Research." *Neotestimentica* 30, no. 1 (1966): 151–68.

Schweitzer, Albert. *The Quest of the Historical Jesus*. 1906. Translated by W. Montgomery. Reprint, Mineola, NY: Dover Publications, 2005.

Scroggie, W. Graham. *A Guide to the Gospels*. London: Pickering & Inglis, 1948.

Searle, John R. *The Construction of Social Reality*. New York: Simon & Schuster, 1995.

———. *Making the Social World: The Structure of Human Civilization*. New York: Oxford University Press, 2010.

Segal, Alan F. *Paul the Convert: The Apostolate and Apostasy of Saul the Pharisee*. New Haven, CT: Yale University Press, 1990.

Seidensticker, Philipp. *Die Auferstehung Jesu in der Botschaft der Evangelisten: Ein Taditionsgeschichtlicher Versuch Zum Problem der Sicherung der Osterbotschaft in der Apostolischen Zeit*. Stuttgarter Bibelstudien 26. Stuttgart, Germany: Verlag Katholisches Bibelwerk, 1967.

Senior, Donald P. *The Passion Narrative According to Matthew: A Redactional Study*. Louvain, Belgium: Leuven University Press, 1975.

Shea, William H. "Literary Structural Parallels between Genesis 1 and 2." *Origins* 16, no. 2 (1989): 49–68.

Shlita, Rabbi Yosef Kalatsky. "Parshas Terumah." (2003). yadavraham.org/documents/shemos/terumah/terumah2003.pdf.

Sim, David C. *The Gospel of Matthew and Christian Judaism: The History and Social Setting of the Matthean Community*. Edinburgh, Scotland: T&T Clark, 1998.

Ska, Jean-Louis. *The Exegesis of the Pentateuch: Exegetical Studies and Basic Questions*. Tübingen, Germany: Mohr Siebeck, 2009.

———. *Introduction to Reading the Pentateuch*. Translated by Sr. Pascale Dominique. Winona Lake, IN: Eisenbrauns, 2006.

Skorupski, John. "Comment on Professor Horton's Paradox and Explanation." *Philosophy of the Social Sciences* 5 (1975): 63–70.

———. "Science and Traditional Religious Thought." *Philosophy of the Social Sciences* 3 (1973): 209–30.

Slade, Darren M. "Properly Investigating Miracle Claims." In *The Case Against Miracles,* edited by John W. Loftus, 114–47. United Kingdom: Hypatia Press, 2019.

Smith, Jonathan Z. *Drudgery Divine: On the Comparison of Early Christianities and the Religions of Late Antiquity*. Chicago, IL: University of Chicago Press, 1990.

Smith, Morton. *Jesus the Magician*. New York: Harper and Row, 1978.

———. "On the Wine God in Palestine." In *Salo Wittmayer Baron, Jubilee Volume*. Vol. 2, 815–29. New York: Columbia University Press, 1974.

Smith, S. H. "'Heel' and 'Thigh': The Concept of Sexuality in the Jacob-Esau Narratives." *Vetus Testamentum* 40, no. 4 (1990): 464–73. http://doi.org/10.1163/156853390x00154.

Snell, Daniel C. "The Invention of the Individual." In *A Companion to the Ancient Near East*, edited by Daniel C. Snell, 357–70. Malden, MA: Blackwell Publishing, 2005.

Sobel, Jordan Howard. "Hume's Theorem on Testimony Sufficient to Establish a Miracle." *The Philosophical Quarterly* 41, no. 163 (1991): 229–37. http://doi.org/10.2307/2219595.

Spencer, W. Baldwin, and F. J. Gillen. *The Northern Tribes of Central Australia*. New York: Macmillan and Company, 1904.

Spinoza, Baruch. *Theological-Political Treatise*. 1670. Translated by Samuel Shirley and Seymour Feldman. Reprint, Indianapolis, IN: Hackett, 1998.

Stager, Lawrence E., and Samuel R. Wolff. "Child Sacrifice at Carthage–Religious Rite or Population Control?" *Biblical Archaeology Review* 10, no. 1 (1984): 31–51.

Stanner, W. E. H. "The Dreaming." In *Reader in Comparative Religion*. 3rd ed, edited by William A. Lessa and Evon Z. Vogt, 269–77. New York: Joanna Colter Books, 1972.

Starbuck, E. D. *The Psychology of Religion: An Empirical Study of the Growth of Religious Consciousness*. 3rd ed. New York: C. Scribner's Sons, 1912.

Stephenson, Paul. *Constantine: Roman Emperor, Christian Victor*. New York: Overlook Press, 2010.

Stevens, Marty E. *Temples, Tithes, and Taxes: The Temple and the Economic Life of Ancient Israel*. Peabody, MA: Hendrickson Publishers, 2006.

Stevenson, Seth William, C. Roach Smith, and Frederic W. Madden. *A Dictionary of Roman Coins*. London: B. A. Seaby, 1964.

Stökl Ben Ezra, Daniel. *The Impact of Yom Kippur on Early Christianity: The Day of Atonement from Second Temple Judaism to the Fifth Century*. Tübingen, Germany: Mohr Siebeck, 2003.

Stone, Christopher D. *Should Trees Have Standing? Law, Morality, and the Environment*. 3rd ed. New York: Oxford University Press, 2010.

Strawson, Galen. *The Secret Connexion: Causation, Realism, and David Hume*. New York: Oxford University Press, 2014.

Stump, Eleonore. *Wandering in Darkness: Narrative and the Problem of Suffering*. New York: Oxford University Press, 2010.

Sumner, Paul B. "The Heavenly Council in the Hebrew Bible and New Testament." *Hebrew Streams* (2012). http://www.hebrew-streams.org/works/hebrew/council.pdf.

Sutherland, C. H. V. *Roman Coins*. New York: G. P. Putnam's Sons, 1974.

Swinburne, Richard. *The Resurrection of God Incarnate*. New York: Oxford University Press, 2003.

———. *Revelation: From Metaphor to Analogy*. New York: Oxford University Press, 2007.

Talbert, Charles H. *What Is a Gospel? The Genre of the Canonical Gospels*. Philadelphia, PA: Fortress Press, 1977.

Tambiah, S. J. "Form and Meaning of Magical Acts: A Point of View." In *Modes of Thought: Essays on Thinking in Western and Non-Western Societies*, edited by Robin Horton and Ruth Finnegan, 199–229. London: Faber and Faber, 1973.

Thomas, Alexander. "Urbanization before Cities: Lessons for Social Theory from the Evolution of Cities." *Journal of World-Systems Research* 18, no. 2 (2012): 211–35. http://doi.org/10.5195/jwsr.2012.479.

Thomas, L. L., J. Z. Kronenfeld, and D. B. Kronenfeld. "Asdiwal Crumbles: A Critique of Lévi-Straussian Myth Analysis." *American Ethnologist* 3, no. 1 (1976): 147–73. http://doi.org/10.1525/ae.1976.3.1.02a00090.

Tobolowsky, Andrew. "Israelite and Judahite History in Contemporary Theoretical Approaches." *Currents in Biblical Research* 17, no. 1 (2018): 33–58. http://doi.org/10.1177/1476993x18765117.

Townsend, Nicholas. "Surveillance and Seeing: A New Way of Reading Mark 12:17, 'Give Back to Caesar…'." *Studies in Christian Ethics* 27, no. 1 (2014): 79–90. http://doi.org/10.1177/0953946813509340.

Turner, Terrence S. "Animal Symbolism, Totemism, and the Structure of Myth." In *Animal Myths and Metaphors in South America*, edited by Gary Urton, 49–106. Salt Lake City, UT: University of Utah Press, 1985.

———. "Narrative Structure and Mythopoesis: A Critique and Reformulation of the Structuralist Concepts of Myth, Narrative, and Poetics." *Arethusa* 10 (1977): 103–63.

———. "Oedipus: Time and Structure in Narrative Form." In *Forms of Symbolic Action: Proceedings of the 1969 Annual Spring Meeting of the American Ethnological Society*, edited by Robert F. Spencer, 26–68. Seattle, WA: University of Washington Press, 1969.

Turner, Victor. *The Forest of Symbols: Aspects of Ndembu Ritual*. Ithaca, NY: Cornell University Press, 1970.

———. *The Ritual Process: Structure and Anti-Structure*. 1969. Reprint, Piscataway, NJ: Aldine Transaction, 1995.

Tylor, Edward B. *Primitive Culture*. 6th ed. Vol. 1. New York: G. P. Putnam's Sons, 1922.

Udoh, Fabian. *To Caesar What Is Caesar's: Tribute, Taxes, and Imperial Administration in Early Roman Palestine (63 B.C.E.–70 C.E.)*. Providence, RI: Brown Judaic Studies, 2005.

van der Toorn, Karel. *Family Religion in Babylonia, Syria, and Israel: Continuity and Change in the Forms of Religious Life*. New York: Brill, 1996.

van Gennep, Arnold. *The Rites of Passage*. 1909. Translated by Monika B. Vizedon and Gabrielle L. Caffee. Reprint, Chicago, IL: University of Chicago Press, 1960.

van Inwagen, Peter. *Material Beings*. Ithaca, NY: Cornell University Press, 1990.

Vauchez, André *Francis of Assisi: The Life and Afterlife of a Medieval Saint*. Translated by Michael F. Cusato. New Haven, CT: Yale University Press, 2012.

Vermes, Geza, trans. *The Dead Sea Scrolls in English*. 3rd ed. London: Penguin Books, 1987.

Vilnay, Zev. *Legends of Jerusalem*. Philadelphia, PA: Wish Publication Society of America, 1973.

Walker, Brent L. *The Conquest of Ainu Lands: Ecology and Culture in Japanese Expansion 1590–1800*. Berkeley, CA: University of California Press, 2001.

Walker, Norman. "The Alleged Matthaean Errata." *New Testament Studies* 9, no. 4 (1963): 391–94. http://doi.org/10.1017/s0028688500002253.

Walton, John H. *Ancient Near Eastern Thought and the Old Testament: Introducing the Conceptual World of the Hebrew Bible.* Grand Rapids, MI: Baker Academic, 2006.

Watkins, J. W. N. "Third Reply to Mr. Goldstein." *The British Journal for the Philosophy of Science* 10, no. 39 (1959): 242–44. http://doi.org/10.1093/bjps/x.39.242.

———. "The Two Theses of Methodological Individualism." *The British Journal for the Philosophy of Science* 9, no. 36 (1959): 319–20. http://doi.org/10.1093/bjps/ix.36.319.

Weatherson, Brian. "Probability in Philosophy." *Rutgers and Arché* (2008). http://brian.weatherson.org/PL4.pdf.

Webb, Robert L. "The Rules of the Game: History and Historical Method in the Context of Faith: The Via Media of Methodological Naturalism." *Journal for the Study of the Historical Jesus* 9, no. 1 (2011): 59–84.

Weeks, Andrew. *German Mysticism from Hildegard von Bingen to Ludwig Wittgenstein: A Literary and Intellectual History.* Albany, NY: SUNY Press, 1993.

Widengren, G. "Early Hebrew Myths and their Interpretation." In *Myth, Ritual, and Kingship: Essays On the Theory and Practice of Kingship in the Ancient Near East and in Israel*, edited by S. H. Hooke, 149–203. Oxford: Clarendon Press, 1958.

Winch, Peter. *The Idea of a Social Science and Its Relation to Philosophy.* New York: Routledge and Keegan Paul, 1958.

———. "Understanding a Primitive Society." *American Philosophical Quarterly* 1 (1964): 307–24.

Winn, Albert C. *Ain't Gonna Study War No More: Biblical Ambiguity and the Abolition of War.* Louisville, KY: Westminster John Knox Press, 1993.

Winter, Paul. *On the Trial of Jesus.* Berlin: Walter de Gruyter, 1961.

Wisdom, J. O. "Situational Individualism and the Emergent Group-Properties." In *Explanation in the Behavioral Sciences*, edited by Robert Borger and Frank Cioffi, 271–96. New York: Cambridge University Press, 1970.

Wolfson, Elliot R. "Circumcision, Vision of God, and Textual Interpretation: From Midrashic Trope to Mystical Symbol." *History of Religions* 27, no. 2 (1987): 189–215. http://doi.org/10.1086/463112.

Wright, G. E. *The Old Testament Against Its Environment*. London: SCM Press, 1950.

Wright, John P. *The Sceptical Realism of David Hume*. Minneapolis, MN: University of Minnesota Press, 1983.

Wright, N. T. *Jesus and the Victory of God*. Vol. 2. Christian Origins and the Question of God. Minneapolis, MN: Fortress Press, 1996.

———. *The New Testament and the People of God*. Vol. 1. Christian Origins and the Question of God. Minneapolis, MN: Fortress Press, 1992.

———. "Paul's Gospel and Caesar's Empire." In *Paul and Politics, Ekklesia, Israel, Imperium, Interpretation*, edited by Richard A. Horsley, 160–85. Philadelphia, PA: Trinity Press International, 2000.

———. *The Resurrection of the Son of God*. Vol. 3. Christian Origins and the Question of God. Minneapolis, MN: Fortress Press, 2003.

Yalman, Nur. "'The Raw : the Cooked :: Nature : Culture'—Observations on *Le Cru et le cuit*." In *The Structural Study of Myth and Totemism*, edited by Edmund R. Leach, 71–89. London: Tavistock Publications, 1967.

Yamouchi, Edwin. "Magic or Miracle? Diseases, Miracles, and Exorcisms." In *Gospel Perspectives*, edited by David Wenham and Craig Blomberg. Vol. 6, *The Miracles of Jesus*, 89–184. Sheffield: JSOT Press, 1986.

Yuval, Israel J. "God Will See the Blood: Sin, Punishment, and Atonement in the Jewish-Christian Discourse." In *Jewish Blood: Reality and Metaphor in History, Religion, and Culture*, edited by Mitchell B. Hart, 83–98. New York: Routledge, 2009.

Yuval, Sinai. "Witness." In *Encyclopaedia Judaica*. 2nd ed, edited by Michael Berenbaum and Fred Skolnik. Vol. 21. New York: Macmillan Reference, 2007.

Index

Abbé de Paris, 60n41, 61n41
Adam and Eve, 76, 180, 289,
    290n12, 292, 308
  childbearing, 287, 288, 297
  compared to Noah, 293n14,
    294, 296, 297, 297n24,
    297n25, 312
  temptation of, 290, 293n14,
    296n23
Aeneid (Virgil), 187, 326n23,
    338–340, 341, 381n43, 422,
    433, 434, 436
akedah, 241, 242, 247, 248, 256,
    262, 271, 272–273, 274, 277–
    278n78, 279, 393n74
altar, Jerusalem Temple, 240,
    244, 246, 251, 253, 254, 256,
    257, 259, 261, 263, 263n46,
    265, 274, 274n72
ancient Israel, 155n38, 176, 177,
    178, 208, 242, 243, 244, 245,
    249, 250, 251n22, 256, 265,
    273, 281, 285, 346, 347, 432
angels, 47n13, 90, 102n25, 113,
    174, 271, 273n70, 286, 290,
    412, 413
  Angel of Death, 371n21, 393
  fallen, 378
  Jacob's combat with, 283, 284
anthropology, 88, 207, 217n16,
    233, 274, 433
  of group intentions and action,
    153n31
  kinship theory, 241
  myth interpretation, 365n14
  of religion, xiv, 11, 20, 99
  structural, 89, 395n79
  Structure-Functionalist School
    in, 172
  study of myth, 191
  study of religious storytelling,
    128
  tools of, 238, 445
apologists, 79, 80, 80n72, 84, 90,
    185, 328n26, 363n11, 364,
    389n60
apostles, 168, 313, 314, 315,
    320n9, 323, 325, 325n20,
    406n98, 416
archaeology, 270, 350n23,
    380n42
arguments to the best explanation
    (abduction), 99, 109, 363,
    421
  abductive reasoning, 56n31,
    110, 111
ark of the covenant, 240, 274n72,
    288
art, works of, 140n6, 145n16,
    146, 146n21, 147, 148,
    149n25, 156n39, 175, 259
artifacts, 13, 74, 144, 145, 148,
    149n25, 168, 196, 201, 232,
    285
Asdiwal myth, 217
ass, Balaam's, 303, 304
Augustine, 361n6, 442, 443n2,
    444n7

Austin, J. L., 13, 14, 16, 31n49
authorities, earthly vs. spiritual, 375n33, 376, 385, 387n54, 393, 401, 413
autochthony, 210, 211, 212, 216, 217, 228
axis mundi, 240, 290, 395n78
Azande, 23, 23n36, 24, 25, 27n42, 30, 38, 170
Azazel, 394, 394n76, 395n79
Balaam, 304n34, 305
  ass of, 303–304
  divine attack on, 303
baptism, 289n9, 299, 316n2, 354, 406n98, 426
  as death and re-birth, 167n59, 296, 425
  to exorcize Satan, 230
  as rite of passage, 267
Barabbas, as scapegoat, 265n54, 394, 394n76, 394n78, 395n79, 396n83
Bayes' Theorem, 64, 65, 87n84
Bayesian conditionalization, 55, 66
Bayesian confirmation, 38, 46, 66, 74
Berengarius of Tours, 264n48
best explanation, reasoning to, xv, 55, 57, 58, 85, 108, 110, 421
Bethany, 194, 371, 385, 389, 390
  chronology of, 386–388
bios (βίος), 200–205, 204–205n32
blood, ritual significance of, 250–251
  for atonement, 252, 254, 254n27, 257, 259, 261, 262, 263n46, 265
  for covenant, 253–254, 255, 255n29, 261, 262, 264n50, 268, 268–269n63, 269
body, immortal, 121, 231, 264, 264n49, 428

Borg, Marcus, 119n51, 416n16, 419
burial grounds, and territorial ownership, 271n22, 371, 384, 389n59, 391, 396, 398
Caesars, legitimacy of, 401, 404, 406n98, 419
Caesar's coin, 343, 351, 354, 445
Caiaphas, 256, 346, 391n64, 392n69, 396, 447
cargo cults, 60n41, 187, 318n6, 403n96, 439n43
carnal nature, human, 411
Castañeda, Carlos, 188, 189
chaos-waters, 240n1, 273, 286, 288–289, 294, 374–376, 378, 406, 435, 436
  and high places, 240, 376n35
  and king, 296
  and rites of passage, 295, 374
  tehom, symbolism, 240, 285, 296, 374, 386, 387, 394n76
charitable/uncharitable explanations, 19n25, 38, 42, 45, 63n47, 85, 110, 145, 160–165, 198, 212, 283
chiasmus, 284n4, 334, 336, 356n36
chiastic structure, as sign of fiction, 284, 341, 446
Christ, the, 251, 259, 261, 261n42, 263, 263n48, 266, 266n56. *see also* Jesus
circumcision, 231, 269n64, 280, 301, 314, 324, 327n25
  of Abraham, 267, 267n60
  commandment of, 269
  covenant of, 280n82
  and paschal lamb, 268
  and Paul, 269n63
  as a "small death," 267, 268–269n63

and Zipporah, 266, 267, 268, 279, 305
City of God, 442
Coady, C. A. J., 6, 6n5, 7, 8, 9, 44
coherence (internal intelligibility), criterion of, 17, 100, 107, 121–123
communication, non-linguistic, 2, 18
conditionalization, 63n47, 65
   Bayesian, 55, 66
conservation, 75, 91n3
   of energy, 40, 40n2, 41n2, 59n40
   of momentum, 40, 50, 59n40
Constantine, 436n39, 439, 439n44, 442, 443, 444, 445
context and expectation, criteria of, 100, 104, 417
contract, social, 141, 142, 142n11, 149, 150, 182, 187, 276
coronation, of Jesus, 115, 117, 406n98
corporation sole, 169n64, 231
cosmos (κόσμος), meaning of, 95, 181, 400, 409, 416
creation, 234, 262, 296, 307, 374
   ex nihilo, 115, 181, 380n42
   goodness of, 289, 291
   second, 173, 286, 294, 297n24, 400, 416n16
   stories, 283, 285, 286, 287, 288, 294, 376
   of the universe, 179, 283–288, 376n35
cross-cousin marriage, matrilateral, 277n78, 298
crucifixion, 93, 109, 194, 258, 327, 378, 392, 393, 403, 447
   time of, 360n3, 369, 370–371, 371n21, 372, 373, 380, 380n42, 387

cultural identity, Israelite, 282, 283, 295, 304n35, 306
cultural relativism, 17, 18, 183, 323
data, underdetermination of theory, 110, 217, 407
de Saussure, Ferdinand, 209, 211
death/resurrection
   of Jesus, 200, 360, 364, 373n23, 402, 446n9
   of kings, 406n98
   role of women in, 380n42
   theme, Hebrew Bible occurrences, 227, 369, 373, 380, 392n70
deity, concept of, 36, 42, 47, 49, 59, 79, 257, 263, 263n46, 324
demons, 90, 113, 114, 171, 318, 366, 412, 415
   Azazel, 394, 394n76
   exorcism of, 97, 111, 438
diamones/genius, 231, 233n43, 414
dietary restrictions, Leviticus, 284, 285, 327n25
diminution principle, 72, 73
Dinka, 29, 30, 34n58, 168
disciples. *see also* apostles
   obtuseness of, 360n2
   post-Easter motivations of, 403
dissimilarity (discontinuity), criterion of, 100, 102, 103, 104, 421
divergent interpretations, substantial agreement, criterion of, 108
divine attacks
   on Balaam, 303
   on Jacob, 282, 283, 298–302, 299n28
   on Moses, 300, 301

Douglas, Mary, 181, 224, 238, 248, 284, 285, 285n6, 334, 335, 336
duality, 394n76, 395n79
  natural/supernatural duality, 50–51n21, 94n8, 367, 378, 412
Durkheim, Emile, 36, 134–135, 156, 157, 157n44, 161, 161n50, 232–233, 366–367
effect, criterion of, 108–109
Elijah, 52n23, 80, 103, 104, 118, 119, 120, 121, 295, 328n27, 342n10, 428, 435
Elisha, 52n23, 103, 104, 118, 295, 342n10
embarrassment
  argument from, 95
  criterion of, 105, 106, 106n31, 107, 417, 421, 428
embellishment, criterion of, 107, 108
embodiment, 145–152, 146n18, 146n21, 148n24
emergence, strong, 139
emergence, weak, 139
empty tomb, 316, 328, 421, 422, 427
  historicity of, 373
  witnesses to, 95, 325, 428
equivalence, mouth to genitals, 280
eschatology, 113, 121, 129, 173, 173n69, 307, 382, 408, 410, 420, 442, 443
Essenes, 94, 94n8, 296, 344
ethics, 246, 247
Eucharist, 69n55, 117, 258, 262, 263, 264n48, 345, 346, 348, 371n21, 380n42
  and embodiment, 259, 261n42
Eusebius, 439n44, 443, 444, 444n7

evangelists, 117, 126, 203, 205, 256, 337, 338, 341n9, 352, 353, 371n21, 374, 379n42, 381n43, 388, 403n95, 404, 409, 411, 428, 434, 436, 437
exchange, 225, 234, 235, 236, 237, 239, 263, 274, 275, 281. *see also* reciprocity
exegesis, 90, 99, 187n5, 361, 385n51, 427
exilic period, 249
exorcism, 104, 105, 111–114, 318
explanations, reductive, 35, 134, 138
Ezekiel, 104, 270, 311n49, 380, 405, 420, 422, 424, 425, 428
fabrication, 75, 102, 105, 108, 124, 149, 191, 388n55
fiction, 14, 121, 142, 170, 171, 173n69, 194, 339
  communicative, 182
  conceptual, 182
  of creation, 179
  historical, 149
  legal, 155n38
  myth as, 185, 192, 204
fig tree, parable of, 353–354n30
First Quest, 96, 199
First Temple, 309n40, 347
  creation of, 243, 289
  destruction of, 249, 346
  rituals of, 234, 247, 250
first-order justification, 144n13
fish, New Testament symbolism of, 343–344, 348, 348n20, 353–354n30
Flood/creation, comparison, 294, 296, 297n24, 376
forty, symbolic significance, 289n9
fraud and folly, 39, 43, 44, 45, 55, 87, 92, 95, 364

Frazer, James, 22, 29, 207, 368n17
Freud, Sigmund, influence of, 159n47, 213, 216
fundamentalism, 12n17, 87, 87n82, 88, 103, 107
Garden of Eden, 175n72, 240, 284, 286, 287, 288–292, 297, 308, 310, 311, 312, 327n23
Gellner, Ernest, 145n15, 164n55
Genesis
  as cosmology, 180, 285
  redaction history, 249, 282, 304n35
  as social charter, 366
Genesis 1-2, chiasmus, 284
genius, 231, 233n43, 414
Gnosticism, 181, 193
gods
  disembodied, 146n19, 182
  false, 79n70, 355n33
  family, 302
  foreign, 243, 300, 302
  national, 176
  royal, 352n28, 377n36, 381
Gomorrah, 282, 292, 309
Guthrie, Woody, 105, 187–188, 188n6, 188n7
Gutting, Gary, 329, 331, 331n34
Hebron, 397, 398n86
Hegel, Georg, influence, 213, 214, 246, 249, 368n16
Hegelian idealism, 213, 214
Hellenistic culture, influence, 92, 93, 94n8, 103, 104, 112, 116
hermeneutics, 1, 21, 38, 42, 44, 88n85, 92, 98, 360
Herodians, 256n34, 349, 350, 352, 353, 355, 434
historicity, 90n1, 96, 97, 98, 100–103, 105, 108, 114, 117, 118, 121, 122

history, criteria for, 188, 191–195, 193n13, 197–200, 203–204, 205–206
Hobbes, Thomas, 150, 150n27, 187
Hollis, Martin, 21, 21n30, 22, 22n34, 23n34, 36, 163, 164
Homer, 197, 422
  literary influence, 338, 339, 340, 341, 341n9, 342
Horton, Robin, 27, 27n42, 28, 28n43, 29, 34, 34n58, 162, 207, 283n2
hot vs. cold societies, 208
hyssop, significance of, 371n21
Incarnation, doctrine of, 177, 180n78
income tax, 242, 245
individualism, 141n10, 143, 145, 150, 234, 292
  metaphysical, 149
  methodological, 134, 138, 138n35, 150n27, 154n35, 157n44
initiation rites, 226, 227, 231, 232, 247, 374n31
  circumcision, 267
intelligibility, conditions of, 13, 18, 21, 107, 160, 182, 183
intentionality, original, 137, 137n4, 146n18, 146n21, 412
interpretation
  figurative, 113
  literal, 12n17, 24, 36, 45, 46, 88n85, 123, 272, 373n24, 402
interpretive charity, xiii, xiv, 4, 7, 40, 365
interpretive method, 1, 13, 88, 95, 165, 184, 193, 196, 200, 342, 368n17, 402
  of Augustine, 361n6
irrationality, 11, 20, 24, 25, 36, 45, 72, 169–172, 182

Isaac
  binding of, 240, 241, 242, 342n10
  structural role of, 251n19, 278n78
Israelite kings, 234, 342n10, 357, 357n38, 375n33, 377n37
  foreign wives of, 243n6, 266, 310n47
  sacerdotal status, 346
Jabbok, River, 298, 299, 300, 300n29
Jacob
  conflict with Esau, 298–300, 301, 304–305
  divine attack on, 282, 283, 298–302, 299n28
  struggle with God, 298–302
Jansenism, 60–61n41
Jerusalem Temple, 241, 247, 248, 281. *see also* altar, Jerusalem Temple
  cleansing of by Jesus, 256–260
Jesus
  anointing of, 194, 371, 375n33, 379n, 383, 384, 387, 389, 390
  appearances after rising, 313, 314, 315, 316n2, 327, 328
  captivity by chaos-waters, 373–377
  cleanses temple, 256–260
  coronation of, 115, 117, 406n98
  death/resurrection of, 200, 360, 373n23, 402, 446n9
  duration of interment, 369
  embalming of, 382, 389
  historical, 127, 129, 199, 200, 204, 407
  hour of, 372n23
  kenosis of, 167n59
  kingdom of, 322n17

  overturns moneychanger tables, 345, 401n92
  as Passover lamb, 117, 260, 261, 268, 271, 371n21, 386, 390, 391
  price of, 390, 390n63, 396
  quests of, 96, 132, 199, 200
  as savior to the Gentiles, 401
  self-conception per Sanders, 408–409, 409n1
  self-conception per Wright, 410–411
  as Son of David, 322n16, 358
  temptations of, 410, 411
  tomb secured by guards, 372n23
  trial of, 380n42, 387, 392n69
  views on family, 293n15, 429–434
Johnathan Apphus, 346
Jonah, sign of, 367, 369–373, 378, 387
Jubilees, Book of, 272, 272n69
Judas, 194, 389n60, 396
  betrayal by, 250n19, 258, 371, 384, 388, 389, 391, 399
  and high priests, 251, 371, 371n22, 384, 392, 395n79
judges of Israel, 243, 320, 400
Kant, Immanuel, 208, 332
Kee, Howard, 112, 113
Keener, Craig S., 70n58, 77, 129–132
Kierkegaard, Søren, 82, 177
Kingdom of God, 101n25, 122, 179, 348, 354, 388, 391, 426, 437, 438
  time of inauguration, 101, 356, 425, 443
kings, immortal body of, 231, 264, 264n49, 428
king's two bodies doctrine, 173n69, 415

kingship vs. kinship, 430, 434, 438
Kuhn, Thomas, 27n42, 100
language learning, 3, 9, 17, 18, 21n30
Larkin, Daniel, xiii, 383n45, 406n98
Last Supper, time of, 258, 371
laws
  agents/representatives, 140, 153, 423
  defeasible, 67, 68n54, 69
  fundamental, 53, 61
  king's immortal body, 169, 178, 231, 264, 264n49, 375n33
  legal traditions, 128, 136, 140, 141n8
  legislative authority, 173n69, 178, 351, 438n42
  of nature, 40n2, 46, 47, 49, 50, 50n20, 51n21, 52, 53, 55, 61, 61n42, 66, 67, 70, 73, 85, 91n3
  presumptive, 48, 49, 54
  social vs. natural, 34–37
  of society, 2, 10, 27, 29–34, 153, 415
  statistical vs. defeasible, 67, 68n54
laying on of hands, symbolism, 257
Leach, Edmund, 248, 294, 371n22, 397
legends, 192, 193, 210, 250, 429
Leviathan/Rahab, 289, 359, 374n29, 375, 382
Lévi-Bruhl, Lucien, 161n50, 207
Lévi-Strauss, Claude, 34, 162, 192n12, 199, 206, 242n4, 246, 293n15, 306, 306n37, 307, 310n46, 367, 368
  on context, 368n17
  contributions of, 207, 208–218, 224, 224n25, 225, 236, 237
  on myth generation, 368n16
  structural myth analysis, 335
Levites, 242, 244n9, 270, 321
Lewis, I. M., 320, 328, 332
  types of mysticism, 171n67, 238, 316, 317, 323, 324
life-of-Jesus research (LOJR), 39, 95, 96n13, 129, 407
  aims and methods, 96–111
  findings of, 111–123
liminality, 226, 230, 267
literal interpretation, 12n17, 24, 36, 45, 46, 88n85, 123, 272, 373n24, 402
Locke, John, 49, 49n18, 150n27, 177, 433, 442
Lukes, Steven, 21, 22, 36
Machpelah, cave purchase by Abraham, 238, 397
Mahanaim, 298, 299, 300, 300n29
Mandelbaum, Maurice, 143n12, 145n15
marriage and the resurrection, 349n21, 357, 357n39
Marx, Karl, 433
Marxism, 242, 249, 385
  Marxist materialism, 246
Mauss, Marcel, xiv, 225, 232, 234, 235, 236, 237, 241, 274
meal at Bethany, time of, 371, 385, 386–387, 389
Melchizedek, 346, 430, 435n38
memory, 120n55, 127
metaphors, 222–225, 227
methodology, xv, 1, 11, 26, 29, 36
metonyms, 213, 222, 223, 258n37
metzizeh b'peh, 279
millenarianism, 187, 318n6, 404, 439n43

Index 489

miracle reports, 5, 10, 43, 64n47, 75, 76, 77, 78, 81, 87, 88, 96, 97, 101, 130, 131–132, 197–198, 364n12
  reliability of, 44, 63
miracle stories, 38, 39, 41, 45, 104, 122, 198, 364n12
miracles, 1, 5, 6, 10, 24, 90n1
  healing, 87n83, 111–114
  modern, 129–132
  nature, 43, 87n83, 111, 112, 121, 122, 364n12
Moby Dick, 120, 121
monsters of the deep, 240, 374, 376n35, 377n36
Moriah, Mount, 240, 247, 255n1, 267, 272, 274n
Moses, divine attack on, 87n, 300, 301
Mount Sinai, 240, 253, 262, 274n72, 276, 277n76, 376n35
multiple attestation, criterion of, 101, 114–118, 417
mystical experiences (MEs), 5, 238, 314, 317, 319, 327n25, 328, 329, 329n30, 330n32, 331, 332, 333
mysticism, 319n7, 324n18, 326n23
  and affliction, 318
  and charisma, 317, 320–321, 323
  public, 319, 320, 323, 324
  types of, 171n67, 238, 316, 317, 323, 324
mystics, 319, 329, 333
  contemporary data, 330
  Paul as, 317, 323
mythemes, 192n12, 193n13, 195, 211n7, 371
  identification across cultures, 368, 368n17, 380
  meaning of, 190, 193, 209–210, 211, 215, 225, 368
  semantic values, 192, 367, 381
mythicist interpretations, 446, 447
mythology, 29, 34, 205n32, 374
myths
  analysis of, 184, 282, 335, 337, 361, 368, 445
  native, 29, 33, 135, 162, 163, 164, 165, 366
  of origin, 152, 186
  as prescriptive, 191, 192
  as social charter, 36, 192, 214, 225
  structural analysis of, xiii, 195, 198, 205, 208, 213, 216, 217, 306
  superposition technique, 214, 215, 216
  traditions, 37, 429
  variants of, 209, 210, 368n17
nation, personhood of, 137, 147n21, 149, 152n29, 155n39, 156
nations, seventy, 412, 413
natural causes, 34n58, 51, 52, 52n25, 55, 59n38, 60n41, 67, 68, 70, 71n59
naturalism, 38, 40, 40n2, 72n60, 86, 87
  metaphysical, 90–91, 91n2
  methodological, 90, 91
  a priori, 90
necessary explanation, criterion of, 108, 109
new heaven/new earth, 173, 294, 295, *312*, 415
New Jerusalem, 310, 394, 401, 442
Nicaea, Council of, 263n48, 439n44, 443, 444

Nixon, Richard, 136, 153, 156, 169n64
Noah, 292–293, 293n14, 312, 428
  compared to Adam and Eve, 293n14, 294, 296, 297, 297n24, 297n25, 312
  compared to Lot, 292, 309, 312
  compared to Sodom, 292, 298, 309
  meaning of name, 297n24
  non-literal meanings, 12, 33n56, 123, 191
Oedipus myth, 208, 210, 211, 216, 218, 219, 220, 221, 222
ontological status, 134, 143, 145n16, 153, 154, 155–156n39, 155n39, 156n39
oppositions, binary, 17n21, 213, 214, 224, 224n26, 308, 310n46, 312
Paradise. *see* Garden of Eden
Paradise/New Jerusalem (Kingdom of God), comparison, 312
parousia (Second Coming), 266, 322n17, 360, 420, 437, 439, 443, 445
paschal/Passover lamb, Jesus as, 117, 260, 261, 268, 271, 371n21, 386, 390, 391
Passion, chronology of, 360, 365, 369, 369–370n18, 370, 371n21, 372, 386, 387, 402
Passover, 117, 241, 242, 263, 269, 271, 272, 272n69, 273, 275, 276
  as explaining the *akedah*, 271–273, 274, 277n78
  and Yom Kippur, 267n60, 393, 394n78, 395n79

Paul
  political motivations of, 317, 320, 321, 322, 322n16, 323, 324, 327, 327n25, 328
  relations with Jerusalem Church, 315, 322, 324–325, 325n21
  sincerity of, 315, 329
  social context of, 317, 318, 319, 320, 329, 336
  visions and authority, 315, 325, 325n21
Pentateuch, 248, 249, 250, 251, 277n78, 309, 427
Pentecost, 297n25, 316n2, 439n44
performatives, 13–16, 29–34, 31n49, 151n28
personage, concept of, 153, 156, 166, 167n59, 168, 169n64, 173, 178–179, 180n78
Pharisees, 349, 352, 353, 353n30, 354n30, 355, 355n33, 358, 392
Philo, 175, 254–255, 255n29, 361n6, 415
Pilate, wife of, 383n45, 385
poison oracle, 23, 25, 27n42
political theory, 149, 152, 224, 246, 288, 351, 369, 403, 406n98
pollution, 104, 250, 285, 302n32, 391, 438
poor, the/sinners, 408, 417–418, 419, 420
Popper, Karl, 141n9, 159n47
possession, 29, 167, 168, 170
  demonic, 111, 170, 318, 319, 326
  divine, 168, 266n56, 317, 319, 326

Potter's Field, purchase of, 384, 389, 389n59, 390, 391, 396, 398
poverty-of-explanations argument, 91
powers of the air, 378, 415
prefiguration, doctrine of, 99, 119, 278, 359, 365, 384n48
presupposition, 53, 86, 90
presuppositionalism, 90, 101, 102, 130
primogeniture, 178, 241, 272, 275, 302, 393n73
probability, 38, 44, 55, 56n30, 61n42, 62, 64, 65n48, 65n49, 66n52, 67, 71, 72, 78, 87–88n84
 antecedent or prior, 42–43, 43n5, 65, 68, 68n54, 69, 70, 77, 82, 110, 448
 epistemic, 68
 objective, 68
 posterior, 8, 81
Promised Land, 244, 267, 276, 301, 342n10, 357n38, 400
 sale of, 371n22, 389n59, 391, 398
properties
 compositional, 138, 139
 holistic, 138, 139
 part, 138, 139
psychology, folk, 36, 105, 158, 222, 283n2
quests, of the historical Jesus, 96, 132, 199, 200
Rahab/Leviathan, 289, 359, 374n29, 375, 382
raising the dead, 92–93, 97, 97n16, 112, 121, 131, 167n59
Rationalism, 3, 87n83
rationality
 criteria for, 21, 24
 of religious beliefs, 11, 15, 19, 20–29
 weak/strong, 26, 27, 114
reasoning to the best explanation, xv, 55, 57, 58, 85, 108, 110, 421
reciprocity, 236, 237, 238, 239, 241, 275, 390, 397n86. *see also* exchange
Red Sea, 177n74, 234, 289n9, 295, 376
 parting of, 41n2, 43n6
reduction, 36, 134, 137, 157n44, 224n26
 diachronic, 139, 140
 of the social, 138–145
 synchronic, 138, 139, 140
reductionism, xiv, 138, 140, 141, 142, 143
 anti-reductionism, 5, 6, 6n5, 10, 145n15, 157n44
 non-reductionist position, 44, 134, 144, 145
Reformation mystics, 171n67, 319, 319n7
relativism, 28, 41n2, 50, 100, 124
 cultural, 17, 183, 323
 radical, 27, 27n42, 36
Religionsgeschichte School, 361
religious/secular distinction, 93, 245, 352, 416
Renan, Ernest, 198, 199
resurrection, 92, 93, 96, 105, 119, 121, 131. *see also* death/resurrection of Jesus
 conception of, 375n34, 421–429
ring composition, 334, 338, 353. *see also* chiasmus
 signs of, 336, 337
risen Jesus, appearances of, 313, 314, 315, 316n2, 327, 328

rites of passage, 225–234, 267, 295, 304, 374, 377n37
ritual purity, 241, 248, 253, 263n46
rituals. *see also* blood, ritual significance of; initiation rites
  death/resurrection, 227, 228, 230, 231, 232, 234
  structural analysis of, 242
Rome
  as Eternal City, 435, 442
  political crises of, 433, 441
rules, constitutive, 140, 141, 143, 151, 266n56
sacrifice, of first-born male, 269, 271, 393
Sadducees, 257n35, 349, 353, 353n30, 354n30, 355, 357, 388, 392
salvation, 39, 43, 76, 265, 266, 276, 324, 339, 359, 387, 388, 391, 408, 411, 417, 418, 419, 435, 440, 445
Sanhedrin, 355, 356, 371, 385, 385n50, 387, 392n69, 395n79, 399, 405
Saussure, Ferdinand de, 209, 211
scapegoat, 257, 265, 394, 394n76, 394n78, 395, 395n79, 396, 396n81, 396n83
Second Coming. *see parousia*
second-order justification, 144n13
semantic information, coding of, 367, 368, 368n17, 381
sex and social chaos, 286, 294
Simon of Cyrene, 194
sin, expiation of, 254, 264n50
Sinai, Mount, 240, 253, 262, 274n72, 276, 277n76, 376n35
sinners/the poor, 417–418, 419, 420

Smith, Jonathan Z., 248, 362, 362n9
Smith, Morton, 112, 200
social contract, myth of, 187
social institutions, 137, 140, 143n12, 146n21, 147n21, 148, 150, 155–156n39, 156, 165, 259, 367, 436
social ontology, xiii, xiv, 1, 135, 152–158, 173–176, 180n78, 234, 242, 413, 423
social systems, 26, 27, 35n61, 144, 164, 217n16, 219, 288, 308n39
social-political context, 112, 119, 128, 132, 133
societies, (in)stability of, 34, 219, 281, 286–287, 291, 341, 376n35, 408
Sodom, 282, 292, 298, 309, 309n45, 310, 310n46
Son of God, political dimensions, 344, 345–346
soteriology, 39, 104, 258, 259, 266, 323, 324, 360, 365, 395n79, 397n85, 406n97, 412, 446
soul
  concept of, 165, 166, 166n56, 166n57, 167, 168
  disembodied, 90, 113, 173, 379n40
Spinoza, Baruch, 48n16, 91n2
stability, social, 219. *see also* societies, (in)stability of
Stanner, W. E. H., 33n56, 35n62
structural analysis, Turner improvements, 208, 218–225
structure, symbolic, 193, 222
style of Jesus, criterion of, 108
supernatural, 135n2, 138, 157, 174, 177, 181

Supreme Court, U.S., 30, 32, 32n55, 34, 34n58, 148n24, 155n38, 171, 244
suspicion, hermeneutics of, 124, 315, 332
synoptics, 82, 83, 101, 117, 204n32, 205, 334, 351, 352, 360n3, 371
tax collecting, political dimensions, 343, 344, 345, 356
tehom, 240, 285, 296, 374, 386, 387
temple. *see also* altar, Jerusalem Temple; First Temple; Jerusalem Temple
   functions of, 241, 242, 243, 244, 245, 247–248, 278
   in Jerusalem, 241, 247, 248, 281
   portable, 263, 433
   sacrifice functions, 241, 244, 245, 247, 253, 263, 264n50, 278
   temple tax, 343, 345, 349, 353, 356
temptations
   of Adam and Eve, 290, 293n14, 296n23
   of Israel, 411
   of Jesus, 410, 411
Teresa of Avila, 319, 319n7, 326
testimony
   epistemology of, 5
   independence of, 5, 47, 60, 84, 85, 114
   witnesses, 8, 9
thematic elements, 192, 194, 209, 305, 338, 339, 340
Theodore of Mopsuestia, 180n78, 264n48
theories of magic, associationist, 29

Third Quest, 132, 200
three days/three nights, implied chronology, 360, 369, 370n20, 372, 372n23
Thucydides, 126
Tophet, valley of, 270, 270n65
Torah, failure of, 418
track-record argument, 91
tribe vs. empire, 433, 438, 441
Trinity, doctrine of, 177, 180n78
truth-value, 14, 16, 19, 21, 32, 161, 192
Turner, Terrence, 218–225, 306
Turner, Victor, 227, 228
two swords, doctrine of, 442, 445
Tylor, Edward, 22, 207
unfruitful tree, parable of, 353–354n30
urbanization and social chaos, 308, 309
valley of Tophet, 270, 270n65
van Gennep, Arnold, xiv, 166, 225, 226, 227, 228, 230, 231, 232, 234
van Inwagen, Peter, xiv, 139n6, 149n25
Virgil, 187, 326n23, 381n43, 422, 423, 433, 436
   literary influence of, 338, 339, 340, 341, 341n9, 342
wedding guests, parable of, 356–357
Wiesel, Elie, 241
Winch, Peter, 24, 27, 162
Wittgenstein, Ludwig, 152n29, 201, 202
women
   role in death/resurrection, 380n42
   role in Passion, 359, 371, 379–387, 379n42, 381n43, 383n45, 389, 390

Wright, N. T., 194, 327, 356n36, 363, 373n27, 375n34, 406n97, 410, 421–429
Yamouchi, Edwin, 112, 113, 114
Yom Kippur, 76, 254, 257, 265, 267n60, 393, 394n78, 395n79
Yuval, Sinai, 272n69
Zechariah, Book of, 357n38, 359, 383n47, 389, 389n59, 390, 391, 398, 399, 400